Behavior Therapy

SERIES IN PSYCHOLOGY

Behavior Therapy

AUBREY J. YATES

UNIVERSITY OF WESTERN AUSTRALIA

JOHN WILEY & SONS, INC.

New York · London · Sydney · Toronto

Library of Congress Catalogue Card Number: 71-88910

SBN 471   97243   6

Printed in the United States of America

To my wife Sylvia
and my children
Julian, Alison, and Stephen

Foreword

IN THE past decade the literature of the behavior therapies has increased enormously. New journals have been founded to make possible the publication of this literature, and contributions have begun to appear with more frequency in journals long accustomed to reporting the views of more traditional psychotherapies. Graduate education in clinical psychology and residency training in psychiatry have introduced training in behavioral techniques into their therapeutic curriculum, associations of behavioral therapists have been formed and, all in all, we see every appearance of a period of exciting and rapid development.

The reasons for this are undoubtedly complex. Among them, we must assume are to be found a serious disillusionment with the shortcomings of the so-called dynamic therapies coupled with the maturity of the generation of clinical psychologists trained after the Second World War. Education designed to produce the scientist-professional has accomplished what it set out to do—the production of a cadre of psychologists dedicated to the principle that applied psychological techniques can only be as viable as their footing in behavioral science.

By far the most powerful reason, however, is the fact that the application of the behavioral therapies to a wide variety of problems has led to results that are distinctly encouraging, especially when considered against the backdrop of the outcome of previously popular methods. Regardless of theoretical persuasion, most clinicians place the welfare of their clients ahead of their personal need to protect an investment in a particular technique or ideology. As evidence of the efficacy of the behavioral therapies continues to appear, there is an increasing demand for systematic information about them. This demand comes from many quarters—clinicians in practical situations, academic theorists, students, psychologists, psychiatrists, and mental health professionals generally. The time has now arrived when it is necessary to provide this kind of information. Professor Yates has undertaken this task with a thoroughness and dedication that has produced a distinguished contribution to the literature of psychology.

In a work of this kind, written at a time such as this, there might well have been a danger that enthusiasm would overpower discretion. However, in keeping with the well-established commitment of behavior therapists to empiricism, Professor Yates' book provides a fine combination of fact, theory, and caution. This characteristic should serve to prevent the excesses of naive enthusiasm so often to be found in the advocates of therapeutic techniques, while providing a solid basis in fact for the confident use of the techniques themselves.

Practicing clinicians will find in the book a comprehensive and detailed resource for the study of the procedures and their empirical validities. Theoreticians will find a sophisticated consideration of the underlying propositions that guide the behavior therapies and their relationship to personality theory. Novices will find a reasoned presentation of a field of endeavor that is rapidly becoming the most prominent in modern psychopathology. Experienced behavior therapists will find this an invaluable compendium of information and a stimulus to lively discussion and debate.

It is a privilege to have the opportunity to offer these comments by way of introduction to this work. Psychology will be indebted to the author for a long time to come.

BRENDAN A. MAHER.

Weston, Massachusetts

May, 1969

Preface

BEHAVIOR THERAPY (as it has come to be called in England) or behavior modification (the term preferred in the United States) has in recent years become perhaps one of the most controversial topics of modern psychology. Breaking away, as it does in certain important respects, from the more established psycho-therapeutic techniques, it has generated much heated dispute as it has trespassed more and more into difficult and controversial areas of behavioral abnormality. How much significant progress has been achieved over this short period of time (about 15 years) is not easy to assess, but certainly it would now be appropriate for an interim report on the achievements, the limitations and defects, and the future prospects of behavior therapy.

In this book, I have attempted to show the historical antecedents of behavior therapy, its development in South Africa, England, and the United States, its allegiance (in principle, at least, if not always in practice) to the experimental approach, its successes and failures, and its future likely lines of development.

The book is divided into three parts. In Part I (Chapters 1 to 4), the historical background of behavior therapy is reviewed, the empirical and theoretical foundations are briefly sketched, the view of abnormality espoused by most behavior therapists is described, and some of the better known techniques used by behavior therapists are indicated. In Part II (Chapters 5 to 17), the wide range of applications of behavior therapy are covered in detail in, it is hoped, a critical fashion. In Part III (Chapters 18 to 20), a more general critical assessment is undertaken in which the major results of behavior therapy are reviewed, recent criticisms are considered, and future trends are assessed.

Work on the book commenced in 1964, but fortunately progress was slow and intermittent until 1967—fortunately, because in the past five years there has been a veritable explosion of work in this area. It would probably not be an exaggeration to estimate that about 300 articles a year are now published concerning behavior therapy, not to mention numerous books and monographs of direct interest. Even so, by the time this book appears in print, several hundred more reports will have appeared. A halt must be called somewhere, however, and this book covers the literature reasonably comprehensively up to October, 1968.

This book shows, no doubt, the influence of many psychologists who may not always agree with the opinions expressed in it about some of their work. A deep debt of gratitude is due Dr. M.B. Shapiro who first set me on the road of the experimental investigation of the single case. Professor H.J. Eysenck has exercised a profound influence without, however, turning me into a disciple—the last thing he would have wished to do (Eysenck has, indeed, indicated that he does not accept entirely the account given of the historical development of behavior therapy at the Institute of Psychiatry, but I have stuck to my guns). Conversations and correspondence with Professor Joseph Wolpe and Professor Arnold Lazarus have thrown further light on their basic contributions, while indebtedness is expressed also to Professor James Inglis and Professor Robert W. Payne, formerly colleagues of mine.

AUBREY J. YATES

Contents

Behavior Therapy

Part I

History, Basic Concepts, Techniques

Historical Development of Behavior Therapy

I. APPROACHES TO THE UNDERSTANDING AND TREATMENT OF BEHAVIOR DISORDER

SINCE THE BEGINNING of this century, two major approaches to the understanding and treatment of disorders of behavior have dominated clinical psychology, at times proceeding quite independently of each other, at times clashing violently. Presently, a spirited and occasionally acrimonious dispute is in progress between the advocates of the "psychodynamic" approach and those of the "behavioristic" approach. The former outlook developed, of course, primarily as a consequence of the work of Freud, while the latter developed primarily from the work of Pavlov, although there have been, as we shall see, attempts to "marry" the two approaches and show that they are translatable into a single, more comprehensive, set of theoretical terms (Dollard and Miller, 1950). In general (though qualifications are necessary), the psychodynamic approach has been characterized by its "clinical" emphasis and is practised by medically trained persons and those psychologists who are nonexperimentally inclined, at least in the sense in which that term is used in referring to "experimental psychology." The behavioristic approach, on the other hand, has been characterised by the attempt to apply laboratory methods and controls to the study and modification of abnormal forms of behavior. The crucial difference between the two approaches seems to lie in the fact that the psychodynamic psychologists may or may not *make use of* knowledge derived from experimental laboratory studies (or may rely on clinical judgment based on experience alone); whereas the behavioristic psychologist will tend to try to investigate and treat abnormal behavior strictly on an experimental basis.

The history and development of psychodynamic psychology and its application to abnormal forms of behavior will not be reviewed here. This tradition has flourished for the last 70 years in unbroken continuity, and its main tenets and methods are well known and have frequently been recorded at length and in detail. The behavioristic approach, in relation to abnormal behavior, which is the subject of this volume, has had a more intermittent history. It is, in fact, only in the last ten years that "behavior therapy," as it is now generally termed, has become a serious alternative to the psychodynamic approach. The purpose of this chapter is to trace the history of this approach and, in particular, to show how behavior therapy developed as it did with particular strength in the early 1950's. In order to do so, however, it is necessary to demonstrate the major sources of dissatisfaction with the traditional psychodynamic approach that influenced the development of behavior therapy.

3

II. SOURCES OF DISSATISFACTION WITH THE TRADITIONAL APPROACHES

Dissatisfaction with the traditional (medical, psychiatric, and psychodynamic) approaches to the diagnosis and treatment of "mental illness" had been expressed forcefully if sporadically throughout the first half of the present century, becoming more widespread as clinical psychologists invaded these areas in strength immediately after the end of World War II. The reasons behind this questioning attitude may be discussed under three broad headings: dissatisfaction with (a) the approach of the orthodox psychiatrist, based on what has been called the "medical model"; (b) the "psychodynamic approach"; and (c) the role assigned to (and often accepted by) the clinical psychologist. We shall discuss each in turn.

1. DISSATISFACTION WITH THE ORTHODOX PSYCHIATRIC APPROACH

(a) THE DISEASE CONCEPT OF MENTAL ILLNESS. The history of the transplantation of the "medical model" into the field of behavior disorders has been clearly described by Ullmann and Krasner (1965, pp. 2–15) and need not be repeated in detail here. Several factors contributed to this emphasis. First, there was the impressive demonstration of the undoubted correlation between abnormal brain function and certain abnormal behavior patterns, the classic examples being general paralysis of the insane and the effects of certain brain injuries in producing aphasia. A second factor, which has largely been ignored, lay in the comparative ignorance on the part of psychiatrists of any but the most elementary psychological facts. The great majority of psychiatrists are physicians with postgraduate training in psychiatry, the latter including what can only be described as a minimal amount of psychology. This state of affairs, unfortunate though it may be, must be recognized as inevitable, in view of the present structure of psychiatric training and, indeed, it is questionable whether psychiatrists should be trained as psychologists at all (this problem is closely related to the role of the clinical psychologist to be discussed below).[1]

The effect produced by the predominantly medical emphasis in the training of psychiatrists has, however, resulted in the transplantation of concepts and methods of proven usefulness in physical illness into the field of "mental illness." Thus, disorders of behavior have been regarded as *diseases* for which an *etiology* must be found, which will ultimately lead to a specific form of *treatment*. Hence the stress on the importance of *diagnosis* and the belief that specific causes would be found for specific *mental illnesses*.

The whole concept of "mental illness" has been severely criticized, particularly by Szasz (1960, 1961a, 1961b). As he points out:

"Mental illnesses" are thus regarded as basically no different than all other diseases (that is, of the body). The only difference, in this view, between mental and bodily diseases is that the former, affecting the brain, manifest themselves by means of mental symptoms; whereas the latter, affecting other organ systems (for example, the skin, liver etc.), manifest themselves by means of symptoms referable to those parts of the body" (Szasz, 1960, p. 113).

The tendency of orthodox psychiatrists to rely on physical methods of treatment (manifested most recently in the use of tranquilizers on a vast scale) is a reflection of the whole approach inculcated in general medical training. A further reflection of this approach is the insistence that the treatment of psychiatric disturbance is fundamentally a *medical* problem, the treatment of which is legitimately the province of the medically trained individual, with the nonmedical psychologist at times barely tolerated as a useful ancillary worker, akin to the biochemist.[2] Some psychologists, it may be added, have accepted the argument that behavior disorder is a disease (e.g., Ausubel, 1961).

It is not necessary to agree with Szasz's own formulation of the essential nature of the problem of "mental illness" (i.e., that it be regarded as an expression of the struggle of the individual with the problem of how he should live and is, therefore, a social, ethical, and legal problem) in order to recognize that a good deal of wasted effort has been poured into the

---

[1] Fortunately, there appears to be a rapidly increasing willingness on the part of psychiatrists to recognize the special knowledge and skills of experimentally-minded clinical psychologists.

[2] If the reader doubts this, he should refer to the fascinating account in the *American Psychologist* of the role of the clinical psychologist *as an expert witness* in legal cases with psychiatric implications (Hoch and Darley, 1962). See also the section below on the role of the clinical psychologist.

problem of behavior disorders as a result of a fundamentally faulty transposition of a medical model into a nonmedical problem. It is, in fact, possible to agree that the medical model may well be appropriate to the etiology and treatment of some disorders of behavior (e.g., the psychoses) where the importance of genetically determined biochemical factors seems certain to be established in the not-too-distant future (see, for example, Watson, 1956, 1965; Woolley, 1962). It seems equally certain, however, that a "psychological model" will prove to be of fundamental significance in dealing with that large group of disorders subsumed under the general heading of "the neuroses." If this should be so, then a training that is basically medically oriented may well prove to be very largely irrelevant, if not inhibiting, and a lack of knowledge of the facts and theories of psychology a fatal bar to progress. It should be pointed out that the "psychodynamic" psychologists have also tended to reject the disease model of abnormal behavior, while at the same time retaining many of its most important concepts (e.g., symptoms as indicators of underlying etiology).

(b) THE PROBLEM OF PSYCHIATRIC DIAGNOSIS. One important consequence of the application of the medical model to abnormal behavior was the attempt to derive a diagnostic or classificatory system for the pigeonholing of patients. There are at least three serious objections which can be brought against any such system: it is unreliable; it is invalid; and, even if it were both reliable *and* valid, it would serve no useful purpose.

(i) *Reliability of Psychiatric Diagnosis.* The unreliability of psychiatric diagnosis is by now well established. Undoubtedly the difficulty arises in part from methodological considerations. Thus, some psychiatrists arrive at a diagnosis from considerations of the symptom-presenting complex alone; others on the basis of psychodynamic formulations arising out of the symptom-complex; still others on some combination of symptoms and dynamic formulation. There are also major differences between psychiatrists on the meaning of the same diagnostic term—what one psychiatrist would lable as shizophrenia, another would label as mania. The attempts that have been made to investigate the reliability of psychiatric diagnosis have frequently foundered on these difficulties alone, so that the question of validity cannot even be considered.

Early studies by Wittson, Hunt, and Stevenson (1946), Ash (1949), and Mehlman (1952) all suggested low interpsychiatrist reliability in diagnosis, but need not be considered further here, since many criticisms can be brought against them on methodological grounds. Schmidt and Fonda (1956) and Kreitman (1961) have carefully delineated the basic requirements of a study of psychiatric diagnosis. These are, as a minimum: a standard, previously agreed upon, psychiatric nomenclature (not easy to obtain); a representative sample of psychiatrists; a representative sample of psychiatric patients; a knowledge of the "base-rates" for each psychiatric category used (to an extent this, of course, begs the whole question of the *validity* of diagnostic classification); an agreed-upon form of psychiatric examination procedure; and independence of assessment and judgment by each psychiatrist. Subsequent studies by Foulds (1955), Schmidt and Fonda (1956), Goldfarb (1959), Kreitman (1961), Kreitman et al (1961) and Zigler and Phillips (1961), to name but a few, have incorporated many of these requirements, with generally more encouraging results, but with a great deal of variability in the amount of agreement relating to various subcategories. Thus, using over 6000 cases, Kreitman (1961) found 89% agreement between psychiatrists for the general category of "functional psychotic" but only 46% agreement for the specific category "paranoid psychosis." Certainly, the reliability of psychiatric diagnosis remains a very real problem, since reliability is a prerequisite for validity.

(ii) *Validity of Psychiatric Diagnosis.* As Ullmann and Krasner (1965) point out, psychiatric classificatory systems "are products of medical sociology and reflect social pressures on physicians in terms of the task imposed upon them in given times and places" (p. 9). More importantly, however, the extraordinary degree of confusion and disagreement among psychiatrists concerning the diagnostic label to be placed on individual patients seems to arise from two main sources: the reliance on clinical experience and judgment as self-validating processes; and the pressure to "put a label" on a patient, which results in a tendency to categorize a patient in an either/or fashion. The latter tendency is, of course, a direct reflection of the influence of the medical model. In general, there has been a deplorable failure even to ask the correct questions in their most elementary form. Typical of basic questions that have been virtually ignored by psychiatrists are: Is neurosis *qualitatively* different from normality?

Is psychosis qualitatively different from normality? Is psychosis qualitatively different from neurosis? Or is there a single dimension of *abnormality*? The answers to these questions have important implications for the kinds of questions that psychiatrists commonly put to their psychological colleagues, such as: Is this patient a hysteric or a schizophrenic? Is this patient depressed or an early schizophrenic? and so on. Now the meaningfulness of these questions clearly depends on the dimensional system that is being employed. If, for example, neurosis and psychosis are orthogonal (i.e., independent or uncorrelated) dimensions, then the question of whether a patient is neurotic *or* psychotic becomes a meaningless one, since clearly there is no reason why the patient who is psychotic should not also be neurotic. It would then become a matter of empirically determining the *degree* of neuroticism *and* psychoticism (which, in each case, will vary independently— thus the patient may be grossly psychotic but only mildly or not at all neurotic; or any possible combination of these variables). Several possible solutions are logically tenable for the problem of the relationship between neurosis and psychosis. Thus, neurosis, normality, and psychosis may be *qualitatively* different, in which case a patient may be neurotic *or* psychotic *or* normal. There are two subpossibilities within this general scheme. Either subjects could be neurotic *or* psychotic, but not both at the same time (i.e., these two categories are mutually exclusive); or he could develop one or both disorders simultaneously. In either event, however, the argument would be analogous to the use of diagnostic categories in physical medicine, that is, a person either has a broken leg or he does not have it, but he may simultaneously have *both* a broken leg *and* pneumonia.[3] An alternative solution would be to argue that there is a single dimension of abnormality from normal through neurotic to psychotic, with the psychotic state being a more severe state of illness than the neurotic. But this argument carries with it the quite different implication that a psychotic individual *must* pass through a neurotic state first (and presumably would pass through it again during the course of recovery).

It will be clear that the resolution of these dimensional problems depends on whether or not a *disease concept* of abnormal behavior is held. Again the medical model is implicated. Clearly, if a particular abnormality is considered to be the product of a single genetic factor, it is reasonable to work in terms of an either/or dimensional system, since the "mental disease" will be present if and only if the specific factor is present. If, however, the determination of abnormal behavior is more akin to the determination of traits such as intelligence (where intellectual differences are determined in much the same way as height and weight, that is, by the effect of a large number of small factors), then clearly a continuous distribution of the abnormality in question must be postulated.

The confusions and contradictions that have resulted from the failure to ask such questions as these on the part of psychiatrists, and the unquestioning adherence in the field of psychiatry to a medical model appropriate to physical disorders, have been well documented, particularly by Eysenck (1947, 1952a, 1953). To give but one striking example, Jung linked introversion with psychasthemia, and extraversion with hysteria; Freud linked neurosis with introversion, while Kretschmer linked both schizophrenia and hysteria with introversion. Thus, in Jung's scheme, the hysteric is extraverted, whereas in Kretschmer's scheme, the hysteric is introverted! These dimensional questions can only be resolved by appropriate empirical studies utilizing proper methods of statistical analysis and not by clinical intuition based on biased and limited samples. The problem is, of course, being increasingly recognized by psychiatrists and, in recent years, some interesting and potentially fruitful new approaches have developed within the medical model framework. Of these, perhaps the most promising is the utilization of computer techniques (e.g., Smith, 1966; Overall and Hollister, 1964, 1968). The usefulness of these procedures remains to be determined.

(iii) *Usefulness of Psychiatric Diagnosis.* Even supposing that psychiatric diagnosis could be made both reliable and valid, the question would arise as to its usefulness. If it is decided that a diagnosis of "schizophrenia" is warranted and if this is agreed upon by all psychiatrists who have examined the patient, the rather rude question may immediately be put: so what? What is the value or purpose of pigeonholing a patient in this way? Again the answer has

---

[3] It should be noted that this argument does *not* imply that all patients classified as neurotic are

equally neurotic any more than all persons suffering from pneumonia are equally sick.

usually involved an analogy with procedures current in physical medicine. In clinical practice a diagnosis is purposeful if it provides information concerning etiology of the disorder involved in the diagnosis or has implications for treatment, or has implications for prognosis. If, however, a diagnosis has no implications for etiology, treatment, or prognosis, then what is the point of making it, except to label the patient with a name?

It is not intended here, of course, to decry entirely the usefulness or value of diagnostic procedures.[4] Indeed, the diagnostic approach is but a variant of the more general dimensional problem discussed earlier. In the field of psychiatry, however, with but a few exceptions, the search for a diagnostic label is completely futile (since it has no etiological or treatment implications) except for research purposes, and serves to draw attention away from far more meaningful and useful activities.

2. DISSATISFACTION WITH THE PSYCHODYNAMIC APPROACH

The psychodynamic approach, developing out of the work of Freud, involved the paradox of the rejection of the medical model (in which it resembles the behavioristic approach) while at the same time retaining many of its most important features. It is assumed that the reader has a considerable degree of familiarity with the history and principles of the psychodynamic approach. Therefore, only the major reasons why some psychologists become dissatisfied with this approach will be indicated here.[5] The following remarks are not intended to denigrate the achievements that have resulted from the psychodynamic approach, but merely to indicate the major sources of discomfort that behavioristic psychologists experience in relation to the model.

(a) SYMPTOMS AND SYMPTOM SUBSTITUTION. One of the basic tenets of the psychodynamic approach has always been that it is necessary to search beyond the presenting behavior of the patient for the underlying "dynamic" causes of that behavior. What the patient complains of (his "symptoms") is not rejected as being of no importance, but his symptoms are regarded as the "surface" indicators of some underlying conflict or disturbance. Thus, enuresis may be regarded as a form of displaced aggression against the parents; stuttering may be regarded as a defense against the uttering of obscene words; and so forth. Some of the psychodynamic formulations have been so extreme as to receive little acceptance, such as the argument that enuresis is a form of "weeping through the bladder" (i.e., a form of depressive reaction). The importance of this formulation of the "meaning" of symptoms for our present purposes is that a very important consequence follows, namely, the adoption of the idea of "symptom substitution." It is argued that, while it may be possible to remove symptoms directly by various means, this is both a futile and possibly even dangerous procedure. For, it is argued, the symptom is essentially a "defense mechanism" which protects the organism against, or temporarily resolves, the underlying conflicts. Therefore, removing the symptom alone will leave the patient with the underlying conflict intact *and with no defenses against it*. From this situation will flow one of two undesirable consequences. Either symptom substitution will occur—that is, the patient will develop new symptoms to replace the ones removed, thus restoring the defensive system and reducing anxiety; or the patient will be left helpless in the face of his inner conflict and, it has even been argued, a psychotic attack may be precipitated. The conclusion that is drawn from this line of argument is that the symptom itself should not be directly attacked by psychotherapy or other means, but that attention should be directed at exposing, analyzing, and resolving the underlying conflict. If this latter approach is successful, the symptom will disappear, since it will no longer have any *raison d'être*.

This formulation was attacked by the present author in a paper (Yates, 1958a) which appears to have stimulated a good deal of subsequent argument. The whole problem of symptoms and symptom substitution, which is a question of crucial significance in behavior therapy, will be considered in detail in a later chapter, from both the empirical and theoretical angle (see Chapter 19). Suffice it to point out here that the question of whether enuresis or stuttering, for example, should be tackled directly or whether attention should be concentrated on the underlying dynamics is one of the points at which the psychodynamic and behavioristic approaches to therapy part company decisively.

---

[4] For a recent comprehensive review of the problem of psychiatric classification, see Zubin (1967).

[5] There are, of course, numerous adequate accounts of the principles of psychodynamic psychology, apart from the original works of Freud and his followers. Perhaps the most balanced and least polemical is that by White (1964).

(b) PSYCHOTHERAPY AND THE PLACEBO
EFFECT. A second major bone of contention
between the psychodynamic and behavioristic
approaches to abnormal behavior appears in
relation to psychotherapy. In the early 1950's
increasing criticism was voiced, not so much of
the efficacy or otherwise of psychotherapy, but
of the apparent "functional autonomy" (Astin,
1961), impervious to criticism, which it had
achieved. The sensitivity of psychotherapists to
any criticism of psychotherapy was clearly
shown by the extraordinary misreadings of
Eysenck's (1952b) celebrated review of the
effects of psychotherapy. It was widely assumed
that Eysenck was arguing that psychotherapy
was of no use and should be abandoned
(Rosenzweig, 1954) whereas, in fact, Eysenck was
merely pointing out that the published evidence
did not, as it stood, indicate that psychotherapy
produced a better remission rate in treated
neurotics, as compared with the spontaneous
recovery rate in untreated neurotic patients;
and that in view of the enormous amount of
money and time involved, methodologically
more sophisticated studies were warranted,
however difficult this might prove to be. Subsequently, similar reviews were carried out with
respect to psychotherapy with children, with
similar results (Levitt, 1957, 1963; Gluck et al,
1964). Eysenck has repeated his criticisms in
much greater detail (Eysenck, 1960a, 1964a,
1964b) and Astin (1961) has satirically and
devastatingly made clear the remarkable resistance to change of fixed ideas in this area. As
Astin (1961) rather savagely put it:

"Eysenck tried again (1954) to promote his
position. This time his claim was that to
squabble over who should do psychotherapy
before its efficacy had been demonstrated is,
in essence, to put the cart before the horse.
Eysenck was answered by Raush (1954) as
follows: 'It is not the point to discuss the
efficacy or lack of efficacy of psychotherapy
here . . . psychotherapy is a method for
studying the human psyche . . . whether it is
a good or a bad method is not at issue.' Thus,
without the bothersome business of first
knowing if, how or under what conditions
psychotherapy might work, we could still
engage in controversies about who should
perform it and also use it to 'study the
psyche'. Who could doubt now that psychotherapy had indeed become functionally
autonomous?" (Astin, 1961, p. 25).

Psychodynamic psychologists seemed curiously reluctant to even consider the possibility
of a massive "placebo effect," a phenomenon
that has been distressingly frequent throughout
medical history (Rosenthal and Frank, 1956;
Shapiro, 1959, 1960a, 1960b, 1964; Liberman,
1962; Lesse, 1964; Steinbook et al, 1965) and the
only protection against which is the consistent use
of the controlled experimental method.

(c) METHODOLOGICAL INADEQUACIES OF
THE MEDICAL MODEL AND THE PSYCHO-
DYNAMIC APPROACH. A final source of dissatisfaction concerned the obvious methodological inadequacies of much that was routinely
accepted as valid by the psychodynamic
psychologists. Three examples will be given.
The validity of the concept of "symptom
substitution" has generally been unquestion-
ingly accepted by this school, in spite of the
absence of any empirical evidence on the
question. Thus White comments that "we must
accept the long-accumulating evidence that
symptomatic treatment can be successful, but
we must not overlook the equally long-
accumulating evidence that symptoms are in
many cases the surface phenomena of more
complex emotional difficulties" (White, 1964,
p. 333). The seeming reasonableness of this
assessment is unfortunately vitiated by the fact
that the two sets of "evidences" are not as equal
as is here implied. For, as we shall see in later
chapters, there is now cogent *empirical* evidence
for the failure of symptom substitution to occur
following symptomatic treatment; whereas
evidence *for* symptom substitution is sparse and
certainly far less frequent than would be
expected if the psychodynamic formulation of
the meaning of symptoms were true.

This brings us to our second example of
methodological inadequacy. Unfortunately for
White, following the quotation just given, he
goes on to illustrate the importance of the
"underlying conflict" and the futility of
symptomatic treatment (in more serious disorders at least) by a brief account of the famous
case of Little Hans.

"The difference can be illustrated by
recalling Freud's case of the five-year-old boy
Hans, who had a phobia of horses. The
history showed certain frights associated with
horses, but Freud became convinced that
these were insufficient to account for the
symptom. He saw the fear of horses as a
somewhat distant displacement of a much
more serious and inescapable dread of the

father, developed out of the conflicts of the Oedipal situation. If the phobia had actually originated in frights connected with horses, it could presumably have been removed by direct counter-conditioning procedures. If it was a displacement, such procedures would not have affected the central cause of anxiety; removal of the phobia would have left this problem unsolved, and a fresh defense against anxiety would presumably have been needed. Thinking about it in this way, Freud advocated treatment that developed the boy's insight into his feelings about his father. Treatment was thus directed at the nuclear fear rather than at the symptom" (White, 1964, p. 333).

Aside from White's begging of the question (since counter-conditioning was not tried and, therefore, we do not know whether it would have succeeded or not), the choosing of this example (which appears always to have been regarded as one of the cornerstones of psychodynamic psychology) was particularly unfortunate, since a critique of the study on methodological grounds which is likely to become a classic had already been published four years prior to the appearance of White's revised edition (Wolpe and Rachman, 1960).

The general tenor of the criticisms of the Little Hans case study by Wolpe and Rachman represents a specific example of the reservations felt by behavioristic psychologists of the whole procedure of psychodynamic psychologists. There is no intention of disputing the insights of Freud and other analysts. Instead, the criticism is directed at the failure to follow up and test the validity of these insights by sufficiently rigorous methods *to permit of their disproof.* Eysenck (1952a) has given an excellent example of this in his comments on a study by Symonds (1949) who obtained correlations *opposite* to those *predicted* on the basis of the dynamic theory being put forward. While such a result would normally lead to the rejection of the hypothesis in question, Symonds introduces the concept of reaction formation to account for the results. Now, in principle, there is nothing illegitimate about the notion of reaction formation. However, it is quite improper to utilize it *ad hoc* as an explanation of unexpected results without at least some further experimentation because otherwise there is no possible way of disproving *any* hypothesis. The major objection, then, to psychodynamic formulations is that they are frequently stated in such a way

as to be impossible of disproof by any *empirical* observations whatever. There can be little doubt that the persistence of psychodynamic formulations in relatively unchanged forms for such a long period is largely a result of the ready availability (and free use!) of convenient concepts to account for discrepant results.

The third example of methodological inadequacy may be treated more briefly and is taken from the medical model. The insulin treatment of schizophrenia has been inflicted over the past 30 years on many thousands of unfortunate patients; yet the hundreds of studies carried out to assess its efficacy are so methodologically inadequate that, until recently, it was quite uncertain whether insulin treatment (like psychotherapy) was of any value at all. This situation persisted basically because clinical psychologists were not permitted to carry out the appropriately designed experiment (which would have involved the use of untreated control groups) on the grounds that it was unethical to withhold treatment from psychiatric patients. This raised the nice question as to which was the more unethical (or ethical, depending on the point of view!): to subject patients to a most unpleasant form of treatment, whose efficacy is unknown, but which may, in some cases, produce severe brain damage; or to withhold the treatment from some patients who will be used as controls in order to find out whether this drastic treatment is a valid one. As Astin (1961) sarcastically put it in connection with psychotherapy:

"A serious ethical objection lodged by the practitioners against 'outcome' research centered around the necessity for using controls in such investigations. Because of the limited usefulness of comparing psychotherapy with other therapies or even with therapy 'wait' groups, an adequately designed outcome study required denying treatment to a comparable group of clients. Practitioners, in their ethical concern for the welfare of their clients, were opposed to the practise of refusing treatment to sick people who ask for it.

In a desperate counterargument, some reactionaries suggested that psychotherapy might conceivably be *detrimental* under certain conditions, and that ethical considerations really *demanded* that controlled outcome studies be done in order to evaluate at least these possibilities" (Astin, 1961, p. 76; italics in original).

It is an unhappy fact that when at last an appropriately controlled study was carried out (Ackner et al, 1957) the results did not give any support to the belief that insulin treatment was of any greater value than the use of certain drugs. In spite of this and earlier severe criticisms of the procedure (e.g., Bourne, 1953, 1958) and in spite of a recent review by Pronko et al (1960), which demonstrated quite clearly the lack of any substantive support for the procedure, this method of treatment is still widely used, though fortunately on a smaller and smaller scale.

3. DISSATISFACTION WITH THE ROLE OF THE CLINICAL PSYCHOLOGIST

The sources of dissatisfaction discussed above were really all parts of the most basic and critical problem, namely, the role that should be played by the clinical psychologist. The central argument of this whole chapter is, in fact, the assertion that this role has been completely misconceived since the end of the war, particularly in the United States.

The question may be best approached by considering the functions that have been traditionally (and often still are) exercised by the clinical psychologist, and then outlining briefly why these functions are, to a large extent, unnecessary and unsatisfactory and what, in this author's view, the clinical psychologist's role *should* be.[6]

(a) TRADITIONAL FUNCTIONS OF THE CLINICAL PSYCHOLOGIST. Watson (1951) has very clearly described the type of work customarily performed by the clinical psychologist under the following headings: mental testing (e.g., the assessment of intelligence); educational assessment (e.g., backwardness in scholastic attainment); personality assessment (particularly by the use of projective techniques); diagnostic testing (the differential assessment between schizophrenia and hysteria, for example); the assessment of intellectual deficit or deterioration and brain damage; the evaluation of methods of treatment; vocational guidance and selection; psychotherapy; and research.

It would be a tedious but revealing exercise to calculate the hundreds of man-hours that were spent in the decade 1950–1960 on diagnostic assessment throughout the United States plus the man-hours spent in attempting to validate various diagnostic tests.[7] It would be equally tedious to calculate the time and effort put into the assessment of personality, mainly by the use of projective techniques which are extremely time-consuming to give, score, and interpret. In the present author's view, the net result of this vast investment of time and effort has been most disappointing. The efforts to devise reliable and valid tests of brain damage, for example, over a period of fifteen years, have been largely fruitless (Yates, 1954, 1966) as have been the attempts to measure intellectual deficit (Yates, 1956). Furthermore, with but few exceptions, clinical psychologists seem to have been content to use such tests as are available without questioning the purpose of the exercise. Once again, the influence of the medical model is apparent, where putting a label on the patient becomes all-important, irrespective of the consequences (or lack of consequences) which flow from such labeling. Altogether apart from the fact that psychological tests of brain damage can usually only identify those patients who are easily identified by less costly means (whereas the tests would be useful only if they identified those brain-damaged subjects *not* readily identifiable otherwise), it is almost always the case that no important consequences (surgical or retraining, for example) flow from such a diagnosis. But, if this is so, why waste precious time to arrive at a diagnosis?

Such criticisms could be multiplied indefinitely. Thus, the battery approach, as advocated by Schafer and Rapaport (Rapaport, Gill, and Schaefer, 1946) has had an immense influence on clinical practice, to the extent that, in many child clinics, for example, it is the automatic practice to administer a battery of tests on admission, irrespective of the disorder—and such testing might occupy at least two full days of intellectual, educational, and projective tests. Yet, if a child is brought to the clinic with a stutter, for example, does it really matter if his I.Q. turns out to be 140 rather than 120 (or even 100)? Of course, various tests may be valuable sources of information under appropriate circumstances, but to administer such tests routinely seems such an incredible waste of valuable time that the question arises: why have clinical psychologists accepted this role of

---

[6] For a rather different viewpoint, see Ausubel (1956), or, more recently, Sundberg and Tyler (1962) and L'Abate (1964).

[7] See, for example, the pages of the *Journal of Consulting Psychology* during this period. Mischel (1968) provides an excellent account of the phenomenon.

diagnostician, supplemented by detailed personality description, usually by means of projective techniques?

There seem to be two broad answers to this problem: one relates to what the present author thinks of as the adoption of the role of pseudopsychiatrist; the second relates to the rejection of the role by which the clinical psychologist capitalizes on and utilizes the special skills and knowledge which he alone possesses by virtue of the fact that *he is trained as a psychologist*. Fundamentally, both of these points reduce to the problem of the relationship between the psychologist and the psychiatrist or physician, a problem that has been the subject of continuous debate throughout the postwar period.[8]

The adoption of the role of diagnostician[9] or pseudopsychiatrist seems to have resulted partly from feelings of professional insecurity on the part of the clinical psychologist, partly from a desire to communicate meaningfully with psychiatrists by means of a supposedly common language, and partly from the demands of psychiatrists for such diagnostic services in line with the tenets of the medical model. The psychiatrist, in fact, has himself perceived the appropriate role of the clinical psychologist as that of a medical ancillary, whose primary purpose in life is to assist in arriving at a diagnostic category into which the patient can be fitted, particularly in the case of doubtful instances. Hence the common request from the psychiatrist to the clinical psychologist: can you help me decide if patient X is brain-damaged or not; or if patient Y is schizophrenic or hysteric; or what the personality structure is of patient Z?

Many clinical psychologists have behaved as if the use of the same terms indicated successful communication. But it is easy to show that this may not be the case at all. A simple example will illustrate the point. One of the most widely used tests in clinical psychology is the Minnesota Multiphasic Personality Inventory (MMPI),[10] and it cannot be denied that this test was most carefully and thoroughly designed and validated. Now let us suppose that the clinical psychologist has been asked to examine patient A and give an opinion as to whether or not he is a schizophrenic (which is the psychiatrist's tentative

diagnosis). The test is administered and scored, and the clinical psychologist reports that the patient obtained an abnormally high score on the schizophrenia subscale of the test, while falling within the normal range on all other subscales. Has there been successful communication between the clinical psychologist and the psychiatrist? The answer, unfortunately, is: probably not. For the use of the same term (schizophrenic) to describe the same patient does not in any way guarantee that the clinical psychologist and the psychiatrist mean the same thing. This is important because there is no doubt that many psychiatrists are not *in detail* acquainted with the individual items which comprise the subscale of schizophrenia. If the psychiatrist were to examine the actual responses of the patient to the individual items, he might well refuse to accept such a pattern as indicative of what *he* means when he places the label "schizophrenic" on a patient. It is a fact which has largely been conveniently ignored by clinical psychologists that, because of the lack of agreement among psychiatrists concerning the defining referents of schizophrenia, the MMPI cannot be validly used outside of its original standardization setting unless either (a) the cooperating psychologist and psychiatrist agree on what they mean by the term "schizophrenia" in relation to diagnostic psychiatric assessment on the one hand, and pattern of performance on the MMPI, on the other; or (b) the test has been completely restandardized (and, indeed, reconstructed) to meet differing conceptions of the characteristics of schizophrenia in the mental hospital in which the patient is. But neither of these conditions is very frequently satisfied. Hence a good deal of miscommunication goes on between the psychiatrist and the psychologist in relation to these diagnostic activities. The psychologist, however, bolsters his insecurity as an independent professional worker by persuading himself that he is successfully communicating with the psychiatrist, who, in turn, feels that he has a useful ancillary worker. The fact that, in assuming the role of pseudopsychiatrist, the clinical psychologist is abdicating the responsibilities deriving from his special qualifications, is ignored. Precisely similar objections can be raised against the widespread use of projective

---

[8] See, for example, the collection of papers on clinical psychology reprinted in Braun (1961).

[9] See Holt (1967) for a comprehensive discussion of the present status and future prospects of diagnostic testing.

[10] It was largely objections to the use of this test that led in 1965 to Congressional investigations of the use of psychological tests. See the entire November 1965 issue of the *American Psychologist*.

techniques where, again, the objective seems to be to achieve some kind of pseudopsychiatric description of the patient in a language which is as much like that of the psychiatrist as possible.

(b) THE FUNDAMENTAL ROLE OF THE CLINICAL PSYCHOLOGIST. If we reject this pseudopsychiatric role as unsatisfactory and unnecessary, what then should be the role (or roles) of the clinical psychologist? The answer must surely follow directly from a consideration of the nature of his training and qualifications. It is a remarkable state of affairs that several years are commonly spent in teaching the embryonic clinical psychologist the fundamental empirical knowledge (of which, in spite of the sceptics, there is now a vast amount) in sensation, perception, learning, motivation, and so forth, together with the principal theoretical systems (which, in spite of their diversity of language, do have a great deal in common), only to find that this basic body of knowledge and theory is virtually ignored as soon as the psychologist moves into the clinical field. It is not, of course, suggested that the application of this knowledge is not extremely difficult, and it is recognized that obstacles are, or would be, placed in the way of psychologists who attempted to do this by unsympathetic or ignorant physicians or psychiatrists. But it is plainly the responsibility of the clinical psychologist to demonstrate that he has something to offer other than a pale copy of psychiatric procedures—and, by and large, clinical psychologists have not met this responsibility.

The contention to be upheld here is that *the most important role which the clinical psychologist can fulfil at this time is that of fundamental research worker*. This contention is derived essentially from the following considerations. In general medicine, it is a truism that the basic discoveries are not usually made by the general practitioner but by fundamental research workers who may not even be medically qualified—and this tradition of basic research work in general medicine is accepted as a natural state of affairs. But no such tradition exists in the field of psychiatry, where basic research, to a great extent, has had to be carried out by the general practitioner in psychiatry (i.e., the fully-employed psychiatrist). Now, two points should be noted. First, the harassed psychiatrist usually does not have the time to carry out this fundamental research, weighed down with his case-

load as he is. But, even if he did have time, he is usually not well qualified to carry out such research,[11] being untrained in the problems of research design. But, if we accept the proposition that many abnormalities of behavior are either biochemically determined (as seems likely in the case of some psychoses) or the result of failures of, or faulty, learning, then it follows that the fundamental research workers in the field of psychiatry are either the geneticists or biochemists, on the one hand, or the clinical psychologists, on the other. The clinical psychologist has (or should have) long and detailed training and experience, not merely in the empirical and theoretical aspects of human behavior (normal and abnormal) but, most importantly, in the design problems of conducting research in these areas.

Thus, it is concluded that, without denying the usefulness of the various roles described above by Watson, the primary and fundamental role of the clinical psychologist must be that of basic research scientist. While there can be no doubt that acceptance of this point of view is slowly gaining ground both among clinical psychologists and psychiatrists, the recognition and implementation of this role will require a much greater effort on the part of clinical psychologists to justify its adoption.

To state that the primary function of the clinical psychologist is research is not to explicate the most important functions within that role which he can perform. At least three aspects may be highlighted. First, the clinical psychologist should be peculiarly well fitted to help in the solution of the persistent diagnostic problems in psychiatry. The use of diagnosis *in the clinical setting* has been criticized earlier in this chapter, but there is no intention of denying the fact, particularly emphasized by Eysenck (1947, 1952a), that, in the long term, the solution of the problem of the basic dimensions underlying abnormal behavior is of fundamental importance. That is, whereas the use of diagnostic categories in the clinical field may at present be largely useless, the specification of the basic dimensions may be of great significance in relation to research, particularly to the formulation of theories concerning individual differences in behavior. Since the ultimate solution of the dimensional problem seems certain to be achieved by statistical techniques applied to appropriately collected data (Lorr et al, 1964), this would appear to be

---

[11] There are, of course, notable exceptions.

an area of research peculiarly suited to the skills of the clinical psychologist. Second, the clinical psychologist should be concerned particularly with the development of theories of abnormal behavior, which clearly can be arrived at only through extensive knowledge of the facts and theories of normal behavior. Third, and perhaps most important, instead of merely copying the procedures and language of the psychiatrist, the clinical psychologist should be vitally concerned with the application of the empirical findings and theories of general psychology to the individual patient. It is here argued that the clinical psychologist far too often has as his major aim the *description* of the patient (either by means of a category placement or by means of a more general personality description), but these are questions for a psychiatrist. The clinical psychologist should, instead, draw on his knowledge of general psychology to define as closely as possible the nature of the disorder from which the patient suffers; to formulate theories concerning the treatment of the disorder; and to carry out *controlled* experiments of a laboratory kind in an effort to modify the behavior of the patient.

The crucial question which each clinical psychologist must ask himself is this: Am I doing anything that could not be done equally as well by a psychiatrist by methods which are little different from those I employ? If he is not attempting to make use of his knowledge of psychology *as a specialist*, then, to a degree, he is wasting his years of training.

In summary, then, the primary role of the clinical psychologist is seen as that of a highly trained specialist research worker, applying empirical knowledge and theories to the understanding and change of abnormal patterns of behavior—a role which can be performed by the clinical psychologist by virtue of his special skills and talents and which could not be performed by anyone without that knowledge and training. Unfortunately, instead of working as such specialists, clinical psychologists far too often are content to adopt the role of pseudo-psychiatrist, basking in the reflected glory and status of the medical profession.

In the next section of this chapter, this delineation of the role of clinical psychologist will be discussed in greater detail by reference to the historical development of behavior therapy.

III. THE DEVELOPMENT OF BEHAVIOR THERAPY

Thus far we have been concerned with what might be termed the "negative" factors which strongly influenced the development of behavior therapy. The reaction of some critics to behavior therapy, however, indicates a belief that this approach is something new, a belief which is quite at variance with the facts. Alternatively, some critics[12] have argued that behavior therapy is nothing but an atavistic regression to the crude punishment - type methods prevalent in mental hospitals in the late 19th century, an argument which simply reveals gross ignorance on the part of the critic. In this section, we shall trace briefly the historical developments which indicate that behavior therapy is by no means a completely new approach, but rather a logical development from a whole series of events in the history of experimental psychology. No attempt will be made at a comprehensive review of the history of experimental psychology and its relationship to the understanding and treatment of abnormalities of behavior, since several excellent accounts of the various strands to be considered already exist.

1. THE INFLUENCE OF RUSSIAN PSYCHOLOGY

As is very well known, the experiments on classical conditioning by Pavlov and his colleagues, on the one hand, and by Bekhterev and his colleagues on instrumental conditioning, on the other hand, exercised an immense influence on the development of experimental psychology in the first three decades of this century.[13] The important point to note, however, for our purposes, is that the *experimental procedures* of these workers began to be applied as far as possible almost immediately to the area of abnormal behavior, both in a general explanatory sense and in explanation of particular disorders. Thus, Pavlov not only published the results of his laboratory experiments on animals (Pavlov, 1927, 1928), but also published extensively on the application of his techniques and theories to abnormal behavior, both in general (Pavlov, 1932, 1941) and in relation to particular disorders, such as hysteria (Pavlov, 1933) and obsessional neuroses and

---

[12] See, for example, the review of Wolpe's (1958) book by Glover (1959).

[13] The terms "classical" and "instrumental" were not used by Pavlov and Bekhterev, of course, and the distinction between the two "types" of conditioning is now known to be strictly untenable. They may still be usefully employed, however, in a general sense.

TABLE I.I. *Early Applications of the Principles of Conditioning To Abnormalities of Behavior*

Source	Disorder Studied
Bekhterev (1923a)	Sexual perversions
Bregman (1934)	Children's fears
Dunlap (1932)	Tics, stuttering, etc.
English (1929)	Children's fears
Harris (1934)	Anxiety
Holmes (1936)	Children's fears
Ichok (1934)	Alcoholism
Ivanov-Smolensky (1928)	Depression
Joncs (H. E.) (1931)	Children's fears
Jones (M. C.) (1924a, 1924b)	Children's fears
Kostyleff (1927)	Sexual aberrations
Krasnogorski (1933a)	Enuresis
Levin (1934)	Narcolepsy
Marinesco (1937)	Hysteria
Marinesco and Kreindler (1935)	Hysteria
Max (1935)	Homosexuality
Meignant (1935)	Sexual aberrations
Moore (1938)	Stuttering
Morgan and Witmer (1939)	Enuresis
Morhardt (1930)	Allergy
Moss (1924)	Children's fears
Mowrer and Mowrer (1938)	Enuresis
Rouquier and Michel (1934)	Anorexia
Rubenstein (1931)	Morphine addiction
Sears and Cohen (1933)	Hysteria
Tinel (1930)	Hysteria
Watson and Rayner (1920)	Children's fears

paranoia (Pavlov, 1934). Likewise, Bekhterev published both his general experimental studies (Bekhterev, 1932) and considered their application to psychiatry (Bekhterev, 1912, 1923a, 1923b). Similarly, a great deal of work along similar lines was published by Ivanov-Smolensky (1925, 1927a, 1927b, 1927c, 1928) and Krasnogorski (1925, 1930, 1931, 1933b). Thus, the possibility of an objective, experimentally-based approach to abnormalities of behavior, derived from knowledge of the principles of conditioning, was recognized very early.[14]

2. INFLUENCE OF RUSSIAN WORK ON AMERICAN PSYCHOLOGY

It is unnecessary here to trace in detail the immense influence that Pavlov's work exercised on the development of American experimental psychology. The possibility of explaining abnormalities of behavior in Pavlovian terminology was explored in two remarkable papers by Watson (1916) and Burnham (1917), while simultaneously Mateer (1917) published a monograph on the application of conditioning techniques to children. Somewhat later, Burnham (1924) expanded his ideas in a book which is now regarded as a classic and a landmark,[15] while Dunlap (1932), several years later, applied behavioristic techniques to a wide range of disorders. In the 1930's, many attempts were made to explore the nature of neurosis by inducing "neurotic behavior" in animals such as the sheep (Liddell, 1938), the pig (Liddell, 1938), the rat (Cook, 1939; Maier, 1939), and

---

[14] The Russian work mentioned here was itself, of course, derived from 19th-century work, particularly in Russia and England. For a clear historical account of the precursors of Pavlov, see Diamond et al, 1963.

[15] Hollingworth's (1930) textbook of abnormal psychology was one of the few to be strongly influenced by these approaches.

the cat (Masserman, 1943). In all of this latter work, the intention was to demonstrate, if possible, whether or not the principles derived from animal studies could usefully be applied to the study of neurotic behavior in human subjects.

3. PARTICULAR APPLICATIONS OF THE PRINCIPLES OF CONDITIONING TO ABNORMALITIES OF BEHAVIOR

Both in Russia and the United States (and to a much smaller degree in England and on the Continent), interest was aroused in the application of the principles of conditioning to the understanding and treatment of behavior disorders. It is the purpose of this chapter to show that behavior therapy did not arise in a vacuum, and it will, therefore, be worthwhile to provide some idea of the extent of the activities relating to conditioning in the area of treatment of abnormal forms of behavior. Table 1.1 provides a selective list of the kinds of particular investigations carried out in the 1920's and 1930's. As will be seen, American and Russian authors predominate. What is especially striking, however, is the wide range of disorders to which conditioning principles were applied. The obvious conclusion to be drawn from this table is that an intense interest was evident throughout the first half of this century in the application of controlled, objective experimentation to the investigation and treatment of a wide variety of forms of abnormal behavior. Furthermore, the interest was clearly not restricted to the investigation of "simple," peripheral phenomena, but embraced more complex forms of behavior disorder, such as anxiety, children's fears, and the psychoses.

4. THE INFLUENCE OF LEARNING THEORY

It will have been noticed that the above studies were mainly concerned with the application of what we have called the "principles of conditioning" and that no mention has been made so far of "learning." A development of major importance in the mid-1930's was that relating to the construction of theoretical models to embrace a much wider range of phenomena than the conditioning situations studied by Pavlov and Bekhterev. Of particular significance in this context was, of course, the work of Hull (1943, 1952) which itself was an attempt to subsume both classical and instrumental conditioning under a single theoretical framework. Hull's work (largely based on the findings of the American "instrumentalists" such as Thorndike) is of great importance because its use of tightly defined theoretical constructs enabled psychologists to begin to make use of theory as well as empirical facts in the field of abnormal behavior. Thus, the use of the term "learning theory" came to be more and more widely used with reference to abnormal behavior. A particularly interesting example of the use of learning theory constructs is to be found in the work of Dollard and Miller (1950) in which they attempted to have the best of both worlds by retaining psychodynamic concepts but, at the same time, translating them as far as possible into the terminology of learning theory. Now, it is important to notice that the application to abnormal behavior of the constructs of psychoanalysis translated into learning theory terms by Dollard and Miller was *essentially nonexperimental* in nature. That is, they worked out a theoretical model of abnormal behavior, deduced from it rational methods of treatment, and then tried to apply these methods of treatment to particular abnormalities. However, whereas their principles of learning were derived from laboratory experimental studies, the application of these principles *did not involve them in carrying out experiments on their patients*. In fact, their *clinical* procedures (their treatment of the patient) differed in no important way from those of the psychodynamic psychologists. To anticipate, they were quite definitely *not* behavior therapists in the sense demanded by the definition of this term which will shortly be given. Nevertheless, there can be no doubt concerning the value of the contribution of Dollard and Miller nor of its profound influence on the development of behavior therapy. Similar approaches at this time were made by Mowrer (1950) and Shoben (1949).

5. THE DEVELOPMENT OF BEHAVIOR THERAPY IN ENGLAND

Since recent critiques of behavior therapy (e.g., Breger and McGaugh, 1965) show a deplorable ignorance of the history of the development of behavior therapy in England,[16] it is important to describe in some detail the way in which behavior therapy was developed

---

[16] An ignorance that is unfortunately not corrected in the recent work on behavior therapy by Eysenck

and Rachman (1965) who ignore completely the contribution of Shapiro.

there.[17] To do this, it is necessary to describe briefly the administrative organization of the Psychology Department at that time in the Institute of Psychiatry. The overall head of the department was, of course, H.J. Eysenck. The department was, however, split into a Research Section and a Clinical-Teaching Section. The Research Section was primarily concerned with work relating to Eysenck's dimensional and, subsequently, theoretical explanatory system in relation to the explanation of abnormal behavior *in general*, with special reference, of course, to the dimensions of neuroticism, psychoticism, and introversion-extraversion. The Clinical-Teaching Section was primarily concerned with the training of clinical psychologists by means of the postgraduate diploma in clinical psychology. In order to achieve this aim, the Clinical-Teaching Section was, of course, closely linked to the Department of Psychiatry located in the Maudsley and Bethlem Royal Hospitals. From this source were obtained patients of every variety (mostly complex and difficult cases, since the Maudsley Hospital was basically a teaching hospital). In return, the Clinical-Teaching Section also provided a clinical service to the hospital, with the usual interaction between clinical psychologist and psychiatrist.

In the early stages of the establishment of the Clinical-Teaching Section, the activities of the clinical staff psychologists were fairly conventional, that is, the usual cognitive and projective tests were administered and interpreted, assessments were made of personality and intellectual deficit, and differential diagnosis was attempted.

It was not long, however, before a change came over the operations of the Clinical-Teaching Section. Four main factors contributed to produce this change. First, there was the general influence exercised by Eysenck's cogent critiques of the validity and reliability of projective techniques and the psychodynamic approach in general. Second, Eysenck also exercised a great influence through his conceptions of the basic role of the clinical psychologist as a fundamental research worker and his rejection of the role of pseudopsychiatrist (diagnostically and therapeutically) so frequently adopted by the clinical psychologist (Eysenck,

1949, 1950). Third, it quickly became clear that the kind of questions put by the psychiatrist to the clinical psychologist reflected the ignorance on the part of the psychiatrist of the special skills and training of the clinical psychologist. It was obvious that one of the primary functions that would have to be rethought by the clinical psychologist related to the formulating of meaningful questions in relation to the patient as he presented himself and that these questions might bear little or no relationship to the kind of questions (usually differential diagnostic ones) put by the psychiatrist, thinking in his own frame of reference and naturally ignorant of *how* the clinical psychologist might be of assistance in terms of his special training and skills. All of these forces were reinforced by a close examination at this time of the validity and reliability of the psychodynamic tests in relation to the aims with which they were used— an examination that revealed with painful clarity their empirical inadequacy and their lack of adequate theoretical rationale. The battery approach (i.e., the administration of a large selection of cognitive and projective tests to *every* patient) was early rejected as a hopelessly wasteful, hit-or-miss procedure which consumed countless man-hours of administration, scoring, and interpretation to very little purpose or result.

All of these influences then tended to lead to the rejection of the traditional approach in clinical psychology. The fourth and most significant factor, however, lay in the brilliant and neglected work of M.B. Shapiro,[18] the head of the Clinical-Teaching Section. Over a period of several years, Shapiro, in a long series of staff seminars, worked out in great detail a new approach to clinical psychological testing which was to have a most profound influence. Some of the flavor of this work (but by no means all) may be found in a long series of publications by Shapiro (Shapiro, 1951, 1961a, 1961b, 1963, 1966; Shapiro, Marks and Fox, 1963; Shapiro and Nelson, 1955; Shapiro and Ravenette, 1959).

In one of his earliest papers, Shapiro (1951) set out clearly the reasons for his dissatisfaction with current clinical psychological procedures, especially those deriving from the "battery" approach of Schaefer. His own views are equally clearly represented in the following

---

[17] The present author had the privilege of being first a student, then a staff member in the clinical teaching section of the Psychology Department from 1951–1957.

[18] Unfortunately, no account of Shapiro's work is to be found in the recent volume by Eysenck and Rachman (1965). Hence the attention paid here to Shapiro's work.

quotation from this paper, describing the procedures he feels should be followed in investigating the single case.

"First of all, the features presented by the patient, his life history and medical history and test results are integrated. In this the discussion between the psychiatrist, social worker and psychologist play an important part. As a result certain formulated problems emerge.

The next move is to advance hypotheses which will explain them. This is in essence what the clinician does, though at times he will not be inclined to admit it.

The third step the clinician takes is to ask himself what effect the truth of each of his hypotheses will have on the treatment and disposal of the patient. If any of these hypotheses are not likely to have an effect on treatment and disposal, he will be disinclined to test them.

Finally, the clinician has to decide how he is going to test the various hypotheses" (Shapiro, 1951, p. 755).

The most important points to note so far are that the clinical psychologist is responsible for formulating his own meaningful hypotheses about a particular patient (utilizing all available knowledge that appears to be pertinent), that he must assess the relevance of what he is proposing to do in relation to treatment and disposal of the patient, and that his hypotheses and procedures may be quite different from those of direct interest to the psychiatrist. Furthermore, he will not necessarily be at all interested in arriving at or considering a formal diagnosis of the patient.

More importantly, Shapiro, in this paper, goes on to suggest that an inevitable corollary of his line of thinking is that the clinical psychologist must be an experimental psychologist, though not of the conventional kind. In testing hypotheses about an individual patient, he must, in effect, treat the patient as the object of an experimental investigation. Shapiro goes on to point out carefully the differences between his approach and that of, for example, Schaeffer, even though, in both cases, hypotheses are being formulated. Shapiro's approach was unique at this time in that it argued that it was not always (or even usually) necessary to derive one's hypotheses about a patient's disorder from the results of the application of a battery of tests. In many instances, the patient would serve as his own control, or it might be necessary to collect special standardization data in order to test a hypothesis. A classic example of this is to be found in the work of Bartlet and Shapiro (1956) dealing with a failure to acquire the skill of reading in a young child. This study involved a careful series of experimental analyses relating to the various modalities involved in learning to read, which required the collection of special standardization data on specially constructed tests.[19]

The significance of this approach lay in subsequent developments. If the experimental method, involving as strict objectivity as possible, and the formulation of meaningful questions derived from knowledge of general psychology could be applied to the elucidation of the basic causal factors underlying abnormalities of function manifested by a single case, then it very soon became obvious that the same techniques could be applied to the *treatment* of the disorder. In other words, by drawing on empirical and theoretical general psychology, it should be possible to carry out controlled, laboratory-type experiments in an effort to manipulate systematically *and change* the abnormal behavior. Early examples of the application of this approach are to be found in studies by Jones (1956), Meyer (1957), and Yates (1958b).

We have paid a good deal of attention to the work of Shapiro because his basic contribution has been largely ignored, possibly because Shapiro himself has not as actively pursued the therapeutic approach as might have been expected. There is no doubt whatever, however, that behavior therapy in England was developed in the Clinical-Teaching Section of the Psychology Department at the Maudsley Hospital under the direct inspiration of Shapiro. It is more than time that his fundamental contribution received due recognition.

6. Development of Behavior Therapy in South Africa

At about the same time that behavior therapy was getting under way in England, a parallel

---

[19] The reader will find much to criticize in this paper (an investigation which was commenced by the present writer and continued by Bartlet). It should be remembered, however, that this was one of the earliest studies of its kind. Other early investigations of this kind are described in Jones (1960). Shapiro's general approach has also been utilized by Hutt and Coxon (1965), Ravenette and Hersov (1963), and Beech (1959).

development was proceeding in South Africa, though there were important differences in the two approaches. Wolpe's rejection of the psychoanalytic theory and technique culminated in the appearance of his book on psycho-therapy by reciprocal inhibition (Wolpe, 1958), certainly the single most influential publication in the field to date. It should be noted, however, that at this stage Wolpe's approach was quite different from that of the English behavior therapists, being more akin to the work of Dollard and Miller (1950). For, like Dollard and Miller, Wolpe's application of the reciprocal inhibition principle in the clinical situation was just that—clinical in nature. Like Dollard and Miller, Wolpe formulated a general (neuro-physiological) theory and then attempted to apply it clinically. But he did not, at this time, carry out controlled experimental investigations of the single case in the sense advocated by Shapiro. This comment is not in any way intended to belittle the major contribution made by Wolpe during this period. Unfortunately, however, as we shall see in a later chapter, some critics (e.g., Breger and McGaugh, 1965) have referred to an "Eysenck-Wolpe school" as if it were representative of one "type" of behavior therapy. But this is to misrepresent the facts completely. Behavior therapy in England developed essentially out of the work of Shapiro on the experimental investigation of the single case and while some of the early studies at the Maudsley (e.g., Meyer, 1957) show the influence of Wolpe's work, the majority do not. Sub-sequently, of course, both movements were to influence each other greatly.

7. Development of Behavior Therapy in America

During the same period also, the work of Skinner gave rise to the application of behavior modification techniques (as they are often called), based on operant conditioning, to abnormalities of behavior. It is interesting to note that the term "behavior therapy" appears to have been used first by Lindsley (1954).[20] Since the use of operant conditioning techniques involved essentially the experimental study of the single case, it would appear that there was no fundamental difference between the approach of Skinner and his colleagues in America and of

Shapiro and his colleagues in England. There were, in fact, two very important differences at this time. First, nearly all of the work of the Americans was carried out on psychotic patients, whereas the English behavior therapists con-centrated mostly on neurotic patients and non-neurotic (but not psychotic) patients with behavior abnormalities (this difference has now disappeared[21]). Second, the English behavior therapists were strongly theory oriented and were willing to make use of hypothetical con-structs, whereas the American behavior thera-pists were not theory oriented, in line with the antitheoretical bias of Skinner.

Mention should also be made here of the monumental work of Voegtlin and his col-leagues during the early 1940's in the con-ditioned reflex treatment of alcoholism. This work will be considered in detail in a later chapter, but it may be remarked here that Voegtlin's contribution has never received adequate recognition and has been criticized by people who appear to have relied mainly on secondary sources.

8. Definition of Behavior Therapy

The definition of behavior therapy which we shall adopt follows directly from the con-siderations discussed earlier in this chapter.

Behavior therapy is the attempt to utilize systematically that body of empirical and theoretical knowledge which has resulted from the application of the experimental method in psychology and its closely related disciplines (physiology and neurophysiology) in order to explain the genesis and maintenance of abnormal patterns of behavior; and to apply that knowledge to the treatment or prevention of those abnormalities by means of controlled experimental studies of the single case, both descriptive and remedial.

Several important points (some of which will be dealt with at greater length in later sections of this book) should be noted about this definition. First, no mention is made of "learn-ing theory" or, indeed, of any theory in the definition. This is in contrast with Eysenck's definition of behavior therapy as 'the attempt to alter human behavior and emotion in a bene-ficial manner according to the laws of modern

---

[20] Since Lindsley does not appear to have used the term subsequently, Lazarus may be correctly credited with introducing the term in 1958.

[21] Eysenck's first book of readings (Eysenck, 1960b) did not contain any studies making use of operant conditioning techniques, though many such papers were already available.

learning theory" (Eysenck, 1964c, p. 1). Second, the stress on the experimental investigation of the single case is intended to stress what is regarded as the fundamental distinguishing characteristic of behavior therapy, the one aspect which clearly and unequivocally distinguishes it from other therapeutic endeavors. This stress is in no way intended to deny that there is much more to behavior therapy than the experimental investigation of the single case. This activity may be regarded as the apex of a pyramid stretching from large-scale empirical studies of the dimensions of personality, through smaller-scale group studies of abnormal behavior, to the treatment of the individual patient. But the behavior therapist's unique contribution lies in what he does in the situation involving an individual patient presenting an abnormality of behavior. It is here that behavior *therapy* is defined as the application of the experimental method to the presenting problem.

REFERENCES

Ackner, B., Harris, A., & Oldham, A.J. Insulin treatment of schizophrenia. *Lancet*, 1957, **1**, 607–611.

Ash, P. The reliability of psychiatric diagnosis. *J. abnorm. soc. Psychol.*, 1949, **44**, 272–276.

Astin, A.W. The functional autonomy of psychotherapy. *Amer. Psychol.*, 1961, **16**, 75–78.

Ausubel, D.P. Relationships between psychology and psychiatry: the hidden issues. *Amer. Psychol.*, 1956, **11**, 99–105.

Ausubel, D.P. Personality disorder *is* disease. *Amer. Psychol.*, 1961, **16**, 69–74.

Bartlet, D. & Shapiro, M.B. Investigation and treatment of a reading disability in a dull child with severe psychiatric disturbance. *Brit. J. educ. Psychol.*, 1956, **26**, 180–190.

Beech, H.R. An experimental investigation of sexual symbolism in anorexia nervosa employing a subliminal stimulation technique; preliminary report. *Psychosom. Med.*, 1959, **21**, 277–280.

Bekhterev, V.M. Die Anwendung der Methode der motorischen Assoziations-reflexe zur Aufdeckung der Simulation. *Zeit. ges. Neurol. Psychiat.*, 1912, **13**, 183–191.

Bekhterev, V.M. Die Perversitäten und Inversitäten vom Standpunkt der Reflexologie. *Arch. Psychiat. Nervenkr.*, 1923, **68**, 100–213 (a).

Bekhterev, V.M. Die Krankheiten der Persönlichkeit vom Standpunkt der Reflexologie. *Zeit. ges. Neurol. Psychiat.*, 1923, **80**, 265–309 (b).

Bekhterev, V.M. *General principles of human reflexology.* New York: Internat. Univer. Press, 1932.

Bourne, H. The insulin myth. *Lancet*, 1953, **2**, 964–968.

Bourne, H. Insulin coma in decline. *Amer. J. Psychiat.*, 1958, **114**, 1015–1017.

Braun, J.R. (ed.). *Clinical psychology in transition: a selection of articles from the American Psychologist.* Cleveland: Howard Allen, 1961.

Breger, L. & McGaugh, J.L. Critique and reformulation of "learning-theory" approaches to psychotherapy and neurosis. *Psychol. Bull.*, 1965, **63**, 338–358.

Bregman, E.O. An attempt to modify the emotional attitudes of infants by the conditioned response technique. *J. genet. Psychol.*, 1934, **45**, 169–198.

Burnham, W.H. Mental hygiene and the conditioned reflex. *Ped. Sem.*, 1917, **24**, 449–488.

Burnham, W.H. *The normal mind.* New York: Appleton, 1924.

Cook, S.W. The production of "experimental neurosis" in the white rat. *Psychosom. Med.*, 1939, **1**, 293–308.

Diamond, S., Balvin, R.S., & Diamond, F.R. *Inhibition and choice.* New York: Harper and Row, 1963.

Dollard, J. & Miller, N.E. *Personality and psychotherapy.* New York: McGraw-Hill, 1950.

Dunlap, K. *Habits: their making and unmaking.* New York: Liveright, 1932.

English, H.B. Three cases of the "conditioned fear response." *J. abnorm. soc. Psychol.*, 1929, **24**, 221–225.

Eysenck, H.J. *Dimensions of personality.* London: Routledge and Kegan Paul, 1947.

Eysenck, H.J. Training in clinical psychology: an English point of view. *Amer. Psychol.*, 1949, **4**, 173–176.

Eysenck, H.J. Function and training of the clinical psychologist. *J. ment. Sci.*, 1950, **96,** 710–725.

Eysenck, H.J. *The scientific study of personality*. London: Routledge and Kegan Paul, 1952 (a).

Eysenck, H.J. The effects of psychotherapy: an evaluation. *J. consult. Psychol.*, 1952, **16,** 319–324 (b).

Eysenck, H.J. *The structure of human personality*. London: Methuen, 1953.

Eysenck, H.J. Further comments on "Relations with psychiatry." *Amer. Psychol.*, 1954, **9,** 157–158.

Eysenck, H.J. The effects of psychotherapy. In Eysenck, H.J. (ed.). *Handbook of abnormal psychology*. London: Pitman, 1960 (a).

Eysenck, H.J. *Behavior therapy and the neuroses*. London: Pergamon, 1960 (b).

Eysenck, H.J. The outcome problem in psychotherapy: a reply. *Psychotherapy*, 1964, **1,** 97–100 (a).

Eysenck, H.J. The effects of psychotherapy. *Internat. J. Psychiat.*, 1964, **1,** 99–144 (b).

Eysenck, H.J. The nature of behavior therapy. In Eysenck, H.J. (ed.). *Experiments in behavior therapy*. London: Pergamon, 1964, pp. 1–15 (c).

Eysenck, H.J. & Rachman, S. *The causes and cures of neurosis*. London: Routledge and Kegan Paul, 1965.

Foulds, G.A. The reliability of psychiatric, and the validity of psychological, diagnoses. *J. ment. Sci.*, 1955, **101,** 851–862.

Glover, E. Critical notice of Wolpe's "*Psychotherapy by reciprocal inhibition.*" *Brit. J. med. Psychol.*, 1959, **32,** 68–74

Gluck, M.R., Tanner, M.M., Sullivan, D.F., & Erickson, P.A. Follow-up evaluation of 55 child guidance cases. *Behav. Res. Ther.*, 1964, **2,** 131–134.

Goldfarb, A. Reliability of diagnostic judgments made by psychologists. *J. clin. Psychol.*, 1959, **15,** 392–396.

Harris, H. Anxiety: its nature and treatment. *J. ment. Sci.*, 1934, **80,** 482–512 and 705–715.

Hoch, E.L. & Darley, J.G. A case at law. *Amer. Psychol.*, 1962, **17,** 623–654.

Hollingworth, H.L. *Abnormal psychology*. New York: Ronald, 1930.

Holmes, F.B. An experimental investigation of a method of overcoming children's fears. *Child Developm.*, 1936, **7,** 6–30.

Holt, R.R. Diagnostic testing: present status and future prospects. *J. nerv. ment. Dis.*, 1967, **144,** 444–465.

Hull, C.L. *Principles of behavior*. New York: Appleton-Century-Crofts, 1943.

Hull, C.L. *A behavior system*. New Haven: Yale Univer. Press, 1952.

Hutt, C. & Coxon, M.W. Systematic observation in clinical psychology. *Arch. gen. Psychiat.*, 1965, **12,** 374–378.

Ichok, G. Les réflexes conditionnels et le traitement de l'alcoolique. *Progr. med., Paris*, 1934, **2,** 1742–1745.

Ivanov-Smolensky, A.G. Uber die bedingten Reflexe in der depressiven Phase der manisch-depressiven Irreseins. *Mschr. Psychiat. Neurol.*, 1925, **58,** 376–388.

Ivanov-Smolensky, A.G. Etudes expérimentales sur les enfants et les aliénés selon la méthode des réflexes conditionnels. *Ann. med.-Psychol.*, 1927, **12,** 140–150 (a).

Ivanov-Smolensky, A.G. Neurotic behavior and the teaching of conditioned reflexes. *Amer. J. Psychiat.*, 1927, **84,** 483–488 (b).

Ivanov-Smolensky, A.G. On the methods of examining the conditioned food reflexes in children and in mental disorders. *Brain*, 1927, **50,** 138–141 (c).

Ivanov-Smolensky, A.G. The pathology of conditioned reflexes and the so-called psychogenic depression. *J. nerv. ment. Dis.*, 1928, **67,** 346–350.

Jones, H.E. The conditioning of overt emotional responses. *J. educ. Psychol.*, 1931, **22,** 127–130.

Jones, H.G. The application of conditioning and learning techniques to the treatment of a psychiatric patient. *J. abnorm. soc. Psychol.*, 1956, **52,** 414–420.

Jones, H.G. Applied abnormal psychology: the experimental approach. In Eysenck, H.J. (ed.). *Handbook of abnormal psychology*. London: Pitman, 1960, pp. 764–781.

Jones, M.C. The elimination of children's fears. *J. exp. Psychol.*, 1924, **7**, 383–390 (a).

Jones, M.C. A laboratory study of fear: the case of Peter. *J. genet. Psychol.*, 1924, **31**, 308–315 (b).

Kostyleff, N. L'inversion sexuelle expliquée par la réflexologie. *Psychol. et Vie.*, 1927, **1**, 8–12.

Krasnogorski, N.I. The conditioned reflexes and children's neuroses. *Amer. J. Dis. Child.*, 1925, **30**, 753–768.

Krasnogorski, N.I. Psychology and psychopathology in childhood as a branch of pediatric investigation. *Acta pediatr. Stockh.*, 1930, **11**, 481–502.

Krasnogorski, N.I. Bedingte und unbedingte Reflexe im Kindesalter und ihre Bedeutung für die Klinik. *Ergebn. inn. Med. Kinderheilk.*, 1931, **39**, 613–730.

Krasnogorski, N.I. Die neue Behandlung der Enuresis nocturna. *Mschr. Kinderheilk.*, 1933, **57**, 252–254 (a).

Krasnogorski, N.I. Physiology of cerebral activity in children as a new subject of pediatric investigation. *Amer. J. Dis. Child.*, 1933, **46**, 473–494 (b).

Kreitman, N. The reliability of psychiatric diagnosis. *J. ment. Sci.*, 1961, **107**, 876–886.

Kreitman, N., Sainsbury, P., Morrissey, J., Towers, J., & Scrivenor, J. The reliability of psychiatric assessment: an analysis. *J. ment. Sci.*, 1961, **107**, 887–908.

L'Abate, L. *Principles of clinical psychology.* New York: Grune and Stratton, 1964.

Lesse, S. Placebo reactions and spontaneous rhythms in psychotherapy. *Arch. gen. Psychiat.*, 1964, **10**, 497–505.

Levin, M. Narcolepsy and the machine age: the recent increase in the incidence of narcolepsy. *J. Neurol. Psychopathol.*, 1934, **15**, 60–64.

Levitt, E.E. Results of psychotherapy with children: an evaluation. *J. consult. Psychol.*, 1957, **21**, 189–196.

Levitt, E.E. Psychotherapy with children: a further evaluation. *Behav. Res. Ther.*, 1963, **1**, 45–51.

Liberman, R. An analysis of the placebo phenomenon. *J. chron. Dis.*, 1962, **15**, 761–783.

Liddell, H.S. The experimental neurosis and the problem of mental disorder. *Amer. J. Psychiat.*, 1938, **94**, 1035–1043.

Lindsley, O.R. *Studies in behavior therapy: status report III.* Waltham, Mass.: Metropolitan State Hosp., 1954.

Lorr, M., McNair, D.M., & Klett, C.J. *Syndromes of psychosis.* London: Pergamon, 1964.

Maier, N.R.F. *Studies of abnormal behavior in the rat.* New York: Harper, 1939.

Marinesco, G. Contribution a l'étude des troubles sensitifs hystériques et le role des réflexes conditionnels dans la physiopathologie de l'hystérie. *Rev. neurol.*, 1937, **68**, 585–600.

Marinesco, G. & Kreindler, A. *Des réflexes conditionnels, études de physiologie normale et pathologique.* Paris: Alcan, 1935.

Masserman, J.H. *Behavior and neurosis.* Chicago: Univer. of Chicago Press, 1943.

Mateer, F. *Child behavior: a critical and experimental study of young children by the method of conditioned reflexes.* Boston: Badger, 1917.

Max, L.W. Breaking up a homosexual fixation by the conditioned reaction technique: a case study. *Psychol. Bull.*, 1935, **32**, 734.

Mehlman, B. The reliability of psychiatric diagnosis. *J. abnorm. soc. Psychol.*, 1952, **47**, 577–578.

Meignant, P. Réflexes conditionnels et psycho-pathologie: quelques remarques concernant les perversions et les anomalies sexuelles. *Gaz. med. Fr.*, 1935, 327–332.

Meyer, V. The treatment of two phobic patients on the basis of learning principles. *J. abnorm. soc. Psychol.*, 1957, **55**, 261–266.

Mischel, W. *Personality and assessment.* New York: Wiley, 1968.

Moore, W.E. A conditioned reflex study of stuttering. *J. Speech Dis.*, 1938, **3**, 163–183.

Morgan, J.J.B. & Witmer, F.J. The treatment of enuresis by the conditioned reaction technique. *J. genet. Psychol.*, 1939, **55**, 59–65.

Morhardt, P.E. Les réflexes conditionells dans les névroses et dans les états allergiques. *Vie med.*, 1930, **11**, 825–828.

Moss, F.A. Note on building likes and dislikes in children. *J. exp. Psychol.*, 1924, **7**, 475–478.

Mowrer, O.H. *Learning theory and personality dynamics.* New York: Ronald, 1950.

Mowrer, O.H. & Mowrer, W.A. Enuresis: a method for its study and treatment. *Amer. J. Orthopsychiat.*, 1938, **8**, 436–447.

Overall, J.E. & Hollister, L.E. Computer procedures for psychiatric classification. *J. Amer. med. Assoc.*, 1964, **187**, 583–588.

Overall, J.E. & Hollister, L.E. Studies of quantitative approaches to psychiatric classification. In Katz, M.M., Cole, J.O., & Barton, W. (eds.). *The role and methodology of classification in psychiatry and psychopathology.* Washington, D.C. Government Printing Office, 1968.

Pavlov, I.P. *Conditioned reflexes* (trans. by G.V. Anrep). London: Oxford Univer. Press, 1927.

Pavlov, I.P. *Lectures on conditioned reflexes* (trans. by W.H. Gantt). New York: Internat. Univer. Press, 1928.

Pavlov, I.P. Neuroses in man and animals. *J. Amer. Med. Assoc.*, 1932, **99**, 1012–1013.

Pavlov, I.P. Essai d'une interprétation physiologique de l'hytérie. *Encéphale.* 1933, **28**, 285–293.

Pavlov, I.P. An attempt at a physiological interpretation of obsessional neurosis and paranoia. *J. ment. Sci.*, 1934, **80**, 187–197.

Pavlov, I.P. *Conditioned reflexes and psychiatry* (trans. by W.H. Gantt). New York: Internat. Univer. Press, 1941.

Pronko, N.H., Sitterly, R., & Berg, K. Twenty years of shock therapy in America, 1937–1956: an annotated bibliography. *Genet. Psychol. Monogr.*, 1960, **62**, 233–329.

Rapaport, D., Gill, M., & Schafer, R. *Diagnostic psychological testing* (2 vols.). Chicago: Year Book Publ., 1946.

Raush, H.L. Comment on Eysenck's "Further comment on 'relations with psychiatry'." *Amer. Psychol.*, 1954, **9**, 588–589.

Ravenette, A.T. & Hersov, L.A. Speed of function and educational retardation: the psychological and psychiatric investigation of an individual case. *J. child Psychol. Psychiat.*, 1963, **4**, 17–28.

Rosenthal, D. & Frank, J.D. Psychotherapy and the placebo effect. *Psychol. Bull.*, 1956, **53**, 294–302.

Rosenzweig, S. A transvaluation of psychotherapy: a reply to Hans Eysenck. *J. abnorm. soc. Psychol.*, 1954, **49**, 298–304.

Rouquier, A. & Michel, J. Anorexie pithiatique élective. *Encéphale*, 1934, **29**, 277–283.

Rubenstein, C. The treatment of morphine addiction in tuberculosis by Pavlov's conditioning method. *Amer. Rev. Tubercul.*, 1931, **24**, 682–685.

Schmidt, H.O. & Fonda, C.P. The reliability of psychiatric diagnosis: a new look. *J. abnorm. soc. Psychol.*, 1956, **52**, 262–267.

Sears, R.R. & Cohen, L.H. Hysterical anesthesia, analgesia, and astereognosis. *Arch. Neurol. Psychiat.*, 1933, **29**, 260–271.

Shapiro, A.K. The placebo effect in the history of medical treatment (implications for psychiatry). *Amer. J. Psychiat.*, 1959, **116**, 298–304.

Shapiro, A.K. A contribution to a history of the placebo effect. *Behav. Sci.*, 1960, **5**, 109–135 (a).

Shapiro, A.K. Attitudes towards the use of placebos in treatment. *J. nerv. ment. Dis.*, 1960, **130**, 200–211 (b).

Shapiro, A.K. A historic and heuristic definition of the placebo. *Psychiatry*, 1964, **27**, 52–58.

Shapiro, M.B. An experimental approach to diagnostic psychological testing. *J. ment. Sci.*, 1951, **97**, 748–764.

Shapiro, M.B. A method of measuring psychological changes specific to the individual psychiatric patient. *Brit. J. med. Psychol.*, 1961, **34**, 151–155 (a).

Shapiro, M.B. The single case in fundamental clinical psychological research. *Brit. J. med. Psychol.*, 1961, **34**, 255–262 (b).

Shapiro, M.B. Clinical approach to fundamental research with special reference to the study of the single patient. In P. Sainsbury & N. Kreitman (eds.). *Methods of psychiatric research*. London: Oxford U. Press, 1963 pp. 123–149.

Shapiro, M.B. The single case in clinical-psychological research. *J. gen. Psychol.*, 1966, **74**, 3–23.

Shapiro, M.B., Marks, I.M., & Fox, B. A therapeutic experiment on phobic and affective symptoms in an individual psychiatric patient. *Brit. J. soc. clin. Psychol.*, 1963, **2**, 81–93.

Shapiro, M.B. & Nelson, E.H. An investigation of an abnormality of cognitive functioning in a co-operative young psychotic: an example of the application of experimental method to the single case. *J. clin. Psychol.*, 1955, **11**, 344–351.

Shapiro, M.B. & Ravenette, A.T. A preliminary experiment of paranoid delusions. *J. ment. Sci.*, 1959, **105**, 295–312.

Shoben, E.J. A learning-theory interpretation of psychotherapy. *Harvard Educ. Rev.*, 1948, **18**, 129–145.

Shoben, E.J. Psychotherapy as a problem in learning theory. *Psychol. Bull.*, 1949, **46**, 366–392.

Smith, W.G. A model for psychiatric diagnosis. *Arch. gen. Psychiat.*, 1966, **14**, 521–529.

Steinbook, R.M., Jones, M.B., & Ainslie, J.D. Suggestibility and the placebo response. *J. nerv. ment. Dis.*, 1965, **140**, 87–91.

Sundberg, N.D. & Tyler, L.E. *Clinical psychology*. New York: Appleton-Century-Crofts, 1962.

Symonds, P.M. *Adolescent fantasy*. New York: Columbia Univer. Press, 1949.

Szasz, T. The myth of mental illness. *Amer. Psychol.*, 1960, **15**, 113–118.

Szasz, T. The uses of naming and the origin of the myth of mental illness. *Amer. Psychol.*, 1961, **16**, 59–65 (a).

Szasz, T.S. *The myth of mental illness*. New York: Hoeber, 1961 (b)

Tinel, J. Les réflexes conditionnels dans les états névropathiques. *Encéphale*, 1930, **25**, 65–81.

Ullmann, L.P. & Krasner, L. Introduction: What is behavior modification? In Ullmann, L.P. & Krasner, L. (eds.). *Case studies in behavior modification*. New York: Holt, 1965, pp. 1–63).

Watson, G. Is mental illness mental? *J. Psychol.*, 1956, **41**, 323–334.

Watson, G. Differences in intermediary metabolism in mental illness. *Psychol. Rep.*, 1965, **17**, 563–582.

Watson, J.B. Behaviorism and the concept of mental disease. *J. Philos. Psychol. Scient. Meth.*, 1916, **13**, 587–597.

Watson, J.B. & Rayner, R. Conditioned emotional reactions. *J. exp. Psychol.*, 1920, **3**, 1–14.

Watson, R.I. *The clinical method in psychology*. New York: Harper and Row, 1951.

White, R.W. *The abnormal personality* (3rd ed.). New York: Ronald, 1964.

Wittson, C.L., Hunt, W.L., & Stevenson, I. A follow-up study of neuropsychiatric screening. *J. abnorm. soc. Psychol.*, 1946, **41**, 79–82.

Wolpe, J. *Psychotherapy by reciprocal inhibition*. Stanford: Stanford Univer. Press, 1958.

Wolpe, J. & Rachman, S. Psychoanalytic "evidence": a critique based on Freud's case of Little Hans. *J. nerv. ment. Dis.*, 1960, **130**, 135–148.

Woolley, D.W. *The biochemical bases of psychoses*. New York: Wiley, 1962.

Yates, A.J. The validity of some psychological tests of brain damage. *Psychol. Bull.*, 1954, **51**, 359–379.

Yates, A.J. The use of vocabulary in the measurement of intellectual deterioration— a review. *J. ment. Sci.*, 1956, **102**, 409–440.

Yates, A.J. Symptoms and symptom substitution. *Psychol. Rev.*, 1958, **65**, 371–374 (a).

Yates, A.J. The application of learning theory to the treatment of tics. *J. abnorm. soc. Psychol.*, 1958, **56**, 175–182 (b).

Yates, A.J. Psychological deficit. *Ann. Rev. Psychol.*, 1966, **17**, 111–144.

Zigler, E. & Phillips, L. Psychiatric diagnosis and symptomatology. *J. abnorm. soc. Psychol.*, 1961, **63**, 69–75.

Zubin, J. Classification of the behavior disorders. *Ann. Rev. Psychol.*, 1967, **18**, 373–406.

Chapter 2

Empirical and Theoretical Foundations of Behavior Therapy

IT WAS pointed out in the previous chapter that, in principle, the behavior therapist should utilize, as appropriate, any part of the empirical and theoretical body of knowledge of psychology in formulating hypotheses about abnormalities of behavior and devising experimental treatment programs. In one sense, therefore, the present chapter is unnecessary and must be unsatisfactory. It would be reasonable simply to request the prospective behavior therapist to familiarize himself with the body of knowledge and refer him to the appropriate textbooks. His success both as a working behavior therapist and in advancing behavior therapy as a rational approach to the treatment of disorders of behavior will then depend on his knowledge of experimental and theoretical psychology and on his ingenuity and ability to relate particular aspects of that body of knowledge to particular problems. In a very real sense, behavior therapy at the present time is both a science and an art in that advancement in devising rational therapeutic procedures for particular problems (many of which will not have been investigated previously by behavior therapists) will depend on individual insightfulness (if the term may be permitted) which produces correlations between experimental procedures, empirical knowledge, and theoretical formulations where none existed before.[1]

This simple solution of the problem by, in effect, eliminating it has been rejected on a number of grounds. First, the material contained in the remainder of this book may well be of interest to nonpsychologists working in the field of abnormal behavior (psychiatrists, medical practitioners, social workers, remedial educationists, and occupational therapists, to name but a few) who would like to know something of the empirical and theoretical background of behavior therapy, but who simply do not have the time to spend becoming trained psychologists. Second, behavior therapists themselves have thus far made only very limited use of the body of psychological knowledge and it is of some interest to note which areas of psychology have been used by behavior therapists.

However, a decision to present some account of the empirical and theoretical basis of behavior therapy presents serious problems. If the account is not to become inordinately long, it must necessarily be highly selective and synoptic and such an account may give a very misleading impression. Nevertheless, the endeavour will be made, subject to a number of important qualifications.

What follows in this chapter is, therefore, really a series of snapshots of certain areas of empirical and theoretical psychology. An attempt has been made to provide a reasonably coherent sequential account, with highlights being chosen for emphasis where these aspects

---

[1] As an example, the present author was recently faced with a behavioral problem (compulsive fire-setting) which behavior therapists thus far do not appear to have dealt with.

have, in fact, been utilized by behavior therapists. Some of the material and some of the concepts would be regarded as outdated by experimental psychologists. However, the important role which they have played in the development of behavior therapy as an experimental approach to disorders of behavior is justification for their inclusion. In the last chapter of this book, an attempt will be made to update this material. Up to the present time, behavior therapists have deliberately made use of the relatively simpler aspects of experimental psychology and have (with notable exceptions) tended to deal with relatively noncomplex disorders of behavior on the grounds that, if rational methods of treatment based on reasonable theories of behavior cannot be developed for these kinds of disorders, it is futile to expect success with more complex disorders. This may or may not be a valid assumption, but it is one which has been widely made by behavior therapists. As we shall see in the final chapter, however, behavior therapists are now moving into the use of more complex theories and procedures and some of the developments which can be expected in the near future will be discussed. The indulgence of the more experimentally sophisticated reader in relation to this chapter is therefore requested, since it is primarily directed at the non-experimental general reader who is interested in behavior therapy.

The first part of the chapter will deal with some empirical and theoretical aspects of conditioning and learning which are of special significance for behavior therapy. Then some account will be given of two approaches to the understanding particularly of sequential (skilled) behavior, namely, the feedback control of skilled behavior and the conceptualization of the human organism as an information-processing organism.

I. CONDITIONING AND LEARNING

In this section, we shall mention briefly the behavioral language of conditioning and learning; the theoretical language we propose to use; and the important distinction between learning and performance.

1. INTRODUCTION: THE BASIC LANGUAGE

(a) THE BEHAVIORAL LANGUAGE. At the direct observational level, psychologists, of course, use the terms *stimulus* and *response*, though the problem of arriving at agreed definitions of these terms remains to be solved.[2] Thus, a distinction is often made between the readily definable *physical stimulus* and the less readily definable *effective stimulus* (i.e., that part of the physical stimulus presented by the experimenter to which the subject actually attends). Within the framework of conditioning experiments, the four terms usually used are now widely familiar to the layman, namely, the *unconditioned stimulus* (US); the *conditioned* (or, more properly, *conditional*) *stimulus* (CS); the *unconditioned response* (UR or UCR); and the *conditioned response* (CR). The US is defined as any stimulus which produces a response (UR) which is unlearned; whereas the CS is defined as any stimulus which, by virtue of its contiguous presentation with a US subsequently evokes a response (CR) which is not naturally evoked by it. It is now generally agreed that the CR and UR are only rarely identical in form, the CR more frequently representing only a fraction of the UR or, indeed, sometimes being completely different from the UR and representing an anticipatory response.

(b) THE THEORETICAL LANGUAGE. For our purposes, we propose in this chapter to adopt the theoretical framework utilized by Hull (1943). Hull identified four basic theoretical constructs which were involved in conditioning[3]: habit strength (sH_R); drive (D); reactive inhibition (I_R); and conditioned inhibition (sI_R), which he linked in the following two fundamental equations:

$$sE_R = (sH_R \times D) \tag{1}$$
$$s\bar{E}_R = (sE_R) - (I_R + sI_R) \tag{2}$$

The theoretical construct, sE_R, *reaction potential*, may be termed the *excitatory strength* of the capacity for responding and is a function of habit strength interacting multiplicatively with drive strength. The theoretical construct, $s\bar{E}_R$, *effective reaction potential*, represents the actual capacity of the organism to respond when not only the excitatory but also the inhibitory forces are taken into account, the latter being represented by the additive strength of reactive and conditioned inhibition. In other words, habit strength (sH_R) refers to the unobservable theoretical strength of association between neural representations of stimulus and

---

[2] For clear discussions of the problems involved in relation to these terms, see Gibson (1960) and Spence (1956).

[3] Hull utilized other theoretical constructs which will be ignored for present purposes.

response and is present whether the organism is actually responding or not. Thus, the capacity for bicycle riding is present in an organism which has acquired the skill, whether that skill is being exercised or not. The drive (D) term is self-explanatory at this level of discourse—here, it may merely be noted that Hull assumed that all drives summate to produce momentary drive strength. Reactive inhibition (I_R) is a theoretical construct which refers to the generation by each response made of states which militate against repetition of the response until the reactive inhibition has dissipated—it is clearly a protective mechanism. Hull tended to think of it in peripheral terms, but it is now generally accepted that the construct refers to events of central origin. Should reactive inhibition accumulate (as it is assumed to do under certain conditions to be described below) the organism will eventually stop responding. During the ensuing involuntary rest period, the reactive inhibition will dissipate and it is assumed that this dissipation will give rise to an increment of conditioned inhibition (sI_R). Conditioned inhibition may be regarded as a kind of negative habit strength or, alternatively, as a habit strength that is incompatible with sH_R. The term inhibition is an unfortunate one, since inhibition is a *positive* process, not merely the absence of responding.[4]

The excitatory ($sH_R \times D$) and inhibitory ($I_R + sI_R$) factors interact together in Hull's system to produce actual performance capacity, i.e., the strength with which a particular response can be performed at a particular moment ($s\bar{E}_R$).

(c) THE LEARNING/PERFORMANCE DISTINCTION. Several famous controversies, especially that over the alleged phenomenon of latent learning, have served to highlight the important distinction between learning and performance. We may note that learning may be defined as the growth of habit strength (sH_R), which is assumed to increase over trials as a negatively accelerated growth curve; and that, usually, *all so-called curves of learning are in fact curves of performance*. Under most conditions, in fact, the performance curve will not accurately represent the learning curve, since it will be a confounded measure of the interacting effects of

rate of growth of habit strength, level of drive, and inhibitory factors—in other words, the curve of performance will represent the end result of the interaction of the excitatory and inhibitory forces in Hull's basic equation. Under very special circumstances, however, the performance curve may coincide with the curve of learning (sH_R), though such conditions are only rarely approximated.[5] The distinction between learning and performance is important in relation to abnormal psychology because absence of a particular response on a particular occasion does not mean that the response has been eliminated in the sense that it cannot be reactivated under appropriate conditions. The situation is not, in other words, analogous to cutting off an arm and throwing it away; rather, it is analogous to the fact that the arm cannot both be flexed and extended simultaneously, since the responses are antagonistic.

2. BASIC PARAMETERS OF CONDITIONING AND LEARNING[6]

As Spence (1956) has pointed out, in studying conditioning and learning phenomena, it is important to make a distinction between the acquisition of a response not already in the repertoire of the subject, and the formation of an associative link between a stimulus (or stimulus-complex) and a response already in the repertoire of the subject. An example of the former type of learning may be seen in the acquisition of a vocabulary by the young child. At birth, the child's vocal repertoire is limited to cries of various kinds. By the age of three years, however, the same child will have a repertoire of several thousand distinct words which he can utter either separately or in meaningful sequences, with varied intonation and loudness, to produce statements or questions, and so on. In conditioning and learning experiments, however, the experimental psychologist usually deals with responses which are already in the organism's repertoire. Thus, in an eyeblink conditioning experiment, the subject is not being taught to blink, a response which he already possesses, but rather to blink to a previously neutral stimulus. Similarly, in training a rat to turn right at the choice-point of a

---

[4] The analogy may be drawn with a train whose engine is shut off. The train is brought to a halt, not because the engine is shut off, but by the operation of *friction*, which is a positive process.

[5] As one possible example, see the study by Yates and Laszlo (1965) where it was claimed that D, I_R

and sI_R were controlled so that $s\bar{E}_R = sH_R$.

[6] For further information, see any good general text; or, in more detail, the well-known monographs of Kimble (1961), Hall (1966), or Hilgard and Bower (1966).

maze, the rat is not being taught to turn right, a response it is perfectly well able to make already, but rather to perform the right-turning response (rather than a left-turning or straight-ahead response), which it already possesses, to a particular stimulus configuration. The distinction we have just made is not entirely valid, perhaps, because attempts have been made to account for the acquisition of novel responses in terms of the same theoretical variables used to explain the attachment of already-acquired responses to neutral stimuli. It is important to remember, however, that in most learning experiments what is being manipulated essentially is associative habit-strength ($_sH_R$). As Spence has also pointed out, it is important to notice further that it is practically impossible to devise an experimental situation in which the only variable is the acquisition of the associative habit strength being manipulated. Even in the simplest situation that can be devised, the organism will bring to it an already acquired repertoire of associative habit strengths, so that learning will nearly always involve the simultaneous (or prior) extinction of competing responses. Finally, it should be remembered, as was pointed out earlier, that most "learning" curves are in fact curves of performance which may or may not represent the true rate of growth of associative habit strength.

In the first part of this section, we will briefly mention some of the basic characteristics of habit strength ($_sH_R$) in so far as it is indexed imperfectly by changes in performance during training; and we will then deal equally briefly with the other main theoretical constructs in Hull's model, namely, drive and inhibition.

(a) THE CURVE OF ACQUISITION. In most experiments on learning and conditioning, the curve of acquisition of the response in question (for example, the conditioned eyeblink response) is negatively accelerated and, if training is continued for a sufficiently long period of time, it will eventually reach asymptotic level. Performance of the response will then remain asymptotic provided the experimental conditions pertaining when asymptotic level is reached remain unchanged. An important theoretical and recently controversial question is whether this empirical fact supports the notion that associative habit strength increases incrementally over trials or whether learning proceeds in an all-or-none fashion. The present writer's view is that this is a pseudocontroversy

and that learning *must* be incremental in nature, the basic question being the conditions under which the increments are large or small.

(b) EXTINCTION. In the usual conditioning experiment, response strength (CR) increases and is then maintained as long as the CS is paired, at least occasionally, with the US, that is, as long as reinforcement is present. If the US is omitted, then the CR will gradually decline and eventually will cease to occur.

(c) SPONTANEOUS RECOVERY. If, when the CR has extinguished, a rest period is introduced and if, following this rest pause, the CS is reintroduced, the CR will spontaneously reappear.

(d) REACQUISITION. Following spontaneous recovery, it is usually found that the CR will attain its maximum strength somewhat faster than during the initial training sequence; and conversely that reextinction will proceed faster when the US is again withdrawn.

(e) GENERALIZATION. Let us suppose that we have trained a human subject to produce a GSR to a tone of 1000 Hz; then it will be found that a GSR will also be produced to a tone of 500 Hz or to a tone of 1500 Hz and that a curve of generalization will be produced, with the strength of the GSR diminishing, the further removed the stimulus is from the originally conditioned stimulus. This important phenomenon is known as *stimulus generalization*. It should be noted carefully that the generalization takes place to stimuli (CS) which have never been directly paired with the US. The classical studies demonstrating stimulus generalization in human subjects are, of course, those of Hovland dealing with the GSR in relation to pitch (Hovland, 1937a) and loudness (Hovland, 1937b). Hovland was also able to demonstrate the phenomena of extinction, spontaneous recovery, and disinhibition of both conditioned and generalized CRs (Hovland, 1937c), as well as the significance of varying amounts of reinforcement (i.e., the strength of shock used as the US) in relation to generalization (Hovland, 1937d). Equally important for our purposes, but unfortunately much less investigated, is the phenomenon of *response generalization*, in which the same stimulus will induce the appearance of a response similar to that originally investigated. Thus, Bekhterev (1932) claimed to have found that a dog conditioned to lift one paw to a CS would lift the other paw, if the one which normally responded to the CS was restricted. An everyday example would be the occurrence of verbal aggression toward a person if direct physical aggression were impossible or inhibited.

(f) DISCRIMINATION. The instances of generalization mentioned above involve positive conditioning, but, as we have seen, it is also possible to extinguish CRs by omission of the US and it is easy to show that generalization of extinguished CRs will also take place to stimuli along a generalization continuum in precisely the same way. If we now combine these two principles, we arrive at the phenomenon of discrimination. Thus, supposing we originally condition the GSR to a tone of 1000 Hz, then a positive CR will also be evoked (of lesser magnitude) to stimuli of 500 Hz and 1500 Hz, as we have seen. Suppose we now repeatedly present the CS of 500 Hz (or, of course, 1500 Hz) without presenting the US, then the positively conditioned, generalized response will be extinguished and this extinction will also generalize. Hence, two generalization curves (one positive, one negative) will be generated. It has been argued (e.g., by Spence, 1936) that the strength of the tendency to react ($_s\bar{E}_R$) to *any* given stimulus along the continuum will be a function of the summation of the positive and negative strengths at that point; and, indeed, Spence claimed that in this manner it was not only possible to account for the results of Kohler's famous transposition experiments (which Kohler claimed provided irrefutable evidence for insightful behavior) behavioristically, but that this kind of analysis led to predictions of a "reversal effect" which could not be predicted by Kohler's model. It is now clear that Spence's formulation, it it applies at all, does so only in relation to low-order nonverbal behaviors. Nevertheless, the empirical facts of generalization and discrimination in relation to CRs seems well established and, as we shall see throughout this book, these phenomena are of crucial significance to many behavior therapy techniques.

(g) HIGHER-ORDER CONDITIONING. A formerly neutral stimulus which has become a CS by being paired with a US may become a reinforcing stimulus for a second neutral stimulus which, in turn, will become a CS although it has never been paired with a true US. Thus, a tone (CS_1), once established as a CS for salivation, may be paired with a black square (CS_2), which will then evoke salivation even though it has never been paired with food (US). This phenomenon, however, proved to be very difficult to demonstrate and even more difficult to maintain once established, a fact which posed grave difficulties for learning theorists, since most human behavior is rather obviously not maintained by primary reinforcement. One possible and very important solution to this basic problem will be described shortly.

(h) THE HABIT-FAMILY HIERARCHY. We have already pointed out that the organism brings with it to any given situation more than one possible response. We may consider any given stimulus complex as having attached to it a range of possible responses, each of which will reflect differential habit strength. Under normal circumstances, the response with the greatest habit strength will be evoked first. If this response is incorrect (if, in effect, it does not resolve the situation), its effective reaction potential ($_s\bar{E}_R$) will decline in magnitude. Should $_s\bar{E}_R$ drop below the strength of $_s\bar{E}_R$ of the response second in the hierarchy through repeated nonreinforcement, then a significant change will have taken place in the habit-family hierarchy. In general terms, a learning situation is one in which the problem of the experimenter is to alter the relative effective reaction potentials so as to raise to the top of the hierarchy that $_s\bar{E}_R$ which is desired to be evoked to the given stimulus. The notion of the habit-family hierarchy is clearly of great importance for the behavior therapist, since it reflects essentially the problem of replacing a maladaptive response (which is, for whatever reason, at the top of the habit-family hierarchy) with another response which, at the beginning of therapy, is lower down in the hierarchy.

To summarize: performance in a given situation is regarded, other things being equal, as a function of the relative strengths of various effective reaction potentials which compete with each other. As we have seen, however, $_s\bar{E}_R$ is a function of variables other than $_sH_R$ alone, namely, drive and inhibitory factors. To these factors we now turn.

3. DRIVE (D)

In Hull's system drive is a motivational construct which interacts multiplicatively with habit strength ($_sH_R$) to produce reaction potential ($_sE_R$). In other words, the vigor or speed with which a particular habit can be produced at any given time will be a function of the level of drive. Hull did not make any distinction between relevant and irrelevant drives but postulated that all drives present at a given time summate to produce a total drive state. An important distinction is made between primary and secondary (or derived) drives, the latter being stimuli which are present when a primary drive is active and which, by association, become learned drives. Of most significance for our purposes is the distinction between fear and anxiety. Many attempts have been made to distinguish these two states of the organism. Here, fear will be defined as a primary aversive drive (US) and anxiety as the learned or conditioned form of fear (CS). It should be noted that this distinction would not be accepted by many experimental psychologists who would regard fear as the conditioned form of the primary drive of pain, but the distinction we have made between fear and anxiety will be adhered to in this book. We shall return to the role of anxiety as drive in a later section of this chapter.

4. Inhibition (I_R and sI_R)

These inhibitory variables played an important role in Hull's system and have been utilized to a considerable degree by behavior therapists; hence careful attention needs to be paid to them.

Hull argued that the evocation of a response generated a state within the organism which militated against repetition of the response until the inhibition so generated had dissipated with time. The need for such a construct (I_R) appeared evident from a number of considerations. Thus, as we have seen, an apparently extinguished response will show spontaneous recovery following a rest period, suggesting that the response had been temporarily suppressed by some factor which dissipated over time. Even more striking is the distinction between massed and spaced practice in motor learning. If two groups of subjects are given an equal number of trials of practice on the pursuit rotor, for example, the group which is given spaced practice (that is, where each trial is separated by a short rest pause) will show a superior level of performance at all stages of practice than the group which is given massed practice (that is, where each trial follows without a rest pause, or at least with a very much shorter rest pause). Performance on the pursuit rotor under conditions of spaced and massed practice highlights, in fact, the distinction made earlier between performance and learning. In both groups, the curves are curves of performance. The performance curve (sE_R) of the spaced practice group, however, is also an indicant of the curve of learning (sH_R), whereas the performance curve of the massed practice group

is a confounded measure of the curve of learning (sH_R) and the depressive effects of the growth of reactive inhibition (I_R) which is unable to dissipate because of the lack of rest periods. Continuing the same experiment a little further provides additional evidence for the necessity of the construct of reactive inhibition, for if both groups are now given a rest period followed by further practice, the spaced practice group will resume at the performance level which it had reached on the last trial before rest, whereas the massed practice group will resume at a higher point than it had reached on the last trial before rest. This phenomenon of reminiscence in motor learning, which has been well documented, is attributed to the effects of the dissipation of reactive inhibition during the rest period.

Now reactive inhibition is assumed to dissipate solely as a function of rest time and if the rest time is sufficiently long it will dissipate entirely. It would be expected, therefore, that if a sufficiently long rest period were given to allow the total dissipation of I_R, the performance of the massed practice group following the rest interval would rise to the level of the spaced practice group. But this, in fact, does not happen. The postrest difference between the spaced and massed practice groups may be explained as follows. Reactive inhibition is regarded as a negative (noxious) drive state, the dissipation of which is reinforcing. It is argued that this reinforcing state of affairs will strengthen whatever responses are being made during the dissipation period. In fact, however, the crucial response which is being made during the rest period is the response of not responding. It should be noted carefully that we are not dealing here with an absence of response, but with an incompatible active state of not responding (the reader will recall that inhibition was earlier characterized as an active process). This "negative habit" (sI_R) could perhaps better be described as a positive habit which is incompatible with the positive habit (sH_R) which has been evoked. The significance of these two constructs for behavior therapists lies in the suggestion that one possible way of eliminating a maladaptive response may be to subject it to extensive massed practice which will generate large amounts of I_R, and give rise to involuntary rest pauses and the consequent generation of a habit (sI_R) of not responding or of performing an incompatible response. If, by this means, sI_R can be increased so that its strength exceeds sH_R, then the latter response will be effectively eliminated, even though it is still potentially available under appropriate circumstances.

One further theoretical inhibition construct should be mentioned here. Spence introduced the notion of I_n to account for response decrement in situations in which I_R and sI_R would be unlikely to operate, notably the area of verbal learning. The construct, I_n, refers to inhibition generated by a nonreinforced trial in verbal learning (and other comparable) situations. Extinction of a habit may be produced then, either by the generation of I_R and sI_R through massed practice; or by the generation of I_n through the use of nonreinforced trials. In verbal learning experiments, a nonreinforced trial is one in which an incorrect, or no, response is made.

5. REINFORCEMENT

What constitutes a reinforcing stimulus and whether reinforcement is essential for learning to occur constitute two of the most enduring problems of experimental psychology. Hull defined a reinforcing stimulus as one which reduced the drive motivating the behavior which produced the reinforcement. Skinner, on the other hand, eliminated the conceptual part of Hull's definition by defining a reinforcing stimulus[7] as one which increased the probability that the response which immediately preceded the reinforcing stimulus would occur again. For a long time Hull also held that reinforcement was necessary for learning to occur (that is, for increments of sH_R to be generated) though he later revised this view. It is now generally held that habit strength does not increase as function of number of reinforced trials but that performance of the habit is a function of reinforcement. For our purposes these problems are less important than the distinction between positive and negative reinforcers; the role of punishment; the distinction between primary and secondary reinforcement; schedules of reinforcement; and the importance of partial reinforcement. In discussing these, we shall be adopting the empirical definition of a reinforcing stimulus as one which increases the probability that a response will be repeated.

(a) POSITIVE AND NEGATIVE REINFORCERS. A positive reinforcer is a stimulus whose *presentation* increases the probability of evocation of the behavior it follows. A negative reinforcer is a stimulus whose *removal* increases the probability of evocation of the behavior it follows. The definition of a negative reinforcer should be carefully noted and should not be confused with an aversive stimulus (punishment) whose presence decreases the probability of evocation of the behavior it follows.[8] The term negative reinforcer is unfortunate because operant conditioners also refer to positive and negative contingencies when speaking of reinforcement. The term negative contingency, of course, refers to an aversive or punishing consequence, not to negative reinforcement. Thus, the same stimulus (e.g., shock) can act as a negative reinforcer (positive contingency) if a response produces (or is followed by) its cessation; and as a punishing or aversive stimulus (negative contingency) if a response produces (or is followed by) its appearance.

(b) PUNISHMENT. The role of punishment in controlling behavior has been hotly debated by experimental psychologists, and opinions have changed markedly over the years. Thorndike (1913) popularized the early view that the effects of punishment were the obverse of the effects of reward; that is, punishment weakened associative strength whereas reward increased associative strength. Twenty years later (Thorndike, 1932) he revised his position on the basis of numerous experiments and concluded that the effects of punishment were extremely complex. Subsequent experimental work, particularly by Estes (1944), led to the position being widely adopted that punishment temporarily suppresses behavior but that the behavior will subsequently reappear. Even more recently, the position has changed again, largely as a result of the brilliant series of studies by Azrin and his colleagues. In a recent comprehensive review of the problem, Azrin and Holz (1966) have shown just how complex are the effects of punishment. They define punishment empirically as:

"... a reduction of the future probability of a specific response as a result of the immediate delivery of a stimulus for that response" (Azrin and Holz, 1966, p. 381).

---

[7] We are, of course, referring to a positive reinforcement.

[8] The recent text by Hall (1966), for example, defines a punishing stimulus as a negative reinforcer (p. 139). One of the leading operant conditioners, on

the other hand, Goldiamond (1965, p. 109) clearly distinguishes a negative reinforcer from an aversive or punishing consequence of a response. We have followed Goldiamond's distinction here.

They note carefully that their definition is an objective one (i.e., not in terms of subjective feeling or experience); that a specific event must be produced by a specific response for the former to be classified as a punishing stimulus (thus distinguishing punishment from satiation); that the definition refers to the *future* probability of the response being lessened (i.e., that reduction during punishment is not sufficient); and they distinguish punishment from an aversive stimulus, the latter requiring a further response which produces escape from the aversive stimulus.

It is impossible here to summarize the extensive empirical and theoretical analysis of punishment provided by Azrin and Holz, but some of their more important conclusions may be mentioned. First, the effects of a punishing stimulus depend upon many factors which interact in a very complex fashion and no doubt account for the inconsistent results of punishment experiments so vividly described by Solomon (1964). Some of these variables are the manner of introduction (sudden or gradual) of the punishing stimulus; its immediacy and intensity; the schedule of punishment over successive trials; whether or not the punished response is also being reinforced (unless reinforcement is continued, the effects of punishment will be confounded with the effects of withdrawal of the reinforcing stimulus, since the latter contingency also reduces response-rate); the reinforcement schedule; and so on. Second, they show beyond doubt that a punished response may be totally suppressed and may not be recoverable, provided the punishment is immediate and severe enough (Thorndike's original Law of Effect thus being shown to be valid but only under stringent conditions). Third, they show that punishment is more effective in eliminating a response when an alternative reinforced response is available (here again, however, the complexity of the phenomenon is apparent, since the effect is much more pronounced with high than with low intensities of punishment). Fourth, they draw attention to the important phenomenon of the punishment contrast effect. When punishment is withdrawn, the response rate recovers to a point higher than the prepunishment rate. But this phenomenon occurs only up to the point at which the intensity of punishment becomes such as to produce complete suppression of the response. Thus, failure of punishment to eliminate a response permanently may be inferred falsely as a general phenomenon

if sufficient intensities of punishment are not used. Fifth, they also draw attention to a punishing stimulus as a discriminative stimulus. This important phenomenon may occur in two forms. On the one hand, a punishing stimulus may become a discriminative stimulus for further punishment and thus reduce response rate. More importantly, if a stimulus which suppresses behavior at high intensities of presentation is introduced at a low level of intensity which is then gradually increased, and if this stimulus is followed by a positive reinforcer, then a stimulus which normally suppresses behavior may actually come to have secondary reinforcing properties, even when subsequently it is presented at high intensity. As we shall see, this phenomenon is of crucial significance for the understanding of both the "neurotic paradox" and masochism.

Azrin and Holz (1966, pp. 426–428) summarize their main findings by stating 14 conditions for making punishment effective in suppressing behavior. Escape from the punishing situation should be impossible; the punishing stimulus should be as intense as possible, continuous, immediate, and should be introduced at maximum strength (not gradually); extended periods of punishment should be avoided; the punishment stimulus should not be allowed to become a discriminative stimulus for reinforcement, but should become a discriminative stimulus for extinction; motivation to emit the punished response should be reduced, as should reinforcement for it; and alternative reinforced responses should be available. It will be evident that the principles laid down by Azrin and Holz are of critical importance to behavior therapy in relation to experimental procedures that utilize punishment procedures. Even more important, the review shows clearly the extraordinary complexity of the factors that determine the precise effects of a punishing stimulus in any given situation.

(c) PRIMARY AND SECONDARY REINFORCEMENT. Just as we distinguished between primary and secondary drive, so we may distinguish between primary and secondary reinforcement. A secondary reinforcing stimulus may be defined as a neutral stimulus which acquires reinforcing properties by virtue of its contiguous occurrence with a primary reinforcing stimulus. In both experimental psychology generally and in behavior therapy in particular, considerable attention has been paid to the use of tokens as secondary reinforcers. It has been shown that animals will work for secondary reinforcers in the form of tokens, provided these can be exchanged later for a primary reinforcement. As we shall see in later chapters, token reinforcement economies have been established in some mental hospitals and other institutions to manipulate and control the behavior of psychotic and mentally defective patients in particular in efforts to increase the range of responses manifested. The distinction is important also because, of course, human behavior is obviously not controlled by primary reinforcement. The instability of secondary reinforcement effects (unless primary reinforcement is presented at regular intervals) poses a serious problem for reinforcement theorists[9].

(d) SCHEDULES OF REINFORCEMENT. A reinforcing stimulus may follow the appropriate response each time the response is emitted, in which case the reinforcement is said to be continuous; or it may occur only on certain occasions, and then it is said to be partial or intermittent. The limiting case of a partial reinforcement schedule is that in which the reinforcing stimulus is never presented, and the process may be said to be one of extinction. Most of the experimental work on schedules of reinforcement has been carried out by operant conditioners who distinguish four fundamental types of schedule. In a *fixed-ratio* (FR) schedule, the organism receives the reinforcing contingency following every *n*th response. Thus, if every 20th response is reinforced, the schedule is said to be a FR-20 schedule. In a *variable-ratio* (VR) schedule the ratio of reinforcement to response varies around a predetermined average. Thus, in the case of a VR-20 schedule, the average ratio of reinforcement to response will be 1:20 but over, say, 200 trials, the ratio may vary from 1:1 to 1:50 by blocks of trials. In a *fixed-interval* (FI) schedule the first appropriate response emitted after a specified time interval is reinforced. Thus, in the case of a FI-20 sec. schedule, an interval of 20 seconds is allowed to occur after the last appropriate response and then the first appropriate response is reinforced. In a *variable-interval* (VI) schedule, the interval between reinforcement of appropriate responses will vary around an average interval so that a VI-20 sec. schedule

will involve blocks of trials in which the VI varies from, say, one second to 60 seconds, the average being, of course, 20 seconds.

It has been shown in animal studies that each of these basic schedules produces characteristic types of response pattern (depending also, of course, on whether the reinforcers are positive or aversive). Thus, for example, a rat on a FR-20 schedule will respond at a slow rate immediately after it has received a reinforcement but will speed up the rate of emission of responses as the total number of responses emitted approaches 20, so that a characteristically fluctuating pattern of response rate is found. On the other hand, a VR schedule produces a more uniform, stable rate of responding.

It should be noted carefully that these schedules of reinforcement must be approached gradually. Thus, if it is desired to achieve a FR-20 schedule, this state of affairs is achieved usually by initially reinforcing every response the organism makes and then gradually omitting reinforcements so that a FR-2 schedule is achieved; then a FR-3 schedule; and so on. Although these schedules can be readily manipulated to produce the required end-result, a breakdown in discrimination on the part of the organism may occur if the changes in schedule are made too rapidly. Quite remarkably, complex schedules of reinforcement can, however, be achieved by skilled experimenters[10] and, indeed, animals can be taught to switch rapidly from one type of schedule to another.

(e) SECONDARY REINFORCEMENT AND STABILITY OF BEHAVIOR. The fact that behavior which is maintained solely on the basis of secondary reinforcement tends to extinguish unless primary reinforcement is intermittently presented represented a serious embarrassment to behavior theorists, since clearly most human behavior is not dependent on the occurrence of primary reinforcement. A possible solution to this problem was suggested by an ingenious experiment by Zimmerman (1957, 1959). Essentially, the problem reduces to one of increasing resistance to extinction. Before considering Zimmerman's experiment, something should be said about the partial reinforcement effect and resistance to extinction. With but few exceptions, a large series of experiments in recent years[11]

---

[9] For a brief review of secondary reinforcement see Myers (1958); for a more comprehensive analysis see Wike (1966).

[10] Candland (1968, p. 406–407) has distinguished seven significant combinations of the four basic schedules.

[11] The literature on partial reinforcement has been reviewed by Jenkins and Stanley (1950) and by Lewis (1960); but the last five years has witnessed a flood of papers on this topic and a further synthesis is urgently required.

has confirmed that resistance to extinction will be greater where the initial training has occurred under a partial reinforcement rather than a continuous reinforcement schedule. The reason for this is quite straightforward. If training is carried out under a continuous reinforcement schedule, then a switch to nonreinforcement when extinction trials are instituted will be readily discriminable. If, however, training is carried out under a partial reinforcement schedule, then a switch to nonreinforcement is less readily discriminable, since the organism has learned that one or more nonreinforced trials are likely to be followed by a reinforced trial. This will be the case particularly where variable schedules of reinforcement have been used in training.

The particular contribution which Zimmerman made was to combine the use of secondary reinforcement with partial reinforcement. His experiment, carried out with rats, involved several stages. In the first stage, the animals were released from a start box by the raising of a door, while simultaneously a buzzer sounded. On running down the straight alley, food was found in the goal box. Commencing with a FR-1 schedule of reinforcement (i.e., food was present in the goal box on each trial), Zimmerman gradually instituted a partial reinforcement schedule until the animals were running on a FR-20 schedule. The second stage of the experiment involved the introduction of a bar into the start box. When the animal pressed the bar, the buzzer sounded and the door rose so that the animal could traverse the runway to the goal box. At this point, however, *the primary reinforcement in the goal box was discontinued*, so that the bar press was followed only by the buzzer and raising of the door (secondary reinforcing stimuli). Furthermore, a partial reinforcement schedule was gradually instituted in this part of the experiment also so that ultimately the bar press was reinforced by the buzzer and door lift on a FR-20 schedule. The animal never received food in the goal box during the second stage of the experiment yet the bar-pressing response was maintained unaltered by the partial reinforcement schedule over many thousands of trials.[12] It may be added that similar striking results have been obtained with children (Myers, 1960; Fox and

King, 1961) and that, as we shall see in a later chapter, Zimmerman's exact technique has been successfully used with psychotic children.

The importance of Zimmerman's technique in producing durable behavior based only on secondary reinforcement, and the importance of the demonstration that training under conditions of partial reinforcement enhances resistance to extinction, can scarcely be overestimated for behavior therapists, since one of the major characteristics of abnormal behavior is often its high degree of resistance to extinction on the one hand and the difficulty of producing equally stable, adaptive, incompatible behavior in therapy on the other. The link between partial reinforcement techniques and durable secondary reinforcement effects provides a possible resolution of these difficulties.

6. CLASSICAL CONDITIONING PARADIGMS

We may distinguish two basic forms of classical conditioning, appetitive and aversive.[13] The paradigm for appetitive conditioning is the well-known experiment of Pavlov in which the CS (usually a bell or buzzer) comes to evoke salivation in the dog (UR and CR) when paired with a US (usually food) and subsequently presented alone. The paradigm for classical aversive conditioning is the somewhat less well-known experiment of Bekhterev (1932) in which a CS paired with a US (usually shock) comes to evoke an involuntary lifting of the paw of the dog when presented alone. The critical point to note about the classical conditioning paradigm is that the US is under the control of the experimenter and that the animal can neither escape from the US nor avoid it by an anticipatory response.

7. INSTRUMENTAL CONDITIONING PARADIGMS

The basic instrumental conditioning situation is represented by the well-known Skinner box situation in which the rat presses the bar and receives food. Reinforcement here is contingent upon the emission of a particular response and, to that extent, the behavior of the animal which it is desired to reinforce is not under the control of the experimenter (hence the distinction between respondent behavior and operant behav-

---

[12] The question whether the secondary reinforcement arises from the buzzer or the opportunity to escape from the start-box has not yet been resolved (Wike et al, 1963).

[13] The taxonomy of classical conditioning is complex and various classifications have been proposed. Grant (1964), for example, has distinguished four subclasses.

ior). A basic distinction may be made between reward learning and escape and avoidance learning. Reward learning involves the strengthening of an approach response by following it with reward. Of more interest for our purposes is aversive instrumental conditioning and learning. If, in the Bekhterev experiment described under classical conditioning, the animal is allowed to escape from the shock by lifting its paw, or to avoid the shock by lifting its paw when the CS occurs but before the US occurs, then we have transformed classical aversive conditioning into instrumental aversive conditioning. The particular experimental example to be discussed here, however, has more important implications for behavior therapy. This is the famous experiment by Miller (1948) on fear as an acquired drive. Miller showed that rats would learn to run from one compartment to the other of a two-compartment box at the sound of a buzzer if that buzzer had previously been paired with shock. In the initial training trials the rats learned to *escape* from the shock by running to the other compartment; if the buzzer preceded the shock by several seconds they would quickly learn to *avoid* the shock by running to the buzzer as soon as it sounded and before the shock occurred. Miller postulated an acquired drive of fear to explain these findings, the conditioned fear (anxiety in terms of the distinction made earlier in this chapter) being reduced by running into the other compartment.

Now let us consider a different situation. Let us suppose an animal runs up a straight runway to a goal containing food; let us suppose further that after the running behavior has been stabilized the animal is shocked at some point in the runway prior to the goal-box. After several trials in which shock is administered, the animal will *escape* from the shock, usually by retreating back down the runway and subsequently will *avoid* the shock by stopping in the runway before the shock point is reached.

These two different experimental paradigms led Mowrer (1960) to make a distinction which is of the greatest interest and significance for experimental abnormal psychology. The Miller paradigm was described by Mowrer as an example of *active avoidance learning* or, alternatively, *nonresponse-correlated* fear learning. In the Miller situation, the animal is initially *passive* with respect to the occurrence of the US (shock), the occurrence of which is uncorrelated with the behavior of the animal, and is rendered *active* by the occurrence of the US and, later, the CS. Thus, on the first

occasion on which it is placed in the box, the animal may be grooming itself when the shock occurs; on the second, it may be roaming about, and so on. The shock occurs at random with respect to the animal's behavior. The other experimental paradigm, however, is described by Mowrer as an example of *passive avoidance learning* since an initially *active* animal (running up the runway) is transformed into a *passive* animal (behavior is inhibited) by the occurrence of shock. Even more importantly, however, the behavior of the animal is correlated with the occurrence of the shock, since on each trial the animal is performing the same response (running up the runway) when the shock occurs. Most interesting of all, the conditioned fear is produced by the animal itself by way of feedback stimuli from the movements involved in running up the runway. In the Miller paradigm the conditioned fear is produced by a stimulus (the buzzer) external to the animal and not under its control; whereas in the runway paradigm the conditioned fear is produced by stimuli arising from movements made by the animal itself. In a very real sense, the animal in the runway carries its own fear-arousing stimulus around with it permanently whereas the animal in the Miller paradigm has to wait for the fear-arousing stimuli to occur in its environment. As we shall see in later chapters, this distinction between response-correlated and nonresponse-correlated conditioned fear furnishes a significant clue to distinguishing between phobias and obsessions, for example.

8. Traumatic Avoidance Learning

An avoidance response that is acquired under conditions of very strong primary aversive stimulation may prove to be highly resistant to extinction even though the US may be omitted for many hundreds of trials (Solomon and Wynne, 1954). The experimental demonstration of this phenomenon is of great importance in view of the fact that responses in human subjects based on conditioned fear (anxiety) also show extreme resistance to extinction in natural circumstances. Solomon and Wynne related this phenomenon to the known fact that autonomic reactions have a longer latency than the avoidance responses which they produce. If the avoidance response comes to antedate the autonomic response and turns off the stimulus-producing fear, then the fear response itself may not receive the opportunity for extinction trials. The experiments on traumatic avoidance learning, suggesting as they do the principles of anxiety conservation and partial irreversibility of anxiety are clearly of crucial importance for the possible understanding of the genesis of some pathological forms of behavior which appear to be based on the persistence of conditioned fear responses.

9. MOWRER'S TWO-FACTOR THEORY

The distinction we have made between classical and instrumental conditioning paradigms has long been known not to be as clear cut as it once seemed. The attempt of Hull (1943) to reduce classical conditioning to an instrumental conditioning paradigm is well known; not so well known is the fact that Pavlov (1932) attempted to do the reverse. More recently, the complex relationship between these two paradigms has received very careful attention (e.g., Grant, 1964). For our purposes, however, the distinction maintained by Mowrer (1947) may be useful to recall, even though Mowrer (1960) later argued that all learning was classical or associative in nature. Mowrer pointed out that classical conditioning may be regarded as logically preceding instrumental conditioning. In the case of escape and avoidance conditioning, for example, Mowrer argued that the acquired drive of fear is based on the contiguity of CS and US and involves drive induction. The induced drive (classically conditioned) sets the organism a problem (that of reducing or terminating the fear), so that the organism indulges in trial-and-error behavior until it hits upon a response which enables it to escape from (later, to avoid) the noxious stimulus and thus reduces the anxiety. The reduction of anxiety serves as a reinforcing event for the escape or avoidance response. Mowrer linked these two forms of learning with the autonomic and central nervous systems, respectively, as well as making other comparisons of interest. Thus, the autonomic fear conditioning was regarded as being based on the reality principle, whereas the instrumentally conditioned escape or avoidance response could be regarded as being based on the pleasure principle. The important point to note is the concept of anxiety as an acquired drive which motivates the organism to produce a response which will reduce the drive (or alternatively, of

course, in terms of the active and passive avoidance paradigms, to stop producing the response) which evoked the noxious stimulation.

10. COMPLEX LEARNING

Ultimately, of course, the experimental psychology of complex learning will probably prove to be more relevant to the explanation and treatment of abnormalities of behavior than the simple situations we have discussed thus far, and some aspects of this area of psychology will be discussed in the final chapter. However, it is pertinent to refer here to some work of Spence (1956) which is of direct relevance to behavior therapy and which may properly be included since the theoretical framework does not depart very much from that utilized here. Spence was particularly interested in the interaction between drive (D) and habit strength (sH_R) in learning. He made an important distinction in this connection between competitional and noncompetitional[14] learning situations. A noncompetitional learning situation is one in which either only a single sH_R is being strengthened or in which the correct sH_R is at the head of the habit family hierarchy. A competitional learning situation is one in which the correct sH_R is weaker at the beginning of learning than a competing sH_R. Spence theorized that in a noncompetitional learning situation high drive would facilitate performance of the response compared with low drive; whereas in a competitional learning situation, high drive would interfere with the performance of the correct response. Fictitious examples may elucidate the point. If the strength of an sH_R is 10 units in 2 organisms, but D is 5 units in O_1 and 10 units in O_2, then sE_R in $O1$ will be 50 and in O_2 will be 100, since D in Hull's system theoretically interacts multiplicatively with sH_R. Now let us suppose that in a competitional learning situation involving 2 organisms, sH_{R_1} (the incorrect response) is 10 units and that sH_{R_2} (the correct response is only 5 units. If D in O_1 is 5 units and in O_2 is 10 units, then sE_{R_1} in O_1 will be 50 and in O_2 will be 100, whereas sE_{R_2} in O_1 will be 25 and in O_2 will be 50. The absolute difference between sE_{R_1} and sE_{R_2} in O_1 will, therefore, be 25 units, whereas in O_2 it will be 50. Hence O_2 will experience more difficulty in

---

[14] The competitional/noncompetitional distinction is sometimes referred to as a distinction between simple and complex task situations. The correlation

is imperfect, however, since task complexity does not necessarily imply competition between responses.

bringing $_sH_{R_2}$ to the head of the hierarchy than will O_1, because of the difference in drive level.

Spence examined these predictions in an ingenious series of experiments which are notable for the methodology of objectively defining competitional and noncompetitional situations. Thus, for example, if we regard eye-blink conditioning as a noncompetitional learning situation, it would be predicted that high drive would facilitate conditioning of the eyeblink response; this was found to be the case by Spence and Farber (1953), using high- and low-drive subjects defined in terms of performance on the Taylor Manifest Anxiety Scale (this being used as a measure of drive rather than as a measure of anxiety). The role of high and low drive in a competitional learning situation was examined by Spence in a stylus maze learning experiment (Farber and Spence, 1953). The maze consisted of ten T-choice-points, the level of difficulty of which had been empirically determined.[15] The prediction was that the high-drive subjects would learn the easier choice points faster, and the difficult choice points more slowly, than the low-drive subjects. The results were somewhat equivocal since the high-drive subjects made more errors on all choice points, but a more detailed analysis of the data did offer some support for the hypothesis.

A more ingenious and satisfactory test of the hypothesis was offered in a two-part study of paired-associate learning by Spence, Farber, and McFann (1956). In the first part of the experiment they operationally defined a non-competitional paired associates list as one in which the association value (empirically deter-mined) *within* stimulus-response pairs was high while the associative value between stimuli and responses in *different* pairs was low. Thus, in the following three pairs:

S_1 adept—skilful R_1
S_2 barren—fruitless R_2
S_3 complete—thorough R_3

the associative values of S_1—R_1, S_2—R_2, and S_3—R_3 are high while the associative values between S_1—R_2, S_1—R_3, S_2—R_3, and so on are low. The prediction that high-drive subjects would learn such a list faster and with fewer errors than the low-drive subjects was con-firmed. In the second part of the study, a competitional paired associates task was con-structed by taking a pair with high associative

value between stimulus and response and then constructing two further pairs with low intra-pair associative value but high interpair associative value. Thus, in the following three pairs:

S_1 barren—fruitless R_1
S_2 arid—grouchy R_2
S_3 desert—leading R_3

S_1—R_1 has high associative value and S_2—R_2 and S_3—R_3 low associative value; but there is a high associative value between S_1—R_2 and S_1—R_3. Thus, learning the association between S_2—R_2 and S_3—R_3 would be interfered with by the existing high associative values between S_1—R_2 and S_1—R_3. The prediction that under these conditions high-drive subjects would take longer to learn the S_2—R_2 and S_3—R_3 asso-ciations was confirmed.

Now it will be apparent that in these experi-ments Spence did not solve the problem of distinguishing between the effects of drive on learning and the effects of drive on performance. An attempt to solve this problem was made by Standish and Champion (1960). They con-structed a noncompetitional learning list and trained their subjects on it to the point of two successive errorless trials. Having reached this criterion, the subject was then given eight further trials which were presumably errorless. Standish and Champion argued that in the errorless trials, a measure of the speed with which responses were produced would demon-strate the effect of level of drive on *performance* with *learning* of the associations themselves controlled. Under these conditions, they did, in fact, find that high-drive subjects produced responses faster than low-drive subjects. It is, however, interesting to note that the perform-ance curves for response speed on the errorless trials were not flat but were negatively acceler-ated and did not, in fact, reach asymptotic level. What this appears to mean is that the learning of paired associate lists involves the acquisition of two sets of habits, not one. First, the correct association must be learned. When this has been achieved to the point at which no further errors are being made, the subject has still to learn to *reproduce* each response to its appropriate stimulus at a uniform speed. Only when this has been achieved can learning be said to be com-plete. Since Standish and Champion's response speed learning curves did not reach asymptotic level, it is impossible to say whether the

---

[15] In such a maze, differential difficulty level of choice-points is found with the easiest choice-points

being at the start and end of the maze.

separation between the high- and low-drive curves would have been maintained at asymptotic levels. Thus, the Standish and Champion experiment is incomplete and would have required further errorless training trials to demonstrate clearly whether high drive facilitates performance of a learned response. In the second part of their study, Standish and Champion examined a further important prediction from Spence's theory. They converted their noncompetitional paired-associates task into a competitional task by the simple expedient of using the same stimulus words but attaching new response words to them, thus creating a competitional task by definition, since to learn the new associations the subject had to overcome the effect of the just-learned associations. Under these conditions, of course, Spence's theory predicts that low-drive subjects will learn the list faster than high-drive subjects. However, the theory also predicts that once the list is learned to a criterion of errorless trials a reversal effect should take place (because the task has now by definition become noncompetitional) and high-drive subjects should perform better than low-drive subjects. The prediction was verified.

The many experiments that have now been carried out within this theoretical framework cannot be reviewed here.[16] Alternative explanations have been put forward to account for the effects of high drive in facilitating noncompetitional learning and interfering with competitional learning. For example, it has been argued that high drive may interfere with performance in a stressful situation by producing task-irrelevant competing responses which distract the subject's attention from the task; and that high drive will facilitate performance even in a competitional learning situation if the drive produces task-relevant behavior. It has also been argued that high drive may facilitate performance on complex tasks provided the task-situation is not seen as threatening by the subject (i.e., is not ego involving). The importance of this approach of Spence for our purposes lies in the possibility that the model may be relevant to the explanation of two very significant facts about neurotic behavior. On the one hand, neurotic patients appear to learn some maladaptive responses very readily; on the other hand, they appear to learn adaptive responses with great difficulty.

Now if it is the case that the opportunity for acquiring maladaptive responses usually occurs in situations where alternative adaptive responses are not available (that is, in a noncompetitional situation) whereas the opportunity for acquiring adaptive responses usually involves situations in which the adaptive response must be chosen from among several possible alternative responses, then Spence's model provides a possible explanation for the two phenomena. Of course, the model is applicable only if the neurotic patient is characterized by high drive; in the next chapter, it will be argued that this is, indeed, the case.

II. SERVOMECHANISTIC CONTROL OF BEHAVIOR

Particular stress was laid in the first chapter on the fact that it is unfortunate that behavior therapy has come to be associated largely with (and, indeed, has been occasionally defined as) the application of learning theory to the understanding and change of abnormalities of behavior. For certain disorders of behavior, other explanatory models of behavior may (and indeed do) turn out to be more useful and appropriate. Of these, one of the most important and interesting is the servomechanistic model. The problem of the sequential control of skilled behavior patterns is one that has received a great deal of attention in experimental psychology. The use of servomechanistic models to account for such control has been quite common in relation to physiological mechanisms such as breathing and, more recently, such models have been advanced to account for skilled motor behavior such as eye-movement control (e.g., Fender, 1964). We will mention briefly here several examples of the importance of servomechanistic models for the control of psychological functions.

Essentially, the servomechanistic model assumes that sequential responding may be considered as consisting of an orderly sequence of discrete units and that orderly progression of these units is achieved by feedback from each of the units to a central monitoring system by which means confirmation is received that each unit has been successfully transmitted. If the feedback signal indicates that transmission is not received, or if the feedback signal indicates that the response unit has been faultily trans-

---

[16] For a recent review of the empirical literature and theoretical problems in this area of research, see Goulet (1968).

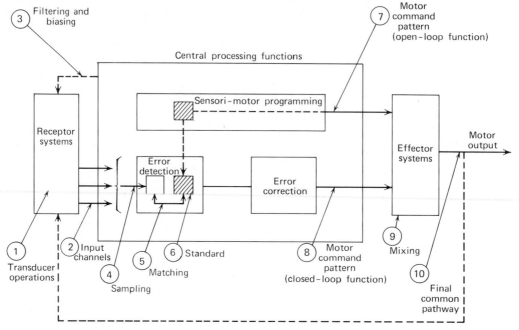

FIG. 1.   Flow diagram of a system for the control of motor activity (Chase, 1965b).

mitted, then the system will either correct the output (by repeating the unit) or the output will halt and transmission recommence at an earlier stage. The question of the size of the units that are monitored and whether monitoring occurs systematically or only when the feedback signals indicate an error exceeding a certain magnitude is a matter around which much controversy has raged. Various feedback control models have been postulated from time to time, of which Chase's (1965a, 1965b), reproduced in Figure 1, is reasonably representative.

As can be seen, Chase's model contains the three basic components of a feedback control system: a receptor system; central processing functions; and an effector system. The principal central processing functions are the error-detection and error-correction functions. The former matches the sensory feedback pattern against an expected feedback pattern which is based on previous experience. Thus, when speaking in an auditorium of given dimensions and acoustic properties, the speaker will, for example, expect to hear the sound of his own voice with a certain time delay and intensity. If the feedback information does not match the expected pattern, then the output will be altered until the match occurs. Of course, correction will also take place if environmental

circumstances change so as to affect the feedback match (such as the sudden appearance of a loud continuous noise).

Now skilled behavior usually involves the close integration and matching of feedback information arising simultaneously from several feedback channels. Thus, for example, the task of keeping a pointer on a target involves both kinesthetic feedback arising from the control movements made by the hand and visual feedback arising from watching the change in the position of the pointer and target. Similarly, walking is monitored not only by kinesthetic stimuli which locate the differential position of the limbs in space but also from visual information provided by seeing the relative position of the limbs in space. If one of the feedback channels is reduced in intensity (e.g., if the subject has to walk wearing a blindfold), there may be little impairment in the skilled behavior provided the environment remains reasonably predictable with respect to changes in kinesthetic feedback. Similarly, if a subject is prevented from hearing the sound of his own voice by a loud masking noise, speech remains relatively unimpaired as in the case of a deaf person, whose voice tends to become flatter and more monotonous but is otherwise relatively unaffected. Serious difficulty in maintaining accuracy of skilled movement will often arise, however, if, instead of attenuating or eliminating one of the feedback channels, one channel is placed out of step with the others so that the subject receives conflicting information about the progress of the individual units which constitute skilled behavior. The effects of introducing asynchrony into one of the feedback channels has been most vividly demonstrated in a remarkable series of experiments carried out by Smith and Smith (1962). Smith's work was, of course, a continuation of a long tradition of similar experimentation, but it has been particularly characterized by important technical innovations, of which two will be mentioned. First, Smith made ingenious use of television cameras to produce delayed or otherwise distorted visual feedback, which produced information that seriously conflicted with information being produced by kinesthetic feedback arising from the movements involved in, for example, drawing. Thus, the subject might be required to write the letter "A" or draw a triangle while watching a visual representation of what he was doing which had been inverted by a television camera (the subject was, of course, unable to see the direct representation of his drawing). In a later series of studies, Smith introduced the use of computer techniques to produce disturbed feedback. For example, the subject might be required to press a very sensitive lever which guided a pen to produce a line on a recorder. The subject's task was to align the pen-record with a pointer set above a moving strip. If the subject was able to see a direct visual representation of the exerted pressure, performance would be within normal limits of finger-tremor; if, however, the subject was able to see only a visual record of the finger tremor which was delayed for three seconds, he would in effect be looking at a record of his tremor which was three seconds behind what his finger was doing at that moment. The delayed visual feedback was achieved by transducing the analogue representation of the finger tremor into a digital representation, taking this into a digital computer, holding it in the computer for three seconds, and then retransducing it back into a visual representation. The placing of the digital computer almost literally into the subject's feedback control system in this way has provided a technique of immense power for investigating the feedback control of skilled behavior, since the perturbations that can be achieved are limited only by the ability to obtain an accurate digital representation of the analogue signal and the arithmetical power of the computer. In the case of speech, for example, the output of the subject can not only be delayed, but can be clipped, interrupted, and even reversed by the computer before being fed back into the subject. The effects of delayed auditory feedback on speech in normal subjects has been well-documented, but in principle there is no limit to the range of skilled behaviors that can be investigated. Henry, Junas, and Smith (1967), for example, have recently shown how breath-pressure control can be greatly disturbed in this way.

It should be noted that while skilled behavior can be seriously disrupted by interfering with the feedback control systems in this way, it is also true that human subjects can be trained to achieve a quite remarkable degree of fine control over skilled movements. This was first shown in detail by Hefferline (1958) whose studies have been carried much further recently by Basmajian (Basmajian, 1963; Basmajian and Simard, 1967).

It is impossible to review the large literature on the feedback control of skilled movement here, but we shall see in later chapters that this kind of model appears much more relevant than learning models to the understanding of some behavior disorders. This is not in any way to deny the importance of learning in such disorders, but it does assume that learning factors are less significant than servomechanistic models for the explanation of the genesis and maintenance of these disorders. A particular example where the servomechanistic model has proved extremely fruitful is that of stuttering (Yates, 1963a, 1963b).

III. INFORMATION PROCESSING IN THE HUMAN ORGANISM

The organism at any given moment is being bombarded with extremely large numbers of stimuli from which appropriate segments must be attended to and the rest (temporarily, at least) ignored if a meaningful relationship to the environment is to be maintained. The problem of selective attention is of very considerable interest and importance to behavior therapy since, as we shall see in later chapters, it is possible to conceptualize certain disorders in terms of a failure of selective attention or as a result of faulty processing of incoming information. It is not possible here to review even a small proportion of the extensive literature on selective attention and short-term memory that has accumulated in recent years,[17] but some remarks may be made about selective attention, dichotic stimulation, and short-term memory, three aspects which are of particular relevance to behavior therapy.

1. SELECTIVE ATTENTION

In a remarkable series of experiments, Cherry and his colleagues (Cherry, 1953; Cherry and Taylor, 1954) investigated the "cocktail party problem." Their technique capitalized on the fact that humans have two ears and involved the presentation of two messages simultaneously, one to each ear. They found that, if the subject was required to "shadow" one of the competing messages, he could do so successfully after very little practice.[18] Under these circumstances, however, at the end of the message the subject would have great difficulty in reporting anything at all about the message which had been simultaneously presented to the other ear. These experiments have been repeated and extended by other workers, notably Treisman (1960, 1964a, 1964b), and various theoretical models to explain the results have been put forward. It is sufficient to note, however, that the experiments offer very strong support for the proposition that the human organism may be regarded as having a very limited channel capacity for handling incoming information and that, under many circumstances, the organism literally cannot do two things at once. It is, of course, true that humans can sing and ride a bicycle simultaneously, but this appears to be possible only when both activities are very familiar and overlearned.

2. DICHOTIC STIMULATION AND SHORT-TERM MEMORY

In some cases where the incoming stimulation overloads the channel capacity of the organism, relevant stimuli may simply not be perceived. The possible disastrous consequences of such overloading with relevant stimulation will be readily apparent in such areas as piloting an aircraft coming in to land in an emergency. A long series of experiments by Broadbent and others, however, have suggested that, in addition to the usual long-term memory store, the organism possesses a short-term memory store which can, by definition, hold information

for very brief periods of time. In a classical experiment, Broadbent (1956, 1957) presented pairs of digits simultaneously to each ear and then required the subject to reproduce what he had heard. Broadbent found that, provided the presentation rate was fast enough to prevent switching of attention between ears the subject would tend to reproduce all of the digits off one ear before any of the digits off the other ear. The results of the experiment were interpreted to mean that the organism's limited channel capacity for processing incoming information led him to place the material coming in at one ear temporarily in short-term memory while the material in the other ear was being processed. Provided the storage period was not too long, the organism could reproduce the stored material from the secondary channel after the material on the first ear had been reproduced. A characteristic of the short-term memory store is, however, that information lost from it is irretrievable. To be retained for eventual processing, the material in the short-term memory system must be periodically retrieved and inspected (rehearsed). If inspection and rehearsal occur often enough, the material may be placed in a long-term memory store. Since the short-term memory store is considered to have a limited capacity, items in the store may be pushed out and lost if processing-channel capacity is exceeded too greatly, resulting in more and more items being pushed into the short-term store.

As we shall see in later chapters, these concepts of limited channel capacity and a limited capacity short-term memory store are of great importance in relation to psychotic disorders.

This brief review of some of the aspects of experimental psychology which may be of particular relevance to behavior therapy at present is perhaps too sketchy and incomplete for comfort. It is hoped it will serve to demonstrate, however, that even at this early stage in the development of behavior therapy, a wide range of empirical findings and theoretical concepts are of relevance to the application of behavior therapy to abnormalities of behavior. It is probably true to say that many other aspects of experimental psychology would be of equal significance and that their application awaits only the knowledge and ingenuity of the behavior therapist.

---

[17] The reader may be referred to the excellent reviews of Broadbent (1958), Adams (1967), and Neisser (1967).

[18] In the shadowing technique the subject repeats the incoming message word by word as immediately as possible. He treads on its heels, as it were; hence the term "shadowing."

REFERENCES

Adams, J.A. *Human memory*. New York: McGraw-Hill, 1967.

Azrin, N.H. & Holz, W.C. Punishment. In Honig, W.K. (ed.). *Operant behavior: areas of research and application*. New York: Appleton-Century-Crofts, 1966, pp. 380–447.

Basmajian, J.V. Control and training of individual motor units. *Science*, 1963, **141**, 440–441.

Basmajian, J.V. & Simard, T.G. Effects of distracting movements on the control of trained motor units. *Amer. J. phys. Med.*, 1967, **46**, 1427–1449.

Bekhterev, V.M. *General principles of human reflexology*. New York: International Press, 1932.

Broadbent, D.E. Successive responses to simultaneous stimuli. *Quart. J. exp. Psychol.*, 1956, **8**, 145–152.

Broadbent, D.E. Immediate memory and simultaneous stimuli. *Quart. J. exp. Psychol.*, 1957, **9**, 1–11.

Broadbent, D.E. *Perception and communication*. London: Pergamon, 1958.

Candland, D.K. *Psychology: the experimental approach*. New York: McGraw-Hill, 1968.

Chase, R.A. An information-flow model of the organization of motor activity: I. Transduction, transmission and central control of sensory information. *J. nerv. ment. Dis.*, 1965, **140**, 239–251 (a).

Chase, R.A. An information-flow model of the organization of motor activity: II. Sampling, central processing and utilization of sensory information. *J. nerv. ment. Dis.*, 1965, **140**, 334–350 (b).

Cherry, E.C. Some experiments on the recognition of speech, with one and with two ears. *J. acoust. Soc. Amer.*, 1953, **25**, 975–979.

Cherry, E.C. & Taylor, W.K. Some further experiments upon the recognition of speech with one and with two ears. *J. acoust. Soc. Amer.*, 1954, **26**, 554–559.

Estes, W.K. An experimental study of punishment. *Psychol. Monogr.*, 1944, **57** (3).

Farber, I.E. & Spence, K.W. Complex learning and conditioning as a function of anxiety. *J. exp. Psychol.*, 1953, **45**, 120–125.

Fender, D.H. Techniques of systems analysis applied to feedback pathways in the control of eye-movements. *Symposium of the Society for Experimental Biology*, 1964, **18**, 401–419.

Fox, R.E. & King, R.A. The effects of reinforcement scheduling on the strength of a secondary reinforcer. *J. comp. physiol. Psychol.*, 1961, **54**, 266–269.

Gibson, J.J. The concept of the stimulus in psychology. *Amer. Psychol.*, 1960, **15**, 694–703.

Goldiamond, I. Stuttering and fluency as manipulative operant response classes. In Krasner, L. & Ullmann, L.P. (eds.). *Research in behavior modification*. New York: Holt, 1965, pp. 108–156.

Goulet, L.R. Anxiety (drive) and verbal learning: implications for research and some methodological considerations. *Psychol. Bull.*, 1968, **69**, 235–247.

Grant, D.A. Classical and operant conditioning. In Melton, A.W. (ed.). *Categories of human learning*. New York: Academic Press, 1964.

Hall, J.F. *The psychology of learning*. New York: Lippincott, 1966.

Hefferline, R.F. The role of proprioception in the control of behavior. *Trans. New York Acad. Sci.*, 1958, **20**, 739–764.

Henry, J.P., Junas, R., & Smith, K.U. Experimental cybernetic analysis of delayed feedback of breath-pressure control. *Amer. J. Phys. Med.*, 1967, **46**, 1317–1331.

Hilgard, E.R. & Bower, G.H. *Theories of learning*. New York: Appleton-Century-Crofts, 1966.

Hovland, C.I. The generalization of conditioned responses: I. The sensory generalization of conditioned responses with varying frequencies of tone. *J. gen. Psychol.*, 1937, **17**, 125–148 (a).

Hovland, C.I. The generalization of conditioned responses: II. The sensory generalization of conditioned responses with varying intensities of tone. *J. genet. Psychol.*, 1937, **51,** 279–291 (b).

Hovland, C.I. The generalization of conditioned responses: III. Extinction, spontaneous recovery, and disinhibition of conditioned and of generalized responses. *J. exp. Psychol.*, 1937, **21,** 47–62 (c).

Hovland, C.I. The generalization of conditioned responses: IV. The effects of varying amounts of reinforcement upon the degree of generalization of conditioned responses. *J. exp. Psychol.*, 1937, **21,** 261–276 (d).

Hull, C.L. *Principles of behavior.* New York: Appleton-Century-Crofts, 1943.

Jenkins, W.O. & Stanley, J.C. Partial reinforcement: a review and critique. *Psychol. Bull.*, 1950, **47,** 193–234.

Kimble, G.A. *Hilgard and Marquis' conditioning and learning.* New York: Appleton-Century-Crofts, 1961.

Lewis, D.J. Partial reinforcement: a selective review of the literature since 1950. *Psychol. Bull.*, 1960, **57,** 1–28.

Miller, N.E. Studies of fear as an acquirable drive: I. Fear as motivation and fear-reduction as reinforcement in learning of new responses. *J. exp. Psychol.*, 1948, **38,** 89–101.

Mowrer, O.H. On the dual nature of learning—a reinterpretation of "conditioning" and "problem solving." *Harvard educ. Rev.*, 1947, **17,** 102–148.

Mowrer, O.H. *Learning theory and behavior.* New York; Wiley, 1960.

Myers, J.L. Secondary reinforcement: a review of recent experimentation. *Psychol. Bull.*, 1958, **55,** 284–301.

Myers, N.A. Extinction following partial and continuous primary and secondary reinforcement. *J. exp. Psychol.*, 1960, **60,** 172–179.

Neisser, U. *Cognitive psychology.* New York: Appleton-Century-Crofts, 1967.

Pavlov, I.P. The reply of a physiologist to psychologists. *Psychol. Rev.*, 1932, **39,** 91–127.

Smith, K.U. & Smith, W.M. *Perception and motion.* Philadelphia: Saunders, 1962.

Solomon, R.L. Punishment. *Amer. Psychol.*, 1964, **19,** 239–253.

Solomon, R.L. & Wynne, L.C. Traumatic avoidance learning: the principles of anxiety conservation and partial irreversibility. *Psychol. Rev.*, 1954, **61,** 353–385.

Spence, K.W. The nature of discrimination learning in animals. *Psychol. Rev.*, 1936, **43,** 427–449.

Spence, K.W. *Behavior theory and conditioning.* New Haven: Yale Univ. Press, 1956.

Spence, K.W. & Farber, I.E. Conditioning and extinction as a function of intensity of anxiety. *J. exp. Psychol.*, 1953, **45,** 116–119.

Spence, K.W., Farber, I.E., & McFann, H.H. The relation of anxiety (drive) level to performance in competitional and noncompetitional paired-associates learning. *J. exp. Psychol.*, 1956, **52,** 296–305.

Standish, R.C. & Champion, R.A. Task difficulty and drive in verbal learning. *J. exp. Psychol.*, 1960, **59,** 361–365.

Thorndike, E.L. *The psychology of learning.* New York: Teachers' College, 1913.

Thorndike, E.L. *The fundamentals of learning.* New York: Teachers' College, 1932.

Treisman, A.M. Contextual cues in selective listening. *Quart. J. exp. Psychol.*, 1960, **12,** 242–248.

Treisman, A.M. Monitoring and storage of irrelevant messages in selective attention. *J. verb. Learning verb. Behav.*, 1964, **3,** 449–459 (a).

Treisman, A.M. The effect of irrelevant material on the efficiency of selective listening. *Amer. J. Psychol.*, 1964, **77,** 533–546 (b).

Wike, E.L. *Secondary reinforcement: selected experiments.* New York: Harper, 1966.

Wike, E.L., Platt, J.R., & Scott, D. Drive and secondary reinforcement: further extensions of Zimmerman's work. *Psychol. Rec.*, 1963, **13,** 45–49.

Yates, A.J. Delayed auditory feedback. *Psychol. Bull.*, 1963, **60,** 213–232 (a).

Yates, A.J. Recent empirical and theoretical approaches to the experimental manipulation of speech in normal subjects and in stammerers. *Behav. Res. Ther.*, 1963, **1,** 95–119 (b).

Yates, A.J. & Laszlo, J.I. Learning and performance of extraverts and introverts on the pursuit rotor. *J. pers. soc. Psychol.*, 1965, **1**, 79–84.

Zimmerman, D.W. Durable secondary reinforcement: method and theory. *Psychol. Rev.*, 1957, **64**, 373–383.

Zimmerman, D.W. Sustained performance in rats based on secondary reinforcement. *J. comp. physiol. Psychol.*, 1959, **52**, 353–358.

Chapter 3

Abnormal Behavior

In this chapter we shall develop briefly some fundamental considerations concerning abnormal behavior. A deliberate decision has been made to deal with a restricted section of the literature in order that a particular point of view may be developed, since it will be impossible to review all of it. For more general reviews of the recent literature on experimental abnormal psychology, the reader must be referred elsewhere.[1] In this chapter, we shall first review the structure of personality as revealed by Eysenck's dimensional analyses; then consider theories that attempt to account for individual differences along these dimensions; and finally relate these dimensions to the concept of abnormality of behavior. No apology is made for concentrating on Eysenck's personality system. In spite of the severe criticisms to which it has been subjected from time to time and the important modifications introduced into it in recent years, it has been and remains the most significant contribution in the field of abnormal psychology in recent years.

I. STAGES IN THE INVESTIGATION OF PERSONALITY

Eysenck (1955a, 1955b, 1956) has pointed out that there are two essential stages in the investigation of personality. The first stage involves the establishment of an objectively determined dimensional framework which will accommodate the main facts and features of behavior relevant to abnormality. On the basis of his own dimensional studies, he maintains that six general statements may be made concerning human behavior.

(i) That human behavior manifests some degree of generality (if this were not so, then general theories of behavior would be difficult, if not impossible, to formulate).

(ii) That different degrees of generality can be discerned, that is, that personality is hierarchically structured.

(iii) That the different degrees of generality can be established by correlational analysis; at the habitual level, by test-retest correlations; at the trait level, by the intercorrelations of habits; at the type level, by the intercorrelations of traits.

(iv) That abnormal behavior is not qualitatively different from normal behavior but represents one end of a continuum from normal to abnormal, with no clearly discernible break between normal and abnormal.[2]

(v) That, once the basic dimensions of personality have been objectively established, it is possible to locate any individual on each of the dimensions, thus producing a parsimonious description of his personality structure.

(vi) That the principal dimensions thus far established are those of neuroticism, introversion-extraversion, and psychoticism.

---

[1] See, for example, the recent text of Maher (1966). For more detailed reviews of particular topics in experimental psychopathology, see Eysenck (1960a). Eysenck's Handbook will appear in a new revised edition in 1970.

[2] Essentially, this represents a rejection of the disease-model of abnormality (see Chapter 1).

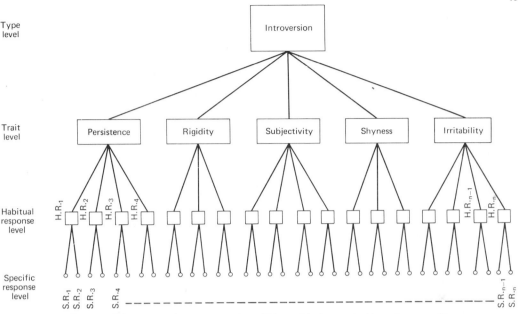

Type
level

Trait
level

Habitual
response
level

Specific
response
level

FIG. 1. Diagrammatic representation of hierarchical organization of personality (Eysenck, 1960b).

Having established the dimensions of personality, the principal task of the personality theorist becomes that of accounting for individual differences manifested along these dimensions. This may be achieved by a dynamic (causal) type of investigation which will have two main aims or functions: first, the already established empirical facts should be deducible from the theories; second, the theories should mediate new predictions which can be confirmed or disconfirmed by experimental investigations.

II. THE DIMENSIONAL ANALYSIS OF PERSONALITY[3]

As is well known, in the area of dimensional analysis of abilities, controversy has raged between the proponents of the single or "g" factor theory of intelligence, through the "g" plus group factor theories, to the multifactoral group factor theories, ranging from the extreme of the original monistic theory of Spearman to the recent postulation of Guilford of more than one hundred intellectual factors. In part, these differences represent real theoretical divergences; however, the differences are to a large extent resolvable into preferential techniques of factor analysis. Similar divergences

have occurred in the field of personality analysis. Eysenck himself has argued that personality structure may most profitably be regarded as being hierarchical in nature, and he has postulated four levels[4] of organization of personality, as shown in Figure 1. At the lowest level are responses that occur on a single occasion but are not systematic in any sense and are produced essentially by random factors present only on that occasion. At the next level we have habitual responses which are characterized by significant reliability (that is, given similar circumstances they are highly likely to occur again). The next level deals with traits that are made up of habitual responses which correlate together to form a cluster that defines the trait (e.g., of persistence). At the highest level we have the type that is made up of a group of traits which intercorrelate to define the type (e.g., neuroticism). In speaking of the fundamental dimensions of personality, Eysenck is referring to the type level, and he considers that (in addition to the nonpersonality factor of intelligence) three personality dimensions have been identified: neuroticism, introversion-extraversion, and psychoticism. Other personality theorists have proposed much larger numbers of dimensions of personality, of course. As was pointed out earlier, the differences

[3] For a more detailed, but simple, introduction to this topic, see Eysenck (1952a, Chapter 2).

[4] These levels correspond to the general, group, specific, and error factors postulated in the area of abilities analysis.

between Eysenck and these other workers can be resolved by, for example, second-order factor analyses of oblique factors.[5] Even where differences still remain after such reanalyses, one major advantage of Eysenck's more parsimonious dimensional system is the degree to which it facilitates the formulation of theoretical models of personality.

III. ESTABLISHMENT OF DIMENSIONS OF NEUROTICISM AND INTROVERSION-EXTRAVERSION[6]

Eysenck's attempt to establish the fundamental dimensions of personality followed a path common in science. He started with a group of patients considered by psychiatrists to be neurotic, factor analyzed a set of ratings of various characteristics made on these patients, and showed that factor-scores on the resulting dimensions did, in fact, discriminate neurotics from nonneurotics. Having established this first crude approximation, the primary empirical task then became one of progressively refining the dimensions with a view to eventually replacing psychiatric diagnostic categories by more meaningful dimensions, less contaminated by "noise."

1. PRELIMINARY OPERATIONAL DEFINITION

In his first large-scale study, Eysenck (1944a) intercorrelated scores of 700 neurotics[7] on a 39-item sheet covering social history, personality, and symptom manifestations. Two factors were extracted in the resulting analysis. The first ("neuroticism") was a general factor accounting for 14% of the variance and was defined by such items as: badly organized personality; dependency; preillness abnormality; lack of energy; poor muscular tone; and lack of group membership. The second bipolar factor (dysthymia/hysteria) accounted for 12% of the variance and contrasted two groups of symptoms and personality traits. The first ("Dysthymia") was defined by such items as: anxiety; depression; obsessional tendencies; irritability; headaches; tremor; and somatic

anxiety. The second ("Hysteria") was defined by such items as: hysterical conversion symptoms; sexual anomalies; hysterical attitude. The two factors were orthogonal[8] to each other, and scores on the two dimensions were normally distributed.

These two factors were initially established by the analysis of data from neurotic patients. Subsequently, it was demonstrated (Eysenck, 1952b; Himmelweit, Desai, and Petrie, 1946) that the same two dimensions appeared when normal subjects were used, thus demonstrating that both dimensions formed a continuum. Hence, the dimensions were named "Neuroticism - Normality" and "Introversion - Extraversion." It was further argued that while an extreme introversion score, for example, did not indicate any abnormal degree of neuroticism, the position of the individual on this dimension determined the kind of neurotic breakdown that would occur. Thus, the dysthymic was the prototype of the neurotic introvert; and the hysteric or psychopath the prototype of the neurotic extravert.

2. EXPERIMENTAL EXPLORATION OF THE DIMENSIONS

The next stage in the investigation involved an attempt to explicate in more detail the nature of these two dimensions. We shall briefly indicate here the nature of some of these explorations.[9]

(a) PHYSIQUE AND CONSTITUTION. As is well known, the study of the relationship between physique, constitution, and personality has been a problem of enduring interest for experimental psychology.[10] Here, we may confine our attention to the work of Kretschmer, Sheldon, and Eysenck. Kretschmer (1948) identified three body types[11]: the pyknic; the athletic; and the leptosomatic. These body types were correlated by Kretschmer with the syndromes of manic-depressive psychosis, epilepsy, and schizophrenia in their extreme form, these syndromes shading off imperceptibly into the normal personality structures of cyclothymia and schizothymia. Later, Sheldon (1940, 1942) also identified, by means of more

---

[5] See, for example, Eysenck (1960b) for a comprehensive review of factor analytic studies of personality structure.

[6] See Eysenck (1947, 1952a) for detailed analysis of these dimensions.

[7] Patients with head injury, epilepsy, CNS organic damage, and physical illness were excluded from the sample.

[8] This means, in effect, that a patient's position on one of the factors cannot be determined (predicted) from knowledge of his position on the other factor.

[9] For fuller details, see Eysenck (1947) or Eysenck (1960b).

[10] See Eysenck (1960b, Chapter 9).

[11] As Eysenck points out, Kretschmer did not conceive of types as discontinuous.

sophisticated experimental measurements and statistical analyses, three body types (endomorph, mesomorph, and ectomorph), relating these to the embryological facts concerning tissue characteristics. The endomorph, for example, was characterized by Sheldon as possessing prominent digestive viscera leading to a predominance of absorptive functions over energy functions; the mesomorph by a predominance of bones, muscles, connective tissue, and heart and blood vessels; and the ectomorph by a predominance of skin, hair, nails, sense organs, and nervous system. Sheldon also related these physique variables to temperamental factors, the endomorph being characterized by viscerotonia (love of physical comfort, love of eating, amiability of disposition, and so on); the mesomorph by somatotonia (love of physical adventure, need for exercise, aggressiveness, and so on); and the ectomorph by cerebrotonia (love of privacy, social inhibition, and so on). Sheldon measured the relative predominance of each of these dimensions in an individual and defined him in terms of his body type (thus 1-1-7 would indicate extreme ectomorphy, 3-3-4 a balanced physique).

The work of Sheldon has been severely criticized for its methodological inadequacies. Of more interest was Eysenck's investigation of the relationship between physique and personality. As we have seen, Kretschmer related physique to psychotic syndromes. An important study by Rees and Eysenck (1945) suggested, first, that two dimensions of physique could more parsimoniously explain the empirical data;[12] and that these factors were related, not to psychotic syndromes, but to the factors of neuroticism and introversion-extraversion. Rees and Eysenck intercorrelated 18 body measures (e.g., length of arm, height, breadth of shoulder and hip, chest circumference, etc.) on 300 soldiers and identified two factors: a general factor of body size, accounting for 40% of the variance; and a bipolar factor of body build, contrasting growth in length with growth in breadth and accounting for 20% of the variance. These factors, it may be noted, were found also in female samples. It was also shown that an Index of Body Size derived from the first (general) factor discriminated between neurotics and normals; while an Index of Body Build derived from the second (bipolar) factor

discriminated between hysterics and dysthymics. Thus, neurotics as a group are characterized by poor physique generally, while dysthymic neurotics tend to be leptosomatic and hysterical neurotics tend to be pyknic.[13]

(b) PHYSIOLOGICAL MEASURES.[14] The possibility that biochemical, physiological, and nervous system (autonomic and central) activities might be fundamentally related to personality has led to much research into these relationships. Physiological traits, if established as relevant to personality, might provide more stable indices of personality structure and might also help to elucidate the role of genetic factors in personality. For example, on the biochemical side, the importance of pituitary-adrenal gland relationships in determining reaction to immediate and continuing stress situations appears to have been demonstrated. Of particular interest, however, has been the work of Wenger (1941, 1942, 1966) on the relationship of autonomic nervous system activity and personality. Wenger advanced the notions of "autonomic unbalance" on the one hand, and of "adrenergic-cholinergic balance" on the other. He hypothesized that activity of the adrenergic branch of the ANS may predominate over the activity of the cholinergic branch (or vice versa); and that autonomic unbalance will be normally distributed in an unselected population.

In a factor analytic study of school children given a battery of autonomic tests, Wenger (1941) identified a factor defined by scarcity of saliva, high percentage of solids in saliva, fast heart rate, little sinus arhythmia, much palmar and volar sweating, high basal metabolic rate, and low blood pressure. In two later studies, Wenger (1948) compared a large group of normal pilots with a group of pilots suffering from operational fatigue and a group of neurotic pilots. The results indicated that the normal and abnormal groups could be clearly distinguished, the neurotic groups manifesting high salivary output, low palmar and volar conductance, long heart period, low oxygen consumption, and low systolic and diastolic pressure. Eysenck (1960b) has carefully examined Wenger's results and suggested tentatively that neuroticism may be associated with autonomic unbalance per se, while introversion-extraversion may be related to the direction of the unbalance towards adrenergic (sympathetic)

---

[12] Reanalysis of Sheldon's data also showed that two dimensions were sufficient to account for the oberserved intercorrelations.

[13] Parnell (1957) criticized the Rees/Eysenck study. For a reply to this criticism, see Eysenck (1959).

[14] See Eysenck (1960b, Chapter 8) for a comprehensive review.

activity (in extraverts) or cholinergic (para-sympathetic) activity (in introverts).

Attempts to relate physiological variables to personality variables, however, have run into serious difficulties as a result of the studies of Lacey and his colleagues (Lacey, 1950; Lacey, Bateman, and Van Lehn, 1953; Lacey and Van Lehn, 1952) on autonomic response specificity. Lacey appears to have made a convincing case for the proposition that human subjects have characteristic individualized physiological response patterns, some of which may be overactive, others underactive, yet others average, in the same stress situation. These specific response patterns tend to be very stable and to be evoked in a similar manner, whatever the nature of the stress. Thus, the present status of the relationship between autonomic variables and personality remains somewhat unclear.

(c) ABILITY AND EFFICIENCY.[15] Eysenck (1947) was able to show that, if sufficiently large groups of neurotics and normals are compared, the intelligence of neurotics as a group will be significantly lower than that of nonneurotics. While such a difference is of some theoretical interest, it has no practical implications. Of considerably greater interest are the results of studies of other aspects of efficiency of functioning. Two only will be mentioned here, the speed-accuracy discrepancy and the level of aspiration.

(i) *Speed-Accuracy Discrepancy.* In a comprehensive study, Himmelweit (1946) applied five tests to 100 neurotic patients (male and female hysterics and dysthymics). The tests[16] could be scored for both speed and accuracy. After partialling out intelligence differences, Himmelweit demonstrated that hysterics trade accuracy for speed (that is, they work quickly but inaccurately) whereas dysthymics trade speed for accuracy.

(ii) *Level of Aspiration.* In this situation, the subject is required to estimate the performance level he will achieve on trial x; on completion of trial x he is required to estimate the level he did achieve and is then required to estimate the level he will achieve on the next trial, y. The maximum possible score on the test is known to the subject when making his estimates. Two main indices of level of aspiration may be derived: *the mean goal discrepancy score* (which is the difference between actual performance on trial x and estimated performance on trial y); and *mean judgment discrepancy score* (which is the difference between estimated and actual performance level on trial x). Himmelweit (1947) applied these measures to both normal and neurotic subjects and demonstrated that dysthymics had higher levels of aspiration than hysterics (that is, their mean goal discrepancy score is higher—they overestimate the score they will obtain on trial y following trial x) but lower judgment scores (that is, their mean judgment discrepancy is lower—they underestimate the score they have just obtained). Put another way, dysthymics appear to have unrealistic goals compared to hysterics; but, at the same time, they undervalue their past performance.

(d) SUGGESTIBILITY.[17] Two problems arise here: first, is suggestibility a unitary trait; second, is there a special relationship between suggestibility and hysteria? The first question was decisively answered by studies by Eysenck (1943) and Eysenck and Furneaux (1945). Factor analysis of eight tests of suggestibility identified two clear uncorrelated factors. Primary (ideomotor) suggestibility was defined by the well-known Body Sway test, the Chevreul Pendulum test, the Arm Levitation test, and the Press-Release test.[18]

The relationship between primary suggestibility and personality was examined in a study by Eysenck (1944b) and confirmed in a later study (Eysenck, 1947). Instead of the often-postulated correlation between suggestibility and hysteria, Eysenck (1944b) found a positive correlation between degree of suggestibility and neuroticism. The later study found the same relationship in a comparison of over 900 neurotics and nearly 400 normal subjects. Amount of sway increased with degree of neuroticism. Not only was suggestibility not correlated with hysteria, there was some evidence that introverted neurotics (dysthymics) were most suggestible of all.

(e) SUMMARY. This brief review of a small selection of the investigations of Eysenck and his colleagues provides some idea of the range of studies that were carried out. Table 3.1 provides a summarizing statement of the overall picture resulting from all of these

---

[15] See Eysenck (1947, Chapter 4) for a detailed review.
[16] Hidden words; cancellation; addition; track tracer; and measuring distance between points.

[17] See Eysenck (1947, Chapter 5; or 1960b, Chapter 3) for a more comprehensive review.
[18] The second factor and a possible third identified in these studies need not be considered here.

TABLE 3.1. *Operational Definition of Introversion-Extraversion Dimension: Summary of Main Results*

Trait	Introversion	Extraversion
Neurotic syndrome	Dysthymia	Hysteria: Psychopathy
Body build	Leptomorph	Eurymorph
Intellectual function	High I.Q./Vocabulary ratio	Low I.Q./Vocabulary ratio
Perceptual rigidity	Low	High
Persistence	Low	High
Speed	High	Low
Speed/accuracy ratio	Low	High
Level of aspiration	High	Low
Intrapersonal variability	Low	High
Sociability	Low	High
Repression	Weak	Strong
Social attitudes	Tender-minded	Tough-minded
Rorschach test	M High	D High
T.A.T.	Low productivity	High productivity
Conditioning	Strong	Weak
Reminiscence	Low	High
Figural aftereffect	Small	Large
Stress Reactions	Overactive	Inert
Sedation threshold	High	Low
Perceptual constancy	Low	High
Time judgment	Longer	Shorter
Verbal conditioning	Good	Poor
Response to therapy	Good	Poor
Visual imagery	Vivid	Weak
Necker cube reversal	Slow	Fast
Perception of vertical	Accurate	Inaccurate
Spiral aftereffect	Long	Short
Time error	Small	Great
Vigilance	High	Low
Motor performance decrement	Little	Much
Problem solving performance decrement	Little	Much
Smoking	No	Yes
Car driving constancy	High	Low
Cheating	No	Yes

Source: Eysenck, 1960c.

studies in relation to the major personality differences between introverts and extraverts. Table 3.2 provides a summarizing statement of the overall picture in relation to neuroticism.[19]

IV. NEUROTICISM—THEORETICAL

Eysenck (1947) has provided a useful discussion of the various classes of theoretical interpretation of the neurotic dimension. He points out that there are three main classes of theory. The first asserts that neurotic phenomena are types of response to which all human beings are equally liable, the determining factor being the degree of stress to which the individual is subjected (the environmental theory). The second asserts that neuroticism is dependent on constitutional, genetically determined factors

---

[19] This summarizing statement was based on studies largely carried out with soldiers.

(the hereditary predisposition theory). Neuroticism may be a function of either a single abnormal gene (the unifactorial version of the theory); or it may be a function of the operation of a large number of separate genes, each having a small but similar effect (the multifactorial version of the theory). The third theory (multiple causation) also has two variants: either a separate gene (or group of genes) is postulated for each form of neurosis (specific form); or separate but overlapping genes are postulated, producing predisposition to more than one type of neurosis (overlapping form). After considering the meager available evidence relating to each of these theories, Eysenck tentatively endorses the multifactorial version of the hereditary predisposition theory but at the same time argues that the appearance of a neurosis is a function of the interaction between strength of hereditary predisposition and amount of environmental stress. Thus, a person with a strong predisposition may not

develop a neurosis if living in a very low stress environment; a person with a weak predisposition may nevertheless develop a neurosis if subjected to an exceptional degree of stress. As to the behavioral nature of the genetic predisposition, Eysenck (1960a) has argued that high neuroticism involves unbalance of the autonomic nervous system:

> "The individual high on neuroticism is conceived to be a person with an overreactive, labile type of nervous system, a person who reacts too strongly, and too persistently to strong external stimuli" (Eysenck, 1960b, p. 28).

This statement is immediately qualified by Eysenck in deference to the demonstration by Lacey and his colleagues of autonomic response specificity, and he suggests that the excessive lability may refer only to subsystems of the ANS and not to ANS reactivity as a whole. It may be noted here that, in other publications,

TABLE 3.2. *Operational Definition of the Neuroticism Dimension*

Method of Assessment	Characteristics
Clinical ratings	Badly organized personality
	Dependent
	Abnormal before illness
	Narrow interests
	Little energy
	Abnormality in parents
	Poor muscular tone
	Unsatisfactory home
	No group membership
Self-assessments	Inferiority feelings
	Touchy
	Nervous
	Autonomic symptoms
	Disgruntled
	Accident-prone
	Effort-intolerant
Constitution	Physique: inadequate
	Effort response: poor
	Dark vision: poor
	Static equilibrium: poor
Test performance	High suggestibility
	Poor persistence
	Slow personal tempo
	Low fluency
	Extreme perseveration

Source (adapted). Eysenck, 1947.

Eysenck has tended to identify autonomic lability with states of high drive (e.g., Eysenck, 1962). In a later section, this question will be considered further.

V. INTROVERSION/EXTRAVERSION —THEORETICAL

Eysenck's theory of introversion/extraversion is derived largely from the work of Hull and Pavlov. It does not seem to be generally realized that Eysenck has, in fact, advanced two versions of the theory, which will be considered in turn.

1. FIRST VERSION OF THE THEORY

In this version (Eysenck, 1955b), three postulates were invoked.

(i) "Whenever any stimulus-response connection is made in an organism (excitation), there also occurs simultaneously a reaction in the nervous structures mediating this connection which opposes its recurrence;"

(ii) "Human beings differ with respect to the speed with which reactive inhibition [I_R] is produced, the strength of [I_R] and the speed with which [I_R] is dissipated. These differences themselves are properties of the physical structures involved in the evocation of responses;"

(iii) "Individuals in whom [I_R] is generated quickly, in whom strong [I_R] are generated, and in whom [I_R] is dissipated slowly are thereby predisposed to develop extraverted patterns of behavior and to develop hysterical disorders in cases of neurotic breakdown; conversely, individuals in whom [I_R] is generated slowly, in whom weak [I_R] are generated, and in whom [I_R] is dissipated quickly, are thereby predisposed to develop introverted patterns of behavior and to develop dysthymic disorders in cases of neurotic breakdown" (Eysenck, 1955b, pp. 96–97).

It will be noted that introversion/extraversion differences are here related to differences in the rate of growth, strength, and rate of dissipation of reactive inhibition (I_R) and that no mention is made of the other variables (D; $_sH_R$; and $_sI_R$) in Hull's basic equation.

2. EXPERIMENTAL EVIDENCE

Eysenck (1957)[20] has reviewed in detail the very large number and range of predictions that were generated by this theory, and it would be impossible to refer here to all of these studies. Some idea of the richness of the predictions generated may be gained from a sampling of the areas of behavior covered.

(a) CONDITIONING OF INTROVERTS AND EXTRAVERTS. It was hypothesized that extraverts would condition slowly and introverts quickly by comparison with a control group whose introversion score was average, since, during conditioning, inhibition (I_R) would build up more rapidly in the extraverts. The prediction was tested by Franks (1956, 1957) in relation to the conditioned eyeblink. He confirmed the hypothesis using hysterics and dysthymics as criterion groups and later replicated these results with normal extraverts and introverts. Similarly, extraverts extinguished more slowly than introverts.

(b) REMINISCENCE. If two groups of subjects are given an equal number of trials on an unfamiliar motor skill learning task, one group practicing under massed practice conditions, the other under spaced practice conditions, usually the spaced practice group will show a superior performance curve compared with the massed practice group. If, however, both groups are given a rest period following which practice is resumed, the spaced practice group will commence at the level of skill it attained on the last prerest trial but the massed practice group will show an increment in performance following rest. This postrest increment in performance is usually attributed to the dissipation of the I_R during the rest period, the accumulation of I_R during the massed practice period preceding rest supposedly having depressed the performance (that is, concealing the true rate of growth of the skill) of the massed practice group. If the theory is correct, then it follows from Eysenck's theory that, under conditions of massed practice, extraverts should show a more depressed performance curve than introverts and should manifest a greater reminiscence effect following rest. These predictions were tested by Eysenck (1956), using the pursuit rotor task with three five-minute periods of massed practice, the first two of which were followed by 10-minute rest periods. Two reminiscence scores were thus obtained. A significant correlation was obtained between the first reminiscence score and extraversion, thus offering some support for the hypothesis.

---

[20] Later experimental evidence will be found in Eysenck (1960d) in particular as well as in numerous separate papers.

(c) VIGILANCE. A task of this kind, which involves essentially a repetitive, monotonous stimulation situation, is clearly one in which I_R would be expected to accumulate over time. If signals are injected periodically and non-systematically into this situation and the subject is required to respond to them, it would be expected that extraverts would miss more signals than introverts, with the number of missed signals increasing in frequency over time. This would be true provided the inserted signals were of low intensity, since clearly sudden strong signals might produce disinhibition. The prediction was tested by Claridge (1960) who used a 30-minute tape recording of digits read at the rate of one per second. A random sequence was used, but at an average interval of 56 seconds, a sequence of three successive odd digits occurred for which the subject was instructed to listen and identify by an appropriate response. There were three such odd sequences which were separated by intervals ranging from three seconds to one minute 41 seconds. The criterion groups were normals, hysterics, and dysthymics. The results supported the hypothesis that hysterics (who detected an average of 15.44 signals) would miss more signals than the dysthymics (24.75 signals detected), with the normals falling in between

(21.06 signals detected). Furthermore, all three groups showed a decline in performance over the 30-minute period, with the hysterics showing a steeper decline than the other two groups, as would be expected. A puzzling, unexplained feature of the data for the normal group, however, was the fact that the normal introverts showed a steeper rate of decline than the normal extraverts and were performing more poorly at the end of the period.

(d) TIME-ERROR AND TIME-JUDGMENT. Claridge (1960) also investigated time-error in extraverts and introverts. If a tone produces both excitation and inhibition, then the latter will reduce the apparent intensity of the tone as a function of its presentation time; hence a following tone of objectively the same intensity will appear louder (negative time error). The prediction follows that extraverts will manifest a larger negative time error than introverts. Claridge also argued that the time error will increase as the time interval between the two tones is increased, though the derivation of this prediction is not so clear. In his experiment on time-error Claridge used a pure tone of 1100 Hz at 75 db for his first stimulus tone. The following tone varied in intensity from 73 to 77 db by 1 db steps, while the interval between the two tones was varied from one to six seconds. The results

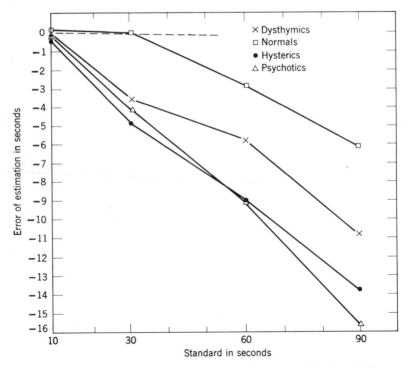

FIG. 2. Time judgment error in extraverts and introverts (Claridge, 1960).

TABLE 3.3. *Mean Time Estimations of Introverts and Extraverts with Positive Feedback Technique*

Trial	Introverts		Extraverts		t
	$\bar{x}$	σ	$\bar{x}$	σ	
1	15.2	4.2	15.4	5.3	NS
2	14.5	2.6	15.0	4.5	NS
3	14.2	6.3	13.5	5.1	NS
4	12.7	4.1	13.0	7.0	NS
5	12.3	6.5	12.5	7.3	NS
6	13.9	6.3	11.8	8.7	NS
7	15.5	7.6	11.6	8.7	NS
8	17.7	7.0	11.3	8.9	0.05
9	17.5	9.4	10.4	8.7	0.05
10	18.4	11.4	10.2	9.6	0.05

Source: Lynn, 1961.

were in accordance with the predictions except for the longest time interval (six seconds).

With respect to time-judgment, Claridge argued that if the subject is required to judge the length of unfilled time-intervals, I_R should accumulate (the situation being a repetitive stimulation one) as a function of the lapse of unfilled time. Hence, the greater the amount of I_R generated the sooner the time interval will be judged as over before it actually is (under-reproduction or overestimation). Extraverts should show greater time overestimation than introverts. The task was to estimate time intervals of 10, 30, 60, and 90 seconds, and the results clearly supported the prediction (Figure 2).

An ingenious extension of Claridge's work was carried out by Lynn (1961), making use of the technique devised by Llewellyn-Thomas (1959). The subject was first required to estimate a time interval of 15 seconds. His actual time judgment on that trial was then used as the interval to be estimated on the next trial. It would be expected, using this procedure, that the time estimations of introverts and extraverts would progressively diverge and this indeed was found to be the case, as the results shown in Table 3.3 indicate.

3. NEGATIVE RESULTS

The studies reviewed above represent only a small fraction of the many attempts made to test Eysenck's theory of introversion-extraversion. By no means all of the attempts have succeeded in providing support for Eysenck's 1955 version of his theory, and some studies (e.g., Rechtschaffen, 1958; Becker, 1960) have resulted in contradictory evidence. The possible reasons for these conflicting results are many but, before considering them, it is necessary to turn to the second version of Eysenck's theory, since this appears to be the one he has held since it was propounded.

4. SECOND VERSION OF THE THEORY

In this version (Eysenck, 1957) asserted that:

". . . individuals in whom excitatory potential is generated slowly and in whom excitatory potentials so generated are relatively weak, are thereby predisposed to develop extraverted patterns of behavior and to develop hysterical psychopathic disorders in cases of neurotic breakdown . . ." (Eysenck, 1957, p. 114).

while the contrary is asserted to be the case for introverted subjects. The postulate concerning the rate of growth, strength, and rate of dissipation of I_R is retained in identical form to that in the 1955 version.

Let us now consider this second version in relation to the basic equation of Hull:

$$s\bar{E}_R = (sH_R \times D) - (I_R + sI_R)$$

The basic difference between the two versions of the theory lies, of course, in the introduction of the postulation of differences in the rate of growth of "excitation" as well as inhibition in extraverts and introverts. Now, as we have seen, Eysenck has linked neuroticism with high drive (D), and he also regards the dimensions of introversion-extraversion and neuroticism as orthogonal to each other. Hence, in terms of Hull's equation, he must be referring to the term sH_R when he talks of excitatory potential. Thus, he has argued that:

"There is no indication in our system that difference in irrelevant drive should produce any differences in conditionability; consequently our prediction points to a correlation between conditionability and extraversion-introversion, but not to any correlation between neuroticism and conditionability" (Eysenck, 1957, p. 115).

He has inferred that normal and neurotic introverts should condition equally well.

In the light of this discussion, it may also be noted now that the attempts reviewed earlier to test the inhibition theory and later attempts to test the later version have been, for the most part, seriously confounded. As an example, consider the prediction that extraverts will show greater reminiscence than introverts. Of necessity, comparison of the postrest performance of groups of introverts and extraverts, while the particular associations under investigation are still being acquired, must confound the rate of growth and strength of sH_R with the rate of growth and strength of I_R, since sH_R by definition is not asymptotic. Hence, at the point at which the rest pause is instituted, extraverts and introverts may not only differ in the amount of I_R generated, but may also differ in the strength of sH_R; indeed, the 1957 version predicts that they will differ with respect to sH_R.

Yates and Laszlo (1965) attempted to resolve these difficulties and provide an unequivocal test of both versions of the theory. In order to test the second version of the theory (that extraverts and introverts will differ in the rate of growth of sH_R), it is clearly necessary to control the other variables (D, I_R, and sI_R) in Hull's equation. It was proposed to do this by matching subjects for D and training them on the pursuit-rotor under conditions of spaced practice. Since

I_R would not accumulate under conditions of spaced practice, sI_R would also not accumulate and, in effect, the actual performance curve obtained would be a true reflection of the rate of growth of sH_R. Thus, if it is true that extraverts build up sH_R more slowly than introverts, then, under spaced conditions of practice, the extraverts will reach the same asymptotic levels as introverts but will approach the asymptote more slowly.

If both groups are trained under these conditions to asymptotic level, it then becomes possible to obtain a direct test of the 1955 version of the theory (that extraverts accumulate I_R more rapidly than introverts) by switching both groups to a condition of massed practice. In this case, sH_R is controlled (since it is asymptotic and cannot be increased by further practice) and D is controlled also, since the groups have been matched on this variable. During massed practice, some growth in the strength of sH_R may be expected to occur, but the 1955 version of the theory can be tested by examining the performance curves for the initial trials where, if I_R is accumulating more rapidly in the extraverts, it would be expected that they would show greater performance decrement than the introverts.

Yates and Laszlo constructed two groups of extraverts and introverts which were clearly differentiated both on the MPI questionnaire measure of extraversion and on another test (time error) of extraversion and which were matched on the MPI Neuroticism Scale (all subjects in both groups falling within $\pm .5\sigma$ of the average neuroticism score.) Thus, there were ten extreme introverts and ten extreme extraverts available from an initial sample of 260 first-year psychology students.

These groups were given forty 12-second spaced[21] practice trials following which they were switched to massed practice trials for seven minutes. The dependent variable was, of course, time on target on the last 10 seconds of each 12-second trial.

The results obtained are shown in Figures 3 and 4 and are quite clear cut. With respect to the acquisition curves, it is clear that the rates of approach both to the asymptote and to the asymptotic levels are virtually identical for both groups throughout training. It is interesting to note that asymptotic level was attained in both

---

[21] A careful review of the literature on spaced and massed practice in relation to the pursuit rotor suggested that work periods of 12 seconds followed

by rest periods of 58 seconds would constitute optimal spaced practice conditions, i.e., that little or no I_R would be generated.

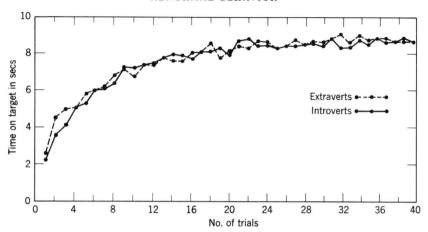

FIG. 3.   Pursuit-rotor learning (spaced practice) of extreme extraverts and introverts (Yates and Laszlo, 1965).

groups by about trial 22 and maintained unchanged through trials 23–40 at about 85–90% time on target. The high level of time on target attained[22] and the fact that no decrement in performance was obtained after asymptotic level was achieved suggests that true spaced practice was accomplished and the growth of I_R prevented. Thus the results for the acquisition phase do not support the hypothesis that sH_R grows more slowly in extraverts. Under massed practice, on the other hand, there was an average decrement of about 30% in time on target during the seven minutes of practice. While, within the theoretical framework here adopted, this decrement may reasonably be attributed to the accumulation of I_R, no

difference was found between the two groups in this respect, throwing doubt on the validity of the 1955 version of the theory (that extraverts build up I_R more rapidly than introverts).

5. COMPLEXITIES OF THE THEORY

The description of the Yates/Laszlo study has been given in some detail, not in order to refute Eysenck's theory but to indicate the methodological complexities involved in attempting to obtain an adequate test of it. That these complexities exist cannot be denied and, indeed, Eysenck himself has spelled them out in considerable detail (Eysenck, 1962, 1965a, 1965b). It should be noted carefully, however, that the

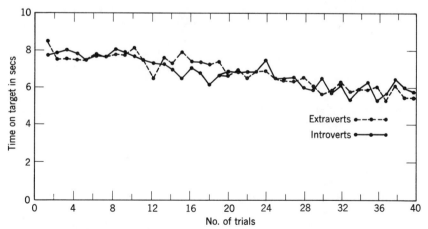

FIG. 4.   Decrement of pursuit-rotor performance from asymptotic level (massed practice) in extreme extraverts and introverts (Yates and Laszlo, 1965).

[22] Under similar conditions of speed of rotation of the turntable, a time on target of about 45–50% is more usually obtained, but spacing of practice

was probably not so successfully achieved in these studies.

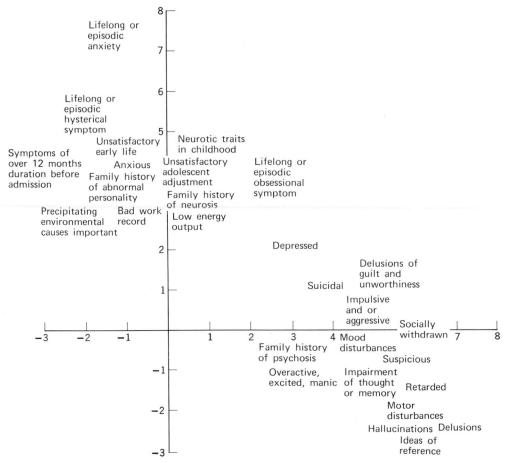

FIG. 5.   Items defining neuroticism and psychoticism factors (Eysenck, 1960a).

existence of these complexities does not render Eysenck's theory of extraversion-introversion untestable in the sense that psychoanalytic propositions are untestable. It will be apparent that the Eysenck, theory is stated in such a way as to enable efforts to be made in a meaningful way to work out the experimental implications of the theory and subject these to empirical test.

It may also be noted at this point that Eysenck, in the face of criticism (e.g., Champion, 1961; Storms and Sigal, 1958), has not been unwilling to modify his position. Thus, Eysenck and Claridge (1962) have conceded that, while the introversion and neuroticism dimensions are orthogonal in normal samples, they appear to correlate negatively in neurotic samples; that hysterics appear to have lower neuroticism scores than dysthymics and do not appear to be significantly more extraverted than normals. While these admissions are damaging to the

general theory, Eysenck has attempted to account for the discrepancies by a rational analysis of the boundary conditions (Spence, 1956) involved. It is not possible to pursue these considerations further here. There is no doubt, however, that Eysenck's theories have justified themselves if only on the grounds that they have mediated such a substantial body of empirical research.

VI. PSYCHOTICISM

The dimensional analyses on the basis of which Eysenck has postulated the existence of a psychoticism factor (Eysenck, 1952b; Eysenck, S.B.G., 1956; Trouton and Maxwell, 1956) will be considered in detail in a later chapter.[23] Here it need only be mentioned that his contention that a single factor of psychoticism may be meaningfully postulated has been subjected to considerable criticism.[24]

---

[23] See Chapter 14.

[24] Chapter 14.

VII. NEUROTICISM, PSYCHOTICISM, AND INTROVERSION-EXTRAVERSION

If, however, a dimension of psychoticism is accepted, then the question arises of the relationship between the three primary dimensions. Basically, Eysenck has argued that the three dimensions are orthogonal (i.e., uncorrelated) and has attempted to demonstrate this by the use of two major statistical techniques, factor analysis and discriminant function analysis. Using the first technique, Trouton and Maxwell (1956) used 45 ratings on over 800 randomly selected patients, correlated the ratings, and factor analyzed them. The analysis identified two orthogonal factors which were labeled neuroticism and psychoticism and defined by the items appearing in Figure 5. Canonical variate analysis of the symptom ratings produced factor scores on each of the dimensions for various clinically diagnosed groups. The results, as shown in Figure 6,

completely separated the psychotic from the neurotic groups, a remarkable result considering the unreliability of psychiatric diagnosis.

A similar degree of separation, using canonical variate analysis was achieved by Eysenck (1955c) and by Eysenck, S.B.G. (1956), Eysenck, S.B.G., et al (1960). The relationship between these two dimensions and introversion-extraversion has not been extensively examined, but a recent study by Eysenck and Eysenck (1968a) has tentatively identified the three orthogonal factors in a large group of normal subjects, using questionnaire measures.[25]

VIII. GENOTYPE AND PHENOTYPE

In the previous discussion the terms "neurosis" and "neuroticism" and "psychosis" and "psychoticism" as well as "constitutional extraversion" and "behavioral extraversion" have been used. Although these terms have been used somewhat interchangeably by Eysenck, it is quite clear that he has always intended to

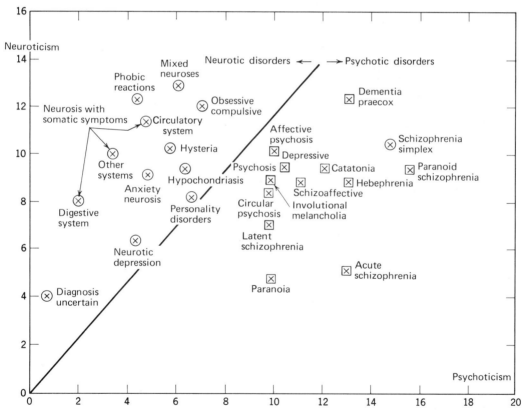

FIG. 6. Position of various clinically diagnosed groups of neurotics and psychotics in two-dimensional framework provided by canonical variate analysis of symptom ratings (Eysenck, 1960a).

---

[25] For fuller details, see also Eysenck and Eysenck (1968b).

draw a clear distinction between them and, more recently, this distinction has been made more explicit. Let us consider, as an example, the extraversion-introversion dimension. The basis for individual differences along this dimension is held by Eysenck to reside in genetically determined properties of the nervous system which, in the case of extraverts, lead to the rapid buildup of reactive inhibition under conditions of repetitive stimulation. This property of the nervous system leads to important behavioral consequences which we have already considered. It also leads to important predictions in other directions, which will be considered in detail in later chapters. For example, the poor conditionability of the extravert will lead to poor socialization and hence to a tendency to break rules and so on. Clearly, however, the genetically determined characteristics of the nervous system provide only a potentiality for the development of these behaviors. Just as height is a function of inherited capacity for growing to a certain maximum height but the actual height attained will be a function also of, for example, nutritional factors,[26] so it may be argued that whether or not a person constitutionally predisposed to extraversion manifests behavioral extraversion depends both on the predisposition and on the environmental influences to which he is subjected. Thus, a person who is constitutionally predisposed to extraversion but who is subjected to a very severe training regimen with respect to socialization may turn out to be a behavioral introvert; whereas a person who is constitutionally predisposed to introversion but whose socialization is seriously neglected may turn out to be behaviorally extraverted.[27] The importance of the distinction between constitutional and behavioral manifestations of extraversion lies in the fact that most of the validation studies of Eysenck's theory of extraversion choose their criterion groups of extraverts and introverts on measures which are confounded. Clearly, a questionnaire measure contains items which refer to the end-product of the interaction between constitution and environment. In fact, Eysenck's theory of introversion-extraversion can be properly tested only by first devising basic measures of constitutional introversion-extraversion; identifying constitutional group of extraverts and introverts as early in life as possible (before, that is, environmental pressures or lack of them have produced significant modifications of the basic predisposition); measuring the type and degree of environmental pressures and training to which these groups are exposed; and predicting in a longitudinal study changes in behavioral extraversion as a result of the iteration of these factors. Such a study has not yet been carried out and would obviously be difficult to perform.

The relationship between the genotype and the phenotype with respect to introversion-extraversion is shown in Figure 7 (Eysenck, 1963). Four levels of organization of the dimension of extraversion-introversion are postulated. The excitation-inhibition balance is the basic, constitutional, genetically-determined theoretical construct which, in principle, could be measured if culture-free tests could be found. At present, this balance can be measured only indirectly and in a contaminated form by such measures as after-image duration, vigilance, conditioning, reminiscence, and figural after-effects. Environmental influences (such as degree of socialization training) produce the behavioral manifestations of introversion-extraversion manifested in such traits as sociability, impulsivity, ascendance, and so on, while at a still more complex level, the interaction of the constitutional and environmental variables produces differential attitudes such as tough-mindedness or tendermindedness, and so on.

The same distinction between constitutional and behavioral individual differences may be applied in relation to the neuroses and psychoses. Thus, individuals may be considered with respect to their degree of neuroticism defined as a genetically determined predisposition to develop a neurosis under appropriate degrees of environmental stress. A large amount of stress would be required to

---

[26] Thus, a person may have the potential to grow to a height of six feet. Poor nutrition may result in growth to a height of only 5ft. 10in.; on the other hand, however favorable the conditions for growth, a height of six feet will not be exceeded. The inherited capacity sets upper limits, but the actual height is a function of the interaction of the predisposition with environmental factors. The fact that London schoolchildren are on average two inches taller and many pounds heavier than they were 50 years ago indicates that improved nutrition and other environmental factors have enabled them to realize their potential more, not that genetic inheritance has changed significantly.

[27] It should be noted that Eysenck has never held that constitutional extraverts are untrainable with respect to socialization; but only that they are more difficult to socialize.

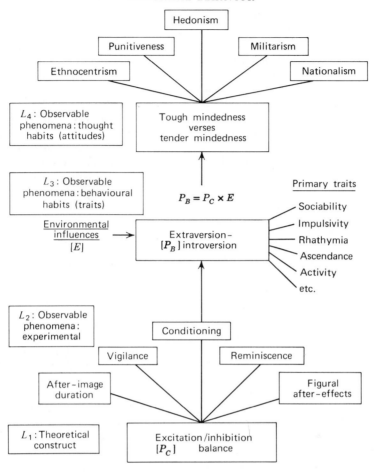

FIG. 7. Relationship between genotype and phenotype in extraversion-introversion (Eysenck, 1963).

produce a neurosis in a person low in neuroticism, whereas only a small amount of stress would be required to produce a neurosis in a person high in neuroticism.[28] One implication of this distinction would be that successful elimination of the neurotic behaviors would leave the neuroticism variable untouched; presumably, the latter could be modified only by the use of chemical agents, such as drugs. It should be noted that there is no implication here of the adoption of a position similar to that of the psychodynamic psychologists, nor is it implied that treatment of neurotic behavior is not worthwhile. Similarly, a distinction can be drawn between psychoticism and psychosis. The distinction between psychoticism and psychosis is not, however, exactly analogous to that

between neuroticism and neurosis. In the case of the neuroses, it may be argued that the primary effort in terms of treatment should be directed toward the neurotic behavior, since this behavior is acquired by learning. It seems likely, however, that in the case of the psychoses, the psychotic behavior is not learned but is a direct byproduct of biochemical disturbance. In other words, in the case of the psychoses, the situation may be more analogous to the psychotic behavior produced by, for example, excessively raised blood sugar level. In the latter case, treatment is directed, not toward the psychotic behavior but toward lowering the blood sugar level; if the latter aim is successfully accomplished, the psychotic behavior disappears.

---

[28] A significant modification of this position will be developed below.

IX. NEUROTICISM, NEUROSIS, AND ABNORMAL BEHAVIOR

In this final section, attention will be drawn to an important distinction which is often overlooked. It is intended to distinguish throughout this book between *neurotic behavior* and *abnormal behavior* and, in particular, to argue that while neurotic behavior is abnormal, not all abnormal behavior is neurotic.

Let us repeat first the definition reproduced earlier in this chapter of Eysenck's conception of neuroticism.

"The individual high on neuroticism is conceived to be a person with an over-reactive, labile type of nervous system, a person who reacts too strongly, and too persistently to strong external stimuli" (Eysenck, 1960b, p. 28).

We propose to modify this definition of neuroticism by arguing that the excessive lability of the autonomic nervous system renders weak (not strong) stimuli threatening to a person with such a labile system and that this perception of the world as threatening obtains from birth in such an individual. The result will be that such an individual will, by means of the conditioning processes described in the previous chapter, build up early in life a wide range of conditioned avoidance responses. The particular form (phobias, obsessions, or whatever) that these avoidance behaviors take will be dependent on environmental circumstances. Thus, a neurosis may be defined as the interaction between high neuroticism and low stress.

A person low on neuroticism will not, of course, tend to develop such avoidance behaviors. However, if stress is excessive (for example, if the individual is subjected to a highly traumatic experience), then a specific abnormal behavior may be instituted in a person who is essentially normal.

The distinction between these two kinds of abnormal behavior and their genesis has a number of important consequences. First, we propose to define as a neurosis the occurrence of polysymptomatic abnormalities. A "normal" person (that is, a person low on neuroticism) who develops an abnormality of behavior will tend to develop a monosymptomatic disorder but should not be called a neurotic. The distinction may most clearly be seen in the phobias. There is no doubt whatever that monosymptomatic phobias occur (e.g., an intense fear of snakes); there is also no doubt that some patients display a wide range of phobias. It is argued that the former situation arises where a person low in neuroticism is subjected to a traumatic experience, whereas the latter situation arises more gradually in a person high in neuroticism. To call both types of patients neurotic is to miss a crucial distinction. Second, it would be expected that treatment of the monosymptomatic disorder would be more successful (or, at least, less time consuming) than treatment of the polysymptomatic disorder and that recurrence of a successfully treated disorder would be less likely in the former case than in the latter, since the presence of high lability of the ANS would make it easier for the latter to develop new symptoms.

It is possible to extend these ideas further by referring to the notions of passive (response-correlated) and active (nonresponse-correlated) avoidance learning discussed in the previous chapter and then by linking these with the dimension of introversion-extraversion. Let us consider the phobias and obsessions. The distinction often drawn between these two disorders is confused by the different levels of terminology used to describe them. Thus, in the former case, we are referring, when using the term "phobia," to the conditioned fear which is part of the disorder; in the latter case, we are referring, when using the term "obsession," to the overt behavior of the patient. In both disorders, however, it is essential to distinguish between the drive which produces the abnormal behavior (which, in turn, reduces the drive) and the behavior itself. In fact, in both phobias and obsessions, we may postulate the existence of conditioned fear which produces avoidance behaviors which reduce the fear. In the case of the phobia, however, the conditioned fear is response correlated and produced by the subject approaching closer to the feared object. The result is passive avoidance behavior. In the case of the obsession, it is argued that the conditioned fear is nonresponse correlated, being produced by the occurrence of fear-inducing conditioned stimuli in the external environment and that, therefore, obsessional behavior represents an instance of active avoidance behavior.

Now, in Eysenck's dimensional system, both obsessions and phobias occur in introverted subjects who are also high on neuroticism. It is meaningful to ask whether a similar distinction can be made in relation to the extraverted neurotic. It is here proposed that the interaction of these variables with extraversion and neuroticism will produce either diminished nonorganic sensory, perceptual, and motor functioning (passive avoidance behavior) such as hysterical blindness, deafness, anesthesia, aphonia, writer's cramp, and so on or heightened nonorganic sensory, perceptual, and motor functioning (active avoidance behavior) such as tics, asthma, excessive frequency of micturition, somnambulism, and so on.

Thus, by the use of the variables of neuroticism, stress, introversion-extraversion, and response / nonresponse - correlated avoidance learning, it is possible to develop a unified theory for the explanation of obsessions, phobias, and the so-called hysterical disorders.

It should finally be repeated that some abnormalities of behavior should not be considered within this framework of the interaction of neuroticism and stress at all but, instead, should be accounted for in terms of other theoretical models. Thus, as we shall see in later chapters, there is no evidence whatever that either enuresis or stuttering is indicative of high neuroticism or that these disorders constitute even examples of traumatic avoidance learning in normal subjects. In the case of enuresis, it will be argued that this disorder involves a failure to acquire a complex set of inhibitory controls; in the case of stuttering, that a defect in the feedback systems controlling speech output is the cause of the disorder.

In summary, it is maintained that there are four great classes of disorder: those which result from a combination of high neuroticism with objectively low stress which is perceived as threatening by the subject; those which appear in persons low in neuroticism but who are subjected to a high degree of stress; those which appear in persons low in neuroticism but who fail to acquire complex skills due to faulty feedback control mechanisms; and those which appear in persons high in psychoticism.

REFERENCES

Becker, W.C. Cortical inhibition and extraversion-introversion. *J. abnorm. soc. Psychol.*, 1960, **61**, 52–66.

Champion, R.A. Some comments on Eysenck's treatment of modern learning theory. *Brit. J. Psychol.*, 1961, **52**, 161–173.

Claridge, G. The excitation-inhibition balance in neurotics. In Eysenck, H.J. (ed.). *Experiments in personality* (Vol. II). London: Routledge and Kegan Paul, 1960, pp. 107–154.

Eysenck, H.J. Suggestibility and hysteria. *J. Neurol. Neurosurg. Psychiat.*, 1943, **6**, 22–31.

Eysenck, H.J. Types of personality—a factorial study of 700 neurotics. *J. ment. Sci.*, 1944, **90**, 851–861 (a).

Eysenck, H.J. States of high suggestibility and the neuroses. *Amer. J. Psychol.*, 1944, **57**, 406–411 (b).

Eysenck, H.J. *Dimensions of personality*. London: Routledge and Kegan Paul, 1947.

Eysenck, H.J. *The scientific study of personality*. London: Routledge and Kegan Paul, 1952 (a).

Eysenck, H.J. Cyclothymia and schizothymia as a dimension of personality: II. Experimental. *J. Pers.*, 1952, **30**, 345–384 (b).

Eysenck, H.J. A dynamic theory of anxiety and hysteria. *J. ment. Sci.*, 1955, **101**, 28–51 (a).

Eysenck, H.J. Cortical inhibition, figural after-effect and the theory of personality. *J. abnorm. soc. Psychol.*, 1955, **51**, 94–106 (b).

Eysenck, H.J. Psychiatric diagnosis as a psychological and statistical problem. *Psychol. Rep.*, 1955, **1**, 3–17 (c).

Eysenck, H.J. Reminiscence, drive and personality theory. *J. abnorm. soc. Psychol.*, 1956, **53**, 328–333.

Eysenck, H.J. *The dynamics of anxiety and hysteria*. London: Routledge and Kegan Paul, 1957.

Eysenck, H.J. The Rees-Eysenck Body Index and Sheldon's somatotype system. *J. ment. Sci.*, 1959, **105**, 1053–1058.

Eysenck, H.J. (ed.). *Handbook of abnormal psychology*. London: Pitman, 1960 (a).

Eysenck, H.J. *The structure of human personality* (2nd ed.). London: Methuen, 1960 (b).

Eysenck, H.J. Levels of personality, constitutional factors, and social influences: an experimental approach. *Internat. J. soc. Psychiat.*, 1960, **6**, 12–24 (c).

Eysenck, H.J. (ed.). *Experiments in personality* (Vols. I and II). London: Routledge and Kegan Paul, 1960 (d).

Eysenck, H.J. Reminiscence, drive and personality—revision and extension of a theory. *Brit. J. soc. clin. Psychol.*, 1962, **1**, 127–140.

Eysenck, H.J. Biological basis of personality. *Nature*, 1963, **199**, 1031–1034.

Eysenck, H.J. Extraversion and the acquisition of eyeblink and GSR conditioned responses. *Psychol. Bull.*, 1965, **63**, 258–270 (a).

Eysenck, H.J. A three-factor theory of reminiscence. *Brit. J. Psychol.*, 1965, **56**, 163–181 (b).

Eysenck, H.J. & Claridge, G. The position of hysterics and dysthymics in a two-dimensional framework of personality description. *J. abnorm. soc. Psychol.*, 1962, **64**, 46–55.

Eysenck, H.J. & Eysenck, S.B.G. A factorial study of psychoticism as a dimension of personality. *Multivariate Behav. Res.* (special issue), 1968, 15–32 (a).

Eysenck, H.J. & Eysenck, S.B.G. *Personality, structure and measurement*. London: Routledge and Kegan Paul, 1968 (b).

Eysenck, H.J. & Furneaux, W.D. Primary and secondary suggestibility: an experimental and statistical study. *J. exp. Psychol.*, 1945, **35**, 485–503.

Eysenck, S.B.G. Neurosis and psychosis: an experimental analysis. *J. ment. Sci.*, 1956, **102**, 517–529.

Eysenck, S.B.G., Eysenck, H.J., & Claridge, G. Dimensions of personality, psychiatric syndromes, and mathematical models. *J. ment. Sci.*, 1960, **106**, 581–589.

Franks, C.M. Conditioning and personality: a study of normal and neurotic subjects. *J. abnorm. soc. Psychol.*, 1956, **52**, 143–150.

Franks, C.M. Personality factors and rate of conditioning. *Brit. J. Psychol.*, 1957, **48**, 119–126.

Himmelweit, H.T. Speed and accuracy of work as related to temperament. *Brit. J. Psychol.*, 1946, **36**, 132–144.

Himmelweit, H.T. A comparative study of the level of aspiration of normal and neurotic persons. *Brit. J. Psychol.*, 1947, **37**, 41–59.

Himmelweit, H.T., Desai, M., & Petrie, A. An experimental investigation of neuroticism. *J. Pers.*, 1946, **15**, 173–196.

Kretschmer, E. *Körperbau und charakter*. Berlin: Springer, 1948.

Lacey, J.I. Individual differences in somatic response patterns. *J. comp. physiol. Psychol.*, 1950, **43**, 338–350.

Lacey, J.I., Bateman, D.E., & Van Lehn, R. Autonomic response specificity: an experimental study. *Psychosom. Med.*, 1953, **15**, 8–21.

Lacey, J.I. & Van Lehn, R. Differential emphasis on somatic response to stress. *Psychosom. Med.*, 1952, **14**, 71–81.

Llewellyn-Thomas, E. Successive time-estimation during automatic positive feedback. *Percept. Mot. Skills*, 1959, **9**, 219–224.

Lynn, R. Introversion-extraversion differences in judgments of time. *J. abnorm. soc. Psychol.*, 1961, **63**, 457–458.

Maher, B.A. *Principles of psychopathology*. New York: McGraw-Hill, 1966.

Parnell, R.W. The Rees-Eysenck Body Index of individual somatoptypes. *J. ment. Sci.*, 1957, **103**, 209–213.

Rechtschaffen, G. Neural satiation, reactive inhibition and introversion-extraversion. *J. abnorm. soc. Psychol.*, 1958, **57**, 283–291.

Rees, L. & Eysenck, H.J. A factorial study of some morphological and psychological aspects of human constitution. *J. ment. Sci.*, 1945, **91**, 8–21.

Sheldon, W.H. *The varieties of human physique*. New York: Harper, 1940.

Sheldon, W.H. *The varieties of temperament*. New York: Harper, 1942.

Spence, K.W. *Behavior theory and conditioning*. New Haven: Yale Univer. Press, 1956.

Storms, L.H. & Sigal, J.J. Eysenck's personality theory with special reference to the dynamics of anxiety and hysteria. *Brit. J. med. Psychol.*, 1958, **31,** 228–246.

Trouton, D.S. & Maxwell, A.E. The relation between neurosis and psychosis. *J. ment. Sci.*, 1956, **102,** 1–21.

Wenger, M.A. The measurement of individual differences in autonomic balance. *Psychosom. Med.*, 1941, **3,** 427–434.

Wenger, M.A. The stability of measurement of autonomic balance. *Psychosom. Med.*, 1942, **4,** 94–95.

Wenger, M.A. Studies of autonomic balance in Army Air Forces personnel. *Comp. Psychol. Monogr.*, 1948, **19,** 1–111.

Wenger, M.A. Studies of autonomic balance: a summary. *Psychophysiology*, 1966, **2,** 173–186.

Yates, A.J. & Laszlo, J.I. Learning and performance of extraverts and introverts on the pursuit rotor. *J. pers. soc. Psychol.*, 1965, **1,** 79–84.

Chapter 4

Techniques of Behavior Therapy

THE DEFINITION of behavior therapy provided in the first chapter implies that there are no standard techniques that can (or should) be employed in a routine fashion. This is not, of course, to deny in any way that, in any particular case, the behavior therapist should build on previous knowledge, both general and specific to the abnormality in question. It has been stressed, however, that essentially each case represents a new problem, to be tackled in its own right.

Thus far, in its short history, a bewildering variety of techniques has been used by behavior therapists. Since many of these have only been used in relation to a single case study, it would be superfluous to describe them in detail in this chapter. However, the technique of systematic desensitization has been so widely used in such a variety of disorders that it is appropriate to pay it some attention here, even though its relative degree of standardized use violates the basic principle enunciated in the first chapter. Following discussion of the technique of systematic desensitization, a brief summary will be given of the other major techniques that have thus far been used by behavior therapists, with more detailed description being reserved for the appropriate place in later chapters.

I. SYSTEMATIC DESENSITIZATION

1. TERMINOLOGY

Considerable confusion has already arisen over the terminology used in relation to this technique. As Evans and Wilson (1968) point out, terms relating to behavioral events, to the

conditions producing these events, and to explanatory concepts have all been confused and often used interchangeably. In relation to systematic desensitization, the following are the principal terms which have become entangled: systematic desensitization, reciprocal inhibition, extinction, and counter-conditioning. Of the four, the term systematic desensitization is the most clear, since it has almost invariably been used to refer to a particular set of procedures which will be described below. The term reciprocal inhibition, on the other hand, has sometimes been used as a synonym for the technique of systematic desensitization (when it is called reciprocal inhibition therapy); sometimes as an "explanation" of the effects obtained by the use of systematic desensitization; and sometimes, especially by Wolpe, to refer to the hypothetical neural events underlying the changes produced by systematic desensitization. Reciprocal inhibition as an explanatory construct has often been contrasted with extinction as an explanatory construct. The term extinction, on the other hand, has also been used to describe a procedure, as has the term counter-conditioning. In turn, the term counter-conditioning has been used as a hypothetical explanatory process. As Evans and Wilson (1968) point out, however, extinction and counter-conditioning are neither alternatives nor are they explanations. The terms refer to experimental procedures that change the probability of evocation of a response.

These terminological problems may perhaps be resolved by adopting the following definitions of the various terms, at least provisionally.

(i) The terms *reciprocal inhibition* and *counter-conditioning* are equivalent terms referring to procedures that strengthen alternative (or new) responses to stimuli to which maladaptive responses are attached.

(ii) The term *extinction* refers to procedures that weaken a maladaptive response to a stimulus without attaching new (or strengthening already attached) responses to the same stimulus.

(iii) The term *systematic desensitization* refers to a general set of experimental procedures that may involve the use of either or both of the procedures defined as counter-conditioning (reciprocal inhibition) and extinction.

Of course, as we have seen in Chapter 2, the question whether extinction procedures *must* include reciprocal inhibition procedures (that is, whether a response already in the repertoire can be weakened or whether only its probability of evocation can be reduced by comparison with the probability of evocation of an alternative response) or not is a matter of much dispute, to which we shall return later in this chapter.

2. Experimental Basis of Systematic Desensitization

The experimental basis of systematic de-sensitization therapy has been described in detail by Wolpe (1952, 1954, 1958). The refusal of cats to eat, even in states of extreme hunger, after conditioned fear had been instilled in them by subjecting them to severe shock while eating in a confined space, was overcome by feeding them in situations on a generalization continuum similar to but far removed from the original situation and then gradually approximating the original fear situation. Progress from one stage to the next was not instituted until all signs of anxiety in the current situation had disappeared. These procedures are summarized in the well-known principle formulated by Wolpe.

"If a response antagonistic to anxiety can be made to occur in the presence of anxiety-evoking stimuli, so that it is accompanied by a complete or partial suppression of the anxiety responses, the bond between those stimuli and the anxiety responses will be weakened" (Wolpe, 1958, p. 71).

Strangely, in view of Wolpe's use of the term reciprocal inhibition, this dictum appears to indicate espousal of the notion that the link between the anxiety response and the stimulus evoking it is actually weakened. Such an assumption is not, of course, necessary, since it could equally be argued that what happens is that the probability of the evocation of an alternative response to the anxiety-evoking stimulus is strengthened to the point at which presentation of the stimulus is now more likely to evoke the new response than the anxiety response. Theoretically, in terms of the latter assumption, the stages involved in systematic desensitization therapy may be represented as in Figure 1. In the pretreatment stage, a stimulus (S_1) evokes a response (r_{a_1}) of maximum strength, which then generalizes to similar stimuli (S_2, S_3, etc.) with strengths r_{a_2}, r_{a_3}, etc. The first stage of training involves the elimination of the diminished anxiety (r_{a_3}) to a remote stimulus (S_3) by training the subject to produce an alternative response (r_{r_1}) to this stimulus to the point at which the probability of evocation of r_{r_1} is greater than the probability of evocation of r_{a_3}. This alternative response then generalizes to other stimuli on the continuum. In the next stage of training, the strength of the anxiety response (r_{a_2}) to S_2 will be found to be reduced as a result of the generalization of the alternative response (r_{r_1}) to S_2 as r_{r_2}. Further training will then increase the probability of evocation of the alternative response (r_{r_2}) to S_2 to the point at which it is more likely to be evoked by S_2 than is the maladaptive response (r_{a_2}). In this way, progress is made along the stimulus similarity dimension, with the subject gradually acquiring alternative adaptive responses. At each stage, the anxiety response (which is increasing) is more able to be tolerated because of the generalization effects of the alternative response from training at points lower down the continuum. Eventually, if all goes well, the stimulus which evokes most anxiety can be presented and will be able to be tolerated by the subject while the strength of the alternative response is increased. When this latter response exceeds the strength of the maladaptive response, therapy could be said to have been completed.

The nature of the alternative (incompatible, in Wolpe's terminology, but not necessarily incompatible according to the viewpoint of Evans and Wilson) response has also given rise to a great deal of confusion. Clearly, in terms of the analysis presented above, the incompatible response must be one which is conceptually at the same level of discourse as the anxiety response. And indeed, Wolpe's technique of

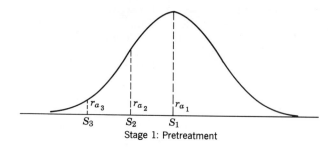

Stage 1: Pretreatment

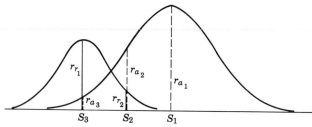

Stage 2: Elimination of anxiety response to S_2

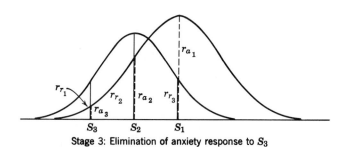

Stage 3: Elimination of anxiety response to S_3

FIG. I. A model for the treatment of anxiety responses by systematic desensitization.

systematic desensitization, as originally formulated, laid major stress (as we shall see) on training in relaxation responses, which would seem to be responses at the same level of discourse as the anxiety responses.[1] Wolpe and his colleagues have, however, repeatedly also referred to the use of assertive responses, sexual responses, and so on as reciprocally inhibiting anxiety. But these responses are at a quite different (peripheral) level of discussion, referring to overt behavioral responses, whereas anxiety and relaxation are internalized, hypothetical constructs (which may, however, be indirectly measured by other response indicators). This problem will be taken up again later.

3. BASIC TECHNIQUE OF SYSTEMATIC DESENSITIZATION

The basic procedures involved here have been fully described in Wolpe (1958, 1961) and Wolpe and Lazarus (1966). The procedure involves three stages: training in deep muscle relaxation (with or without the aid of hypnosis or drugs); the construction of anxiety hierarchies; and the application of desensitization procedures by moving through the anxiety hierarchies step by step while practicing the relaxation responses.

The relaxation technique is based on the work of Jacobson (1938) but is much less intensive in nature. However, it may involve as

[1] One is reminded of Mowrer's (1960) distinction between "fear" and "hope."

many as six sessions (Wolpe and Lazarus, 1966). During this period, construction of the anxiety hierarchies may begin, a procedure which is not nearly as simple as it may seem. The anxiety hierarchies are constructed from four main sources: the case history of the patient; his responses (amplified by questioning) to the Willoughby questionnaire and, more recently, the Fear Survey Schedule; and special investigations into areas of difficulty. It will be noted that the therapist does not necessarily (or even usually) restrict himself to those areas verbally indicated by the patient as troublesome but, instead, attempts to identify all sources of disturbance.[2] Hierarchy construction is carried out while the patient is not relaxed. Many technical problems arise, such as the spacing of items in a particular hierarchy, which are discussed at length in Wolpe (1958) and Wolpe and Lazarus (1966). Some of these will be considered later.

The desensitization procedure itself commences when the relaxation training and the hierarchy construction have been completed and involves essentially the steps already detailed. Wolpe stresses that it is important that the stimulus presented should arouse some degree of anxiety but that too much anxiety should not be aroused as otherwise, of course, the patient, instead of being desensitized, may be further sensitized to the particular stimulus. Again, many technical problems arise (number of presentations of a particular scene, rate of progression through a hierarchy, and so on), some of which will be considered shortly.

4. IMAGINAL VERSUS IN VIVO DESENSITIZATION

At this point, an important distinction between two fundamental techniques of systematic desensitization should be mentioned, a distinction that will recur throughout this book. Wolpe has always favored the technique that involves the reproduction by the subject in imagination of the anxiety-arousing objects or situations. It will be apparent, however, that an alternative procedure would be one in which the hierarchy consisted of real objects or situations, graded according to the amount of anxiety that they aroused. The former procedure may be termed imaginal desensitization (SD—I); the latter real-life or in vivo desensitization (SD—R).

While it might be thought that the natural tendency of behavior therapists would be to use the SD—R technique, in fact, the vast majority of SD studies have utilized the SD—I technique. The principal reason for preferring the SD—I technique is, of course, one of economy. It is clearly easier to work with complex hierarchies of objects and situations if these only have to be visualized as opposed to actually setting up real-life situations or building objects. Wolpe has, however, always maintained that the beneficial effects of the SD—I procedure generalize to the real-life situation they represent fully, though this assumption does not appear to be deducible from the general theory of generalization—at least some reduction in transfer to the real-life situation would be expected and has, in fact, been reported (Rachman, 1966b).

Nevertheless, the use of the SD—R technique has undoubtedly been increasing rapidly in recent years and many examples will be discussed in later chapters. Here, mention may be made of a few such studies, such as the famous cat phobia case of Freeman and Kendrick (1960); Meyer's (1957) study of two phobic patients; Bentler's (1962) elimination of a bathphobia in a one-year-old child; and Murphy's (1964) treatment of an incapacitating fear of earthworms. Only one study (Cooke, 1966) appears to have directly compared SD(I) with SD(R); he found no difference in the efficaciousness of the two techniques. As we shall see in later chapters, many studies using the SD(I) technique have failed to determine whether the reduction in anxiety in the laboratory situation has generalized to real-life situations, relying often on verbal reports from the patient.

5. TECHNICAL (PROCEDURAL) PROBLEMS IN SYSTEMATIC DESENSITIZATION

Procedural problems in carrying out systematic desensitization have been widely discussed by various authors, but little empirical research has thus far been carried out.

(a) TRAINING IN MUSCULAR RELAXATION. The problem of the patient who is difficult to train in muscular relaxation has been discussed by Wolpe and Lazarus (1966). Attempts to overcome the difficulty include the use of hypnosis and drugs, or even variants of systematic desensitization procedures.

---

[2] A quite different procedure, of course, from that adopted by the early English behavior therapists

(Chapter 1).

(b) CONSTRUCTION OF HIERARCHIES. There are two major problems here. First, as Wolpe and Lazarus (1966) point out, the construction of the hierarchies is, in some respects, the most vital part of the whole procedure. Irrelevant items may be included if, for example, the patient's own construction is wholly relied on, while important items may be omitted altogether. Lazarus (1964) has considered these problems in some detail. A second problem, which has been little explored to date, concerns the question whether hierarchies must be constructed for each individual or whether, in some circumstances, standardized hierarchies might be used. The former procedure has been strongly emphasized by Wolpe (1958) who argues that a standardized hierarchy (relating, for example, to fear of spiders and used with all subjects expressing such fears) may have individual items which are quite incorrectly scaled for a particular subject and thus may be either too "hard" (inducing a level of anxiety which cannot be controlled) or too "easy" (including items which fail to elicit any anxiety). On the other hand, the development of group desensitization obviously requires the use of a common hierarchy. Emery and Krumboltz (1967) specifically compared the two procedures and found no significant difference in the results obtained with each. This result is supported by other studies (to be reported in later chapters) which have used standard hierarchies with apparent success.

(c) DESENSITIZATION PROCEDURE. The rate at which a patient can be taken through a particular hierarchy has given rise to some difference of opinion. Wolpe (1958) stressed the importance of not leaving an item until the anxiety associated with it was no longer being manifested. There is now, however, cogent evidence that this position may have to be modified. Ramsay et al (1966), for example, found no difference between the effects of massing and spacing of SD(I). More specifically, Rachman and Hodgson (1967) compared the effects of reducing anxiety to zero for each item at each step in the hierarchy with the effects of reducing anxiety by half. Not only did they find no difference between the two groups so treated, but the latter group received fewer treatment sessions than the former.

Lazarus (1964) and Wolpe and Lazarus (1966) have discussed in considerable detail the many problems arising in the conduct of desensitization sessions. These include: the duration a visualized scene should last when no anxiety is evoked by the stimulus; the relaxation interval duration between scenes; the number of scenes that should be presented in a single session; the number of times a scene should be repeated; the number of hierarchies that should be used during a session; the length of time a session should last; and the time interval between sessions. Their suggestions in relation to these problems are, however, based entirely on their own clinical experience, and systematic investigation of these important questions can scarcely be said to have begun. A final problem is the customary practice of requiring the patient to signal excessive anxiety during visualization by means of a nonverbal response (raising of the finger). Lazarus (1968) has suggested that there may be certain advantages in requiring a verbal communication for this purpose.

6. METHODOLOGICAL PROBLEMS IN
SYSTEMATIC DESENSITIZATION

Systematic desensitization, it will be recalled, involves the use of relaxation techniques and, indeed, in terms of the model presented earlier, the technique essentially appears to involve the strengthening of such responses so that the anxiety-evoking stimuli now come to evoke relaxation responses with a higher degree of probability than they evoke anxiety responses. The relaxation responses then serve as stimuli, evoking adaptive behavior in the same way that the anxiety responses as stimuli formerly evoked maladaptive responses. If, on the other hand, the systematic desensitization procedure merely reduces the probability of evocation of the anxiety responses, then training in relaxation may be unnecessary. The role of relaxation training as a part of the systematic desensitization procedure has, therefore, not unnaturally, received a good deal of attention, particularly in recent years.

Lang and Lazovik (1963) investigated the effects of training in relaxation alone on reduction of the expression of real-life fears and found no reduction. But this is an inconclusive test, since such relaxation responses would not be expected to be related in any way to the anxiety-arousing stimuli which were not presented during the relaxation training. Moore (1965) compared the effects of three procedures in relation to the treatment of bronchial asthma: relaxation training alone; relaxation training with suggestion; and relaxation training with SD(I). She found that only the third condition produced significant change. A rather similar approach (dealing with severe phobia for spiders) by Rachman (1965) compared the effects of: relaxation alone; relaxation with SD(I); SD(I) alone; and no treatment. Significant change was produced only by the relaxation with SD(I) condition. Wolpin and Raines (1966), on the other hand, claimed that SD(I) alone was effective in producing change, while the same authors and Lazarus (1965) showed that directed muscular *activity* combined with SD(I) or alone was effective.[3] All of these observations and other considerations led Rachman (1968) to revise his earlier view (Rachman, 1967) that *muscular* relaxation was essential to the success of SD(I). He argued rather that "mental" relaxation was the essential factor, a position which is in line with that advanced earlier in this chapter, namely, that relaxation training involves a response antagonistic to the anxiety response; however, this response need not necessarily involve peripheral muscular relaxation but may be a phenomenon central in origin.

Several recent studies by Davison have contributed significantly to this issue. Davison (1965), using SD(R) procedures with students with an intensive fear of beetles, compared the relative effectiveness of three variations: relaxation training with SD(R); SD(R) alone; and no treatment. The results suggested tentatively that while the use of SD(R) alone might enable the subject to change his *overt behavior* toward the feared stimulus (e.g., he might now be prepared to pick up the beetle), the use of this technique without relaxation appeared to have little effect on reported fear in the real-life test situation. This conclusion certainly makes sense in relation to the model put forward in this chapter. In a more recent study, Davison (1968) formed four groups of subjects with intense fear of snakes. Two groups were treated by SD(I) with relaxation training. However, for one of the two groups, the SD(I) involved the presentation of stimuli which were relevant to the fear (desensitization group), whereas for the other group, the SD(I) involved the presentation of stimuli which were irrelevant to the fear (pseudodesensitization group). A third group was given SD(I) without relaxation training (but with relevant stimuli), while the fourth group was a no-treatment control. Davison found that the only group to show a significant reduction

in avoidance behavior was the one which was given SD(I) with relaxation in which the stimuli were relevant to the fear. This result strongly suggests that the relaxation responses must be trained in the presence of the anxiety-evoking stimuli and produce their effect by becoming evoked by the originally anxiety-producing stimuli.

Further evidence against Wolpe's view that relaxation training *inhibits* anxiety was provided by Davison (1966a) in a review of this problem, in which he points out, for example, that muscular paralysis by curarization does not prevent the formation of conditioned fear, as manifested by the subsequent appearance of conditioned avoidance responses. Davison postulates that relaxation training induces a state antagonistic to the state of anxiety; in effect, as we have stated before, that the relaxation-responses become elicitable by the stimuli that formerly evoked the anxiety responses, the latter now having a lower probability of evocation than the relaxation responses.

7. THEORETICAL PROBLEMS IN SYSTEMATIC DESENSITIZATION

The controversy over relaxation discussed in the previous section was partly a theoretical, as well as a methodological problem. The basic theoretical dispute which has arisen in relation to systematic desensitization therapy[4] relates to the question whether counter-conditioning procedures are both a necessary and a sufficient condition of desensitization. Put differently, does systematic desensitization therapy involve reduction in the habit strength of the anxiety responses only; does it involve the induction of alternative responses to the anxiety-arousing stimuli (or the strengthening of already present alternative responses which are weaker than the anxiety responses); or does it involve both procedures? The material we have already discussed relating to the need for relaxation training is, of course, relevant to the question. Here we will consider some further evidence.

Agras (1965) demonstrated the occurrence of spontaneous recovery of diminished anxiety responses and claimed that this result indicated that SD(I) at least involves classical conditioning. This finding is not, of course, decisive

---

[3] As Rachman (1967) has pointed out, the SD(R) technique involves action rather than relaxation on the part of the subject.

[4] It could, of course, be regarded as a methodological problem, rather than a theoretical problem.

evidence against the role of alternative responses. On the other hand, a good deal of experimental evidence suggests rather strongly that counter-conditioning procedures do form an essential part of the SD(I) paradigm. We have already mentioned the studies of Davison (1965, 1966a, and 1968), Rachman (1965), and others in this connection and here may additionally refer to studies by Lomont (1965) and the review of the problem by Lomont and Edwards (1967), as well as the work of Gale et al (1966) with rats. Of particular interest is the recent work on "flooding" and "implosive therapy" (Hogan and Kirchner, 1967, 1968; Stampfl and Levis, 1967) in which, instead of proceeding cautiously through the hierarchy from the least to the most anxiety-evoking stimuli, the subject is exposed, either in imagination or in vivo, to the most anxiety-evoking stimuli continuously in conditions which are similar to those of massed practice and from which escape is impossible. The principal argument against this procedure is the belief that the amount of anxiety generated will be greater than the patient can handle and that the conditioned fear response may thereby be exacerbated. Essentially, flooding or implosive therapy represents a form of forced reality testing; that is, if the subject is prevented from making his usual avoidance response to reduce the anxiety generated by the CS, and if, in fact, the anticipated traumatic event does not occur, then the conditioned anxiety response will extinguish, since it is no longer reinforced by drive reduction resulting from the avoidance response.

The empirical evidence thus far is conflicting. Lang and Lazovik (1963) and Rachman (1966a) did not find a "flooding procedure" effective, whereas Wolpin and Raines (1966) did. The difference of opinion between Rachman (1966a) and Wolpin and Raines (1966) has produced an interesting and perceptive comment by Wilson (1967) who noted that Rachman's instructions to his subjects required them to rehearse the anxiety responses to the feared stimulus, whereas the instructions of Wolpin and Raines required their subjects to rehearse adaptive responses to the feared stimulus. Staub (1968) has further commented that Rachman perhaps did not keep his subjects in the "flooding" situation long enough for extinction to take place and contrasts the short period used by Rachman with the much longer exposure periods to the feared stimulus utilized by the

"implosive" therapists. In any event, the "flooding" procedure by itself is incapable of resolving the dispute which requires experimental designs of the kind used by Davison, discussed earlier. Much more careful experimentation is required to clarify this particular problem.

8. VARIATIONS OF SYSTEMATIC DESENSITIZATION

The distinction between SD(I) and SD(R) procedures has already been considered, but there are several other variants of systematic desensitization therapy that are of interest and may be mentioned here.

(a) GROUP DESENSITIZATION. Lazarus (1961) introduced this procedure in relation to the treatment of phobias and sexual disorders. The technique involves the use of standard hierarchies, with an upward step in the hierarchy being taken only when each patient indicated reduction of anxiety to the previous step. The technique has been more recently applied by Paul and Shannon (1966)[5] who found it equally as effective as individualized SD(I).

(b) "ENRICHED" SD(I). Lazarus (1968) has explored the possibility of adding alternative responses to the relaxation responses in attempts to eliminate the anxiety responses and, in so doing, has come very close to Davison's position that SD(I) involves counter-conditioning.

(c) EMOTIVE-IMAGERY TECHNIQUE. These "enriched" SD(I) techniques include the use of the emotive-imagery technique first reported by Lazarus and Abramovitz (1962). The term emotive imagery refers to:

"those classes of imagery which are assumed to arouse feelings of self-assertion, pride, affection, mirth, and similar anxiety-inhibiting responses" (Lazarus and Abramovitz, 1962, p. 191).

The technique, which has mainly been used with children, involves getting the child to imagine sequences or stories involving his heroes or other positive figures. During the course of the sequence, a minimally anxiety-arousing stimulus from a hierarchy is introduced into the story by the therapist at the point at which positive responding is maximal.

(d) COGNITIVE SD(I). Lazarus (1968) has also discussed the addition of "cognitive" variables to the SD(I) procedure, and this may also be considered as an "enrichment" variable. As

---

[5] See Chapter 17.

TABLE 4.1. *Some Techniques Used by Behavior Therapists and Abnormalities to which They Have Been Applied*

Technique	Abnormalities
I. *Classical aversive conditioning*	
1. Drugs	Fetishism; transvestism; homosexuality; alcoholism.
2. Shock	Writer's cramp; fetishism; transvestism; sadistic fantasies; voyeurism; alcoholism; smoking; gambling.
3. Paralysis	Alcoholism.
II. *Instrumental escape conditioning* (*shock*)	Homosexuality; alcoholism; smoking.
III. *Instrumental avoidance conditioning* (*shock*)	Homosexuality; alcoholism.
IV. *Massed practice*	Tics; smoking; stuttering.
V. *Aversive imagery* (*covert sensitization*)	Obsessional behavior; homosexuality; alcoholism; smoking.
VI. *Aversion—relief*	Phobias; obsessional behavior; fetishism; transvestism; smoking.
VII. *Operant procedures*	1. Childhood psychoses—elimination of undesirable behaviors (time out, etc.) strengthening of desirable behaviors — teaching speech, cognitive and social skills.
	2. Adult psychoses—reinstatement of speech, control of ward behavior, etc.
	3. Mental deficiency—toilet training, ward behavior, self-care, remedial education, etc.
	4. Children's behavior problems — temper tantrums, operant crying, head-bumping, thumbsucking, excessive scratching, excessive verbal demands, rebellious behavior, isolate behavior, regressed crawling, hyperactivity, social interaction with peers, educational retardation (classroom orientation, reading, etc.)
	5. Obsessional rituals; anorexia nervosa, neurodermatitis, tics, stuttering.
	6. Delinquent and antisocial behavior.
VIII. *Special techniques*	Obsessional eyebrow plucking; functional blindness, deafness, analgesia, astereognosis, anesthesia, motor paralysis, aphonia and dysphonia, retention of urine, excessive frequency of micturition, somnambulism.
IX. *Feedback control techniques*	Stuttering.

used by Lazarus in a preliminary study of SD(I) with patients with so-called cardiac neuroses, the subject is instructed, while going through a hierarchy under desensitization, to think about all of the benign explanations they had learned about pains in the chest. "Cognitive restructuring" has been utilized by Davison (1966b) in a study of a paranoid schizophrenic.[6]

(e) "AUTOMATED" SD. Migler and Wolpe (1967) and Migler (1968) have described the use of a tape recorder to enable a patient to practise SD(I) at home. The tape recording includes relaxation instructions (using the patient's own voice) and hierarchy scenes for self-presentation.

(f) ASSERTIVE AND SEXUAL RESPONSES. Both Wolpe (1958) and Wolpe and Lazarus (1966) treat the use of assertive responses and sexual responses in chapters separate from those dealing with systematic desensitization. Furthermore, contrary to their general adherence to the SD(I) technique in preference to the SD(R) technique, their training in assertive and sexual responses involves essentially the use of SD(R) without the concommitant use of relaxation training, although in many instances assertive training may be initially conducted through the use of SD(I) technique (that is, imagining scenes in which assertive responses occur) or, alternatively, the "behavior rehearsal" technique described by Lazarus (1966). Nevertheless, they describe assertive and sexual responses as reciprocally inhibiting anxiety responses. Their position appears to be based on the fundamental misconception described earlier in this chapter, since clearly these assertive and sexual responses are peripheral, behavioral responses and, therefore, are at a different level of discourse than the anxiety responses. It is difficult to see why a patient who is afraid of his boss should be instructed to practise assertive responses (albeit in a hierarchical fashion) directly in the presence of his boss (thus risking a severe rebuff) while a patient with a phobia for snakes should be required to undergo SD(I). In fact, to be consistent, it should be argued that training in relaxation responses will enable assertive or sexual responses to be exercised where formerly the anxiety response produced avoidance behavior in such situations. There seems no logical reason whatsoever for treating assertive and sexual responses as distinct categories from other kinds of positive behavioral responses which become possible when relaxation responses replace anxiety responses.

II. SOME OTHER BEHAVIOR THERAPY TECHNIQUES

As was pointed out earlier in this chapter, most of the other techniques used by behavior therapists will be described in the appropriate chapter in which they are introduced. Their use has not been sufficiently extensive as yet to justify a separate description in full here. However, some indication should be given of the range of techniques that have been used, without any attempt to be exhaustive. Table 4.1 shows some of the techniques that have been employed by behavior therapists and the range of abnormalities to which they have been applied. The second part of this book is devoted to describing in detail the application of systematic desensitization procedures and these other techniques to the very wide range of abnormalities that have been investigated up to this point by behavior therapists.

[6] See Chapter 14.

REFERENCES

Agras, W.S. An investigation of the decrement of anxiety responses during systematic desensitization therapy. *Behav. Res. Ther.*, 1965, **2**, 267–270.

Bentler, P.M. An infant's phobia treated with reciprocal inhibition therapy. *J. child Psychol. Psychiat.*, 1962, **3**, 185–189.

Cooke, G. The efficacy of two desensitization procedures: an analogue study. *Behav. Res. Ther.*, 1966, **4**, 17–24.

Davison, G.C. Relative contributions of differential relaxation and graded exposure to in vivo desensitization of a neurotic fear. *Proc. 73rd Ann. Conv. A.P.A.*, Washington, D.C., 1965, pp. 209–210.

Davison, G.C. Anxiety under total curarization: implications for the role of muscular relaxation in the desensitization of neurotic fears. *J. nerv. ment. Dis.*, 1966, **143**, 443–448 (a).

Davison, G.C. Differential relaxation and cognitive restructuring in therapy with a "paranoid schizophrenic" or "paranoid state." *Proc. 74th Ann. Conv. A.P.A.*, Washington, D.C., 1966, pp. 177–178 (b).

Davison, G.C. Systematic desensitization as a counter-conditioning process. *J. abnorm. Psychol.*, 1968, **73**, 91–99.

Emery, J.R. & Krumboltz, J.D. Standard versus individualized hierarchies in desensitization to reduce test anxiety. *J. counsel. Psychol.*, 1967, **14**, 204–209.

Evans, I. & Wilson, T. Note on the terminological confusion surrounding systematic desensitization. *Psychol. Rep.*, 1968, **22**, 187–191.

Freeman, H.L. & Kendrick, D.C. A case of cat phobia. *Brit. med. J.*, 1960, **2**, 497–502.

Gale, D.S., Sturmfels, G., & Gale, E.N. A comparison of reciprocal inhibition and experimental extinction in the psychotherapeutic process. *Behav. Res. Ther.*, 1966, **4**, 149–155.

Hogan, R. & Kirchner, J. Preliminary report of the extinction of learned fear in a short-term implosive therapy. *J. abnorm. Psychol.*, 1967, **72**, 106–109.

Hogan, R.A. & Kirchner, J.H. Implosive, eclectic verbal and bibliotherapy in the treatment of fears of snakes. *Behav. Res. Ther.*, 1968, **6**, 167–171.

Jacobson, E. *Progressive relaxation.* Chicago: Univer. Chicago Press, 1938.

Lang, P.J. & Lazovik, A.D. Experimental desensitization of a phobia. *J. abnorm. soc. Psychol.*, 1963, **66**, 519–525.

Lazarus, A.A. Group therapy of phobic disorders by systematic desensitization. *J. abnorm. soc. Psychol.*, 1961, **63**, 504–510.

Lazarus, A.A. Crucial procedural factors in desensitization therapy. *Behav. Res. Ther.*, 1964, **2**, 65–70.

Lazarus, A.A. A preliminary report on the use of directed muscular activity in counter-conditioning. *Behav. Res. Ther.*, 1965, **2**, 301–303.

Lazarus, A.A. Behavior rehearsal vs. nondirective therapy vs. advice in effecting behavior change. *Behav. Res. Ther.*, 1966, **4**, 209–212.

Lazarus, A.A. Variations in desensitization therapy. *Psychotherapy*, 1968, **5**, 50–52.

Lazarus, A. & Abramovitz, A. The use of "emotive imagery" in the treatment of children's phobias. *J. ment. Sci.*, 1962, **108**, 191–195.

Lomont, J.F. Reciprocal inhibition or extinction? *Behav. Res. Ther.*, 1965, **3**, 209–219.

Lomont, J.F. & Edwards, J.E. The role of relaxation in systematic desensitization. *Behav. Res. Ther.*, 1967, **5**, 11–25.

Meyer, V. The treatment of two phobic patients on the basis of learning principles. *J. abnorm soc. Psychol.*, 1957, **55**, 261–266.

Migler, B. A supplementary note on automated self-desensitization. *Behav. Res. Ther.*, 1968, **6**, 243.

Migler, B. & Wolpe, J. Automated self-desensitization: a case report. *Behav. Res. Ther.*, 1967, **5**, 133–135.

Moore, N. Behavior therapy in bronchial asthma: a controlled study. *J. psychosom. Res.*, 1965, **9**, 257–276.

Mowrer, O.H. *Learning theory and behavior.* New York: Wiley, 1960.

Murphy, I.C. Extinction of an incapacitating fear of earthworms. *J. clin. Psychol.*, 1964, **20**, 396–398.

Paul, G.L. & Shannon, D.T. Treatment of anxiety through systematic desensitization in therapy groups. *J. abnorm. Psychol.*, 1966, **71**, 124–135.

Rachman, S. Studies in desensitization: I. The separate effects of relaxation and desensitization. *Behav. Res. Ther.*, 1965, **3**, 245–252.

Rachman, S. Studies in desensitization: II. Flooding. *Behav. Res. Ther.*, 1966, **4**, 1–6 (a).

Rachman, S. Studies in desensitization: III. Speed of generalization. *Behav. Res. Ther.*, 1966, **4**, 7–16 (b).

Rachman, S. Systematic desensitization. *Psychol. Bull.*, 1967, **67**, 93–103.

Rachman, S. The role of muscular relaxation in desensitization therapy. *Behav. Res. Ther.*, 1968, **6**, 159–166.

Rachman, S. & Hodgson, R.J. Studies in desensitization: IV. Optimum degree of anxiety-reduction. *Behav. Res. Ther.*, 1967, **5**, 249–250.

Ramsay, R.W., Barends, J., Breuker, J., & Kruseman, A. Massed versus spaced desensitization of fear. *Behav. Res. Ther.*, 1966, **4**, 205–207.

Stampfl, T.G. & Levis, D.J. Essentials of implosive therapy: a learning theory based psychodynamic behavioral therapy. *J. abnorm. Psychol.*, 1967, **72**, 496–503.

Staub, E. Duration of stimulus-exposure as determinant of the efficacy of flooding procedures in the elimination of fear. *Behav. Res. Ther.*, 1968, **6**, 131–132.

Wilson, G.D. Efficacy of "flooding" procedures in desensitization of fear: a theoretical note. *Behav. Res. Ther.*, 1967, **5**, 138.

Wolpe, J. Experimental neurosis as learned behavior. *Brit. J. Psychol.*, 1952, **43**, 243–268.

Wolpe, J. Reciprocal inhibition as the main basis of psychotherapeutic effects. *Arch. Neurol. Psychiat.*, 1954, **72**, 205–226.

Wolpe, J. *Psychotherapy by reciprocal inhibition.* Stanford: Stanford Univ. Press, 1958.

Wolpe, J. The systematic desensitization treatment of neuroses. *J. nerv. Ment. Dis.*, 1961, **132**, 189–203.

Wolpe, J. & Lazarus, A.A. *Behavior therapy techniques.* Oxford: Pergamon, 1966.

Wolpin, M. & Raines, J. Visual imagery, expected roles and extinction as possible factors in reducing fear and avoidance behavior. *Behav. Res. Ther.*, 1966, **4**, 25–38.

Part II

Applications of Behavior Therapy

Chapter 5

Enuresis and Encopresis

A. Enuresis

I. DEFINITIONS, MEASUREMENT, INCIDENCE

1. DEFINITION OF ENURESIS

CROSBY (1950, p. 534) defined essential enuresis as:

"the involuntary and unconscious passing of urine after an arbitrary age limit of three years, in the absence of significant congenital or acquired defect or disease of the nervous and uro-genital systems, and in the absence of significant psychological defects."

Michaels (1955, p. 7) defined enuresis as:

"uncontrolled, unintentional voiding of urine at one expulsion usually occurring during sleep; it may be considered to be present if bed-wetting occurs past the age of three, a liberal time for control or urination to have been established in so-called normal individuals."[1]

These definitions immediately pose a problem, since both appear to argue that any child who even intermittently wets the bed after the arbitrary age of three years may be termed an enuretic; furthermore, the arbitrary use of age three as a watershed, as it were, ignores the fact (which will be demonstrated later) that there is no arbitrary point at which bed-wetting ceases in normal children. If control of nocturnal micturition is an acquired skill, then, like any other skill, its acquisition will be expected to follow the normal curve of acquisition, which is characteristic of the learning of new skills, with "relapses" being quite normal and with final control being achieved over a period of time. Furthermore, large individual differences in the time taken to acquire the skill would be expected. The definitional problem is clearly related to the natural history of micturitional control and, therefore, to the known *incidence* of bed-wetting at different age-levels in unselected samples. Before turning to this question, however, it should be pointed out that it may prove to be important to distinguish *subcategories* of enuresis, since not all forms may prove to have the same explanation. Perhaps the most important distinction that has been made is that between *primary enuresis* (where the child has never gained control of nocturnal micturition) and *secondary enuresis* (where the child reverts to bed-wetting after a period of dryness). Secondly, a distinction may be made between children who are *regularly* and those who are *intermittently* enuretic. Thirdly, of course, it is necessary to distinguish enuretic children who are so because of organic abnormalities (such as physiological disease affecting the muscular processes involved in micturition) from those who have no demonstrable organic malfunction. (It seems to be generally agreed that not more than 10% of enuretics suffer from

---

[1] Since Michaels clearly distinguishes enuresis from *incontinence* ("primarily a neurological symptom"), he would obviously accept Crosby's more comprehensive definition.

organic disease.) Crosby (1950, p. 536) has additionally distinguished what he calls *essential enuresis* (usually due to lack of training in infancy) from *complicated enuresis* (where the wetting is caused primarily by faulty training). All of these distinctions imply, first, that there are a number of *dimensions* of enuresis and, second, that there is a good deal of individual variability within these dimensions.

2. THE INCIDENCE OF ENURESIS

Establishment of the incidence of enuresis is fraught with serious difficulties. First, different authors have used quite different criteria in their definition. Should one, for example, define as a bed-wetter a child of four who wets, on average, two nights per week? Or a child of seven who wets, on average, one night per week? Or a child of ten who wets, on average, once a month? Certainly, it seems reasonable to regard a child of four wetting once a month as less of a problem than an adolescent of fifteen who wets once a month. Second, very few sample surveys (if any) are based on *direct* observation of the incidence of wetting; rather, the tendency is to rely on verbal reports from the child or parents of events that have taken place in the past. Third, it is obviously unwise to rely on information available from clinical samples, since these are invariably seriously biased. Enuresis is, of course, a serious social problem, but the disfavor with which parents regard it certainly differs in different social strata. Thus, in the lower social class strata, continuous bed-wetting after the age of three years is often viewed with great tolerance and many such children simply are never brought to the child clinic for treatment. In other social groups, the child may be regarded as a problem if he wets the bed once a week after his second year, and help may be sought at this early age. Late bed-wetting is not uncommonly first detected when the adolescent enters the Armed Forces (e.g., Plag, 1964).

Bearing in mind the different criteria used by various investigators, Jones (1960) constructed graphs of the probable incidence of bed-wetting at different ages, based on data from Crosby (1950), Bransby, Blomfield and Douglas (1955), and Hallgren (1956, 1957). Surveys have, of course, been carried out in many countries, for example, England (Blomfield and Douglas, 1956), Australia (Hawkins, 1962), Norway (Hallgren, 1956, 1957), France (Lobrot, 1963), and Germany (Hoppner, 1952). Lobrot (1963)

confirmed the existence of large regional variations in France, while nearly all investigators have confirmed the existence of a sex difference, with boys apparently having more difficulty in achieving nocturnal control than girls (Stalker & Band, 1946; Blomfield and Douglas, 1956). Little information is available concerning the differential incidence of primary as compared with secondary enuresis, though Freyman (1963) found 53 cases of primary enuresis (wet continuously since birth) in a sample of 71 enuretics.

Jones' analysis of the available data indicated that probably at least 20% of all children still wet the bed at age five with a frequency sufficient for the fact to be commented on by the mother when questioned by survey techniques. The curves shown in Figure 1 indicate that the incidence of bed-wetting declines steadily up to adulthood and, further, that the incidence-curve of secondary (or acquired) bed-wetting follows a different pattern, rising to a peak at 5 years of age and declining practically to zero by 10.

II. ETIOLOGY OF ENURESIS

Since the *overt* disorder (bed-wetting) is so clear cut in its manifestations, it is not surprising that enuresis has proved a happy hunting-ground for theoretical formulations. The disorder, in fact, constitutes a critical area for resolution of many of the disputes between behavior therapists and psychodynamic therapists, particularly in relation to the question of

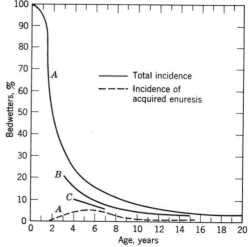

FIG. 1.   Incidence of bed wetting at different ages (Jones, 1960, modified). *A*. From Crosby (1950). *B*. From Bransby, Blomfield, and Douglas (1955). *C*. From Hallgren (1956).

symptom substitution. We shall consider in turn psychoanalytic and psychodynamic formulations; medical and physiological formulations; and behavioristic formulations.

1. PSYCHOANALYTIC AND PSYCHODYNAMIC FORMULATIONS

For these workers, enuresis is a classical example of the symptomatic theory and is invariably regarded as the overt symptom of some basic underlying disturbance. However, as we shall see, there has been little agreement regarding the nature of the basic disturbance.

As usual, we may begin with the views of Freud (though it is doubtful if Freud ever actually observed enuretic children directly, and certainly not in any numbers), who argued that "whenever enuresis nocturna does not represent an epileptic attack, it corresponds to a pollution" (Freud, 1905)—i.e., masturbation.[2] This idea was elaborated by Fenichel.

"Infantile (nocturnal or diurnal) enuresis is a sexual discharge. Urinary excretion originally served as an autoerotic activity which gave the child urethral-erotic (and cutaneous) satisfaction. . . . Between the infantile autoerotic wetting and the later symptom of enuresis there was a time of masturbation; and the enuresis represents a substitute and equivalent of suppressed masturbation . . . bedwetting is very often an expression of sexual fantasies proper to the opposite sex. Girls in whom urethral eroticism is well marked are almost always dominated by an intense envy of the penis. Their symptom gives expression to the wish to urinate like a boy. In boys the incontinence usually has the meaning of a female trait; such boys hope to obtain female kinds of pleasure by 'urinating passively' " (Fenichel, 1946, pp. 232–233).

The "evidence" for this interpretation has been reviewed by Campbell (1918) and many other psychoanalytic writers have put forward somewhat similar views. Thus, Berezin (1954) stressed the active and passive (male/female) aspects of the enuretic act and argued that it may represent a prototypical sexual experience so that, later in life, it may act as a determinant in masturbation and coital fantasies. Sometimes, these interpretations can only be described as bizarre. Thus, Robertiello (1956) agreed that enuresis represents gratification of a mastur-

batory wish via the urinary system, but went much further in declaring that the function of bed-wetting was the cooling-off of the penis, the fire (i.e., sexual drive) of which was condemned by the super-ego (hence, bed-wetting is, as it were, an agent of the super-ego). Imhof (1956) considered that the neurotic type of enuresis resulted from emotional conflicts (usually of the mother-child relationship). Enuresis, in his view, expresses a demand for love and may be characterized as a form of "weeping through the bladder" (i.e., a form of depressive reaction).

Somewhat less extreme is the view of Grunewald (1954). He argues that the morning erection arising from awakening with a full bladder (a quite common phenomenon in the young child) gives rise to disapproval, on the part of the parents, who regard it as a manifestation of sexual drive. Their disapproval results in bed-wetting which has the effect of producing a flaccid penis on awakening but also induces a double avoidance conflict in the child (i.e., fear of an erection on waking versus fear of wetting) and so produces anxiety and sleep disturbance. Hermann (1961) postulated a relationship between hunger and enuresis and additionally conceptualized bed-wetting as a "mocking" identification with enuretic siblings.

Enuresis has also been regarded as a conversion symptom by Fenichel (1946) (a viewpoint consistent, of course, with the implied sexual content of all conversion hysterias) and as a form of aggression against the parents whom the child is too weak to assault directly (it is, therefore, in this view, a displaced activity, but not necessarily with sexual content). More generally, it has been regarded as a symptom of anxiety, restlessness, and inner conflicts (Decurtins, 1957). Vox (1962) considers enuresis to be a reactive psychosis against familial or societal deprivations and frustrations.

In summary, therefore, psychodynamic formulations run the whole gamut from highly specific to very general conceptualizations of its symptomatic nature, but all agree that enuresis is a *symptom* of some underlying disturbance of a fundamentally more important nature. They further agree that direct symptomatic treatment is not only futile but, even if successful, may lead to displacement to other more harmful symptoms, such as neuroses, compulsive firesetting, or premature ejaculation, to name but a

---

[2] The reference to enuresis as an epileptic attack probably is a lingering remnant of Freud's earlier neurological approach to abnormal behavior.

few of the dire consequences predicted if symptomatic treatment is undertaken (De Curtins, 1957; Muller, 1957). Whether these dire consequences do actually occur will be considered later.[3]

2. MEDICAL AND PSYCHIATRIC FORMULATIONS

Medical and psychiatric formulations of the etiology of enuresis have been less extreme than the psychoanalytic formulations discussed above. Generally speaking, they have stressed two points: first, that enuresis is part of a *physiological syndrome* and, second, that enuresis is part of a *personality syndrome*. The two viewpoints are, however, frequently taken together.

With respect to enuresis as a physiological syndrome, Crosby (1950) quite bluntly held that:

"essential enuresis is not primarily a symptom, but that it is an entity or state arising from physiological activity, and is not of anatomical, pathological or psychological origin" (Crosby, 1950, p. 534).

He further held that "conversion from enuresis to continence usually occurs by physiological responses" and that "a further reversal from continence to enuresis is always possible" (Crosby, 1950, p. 534). By this, Crosby appears to mean that the process of achieving micturitional control is basically a process of physiological maturation at progressively higher brain centers, *a process which is not normally dependent for its success on training*, though he does not at all deny that training techniques may influence (often deteriously) this process. Crosby argues that for nocturnal continence to be obtained, two conditions must exist: first, inhibition of detrusor activity coupled with increased bladder capacity, so that reflex micturition is not precipitated at low bladder volumes; and second, increased prepotency of this inhibition over the visceral afferent stimuli tending to initiate micturition, to the point at which stimulation from the filling bladder will initiate waking before it initiates reflex voiding. Basically, Crosby's theory is one of feedback rather than learning.

Crosby's theory of essential enuresis is, however, difficult to follow, for he goes on to argue that the inhibitory stimulus that produces waking is the wet, urinous state which, following wetting, causes discomfort and that reinforcement from this repeated urinous state in the infant produces a gradual increase in the inhibitory tone of the bladder. It is difficult to see why this aspect of his formulation, at least, should not be regarded as involving the learning process.

A rather similar viewpoint is put forward by Gillison and Skinner (1958) who argue that failure to achieve control of micturition is "mainly a failure of development—a failure, that is, to substitute cerebral control for the spinal control of infancy" (Gillison and Skinner, 1958, p. 1271), and they specifically reject the conditioning model. However, in arguing that "we are here dealing with the establishment of a normal physiological inhibitory mechanism," these authors simply beg the question of how the establishment is achieved.

Other writers have suggested that failure to achieve micturitional control is primarily a result of inadequate development of cortical control over subcortical reflex circuits (e.g., Hodge and Hutchings, 1952; Gunnarson and Melin, 1951) without, however, denying the possibility that complex sequences of conditioned responses may constitute the basis of cortical control.

It has also been argued that enuresis is only part of a larger physiological syndrome. Thus, Stalker and Band (1946) consider enuresis to be but one part of a local autonomic symptom complex, consisting of nocturnal enuresis, rising at night, diurnal enuresis, diurnal frequency and urgency, and encopresis. Similarly, Pierce and Lipcon (1956) speak of a syndrome of "biophysical aberrancy" consisting of enuresis, sleepwalking, and epilepsy. Braithwaite (1955) has, however, indicated the obvious need for control data from nonenuretic children and has actually shown, in several instances, that physiological disturbances supposedly related to enuresis are just as frequently found in nonenuretic children.

All of this work suggests that maturation of the highest nervous centers is of great significance in relation to achievement of control. There is no reason to suppose that this view is incorrect.

It has also been argued that enuresis is a neurotic trait and is normally found in accompaniment with other common so-called neurotic traits of childhood, such as thumb-sucking,

---

[3] For a cogent critique of the psychodynamic approach, see Werry (1967).

temper tantrums, and the like. The most out-spoken advocate for this position is Michaels (1955).[4] For Michaels, enuresis is primarily the reflection of a poorly integrated and developed personality. He further considered that *persistent* enuresis reflected a failure of the development of inhibitory controlling mechanisms and linked it, when it persisted into adolescence, with juvenile delinquency and psychopathic personality. Michaels also considered that there was a strong hereditary factor, since enuresis is usually accompanied by an increased incidence in the families of enuretics as compared with the families of nonenuretics, a finding that has been replicated many times (e.g., Pierce and Lipcon, 1956; Young, 1963).[5]

Two points need to be made, however, concerning the possible relationship between enuresis and personality. First, the evidence is highly contradictory, no doubt because of the wide variation in samples studied. In many clinic samples, for example, the initial reason bringing the child to the clinic is often not (in the parent's view) related to the existence of enuresis, but rather the existence of enuresis is discovered incidentally during the anamnestic interview. As was pointed out earlier, there is no doubt that many enuretic children (with or without personality disturbance) are not referred to a clinic, which therefore sees an extremely biased sample. Thus, Pierce et al (1956) studied 60 enuretic and 60 nonenuretic recruits to the Armed Services and found that the enuretics showed a wide variety of neurotic traits and special sexual fears. The enuretics were less successful in all areas of adjustment, had more sibling rivalry, stricter parents, and were prone to chronic illness. These findings are consonant with those of Michaels (1955) and might even be considered as support for the psychodynamic formulations discussed earlier. Similarly, Stalker and Band (1946) concluded that anxiety and psychopathic features were characteristic of enuretics, their major conclusion (that enuresis is associated with psychopathy) being very similar to that of Michaels (1955).

On the other hand, Lickorish (1964) compared 100 enuretics with 100 nonenuretics on 30 characteristics and could find very few differences.

This brings us to the second point to be noted about the personality studies. First, the studies by Michaels, Pierce, et al and Stalker and Band were all conducted on adolescent or adult enuretics, whereas the study by Lickorish (1964) covered an age range of 2–18 years. Second, it is clearly impossible to determine from these studies whether (a) the personality deficiencies have arisen independently of the enuresis; or (b) the personality deficiencies are a reaction to the difficulties and conflicts resulting from parental disapproval of the enuresis over a long period of time; or (c) whether the enuresis is a reaction to personality difficulties of long-standing. It has too generally been assumed that enuresis is a symptom of underlying personality problems, whereas it is equally reasonable to assume that *persistent* enuresis leads to disturbed family relationships which, if they last long enough, may well produce more general deterioration of personality traits and an increase in aggressiveness, etc.

3. Behavioristic Formulations

The essence of the behavioristic approach to the etiology of enuresis may be stated most helpfully in a series of propositions.

(i) That, in the newborn child, the voiding reflex is an extremely powerful natural reflex and that this is essential if the infant is to survive.

(ii) That the problem faced by the growing child is to develop the higher nervous centers, by both maturation and learning, to the extent that inhibitory factors are strong enough to hold in check the natural reflex until voluntary voiding can be achieved.

(iii) That this achievement represents a high-level skill of considerable complexity and that it is not, therefore, surprising that some children have difficulty in achieving such control (indeed, it may be argued that the really surprising fact is not that some children fail to achieve such control, but that most children do achieve it).

The problems to be solved, therefore, are: how is normal micturitional control established, both nocturnal and diurnal, and what factors are involved in the failure to achieve such control?

It is necessary, therefore, to examine two aspects of micturitional control: first, the

---

[4] Michaels' book is, in effect, a summary of a long series of individual studies, originally published in journal form.

[5] Young (1963) has reviewed the hereditary evidence which need not be repeated here, since it is obviously inconclusive.

TABLE 5.1. *Initiation of Involuntary Micturition Reflex*

Reflex	Adequate Stimulus	Pathways		Level of Control
		Afferent	Efferent	
I. Detrusor contraction Internal sphincter relaxation	Bladder distention	Pelvic nerve	Pelvic nerve	Hind brain
II. Detrusor contraction	Urethral fluid	Pudic nerve	Pelvic nerve	Hind brain
III. External sphincter relaxation	Urethral fluid	Pudic nerve	Pudic nerve	Spinal sacral
IV. External sphincter relaxation	Bladder distention	Pelvic nerve	Pudic nerve	Spinal sacral
V. Internal sphincter relaxation	Bladder distention	Pelvic nerve	Pelvic nerve	Spinal sacral

physiological processes involved; second, the part played by learning.

(a) PHYSIOLOGICAL BASIS OF MICTURITIONAL CONTROL. The physiology of normal *reflex* micturition is extremely complex.[6] Briefly, urine passes from the kidney through the ureters (by peristaltic action) into the bladder. The wall of the bladder contains the detrusor muscle which does not respond linearly to increased volume of urine but maintains a steady level of pressure until the volume exceeds about 200 ml. Above this point, the detrusor muscle is less successful in maintaining tone[7] and begins to contract rhythmically, leading ultimately to the micturition reflex, which involves strong contractions of the detrusor muscle and relaxation of the internal followed by the external sphincters, and involuntary voiding of urine.

The micturition reflex is, in fact, made up of the coordinated sequential "firing" of several simple reflexes. Table 5.1 shows the individual reflexes involved, together with the afferent and efferent pathways involved and the level of nervous system control.

(b) DEVELOPMENT OF CORTICAL CONTROL OF MICTURITION. It is clear that the child is faced with a major task in developing voluntary control over what is a powerful and complex natural reflex. There are several aspects to this problem which should be kept quite separate.

(i) The child must acquire the skill of inducing voluntary urination when the act is required to be performed and, further, *must be able to do this at low volumes and pressures of urine in the bladder.* The crucial question involved here is the relative contribution of neural maturation and high-level learned stimulus-response sequences eventuating in successful micturition. The evidence suggests that the controlled initiation of the natural reflex is achieved *indirectly*; voluntary direct contraction of the detrusor muscle is an unlikely explanation since smooth muscle function is involved. An alternative explanation, that detrusor contraction is normally inhibited through cortical inhibition, release of which enables detrusor contraction to take place, is unlikely to be a complete explanation since urine can be voided at very low bladder pressures. Muellner (1951, 1958, 1960), basing his ideas on fluoroscopic observations, has suggested that, by voluntarily steadying the diaphragm, contracting the lower abdominal muscles, and relaxing the pubococcygeus of the levator ani, a rapid lowering of the bladder neck is achieved. This, in turn, leads to an increase in intraabdominal pressure, followed by detrusor contraction and micturition. Muellner suggests that this skill is achieved in four stages: first, the child must perceive stimulation arising from increasing bladder function; second, he must be able to

---

[6] The most recent survey of the experimental literature will be found in the paper by Kuru (1965).

[7] Detrusor muscle tone is controlled by the antagonistic action of the pelvic and hypogastric nerves, which are parts of the parasympathetic and sympathetic divisions of the autonomic nervous system, respectively.

hold urine briefly when the bladder is full; third, he must develop the ability to start the urine flow from a full bladder; and fourth, he must be able to start the urinary stream from a bladder that is much less than full.

Now Muellner has argued strongly that parental training techniques and environmental conditioning are irrelevant to the explanation of how this complex skill is achieved; and he is unquestionably right in this viewpoint, except in so far as parental pressures may increase drive level in the child, thus interfering with the acquisition and performance of the skill (see below). As Muellner points out, in a very real sense, "the process is . . . self-learned, and . . . the skills which the child must learn cannot be taught by others" (Muellner, 1960, p. 714). It does not seem unreasonable, however, to suppose that the voluntary muscular activities that initiate the final reflex act (and the modifications that may occur *during* the act of micturition, such as the slowing of the voiding rate) are not merely a function of neural maturation but involve also conditioning. Thus, the increased tension of the bladder as it fills presumably becomes a conditioned stimulus producing the muscular responses referred to above, these muscular responses themselves then becoming unconditioned stimuli for detrusor contraction. The importance of maturation can scarcely be overstressed, however, since the relationship between urinary volume in the bladder and pressure sensations will almost certainly change as the bladder increases its capacity as a result of maturation.

(ii) Even more important than cortical control of the act itself is development of the capacity to *inhibit* detrusor activity with increasing volumes and pressures of urine, to the point at which reflex voiding is unlikely to take place even when the bladder is full and the urgency to micturate is very great. Here very little is known except that it seems clear that high-level inhibitory controlling centers must be gradually established.

(iii) Having established control of the act itself, and having developed the capacity to delay initiation of the conditioned sequences leading to micturition, the child must also acquire the ability to exercise this control during sleep. There are two aspects to this achievement. First, the child must transfer the daytime inhibitory control to sleep; second, if bladder pressures increase during sleep to the point at which reflex voiding becomes imminent, the bladder pressures must be capable of waking the child before the reflex is triggered and automatic voiding occurs. Here again, the process is undoubtedly complex and involves both maturation and learning, the mechanisms being little understood, although Jones (1960) has stressed the importance of the establishment of cortical "sentinal" points.

(iv) Finally, the child must learn to attach *situational* cues to the whole micturitional sequence, so that the need to micturate will be suggested not only by internal sensations but also by external factors. Here, undoubtedly, factors of parental training and the conditioning of situational stimuli become of great significance—but these, of course, are events *prior* to the actual act itself. The processes involved here have been carefully analysed by Ellis (1963) who has proposed the following paradigm:

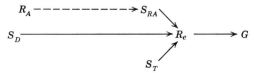

where S_D refers to tension in the bladder, R_A is the approach response elicited by S_D, S_T are cues associated with the toilet, and S_{RA} are cues generated by the approach response. Thus, stimuli from the bladder produce an initial approach response (or an "alerting"), and the feedback stimuli resulting from the alerting response summate with those from the environment (e.g., the sight of the toilet) to produce elimination (R_e), which achieves a goal that is rewarding (reduction of aversive stimulation from the full bladder). In this way, through generalization, situational stimulation may produce urinatory activity at lower bladder pressures than those normally initiating the sequence of events described by Muellner.

Thus, it may be concluded that successful control of urination is both a function of the acquisition of control of the *mechanics* of the act itself and the learning of situational cues which enable the child to *anticipate* its needs. That situational cues may be of vital importance and that failure to respond to these may give the false impression that the mechanics of voluntary control have *not* been acquired is illustrated by a study of Madsen (1965). He trained a normal child of 19 months to use the toilet successfully for both urination and defecation in one month by using reward for successful performance. This study suggests that inappropriate urination (apparent incontinence) may occur simply because situational learning has not taken place;

and, indeed, this argument may be particularly relevant to continence training in severe mental defectives. It would appear from some studies (e.g., Hundziak et al, 1965) that the problem here is not the control of the act itself so much as the failure to respond to situational cues that is the source of the difficulty. That is, many severe mental defectives, who are apparently voiding reflexly, are, in fact, able to control elimination voluntarily *once they are placed in the appropriate situation*. However, they have great difficulty in initiating movement toward the appropriate situation because of their difficulty in discriminating *situational* anticipatory cues.

(c) FAILURE TO ACQUIRE VOLUNTARY CONTROL OF MICTURITION. It will be obvious from what has already been said that acquiring control of micturitional behavior (both diurnal and nocturnal) is a complex skill, involving physiological maturation (e.g., increased bladder size so that increased volumes and pressures of urine can be tolerated), the development of high-level cortical control (so that the delicate adjustments required both to inhibit involuntary micturition and initiate and control the complex series of events leading to the micturition reflex at the right place and time can be made), and the development of the ability to discriminate environmental cues which will summate with minimal internal feedback cues from the filling bladder so that micturition can be induced voluntarily in appropriate places before the urgency becomes too great in settings where micturition may be socially inappropriate.

There seems little doubt that development of high-level cortical control is the most important factor involved. But the evidence of how this is achieved and the role of conditioning factors is unfortunately very sketchy indeed. Most of the evidence is both indirect and negative, rather than positive. Thus, Stalker and Band (1946) obtained cystometrographic records of bladder pressure and detrusor activity from a group of enuretics and claimed that most enuretics show the uninhibited neurogenic[8] type of bladder, with high pressure, low capacity, and early uninhibited contractions, these being accompanied by a strong urge to urinate at low bladder

pressure and volumes. Whereas the normal cystometrogram is characterised by initial strong detrusor activity as the bladder fills, followed by inhibition of the activity and then positively accelerated contractions to the voiding point, the enuretic cystometrogram shows uncontrolled and widely variable detrusor activity, with strong peaks at very low bladder volumes. After careful consideration of all the evidence from anatomical studies, they rejected explanations at the spinal level and concluded that the results indicated a failure of cerebral control. But this evidence is clearly indirect, since no correlations were attempted with cortical activity. Other studies have, however, more directly implicated inefficient cortical control. Thus, EEG studies of 90 enuretic children led Gunnarson and Melin (1951) to suggest immaturity of the nervous system as an important factor. In 100 cases of severe enuresis, Turton and Spear (1953) found that one-third showed a too slow ("immature") wave-type, while Temmes and Toivakka (1954) found that only 11 out of 54 enuretics showed no evidence of EEG abnormality, suggesting disturbances of cerebral origin.

Many investigations have been made of the relation of sleep to enuresis, the suggestion being that the deep sleep supposedly characteristic of the enuretic makes him less sensitive to the stimulation reaching the cortex from the filling of the bladder—hence, involuntary micturition occurs before the subject wakes. The evidence is, however, contradictory. Pierce et al (1961) found that wetting during sleep was accompanied by deep sleep (as indicated by delta high amplitude EEG waves). Boyd (1960), on the other hand, using a standard procedure to awaken subjects from sleep, could find no difference in waking time between enuretics and nonenuretics, nor could she find any relationship between depth of sleep and EEG abnormality. No attempt will be made to review the literature here, because of these contradictions.[9]

The most likely possibility seems to be that inefficient activity of the detrusor muscle produces involuntary voiding of urine at quite low bladder pressures and volumes and that, during sleep, stimulation from these events is

---

[8] The use of the term "neurogenic bladder" is unfortunate, since it is more customarily used to describe failure of micturitional control resulting from congenitally or organically determined causes (Boyarsky, 1967) and thus excludes enuresis.

[9] See Boyd (1960) for a comprehensive review of the literature. Browning (1967) has recently shown that operant conditioning techniques may be successfully used to produce waking to the bell in heavy sleepers as a preliminary to training with the Mowrer technique.

insufficiently strong to awaken the child before the reflex occurs. This explanation would *not* require that the enuretic be a heavy sleeper, nor that the occurrence of the reflex itself should awaken him, since the events may all involve relatively low levels of feedback stimulation. It would then be argued that, essentially, the child with nocturnal enuresis fails to transfer to sleep the conditioned alerting stimulus-response connections established during waking hours because while these stimuli are strong enough to "alert" the child to the imminence of micturition during the day, they are not strong enough to penetrate the general inhibition induced during sleep over the whole cortex. Unfortunately, very little study has been made of the bladder capacity of enuretics. Crosby (1950) did devise an apparatus to collect urine from his enuretic subjects and tested the samples obtained for pH, specific gravity, and chloride and urea concentrations, as well as the amount secreted. However, he did not present any comparative results for nonenuretic children. Braithwaite (1955) did, however, demonstrate that in only 4 out of 117 enuretics studied by him, did the micturition urge occur at volumes *exceeding* 100 ml of urine; while in 58 cases the volume was less than 10 ml.

Crosby's explanation of the occurrence of involuntary micturition during sleep is essentially the same as that suggested here: in essential enuresis, "the filled[10] bladder initiates micturition before the discomfort of the distending bladder reaches the threshold to disturb sleep" (p. 536).

This explanation suggests, of course, that enuresis represents a form of *habit deficiency*, i.e., a failure to develop cortical control. Crosby, however, suggested that most cases of enuresis involve *inappropriate conditioning*, rather than a failure of conditioning. That is, he argued, the child learns to micturate to a large range of stimuli which do not produce the micturition reflex in nonenuretic children. Thus he writes that:

"A common history is that it is almost impossible to go to the child during sleep without finding him urinating in his sleep or just having completed the act. In these cases, light, noise, or physical disturbances from early training have been the conditioning stimuli which initiate micturition . . ." (Crosby, 1950, p. 536).

He goes on to argue against the common training procedures used by most mothers (e.g., placing the child on the toilet at regular intervals or lifting him at night for the same purpose), since in his view, far from training the child to control urination, it merely succeeds in teaching the child to urinate at regular intervals, whereas the primary goal is, of course, inhibition of micturition during sleep. There is much to be said for this point of view, and certainly the whole question of how far toilet training practices facilitate or interfere with continence achievement is a very vexing one. Thus, Young (1964a), in a careful retrospective study, found that nonenuretic children achieved continence earlier if they were "trained" earlier by the parents, but that in enuretic children, it made no difference whether training procedures were indulged in by the parents or not.

An interesting hypothesis was put forward by Young (1965c) in which he argued that the Yerkes-Dodson law was relevant to the achievement of micturition control. If we regard the achievement of continence as involving the acquisition of a complex skill, then it follows that high drive levels would interfere with the initial acquisition of the skill, and, further, where the skill had been achieved, but only tenuously, the subsequent introduction of high drive levels would tend to break down the skill. From this, he deduced that coercive training on the part of the parents, with punishment or threats for wetting, would make it more difficult for the child to acquire control and would produce a reversion to wetting (the acquired enuresis cases) in children who had reached a stage of apparent control, but where overlearning was minimal.

Thus we reach the general conclusion that acquisition of diurnal and nocturnal control of micturition is a high-level skill, involving complex cortical sequences of conditioned inhibition and controlled release, a skill which may fail to be acquired either because of inadequate physiological and neural maturation, or because of the learning of inadequate patterns of micturition, or because of interference through the induction of aversive drive states, or indeed, through a combination of several of these factors. In any event, it is clear that the resolution of these difficulties will involve assisting the child to achieve the required delicate control by systematic experimental studies. There is, therefore, every justification

---

[10] Crosby should probably have used the term "filling" rather than "filled."

for applying knowledge of techniques derived from learning theory to the resolution of the difficulties.

III. TYPES OF TREATMENT (NONBEHAVIORISTIC)

Before proceeding further, however, it is worth glancing briefly at nonbehavioristic methods of treatment of enuresis. In this regard, one cannot do better than to quote, from Mowrer's study, the bewildering and often wildly improbable methods that have been tried at one time and another.[11]

"Innumerable drugs and hormones; special diets (including fresh fruit, caviar, and colon bacilli); restriction of fluids; voluntary exercises in urinary control; injections of physiological saline, sterile water, paraffin, and other inert substances; real and sham operations (passage of a bougie, pubic applications of cantharides plasters, cauterization of the neck of the bladder, spinal punctures, tonsillectomy, circumcision, clitoridotomy, etc.); high-frequency mechanical vibration and electrical stimulation of various parts of the body; massage; bladder and rectal irrigations; Roentgen and other forms of irradiation; chemical neutralization of the urine; sealing or constriction of the urinary orifice; hydrotherapy; local 'freezing' of the external genitalia with ice or 'chloratyl', elevation of the foot of the patient's bed[12]; sleeping on the back; not sleeping on the back; and the use of a hard mattress" (Mowrer and Mowrer, 1938, p. 436).

In addition, more "modern" methods include psychotherapy, arousing at intervals, psychodrama, and so on and so forth. No comment seems necessary.

IV. BEHAVIOR THERAPY AND ENURESIS

1. HISTORICAL DEVELOPMENT OF CONDITIONING TECHNIQUES

Although the use of conditioning methods in the treatment of enuresis is usually considered to have originated with the paper by Mowrer and Mowrer (1938), these authors themselves

indicated the use of similar techniques by earlier authors. Thus, Pfaundler (1904) devised a method that involved the ringing of a bell when the infant wet, but the intention was to facilitate the changing of the child and prevent skin irritation, rather than to teach the child to achieve dryness. He did, however, observe therapeutic consequences of the procedure. Genouville (1908) used Pfaundler's method with the specific intention of diminishing incontinence and, in fact, verbally described the mechanics of the process later formalized in terms of conditioning processes by Mowrer.[13] The method seems to have been independently rediscovered simultaneously by Mowrer and Mowrer (1938) and by Morgan and Witmer (1939), though major credit must be given to Mowrer and Mowrer for their extensive survey of the literature on enuresis and their more comprehensive attempt to provide a rational theory for the method.

In considering the development of the theory and technique of the conditioning treatment of enuresis, we may conveniently divide the literature into three phases: (1) the use of classical conditioning theory and the "bell method" following the work of Mowrer and Mowrer (1938), together with modifications of apparatus; (2) the development of a supposedly different method, based on electric shock by Crosby (1950); and (3) the more recent reformulation of the theory in terms of instrumental avoidance conditioning together with the elaboration of a modified method of treatment by Lovibond (1963, 1964).

2. THEORY AND TECHNIQUE: (1) THE MOWRER APPROACH

(a) THEORY. Mowrer and Mowrer argued that:

"If the child is repeatedly awakened at a time when the bladder is partially filled, but not so distended as to produce reflex emptying, the attendant bladder stimulation will eventually become specifically associated with the response of awakening, before the point has been reached at which voiding tends to occur automatically . . . would it not be advantageous from the point of view of most efficient habit formation if the awakening could always occur at a time when bladder

backwards?(!)

[11] See Glicklich (1951) for a historical review of research on enuresis.

[12] With the idea of inducing the urine to run

[13] See the quotations from the paper by Remy-Roux in Mowrer and Mowrer (1938, p. 448–449).

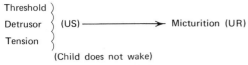

(Child does not wake)

FIG. 2. Pretraining stage.

Stage II consists of *training the child to awake immediately after the onset of micturition*. The theoretical process is represented in Figure 3. It is important to note that the process involves *two* unconditioned stimuli and *three* unconditioned responses. Threshold detrusor tension (US_1), produces micturition (UR_1) which in turn rings the bell (as will be described later). The bell (US_2) awakens the child[14] and produces two unconditioned responses (UR_2—awakening, and UR_3—inhibition of micturition). Threshold detrusor tension, however, also serves as a CS for waking (CR_1) and inhibition of micturition (CR_2). Thus, it is argued, the use of the method will condition waking and inhibition of micturition to increasing detrusor contractions.

distention is maximal and only at such a time, instead of at more or less arbitrarily determined intervals during the night, when bladder-filling may be at any of various stages? If some arrangement could be provided so that the sleeping child would be awakened *just after the onset of urination*, and only at this time, the resulting association of bladder distention and the response of awakening and inhibiting further urination should provide precisely the form of training which would seem to be most specifically appropriate" (Mowrer and Mowrer, 1938, p. 445).

The theory needs to be more complicated than this, as has been clearly shown by Jones (1960). Several stages in the acquisition of bladder control need to be distinguished.

In the *pretraining stage*, the model may be described as shown in Figure 2. When detrusor tension (US) exceeds a given threshold (there will be individual differences, of course, in the appropriate threshold), involuntary urination (UR) will occur, without the child waking.

Stage III consists of *the child awakening to increased detrusor contractions before the bell rings and therefore before wetting occurs*. The theoretical explanation of this stage (which unquestionably occurs in *practice*) is more difficult. Mowrer and Mowrer (1938) argue that the functional connection between bladder-distention stimulation and the waking/inhibition response "should become sufficiently well-established to cause the awakening response and the contraction of the bladder sphincter to 'come forward' in time and occur actually in advance of the onset of urination, instead of afterwards" (Mowrer and Mowrer, 1938, p. 446).

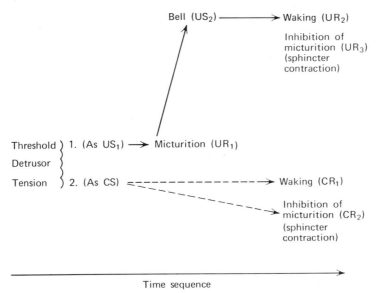

FIG. 3. Training the child to wake to onset of micturition.

[14] An unfortunate association of ideas with the classical conditioning of the salivary response (where the bell is a CS) has misled some authors to regard the bell in the Mowrer technique as a CS. In this technique, however, the bell is a US for awakening.

It is clear that gradients of stimulus generalization must be involved in this process, and Jones (1960, pp. 393–396) has attempted to work out in detail how this occurs. Briefly, Jones argues that both the micturition and waking *thresholds* are distorted by the generalization gradients of the contrary tendencies conditioned on the first trial when reflex voiding occurs and the bell wakes the child. On successive trials, the whole process moves backward, as it were, in time, and both inhibition and wakening occur to increased bladder tension *before* micturition occurs. Hence, the child wakes before the bell rings and before wetting occurs. This process is, of course, a learning process and hence follows a curve of learning with occasional failures and gradual strengthening of the tendency to wake before wetting (again, empirically, there is no doubt that the course of increased control does follow this pattern).

The final stage involves a continuation of inhibitory control (sphincter contraction to increasing bladder pressure) but also the *inhibition of the waking response*, so that the child sleeps through the night while remaining dry. If this stage is achieved the child is now nonenuretic.[15] The explanation of this stage is by no means clear. It is conceivable that the conditioning process improves the "tone" of the bladder causing increasing changes in volume of urine not to produce increased bladder pressures so that, whereas these are strong enough to induce sphincter contraction, they are not strong enough to produce wakening as well.

(b) TECHNIQUE. The apparatus constructed by Mowrer for the conditioning technique is sufficiently well known not to require elaborate description. It consisted of a pad made up of two layers of heavy cotton fabric separating two pieces of bronze gauze, together with a third layer of cotton. The sheets of gauze were connected in series to a battery and a sensitive relay. Since urine has electrolytic properties, when contact is made with the gauze, the relay is activated and the bell rings until the child wakes (or is woken by the parent) and turns it off. Practically all researches have utilized this method, though the construction of the pad, in particular, has been modified in the direction of efficiency and simplicity (Davidson and

Douglass, 1950; Coote, 1965; Freyman, 1963). There are a number of important points to note about the Mowrer-type apparatus. It is designed specifically so that the child's sleep will not be disturbed by the fact that he is lying on the pad, that he will have freedom of movement and be able easily to rise from bed to visit the toilet. The child does not at any stage receive a shock (though electrolysis of the urine may cause skin irritation). Mowrer laid particular stress on the importance of the child waking to the bell (or being woken by the parents).

One point which has not perhaps been stressed sufficiently is the fact that a great deal of evidence suggests that, for the most satisfactory results, the method should be used under close supervision and that even the most careful instructions may not prevent inadequate use of the instrument in the home. Bostock and Shackleton (1957) have given an alarming account of pitfalls in the use of the apparatus, most of which relate to adequacy of parental supervision, though the child himself may interfere with the apparatus, and the latter is itself subject to various kinds of breakdown. It cannot be too strongly emphasized that the application of the method to the treatment of enuresis is not a simple, routine procedure and that the first consideration in *any* apparent failure is to investigate the various causes that may produce failure rather than conclude that the technique as such has failed. This problem so concerned Lovibond that he devoted a separate chapter in his book to the procedures to be followed (Lovibond, 1964, Ch. 14). Reasons for failure with the technique will be discussed in more detail below.

3. THEORY AND TECHNIQUE: (2) THE CROSBY APPROACH

(a) THEORY. Crosby's (1950) method of treatment is derived (though the line of argument is by no means clear) from his theory of how the normal child achieves control of micturition. He argues that:

"the wet urinous state, which I term 'somatic discomfort', acts as an inhibitory stimulus, and that this, at the onset of micturition, causes an unconditioned response tending to inhibit continuation of

---

[15] It should be pointed out that not all enuretic children would be expected to achieve this final stage. Many nonenuretic children (and adults!) are unable to sleep through the night without rising

to urinate, though no reliable data on the incidence of night-rising are available. Achievement of all but the final stage would however obviously be a satisfactory outcome.

urination by inhibiting the detrusor and contracting the sphincter. . . . Reinforcement of
this inhibition from repeated soiling would be
expected to produce a gradual increase in the
tone of inhibition of the bladder, so that the
volume of urine necessary to initiate urination
would increase also. . . . In the sleeping child,
then, the filling bladder is producing stimuli
which are active at two separate 'centers', the
bladder reflex center and the 'sleep center',
and the resultant effect is determined by three
coexisting factors, depth of sleep, inhibitory
tone, and stimulation of bladder efferents. If
the inhibitory tone is sufficiently prepotent,
the discomfort of a filled bladder will
dispense sleep before the bladder afferents
initiate micturition as a reflex act" (Crosby,
1950, p. 536).

Crosby appears then to be arguing that the
discomfort of a filling bladder becomes a CS by
association with the inhibition arising as a US
from the discomfort experienced on wetting, but
he does not explain how the child eventually
comes to sleep through the night, nor does he
invoke the principle of generalization. His
actual treatment, in fact, seems more directed
towards his contention that, in most cases of
enuresis, wetting occurs, not as an unconditioned
reflex but rather as a conditioned response and,
indeed, he specifically states that his treatment is
aimed "at extinguishing any conditioned responses which initiate micturition, and at
reinforcing the natural method of building up
the 'inhibitory' tone, which is considered
necessary for continence" (Crosby, 1950, p. 538)
though he does not indicate how his method is
supposed to achieve this end.

(b) TECHNIQUE. Unlike the Mowrer technique, that used by Crosby does involve electric
shocks to the subject. The stimulating electrodes
are attached to the loin region and are kept in
place by means of a belt, the intensity of the
stimulus being variable by the experimenter or
the patient. In the male, the emission of urine is
detected immediately by means of a urine
electrode screwed into a plastic tube which is
fastened to the penis to make a leak-tight join.
A modified method is used with females. When
urine is voided, the contact electrodes result in
the delivery of an electric shock to the loin of
the child, sufficient to wake it.

There are a number of important points to
be noted about the Crosby technique. A grave

weakness in the method as such is that it is
possible for the batteries producing the shock to
run flat and hence for no electrical stimulus to be
delivered. To avoid this possibility (which may
not be apparent) Crosby arranged for the
voiding of urine also to activate a bell which
was intended to alert the attendant. As Crosby
puts it, "if the patient is alone, then it is
essential that the stimulus[16] be sufficient to
ensure waking, otherwise small points of
electrolysis can appear at the stimulating
electrodes and, of less importance, the batteries
will run flat" (Crosby, 1950, p. 539). But
Crosby does not appear to have realized that the
introduction of this device *confounds his technique with that of Mowrer, since in both methods,
the subject is awakened by the bell.* In other
words, any positive results obtained by Crosby
could be due to the operation of the bell in
waking the patient, rather than to the effect of
the electrical stimulus.[17] Hence, we are forced
to conclude that the Crosby technique cannot
be clearly distinguished from the Mowrer
technique except by special investigations, one
of which will be discussed below.

4. THEORY AND TECHNIQUE: (3) LOVIBOND'S APPROACH

(a) THEORY. Lovibond (1963, 1964), following
up unpublished observations by Place, criticized
the classical conditioning model put forward by
Mowrer and adumbrated by Jones. First, he
argued that the paradigm (as outlined above)
was different from the classical Pavlovian model
for salivary conditioning in that the supposed
CS (bladder distention) was *not* originally (i.e.,
before conditioning) a *neutral stimulus* but was
rather a natural (unconditioned) stimulus for
sphincter relaxation and, therefore, for involuntary micturition. Second, he argued that,
if the classical conditioning model is correct,
then the method of treatment based on it
should be unsuccessful, or, at least, very
inefficient, since in classical conditioning the
CS-CR connection should extinguish when the
stage of training is reached at which reinforcement (the ringing of the bell) no longer occurs.
But extinction does not usually take place if the
experimental procedure is adequately carried
out—hence, the model must be incorrect.

Now, it is, in fact, arguable that Lovibond's
criticisms are both incorrect. In the first place, it
has been shown that an unconditioned stimulus

---

[16] I.e., the *auditory* stimulus.

[17] This critical point does not appear to have been
remarked upon previously.

may become a conditioned stimulus under certain conditions.[18] Thus, a pain stimulus of a severe kind (electric shock), which will normally produce an unconditioned response of withdrawal, may become a conditioned stimulus producing approach behavior provided it is introduced gradually, in association with a positive reinforcing stimulus (Pavlov, 1927). And, in the second place, whether or not a classically conditioned response will extinguish easily when the reinforcing stimulus is withdrawn depends in part on the method by which the classically conditioned response is established. As we have already seen (Chapter 2), the use of partial reinforcement techniques may lead to very strong resistance to extinction. Hence, neither of Lovibond's criticisms are fatal to the classical conditioning theory.

As a result of his reasoning, however, Lovibond produced an interesting alternative model based on instrumental avoidance conditioning. In an experiment by Konorski, passive leg flexion was followed by shock and, after several pairings, it was found that the dog would actively resist leg flexion and instead extend the leg (an antagonistic response). The interpretation placed on this experiment was that kinesthetic stimuli from leg flexion served as a CS (the signal for shock) which produced an avoidance response (CR).[19]

Applying this model to the theoretical explanation of the processes involved in the treatment of enuresis, Lovibond argued that the process could be conceptualized as follows.

(i) Detrusor contraction and sphincter relaxation lead to the occurrence of the noxious stimulus (bell in the Mowrer method; bell + shock in the Crosby method).

(ii) Kinesthetic stimuli from sphincter relaxation come to be a signal (CS) for the imminent noxious stimulus and hence induce the antagonistic response of sphincter contraction (CR).

(iii) Generalization moves the process back in time, that is, the onset of relaxation (but prior to wetting) leads to sphincter contraction (and may also generalize to detrusor contraction).

The major importance of Lovibond's reformulation (apart from its intrinsic theoretical interest) lies in the implication that *waking is not essential to the success of the treatment*, since the bell, as an aversive stimulus need not wake the subject to be effective, but needs only to produce detrusor relaxation and sphincter contraction.

(b) TECHNIQUE. Lovibond's reanalysis also suggested to him that it might be possible to increase the efficiency of the conditioning method of treatment by designing an instrument which permitted escape from the aversive stimulus (the bell). Accordingly, he devised what he called the twin-signal apparatus, which differs from the Mowrer technique in making use of two auditory stimuli. The first auditory stimulus (a loud hooter) occurs on initial wetting, but lasts for a period of only one second, followed by a silent period of one minute. An ordinary buzzer then sounds continuously until switched off. The duration of the first auditory stimulus exceeds slightly the latency plus duration of the response of sphincter contraction. Hence, sphincter contraction to the hooter would be followed immediately by the latter's cessation, thus providing escape from the aversive stimulation. Lovibond argued that this method would be successful even if the subject was not wakened by the hooter.[20] Lovibond (1964) has buttressed his theoretical analysis by a careful review of the experimental literature on avoidance training in animals, which we shall have occasion to refer to later in this chapter.

It should be noted in passing that Lovibond does not attempt to incorporate "sleeping through the night without wetting" into his theoretical reformulation but, as was already indicated, this stage presents difficulties for all theorists.

5. EFFICACY OF CONDITIONED RESPONSE TREATMENT OF ENURESIS

In evaluating the results of the conditioned response treatment of enuresis, it is necessary to bear in mind several methodological points which are often overlooked or vary from one experimenter to another. It is most unfortunate that, thus far, no standard procedure has been followed. In many instances vital information is not provided. The major points to be considered in the evaluation of any study are these:

---

[18] See Chapter 2.
[19] Compare Mowrer's response-dependent avoidance learning (Chapter 2).
[20] The subsequent buzzer is not primarily intended to waken the subject but rather to summon the attendant. (This second auditory signal would appear to be unnecessary and indeed better omitted altogether.)

(i) *Composition of the sample.* The major variable here is the degree of severity of the enuresis. This has varied in different studies; some samples have largely consisted of enuretics who are incontinent nightly (and often several times a night); others have included a wide range of severity. A second variable is the proportion of enuretics who are primary (wet from birth) as opposed to secondary (achieved dryness, then relapsed). Little systematic study of these variables has been carried out, and often the criteria dictating choice of sample are not stated.

(ii) *Initial success criterion.* The criterion which has been used *usually* refers to a stated number of *successive* dry nights, after which the apparatus is removed (in some cases a second set of successive dry nights is required under increased fluid intake). Quite variable requirements have been used by different workers, as shown in Table 5.2. A second measure occasionally reported is the *number of reinforcements* required to achieve the criterion (i.e., the number of times the bell rings or shock is given).

(iii) *Final success criterion.* This refers to the percentage of subjects remaining dry for a given follow-up period. Again, this has proved to be very variable, both within and across studies. A major problem here is the definition of "dry." A strict criterion would require complete dryness between achievement of the initial criterion and the end of the follow-up period. A more lenient criterion would require the subject not to wet more than, say, once a month. The strict criterion seems very severe, since it is well known that occasional wetting is found in many children who are not considered enuretic.

(iv) *Assessment of failures.* This is a most important problem, which has not so far been adequately dealt with in most studies. Should subjects who relapse after reaching the initial criterion and *who are not retrained* be considered as failures? If we view the process as one of training in a complex habit, it seems reasonable to argue that failure should not be recorded until at least one further attempt at retraining has been given. The initial criterion of seven dry nights, which is often used, may well be a much too lenient one for such a complex skill, and overlearning might be very important.

(v) It should be recognized that the technique has been applied to a very wide range of age-groups, and it is rare for the results to be broken down by age. Sex differences also seem to be important.

(vi) In assessing the results, it is important to bear in mind that, in many studies, the procedure has not been carried out under the direct control of the experimenter. Initial (often careful) instructions have been given and then the procedure carried out in the home. In view of the difficulties outlined by Bostock and Shackleton (1957) and the results of investigations into "failures" by Young (1965b) and Geppert (1953), a truly accurate appraisal of the CR treatment of enuresis could be achieved only in a study where the use of the apparatus

TABLE 5.2. *Initial Criteria for Arrest of Wetting*

Study	Initial Criterion (Number of dry nights)
Baller and Schalock (1956)	10 (after last accident)
Behrle et al (1956)	7 (consecutive)
Crosby (1950)	5 (consecutive)
De Leon and Mandell (1966)[a]	13 (consecutive)
Freyman (1963)	15
Geppert (1953)	7 (more in difficult cases)
Gillison and Skinner (1958)	14–21 (at least)
Mowrer and Mowrer (1938)	7 (consecutive) +7 (with increased fluid intake)
Seiger (1952)	14+ (minimum)
Young and Turner (1965)	14

[a] Seven with apparatus connected; three with apparatus disconnected; and three with apparatus removed.

TABLE 5.3. *Results of CR Treatment of Enuresis*

Study	N		Age Range	Percentage Achieving Initial Criterion	Relapse Rate (%)		Follow-up Period (Months)	Success Rate (% dry at follow-up including those retained)	Posttreatment Adjustment (+ improvement; O no change; − deterioration)	Symptom Substitution
	M	F			No Retraining	After Retraining				
Baller and Schalock (1956)	43	12	5–26	98	23	0	24–40	70	+	No
Behrle et al (1956)	12	8	5–14	Not stated	15	5	18–40	75	0	No
Crosby (1950)	17 5 15	12 1 8	3½–10½ 3½–10½ 11–38	Not stated	3.5 20.0 13.0	— — —	Not stated	96.5 80.0 87.0	Not stated	Not stated
Davidson and Douglass (1950)	17	3	5–30	Not stated	—	0	1–13	100	+	No
De Leon and Mandell (1966)	42	14	5½–14	86	79.6[a]	—	1–22	21.4	Not stated	Not stated
Forrester et al (1964)	7	9	8–14	Not stated	Not stated	—	6	62	Not stated	Not stated
Freyman (1959, 1963)	47	24	5–15+	72	35	20	10	80	Not stated	No
Geppert (1953)	30 (approx.)	12	5–10+	90	—	20	Not stated	90 (?)	+	Not stated
Gillison and Skinner (1958)	64	36	3½–21	Not stated	—	0	No systematic follow-up	90 (?)	+	No
Martin and Kubly (1955)	(79)[b]	(35)	3½–18	Not stated	26	—	14 (average)	74	Not stated	Not stated
Mowrer and Mowrer (1938)	30		3–13	100	—	—	Up to 30	100	+	No
Seiger (1952)	73	33	2½–29	—	11	—	2–many years	89	Not stated	Not stated
Taylor (1963)	62	38	5–15	64	16	—	6+	53	Not stated	Not stated
Wickes (1958)[c]	81	19	5–17	Not stated	26	—	Not stated	74	+	Not stated
Young and Turner (1965)	105		4–15	65 (93)[d]	13	—	12	53 (81)[d]	+	No

[a] The relapse criterion was very severe—a single wet night.

[b] In four cases sex was unknown (study was carried out by questionnaire on commercial users).

[c] Wickes (1963) reported a success rate of 74% (dry) in a series of 445 cases; but insufficient details are given to justify inclusion in the table.

[d] 93% rate if cases where treatment was discontinued are excluded; 65% if they are included. Same comments apply to success rate.

TABLE 5.4. *Percentage "Cured" (i.e., at least 6 Dry Nights per Week) with at least 6 Months Follow-Up*

Study	N	Percent "Cured"	Follow-up Period
Baller and Schalock (1956)	55	70	24–40 months
Behrle et al (1956)	20	75	18–40 months
Davidson and Douglass (1950)[a]	15	93	6–13 months
Forrester et al (1964)	16	81	6 months
Freyman (1963)	37	80	10 months
Taylor (1963)	100	53	6 months
Turner and Young (1966)[b]	41	63	40–63 months
Young and Turner (1965)	68	100	12 months

[a] Includes only those followed up for at least six months.
[b] Data for conditioning group only.

and the recording of results are carried out by an expert directly supervising each subject.

(a) GENERAL RESULTS OF CR TREATMENT. It will be clear from the above that most of the studies leave much to be desired methodologically. Despite this, the results are undeniably impressive, as indicated in Table 3. The final success rate (percentage dry or practically dry at the end of the follow-up period—including those relapsed and retrained) varies from 100% in two studies to a low point of 21%.

The column showing success rate must be viewed cautiously, however, since it can be seen that the length of follow-up varies enormously. Thus, in the study by Davidson and Douglass (1950), for example, the figure of 100% success rate is practically meaningless, since the follow-up period varied from as little as one month to as long as 13 months. Clearly, if some of the subjects had been followed up for longer periods, they may well have relapsed. In order to evaluate the long-term effect of the treatment, it is important only to include those cases satisfying a minimal follow-up period. Table 5.4 lists studies where information was available for subjects with a minimum of six months' follow-up and where the subject was dry at least six nights out of seven. Taking these studies as a whole, it can be seen that, for a follow-up period of this length, a minimal figure of 53% success is obtained. The actual (or true) figure would undoubtedly be much higher (probably

of the order of 90–95%) if more adequate control over the process were maintained by the experimenter, as suggested above. Considering the severity of many of the individuals treated, the results are extremely gratifying.[21]

Recent studies by Lovibond (1964), however, to be discussed shortly, suggest that, with follow-up extending to 2 years or more, the relapse rate may reach 35–40%, a figure which still justifies use of the method but which, as we shall see, suggests the urgent necessity for further experimental study. Similar figures were found by Turner and Young (1966) with a follow-up period of 3–5 years, as shown in Table 5.4.

It should also be pointed out that these figures are attained over a relatively short period of treatment. Figures given by Mowrer and Mowrer (1938), Geppert (1953), and Martin and Kubly (1955) suggest that the training period to achieve the initial criterion of 14 dry nights rarely exceeds 8 weeks and, on average, is as low as 4–6 weeks.

(b) REASONS FOR "FAILURE." Why do some subjects fail to achieve the initial criterion? While, in a few instances, there is no doubt that conditioning genuinely fails to occur, specific investigations have demonstrated beyond doubt that failure to supervise the process directly on the part of the experimenter is the main cause of failure. Thus Young (1965b) listed the following reasons for failure in 37 out of 105 cases: lack of parental cooperation (18 cases);

---

[21] De Leon and Mandell (1966) followed up 75% of their cases for at least six months, and found a very high relapse rate (80%); but their criterion was

exceptionally severe (a single wet incident) and, as they point out, no data is available on the frequency of such incidents in normal children regarded as dry.

poor housing and sleeping conditions (3); child frightened by machine (2); machine not awakening child (6); preferred treatment in hospital (1); too far to come to clinic (1). And he concludes that "lack of parental cooperation is undoubtedly the chief cause of uncompleted treatment" (Young, 1965b, p. 559). This conclusion is strengthened by the finding of Geppert that "the chief causes of failures unquestionably was poor parental cooperation" (Geppert, 1953, p. 383), and by Freyman (1963) and Taylor (1963), who investigated and found factors similar to those of Young. It seems that these difficulties are *not* overcome by even the most careful instructions and that, ideally, direct control of the process by the experimenter is most desirable.

(c) COMPARATIVE AND CONTROL STUDIES. The use of a standard procedure, of course, necessitates a comparison of the results of this treatment with alternative forms and with the "spontaneous recovery" rate (which, in this case, probably refers to the "untreated" gaining of control of micturition which, as was indicated in Figure 1, is a continuous process throughout childhood). Fortunately, a good deal of evidence is now available that indicates the usefulness of the CR method.

(i) *The Effectiveness of Drugs.* Many attempts have been made to use drugs in the treatment of enuresis. Thus Vignec et al (1957) treated chronic enuretics with a drug consisting of a mild sedative, belladonna alkaloids, and vitamin B complex, and claimed it was effective in 42% of cases. However, most drug studies have resulted in much poorer results. Representative of these is the study by Browne and Ford-Smith (1941) who tried a dozen different medications including ephedrine sulphate, belladonna, bar-

bital derivatives, diuretics, etc., and could find no difference in the effect on enuresis of any of these drugs as compared with a placebo. On the whole then, the effects of drug treatment alone appear to have been inconsistent and disappointing (Braithwaite, 1955).

(ii) *Drugs Compared with CR Treatment.* Forrester et al (1964) compared the effects of amphetamine with the effects of CR treatment on 37 schoolchildren over the age of eight years who were allocated at random to either treatment. The follow-up period was six months. They found that the CR treatment was significantly superior to the amphetamine treatment, the latter proving no different from the natural remission rate. Even more striking were the results of a very careful study by Young (1965b). He compared 273 enuretic children receiving one of a number of drug treatments[22] with 105 enuretic children receiving CR treatment. The results (Table 5.5) indicated quite clearly that the conditioning method was more successful, was faster, and involved a smaller relapse rate as compared with the drug treatment.

(iii) *Combination of Drugs and CR Treatment.* The interesting possibility that drugs may *facilitate* training when used *in combination with* the CR technique was investigated by Young and Turner (1965). They compared the effectiveness of CR treatment alone with effectiveness of CR treatment used in conjunction with dexedrine or methedrine, using large numbers of subjects. The results are shown in Table 5.6. These results suggested that CR treatment alone produces a higher discontinuance rate and that the use of excitatory drugs facilitates the conditioning process. Young and Turner also found that, with a uniform follow-up period of one year, the use of dexedrine produced a higher

TABLE 5.5.   *Results Obtained with Conditioning Treatment and with Drugs*

Method of Treatment	Number of Cases	Successfully Treated		Average Duration of Treatment (Months)	Relapsed	
		N	Percent		N	Percent
Conditioning	105	68	65	2.2 (range 1–6)	9	13
Drugs	273	98	36	5.2 (range 1–19)	27	28

Source: Young, 1965b.

---

[22] Posterior-pituitary gland snuff (dispidin); dexedrine; drinamyl; tyrimide; or a mixture of potassium citrate, hyoscyamus, and belladonna.

TABLE 5.6.   *Comparative Efficiency of CR Treatment with CR Treatment combined with Drugs*

Treatment Groups	N	Reached Initial Criterion		Discontinued Treatment		Number of Failures	
		N	Percent	N	Percent	N	Percent
I. CR treatment only	105	68	65	31	29	6	6
II. CR + dexedrine	84	64	76	12	14	8	9
III. CR + methedrine	110	90	82	13	12	7	6
Totals	299	222	74	56	19	21	7

Source: Young and Turner, 1965.

relapse rate (26.7%) than either CR treatment alone (13.2%) or CR treatment combined with amphetamine (13.3%). These findings regarding differential relapse rate were confirmed in a long-term follow-up study (Turner and Young, 1966).

This study is particularly interesting because of its relevance to the theoretical possibilities that (a) drugs may facilitate the conditioning process and (b) personality factors may be important in relation to the rate of conditioning (where these factors slow down the conditioning process, the use of appropriate drugs may facilitate conditioning). The study by Young and Turner indicates the importance of the drug variable per se, while the importance of personality factors is clearly shown in a study by Young (1965a) who predicted and found that enuretic children with high extraversion scores will show a higher relapse rate than children with high introversion scores, as measured by the Junior Maudsley Personality Inventory.[23]

The importance of appropriate drugs used in conjunction with CR treatment and personality score on the I-E dimension therefore seems undoubted.

(iv) *CR Treatment compared with Psychotherapy.* The only study of this kind appears to be that of De Leon and Mandell (1966). They used an initial success criterion of 13 successive dry nights and found that this was achieved by 86% of 51 children treated by the Mowrer technique compared with only 18% of 13 children treated by psychotherapy. Those

children achieving the criterion via conditioning did so in about half the time of those achieving it by psychotherapy.

(v) *Spontaneous Remission Rate.* This can be roughly estimated from the age-incidence curves shown in Figure 1. However, little direct work on this problem has been done, where the appropriate comparison would be between treated and untreated groups of enuretics over the same period of time, with variables (such as sex, severity of wetting, and so forth) carefully controlled. Freyman (1963), however, did follow up 46 cases referred for enuresis but not treated over the same period as the cases he did treat by conditioning. He found that 11 (24%) of the untreated cases had stopped wetting completely, or almost so, during the follow-up period.[24] Blomfield and Douglas (1956) reported that 59% of a large sample of children who were regularly wetting at $4\frac{1}{4}$ years of age were dry at $7\frac{3}{4}$ years, with remission apparently unrelated to treatment. De Leon and Mandell (1966) found that only 2 out of 18 untreated controls achieved the criterion of dryness used by them.

(vi) *The "Staggered-Wakening" Procedure.* Young (1964b) studied 58 enuretic children who were wakened at different times each night for 4 weeks at fixed but arbitrary times (i.e., unrelated to the time of wetting) and found that 67% were "improved" on follow-up, 10 children being completely continent after 2–3 treatments. He suggested this procedure might

---

[23] Unfortunately, the hypothesis that extraverted enuretics would also condition more poorly was not tested in this study.

[24] In some of these cases, some form of treatment (e.g. play therapy) was given but it was apparently non-systematic.

be useful where there was a waiting list for the CR apparatus.[25]

(vii) *Direct Diurnal Training in Bladder Control.* Several authors (e.g., Muellner, 1960) have tried the effect of training the child during the daytime to increase bladder capacity and control through the ingestion of increased amounts of fluid, on the assumption the increased control would generalize to sleep, and have reported good results.

We may conclude, therefore, that the various control studies discussed above do not in any way detract from the reported results of the efficacy of CR training by use of the apparatus, and that the results offer a number of interesting suggestions for further work.

(viii) *Comparison of Various CR Methods.* The question whether the Mowrer, the Crosby, or the Lovibond Twin Signal Apparatus are equal in efficacy has been studied by Lovibond (1964). Twelve enuretic children in each of three age groups ($6-7\frac{1}{2}$, $7\frac{1}{2}-10\frac{1}{2}$, and $10\frac{1}{2}-14$) were allocated at random to one of the three treatment groups (Mowrer, Crosby, or Lovibond apparatus).[26] Lovibond found that the Twin Signal apparatus was the most efficient in producing initial arrest, involving a median number of 14.5 stimuli compared with 20.0 for the Crosby and 30.5 for the Mowrer. However, subsequent studies (Lovibond, 1964) suggested that these differences were not replicable and that there was no important difference between the three instruments when used in the standard way.

(d) SYMPTOM SUBSTITUTION AND PERSON-ALITY CHANGES FOLLOWING CR TREATMENT. As was pointed out earlier, the CR treatment of enuresis is a critical area for the problem of symptom substitution, since all psychodynamic writers have predicted the occurrence of symptom substitution (often of a baleful nature) if direct treatment of the "symptom" is success-ful. Behavioristic writers, on the contrary, have argued that personality disturbance and emo-tional conflict either are generated independently of the enuresis or are a result of the intrafamily difficulties which enuresis produces. Thus, the psychodynamic psychologists predict that symp-tom substitution or deleterious personality changes will occur, whereas the behavior

therapists predict either no change in person-ality or an improvement and, further, that symptom substitution will not occur. The differential predictions could scarcely be clearer.

Nor, indeed, the results. In paper after paper, there is a clear indication that no symptom substitution was observed and that personality characteristics either did not change or altered for the better. A few quotations will suffice.[27]

"A surprisingly high proportion showed positive personality changes after acquiring the dry habit" (Davidson and Douglass, 1950, p. 1347).

"No substitution of symptoms has been reported by any of the parents of children treated by us with the enuresis apparatus" (Freyman, 1963, p. 206).

"Personality difficulties improved con-siderably in the majority of patients, indi-cating that such maladjustments may often be the effect rather than the cause of enuresis" (Geppert, 1953, p. 383).

"No adverse psychological effects, or substitution symptoms, have been observed either during or subsequent to treatment. Indeed, parents have spontaneously remarked how much brighter and happier the child has been since he became dry . . . we know of no published evidence which refutes this view" (Gillison and Skinner, 1958, p. 1270).

"Personality changes, when any have occurred as a result of the application of the present method of treating enuresis, have uniformly been in a favourable direction. In no case has there been any evidence of 'symptom substitution' " (Mowrer and Mowrer, 1938, p. 451).

Most of these reports are anecdotal, of course, but the consensus of opinion seems overwhelming. However, studies in which *experi-mental* measures of personality change have been made before and after treatment reach essentially the same conclusion (e.g., Baller and Schalock, 1956) or conclude that personality disturbances and changes are usually unrelated to the existence of enuresis or its disappearance with treatment (e.g., Behrle et al, 1956).

---

[25] Similar results with institutionalized children have been reported by Dewdney and Dewdney (1965).
[26] The Crosby apparatus was, however, used in modified form, the genital electrode being replaced

by a pad electrode.
[27] Many of these comments emanate, not from behavioristic psychologists, but from psychiatrists or physicians on the alert for evidence of change in accordance with the psychodynamic viewpoint.

Finally, mention should be made of an important study by Tapia et al (1960). They rated 824 3rd-grade children as well-adjusted (167); no significant problems (429); marginally disturbed (166); or clinically disturbed (68). They also rated the children for the presence or absence of 21 common symptoms. Of the sample, 10.1% were categorized as enuretic, using the very liberal criterion of wetting at least once a month. They found no correlation between enuresis and adjustment category or occurrence of symptoms and concluded that enuresis is not an emotional symptom.

Hence, it may confidently be concluded that there is no evidence whatsoever that enuresis is a symptom of some underlying conflict or disturbance; that successful treatment of the enuresis does not produce adverse personality changes; and that it does not produce symptom substitution. The more rational explanation would appear to be that enuresis represents the failure to acquire a skilled behavior pattern and that this failure may result in intrafamily conflict and disturbance. If the enuresis persists over a long period the child *may* develop personality disturbance, but successful treatment of the disorder, far from leading to symptom substitution, may lead to a dramatic improvement in the child's personal relationships and general adjustment.

V. FUTURE RESEARCH DIRECTIONS

In spite of the optimistic conclusion arrived at regarding the efficacy of behavior therapy for enuresis, there can be no doubt that much future research remains to be carried out. We shall group these tasks under four headings.

1. REDUCTION OF THE RELAPSE RATE

A subject may be properly considered to have relapsed, and the treatment to have failed, where, following attainment of the initial criterion,[28] complete, or virtually complete, dryness is not maintained. Table 5.3 shows that widely varying relapse rates (without retraining) have been reported, this being due, in part no doubt, mainly to varying lengths of follow-up. The reduction of the relapse rate is an important and neglected topic. The most obvious ways of reducing the relapse rate would consist of: (a) overlearning during the original

training (that is, increasing the initial success criterion beyond the seven or 14 days normally used) and (b) retraining the subject immediately on relapse. Use of the latter technique has been reported by several authors, usually with encouraging results, though Lovibond (1964, p. 130) reports somewhat variable results in the only systematic study that has been reported. Contrary to theoretical expectation, he found that 30% of the retreated cases responded *more slowly* than they had to the initial treatment and that 20% of the retreated cases relapsed a second time (with a follow-up period of one to three years). It does appear, however, that persistence with retreatment will pay off ultimately.

Lovibond (1964) carried out several other investigations relating to attenuation of the relapse rate. These included the effects of random presentation of the auditory stimulus at times when the subject was not wetting;[29] the modification of the Twin-Signal method to produce a long-duration, less intense auditory stimulus *immediately* following the intense short-duration auditory stimulus which is triggered off by wetting; and the use of the auditory stimulus alone without the child being wakened. Most importantly, however, Lovibond investigated the effects of partial reinforcement during training. It will be recalled (see Chapter 2) that the acquisition of a response under conditions of partial reinforcement increases resistance to extinction, since an extinction trial, under these circumstances, becomes more difficult to discriminate from an acquisition trial. Although Lovibond's experiment could not be described as definitive, his results suggested that this schedule of training reduced the relapse rate during the first three months of follow-up and may have maintained this effect over a 12-month follow-up. More systematic experimentation is certainly called for here.

2. CHANGES IN BLADDER FUNCTIONING

It is most unfortunate that so little attention has been paid to volume/pressure relationships in the bladders of enuretics compared with those of controls. Crosby (1950) did collect samples of urine voided by enuretics but did not report on the volumes voided and did not directly measure volume/pressure relationships. Gillison and Skinner (1958) reported that test measurements made at the time of wetting

---

[28] With properly supervised control, practically 100% subjects achieve the initial criterion (Lovibond, 1964).

[29] By analogy with the finding that avoidance behavior in animals could be maintained by the presentation of "free" shocks.

indicated that the bladder of enuretics was usually less than half full when wetting occurred. These results certainly suggested an abnormality of bladder volume/pressure relationships, but again no direct measurements were made. The most direct evidence comes from Stalker and Band (1946) who, as discussed above, reported a high incidence of abnormal cystometrograms in enuretics, and from Braithwaite (1955) (see results reported earlier).

Even less evidence is available concerning changes in volume/pressure relationships following CR training. Crosby (1950) considered that a real increase in bladder capacity occurred as a result of training but presented no evidence to support his contention. The question whether enuretics do, in fact, develop a large-volume low-tension bladder with training is obviously in need of urgent investigation.

3. STUDIES OF CORTICAL PHYSIOLOGY

The finding, already referred to, that abnormal cerebral patterns, as measured by the EEG, may be present in many enuretics, and the suggestion that CR treatment develops cortical control over lower reflex centers (Bental, 1961; Labar, 1965; Temmes and Toivakka, 1954; Turton and Spear, 1953; Gunnarson and Melin, 1951) suggests the need for much more extensive and careful investigation of cortical activity before, during, and after CR treatment. The cerebral basis for the establishment of conditioned responses is now being investigated and elucidated by modern neurological techniques, and it might well be that these techniques could be adapted for use in studies of the cortical physiology of enuretics. Similarly, the more careful study of the depth of sleep in enuretics (Boyd, 1960; Ditman and Blinn, 1955; Pierce and Lipcon, 1956; Pierce et al, 1961) is important because of the possibility of combining the use of drugs with CR treatment in appropriate cases (Young and Turner, 1965).

4. PERSONALITY FACTORS AND CR TREATMENT

The encouraging results of the careful study by Young (1965a) suggest that this area of research may pay dividends, if systematically pursued. It is perhaps not too fanciful to suggest that a composite area of research embracing personality factors, drugs, and cortical physiology may prove to be the one which will produce the most important advances in the immediate future.

VI. CONCLUSIONS

The etiology and treatment of enuresis nocturna may be described as a classic area of conflict between the psychodynamic and behavioristic approaches to behavior disorders. The disorder manifests itself as a clearly defined, readily measurable response. The respective explanations of the cause of the disorder are manifestly very different, the preferred methods of treatment are poles apart, and the issue of symptom substitution or more serious disturbance, if CR treatment is used, is starkly clear.

The survey above would seem to clearly indicate the superiority of the behavioristic position, with respect both to theory and treatment, a conclusion arrived at by Lovibond (1964). More significantly, however, the behavioristic approach to enuresis illustrates very clearly the essence of the behavior therapists' approach, which is the interplay of theory and practice, and the refusal to allow any model, however convincing it might seem, to achieve the status of a "truth." For here we have a very clear example of experimental and theoretical laboratory psychology furnishing an apparently clear-cut theoretical model for enuresis and its treatment (the classical conditioning model and the Mowrer technique). Yet, in spite of its apparent success, a careful examination by Lovibond led him to the conclusion that the classical conditioning model could not be correct, to the reformulation of the explanation in terms of an avoidance conditioning model, and consequently to the derivation of a modified method of treatment. The important point is not, in fact, whether *either* model is entirely satisfactory but the application of knowledge of conditioning theory to a real-life problem in a systematic fashion.

B. Encopresis

I. DEFINITION AND INCIDENCE OF ENCOPRESIS

1. DEFINITION OF ENCOPRESIS

Kanner (1950) defines encopresis as "an act of involuntary defecation which is not directly due to organic illness." This definition is not entirely satisfactory and a more adequate one is that provided by Warson et al (1954) who define encopresis as a "disturbance in regulation of bowel evacuation." The distinction is important because, as Warson et al (1954), Pick (1963), and others have stressed, encopresis is very frequently associated with (and may, in fact, result from) the simultaneous presence of constipation, or fecal retention. For this reason, it is particularly important to notice carefully the various subcategories of encopresis which have been suggested. Garrard and Richmond (1952) defined what they called the "psychogenic megacolon syndrome" in which massive retention of fecal material is found and which must be carefully distinguished from Hirchsprung's disease ("neurogenic megacolon") in which the cause of fecal retention is organic in nature. Whereas the latter syndrome is now operable, the former is unaffected by surgical procedures. Richmond et al (1954) have presented a number of criteria for distinguishing the two syndromes.[30] Hirchsprung's disease is usually associated with: severe constipation; absence of fecal soiling; onset at birth or very soon after; use of toilet for defecation; attempted defecation in the sitting position; pellet-like or ribbon stools; frequent episodes of intestinal obstruction; an empty rectum; and presence of a spastic segment of rectum or rectosigmoid using Neuhauser's fluoroscopic technique. Psychogenic megacolon, on the other hand, is characterized by fecal soiling; onset after neuromuscular control is usually achieved; infrequent use of the toilet for defecation; defecation in standing or supine positions; inhibition of the stool; periodic voluminous stools; no intestinal obstruction; a feces-packed rectum; and absence of a spastic segment of rectum.

Hall (1941) distinguished three groups of encopretics; those in whom control had never been established; those in whom control had been established and then lost;[31] and those in whom encopresis was associated with coprophagia (i.e., playing with and smearing of feces over the person and objects). The first two groups have been clearly distinguished by Anthony (1957) as "continuous" and "discontinuous" types.

2. INCIDENCE OF ENCOPRESIS

Practically nothing is known concerning the incidence of encopresis, except that it is almost certainly, as in the case of enuresis, considerably more frequent in boys than in girls (Anthony, 1957; Shirley, 1938). Shirley (1938) reported that, in a sample of children referred to a psychiatric clinic, there was an incidence of about 3%, but this clearly is not a reliable indication of the true incidence of the disorder.

II. ETIOLOGICAL THEORIES OF ENCOPRESIS

As in the case of enuresis, there have been widely conflicting theories regarding the etiology of encopresis.

1. PSYCHOANALYTIC AND PSYCHODYNAMIC FORMULATIONS

While psychoanalytic writers, following Freud, have laid very considerable stress on the anal developmental stage (in which the child progresses from initial autoerotic pleasurable elimination to the anal retentive and anal sadistic stages, and so forth), particularly in its supposed relationship to later personality traits (e.g., obsessive-compulsive behavior), they have not paid much attention to encopresis as such,[32] with a few exceptions, such as Sterba (1949) who related encopresis to fears of castration. Burns (1941) and Pinkerton (1958) considered encopresis to be a form of aggression against a hostile and threatening environment. The most systematic development of the psychodynamic viewpoint, however, is that of Warson et al (1954) who, basing themselves largely on a single intensive case study, traced the problem to an originally mutually enjoyable somatic relationship between the mother and the child in infancy, traumatic separation experiences during the transition stage between oral and anal organizations, and the neurotic use of the child by the mother to express resentments, receive gratifications, etc.

Much the most important psychodynamic psychologist in the study of encopresis is Anthony (1957). Since his formulation, on examination, turns out to be entirely compatible with the behavioristic approach, however, his work will be considered below.

2. BEHAVIORISTIC FORMULATIONS

(a) THE PHYSIOLOGY OF BOWEL CONTROL. As in the case of control of micturition,

---

[30] The distinction is vital since Hirchsprung's disease will usually result in death if not treated surgically.

[31] It will be recalled that these two categories were distinguished also in enuresis.

[32] Thus, in Fenichel (1946) the very comprehensive index does not mention encopresis as such.

elimination of fecal material is originally produced by complex coordinated involuntary reflex action.[33] In the untrained child, food intake is an important stimulus in triggering off intestinal mobility, the rate of which depends on the fluidity and viscosity of the intestinal contents (which, in turn, depend on the type of food consumed and the efficiency of the mechanisms producing the intestinal juices and bile). Three types of intestinal movements have been distinguished—the segmentary and pendular (which are intrinsic nervous reflexes modified by extrinsic sympathetic and vagal activity), and the peristaltic (which are extrinsic nervous reflexes controlled by the medullary centers and the abdomino-pelvic autonomic pathways).

The act of defecation itself commences with the passage of feces across the pelvirectal flexure. This produces sphincter relaxation and the feces enter the rectum, leading to distention of the rectum and a consequent rise in pressure. When the intrarectal pressure exceeds about 40 mm Hg, reflex centers in the medulla and spinal cord (sacral segments 2, 3, and 4) trigger off a coordinated reflex, involving descent of the diaphragm, closing of the glottis, and contraction of the abdominal muscles and levator ani. Waves of peristalsis pass over the distal part of the colon, the sphincter ani relax, and the feces are expelled.

(b) DEVELOPMENT OF CORTICAL CONTROL OF BOWEL FUNCTION. Unfortunately, virtually nothing is known of how voluntary initiation of defecation or its inhibition is achieved. Quarti and Renaud (1962) suggest that perineal sensations produced by the distention of the rectum may be important; presumably these sensations could become conditioned stimuli for initiation of the act. They also suggest that inhibition of defecation results from paretic relaxation of the rectal wall, or a failure of the pressure and stretch receptors to respond to their specific stimulus. However, no attempt is made by Quarti and Renaud to explain the cortical mechanisms involved in this achievement[34] and recent textbooks of physiology (e.g., Langley et al, 1963) throw no light on the matter. It will be apparent, however, that the entire process is very similar to that involved in urination, a fact the importance of which will

become apparent when we consider methods of treatment.

(c) FAILURE TO ACQUIRE CONTROL OF BOWEL FUNCTION. As in the case of enuresis, it is important to make a distinction between control of the act of defecation itself, once it has been initiated (at whatever point in the sequence from the ingestion of food), and the failure to respond to situational cues.

(i) Control of the Act of Defecation. Neale (1963) has suggested that if, for any reason, the sensation of fullness produced by the fecal mass moving into the rectum does not lead to defecation, then the subject may adapt to the sensation and be no longer aware of the need to defecate.[35] As the rectum distends, overflow incontinence may take place involuntarily. We have already mentioned that constipation is a common accompaniment of encopresis, and it may therefore well be the case that the sensation of fullness arising from accumulation of feces is defective in encopretics. This explanation would differ from that of Neale in arguing that, rather than the subject *adapting* to sensations of fullness, *these sensations are not perceived.* Indeed, Neale himself states that none of his subjects experienced the sensation of rectal fullness. Again by analogy with enuresis, it would seem possible that there is a failure of conditioning, that is, conditioned stimuli fail to alert the subject before automatic voiding occurs. The situation is clearly more complex in encopresis, however, due to the fact that *inhibition* of the reflex (constipation) sequence appears to be important, whereas in enuresis this is not the case. Warson et al (1954) have also stressed the fact that the bowel appears to accommodate itself to retention through dilation beginning above the anal sphincter and leading to megacolon in severe cases.

It will be clear that the learning processes involved in voluntary initiation or inhibition of the act of defecation have not been worked out satisfactorily as yet.

(ii) Situational Factors. The external (situational) factors that interfere with bowel function have, however, been given a good deal of attention. Anthony (1957), in a very comprehensive study, has distinguished clearly between "continuous" and "discontinuous" encopresis. The former results from a lack of

---

[33] See Gaston (1948), Goligher and Hughes (1951).

[34] The importance of such mechanisms is, of course, clearly indicated by the loss of control which occurs when the spinal cord is severed.

[35] The obvious analogy is with hunger sensations, which may disappear over time even if the subject ingests no food.

training on the part of the mother; the latter from a too intense form of training. In essence, Anthony argues that both the form encopresis takes (continuous or discontinuous) *and* the emotional attitudes towards bowel function (pleasure or disgust) are determined by the situational training method used by the mother. In normal children, bowel elimination is fundamentally pleasurable and the task of society (usually exercised through the mother) is to attach a just sufficient degree of aversion to the act of defecation so that elimination will take place only in the appropriate place. The mothers of encopretics, however, tend to fall into one of two groups. Either they are *too relaxed* in their training methods, so that defecation remains a pleasurable act, or they are *too coercive*, so that an excessive amount of disgust is associated with the act. These training methods are determined in part by changes in society's views on training methods, but also by the influence of more conservative pressures, especially the influence of the maternal grandmother.

Anthony carried out a very careful investigation of these two types of encopresis (resulting from too lax and too severe training, respectively) and produced evidence in support of his contention by the use of experimental measures of degree of aversion to olfactory, auditory, visual, touch, etc. stimuli ranging from pleasant to very unpleasant. He also laid a great deal of stress on the complex requirements of society in relation to toilet training, making use of Huschka's (1942) scales of coerciveness in training. It is quite clear from his account that he would agree that achievement of fecal continence is a complex skill involving mother-child relationship (the "potting" couple), responsiveness to cues by both mother and child, consistency of training, and so forth. Coercive training may be regarded as the imposition of high stress on the child in a complex learning situation.[36] He found that the coercive mothers were characterized by a high level of aspiration in relation to toilet training and, interestingly, that these mothers had successfully trained their first child, a success that raised their level of aspiration in relation to their encopretic child. He also found that the coercively trained encopretic child was usually of the discontinuous type, that is, the mother had had initial training success, but the child had then relapsed. In the case of the lax mother,

on the other hand, the child was usually encopretic from birth and these mothers manifested a low level of aspiration in regard to toilet training.

We are faced here, however, with precisely the same problem as in the case of enuresis. Are these situational defects merely producing inappropriate defecation while the capacity of the child to perform the act itself is unimpaired; or is there, as Muellner (1960) argued in the case of enuresis, a failure of *internal* control of the complex act? There is every reason to suppose that, in most cases of encopresis, the act itself is disorganized (Neale, 1963) but as Young (1965c) pointed out in relation to enuresis, this could be produced by the interference on a complex response of *externally* imposed high drive. Anthony's distinction between "continuous" and "discontinuous" encopretics is vital here, since, although he always seems to be referring to situational factors, it is possible that the continuous encopretic represents a failure to acquire internal control, whereas the discontinuous encopretic represents loss of internal control through externally imposed environmental stress. Muellner's argument that achievement of control of the act of micturition itself is unrelated to training procedures is as difficult an objection in the case of encopresis.

III. TYPES OF TREATMENT (NONBEHAVIORISTIC)

As Anthony wittily observes:

"The instrumentalists of the back passage had been accustomed to wash out the colon religiously, the rationale of which it was difficult to understand. . . . Clinicians on the whole, perhaps out of disgust, prefer neither to treat them nor to write about them. The literature as compared with enuresis is surprisingly scanty, and what there is seems superficial, as if the children had been observed from a respectable distance" (Anthony, 1957, p. 157).

Anthony himself considered that the "continuous" encopretic is in need of habit training rather than psychotherapy, but that the "discontinuous" encopretic was a more serious problem, being a deeply disturbed child, needing prolonged psychotherapy and protection from his coercive mother. In general, encopresis has been considered a difficult

---

[36] Compare the above argument of Young (1965c) in relation to enuresis.

problem and intensive psychotherapy is usually considered essential. There is an almost complete absence of data concerning the success of such therapy or the natural remission rate.

IV. BEHAVIOR THERAPY AND ENCOPRESIS

The application of systematic retraining schedules, using operant conditioning techniques, is a relatively recent development, and the results obtained must naturally be viewed with much more caution than is the case with enuresis.

The first important contribution was made by Neale (1963). He stressed the retentive aspect of encopresis and considered that the initiation of the reflex was disrupted by fear following punishment. Using Anthony's distinction, his four cases would not be considered promising material for operant conditioning techniques, since they were all "discontinuous" encopretics. Since they were aged between $7\frac{1}{2}$ and 11 years on admission, they were obviously severe cases, whose incontinence had not been affected by hospitalization.

Neale's technique involved primarily the use of a graded series of reward-training for expulsion at the appropriate time in the right place. Initially, they were placed on the toilet four times daily with varying rewards for suitable performance. A shift was then made from experimenter to self-control, the subject being told to take himself to the toilet and being rewarded for doing so. Careful quantitative records were kept of incontinence and appropriate defecation. Of the four subjects, three achieved control, one did not, the average training period being 14 weeks. The children were not punished for soiling, nor were they rewarded for having clean clothes. Fairly short follow-ups showed no tendency to relapse. In the one case of failure, Neale considered that a full rectum produced pleasurable sensations which were stronger than the pleasure produced by reward for evacuation.

Gelber and Meyer (1965), on the other hand, used operant conditioning techniques to successfully treat long-standing encopresis in a boy of 14 who would be classified by Anthony as of the continuous type (he had been encopretic since birth). They stress particularly the need for discovering an *appropriate* reward, which may well be different from one subject to another. In this case, the only appropriate reward was found to be the granting of access to the hospital grounds. The total treatment time was 62 days. A six-month follow-up revealed only minor relapses and no evidence of symptom substitution. Keehn (1965) reported immediate success with operant conditioning in a 5-year-old boy with encopresis. Peterson and London (1964) also successfully treated a 3-year-old male child with fecal retention resulting from fear of painful defecation. They used operant reward and hypnotic suggestion with a follow-up of one year. Curiously, Peterson and London interpret their results in terms of cognitive insight as much as retraining. This is curious, not because there is any basic objection to what they call their "neobehavioristic psychotherapy" (in which they attempt to take cognitive factors into account), but simply because their experimental procedures (operant conditioning and hypnosis with suggestion) are so hopelessly confounded as to make it quite impossible to sort out the respective contribution of each of the two methods.

Several points should be noted carefully about the treatment methods described above. First, the results obtained by Neale (1963) suggest rather strongly that encopresis of the discontinuous type can be successfully treated without the necessity for deep psychotherapy. Second, *all of the treatments are situational in nature* and, in this respect, contrast strikingly with the usual methods of treatment in enuresis. As was pointed out earlier, it is quite feasible to analyze encopresis theoretically along the same lines as has been done for enuresis. Yet, with one notable exception, this has never been done. The plain inference from this is that the skilled control of the mechanism of defecation itself is intact and the defective or maladaptive learning relates to the acquisition of situational cues. On the face of it, this seems most unlikely to be the case, at least with reference to the continuous encopretics where an explanation similar to that for continuous enuresis seems preferable. There seems no reason why an apparatus for treating encopresis along conditioned response lines should not be developed, together with a theoretical explanation of the conditioning process. It may be pointed out in this connection that the operant conditioning technique used by Neale (1963) does not in any way satisfactorily explain how the disordered function referred to by Neale is overcome by what is essentially situational training.

The one exception is the study of Quarti and Renaud (1962) which deals with constipation, rather than encopresis. They argued that the US for defecation is stimulation of the walls of the rectum, which originally leads to a mass reflex in the colon (UR). In their method of treatment, they utilized laxatives to produce reflex defecation and electrode stimulation (nonaversive) from two electrodes applied on each side of the lumbar spine (the intensity of the stimulation was controlled by the subject) as the initial CS for defecation. If this pattern of laxative → electrode stimulation just prior to defecation → defecation is repeated often enough, then it is found that the subject can "voluntarily" induce defecation by electrode stimulation alone; and if this association is strengthened sufficiently, then eventually a higher-order conditioned stimulus (time) eventually produces defecation alone, thus producing the normal common experience of desire to defecate at regular times.

There is no need for any elaborate account of future research directions in the study of encopresis, since these have already been clearly indicated. The main need is for a clearer delineation of the degree to which encopresis is a result of a failure of cortical control of a complex act as compared with the significance of situational factors. The possibility of an interaction between the two must also be considered.

REFERENCES

Anthony, E.J. An experimental approach to the psychopathology of childhood encopresis. *Brit. J. med. Psychol.*, 1957, **30**, 146–175.

Baller, W. & Schalock, H. Conditioned response treatment of enuresis. *Except. Child*, 1956, **22**, 233–236 and 247–8.

Behrle, F.C., Elkin, M.T., & Laybourne, P.C. Evaluation of a conditioning device in the treatment of nocturnal enuresis. *Pediatrics*, 1956, **17**, 849–854.

Bental, E. Dissociation of behavioral and electroencephalographic sleep in two brothers with enuresis nocturna. *J. psychosom. Res.*, 1961, **5**, 116–119.

Berezin, M.A. Enuresis and bisexual identification. *J. Amer. Psychoanal. Assoc.*, 1954, **2**, 509–513.

Blomfield, J.M. & Douglas, J.W.B. Bedwetting: prevalence among children aged 4–7 years. *Lancet*, 1956, **1**, 850–852.

Bostock, J. & Shackleton, M. Pitfalls in the treatment of enuresis by an electric awakening machine. *Med. J. Aust.*, 1957, **2**, 152–154.

Boyarsky, S. (ed.). *Neurogenic bladder*. Baltimore: Williams and Wilkins, 1967.

Boyd, M.M. The depth of sleep in enuretic school-children and in non-enuretic controls. *J. psychosom. Res.*, 1960, **4**, 274–281.

Braithwaite, J.V. Some problems associated with enuresis. *Proc. Roy. Soc. Med.*, 1955, **49**, 33–38.

Bransby, E.R., Blomfield, J.M., & Douglas, J.W.B. The prevalence of bed-wetting. *Med. Offr.*, 1955, **94**, 5–7.

Browne, R.C. & Ford-Smith, A. Enuresis in adolescents. *Brit. med. J.*, 1941, **2**, 803–805.

Browning, R.M. Operantly strengthening UCR (awakening) as a prerequisite to treatment of persistent enuresis. *Behav. Res. Ther.*, 1967, **5**, 371–372.

Burns, C. Encopresis (incontinence of feces) in children. *Brit. med. J.*, 1941, **2**, 767–769.

Campbell, C.N. A case of childhood conflicts with prominent reference to the urinary system: with some general considerations on urinary symptoms in the psychoneuroses and psychoses. *Psychoanal. Rev.*, 1918, **5**, 269–290.

Coote, M.A. Apparatus for conditioning treatment of enuresis. *Behav. Res. Ther.*, 1965, **2**, 233–238.

Crc~by, N.D. Essential enuresis: successful treatment based on physiological concepts. *Med. J. Austr.*, 1950, **2**, 533–543.

Davidson, J.R. & Douglass, E. Nocturnal enuresis: a special approach to treatment. *Brit. med. J.*, 1950, **1**, 1345–1347.

Decurtins, F. Bettnässen in psychiatrischer Sicht. *Heilpädag. Werkbl.*, 1957, **26**, 197–201.

De Leon, G. & Mandell, W. A comparison of conditioning and psychotherapy in the treatment of functional enuresis. *J. clin. Psychol.*, 1966, **22**, 326–330.

Dewdney, J.C. & Dewdney, M.S. Wake them at night: incidence of nocturnal enuresis among a group of institutionalized boys, effect of spaced arousal program. *Child Care Quart. Rev.*, 1965, **19**, 96–101.

Ditman, K.S. & Blinn, K.A. Sleep levels in enuresis. *Amer. J. Psychiat.*, 1955, **111**, 913–920.

Ellis, N.R. Toilet training the severely defective patient: an S-R reinforcement analysis. *Amer. J. ment. Def.*, 1963, **68**, 98–103.

Fenichel, O. *The psychoanalytic theory of neurosis*. London: Routledge and Kegan Paul, 1946.

Forrester, R.M., Stein, Z., & Susser, M.W. A trial of conditioning therapy in nocturnal enuresis. *Develop. Med. & Child Neurol.*, 1964, **6**, 158–166.

Freud, S. *Three contributions to the theory of sex* (1905). London: Hogarth, 1962.

Freyman, R. Experience with an enuresis bell-apparatus. *Med. Offr.*, 1959, **101**, 248–250.

Freyman, R. Follow-up study of enuresis treated with a bell apparatus. *J. child Psychol. Psychiat.*, 1963, **4**, 199–206.

Garrard, S.D. & Richmond, J.B. Psychogenic megacolon manifested by fecal soiling. *Pediatrics*, 1952, **10**, 474–483.

Gaston, E.A. The physiology of faecal incontinence. *Surg. Gynec. Obstet.*, 1948, **87**, 280–290.

Gelber, H. & Meyer, V. Behavior therapy and encopresis: the complexities involved in treatment. *Behav. Res. Ther.*, 1965, **2**, 227–231.

Genouville, –. Incontinence d'urine. *L'Assoc. franc. d'urol.*, 1908, **12**, 97–107.

Geppert, T.V. Management of nocturnal enuresis by conditioned response. *J. Amer. med. Assoc.*, 1953, **152**, 381–383.

Gillison, T.H. & Skinner, J.L. Treatment of nocturnal enuresis by the electric alarm. *Brit. med. J.*, 1958, **2**, 1268–1272.

Glicklich, L.B. An historical account of enuresis. *Pediatrics*, 1951, **8**, 859–876.

Goligher, J.C. & Hughes, E.S. Sensibility of the rectum and colon. *Lancet*, 1951, **1**, 543–548.

Grunewald, E. Kastrationsdrohung und Bettnässen. *Jahrb. Psychol. Psychother.*, 1954, **2**, 364–367.

Gunnarson, S. & Melin, K.A. The electroencephalogram in enuresis. *Acta Paediat.*, 1951, **40**, 496–501.

Hall, M.B. Encopresis in children. *Brit. med. J.*, 1941, **2**, 890–892.

Hallgren, B. Enuresis: I. A study with reference to the morbidity risk and symptomatology. II. A study with reference to certain physical, mental and social factors possibly associated with enuresis. *Acta Psychiat.*, Kbh., 1956, **31**, 379–436.

Hallgren, B. Enuresis: a clinical and genetic study. *Acta psychiat.*, *Kbh.*, 1957 (Supplement 114).

Hawkins, D.N. Enuresis: a survey. *Med. J. Austr.*, 1962, **1**, 979–980.

Hermann, I. Zur Frage des Bettnässens. *Acta paedopsychiat.*, 1961, **28**, 308–311.

Hodge, R. & Hutchings, H.M. Enuresis: a brief review, a tentative theory and a suggested treatment. *Arch. Dis. Child.*, 1952, **27**, 498–504.

Hoppner, E. Die Häufigkeit der Enuresis bei Berliner Schulkindern. *Prax. Kinderpsychol. Kinderpsychiat.*, 1952, **1**, 265–267.

Hundziak, M., Maurer, R.A., & Watson, L.S. Operant conditioning in toilet training of severely mentally retarded boys. *Amer. J. ment. Def.*, 1965, **70**, 120–124.

Huschka, M. Child's response to coercive bowel training. *Psychosom. Med.*, 1942, **4**, 301–308.

Imhof, B. Bettnässer in der Erziehungsberatung. *Heilpädag.*, *Werkbl.*, 1956, **25**, 122–127.

Jones, H.G. The behavioral treatment of enuresis nocturna. In Eysenck, H.J. (ed.). *Behavior therapy and the neuroses*. Oxford: Pergamon, 1960, pp. 377–403.

Kanner, L. *Child psychiatry*. Springfield: C.C. Thomas, 1950.

Keehn, J.D. Brief case-report: reinforcement therapy of incontinence. *Behav. Res. Ther.*, 1965, **2**, 239.

Kuru, M. Nervous control of micturition. *Physiol. Rev.*, 1965, **45**, 425–494.

Labar, P. L'enurésie nocturne chez l'enfant; premiers essaies d'un traitement basé sur la neurophysiologie du sommeil. *Acta neurolog. et psychiat. Belgica*, 1965, **65**, 127–133.

Langley, L.L., Cheraskin, E., & Sleeper, R. *Dynamic anatomy and physiology* (2nd ed.). New York: McGraw-Hill, 1963.

Lickorish, J.R. One hundred enuretics. *J. psychosom. Res.*, 1964, **7**, 263–267.

Lobrot, M. Etude sur les enfants enurétiques. *Enfance*, 1963, No. 3, 209–231.

Lovibond, S.H. The mechanism of conditioning treatment of enuresis. *Behav. Res. Ther.*, 1963, **1**, 17–21.

Lovibond, S.H. *Conditioning and enuresis*. Oxford: Pergamon, 1964.

Madsen, C.H. Positive reinforcement in the toilet training of a normal child. In Ullmann, L.P. & Krasner, L. (eds.). *Case studies in behavior modification*. New York: Holt, 1965, pp. 305–307.

Martin, B. & Kubly, D. Results of treatment of enuresis by a conditioned response method. *J. consult. Psychol.*, 1955, **19**, 71–73.

Michaels, J. *Disorders of character*. Springfield: C.C. Thomas, 1955.

Morgan, J.J.B. & Witmer, F.J. The treatment of enuresis by the conditioned reaction technique. *J. genet. Psychol.*, 1939, **55**, 59–65.

Mowrer, O.H. & Mowrer, W.A. Enuresis: a method for its study and treatment. *Amer. J. Orthopsychiat.*, 1938, **8**, 436–447.

Muellner, S.R. The physiology of micturition. *J. Urol.*, 1951, **65**, 805–810.

Muellner, S.R. The voluntary control of micturition in man. *J. Urol.*, 1958, **80**, 473–478.

Muellner, S.R. Development of urinary control in children: a new concept in cause, prevention and treatment of primary enuresis. *J. Urol.*, 1960, **84**, 714–716.

Muller, E. Zur Behandlung der Bettnässer in den Erziehungsheim fur Schwererziehbare. *Heilpädag. Werkbl.*, 1957, **26**, 202–205.

Neale, D.H. Behavior therapy and encopresis in children. *Behav. Res. Ther.*, 1963, **1**, 139–149.

Pavlov, I.P. *Conditioned reflexes*. London: Oxford Univer. Press, 1927.

Peterson, D.R. & London, P. Neobehavioristic psychotherapy; quasi hypnotic suggestion and multiple reinforcement in the treatment of a case of postinfantile dyscopresis. *Psychol. Record*, 1964, **14**, 469–474.

Pfaundler, M. Demonstration eines Apparatus zur Selstättigen Singalisierung Stattgehabter Bettnässung. *Verhandl. der Gesellsch. für Kinderhlk.*, 1904, **21**, 219–220.

Pick, W. Fecal soiling due to paradoxic constipation. *Amer. J. Dis. Children*, 1963, **105**, 229–233.

Pierce, C.M. & Lipcon, H.H. Clinical relationship of enuresis to sleepwalking and epilepsy. *Arch. Neurol. Psychiat.*, 1956, **76**, 310–316.

Pierce, C.M., Lipcon, H.H., McLary, J.H., & Noble, H.F. Enuresis: psychiatric interview studies. *U.S. Armed Forces med. J.*, 1956, **7**, 1265–1280.

Pierce, C.M., Whitman, R.M., Maas, J.W., & Gray, M.L. Enuresis and dreaming: experimental studies. *Arch. gen. Psychiat.*, 1961, **4**, 166–170.

Pinkerton, P. Psychogenic megacolon in children. *Arch. Dis. Childh.*, 1958, **33**, 371–380.

Plag, J.A. The problem of enuresis in the naval service. *U.S. Navy Med. Neuropsychiat. Res. Unit, San Diego*, Rep. No. 64–3, 1964.

Quarti, C. & Renaud, J. Note préliminaire sur un nouveau traitement des constipations par réflexe conditionnel. *La Clinique (Paris)*, 1962, **57**, 577–583.

Remy-Roux, –. Nouvel appareil électrique contre l'incontinence nocturne d'urine. *Bull. et Mem. de la Soc. de Méd. de Vaucluse*, 1908, **2**, 337–340.

Richmond, J.B., Eddy, E.J., & Garrard, S.D. The syndrome of fecal soiling and megacolon. *Amer. J. Orthopsychiat.*, 1954, **24**, 391–401.

Robertiello, R.C. Some psychic interrelations between the urinary and sexual systems with special reference to enuresis. *Psychiat. Quart.*, 1956, **30**, 61–62.

Seiger, H.W. Treatment of essential nocturnal enuresis. *J. Pediat.*, 1952, **40**, 738–749.

Shirley, H. Encopresis in children. *J. Pediat.*, 1938, **12**, 367–380.

Stalker, H. & Band, D. Persistent enuresis: a psychosomatic study. *J. ment. Sci.*, 1946, **92**, 324–342.

Sterba, E. Analysis of psychogenic constipation in a two-year-old. In Freud, A., Hartmann, H. & Kris, E. (eds.). *Psychoanalytic Study of the Child*, Vol. 3–4. New York: Internat. Univ. Press, 1949, pp. 227–252.

Tapia, F., Jekel, J., & Domke, H.R. Enuresis: an emotional symptom? *J. nerv. ment. Dis.*, 1960, **130**, 61–66.

Taylor, I.O. A scheme for the treatment of enuresis by electric buzzer apparatus. *Med. Offr.*, 1963, **110**, 139–140.

Temmes, Y. & Toivakka, E. Uber die EEG-Befunde bei Enuresis. *Acta paediatr., Stockh.*, 1954, **43**, 259–263.

Turner, R.K. & Young, G.C. CNS stimulant drugs and conditioning treatment of nocturnal enuresis: a long-term follow-up study. *Behav. Res. Ther.*, 1966, **4**, 225–228.

Turton, E.C. & Spear, A.B. EEG findings in 100 cases of severe enuresis. *Arch. Dis. Child.*, 1953, **28**, 316–320.

Vignec, A., Moser, A., & Julia, J.F. Treatment of chronic enuresis, poor weight gain, and poor appetite in institutional children. *Arch. Ped* *iat.*, 1957, **74**, 119–130.

Vox, C.A. L'enuresi e il suo valore medico-sociale. *Difesa soc.*, 1962, **41**, 93–111.

Warson, S.R., Caldwell, M.R., Warriner, A., Kirk, A., & Jensen, R.A. The dynamics of encopresis. *Amer. J. Orthopsychiat.*, 1954, **24**, 402–415.

Werry, J.S. Enuresis: a psychosomatic entity? *Canad. med. Assoc. J.*, 1967, **97**, 319–327.

Wickes, I.G. Treatment of persistent enuresis with an electric buzzer. *Arch. Dis. Childhood*, 1958, **33**, 160–164.

Wickes, I.G. Enuresis. *Brit. med. J.*, 1963, **2**, 1199–1200.

Young, G.C. The family history of enuresis. *Journal R.I.P.H.*, 1963, **26**, 197–201.

Young, G.C. The relationship of "potting" to enuresis. *Journal R.I.P.H.*, 1964, **27**, 23–24 (a).

Young, G.C. A "staggered-wakening" procedure in the treatment of enuresis. *Med. Offr.*, 1964, **111**, 142–143 (b).

Young, G.C. Personality factors and the treatment of enuresis. *Behav. Res. Ther.*, 1965, **3**, 103–105 (a).

Young, G.C. Conditioning treatment of enuresis. *Develop. Med. Child. Neurol.*, 1965, **7**, 557–562 (b).

Young, G.C. The aetiology of enuresis in terms of learning theory. *Med. Off.*, 1965, **113**, 19–22 (c).

Young, G.C. & Turner, R.K. CNS stimulant drugs and conditioning treatment of nocturnal enuresis. *Behav. Res. Ther.*, 1965, **3**, 93–101.

Chapter 6

Stuttering

As in the case of enuresis and encopresis, the most striking thing about stuttering is not the fact that some people stutter, but rather that most people do not. The newborn child can indicate its needs only by a limited range of vocal sounds; yet, by the age of five, it not only has a vocabulary of several thousand words but can order these sequentially and with a wide variety of intonations and meanings in interacting with other humans. If we regard the control of speech as a form of highly skilled behavior, it is not at all surprising that, in some children, the skill fails to be adequately acquired. Since speech is one of the most accessible of behaviors, a vast amount of experimental work has been carried out on conditions affecting the speech of both nonstutterers and stutterers, and it will be shown that the results add up to a very clear-cut picture.[1]

I. THE CONTROL OF NORMAL SPEECH

Speech may be regarded either as a form of tracking behavior, dependent for its smooth execution on feedback control, or as an operant dependent for its execution on the environmental and internal contingencies that it produces. Both conceptualizations (which are by no means as antithetical as they might seem) have, in recent years, led to a very large amount of empirical work which is highly relevant to the understanding and modification of stuttering behavior. We shall consider first empirical studies of the control of normal speech and then briefly review theoretical models which have been derived from this work.

1. Empirical Studies of the Control of Normal Speech

We are concerned here, of course, not with the acquisition of a *vocabulary* by the child but with how speech *as a sequential skill* is controlled. That is, the problem is similar to explaining the acquisition and use of the skill of driving, or of walking, or of any other form of skilled behavior. The problem really takes two forms: how the skill of speaking itself is executed and controlled and how the execution of the skill may be affected by extraneous factors.

(a) FEEDBACK CONTROL OF NORMAL SPEECH. It must be admitted at once that very little indeed is known about how the young child achieves sequential control of normal speech. Two problems are involved: (1) the co-ordinated control of the act of speech and (2) the monitoring of the speech output so that errors can be corrected. Although much is known about the coordinated control of the act of speech at the behavioral level, much less is known about the cortical control. However, a great deal of work has been carried out relating to the monitoring of speech. Of particular interest in this connection is the phenomenon known as delayed auditory feed-

---

[1] Parts of this chapter are reproduced verbatim or in altered form from Yates (1963b) by permission of Pergamon Press.

back (DAF) (Yates, 1963a). Although speech is a greatly overlearned skill, it turns out to be surprisingly susceptible to interference in non-stuttering subjects.

Interest in the phenomena resulting from DAF stems primarily from the work of Lee (1950a, 1950b, 1951) and Black (1951) in the United States, who apparently began their investigations independently at the same time. It is known that speech is monitored in three main ways. Kinesthetic and sensory feedback from the speech organs provide some information. A second source is provided by the transmission of the speech sounds to the cortex via the bony structures of the body, especially the bones of the head. A third source is provided by the transmission of the speech sounds to the cortex via the air to the ear.[2]

The airborne transmission of feedback can be interfered with by modifying a magnetic tape recorder in such a way that the voice production of S may be recorded on the tape and then stored in the tape recorder for brief periods of time, after which it is returned to S's ears through closely fitting headphones which attenuate normal airborne feedback. The delay is usually varied from very short time intervals up to about 300 milliseconds (though longer delay times have been used), the optimal time interval for producing disturbance being 180–200 msecs. The intensity of the feedback at S's ear is set at a level which is high enough to mask veridical airborne and bone-conducted feedback.

The principal independent variables that have been manipulated in experiments on DAF have been delay-time and the intensity of the feedback at S's ear. The principal dependent variables have been duration of phrase (the time taken to read a standard passage of prose, or a phrase, or even a word) and intensity of utterance (changes in the level at which S speaks). Other dependent variables (which probably overlap with the two principal ones) have included fundamental frequency, intelligibility and articulatory changes (repetitions of syllables and continuant sounds, mispronunciations, omissions, substitutions, etc.), and phonation-time rates.

The task which S has to accomplish under DAF usually involves reading a passage of prose, but spontaneous speech and recitation have also been used (Lotzmann, 1961). The

degree of standardization of the material has varied widely, from uncontrolled material to phonetically balanced passages or ones which have been equated for difficulty level, or which contain all English speech sounds. A quite different task, which has important advantages over prose material, was that used by Butler and Galloway (1957) in which five two-digit numbers were successively flashed at random on a screen in one of five different positions at a fast presentation-rate.

The literature relating to the effects of DAF on normal speech is now very extensive and cannot be reviewed here.[3] We will mention here only those facts which are of particular relevance in relation to the subsequent discussion of stuttering.

Early studies demonstrated that, with intensity of feedback held constant and delay varied from 30 to 300 msecs., duration of phrase increased as a function of delay up to about 180 msecs., then declined, a discrete increment in breakdown being manifested at 60 msec. and a linear trend between 60 and 180 msecs. (Black, 1951). Tiffany and Hanley (1952) showed that, with delay held constant, a reduction in reading rate resulted from increased feedback intensity, while Butler and Galloway (1957) demonstrated an interaction between delay and intensity when the level of the latter at S's exceeded 80 db above sensation level. The number of errors increased at all delay times compared with 50 db, but a delay of 170 msec. produced a significantly greater effect than any other delay time. Intensity of utterance is also affected by delayed feedback, while various "qualitative" changes in speech (repetition of syllables and continuant sounds, mispronunciations, omissions, substitutions, and number of word endings omitted) have also been observed.

Two important studies have thrown a good deal more light on the conditions producing breakdown in speech. Winchester and Gibbons (1957) divided 160 normally hearing adults into four groups, which were allocated to one of four conditions involving DAF presented: biaurally; uniaurally; uniaurally with a masking tone in the other ear; and no DAF or masking tone. The results indicated that uniaural delay without masking of the other ear produced less disturbance than uniaural delay

---

[2] The relative importance of each of the three channels in normal speech monitoring is a matter of much dispute.

[3] See Yates (1963a, 1963b) for reviews of the literature through 1962.

with the masking, although all three delay conditions produced significantly more disturbance than the control condition. Chase and Guilfoyle (1962) presented delayed and undelayed feedback simultaneously to both ears. The gain of the undelayed feedback was varied from one-third, two-thirds, or equal to that of the delayed feedback. However, speech was still disturbed compared with normal conditions when the gain of the undelayed feedback was made equal to that of the delayed feedback.

It has also been shown that rhythmic handclapping (Kalmus, Denes, and Fry, 1955), tapping, even by skilled operators (Yates, 1965), and whistling (Hanley and Tiffany, 1954) may be severely disturbed by DAF.

Unfortunately, in view of its special interest in relation to stuttering, as we shall see, virtually no work has been carried out on boneconducted DAF, although Cherry and Sayers (1956) report[4] that the effect of DAF transmitted to the ear through a bone-conduction channel appears to be considerably more severe than the effect of DAF transmitted through headphones by air conduction and, in fact, may be quite distressing.

All of these studies indicate that normal speech may break down severely if the time relationships normally obtaining between the three major feedback channels are disrupted by artificially delaying the transmission of the feedback in one of the channels beyond its normal time. It may be noted that there are marked individual differences in degree of susceptibility to DAF, and different strategies seem to be adopted in efforts to overcome the initial disruption of speech.

(b) OPERANT CONTROL OF NORMAL SPEECH. In speaking of the operant control of normal speech, we are not referring to what may be called the "control of the content of conversation" but to the control of the *form* of speech, that is, the smooth sequential execution of a skilled act. That such control can be achieved to a very high degree has been demonstrated by the extensive studies of Goldiamond and his colleagues.[5] For example, Flanagan et al (1959) produced chronic stuttering-like speech in normally fluent individuals when shock termination was made

contingent upon the occurrence of nonfluency. Furthermore, the nonfluency (which originally produced *escape* behavior via nonfluency) developed all of the characteristics of extinction-resistant *aversive* behavior, since it persisted in the *absence* of shock.[6] On the other hand, Siegel and Martin (1965a; 1965b; 1966) and others have shown that disfluencies in normal subjects will decrease if they produce an aversive stimulus (shock or verbal punishment). These experiments indicate quite clearly that speech fluency may be drastically altered by learning factors.

2. THEORETICAL MODELS FOR THE CONTROL OF NORMAL SPEECH

As we shall now see, the disruption of normal speech under experimental conditions has been interpreted in two ways: as the failure of a servomechanism and as the result of changes in reinforcement contingencies.

(a) SERVOMECHANISTIC MODELS. It is extraordinary how little attention has been directed to the problem of how continuous speech is monitored and adjusted or corrected in relation to events occurring within the speaker. The majority of the standard texts on speech and hearing are completely silent on this important question, although they consider in detail the problem of the maintenance of communication (intelligibility or articulation accuracy) under changing environmental conditions, such as an increase in the level of noise. No doubt this is in part because of the very scanty amount of knowledge presently available concerning the neurological events concerned in speech and hearing. Any model of a speech control mechanism must, of necessity, be of a hypothetical nature at present. The neglect is the more surprising, since there has been no lack of interest in the more general question of the control of high-level skills. A good deal of controversy has occurred, for example, over the question of whether high-level skilled performance is continuously or only intermittently monitored. Thus, whereas Lashley (1951) has argued that continuous monitoring (in the sense that peripheral feedback from one response can influence the next response) is impossible at least in certain types of skilled performance,

---

[4] The observations of Cherry and Sayers were made informally, and their reliability is uncertain.

[5] For a recent review of much of this work, see Goldiamond (1965).

[6] Many subjects, in fact, believed that the shock had nothing to do with the experiment, being due to faults in the apparatus on the initial trials.

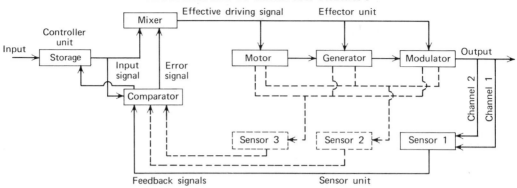

FIG. 1. Model of a closed cycle control system for speech (Fairbanks, 1954).

such as piano-playing, Gibbs (1954) has argued that continuous monitoring is possible. Although the problem has not been solved, it is clearly of crucial importance for any theory of the self-monitoring of speech. It will be obvious that DAF could be extremely useful in obtaining more empirical information about this question.

Lee (1951) suggested that the speech mechanism operates like a machine gun, repeating aurally monitored units as long as the "trigger" is held down. More generally, he conceived of continuous speech as constituting a closed loop feedback system and he argued that: "A mechanism which depends on feedback for continuation or procedure into the next cycle may halt for either of two reasons: (1) the impulse or initiating phase may fail, or (2) the feedback may fail, and thus, lacking the necessary returning signal, the machine will also halt. Yet another result of feedback failure or delay might be repetition of the initiating impulse over and over until the mechanism is satisfied to proceed to the next cycle by the returned signal or feedback."

Chase (1958) has argued that DAF "facilitates the circulation and recirculation of speech units in the speech-auditory feedback loop." If this assumption is correct, it follows that it should be possible to repeat a sound more times under DAF than under normal conditions. Chase found an average increase of 3.3 in the number of times the speech sound [b] could be repeated under a delay of 216 msec. during a 5-second period compared with a control period of similar duration. Thus, it seems that a delay in the feedback does facilitate repetition of speech units, and this could well result in the kinds of

disturbances which we have found to result from DAF.[7]

A more comprehensive model of how a self-monitoring feedback mechanism for speech might be conceived has been provided by Fairbanks (1954).[8] He stresses the importance, not merely of estimating and correcting the present state of the system but also of predicting the future course of events. The model proposed by Fairbanks is shown in Figure 1. Essentially, his closed cycle system involves: an effector unit (which produces an output); a sensor unit (which picks up the output); a storage unit, which contains the short-term instructions for a set of speech units that must be displayed through the effector unit in a definite sequence—when the sequence is completed a new set of instructions appears; a comparator, which matches the feedback signals from the effector unit with the input information received from the storage unit; and a mixer unit, which receives the input and error signals and combines them so as to reduce the error signal to zero.

The comparator, however, also contains a predicting device which continuously indicates the future point at which the error signal will be zero. Thus, the input may be changing even before the transmission of the current speech unit is completed.

Under normal speech conditions, it may be assumed that the control system has "learned" how to correct rapidly and effectively for minor deviations (such as faults in articulation, etc.) from the normal speech pattern and for familiar changes in environmental conditions (such as a sudden rise in noise level). The

---

[7] Unpublished studies in the author's laboratory have, however, thrown some doubt on the reliability of Chase's finding. Chase did not test the significance of the increase he found.

[8] As we saw in Chapter 2, models are now available for the feedback control of motor activity more generally (e.g., Chase, 1965a, 1965b).

mechanism has, as it were, stored "experiences" against which the current output can be matched and corrected if necessary. If, however, as occurs in the case of DAF, the time relationship between the various types of feedback is severely distorted, the controller mechanism may not be able to handle the situation immediately. The whole system may be brought temporarily to a halt, the signal may be repeated, or the organism may be reduced to trial-and-error behavior. Goldiamond et al (1962) have pointed out that the repetitions and prolongations characteristic of the response to DAF may well represent the attempt of the organism to restore the customary overlap of output/feedback relationships in normal speech.

Fairbank's model is of particular interest in that it does seem to overcome some of the problems associated with the question of continuous monitoring of skilled behavior. His model suggests that units of speech run off automatically and without further direct monitoring unless the error signal exceeds certain limits. Only then would the self-correcting mechanism actually be called into action. The model also suggests that the error concerns the asynchrony between air-conducted and other types of feedback. However, it is conceivable that the asynchrony also relates to the disparity between the time delay expected on the basis of previous experience and that actually being experienced. In either case the model helps to explain why there are such marked individual differences in degree of susceptibility to DAF. It suggests that whether or not an individual is highly susceptible to DAF depends on the relative degree to which he utilizes the auditory feedback channel in monitoring his speech as compared with the other channels. Individuals who are highly dependent on auditory feedback will be subject to severe breakdown under DAF, whereas individuals who rely mainly on bone-conducted or kinesthetic feedback will show less breakdown.

However, as a recent study by Stromsta (1962) shows, the whole problem of feedback is likely to prove extremely complex. Stromsta reviewed the scanty evidence concerning the differential transmission rates of air-, bone-, and tissue-conducted sound which suggested that there are remarkable differences in speed of transmission of sound through bone and tissue that are additional to disparities arising from

spatial distances to the auditory receptors. His own study fully confirms and extends these earlier findings. He measured the minimum delay times (using male Ss only) in the following pathways: a bone pathway (from the superior medial incisors to the mastoid process); a tissue pathway (from the vocal chords to the mastoid process); the internal pathway of minimum delay (from the vocal chords to the mastoid process irrespective of media); and the air pathway (from the vocal chords through the pharynx and oral cavity to the tympanic membrane). His basic procedure may be illustrated by reference to the bone pathway measurements. He stimulated the incisors with each of a series of rectangular pulses representative of 13 frequencies ranging from 125 to 2000 cps. The transmitted impulses were picked up at the incisors and mastoid process, and the arrival time difference was electronically determined. Two striking findings emerged. First, there are large differences between the various media in the extent to which they resist the passage of sound; second, within a particular medium (except, of course, for air-conduction), the resistance varies according to the frequency being transmitted.

Stromsta's results suggest that, for normal speech, the feedback via the various transmission media is delayed naturally by varying amounts. This indicates, first, that the brain must be receiving information relating to any particular speech unit spread over a time period which is greater than that involved in producing it and, second, that the integration of these disparate sources of information in normal speech must be central in nature, rather than peripheral.

Fairbank's model is purely fictional in our present state of knowledge of how central controlling processes operate.[9] This is not to deny its usefulness or importance, however. But it is clear from what has been said thus far that a great deal more work of a very precise nature will be required before sufficient information of a basic kind is available which will enable a mathematical model to be constructed or, indeed, before the essential controlling factors can be specified. This work, in relation to speech, will need to proceed along at least three lines. Some progress of a qualitative kind has already been made. First, the work of Stromsta, of a physical and physiological nature, needs to

[9] Fairbank's model has been considerably extended by several authors (Mysak, 1959, 1960; Wolf and Wolf, 1959; Butler and Stanley, 1966).

be continued and extended. Second, careful studies concerning the perception of successive sounds are urgently needed. Hirsh (1959, 1961) has done important work in this area. He has shown that two brief sounds can be distinguished separately with temporal intervals as small as 2 msec. However, an interval as long as 17 msec. is required if the order in which the sounds occurred is to be correctly reported. Hirsch concluded from his studies that, for temporal order judgments, a peripheral mechanism is probably insufficient. Third, much more information is required concerning the time relationship involved when the organism is simultaneously receiving and transmitting information. Thus, it is known that skilled operators will make many more errors on Morse code letters involving three or four symbols than on those letters involving only one or two when transmitting randomly constructed lists of letters continuously under a delay of 180 msec. The error score increases as a function of whether the letters are being transmitted individually, continuously at a preferred rate, and continuously as fast as possible (Yates, 1965).

One other area of investigation may be mentioned briefly in which the empirical results and theoretical formulations should prove to be of fundamental significance for any servomechanistic model of speech control. This concerns the large series of investigations carried out on the simultaneous reception and transmission of signals. Cherry (1953) investigated the ability of Ss to separate simultaneously presented messages. He found that, if the S were not allowed to write anything down, he had great difficulty in separating two simultaneously spoken messages emanating from a single source. However, the task could be accomplished successfully unless the messages consisted of cliches or contained units which could be transposed with little loss of meaning from one message to another. More importantly, he showed that if one message were presented through headphones to one ear and the second message simultaneously to the other (with the messages being recorded by the same voice), the S was able to reproduce, by shadowing, either of the messages without error—but he would be unable to say what was happening in the other ear and would not even perceive a change in language or be able to say what language had been spoken. It should be noted carefully that this finding applies only to continuous speech. Other studies have shown (e.g., Broadbent, 1956) that if dichotic stimu-

lation is employed with short lists of numbers (three successively in one ear with another three successively in the other, the two sets being presented simultaneously), the S will be able to reproduce all six correctly, but will produce the three from one ear first, followed by the other three. He will not produce the digits in a mixed form. These results, and others resulting from a long series of experiments by Broadbent (1958) on simultaneous listening and speaking, led that author to postulate a filter mechanism which enabled a subject to deal successfully with multiple information arriving simultaneously by storing or holding in a short-term memory system some of the information while other material was being processed. It is impossible to consider in detail here the large body of evidence resulting from the experiments of Broadbent and his colleagues, but it is obvious from this brief discussion that experiments of this nature will be of great significance for the elucidation of the mechanisms controlling continuous speech.

(b) OPERANT CONTROL MODELS. As an operant, speech may be regarded as being under the control of its contingencies, that is, of the effects it produces on the environment; this has generally been the approach adopted in discussions of verbal behavior. That is, changes in speech production have usually been attributed to the positive or negative effects that they produce on other people (Skinner, 1957). Not so much attention has been paid to the internal contingencies of speech, that is, to the feedback stimulation resulting from the emission of the speech units (the self-motivated, or feedback control of speech).

Individual differences in speech characteristics no doubt result in part from the contingencies they produce in the environment, such as parental reaction. By this means, the *form* as well as the *content* of speech may be subject to change. The ways in which, for example, natural nonfluencies in early speech may be reinforced (particularly on a partial reinforcement basis) have been outlined in some detail by Shames and Sherrick (1963). However, it must be admitted that a detailed account of how speech control is modified by operant learning is still a matter for the future.

II. STUTTERING—INTRODUCTION

1. THE DEFINITION OF STUTTERING

It is important to note that it is not easy to make a clear distinction between the speech of

TABLE 6.1. *Average Number of Nonfluencies of Various Types per 100 Words in the Speech of 42 Stutterers and 42 Nonstutterers (Average Age—5 Years)*

Type of Nonfluency	Stutterers	Nonstutterers
Interjection	2.9	2.7
Part-word repetition	4.2	0.4
Whole-word repetition	4.5	1.2
Phrase repetition	1.4	0.5
Revisions	1.4	1.5
Incomplete phrases	0.2	0.05
Broken words	0.1	0.03
Prolongations	1.5	0.15

Source: Johnson, W., 1956.

stutterers and nonstutterers. If stuttering behavior is scored for various types of nonfluency, a considerable degree of overlap is found between the characteristics of the speech of individuals classified as nonstutterers and those classified as stutterers. This finding applies both to adults and children, with the differences being even less for children than they are for adults. Representative results are shown in Table 6.1. Recent data presented by Johnson (1961) show, in detail, the degree of overlapping in adults, for various categories. Indeed, if the records of the most fluent stutterers and the most nonfluent nonstutterers are presented in random order, even speech experts find it very difficult to classify them correctly (Johnson, 1956). It is clear that we are dealing with a continuum of fluency-nonfluency and that, while individuals labeled as stutterers will tend to fall toward the nonfluent end of the continuum, there will be many labeled stutterers whose fluency will be greater than that of individuals who have never been so labeled. Johnson, in fact, has argued that a truly objective definition of stuttering is impossible and that a child *becomes* a stutterer when he is so labeled by his parents or peers. Thus, a child may be brought to a speech clinic as a stutterer by his parents, even though his speech difficulties may not, in fact, exceed the speech nonfluencies characteristically found in children of his age level.

Johnson's viewpoint has not, however, gone unchallenged. Wendahl and Cole (1961) showed that the speech of severe stutterers may be clearly distinguished from that of nonstutterers, even when the stuttered speech is removed from the tape recording. Furthermore, it has been demonstrated that the "normal" disfluencies of nonstuttering children involve the repetition of whole words and phrases (a characteristic which, in some cases, persists into adulthood) rather than the repetition of sounds and syllables which is characteristic of the stuttering child (Metraux, 1950; Voelker, 1944; Van Riper, 1954).

The difficulty of reaching an agreed definition of stuttering has not, of course, precluded the development of measures of speech nonfluency. Thus, Sherman and her colleagues have investigated very thoroughly a number of scaling techniques for estimating speech breakdown, concluding that the method of equal-appearing intervals is the most appropriate (Lewis and Sherman, 1951; Sherman, 1952; Sherman and McDermott, 1958; Sherman and Moodie, 1957). A more recent study by Cullinan et al (1963) indicates that the difficulties are by no means easily overcome in relation to intrajudge reliability. The recent development of the Iowa Speech Disfluency Test (Johnson, 1961; Sander, 1961; Young, 1961) appears, however, to have overcome many of these difficulties.

2. INCIDENCE OF STUTTERING

The incidence of stuttering appears to be roughly seven per thousand of the population (Schindler, 1955), though the figure varies, of course, according to whether the incidence is calculated for a single age group or over the entire age range. One of the most careful epidemiological surveys of recent years is that by Andrews and Harris (1964). In a survey of over 1000 schoolchildren, they found an incidence of 3%, rising to 4.5% if cases of transient stuttering lasting up to six months were included. Significant cultural differences have been observed and it has been suggested that the highest incidence of stuttering may be found in "upwardly mobile" areas (Darley, 1955). It seems indisputable that stuttering is found more frequently in boys than in girls (Schuell, 1946; Andrews and Harris, 1964), the ratio being of the order of about four boys to every girl.

3. TYPES OF STUTTERING

Distinctions made between stuttering and stammering, stuttering and cluttering, and so forth have generally fallen into disuse and need not be further mentioned here. Andrews and Harris (1964), however, identified three "types" of stuttering. The first they called "developmental," being of early onset (2–4 years) but lasting only a few months. "Benign" stuttering is characterized by late onset (mean of $7\frac{1}{2}$ years) and tends to remit spontaneously after about two to three years. "Persistent" stuttering has its onset between $3\frac{1}{2}$ and 8 years.

4. CHARACTERISTICS OF STUTTERERS

The number of facts that have been established in relation to stuttering must by now, run into thousands. Practically every possible factor that could conceivably throw light on stuttering has been subjected to examination. We will present only a small selection of those facts.

The onset of stuttering is usually, though not always, early in life, with ages three to four being a focal point, with a secondary rise at seven to eight (Johnson, 1956).

There is no evidence that, except for rare special cases, there is any defect of the motor structures involved in speaking; indeed, there is good evidence that stutterers are equally as good as nonstutterers in executing voluntarily skilled movements of the speaking and breathing musculature (Strother and Kriegman, 1943, 1944). This is not to deny, of course, that stutterers often exhibit quite severe motor disturbances while speaking.

There is no evidence that stutterers are in any way different from nonstutterers in physiological or biochemical characteristics (Hill, 1944a, 1944b).

There is no evidence that stutterers are any different from nonstutterers in personality characteristics (Sheehan, 1953; Goodstein, 1958). The notion that stuttering is a symptom of some underlying neurotic conflict or is an indication of serious personality disturbance appears to have no basis in fact. Stutterers appear to differ in much the same way as do normals from neurotic or psychotic patients. Such differences on personality tests as are found would seem to reflect a normal reaction to a severe social disability. As Johnson puts it:

"They differ in tending to be a bit more depressed or discouraged, a bit more anxious or uneasy or unresponsive, especially in speech situations, and somewhat more socially withdrawn. The kinds and degrees of difference indicate, not a serious personality maladjustment, but rather a normal kind and amount of emotional reaction to the sorts of frustrating, threatening and unpleasant experience that stuttering involves" (Johnson, 1956).

In fact, it is extraordinary that more stutterers do not develop severe personality disturbances.

Contrary to the often expressed opinion of stutterers themselves, there is no evidence that stuttering increases with fatigue (Curtis, 1942).

There is no evidence at present that will stand up to critical examination of any relationship between stuttering and handedness.[10]

Close examination of the stuttering behavior itself has shown that stuttering tends to occur on no more than 10% of the total number of words spoken; that a stuttering "sequence" lasts usually no more than one to two seconds; that the loci of stuttering is partly a function of word position and word information value (Conway and Quarrington, 1963; Quarrington, 1965; Schlesinger et al, 1965), but apparently not of the phonetic structure of the material (Soderberg, 1962); and that, if stutterers are asked to read a passage several times, they tend to stutter on the same words in successive readings (consistency response). It may also be noted that while interjections comprise about 35% of nonfluencies of stutterers in speech, they comprise only 12% of reading nonfluencies. The comparable figures for part-word repetitions are 25% (speech) and 45% (reading).

Finally, it may be noted that there are very considerable individual differences in the type of stuttering from which different individuals suffer.

---

[10] The majority of the negative findings were confirmed in the recent large-scale study of Andrews and Harris (1964)

5. PSYCHOANALYTIC AND PSYCHODYNAMIC THEORIES OF STUTTERING

As might be expected, the psychodynamic psychologists have had a field day with stuttering which, like enuresis, is regarded as a symptom indicative of more deep-seated underlying conflict or disturbance. As so often, Fenichel (1946) has put the psychoanalytic viewpoint most clearly. According to him, *persistent* stuttering must be regarded as a pregenital conversion neurosis in which the function of speech itself represents an objectionable instinctual impulse:

"Psychoanalysis of stutterers reveals the anal-sadistic universe of wishes as the basis of the symptom. For them, the function of speech regularly has an anal-sadistic significance. Speaking means, first, the utterance of obscene, especially anal, words, and, second, an aggressive act directed against the listener" (Fenichel, 1946, p. 312).

Somewhat more crudely put, speech represents to the stutterer sexualized defecation:

"The expulsion and retention of words means the expulsion and retention of feces, and actually the retention of words, just as previously the retention of feces, may be either a reassurance against possible loss or a pleasurable autoerotic activity. One may speak, in stuttering, of a displacement upward of the functions of the anal sphincter" (Fenichel, 1946, p. 312).

In its aggressive function, stuttering represents a desire to harm the person being spoken to and may, therefore, be considered as a displaced form of aggression.[11] The reader is invited to work out for himself the further implications of Fenichel's theory (Fenichel, 1946, pp. 311–317).

In more general terms psychodynamic theories have regarded stuttering as an indicator of conflict or personality disturbance or hostility (Santostefano, 1960). As was pointed out earlier, there is no evidence whatsoever that stutterers are more or less neurotic than nonstutterers. Yet studies attempting to demonstrate this continue to be carried out. Thus, Adams and Dietze (1965) found that stutterers had significantly longer latency times for words indicating guilt. Once again, it should be pointed out that these kinds of disturbances are just as likely to result from stuttering as to be the cause of it. In this connection, the painstaking investigations of Bloodstein (1960a, 1960b, 1961) are worthy of mention. As a result of careful analysis of the records of many hundreds of stutterers, he concluded that stuttering developed in four stages. In the first two of these stages, the actual speech defect develops without any preceding or concomitant personality disturbance. In the final two stages, however, the stutterer comes to realize that he is different from others and experiences difficulty in social communication. It is only at this stage that personality difficulties and inadequate social behavior begin. In the light of this evidence and that reviewed earlier, it seems reasonable to conclude that the personality disturbance results from the stuttering, and not vice versa.[12]

6. MEDICAL AND PHYSIOLOGICAL THEORIES OF STUTTERING

The idea that stutterers may be distinguished from nonstutterers on an *organic* basis (disorders of the vocal musculature; disturbances in the coordination of breathing; blood volume; endocrine disturbance; metabolism; and so forth, *ad infinitum*) may, with one important possible exception to be discussed later, be dismissed without further consideration. As pointed out earlier, there is no evidence whatever that stutterers differ significantly from nonstutterers in physiological, biochemical, or neurological characteristics, although disturbances in some of these functions may *result* from stuttering (e.g., persistent stuttering may lead eventually to disorganization of motor movements involved in speech, resulting from the stutterer's efforts to overcome his stutter).

7. TYPES OF TREATMENT (NONBEHAVIORISTIC)

The various *medical* treatments that have been tried for the amelioration of stuttering make up almost as horrifying a list as in the case of enuresis.

---

[11] Cf. Alexander Pope's famous phrase: "willing to wound, yet afraid to strike," and the common expression: "words can kill."

[12] It is impossible to do justice to the many variants of the psychodynamic approach. The reader is referred to Hahn (1956) for brief statements of their position by leading theorists in the field.

"Wedge-shaped portions were cut from the back of the tongue; the hypo-glossal nerve, the lingual frenum, and the various extrinsic and intrinsic muscles of the tongue were severed. The tongue was pierced with needles, cauteries, blisters, and embrocations of petroleum, also inoculations of croton oil were administered. Tincture of rectified alcohol, peppermint oil, and chloroform were applied. Wooden wedges were placed between the teeth. Smoking was recommended as a sedative to the vocal chords" (Hollingworth, 1931, p. 405).

On the psychological side, the list of "training" methods is endless—relax or yawn before speaking; speak in a low-pitched voice; grunt before speaking; whistle before difficult words; practice vocal gymnastics with dumbbells; follow Christian Science; and so on and so forth.

The use of psychotherapy (Barbara, 1962; Hejna, 1960), play therapy (Murphy and Fitzsimmons, 1960), group psychotherapy (Barbara et al, 1961; Sadoff and Siegel, 1965) and mother-child relationship therapy (Wyatt and Herzan, 1962) represent but a few of the psychodynamic methods used in stuttering. In spite, however, of the thousands of man-hours which must have been spent both in the retraining of stutterers and their psychotherapy, the amount of published data concerning the results of these various forms of treatment is ludicrously inadequate. Williams (1955), reviewing the psychotherapy literature from 1920–1949 could find almost nothing of value to report, and his own study was confined to reports on four male stutterers given both counselling and direct speech therapy over a period of 6–8 weeks.[13]

One of the few *experimental* studies of the effects of psychotherapy is that by Lanyon (1965) who measured adaptation and consistency in 33 stutterers before therapy and predicted that high adaptation and low consistency scores would correlate positively with speech improvement following therapy. Using as his criteria for improvement increase in the rate of utterance, decrease in frequency of disfluencies, and decrease in judged severity, he found moderate support for his hypothesis after a period of one year's therapy.

It may be added that the use of carbon dioxide therapy, tranquilizers, and other drugs has not been shown to affect stuttering in any significant way (Kent, 1961, 1963), nor is there any satisfactory evidence that hypnosis is of any real value (Falck, 1964).

It is, of course, well known that stuttering has proved to be highly resistant to *any* form of treatment, in which case it would appear obvious that quantitative studies are essential in order that valuable time is not lost pursuing worthless leads. Bearing this in mind, a situation in which countless man-hours have been spent on particular techniques or methods without any attempt at measurement of pre- and post-treatment changes can only be described as disgraceful.

III. BEHAVIORISTIC APPROACH TO STUTTERING

In this section we will consider empirical studies relating to the control of stuttering behavior and theoretical models relating to the explanation of the genesis and maintenance of stuttering.

1. Empirical Studies of the Control of Stuttering

There is abundant evidence that the speech of stutterers can be experimentally modified to a truly remarkable degree. The early evidence has been reviewed in detail by Bloodstein (1950). We shall concern ourselves, however, with only a selected portion of the evidence, i.e. that which seems to be particularly relevant to the theoretical formulations which follow.

(a) FEEDBACK CONTROL OF STUTTERING. Stuttering may be totally or very substantially attenuated by a technique known as speech shadowing (Cherry and Sayers, 1956). With this method the stutterer, speaking aloud, follows as closely as possible behind another speaker who is reading from a prose passage which the stutterer does not see. Severe stutterers may achieve very high speaking speeds by this method. The present author has found that equally striking results are obtained if a tape recording or a speaker's voice on the radio is shadowed.

Even more simply, stuttering may be abolished by means of simultaneous reading, in which the stutterer and another person read

---

[13] Undoubtedly, one reason for the lack of quantitative data lies in the psychodynamic viewpoint that the stutter itself is unimportant (though few stutterers would be very happy with this.)

from the same book. Furthermore, the stutterer will usually continue to read without fault even if the second reader switches to a different part of the passage or starts reading gibberish. However, if the second reader stops reading, the stutterer will gradually return to his usual hesitant reading (Cherry and Sayers, 1956). It should be emphasized that in nearly all instances, the suppression of the stutter, by shadowing or simultaneous reading, is total, and the speech, if recorded, is usually indistinguishable from normal superior fluency. This total suppression can be achieved by not more than 40 or 50 words of practice in the case of simultaneous reading. (By the use of headphones and appropriately placed microphones, it is possible, with simultaneous reading, to record the stutterer's voice clearly with the other reader's voice heard faintly in the background. In this way, the various effects outlined above may be readily demonstrated.) Shadowing may take a little longer to master, but this is usually because of lack of skill in "pacing" the stutterer by the reader.

Stuttering may also be abolished or substantially reduced if the stutterer reads aloud as one of a group of normal readers or stutterers (Barker, 1939); during singing or whispering; and during states of high emotion, e.g., if the stammerer becomes very angry.

A series of experiments by Cherry and Sayers (1956) showed that stuttering is very substantially reduced if the stutterer is prevented from hearing the low-frequency components (which are mainly bone-conducted) of his own voice while speaking. This conclusion was reached as the result of a series of experiments that demonstrated that elimination of air-conducted feedback alone did not affect stuttering; elimination of both air-conducted and bone-conducted feedback by masking white noise approaching the pain threshold in intensity produced almost complete suppression of stuttering; elimination, by means of a filter, of the high-frequency components of speech feedback only, did not affect stuttering; elimination, by means of a filter, of the low-frequency components of speech feedback only (within the range 120–180 cps) resulted in the almost complete suppression of stuttering. These low frequency components are mainly bone conducted and emanate principally from the larynx. Cherry and Sayers (1956) also showed that the stuttering was suppressed if the stutterer

whispered under masking conditions, thus ruling out the possibility that the stutter disappeared merely because the intense feedback made the stutterers speak more loudly than usual. The very few breakdowns that occurred under a high energy 140 cps masking tone arose from momentary difficulties in starting. It is again emphasized that these results were obtained with virtually no practice. They have been confirmed independently by Shane (1955) and by Maraist and Hutton (1957); the latter showing that stuttering decreased as a function of increase in intensity of the masking white noise.

May and Hackwood (1968), however, found that stuttering was equally reduced in conditions of simultaneous reading, whispering, and both low- and high-frequency masking. This study was rather poorly controlled, however, and can scarcely be considered to refute the evidence of the three earlier investigations. Sutton and Chase (1961) used a voice-actuated relay to control the presentation of white noise during reading. Nine stutterers were presented with each of the following conditions: normal reading, with and without headphones; reading in the presence of continuous white noise (the Cherry and Sayers condition); reading under white noise which was present only while they were speaking; and reading under white noise which was present only while they were silent. Sutton and Chase reported that the three white noise conditions were equally effective in reducing stuttering and concluded that white noise did not produce its effect by preventing the speaker from listening to his own voice. This study was criticized on technical grounds by Yates (1963b) and Webster and Lubker (1968)[14] and must be regarded as inconclusive.

(b) OPERANT CONTROL OF STUTTERING. That the modification of stuttering behavior can be achieved by controlling its *consequences* has been abundantly demonstrated. Thus, Flanagan et al (1958) produced a significant decline in stuttering if each stutter produced a one-second blast of high intensity white noise (used as an aversive stimulus). They also showed that the stuttering could be reinstated if stuttering *turned off* otherwise continuous white noise. In later studies, Goldiamond (1965) utilized DAF for similar purposes, with extremely interesting and important results. When DAF was used as an aversive stimulus which could be turned off by cessation of stuttering,

---

14 See also the reply by Chase and Sutton (1968).

the effect was as predicted, i.e., decline in stuttering and an increase in reading rate. When, however, DAF was continuously presented until eliminated by stuttering, the effect was quite unexpected. Instead of increasing, the stuttering was either *eliminated* altogether or a new pattern of speech resulted involving prolongation of speech units (the effect was the same as that found in many normal subjects under DAF, where it represents, as was pointed out earlier, an attempt to restore the overlap between output and feedback found in normal speech). As we shall see later, Goldiamond utilized this unexpected finding for therapeutic purposes.

In a quite different kind of experiment, Sheehan (1951) required stutterers to repeat a stuttered word over and over until it was pronounced without error before proceeding to the next word.[15] With the stutterers being used as their own controls, a significant drop in stuttering was produced over a number of trials.[16]

2. THEORETICAL EXPLANATIONS OF STUTTERING

Within the general behavioristic framework, three approaches have been made to the explanation of the genesis and maintenance of stuttering behavior: it has been regarded as a defect in feedback control analogous to the breakdown of a servomechanistic system; as an acquired defect based on the principles of learning theory; and as an acquired set of operant responses. We shall consider each in turn.

(a) STUTTERING AS A PERCEPTUAL DEFECT. As we have seen, the human organism reacts very rapidly to changes in external or internal stimulus conditions. Either continuously or periodically (i.e., when a significant change occurs), ongoing behavior is modified to produce performance which is optimal for the current demands being made—the adjustments being effected by reference to a storehouse of information which is based on past experience. As a result of a vast amount of experience, the organism builds up certain patterns of expectations. Thus, in relation to speech, the return of feedback via the shortest airborne pathway can be expected within about one-thousandth of a

second. Any deviation of a marked kind from the expected pattern of feedback will lead to an attempt to restore the usual relationship. Furthermore, the brain presumably integrates the various feedback patterns arising from the triple media (air, bone, and kinesthetic) into a unitary whole. Now it is clear that the disturbance in the speech of nonstutterers under DAF results primarily from a conflict of feedback information, since the absence of feedback does not produce these disturbances (though it does produce some changes), while the effect of DAF is reduced (though not entirely abolished) in proportion as the intensity of the alternative undisturbed feedback signals approach the intensity level of the DAF.

It is tempting to argue that a similar asynchrony of feedback signals is present in stuttering. If the stutterer is, in fact, suffering essentially from a perceptual defect, as Cherry and Sayers (1956) argued, that is, if he is continually receiving false or conflicting information concerning the progress of emitted speech units, then it would not be surprising if he continually repeated signals or ground to a halt from time to time. The stutterer thus has been regarded as suffering from an instability of the feedback loop, similar to that which is artificially induced in nonstutterers by DAF. It is important to note that, following Cherry and Sayers (as was discussed earlier), the instability would be related to the bone-conducted rather than the air-conducted feedback loop. If this reasoning is correct, then it would seem very likely that the auditory defect may ultimately be shown to have a genetic basis.

We have already seen that DAF used as an aversive stimulus can control stuttering rate. Goldiamond (1965), however, did not use DAF continuously with stutterers,[17] nor did he vary the delay time. If, however, there is an asynchrony between air- and bone-conducted feedback in stutterers, then it could be argued that, if this asynchrony could be artificially abolished, normal speech would result. Should this be so, an important breakthrough would have been achieved, as it might well prove possible to manufacture miniature delay systems which could be permanently worn by the stutterer, in much the same way as hearing aids are worn by the deaf.

---

[15] Thus, the subject would be required to say, for example, "b-b-b-but but it" instead of his usual "b-b-b-but it."

[16] Similar effects have been demonstrated by

Martin and Siegel (1966a; 1966b) using response contingent shock.

[17] Except as a *control* condition, and he did not examine the effect of *different* delay times.

Studies of the effects of DAF on stuttering are relatively few,[18] and the results are by no means clear or consistent. Thus, Ham and Steer (1967) and Neelley (1961) reported that DAF produced similar effects on the speech of both stutterers and nonstutterers, with wide individual differences in both groups, and Neelley concluded that the hypothesis that stuttering may be related to a delay in the bone-conduction feedback channel is untenable. Neelley's study was severely criticized by Yates (1963b), however, who pointed out that Neelley's technique was an inappropriate way of testing the hypothesis, since the speech of normal subjects under DAF represents a novel reaction to an unfamiliar situation, whereas the speech of stutterers represents the final adjustment worked out over many years.

The monumental study of Lotzmann (1961), on the other hand, found much more positive results. Lotzmann investigated the effects of delays ranging from 50 to 300 msec on the speech of 60 stutterers and found marked reduction of stuttering in all cases. Of particular interest is his finding that, for each stutterer, there was an optimal individual delay time which produced the greatest attenuation of stuttering. The ameliorative effects of DAF were most marked with severe stutterers; the effect on mild stutterers was often similar to that found with nonstutterers. Thus, the discrepancy between the results of Lotzmann and the American studies may be due in part at least to the severity of stuttering in the cases used.

(b) STUTTERING AS LEARNED BEHAVIOR. The interpretation of stuttering phenomena in learning theory language has been made in general terms by Johnson (1959) and others, and developed in detail by Wischner (1950), by Sheehan (1953, 1958), and more recently by Brutten and Shoemaker (1968).

We have already pointed out that the speech of normal young children contains many and varied disfluencies which gradually disappear as the skill develops. It has been argued that these nonfluencies cause the child no concern, provided his attention is not drawn to them. However, a minority of parents interpret these normal nonfluencies as an indication that the child is beginning to stutter, and in their own anxiety to eliminate the "errors," correct the child's speech, reprove him, or even punish him. Not unexpectedly, the effect of this is to make the child aware of, and anxious about, his speech at a critical stage in his development. This anxiety acts as a drive motivating instrumental avoidance behavior which seeks to reduce the anxiety drive. Any behavior that accomplishes this will be reinforced. Johnson argued that stuttering represented just such an example of avoidance response to anxiety, in that it represented an attempt to avoid nonfluency. An alternative type of "response" would presumably be silence. Wischner (1950) argues, however, that the stuttering represents an attempt to avoid the consequences of non-fluency, that is, parental disapproval.

Let us assume for the moment that the stutter has been successfully established and turn to the question of its maintenance. Sheehan (1951) has argued that, in the case of normal speech, the word as stimulus evokes a normal speech response, the successful execution of which achieves the goal of terminating that particular sequence (i.e., communication). Thus:

$$S \longrightarrow R \longrightarrow G \text{ (saying word)}$$
$$\text{word} \quad \text{normal speech}$$
$$\text{response}$$

In stuttering, however,

$$S \longrightarrow R \longrightarrow$$
$$\text{word} \quad \text{anxiety}$$
$$S \longrightarrow R \longrightarrow G \text{ (saying word)}$$
$$\text{anxiety} \quad \text{stuttering}$$

That is, the perception of the word (in reading) or the anticipation of saying it produces anxiety responses which serve as stimuli for the stuttering. The stuttering is reinforced because it immediately precedes the saying of the word correctly.

Sheehan has significantly extended this approach by introducing the notion of conflict in relation to stuttering. Johnson and Knott (1936) described the essentials of such a theory, as did Wischner (1950) but Sheehan has notably extended its use. We shall assume that the reader is generally familiar with the principal features of conflict theory (Yates, 1962) and proceed at once to Sheehan's application of the theory to stuttering. According to Sheehan, the two principal facts which any theory of stuttering must explain are the momentary blocking (whether this involves silence or the repetition of part of a word) and the release from the blocking, i.e., the fact that the stutterer eventually does say the word.

The momentary blocking is accounted for by conceptualizing the stutterer as being placed in

---

[18] Soderberg (1968) has recently reviewed 11 such studies.

a double approach-avoidance conflict situation of increasing magnitude as he approaches a particular word. Two types of conflict are involved, that between speaking (approach) and not speaking (avoidance), and that between not speaking (approach) and speaking (avoidance). In other words, speech is both a desired and a feared goal; similarly, silence is both a feared and a desired goal. As Sheehan puts it:

"Speaking holds the promise of communication, but the threat of stuttering; silence eliminates temporarily the threat involved in speaking, but at a cost of abandonment of communication . . ." (Sheehan, 1958).

Sheehan distinguishes five levels of conflict in stuttering. At the word level, the conflict is between the desire to say and avoid saying a particular word. At the situation level, the conflict is between speaking and not speaking in a situation arousing anxiety about stuttering. At the emotional level, the conflict relates to the content of the utterance. At the relationship level, the conflict relates to conversation with particular individuals. At the ego-protective level, the conflict relates to speech in threatening situations, involving particularly level of aspiration.

The experimental evidence in favor of the formulation of stuttering as an approach-avoidance conflict, involving different levels, is presented in detail by Sheehan (1958) and need not be repeated here. Sheehan's formulation certainly makes "good sense" and seems to be supported by the rather meagre evidence available at present.

A more difficult question concerns the problem of accounting for the release of the stutterer from a momentary blocking. How does the equilibrium which produces blocking come to be broken? Sheehan's hypothesis is that:

"the occurrence of stuttering reduces the fear which elicited it, so that during the block there is sufficient reduction in fear-motivated avoidance to resolve the conflict, permitting release of the blocked word" (Sheehan, 1958).

But how does the fear reduction take place? Sheehan suggests that three factors influence the change. First, the sheer occurrence of the stuttering reduces the anticipatory fear by bringing the whole process into the open.

Second, the occurrence of the stuttering provides more proprioceptive information about the block and reduces anxiety. Third, if we regard stuttering as a form of aggression, then the occurrence of the stuttering reduces the aggressive drive and hence permits speech to proceed.

It must be admitted that here Sheehan's arguments are very weak. However, in fairness, it must also be stated that the general problem of the resolution of conflict when all forces are in equilibrium has never been satisfactorily solved by any of the major theorists on conflict (Yates, 1962). The experimental evidence purporting to support this part of the theory has also been reviewed by Sheehan (1958), though its relevance to the theory is much less obvious than in the case of the blocking itself.

We may conclude that although the maintenance of stuttering may be satisfactorily accounted for in terms of learning theory, no satisfactory explanation has so far been put forward to account for the genesis of stuttering. A consideration of the theory of the genesis of stuttering as presented at the beginning of this section at once reveals its total inadequacy.[19] We may readily agree that the child's nonfluencies may be criticized by the parents or others, and that this will arouse anticipatory anxiety in relation to speech in the child. However, it is quite impossible to see why the child should successfully reduce this anxiety either by continuing to be nonfluent or developing a stutter. In either case, the child is likely to receive more, not less, "punishment" (we are, of course, dealing with the learning of the stutter, not its maintenance). Wischner's attempts to circumvent this basic difficulty are wholly unconvincing (Wischner, 1950). The author can think of only one possible resolution of the difficulty, which runs somewhat as follows. Clearly, the learned nonfluency or stutter must (in terms of the theory) reduce the anxiety by preventing the appearance of the noxious unconditioned stimulus (parental disapproval). It is possible that many parents, after initially drawing the child's attention to his nonfluencies, and thus inducing anxiety, subsequently react with a policy of withdrawing attention to the child's speech as soon as he begins to stutter. Thus, where previously parental reproof has followed nonfluency, and

---

[19] Wingate (1962a, 1962b, 1962c) has recently examined the empirical evidence for Johnson's "evaluative" theory of the genesis of stuttering, concluding that the evidence was contradictory and unconvincing.

while the parents observe the child's speech closely (to the discomfiture of the child) until he stutters, the act of stuttering removes this embarrassing scrutiny and hence reduces the anticipatory anxiety. Hence the stuttering is rewarded. While this *ad hoc* explanation is not entirely unreasonable, the author feels little confidence in it, especially as Wischner adduces what is virtually the opposite (i.e., that the stuttering is reinforced because it produces attention from the parents which was previously lacking).

Recently, however, Brutten and Shoemaker (1968) have advanced a two-factor theory of the genesis of stuttering. Essentially, they argue that stuttering per se is not anxiety reducing but represents disorganization of a complex motor response in situations involving the induction of high states of emotion. This disorganization is initially an unlearned reaction of nonfluency but eventually it becomes a learned reaction which is intensified because it produces negative audience reactions which, in turn, heighten the anxiety. Response-produced cues arising from speech may also then become anxiety eliciting stimuli. It should be noted carefully that the disorganized speech response is not regarded as reducing the anxiety that produces it. Rather, the anxiety is reduced by other instrumental behaviors. The implications of this theory for the treatment of stuttering by a two-stage attack will be discussed later.

(c) STUTTERING AS AN OPERANT. The explanation of the *maintenance* of stuttering as a form of operant conditioning would be rather similar to that put forward by Sheehan and others. In one of his earlier papers, Sheehan (1951), in fact, put forward an explanation in terms of the contingencies produced by stuttering. He argued that stuttering is reinforced because it *immediately precedes a reinforcing event*, which in this case is *proceeding to the next word*. Goldiamond (1965) has pointed out that stuttering may be reinforced by one of two possible contingencies: either it brings about a *rewarding* state of affairs or it forestalls the *threat* of punishment. For example, the threat of punishment if an immediate answer to a question is not forthcoming may be forestalled if the subject stutters, thus both giving himself more time to formulate a reply and enlisting sympathy instead of censure.[20]

From the foregoing evidence, it might appear that there is considerable (if not fundamental) disagreement among behavior theorists concerning the genesis and maintenance of stuttering behavior. But these differences are almost certainly more apparent than real. A composite formulation may be made along the following lines. Speech is a complex skilled act, involving both internal feedback controlling factors via the air, bone, and kinesthetic feedback channels. In the course of acquiring this skill, all children evidence a marked degree of nonfluency in their speech. Elimination of the nonfluencies involves essentially the integration of the feedback channels controlling speech. In some children there is probably a genetically-determined constitutional abnormality in the bone-conduction channel which makes it exceptionally difficult for them to achieve this integration. Whether these constitutionally defective children do, however, in fact develop a stutter (and, if so, its severity) is not solely a function of the constitutional defect, but also of whether or not their nonfluencies arouse anxiety in their parents or other listeners that the child is developing a stutter. It is clear that *skilled behavior becomes skilled precisely in so far as its control becomes automatic*. If, however, at the precise moment when this automatic control is being achieved the parents begin to correct or reprove or punish the child's errors of speech, they are drawing the attention of the child to the execution of the skill at the worst possible time. Not only does this make the achievement of automatic control much more difficult, but *it also introduces the opportunity for these errors to be strengthened on an operant conditioning basis*, in the ways outlined earlier.

We may go further than this and argue that not all children with the constitutional defect will develop a stutter. If the nonfluencies are ignored by the parents, such a child may eventually achieve relatively normal speech, though perhaps with great difficulty.[21] Conversely, it would follow that not all children whose normal disfluencies are punished by the parents will develop a stutter—since the basic constitutional defect must also be present. Furthermore, it will be clear that the wide variability in type of stutter which is such a striking feature of the disorder must imply a significant contribution on the part of learning.

---

[20] There is no necessary implication that the stutter is deliberate.

[21] It is tempting to speculate that adults with non-fluent speech (but who are not regarded as stutterers) are people who *would* have been stutterers but who were fortunate in their parents; and that these are the people most susceptible to DAF.

Hence we conclude that there is no necessary incompatibility between the perceptual-defect theory and the learning theory and operant approaches to stuttering. The basic defect would appear to be perceptual in nature but grafted on to this are the numerous contingencies which stuttering produces and which in turn modify both the frequency and type of stuttering which is the end-product.

IV. BEHAVIOR THERAPY AND STUTTERING

The application of behavior therapy techniques to the treatment of stuttering has not been very extensive or intensive. Nevertheless, such results as have been obtained are of considerable interest, both empirically and theoretically. We shall discuss several approaches: shadowing; masking; negative practice; rhythmic speaking; operant techniques; and the use of systematic desensitization.

1. SHADOWING

As was pointed out earlier, a number of techniques (shadowing, high-intensity white noise, and simultaneous reading) markedly reduce stuttering and reinstate normal speech. Now, it might be argued that, even though capable of normal speech under special circumstances, the normal feedback controlling factors are defective in that the abnormal channel (bone-conduction) is prepotent over the normal feedback channel (air-conduction). If we add to this the assumption that the *relative* potency of these two channels in the monitoring of speech can be altered, then it is feasible to argue that, *provided the stutterer could be given enough practice in normal speech under artificial conditions*, he would be able to shift from his dependence on the normal air-conduction channel. The stutterer cannot, however, achieve this himself because he cannot stop stuttering. Hence, it was hoped that, if the stutterer were given continuous practice in normal speech under artificial conditions, he might eventually build up normal airborne feedback control and could come to rely on this alone. The use of the shadowing technique is one way in which this might be achieved.

Both Cherry and Sayers (1956) and Maclaren (1956) made use of the shadowing technique for therapeutic purposes, with apparently encouraging results. The subsequent pessimistic conclusions of Meyer and Mair (1963) regarding this technique, however, have been somewhat offset by two recent studies. Kondas (1967) used the technique with 19 child and one adult stutterers with a follow-up of three years on the average. About 70% showed highly significant improvement (as assessed in relation to real-life speech) at the termination of treatment, the improvement being maintained on follow-up in about 59% of the cases. Kelham and McHale (1966) not only used the shadowing technique but applied it in situations which progressively approximated the real-life social situations in which the stuttering was most severe. Three different therapists, working independently with 38 child and adolescent stutterers, obtained "success" rates of 67–75%, though the criteria of success were not very satisfactory. Success was greatest with the younger subjects; there was no relation between degree of success and intelligence, and no evidence of symptom substitution was found.

2. MASKING

The use of white noise for therapeutic purposes has been neglected because of the high level of intensity that is required to completely attenuate bone-conducted feedback and the possible undesirable side effects. However, it seems clear that the dangers and difficulties of this technique may be less than previously thought, since it is now evident that the masking noise may need to be used only intermittently and for short periods. Parker and Christopherson (1963) have reported on the use of a portable apparatus for producing white noise, while Trotter and Lesch (1967) have described a similar instrument. In the former study, encouraging results were obtained with three severe stutterers, while Trotter has given a detailed account of the use of the technique on himself. Further work with this method should be encouraged.

3. NEGATIVE PRACTICE

Use of the negative practice technique derives from the work of Dunlap (1932) and may be considered as a form of massed practice. Fishman (1937) reported on the effects of negative practice on the speech of five stutterers who were required to stutter words deliberately (that is, words on which they normally stuttered). The three cases who tended to repeat words and initial letters showed improvement, whereas the two who displayed mainly blockages did not improve. More recently, Case (1960) reported that this method was effective in about one-third of his stutterers.

The method of negative practice, if interpreted as massed practice, is open to serious objections as used in therapy. For, in fact, it is clear that it does not constitute massed practice at all. In massed practice, the subject is required to repeat the stuttered word over and over again with no or very little time interval between repetitions. In negative practice, however, the stutterer repeats whole sentences in which the stuttered words are embedded. Hence, there are appreciable time intervals between repetitions of the stuttered material. In fact, massed practice does not appear to have been used with stutterers in any genuine sense. It might be added at this point that the same criticism can be brought against the interpretation of adaptation studies in relation to stuttering.[22] That adaptation takes place with repeated reading of the same passage is undoubted (Cullinan, 1963a, 1963b; Donohue, 1955; Johnson and Knott, 1937; Jones (E.L.), 1955; Tate and Cullinan, 1962; Tate et al, 1961), and the effect has been demonstrated over very long periods of speaking (Rousey, 1958). Two competing interpretations have been put forward to account for the effect: that it is a result of a decline in anxiety relating to the material read; and that it is because of the growth of reactive inhibition. The anxiety interpretation was postulated to explain the differential effects found when stutterers read alone as opposed to before an audience (Dixon, 1955; Shulman, 1955; Siegel and Haugen, 1964) but was effectively refuted by Gray and Brutten (1965) who preferred the reactive inhibition theory (Gray, 1965a, 1965b). This interpretation was supported by findings such as that of Golub (1955) who showed that the adaptation effect occurred on repeated words and not on different words; and those relating to spontaneous recovery by Frick (1955) and Jamison (1955). The explanation is untenable, however, partly for the reason given above that repetition of the same passage does not constitute massed practice (where repetition of the same word over and over again would) and partly by experimental findings such as those of Van Riper and Hull (1955). They found that if, after several adaptation trials, the subject read the same passage *backwards*, the adaptation effect did not disappear.

4. RHYTHMIC AND SYLLABLE-TIMED SPEECH

It has, of course, been known for a very long time that the imposition of rhythm on speech may attenuate stuttering to a very significant degree. Empirical demonstrations of this were provided by Johnson and Rosen (1937) who found stuttering reduced virtually to zero under a variety of conditions involving rhythmic speech of one kind or another (speaking in time to a slowly beating metronome; speaking in time with arm swinging; and reading in a sing-song voice). Van Dantzig (1940) produced a similar reduction with finger tapping. While rhythmic speech has been used clinically in therapy for an equally long period, it is only recently that systematic investigation of the phenomenon has been carried out in relation to the therapeutic usefulness of the technique.

Meyer and Mair (1963), after confirming that speaking in time with a metronome eliminated stuttering and, further, that each stutterer had a preferred metronome rate for rhythmic speaking, constructed a miniature apparatus which the stutterer could wear like a hearing aid and switch on whenever he felt he was going to stutter. As in the case of shadowing, it was hoped that the procedure would not merely serve as a crutch but that normal speech patterns could gradually be acquired with the metronome being progressively discarded. Encouraging results in real-life situations were obtained by Meyer and Mair, and there appears to be no doubt that for those stutterers who are willing to wear the apparatus and use it appropriately, stuttering in social situations can be virtually abolished. It is important to note that Fransella and Beech (1965) and Fransella (1967) have demonstrated that the use of the metronome in this way is not simply an exercise in distraction. They found that an *arhythmic* metronome did not have the same effect as speaking in time with a rhythmic metronome.

More recently, Andrews has developed the technique of syllable-timed (ST) speech. It is important to note that ST speech differs in important ways from rhythmic speech. Indeed, it appears to eliminate the "rhythm" from rhythmic speech, though its precise relationship to metronome-paced speech is not yet clear. In ST speech, the speech output is evenly produced with clear separation between each speech unit,

---

[22] For a recent cogent critique of adaptation studies of stuttering as learned behavior, ees Wingate (1966a, 1966b).

yet with the aim being smooth enunciation. Andrews and Harris (1964) and Holgate and Andrews (1966) have reported the results of three studies using ST speech with stutterers, in each case with encouraging results. It should be noted that Andrews has argued that the elimination of stuttering with this technique produces problems of adjustment, not only in the stutterer but often in the stutterer's family since, in long-term stutterers, social intercourse has been organized to take account of the speech difficulty. Fluent speech in a stutterer apparently produces its own problems.[23] Like Goldiamond (see below), Andrews considers that essentially the stutterer is being taught a new form of speech which is then gradually shaped toward normal speech. Brandon and Harris (1967) have also used ST speech, finding 64% of a group of 28 stutterers still showing significant speech improvement on a follow-up of at least 18 months. Horan (1968) has combined the metronome technique of Meyer and Mair with the ST speech technique of Andrews. All of these workers agree in finding that ST speech can be rapidly acquired by even severe stutterers.

Why ST or metronome-controlled speech should reduce stuttering so dramatically is by no means clear as yet. It is possible that, by reducing the length of the speech units and increasing the length of the interval between them, feedback from each speech unit falls entirely within the interval between speech units. The effect would then be the same as that achieved by white noise—the feedback would be irrelevant to the output and the stutterer would be speaking, in effect, without airborne and bone-conducted feedback.

5. OPERANT TECHNIQUES

In some respects, the most interesting and important treatment techniques are those recently reported by Goldiamond (1965) and by Rickard and Mundy (1965). Rickard and Mundy (1965) used extrinsic (ice-cream) and intrinsic (achieving better than stuttering baseline) rewards in a nine-year-old boy and achieved satisfactory results in both the laboratory training and its transfer to real life. Especially noteworthy are their cooption of the parents of the child as reward-givers and the grading of the experimental and real-life speech tasks for difficulty level.

As was pointed out earlier, the use of operant procedures in behavior therapy has mainly been confined to varying *environmental* contingencies in attempts to alter behavior, as in the study by Rickard and Mundy. The recent work of Goldiamond (1965) is important because it applies operant procedures to *internal* controlling stimuli, not normally under the control of the experimenter in a precise way. As we noted earlier, Goldiamond found, unexpectedly, that if elimination of aversive stimulation (DAF) was made contingent upon stuttering, the stuttering *declined* rather than increased. Goldiamond argued that this effect was produced because DAF used in this way produced a new pattern of speech, which was not like normal speech but not like stuttering either. In effect, DAF alters the normal proprioceptive and auditory feedback relations. Now, the subject may attempt to restore the status quo in one of a number of ways: by reducing the auditory component (whispering); by "tuning-out" the auditory component altogether and relying on the undisturbed proprioceptive feedback; or by prolonging the speech units to restore as far as possible the overlap between output and feedback. The latter stratagem produces a new form of speech and Goldiamond considered that this form of adaptation to DAF could be utilized therapeutically. This new form of speech could itself then be brought under operant control so that it could be utilized outside the laboratory situation. More importantly, it could also be shaped so that emission of these speech units could be speeded up and approximate more and more the formal characteristics of normal speech. Finally, the subject could be taught simple operant procedures to apply by himself in real-life situations. During these procedures, DAF itself as a controlling stimulus may be gradually faded out so that the new speech pattern is no longer dependent on it.

These procedures were applied to eight chronic stutterers by Goldiamond (1965). Once the new form of prolonged speech was established by the use of elimination-avoidance DAF, a Percepto-Scope (which presents successive displays of reading materials at controlled rates) was used to speed up reading, the DAF was decreased progressively by increments of 50 msec and eventually faded out altogether, and the subject was trained to extend the new speech patterns to situations outside the laboratory. In all eight cases, the stuttering was

---

[23] Andrews handles this problem by the use of group psychotherapy.

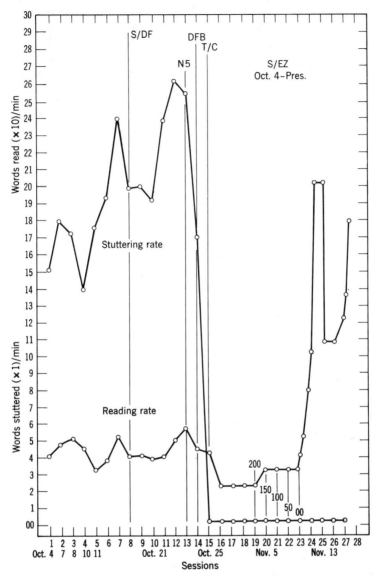

FIG. 2. Laboratory elimination of stuttering and quadrupling of reading rate in a very severe stutterer (Goldiamond, 1965).

totally eliminated within the laboratory situation, reading rate was speeded up to a remarkable degree, and in some cases the results carried over into real-life situations.[24] The results for one subject are shown in Figure 2. The natural stuttering and reading rates are shown in the left-hand portion of the graph. The section, S/DF, shows the stutterer's self-definition of stuttering and reading rate. The introduction of DAF at session 14 produced a drop in stuttering and a slight drop in reading rate, while the introduction of timer-controlled reading rate eliminated stuttering completely. The reading rate (as controlled by the Percepto-Scope) was deliberately reduced at session 16 for four days, then gradually increased while DAF was faded out. Over a comparatively short period of time, it proved possible to increase the reading rate to 204 words per minute, with stuttering rate remaining zero.

[24] It should be realized that this part of the therapy is still in its early stages, but the results are extremely promising.

6. USE OF SD(I) AND SD(R)

The adoption of a model that regards stuttering as caused by a fault in the feedback control system for speech does not, of course, rule out the possibility that stuttering may occasionally be an anxiety-reducing response, especially in those cases where the stuttering appears to be attached to relatively specific stimulus situations such as speaking on the telephone. Rosenthal (1968) has successfully treated an exceptionally severe stutterer by the use of SD(I) applied to situations in which stuttering occurred, while Brutten and Shoemaker (1968) specifically argue that a two-pronged attack on the stuttering problem is essential. SD techniques should be used, they argue, to reduce anxiety associated with stuttering, while other techniques (such as those described above) may be appropriate for treating the stutter itself. Andrews' use of group psychotherapy, in which the stutterers meet as a group to discuss their problems of adjustment, both with and without their stutter, can be regarded as an example of the procedures advocated by Brutten and Shoemaker.[25]

In principle, the servomechanistic and the learning models are not incompatible with each other. A defect in the feedback control system may produce instability in the feedback loop, thus producing an excessive degree of non-fluency. Onto this, however, is grafted a very large amount of learning so that the final product, behavioristically, is a complex resultant of interacting forces. An attack on any point in the chain of events which represents stuttering may produce therapeutic dividends. The precise relationship between the feedback control defect and learning processes in stuttering appears to have been misconceived in the past, however, and cannot yet be said to have been satisfactorily resolved.

REFERENCES

Adams, M.R. & Dietze, D.A. A comparison of the reaction times of stutterers and non-stutterers to items on a word-association test. *J. Speech Hear. Res.*, 1965, **8**, 195–202.

Andrews, G. & Harris, M. *The syndrome of stuttering* (*Clinics in developmental medicine, No. 17*). London: Heinemann Medical Books, 1964.

Barbara, D.A. (ed.). *The psychotherapy of stuttering*. Springfield: C.C. Thomas, 1962.

Barbara, D.A., Goldart, N., & Oram, C. Group psychoanalysis with adult stutterers. *Amer. J. Psychoanal.*, 1961, **21**, 40–57.

Barker, V. Chorus reading as a distraction in stuttering. *J. Speech. Dis.*, 1939, **4**, 371–383.

Black, J.W. The effect of delayed side-tone upon vocal rate and intensity. *J. Speech Hear. Dis.*, 1951, **16**, 56–60.

Bloodstein, O. Hypothetical conditions under which stuttering is reduced or absent. *J. Speech Hear. Dis.*, 1950, **15**, 142–153.

Bloodstein, O. The development of stuttering: I. Changes in nine basic features. *J. Speech Hear. Dis.*, 1960, **25**, 219–237 (a).

Bloodstein, O. The development of stuttering: II. Development phases. *J. Speech Hear. Dis.*, 1960, **25**, 366–376 (b).

Bloodstein, O. The development of stuttering: III. Theoretical and clinical implications. *J. Speech Hear. Dis.*, 1961, **26**, 67–82.

Brandon, S. & Harris, M. Stammering: an experimental treatment programme using syllable-timed speech. *Brit. J. Disord. Commun.*, 1967, **2**, 64–68.

Broadbent, D.E. Successive responses to simultaneous stimuli. *Quart. J. exp. Psychol.*, 1956, **8**, 145–152.

Broadbent, D.E. *Perception and communication*. Oxford: Pergamon, 1958.

Browning, R.M. Behavior therapy for stuttering in a schizophrenic child. *Behav. Res. Ther.*, 1967, **5**, 27–35.

Brutten, E.J. & Shoemaker, D.J. *The modification of stuttering*. Englewood Cliffs: Prentice-Hall, 1968.

---

[25] A similar double approach was used successfully by Browning (1967) with a schizophrenic child who stuttered.

Butler, R.A. & Galloway, F.T. Factoral analysis of the delayed speech feedback phenomenon. *J. acoust. Soc. Amer.*, 1957, **29**, 632–635.

Butler, B.R. & Stanley, P.E. The stuttering problem considered from an automatic control point of view. *Folia phoniat.*, 1966, **18**, 33–44.

Case, H.W. Therapeutic methods in stuttering and speech blocking. In Eysenck, H.J. (ed.). *Behavior therapy and the neuroses.* Oxford: Pergamon, 1960, pp. 207–220.

Chase, R.A. Effect of delayed auditory feedback on the repetition of speech sounds. *J. Speech Hear. Dis.*, 1958, **23**, 583–590.

Chase, R.A. An information-flow model of the organization of motor activity: I. Transduction, transmission, and central control of sensory information. *J. nerv. ment. Dis.*, 1965, **140**, 239–251 (a).

Chase, R.A. An information-flow model of the organization of motor activity. II. Sampling, central processing, and utilization of sensory information. *J. nerv. ment. Dis.*, 1965, **140**, 334–350 (b).

Chase, R.A. & Guilfoyle, G. Effect of simultaneous delayed and undelayed auditory feedback on speech. *J. Speech Hear. Res.*, 1962, **5**, 144–151.

Chase, R.A. & Sutton, S. Reply to "Masking of auditory feedback in stutterer's speech." *J. Speech Hear. Res.*, 1968, **11**, 222–223.

Cherry, E.C. Some experiments on the recognition of speech, with one and with two ears. *J. acoust. Soc. Amer.*, 1953, **25**, 975–979.

Cherry, C. & Sayers, B.McA. Experiments upon the total inhibition of stammering by external control and some clinical results. *J. psychosom. Res.*, 1956, **1**, 233–246.

Conway, J.K. & Quarrington, B.J. Positional effects in the stuttering of contextually organized verbal material. *J. abnorm. soc. Psychol.*, 1963, **67**, 299–303.

Cullinan, W.L. Stability of adaptation in the oral performance of stutterers. *J. Speech Hear. Res.*, 1963, **6**, 70–83 (a).

Cullinan, W.L. Stability of consistency measures in stuttering. *J. Speech Hear. Res.*, 1963, **6**, 134–138 (b).

Cullinan, W.L., Prather, E.M., & Williams, D.E. Comparison of procedures for scaling severity of stuttering. *J. Speech Hear. Res.*, 1963, **6**, 187–194.

Curtis, J.F. A study of the effect of muscular exercize upon stuttering. *Speech Monogr.*, 1942, **9**, 61–74.

Darley, F.L. The relationship of parental attitudes and adjustments to the development of stuttering. In Johnson, W. (ed.). *Stuttering in children and adults.* Minneapolis: Univer. Minnesota Press, 1955, pp. 74–153.

Dixon, C.C. Stuttering adaptation in relation to assumed level of anxiety. In Johnson, W. (ed.). *Stuttering in children and adults.* Minneapolis: Univer. Minnesota Press, 1955, pp. 232–236.

Donohue, I.R. Stuttering adaptation during three hours of continuous oral reading. In Johnson, W. (ed.). *Stuttering in children and adults.* Minneapolis: Univer. Minnesota Press, 1955, pp. 264–267.

Dunlap, K. *Habits: their making and unmaking.* New York: Liveright, 1932.

Fairbanks, G. Systematic research in experimental phonetics: I. A theory of the speech mechanism as a servo system. *J. Speech Hear. Dis.*, 1954, **19**, 133–139.

Falck, F.J. Stuttering and hypnosis. *Internat. J. clin. exp. Hypnosis*, 1964, **12**, 67–74.

Fenichel, O. *The psychoanalytic theory of neurosis.* London: Routledge and Kegan Paul, 1946.

Fishman, H.C. A study of the efficiency of negative practice as a corrective for stammering. *J. Speech Dis.*, 1937, **2**, 67–72.

Flanagan, B., Goldiamond, I., & Azrin, N. Operant stuttering; the control of stuttering behavior through response-contingent consequences. *J. exper. anal. Behav.*, 1958, **1**, 173–177.

Flanagan, B., Goldiamond, I., & Azrin, N. Instatement of stuttering in normally fluent individuals through operant procedures. *Science*, 1959, **130**, 979–981.

Fransella, F. Rhythm as a distractor in the modification of stuttering. *Behav. Res. Ther.*, 1967, **5**, 253–255.

Fransella, F. & Beech, H.R. An experimental analysis of the effect of rhythm on the speech of stutterers. *Behav. Res. Ther.*, 1965, **3**, 195–201.

Frick, J.V. Spontaneous recovery of the stuttering response as a function of the degree of adaptation. In Johnson, W. (ed.). *Stuttering in children and adults.* Minneapolis: Univer. of Minnesota Press, 1955, pp. 249–255.

Gibbs, C.B. The continuous regulation of skilled response by kinaesthetic feedback. *Brit. J. Psychol.*, 1954, **45**, 24–39.

Goldiamond, I. Stuttering and fluency as manipulatable operant response classes. In Krasner, L. and Ullmann, L.P. (eds.). *Research in behavior modification.* New York: Holt, 1965, pp. 106–156.

Goldiamond, I., Atkinson, C.J., & Bilger, R.C. Stabilization of behavior and prolonged exposure to delayed auditory feedback. *Science*, 1962, **135**, 437–438.

Golub, A. The cumulative effect of constant and varying reading material on stuttering adaptation. In Johnson, W. (ed.). *Stuttering in children and adults.* Minneapolis: Univer. Minnesota Press, 1955, pp. 237–244.

Goodstein, L.D. Functional speech disorders and personality: a survey of the research. *J. Speech Hear. Res.*, 1958, **1**, 359–376.

Gray, B.B. Theoretical approximations of stuttering adaptation. *Behav. Res. Ther.*, 1965, **3**, 171–185 (a).

Gray, B.B. Theoretical approximations of stuttering adaptation: statement of predictive accuracy. *Behav. Res. Ther.*, 1965, **3**, 221–228 (b).

Gray, B.B. & Brutten, E.J. The relationship between anxiety, fatigue and spontaneous recovery in stuttering. *Behav. Res. Ther.*, 1965, **2**, 251–259.

Hahn, E. (ed.). *Stuttering: significant theories and therapies.* Stanford: Stanford Univ. Press, 1956.

Ham, R.E. & Steer, M.D. Certain effects of alterations in the auditory feedback. *Folia phoniat.*, 1967, **19**, 53–62.

Hanley, C.N. & Tiffany, W.R. An investigation into the use of electro-mechanically delayed side tone in auditory testing. *J. Speech Hear. Dis.*, 1954, **19**, 367–374.

Hejna, R.F. *Speech disorders and nondirective therapy.* New York: Ronald, 1960.

Hill, H. Stuttering: I. A critical review of biochemical investigations. *J. Speech Dis.*, 1944, **9**, 245–261 (a).

Hill, H. Stuttering: II. A review and integration of physiological data. *J. Speech Dis.*, 1944, **9**, 289–324 (b).

Hirsch, I.J. Auditory perception of temporal order. *J. acoust. Soc. Amer.*, 1959, **31**, 759–767.

Hirsch, I.J. & Sherrick, C.E. Perceived order in different sense modalities. *J. exp. Psychol.*, 1961, **62**, 423–432.

Holgate, D. & Andrews, J.G. The use of syllable-timed speech and group psychotherapy in the treatment of adult stutterers. *J. Austr. Coll. Speech Ther.*, 1966, **16**, 36–40.

Hollingworth, H.L. *Abnormal psychology.* London: Methuen, 1931.

Horan, M.C. An improved device for inducing rhythmic speech in stutterers. *Austr. Psychol.*, 1968, **3**, 19–25.

Jamison, D.J. Spontaneous recovery of the stuttering response as a function of the time following adaptation. In Johnson, W. (ed.). *Stuttering in children and adults.* Minneapolis: Univer. Minnesota Press, 1955, pp. 245–248.

Johnson, W. Stuttering. In Johnson, W., Brown, S.J., Curtis, J.J., Edney, C.W., & Keaster, J. (eds.). *Speech handicapped schoolchildren.* New York: Harper, 1956, pp. 202–300.

Johnson, W. (ed.). *The onset of stuttering.* Minneapolis: Univer. Minnesota Press, 1959.

Johnson, W. Measurements of oral reading and speaking rate and disfluency of adult male and female stutterers and nonstutterers. *J. Speech Hear. Dis. Monogr. Suppl.*, 1961, **7**, 1–20.

Johnson, W. & Knott, J.R. The moment of stuttering. *J. genet. Psychol.*, 1936, **48**, 475–480.

Johnson, W. & Knott, J. Studies in the psychology of stuttering: I. The distribution of moments of stuttering in successive readings of the same material. *J. Speech Dis.*, 1937, **2**, 17–19.

Johnson, W. & Rosen, L. Studies in the psychology of stuttering: VII. Effect of certain changes in speech pattern upon frequency of stuttering. *J. Speech Dis.*, 1937, **2**, 105–109.

Jones, E.L. Explorations of experimental extinction and spontaneous recovery in stuttering. In Johnson, W. (ed.). *Stuttering in children and adults.* Minneapolis: Univer. Minnesota Press, 1955, pp. 226–231.

Kalmus, H., Denes, F., & Fry, D.B. Effect of delayed acoustic feedback on some nonvocal activities. *Nature*, 1955, **175**, 1078.

Kelham, R. & McHale, A. The application of learning theory to the treatment of stammering. *Brit. J. Disord. Commun.*, 1966, **1**, 114–118.

Kent, L.R. Carbon dioxide therapy as a medical treatment for stuttering. *J. Speech Hear. Dis.*, 1961, **26**, 268–271.

Kent, L.R. The use of tranquilizers in the treatment of stuttering. *J. Speech Hear. Dis.*, 1963, **28**, 288–294.

Kondas, O. The treatment of stammering in children by the shadowing method. *Behav. Res. Ther.*, 1967, **5**, 325–329.

Lanyon, R.I. The relationship of adaptation and consistency to improvement in stuttering therapy. *J. Speech Hear. Res.*, 1965, **8**, 263–269.

Lashley, K.S. The problem of serial order in behavior. In Jeffress, L.A. (ed.). *Cerebral mechanisms in behavior.* New York: Wiley, 1951, pp. 112–136.

Lee, B.S. Effects of delayed speech feedback. *J. acoust. Soc. Amer.*, 1950, **22**, 824–826 (a).

Lee, B.S. Some effects of side-tone delay. *J. acoust. Soc. Amer.*, 1950, **22**, 639–640 (b).

Lee, B.S. Artificial stutter. *J. Speech Hear. Dis.*, 1951, **16**, 53–55.

Lewis, D. & Sherman, D. Measuring the severity of stuttering. *J. Speech Hear. Dis.*, 1951, **16**, 320–326.

Lotzmann, G. Zur Anwendung variierter Verzögerunszeiten bei Balbuties. *Folia phoniat.*, 1961, **13**, 276–312.

Maclaren, J. The treatment of stammering by the Cherry-Sayers method: clinical impressions. In Eysenck, H.J. (ed.). *Behavior therapy and the neuroses.* Oxford: Pergamon, 1960, pp. 457–460.

Maraist, J.A. & Hutton, C. Effects of auditory masking upon the speech of stutterers. *J. Speech Hear. Dis.*, 1957, **22**, 385–389.

Martin, R.R. & Siegel, G.M. The effects of response-contingent shock on stuttering. *J. Speech Hearing Res.*, 1966, **9**, 340–352 (a).

Martin, R.R. & Siegel, G. The effects of simultaneously punishing stuttering and rewarding fluency. *J. Speech Hearing Res.*, 1966, **9**, 466–475 (b).

May, A.E. & Hackwood, A. Some effects of masking and eliminating low frequency feedback on the speech of stammerers. *Behav. Res. Ther.*, 1968, **6**, 219–223.

Metraux, R.W. Speech profiles of the preschool child 18 to 54 months. *J. Speech Hear. Dis.*, 1950, **15**, 37–53.

Meyer, V. & Mair, J.M.M. A new technique to control stammering: a preliminary report. *Behav. Res. Ther.*, 1963, **1**, 251–254.

Murphy, A.T. & Fitzsimmons, R.M. *Stuttering and personality dynamics: play therapy, projective therapy and counseling.* New York: Ronald, 1960.

Mysak, E.D. A servomodel for speech therapy. *J. Speech Hear. Dis.*, 1959, **24**, 144–149.

Mysak, E.D. Servo-theory and stuttering. *J. Speech Hear. Dis.*, 1960, **15**, 188–195.

Neelley, J.M. A study of the speech behavior of stutterers and nonstutterers under normal and delayed auditory feedback. *J. Speech Hear. Dis. Monogr. Suppl.*, 1961, **7**, 63–82.

Parker, C.S. & Christopherson, F. Electronic aid in the treatment of stammer. *Med. Electron. biol. Engin.*, 1963, **1**, 121–125.

Quarrington, B. Stuttering as a function of the information value and sentence position of words. *J. abnorm. soc. Psychol.*, 1965, **70**, 221–224.

Rickard, H.C. & Mundy, M.B. Direct manipulation of stuttering behavior: an experimental-clinical approach. In Ullmann, L.P. & Krasner, L. (eds.). *Case studies in behavior modification.* New York: Holt, 1965, pp. 268–274.

Rosenthal, T.L. Severe stuttering and maladjustment treated by desensitization and social influence. *Behav. Res. Ther.*, 1968, **6**, 125–130.

Rousey, C. Stuttering severity during prolonged spontaneous speech. *J. Speech Hear. Res.*, 1958, **1**, 40–47.

Sadoff, R.L. & Siegel, J.R. Group psychotherapy for stutterers. *Internat. J. Group Psychother.*, 1965, **15**, 72–80.

Sander, E.K. Reliability of the Iowa Speech Disfluency Test. *J. Speech Hear. Dis. Monogr. Suppl.*, 1961, **7**, 21–30.

Santostefano, S. Anxiety and hostility in stuttering. *J. Speech Hear. Res.*, 1960, **3**, 337–347.

Schindler, M.D. A study of educational adjustments of stuttering and nonstuttering children. In Johnson, W. (ed.). *Stuttering in children and adults.* Minneapolis: Univer. Minnesota Press, 1955, pp. 348–357.

Schlesinger, I.M., Forte, M., Fried, B., & Melkham, R. Stuttering, information load, and response strength. *J. speech Hear. Dis.*, 1965, **30**, 32–36.

Schuell, H. Sex differences in relation to stuttering. *J. Speech Dis.*, 1946, **11**, 277–298.

Shames, G.H. & Sherrick, K.E. A discussion of nonfluency and stuttering as operant behavior. *J. Speech Hear. Dis.*, 1963, **28**, 3–17.

Shane, M.L.S. Effect on stuttering of alteration in auditory feedback. In Johnson, W. (ed.). *Stuttering in children and adults.* Minneapolis: Univer. Minnesota Press, 1955, pp. 286–297.

Sheehan, J.G. The modification of stuttering through nonreinforcement. *J. abnorm. soc. Psychol.*, 1951, **46**, 51–63.

Sheehan, J.G. Theory and treatment of stuttering as an approach-avoidance conflict. *J. Psychol.*, 1953, **36**, 27–49.

Sheehan, J.G. Projective studies of stuttering. *J. Speech Dis.*, 1958, **23**, 18–25.

Sherman, D. Clinical and experimental use of the Iowa scale of severity of stuttering. *J. Speech Hear. Dis.*, 1952, **17**, 316–320.

Sherman, D. & McDermott, R. Individual ratings of severity of moments of stuttering. *J. Speech Hear. Res.*, 1958, **1**, 61–67.

Sherman, D. & Moodie, C.E. Four psychological scaling methods applied to articulation defectiveness. *J. Speech Hear. Dis.*, 1957, **22**, 698–706.

Shulman, E. Factors influencing the variability of stuttering. In Johnson, W. (ed.). *Stuttering in children and adults.* Minneapolis: Univer. Minnesota Press, 1955, pp. 207–217.

Siegel, G.M. & Haugen, D. Audience size and variations in stuttering behavior. *J. Speech Hear. Res.*, 1964, **7**, 381–388.

Siegel, G.M. & Martin, R.R. Experimental modification of disfluency in normal speakers. *J. Speech Hear. Res.*, 1965, **8**, 235–244 (a).

Siegel, G.M. & Martin, R.M. Verbal punishment of disfluencies in normal speakers. *J. Speech Hear. Res.*, 1965, **8**, 245–251 (b).

Siegel, G.M. & Martin, R.R. Punishment of disfluencies in normal speakers. *J. Speech Hear. Res.*, 1966, **9**, 209–217.

Skinner, B.F. *Verbal behavior.* New York: Appleton-Century-Crofts, 1957.

Soderberg, G.A. Phonetic influences upon stuttering. *J. Speech Hear. Res.*, 1962, **5**, 315–320.

Soderberg, G.A. Delayed auditory feedback and stuttering. *J. Speech Hear. Dis.*, 1968, **33**, 260–267.

Stromsta, C. Delays associated with certain sidetone pathways. *J. acous. Soc. Amer.*, 1962, **34**, 392–396.

Strother, C.R. & Kriegman, L.S. Diadochokinesis in stutterers and nonstutterers. *J. Speech Dis.*, 1943, **8**, 323–325.

Strother, C.R. & Kriegman, L.S. Rhythmokinesis in stutterers and nonstutterers. *J. Speech Dis.*, 1944, **9**, 239–244.

Sutton, S. & Chase, R.A. White noise and stuttering. *J. Speech Hear. Res.*, 1961, **4**, 72.

Tate, M.W. & Cullinan, W.L. Measurement of consistency of stuttering. *J. Speech Hear. Res.*, 1962, **5**, 272–283.

Tate, M.W., Cullinan, W.L., & Ahlstrand, A. Measurement of adaptation in stuttering. *J. Speech Hear. Res.*, 1961, **4**, 322–339.

Tiffany, W.R. & Hanley, C.N. Delayed speech feedback as a test for auditory malingering. *Science*, 1952, **115**, 59–60.

Trotter, W.D. & Lesch, M. Personal experiences with stutter-aid. *J. Speech Hearing Dis.*, 1967, **32**, 270–272.

Van Dantzig, M. Syllable tapping: a new method for the help of stammerers. *J. Speech Dis.*, 1940, **5**, 127–131.

Van Riper, C. *Speech correction: principles and methods.* Englewood Cliffs: Prentice-Hall, 1954.

Van Riper, C. & Hull, C.J. The quantitative measurement of the effect of certain situations on stuttering. In Johnson, W. (ed.). *Stuttering in children and adults.* Minneapolis: Univer. Minnesota Press, 1955, pp. 199–206.

Voelker, C.H. A preliminary investigation for a normative study of fluency: a clinical index to the severity of stuttering. *Amer. J. Orthopsychiat.*, 1944, **14**, 285–294.

Webster, R.L. & Lubker, B.B. Masking of auditory feedback in stutterer's speech. *J. Speech Hear. Res.*, 1968, **11**, 221–223.

Wendahl, R.W. & Cole, J. Identification of stuttering during relatively fluent speech. *J. Speech Hear. Res.*, 1961, **4**, 281–286.

Williams, D.E. Intensive clinical case studies of stuttering therapy. In Johnson, W. (ed.). *Stuttering in children and adults.* Minneapolis: Univer. Minnesota Press, 1955, pp. 405–414.

Winchester, R.A. & Gibbons, E.W. Relative effectiveness of three modes of delayed sidetone presentation. *Arch. Otolaryngol.*, 1967, **65**, 275–279.

Wingate, M.E. Evaluation and stuttering: Part I. Speech characteristics of young children. *J. Speech Hear. Dis.*, 1962, **27**, 106–115 (a).

Wingate, M.E. Evaluation and stuttering: II. Environmental stress and critical appraisal of speech. *J. Speech Hear. Dis.*, 1962, **27**, 244–257 (b).

Wingate, M.E. Evaluation and stuttering: III. Identification of stuttering and the use of a label. *J. Speech Hear. Dis.*, 1962, **27**, 368–377 (c).

Wingate, M.E. Stuttering adaptation and learning: I. The relevance of adaptation studies to stuttering as "learned behavior." *J. Speech Hear. Dis.*, 1966, **31**, 148–156 (a).

Wingate, M.E. Stuttering adaptation and learning: II. The adequacy of learning principles and the interpretation of stuttering. *J. Speech Hear. Dis.*, 1966, **31**, 211–218 (b).

Wischner, G.J. Stuttering behavior and learning: a preliminary theoretical formulation. *J. Speech Hear. Dis.*, 1950, **15**, 324–335.

Wolf, A.A. & Wolf, E.G. Feedback processes in the theory of certain speech disorders. *Speech Path. Ther.*, 1959, **2**, 48–55.

Wyatt, G.L. & Herzan, H.M. Therapy with stuttering children and their mothers. *Amer. J. Orthopsychiat.*, 1962, **32**, 645–659.

Yates, A.J. *Frustration and conflict.* New York: Wiley, 1962.

Yates, A.J. Delayed auditory feedback. *Psychol. Bull.*, 1963, **60**, 213–232 (a).

Yates, A.J. Recent empirical and theoretical approaches to the experimental manipulation of speech in normal subjects and in stammerers. *Behav. Res. Ther.*, 1963, **1**, 95–119 (b).

Yates, A.J. Effects of delayed auditory feedback on morse transmission by skilled operators. *J. exp. Psychol.*, 1965, **69**, 467–475.

Young, M.A. Predicting ratings of severity of stuttering. *J. Speech Hear. Dis. Monogr. Suppl.*, 1961, **7**, 31–54.

Chapter 7

Phobias

A. Fears and Phobias[1]

I. DEFINITIONS, MEASUREMENT INCIDENCE

No ATTEMPT will be made at this stage to provide a formal definition of a fear or a phobia; as will be seen later, the terms are ambiguous as to their referents. Rather, the meaning of the terms will become clear from a discussion of attempts to measure fears and phobias in normal and psychiatric subjects.

1. MEASUREMENT OF FEARS IN NONPSYCHIATRIC SUBJECTS

The systematic attempt to assess fears in normal subjects is a relatively recent development and may be considered in relation to *assessment techniques* and *dependent measurements*.

(a) ASSESSMENT TECHNIQUES. The most obvious way of assessing whether a person is afraid of something is to expose him to it and note his behavior. Curiously, psychologists have shown a marked reluctance to do this, preferring more indirect methods for the most part. Some of the earliest workers did, however, use the *direct exposure* technique. Thus, Jones (1924a) exposed children to presumably frightening situations such as a dark room, being left alone, being suddenly presented with a snake,

and so on. Jersild and Holmes (1935a) used a wide range of similar situations, while Holmes (1936) used a high bar and a dark room. More recently, Lanyon and Manosevitz (1966), for example, have utilized exposure to spiders where it is known from verbal report that the subject has an intense fear of spiders; while the use of snakes is now quite common.

If the direct presentation of the feared object is regarded as undesirable, then an *indirect representation* of it (e.g., a picture) may be used (Geer, 1966).

Most popular of all in recent years, however, has been an even more indirect approach, the use of questionnaires which, of course, rely on the subject's verbal report of his fears. The use of the questionnaire has the enormous advantage that a very rapid survey can be made of a wide range of *possible* fears from which a person may suffer. On the other hand, whether it can be considered a satisfactory substitute for direct exposure to the feared object where, as will shortly be seen, more comparable estimates of the strength of particular fears in particular individuals can be obtained, is an empirical question for which evidence is lacking at present.

(i) *Development of the Fear Survey Schedule* (*FSS*). The situation here is well on the way to becoming confused, since no less than four versions of the FSS are extant. FSS-I refers to the form used by Lang and Lazovik (1963).

---

[1] Errera (1962) has reviewed the historical literature through 1872, showing clearly that there was an intensive interest in phobias long before Freud's famous cases. Rachman and Costello (1961)

have reviewed the literature relating to children's phobias. Snaith (1968) has recently produced a well-balanced review of both the psychodynamic and behavioristic positions.

This schedule was developed into a 72-item questionnaire by Wolpe and Lang (1964), and this version of the schedule was labeled FSS-III by Geer (1965) who, in the meanwhile, had developed his own schedule from the Lang/Lazovik one and which he labeled FSS-II. Wolpe and Lang (1964) did not publish any empirical data on FSS-III, but Geer (1965) developed his version on an empirical basis by asking males and females to list their fears and rate them for intensity. FSS-II was made up of 51 fears occurring more than twice. This scale was then given to a new and larger sample of males and females who checked a 7-point rating scale for each item. The internal consistency of the scale was found to be high (0.939 for males and females combined); it was found to correlate significantly with Bendig's N-scale and Taylor's MAS, but not with Bendig's E-scale. Validity was assessed by choosing subjects on the basis of high, medium, and low questionnaire scores and comparing their performance on tasks requiring approach to objects indicated on the questionnaire as feared objects. More recently, Scherer and Nakamura (1968) have developed a children's version (FSS-FC).

Using the Wolpe/Lang FSS-III, Grossberg and Wilson (1965) also found a significant correlation with the Taylor MAS and that the subscales of FSS-III correlated highly. Finally, it should be noted that Manosevitz and Lanyon (1965) used a *modified* version of FSS-III (increasing the number of items and providing five alternative responses for each item). Again, the correlation with the Taylor MAS was significant.

In summary, the present position is that the most extensive standardization data are available for FSS-II. It is certain that all three adult versions would intercorrelate very highly, but it would, nevertheless, be a pity if the three different versions continued to be used by different investigators.

(ii) *Other Indirect Measures.* Several other indirect measures of fear may be briefly mentioned. These have been mostly developed by Lanyon and Manosevitz (1966) and include task-oriented check lists (TC); general check lists (GC); and, of course, interviews (IV). Walk (1956) developed a simple 0–100 rating scale of fear, which has subsequently been given the exotic title of a *Fear Thermometer* and has been used in several recent studies.

As was pointed out earlier, all of these indirect measures are substitutes for the direct measurement of fear in a real-life situation. As we have seen, Geer (1965) validated his questionnaire results against real-life performance and, indeed, Walk's Fear Thermometer was developed in a very real fear situation, the subjects rating their degree of fear just prior to taking part in a parachute jump. There is, of course, a very real problem as to the relationship between verbal reports of fear in a given situation and other measures (behavioral and physiological). This problem will be considered later on.

(b) DEPENDENT MEASURES. Most of these have already been mentioned in the preceding section. They may be divided into the use of *objective* and *subjective* measures of fear.

(i) *The Use of Objective Measures of Fear.* Here we may measure either the subject's *behavior* in relation to the feared object or we may take *physiological* measures. As we shall see later in relation to the evaluation of the effects of treatment, it is surprising how little use has been made of objective measures of the subject's behavior in vivo. As an example of direct behavioral measurement, however, the technique used by Lang and Lazovik (1963) may be quoted:

"A direct estimate of S's avoidance behavior was obtained by confronting him with the phobic object. S was informed that a non-poisonous snake was confined in a glass case in a nearby laboratory. He was persuaded to enter the room and describe his reactions. The snake was confined at a point fifteen feet from the entrance to the room. On entering the room with S, E walked to the case and removed a wire grill that covered the top. S was assured that the snake was harmless. E then requested that S come over and look down at the snake as he was doing. If S refused, he was asked to come as close as he felt he could and the distance was recorded. If S was able to come all the way to the case, he was asked to touch the animal (a five-foot black snake) after he had seen the experimenter do this. If S succeeded in this, the experimenter picked up the snake and invited S to hold it" (Lang and Lazovik, 1963, pp. 520–521).

Geer (1965) has further objectified Lang and Lazovik's technique by measuring the latency of approach, distance from the feared object at which S stopped, and so on. The advantages of using such readily quantifiable real-life measures of fear will be obvious.

The use of physiological indices of fear, such as GSR, has not so far been very common, but an example may be found in the study by Geer (1966).

(ii) *The Use of Subjective Measures of Fear.* Here we include the responses to questionnaires, self-ratings of fear, and so on.

2. Measurement of Phobias in Psychiatric Patients

Very little may be added here, since, in general, very similar methods have been used to measure the existence and strength of phobias in psychiatric patients, but in a less systematic way. Three studies of special interest may be mentioned. Dixon, de Monchaux, and Sandler (1957) administered an inventory of 26 phobic items[2] to 250 unselected psychiatric patients. The items are shown in Table 7.1. Lazarus (1961) directly tested the strength of a phobia by requiring the patient to perform the feared activity to the best of his ability (an acrophobic patient, for example, would be required to climb a fire-escape; a claustrophobic patient would be required to remain in a small cubicle whose size was gradually reduced by moveable screens). Hoenig and Reed (1966) measured physiological concomitants of exposure to the feared objects or situations.

TABLE 7.1.   *Phobic Items Used by Dixon, de Monchaux, and Sandler*

1. I have an intense dislike of snakes
2. I am rather afraid of water
3. The thought of a surgical operation would terrify me
4. I am very uneasy when alone in a large open space
5. I am afraid of the dark
6. I worry about getting accidentally hurt
7. I sometimes have the fear of finding myself in a small enclosed space
8. I am very nervous of knives
9. I am nervous when I am left alone
10. I feel uneasy when I am in a crowded space
11. I sometimes fear that I might drown
12. I hate dirt or dirty things
13. It generally makes me uneasy to cross a bridge or a main street
14. There is some situation or thing of which I am particularly frightened
15. I sometimes worry in case I might be involved in a street accident
16. I worry about the prospect of having to bear pain
17. I am frightened of mice or spiders
18. I dislike and distrust dogs
19. I dislike having my hair cut
20. For some reason I am very frightened of insects
21. Hospitals make me very nervous
22. I am very afraid of going to the dentist
23. I feel nervous when I have to go on a train journey
24. There are certain things I cannot bear to touch
25. I am rather frightened of cats
26. I worry about picking up germs or dirt from door handles

Source: Dixon, de Monchaux, and Sandler, 1957, p. 36.

3. The Classification of Fears

Jersild and Holmes (1935b) distinguished between real and imaginary fears in children. It should be noted, however, that the distinction refers to fears related to specific objects, situations, or activities as opposed to imaginary fears. The first type of fear is not intended, of course, to include fear in situations which are genuinely dangerous. Wolpe and Lang (1964), in constructing FSS-III, divided fears into a

---

[2] The phobic items were part of an 876-item inventory.

number of categories: animal; social interpersonal; tissue-damage, illness, and death; noises; other classical phobias; and a miscellaneous category. Psychiatric classifications of phobias have listed well over 100 separate types of phobia.

Several factor analyses of the Fear Survey Schedule or similar scales have been carried out recently (Rubin et al, 1968; Scherer and Nakamura, 1968; Wilson and Priest, 1968). While the results are not directly comparable, these analyses all agree that the Schedules cover a limited number of areas. Rubin et al (1968), for example, identified two factors (fear of water and fear of death, illness, or injury) which were common to males and females; and two factors (fear of interpersonal contacts and fear of discrete objects) which were less stable across sex differences, as might be expected.

The question of the degree of specificity of phobias, however, is one which has been relatively neglected, in spite of the fact that considerable theoretical interest awaits its resolution. Using the items and subjects mentioned earlier, Dixon, de Monchaux, and Sandler (1957) carried out a centroid factor analysis which revealed seven factors, of which the first two were interpreted. The first was a general factor, loading positively on all of the items and accounting for 18.42% of the variance. The second factor contrasted two types of phobias—those relating to fears of separation and those relating to fears of injury, hurt, or pain. From this analysis, the authors concluded that monosymptomatic phobias (that is, the existence of a single, relatively uncircumscribed phobia) would be the exception rather than the rule and that most patients would manifest a wide range of phobias. This conclusion is premature, however; it may or may not prove to be correct with respect to psychiatric patients. Even so, of course, it would not preclude the possible importance of monosymptomatic phobias occurring in nonpsychiatric subjects. It will be shown later on in this section that the situation is much more complex than the conclusion of Dixon et al would imply.

4. Incidence of Fears and Phobias

In any definitive sense, the incidence of fears and phobias in normal and psychiatric subjects is unknown, but some sketchy information is available that is gradually increasing in precision, at least in relation to nonpsychiatric subjects.

(a) IN NONPSYCHIATRIC SUBJECTS. Geer (1965), Grossberg and Wilson (1965), Manosevitz and Lanyon (1965), and Scherer and Nakamura (1968) have all provided data relating to the incidence of fears of various kinds and to sex differences in the incidence. In the first three studies, college students were used, so generalization of the results to other samples would be dangerous. The results of Grossberg and Wilson (1965) may be taken as representative of the results obtained with college students. Table 7.2 shows the frequency of occurrence of the ten most disturbing fear items for men and women. Many of these items are also significant sources of fear in the study of Manosevitz and Lanyon (1965), but the overlap with Geer's results is somewhat less. All three studies agree in finding that women report a greater number of intense fears than men.[3] This difference is maintained in relation to specific fears, even when the overall tendency is allowed for. It may be noted that several of the fears shown in Table 7.2 refer to events that have probably never actually been experienced by the subjects (e.g., witnessing surgical operations). The data also indicate the very wide range of expressed fears that will result from an investigation of this kind.

(b) IN PSYCHIATRIC PATIENTS. Unfortunately, Dixon et al (1957) did not provide an analysis of the incidence of phobias in their relatively large sample of patients. A distinction must be made, of course, between the incidence of *phobic patients* in a psychiatric sample and the variety and intensity of *phobias* in a given sample. Two studies have reported on the incidence of phobic patients. Terhune (1949) found an incidence of 2.5% in 3100 cases seen, while Errera and Coleman (1963) found an incidence of 2.8% in a four-year sample of psychiatric patients. In view of the higher incidence of fears in normal women than in men, it is worth noting that Terhune (1949) reported that the phobic syndrome was twice as frequent in women as compared with men. It is very likely, of course, that the true incidence of quite severe phobias, which do not result in hospitalization, is very much higher.

---

[3] But Wilson (1967) has provided evidence that females may be more willing to report certain fears than males, suggesting the importance of "social desirability" in assessing incidence.

TABLE 7.2.   *The Ten Most Disturbing Fear Survey Schedule Items and Their Frequency of Occurrence*

	Men (n = 203)			Women (n = 302)	
Item	Frequency	Percent of group	Item	Frequency	Percent of group
Failure	51	25.1	Failure	104	34.4
One person bullying another	34	16.7	Dead people	85	28.1
Looking foolish	32	15.8	Feeling rejected by others	78	25.8
Dead people	28	13.8	Speaking in public	70	23.2
Speaking in public	28	13.8	Parting from friends	66	21.8
Feeling rejected by others	27	13.3	Prospect of a surgical operation	66	21.8
Prospect of a surgical operation	26	12.8	Feeling disapproved of	60	19.9
Feeling disapproved of	21	10.3	One person bullying another	59	19.5
Making mistakes	20	9.8	Dead animals	56	18.5
Witnessing surgical operations	16	7.9	Witnessing surgical operations	56	18.5

Source: Grossberg and Wilson, 1965.

II. GENESIS AND MAINTENANCE OF FEARS AND PHOBIAS

We have reviewed in an earlier chapter the empirical evidence relating to fear as an acquired drive and its mediation of skeletal drive-reducing responses which remove the conditioned fear stimulus. In this section, we shall concern ourselves with two questions only: first, is there evidence that fears and phobias can be generated in human subjects under controlled laboratory conditions; second, is there convincing evidence that some phobias have been acquired under traumatic learning conditions?

1. LABORATORY STUDIES OF THE ACQUISITION OF FEARS IN HUMANS

The most famous demonstration of the acquisition of a fear under controlled laboratory conditions is, of course, the case of Albert and the white rat reported by Watson and Rayner (1920). Even at this early stage, Watson and Rayner were able to formulate the four basic questions in relation to this kind of research: Can conditioned fear be established? Will the

fear generalize to other objects? Will the fear diminish spontaneously with time? How can the induced fear be removed experimentally? Watson and Rayner tackled the first three of these questions. With respect to the establishment of conditioned fear, they first showed that the CS (a white rat) did not produce spontaneous fear. The rat was then paired with a loud noise (US)[4] and seven joint stimulations produced a marked fear response to the sight of the rat, a fear which generalized to similar animals (rabbit and dog) and to objects with certain common characteristics (fur). Furthermore, the fear response persisted over a period of one month, with slightly lessened intensity. The child was described as a very stolid and passive child, in no way normally anxious or easily upset. Watson and Rayner did not actually attempt to remove the conditioned fear, since the child unexpectedly left the hospital. As we shall see later, however, they suggested most of the experimental means which were to be used in the treatment of phobias.

Several later studies obtained results that appeared to support Watson and Rayner's analysis. Thus, Moss (1924) found a conditioned

---

[4] A loud noise was one of the principal situations found by Watson and Morgan (1917) to call out a fear response.

aversion reaction was produced to the click of a telegraph key (CS) after it had been paired with the taste of vinegar (US), the aversive qualities of the latter being enhanced by prior presentation of very sweet orange juice. Although unable to replicate this conditioning with a second child (for whom vinegar did not appear to be an aversive stimulus), he did obtain similar conditioning with this second child by the use of electric shock, obtaining an escape response to the click of the telegraph key. Similarly Jones (1931) obtained conditioning, extinction, reestablishment of conditioning, generalization, and discrimination of emotional responses to stimuli associated with mild shock in a stable 15-month-old child.[5]

These promising beginnings were not, however, to be followed up intensively, the reason probably being the publication shortly after these studies of two apparently negative findings. In the first of these (English, 1929), the observations were uncontrolled and anecdotal. The second study by Bregman (1934), however, deserves careful examination, both because of its virtues as a careful experimental study and for its fatal flaw, which renders it invalid as a negative finding for the conditioning of fear.

Bregman made use of 15 infants aged 8–16 months. She used as US both stimuli which would arouse fear (an electric bell placed immediately behind the child) and pleasure (a small red celluloid rattle and a melody of 10 sec duration). As originally neutral stimuli (CS), she associated with the aversive US a wooden rectangular block and a wooden triangle; and with the pleasant US a rectangular flat of wood, painted gold, a grey wooden ring, and a yellow cloth curtain. She devised a very careful training and test program, classified and scaled the responses into three categories (negative, positive, and indifferent), and presented evidence convincingly showing that the aversive stimulus did produce mainly negative responses which persisted throughout the experiment (though with decreasing intensity) while the positive stimuli produced more positive responses initially than the neutral stimuli with which they were paired. Since she also found that, following training, there was no consistent tendency for aversive or positive responses to become attached to the appropriate formerly neutral objects, it might well appear that cogent evidence was available to justify her conclusion that "changes in emotional behavior, in attitude and interest, are not as a general rule, at least, readily brought about by joint stimulation in early life, and that conditioning *per se* cannot be accepted as the cover all (sic) explanation of the emotional modifications which take place during that period" (Bregman, 1934, p. 196).

There can be no doubt that this is an important and, in many ways, admirable experiment. A careful examination of the paper, however, reveals that a number of serious objections can be raised against it as an adequate test of Watson's hypothesis. First, and most important, the introduction of both positive and negative unconditioned stimuli, while admirable in principle as a necessary control, introduced a degree of complexity which was almost certainly undesirable. For, in both training and test sessions, the aversive and positive US were presented in sequence. Now since the CS paired with the two types of US were very similar (see above), *the task was in effect made an exceedingly difficult discrimination one*.[6] Thus, the child was required to attach an aversive response to a rectangular wooden block while almost simultaneously attaching a positive response to a rectangular flat wooden block and, similarly, it had to discriminate between the other CS pairs. It is extremely doubtful whether children of this age would, in fact, be capable of making such discriminations.[7] Furthermore, since it is very likely that the unconditioned aversive responses were stronger than the unconditioned positive responses, a good deal of generalization and failure of discrimination would be certain to take place. Indeed, Bregman herself states that "the negative reaction which followed S[8] in the first period tended to persist as a generalized response throughout the balance of the period and to appear again in subsequent experimental periods" (Bregman, 1934, p. 193).

Again, in examining the status of the rattle as a positive US, Bregman states quite unequivocally that, during the pretraining period, the rattle was presented immediately following

---

[5] The famous study of Peter by Mary Cover Jones (1924b) is not included here as Peter's fear of white rats had not been experimentally produced but had developed in unknown circumstances.

[6] It will be recalled that the subjects of this experiment were aged 8–16 months!

[7] The testing schedule (carefully described in detail by Bregman, 1934, pp. 173–175) was extremely complex.

[8] The electric bell stimulus.

two successive presentations of the bell and that in 55/60 such instances *the child was crying.* The effect of this would obviously be to attach some degree of negative reaction to the supposedly positive US.

We may conclude, therefore, that the major reason for the negative results obtained by Bregman can probably be accounted for by postulating that she had made the task too difficult for the child. A better approach would have been to have kept the positive and negative conditioning procedures quite separate and to have more clearly differentiated the objects to which a positive or negative response was to be attached. Bregman's study cannot be regarded as providing any evidence against the hypothesis put forward by Watson.

It is unfortunate in the extreme that Bregman's study should have virtually brought to a halt the promising leads initiated by Watson and others. This field of research has remained virtually moribund since the early experiments. Recently, Galibert (1963) has put forward a detailed *theoretical* account (based on a case history of the development of a phobia) of the acquisition of phobias based on a conditioning model, but such efforts are few and far between.

2. ACQUISITION OF FEARS AND PHOBIAS IN REAL LIFE

The laboratory work just described was based on the assumption that the fears and phobias complained of by normal subjects and by psychiatric patients were generated in essentially the same way, that is, by the attachment of intense fear responses to specific neutral stimuli present at the moment an unconditioned fear-producing situation or object was experienced. While is it certainly true that by no means all fears and phobias can be accounted for in this dramatic way, there is equally no doubt now that *some* phobias may reasonably be supposed to have arisen in traumatic situations. The inference is indirect, of course, but the weight of evidence is by now overwhelming. From a large number of clear-cut reports of precipitating traumatic experiences, reference may be made to extremely frightening experiences (followed by the appropriate phobia) with dogs (Lazarus and Rachman, 1957; Friedman, 1966b; Kraft and Burnfield, 1967); cats (Freeman and Kendrick, 1960); birds (Clark, 1963c); and traffic accidents (Wolpe, 1962; Kraft and Al-Issa, 1965; Kraft and Burnfield, 1967; Kushner, 1965). It is interesting to note, in this connection, that Freud's notorious Little Hans apparently underwent at least four traumatic experiences with horses while developing his phobia (Freud, 1955; Wolpe and Rachman, 1960).

III. BEHAVIOR THERAPY APPLIED TO FEARS AND PHOBIAS

1. METHODS OF TREATMENT

The most preferred method for the treatment of fears and phobias has, of course, been the use of systematic desensitization, following the procedures advocated by Wolpe (1961a) and described in detail in an earlier chapter: training in relaxation, the construction of anxiety hierarchies, and the application of desensitization by working through the hierarchies systematically and with the usual precautions. However, it will be remembered that the same alternative arises here as in the case of the measurement of the strength of a phobia. That is, the desensitization procedure may be carried out in the absence of the real objects of fear by imagining the objects visually (SD-I); or it can be carried out by direct exposure (on a generalization gradient) to real objects which approximate successively the object producing the greatest amount of fear. Wolpe has argued generally that the reduction in anxiety generated by SD(I) will generalize to real situations almost completely. If this is really so, then clearly SD(I) would probably be more economical than SD(R). However, no real evidence has ever been presented to support this position and the SD(R) technique has been used increasingly in recent years.

We will confine our attention here to a consideration of some special techniques that vary the standard procedures recommended by Wolpe. Of course, it should be recognized that reciprocal inhibition techniques are quite old but a glance at some of the earlier reports show quite clearly the relative sophistication of Wolpe's approach. Thus, McLaughlin and Millar (1941) and Schwartz (1945) presented visual-auditory battle stimuli in attempts to decondition battle fears. While Schwartz did use a graded presentation (". . . the more innocuous sound films are introduced first"), the techniques were extremely crude. Even earlier, Jones (1924a) used repeated presentation of the feared object at short or long intervals of time, but the presentation was not graded.

Several studies have utilized special responses that *actively* inhibit the anxiety responses. A classic example of this is the use of the eating response in the presence (initially at a respectful distance!) of the feared stimulus (Watson and Rayner, 1920; Jones, 1924a; Lazarus, 1959; Cautela, 1965). As has often been pointed out, the danger (more apparent than real as no instance of it happening has been reported) here is that the anxiety may become attached to the food. It may be noted that the eating activity is completely unrelated to any responses of a positive kind that could in principle be made toward the feared object, and this applies also to Lazarus' recent use of forceful muscular activity (by comparison with the more usual relaxation response utilized) to counteract anxiety. Holmes (1936), however, was very critical of any techniques for combatting fear which involved *passivity* on the part of the subject. She insisted that the subject must be helped to manipulate the feared object directly and proposed to achieve this essentially by an active desensitization procedure; in this case, the experimenter and the subject would, for example, approach the feared object together.

Mention may also briefly be made here of the concomitant use of drugs (to reduce anxiety) with SD-I (Lazarus, 1959; Galibert, 1960; Friedman, 1966a, 1966b); the use of aversion-relief therapy in a number of different variations (Wolpe, 1958; Lazarus, 1959; Thorpe et al, 1964); and of group SD-I (Lazarus, 1961). Finally, we may mention the unsuccessful approaches to the treatment of fears and phobias. Of seven methods used by Jones (1924a), five were found to be unsuccessful—repeated representation of feared object at short or long intervals, verbal talk about the feared object, the use of social ridicule, and distraction. Jones found two methods to produce a high probability of success. The first she described as *"direct conditioning"* in which the feared object is presented in the presence of a positive object (e.g., food). The second technique was described as *social imitation* in which an incompatible motive is evoked to overcome fear. Thus, if the "social drive" is evoked by having other children approach the feared object, the child who fears the object may be driven to approach it also. The presence of the other children will reduce the anxiety level of the frightened child and allow positive responses to be made.

It may be noted also that most of the techniques described here have been used by parents, although under relatively uncontrolled conditions (Jersild and Holmes, 1935b).

2. Early Studies

It is a historical fact that most of the techniques now employed under the rubric of behavior therapy were applied in one form or another over 40 years ago, almost entirely in attempts to treat children's fears. Watson and Rayner (1920), in their famous study of "Little Albert," did not actually get round to attempting to remove the fear they had produced in the child, but they did suggest four ways in which the conditioned fear response *might* be eliminated. The first of these involved the repeated presentation of the feared object, in the expectation that this procedure might lead to habituation. The remaining three techniques they suggested all involved the technique of reciprocal inhibition, namely, stimulation of erogenous zones while showing the feared object, feeding while showing the feared object, and building up constructive activities around the feared object by, for example, manipulation of it with the hands (obviously, all of these methods, but particularly the last, would also have required desensitization procedures). This and subsequent studies along the same lines (Jones, 1924a; 1924b; Jones, 1931; Jersild and Holmes, 1935b; Holmes, 1936) were all essentially laboratory studies and will be considered later. An early application of desensitization procedures with adult phobics is to be found in a study of Terhune (1949). The second phase of his treatment involved what he called the reconditioning of specific fears. That Terhune's technique involved a form of SD(R) is made clear by the following quotation:

"3. The patient must cooperate in specific undertakings that involve placing himself in situations of which he is afraid. For example, after he has several times walked a country road with others, he takes this walk alone. To divert his attention from himself and his fears, he is given an objective project—he makes a rough but fairly accurate map of the road he travels, indicating houses, lakes and side roads. When he has successfully accomplished this task, his confidence is greatly increased. He is then assisted to take a short train trip alone, with 'doctor's orders' to make certain definite purchases while in town, these purchases involving considerable planning en route. Next he is to take an elderly relative or friend to church. Then he is instructed to go to a moving picture, to keep notes and to bring the doctor a written resume of the plot, with names and descriptions of the actors and actresses. Later, he makes a trip to the city, perhaps to a famous restaurant for an unusually good luncheon, and then to an amusing matinee" (Terhune, 1949, p. 170).

For reasons which will become apparent later, we shall divide consideration of behavior therapy with fears and phobias into two parts, dealing with monosymptomatic and polysymptomatic phobias separately. At this stage, attention will also be confined to what are essentially case studies.

3. BEHAVIOR THERAPY OF MONOSYMPTOMATIC FEARS AND PHOBIAS

Table 7.3 presents a representative sample of single case studies of the application of behavior therapy techniques to relatively circumscribed fears and phobias. No attempt will be made to assess the overall degree of success claimed, though in most studies it was, in fact, claimed either that the phobia disappeared completely or that it was very much lessened in intensity. Several points about the information contained in the table are, however, worthy of note.

(i) A very wide range of specific phobias has been treated by behavior therapy techniques, ranging from traffic phobias through animal phobias to intense fear of earthworms. Some of the phobias may seem trivial or even amusing; in fact, however, they were almost all of crippling severity and severely inconvenienced the patient socially. Thus, the patient with a phobia for earthworms was effectively and severely hindered from moving about on grass or other areas where earthworms might be found.

(ii) It will be noticed particularly that SD(I) has been used much more often than SD(R), even though there is no evidence to suggest that SD(I) is superior in its effects to SD(R).

(iii) Nearly all of the studies were essentially nonexperimental in nature. That is, there was a strong tendency to apply a standard technique (almost always systematic desensitization of the imaginal or real variety) and then assess any change in the patient's phobic state.

(iv) One of the most striking features of the majority of these studies is their failure to carry out pre- and posttreatment real-life tests for the

strength (before treatment) and change in strength (after treatment) of the phobia, in spite of the fact that, in many instances, direct testing would have been relatively simple and inexpensive. Thus, Murphy (1964) apparently relied entirely on the patient's verbal report concerning the diminution in strength of his fear of earthworms, while neither Kraft and Al-Issa (1965a) nor Kushner (1965) directly tested the strength of the patients' alleged traffic phobias. In such situations, the failure to reality-test is quite inexcusable.

(v) It will be apparent from inspection of the table that, while in many instances the phobia was of long standing, the length of follow-up was often very unsatisfactory. Freeman and Kendrick (1960) not only reality-tested their cat-phobic patient, but reported briefly and favorably on her status three years later. The majority of the follow-up reports, however, not only generally involved indirect assessment of the strength of the phobia but covered a most unsatisfactory short period.

In spite of these criticisms, a careful study of the evidence in these case studies does suggest very strongly that severe, long-lasting monosymptomatic phobias can be significantly ameliorated by the application of systematic desensitization procedures, whether the method of treatment involves imaginal visualization or direct approach to the feared object. Where the assessment and follow-up is carefully carried out, long-term amelioration may be achieved.

4. BEHAVIOR THERAPY OF POLYSYMPTOMATIC FEARS AND PHOBIAS

Only one study will be mentioned here, but it provides a striking contrast with the results reported above. Meyer and Gelder (1963) gave prolonged (average of 80 hours per case) SD-R to five very severe cases of phobic symptoms, all of them polysymptomatic. They achieved only a very limited success. In particular, they found that, where they did succeed in ameliorating a particular phobic symptom, little, if any, generalization occurred to others. This study indicates clearly that it would be rash indeed to conclude optimistically from the study of monosymptomatic phobias that the same techniques will be equally successful with polysymptomatic phobias.

Nevertheless, it remains true that in this study, as well as in the monosymptomatic case studies considered earlier, the basic experimental approach has been lost sight of and the treat-

TABLE 7.3. *Studies of Real-Life Monosymptomatic Phobias Treated by Behavior Therapy*

Source	Sex	Age	Phobia	Duration	Method of Treatment	Follow-up Period	Method of Assessment of Results of Treatment
Lazarus and Rachman (1957)	M F	14 29	Ambulances/hospitals Dogs	4 years 4 years	SD(I) SD(I)	3 months 1 year	Subject report Subject report
Meyer (1957)	F M	48 42	Going out alone Enclosed spaces	4 years 20 years	SD(R) SD(R) plus Anxiety/relief Conditioning with use of conditioning drug	5 months 4 months	Real-life test by E Real-life test by E
Rachman (1959)	F	24	Injections Insertion of sanitary pads	18 years 1½ years	SD(I) SD(I)	3 months 3 months	Real injections Subject report
Freeman and Kendrick (1960)	F	37	Cats	30 years	SD(R)	3 years	Real-life test by E
Walton (1960b)	M	22	"Sexual" material	Not stated	SD(R)	1 year	Subject report
Bentler 1962)	F	1	Bathwater	< 1 month	SD(R)	1½ years	Real-life test by E
Cowden and Ford (1962)	M	27	Talking to people	Not stated	SD(I)	Not stated	Observation by E
Wolpe (1962)	F	39	Car and traffic	2 years	SD(I)	1½ years	Real-life test by E
Ashem (1963)	M	27	Atomic disaster	> 5 years	SD(I)	3 months	Subject/wife reports
Clark (1963a)	F	31	Birds/feathers	25 years	SD(R)	Not stated	Real-life test by E and GSR change
Clark (1963b)	F	30	Going out	Not stated	SD(R)	Not stated	Subject and husband report
Galibert (1963)	M	37	Travel (alone or accompanied)	10 years	Subnarcosis	4 years	Subject report
Walton and Mather (1963a)	M M	34 40	Social situations Speech	2 years Many yrs.	SD(R) SD(I)	1 year 6 months	Subject report Subject report
Geer (1964)	F	17	Lice hair-infection	1½ years	SD(I)	3 months	Subject report
Murphy (1964)	F	19	Earthworms	11 years	SD(R)	12 months	Subject report
Thorpe et al (1964)	M	43	Clouds Tunnels Lifts	10 months 4 years 10 years	Aversion-relief in all cases	Incomplete	Subject report (incomplete)
Brough et al (1965)	F	39	Wasps	5 years	SD(I)	1 year	Subject report
Cautela (1965)	M	33	Return to work	2 years	SD(I) + Watson method	6 months	Subject report
Kraft and Al-Issa (1965a)	M	37	Traffic phobia	7 years	SD(I)	6 months	Subject report
Kraft and Al-Issa (1965b)	F	24	Hot objects	19 years	SD(I)	1 year	Real-life test
Kushner (1965)	M	17	Traffic phobia	1 month	SD(I)	3 months	Subject report
Perinpanayagam (1965)	F	65	Being left alone	59 years	SD(I)	Not stated	Subject and relative report
Wolpin and Pearsall (1965)	F	40	Snakes	Not stated	SD(I)	3 weeks	Real-life test by E Pre- and posttreatment
Friedman (1966b)	M	66	Dogs	8 months	SD(I) + drug to relax	6 months	Subject and relative report
Kraft (1967)	F	30	Going out	6 years	SD(I) + drug to relax	9 months	Subject report
Kraft and Burnfield (1967)	M F	43 26	Driving bus Dogs	< 1 year 21 years	SD(I) + SD(R) SD(I) + SD(R)	3 months 6 months	Real-life tests Real-life tests

ment carried out largely on an *ad hoc* basis and under the assumption that standard procedures exist. In the absence of systematically controlled experiments on *individuals*, it becomes important to consider carefully laboratory-based *group* studies of the modification of fears and phobias, particularly to see if the standard format for systematic desensitization therapy is tenable. To these studies we now turn.

5. LABORATORY STUDIES OF THE MODIFICATION OF FEARS AND PHOBIAS

Some recent very careful laboratory work has elucidated some of the crucial variables involved in the diminution of fears and phobias by behavior therapy techniques, particularly the use of SD-I.

First, Lazovik and Lang (1960) were able to produce a significant reduction in snake phobia under laboratory controlled conditions in four subjects with an intense fear of snakes. They used a laboratory analogue of Wolpe's SD-I procedure, involving hierarchy building of feared snake situations; training in muscle relaxation and hypnosis; and systematic desensitization, using visualized scenes and hypnotically-produced relaxation. They then turned their attention to a more careful investigation of the relative significance of the procedures outlined above (Lang and Lazovik, 1963). The experimental design they utilized is shown in Table 7.4. The experimental groups were both given training (which involved the construction of phobic hierarchies, training in relaxation, and training in visualization under hypnosis) and systematic desensitization. The first experimental group was given three real-life tests of the intensity of the snake phobia; the first of these tests was omitted for the second experimental group. The control groups were used to test for the effect of repeated exposure to the feared stimulus. The results indicated clearly that training in hierarchy construction, relaxation, and hypnotic visualization per se did not affect the strength of the phobia (as shown by

comparing test 1 with test 2); nor did repeated exposure to the feared stimulus (tests 1, 2, and 3 comparisons in the control groups). Desensitization therapy, however, did produce a reduction in fear, the experimental groups showing a significant change from test 2 to test 3, while the control groups did not. These gains were maintained over a six-month follow-up, with no evidence of symptom substitution. In a further study, Lang et al (1965) studied 44 subjects (including those from the previous studies) who were divided into three groups. The two experimental groups were alike in having been given training in relaxation, hierarchy building, and hypnosis. The experimental group, however, was additionally given SD-I, whereas the "pseudo-therapy" group was additionally given discussion of fears in general (but no desensitization program). An untreated control group was also used. Utilizing again pre- and postreal life tests, it was found that the experimental (desensitization) group showed significantly more change (in a positive direction) than the control or pseudotherapy groups, which did not differ from each other. Within the SD-I group, it was found that better results were obtained with subjects completing more than 15 hierarchy items, whereas those subjects completing less than 15 hierarchy items did not differ from the controls.

From these studies, Lang and Lazovik concluded that the results of systematic desensitization therapy could not be accounted for in terms of general therapeutic effects of interacting with or establishing a relationship with the therapist. They also ruled out the possibility of suggestion as a significant variable and argued that hypnosis, relaxation, and hierarchy building are not *sufficient* causes of the changes produced by SD(I), though they might be *necessary* concomitants of change. This conclusion has received some support from the work of Wolpin and Raines (1966) who found that relaxation was not a necessary part of the desensitization procedure.[9]

TABLE 7.4.   *Design of Experiment of Lang and Lazovik (1963)*

Group	Experimental Procedures				
E1	Test 1	Training	Test 2	Desensitization	Test 3
E2	—	Training	Test 2	Desensitization	Test 3
C1	Test 1	—	Test 2	—	Test 3
C2	—	—	Test 2	—	Test 3

[9] See Chapter 4 for a fuller discussion of this problem.

6. Comparative and Control Studies of Treatment

We shall consider here the results of psychotherapy or no treatment; the results of behavior therapy; and the results obtained in a number of comparative studies.

(a) RESULTS OF PSYCHOTHERAPY OR NO TREATMENT. Very little quantitative material is available concerning the results of psychotherapy with phobic states and, in relation to what information is available, the therapy given was usually of such a transitory nature as to render the follow-up assessment virtually one relating to the effects of no treatment. Nevertheless, the meagre results do support the hypothesis that monosymptomatic phobias are more likely to yield to treatment than polysymptomatic phobias. Friedman (1950) reported on the effects of short-term therapy with 50 cases of travel phobia (excluding sea and air travel phobias) and found 23 completely recovered, 15 improved, and 12 unimproved. On the other hand, Errera and Coleman (1963) found that 18/19 phobics followed up by personal interview 22–24 years after treatment were essentially unchanged. Only minimal treatment had been given. A similar pessimistic result was reported by Kringlen (1965), with a follow-up at a mean interval of 30 years from the time of onset. Kringlen's group is also virtually an untreated control group as the mean treatment duration was only 2 months.[10] Little and James (1964) have recently reported the successful ether abreaction of a battle phobia 18 years after its onset, using the techniques described by Shorvon and Sargant (1947). The conclusion from this work, unsatisfactory though most of it is, seems to be that polysymptomatic phobias are extremely resistant to psychotherapy.[11]

(b) OVERALL RESULTS OF BEHAVIOR THERAPY. We have already seen that behavior therapy appears to have good prospects of success with monosymptomatic phobias, particularly if these occur in otherwise normal people; but that much more difficulty is experienced in relation to polysymptomatic phobias. All of these studies were, however, carried out as individual case studies. Here we shall report the results of the accumulation of results on much larger numbers of subjects. Wolpe (1958) consolidated the results of

behavior therapy with three series of patients (Wolpe, 1952, 1954, 1958). Included in the 210 patients were 135 anxiety states (including phobics). The improvement rate for phobic patients was not separated out from the other subcategories. Wolpe (1958) claimed that roughly 90% of the total group ($n = 210$) fell into the categories of "apparently cured" or "much improved" after an average time in therapy of 10 months, and it may be presumed that the figure would not be significantly different for the 135 anxiety states or the phobic subgroup. Wolpe also obtained follow-up data 2–7 years after cessation of treatment on 45 of the "apparently cured" or "much improved" patients and claimed that all but one had maintained or improved on their status at the end of treatment. Apart, however, from his own ratings of the patients, the only objective evidence Wolpe produced for the effectiveness of his methods was a very significant drop in Willoughby questionnaire score at the end of treatment and the fact that the drop was significantly greater for the "apparently cured" than for the "much improved group." No information is given concerning methods of determining the strength of the phobia in a real-life situation as opposed to the subject's verbal report.

In a later study, Wolpe (1961) used SD-I with 39 cases and reported that, of 68 phobic and anxiety responses shown by the patients, 45 were eliminated and 17 markedly reduced. With a 6-month to 4-year follow-up on 20 successfully treated cases, no relapses or symptom substitutions were apparent. In this paper, Wolpe reports that he did not regularly check the outcome by real-life observation, but that wherever he did, the patient's verbal report was invariably confirmed. Such a casual statement can, however, scarcely be considered an acceptable substitute for properly evaluated and controlled outcome observations.

Two studies, by Lazarus (1959) and Lazarus and Abramovitz (1962), report striking success with children and adolescents. Lazarus (1959) used four variants of reciprocal inhibition (feeding responses, relaxation, drug-induced relaxation, and a special form of aversion-relief therapy) with 18 children aged $3\frac{1}{2}$–12 years. With a follow-up period varying from 6 months to $2\frac{1}{2}$ years, he claimed that all of the

---

[10] Kringlen was reporting on "obsessional" cases, but he classified patients with phobias under this category.

[11] Sim and Houghton (1966) have reported much more successful results, using acetylcholine chloride combined with nonspecific therapy.

children recovered or were much improved. Lazarus and Abramovitz (1962) used the emotive imagery technique with 9 children aged 7–14 years and claimed that 7 recovered with a mean of 3.3 sessions. In both these studies, illustrative case histories are given, but the assessment of the results is inadequately described in relation to the groups as a whole. The procedure for assessing results of the treatment seems to have been the same as that of Wolpe in his assessments.

Three other studies have also reported overall results of the treatment of phobias by behavior therapy. Friedman (1966a) used SD-I with 25 cases of "phobic anxiety." Relaxation was induced by intravenous administration of barbiturate methohexitone sodium in 2.5% solution. All cases were said to be free of symptoms at the end of treatment. However, the sample is very inadequately described, the criteria of "symptom-free" status are not stated, and there was no control for possible effects of administration of the drug alone. In a subsequent study, Friedman and Silverstone (1967) used a similar technique with 20 phobic patients whose mean symptom duration was 4–7 years. At the end of treatment, all of the patients were "much improved" and five were "completely symptom-free." On an average follow-up of $10\frac{1}{2}$ months, the improvement (patient report) was maintained in 83% of the patients. Hain et al (1966) reported on the results of SD-I with 27 patients, mostly with phobias. This study did attempt to establish objective indices of change after treatment. Ratings before and after therapy were made on a symptom severity scale, a scale of general improvement, and a functional status scale by the therapists (a contaminated measure, of course) and by one independent worker using the case summaries (since the case summaries were undoubtedly written by the therapists, this measure would also be in doubt). The cases treated were fairly severe, with a mean symptom duration of nearly 9 years. The results indicated that 70% showed "improvement" on the General Improvement Scale; 78% showed "improvement" on the Symptom Improvement Scale; and there was little change on the Functional Status Scale (which measured such variables as sexual adjustment). However, no correlation was found between any of these indices and number of therapy sessions, frequency of therapy, or duration of treatment. More than half of the patients were followed up at an average of 12 months. Of those showing improvement at the end of treatment, 20% were even more improved, while 47% had maintained their gains. There was no evidence of symptom substitution. It is interesting to note that in two cases where SD-I produced no change in symptoms, a switch to SD-R apparently led to rapid success. These results of Hain et al are, however, hopelessly confounded, since the authors stress the fact that various other forms of therapy were used at the same time as SD-I or SD-R. While other factors are undoubtedly at work in most studies using SD-I and SD-R, it is hardly helpful to introduce these deliberately in what purports to be an experimental study of the effects of SD-I.

A study by Weinberg and Zaslove (1963) is one of the few to report difficulties experienced with desensitization therapy of monosymptomatic phobias. Among the factors were: direct resistance caused by fluctuations of the hypnotic state and imaginal stimuli; indirect resistance caused by the failure of the subject to practice on his own, follow instructions, and so on; and resistance related to factors such as intrafamily quarrels, doubtful motivation for volunteering for the experiment, and so on. In spite of these unfavorable factors, it was reported that all three subjects showed some improvement. Two other points are also relevant: all three subjects were highly extraverted, and the experimenter was inexperienced.

Mention should also be made of the study by Solyom and Miller (1967) who used a modified form of aversion-relief therapy involving the pairing of relief produced by shock termination with presentation of anxiety-evoking verbal stimuli. The results with eight phobic patients were not particularly clear cut or encouraging, in spite of the rather optimistic conclusions of Solyom and Miller.

(c) COMPARATIVE STUDIES OF BEHAVIOR THERAPY AND OTHER TECHNIQUES. The above studies can scarcely be said to throw any serious light on the efficacy of behavior therapy in relation to the use of standard techniques such as SD-I by comparison with more traditional approaches. A recent series of studies does, however, more nearly provide the possibility of direct comparison of different approaches. It should be reiterated at this point that, at a later stage of this book, the essential irrelevance of the studies to be reviewed to the question of the validity of behavior therapy will be demonstrated. However, at this point, these criticisms will be ignored and the studies taken at their face value.

In the first of these studies, by Marks and Gelder (1965), 20 agoraphobics and 11 other phobic states who had been treated by behavior therapy were carefully matched with similar cases treated by psychotherapy and rated blind on change in phobic symptoms and general improvement at five points in time: on admission; at the end of treatment; and one, three, and 12 months after the end of treatment. The results indicated no difference in outcome for agoraphobic patients (either symptomatic or general). Behavior therapy produced better results at the end of treatment for the other phobias, but this difference had disappeared at the one-year follow-up. Other results included: no differential occurrence of fresh symptoms; the behavior therapy patients had more and longer treatment; no important correlations were found between patient characteristics (age at treatment, symptom duration, and severity) and outcome; and no relationship was found between the success of either treatment and dependency of the patients.

From this "controlled retrospective study" of behavior therapy, as they called it (since the patients' treatments were completed before it was commenced), Gelder and Marks drew pessimistic conclusions. The paper led to a fierce and somewhat acrimonious correspondence, which we shall ignore since subsequent work has rendered the dispute somewhat irrelevant.[12]

This initial study was quickly followed by a "controlled prospective study" (Gelder and Marks, 1966) in which 20 agoraphobic patients (mean duration of symptoms, seven years) were allocated at random to a behavior therapy or psychotherapy group. Behavior therapy consisted of graded retraining (SD-R) and systematic desensitization (SD-I) three times weekly for three-quarters of an hour; psychotherapy consisted of brief reeducative interviews. All of the therapists were psychiatric registrars. Clinical ratings (symptom ratings and social adjustment ratings) were completed by therapists, patients, and a second medical assessor every two weeks during treatment and every three months during follow-up. Various other measures of symptoms and adjustment were also used. The results of this study were disappointing to the authors. 70% of the patients in each group did show improvement

at the end of treatment (on average 23 weeks for the behavior therapy group, 19 weeks for the controls) but phobic symptoms still interfered significantly with social adjustment. Behavior therapy tended to improve work adjustment while psychotherapy tended to improve social adjustment. At a one-year follow-up there was a disturbing tendency for the phobias to increase in strength. There was no evidence of symptom substitution.

Undaunted by these results, Gelder et al (1967) carried out an even more formidable experiment, involving three groups of phobic patients (including both agoraphobic and other phobic patients). The three groups were matched as carefully as possible on age, sex, duration of symptoms, verbal IQ, severity of phobias, and so on. The first group ($n=16$) was treated by SD-I, the second ($n=16$) by group psychotherapy, and the third ($n=10$) by individual psychotherapy. Among the most important features of this study were the very careful specification and description of the dependent variables (symptom change, social adjustment, and interpersonal relations) and the fact that the ratings were carried out at the start, during, and at the end of treatment by the patient, the therapist, and an independent assessor, while a follow-up assessment was made seven and 18 months after the end of treatment by a psychiatric social worker who had no knowledge of which treatment a patient had received, nor of the results of his previous assessments. One of the worst features, on the other hand, was the utilization of five psychiatrists as the behavior therapists, four of them having had no prior experience of carrying out behavior therapy. Gelder et al comforted themselves with the remark that behavior therapy was so simple that no special training or experience in its use was required.

Granted this extraordinary assumption, the results turned out to be rather more clear cut than in the two previous efforts. *During treatment*, the use of desensitization led to a more significant drop in the intensity of the main phobia. This difference tended to become less significant on follow-up, but this appeared to be because of improvement in the psychotherapy groups rather than relapse in the behavior therapy groups. (It should be noted that, this time, the treatment period was shorter

---

[12] See the correspondence by Snaith, Eysenck, Rachman, and Gelder and Marks in *Brit. J. Psychiat.*, 1965, **111**, 1007–1010. It will be shown later that *all*

of the correspondents betrayed fundamental ignorance of the essential nature of behavior therapy.

with behavior therapy than with individual or group therapy.) On *final rating* (at cessation of treatment), 9/16 behavior therapy patients were rated as much improved on phobic symptoms, compared with only 2/16 group and 3/10 individual therapy patients. Similarly, the results for behavior therapy were better than for individual or group psychotherapy at the time of follow-up by the psychiatric social worker. Once again, no evidence of symptom substitution was found. An interesting side-light was the suggestive finding that those subjects whose phobic symptoms lessened under behavior therapy also showed much benefit in other ways, but that this was not found with the improved cases provided with individual or group psychotherapy.

Lazarus (1966) has quite properly criticized the earlier studies by Marks and Gelder, but on grounds which will be discussed later in this book. To summarize these studies, the overall results indicate a slight but consistent superiority of behavior therapy over other methods of treatment. Considering that untrained behavior therapists (with, no doubt, ingrained psychiatric habits to confound their activities) were used in the treatment of severe phobic cases, and that the method of assessing the efficacy of behavior therapy by these group comparisons reflected a basic misunderstanding of behavior therapy, the results achieved with the systematic desensitization technique were remarkable.

7. DISCUSSION

No extended discussion of the results of behavior therapy with fears and phobias is required. Most of the studies provide no convincing evidence whatsoever of the efficacy of behavior therapy since, almost without exception, they reflect the influence of either (a) the uncontrolled case study, or (b) the medical-model paradigm for the assessment of the effects of a particular standard technique. These points will be discussed in detail in a later chapter, but it should be stressed that very few of the studies reviewed above could be said to be *experimental* studies of changes in the behavior of *single subjects* with *clearly-defined disorders* under *controlled conditions*. This is not, of course, to deny the value of these studies on other grounds. The weight of evidence *does* suggest that behavior therapy may be successful

very rapidly with monosymptomatic phobias, but that polysymptomatic phobias will be a much harder nut to crack. They also, of course, provide valuable information on many different techniques and variations of technique.

One other significant study should be mentioned here. Lang et al (1965), in a study already referred to, found that a "pseudo-therapy" group of phobics did not differ in posttreatment status from an untreated control group, whereas a "desensitization" group showed significantly more change (improvement in real-life ability to handle snakes) than either of the other groups. The study is important because of the degree achieved of quantification of the intensity of the fear, thus making group comparisons of this kind more valid.

IV. METHODOLOGICAL PROBLEMS

We shall consider here a number of problems that have arisen in the course of the studies referred to above. Two of these problems are quite important, the other is relatively minor.

1. THE RELATIONSHIP BETWEEN VARIOUS MEASURES OF FEAR

There are three ways in which attempts have been made to measure the strength of fear in relation to a particular situation or object. First, the subject's own *verbal report or rating* of the degree of fear may be taken as an indicator. Second, *physiological changes* in the presence of the feared object may be recorded. Third, the subject's *behavior* in the physical presence of the object may be assessed in ways that have been mentioned earlier. Recent research has demonstrated quite clearly that these measures may not always agree with each other as indicators of the intensity of fear.[13] Lang and Lazovik (1963), for example, reported that measures of fear obtained from the FSS did not necessarily reflect accurately changes in rated fear after exposure to the feared object following treatment. On the other hand, Geer (1965) found that verbal and behavioral indicators of fear correlated highly, and the same author (Geer, 1966) reported that verbal and physiological indicators also correlated significantly. Lanyon and Manosevitz (1966), however, although they found that behavioral

---

[13] See, for example, the comprehensive study by Mandler et al (1961) of the relationships among

verbal and physiological indices of response to threat.

measures of fear correlated positively with verbal reports of several different kinds, also reported that the feared task might be carried out (e.g., approaching a snake) even though the verbal report indicated intense fear. Wolpin and Raines (1966) argued, on the basis of their results, that such a discrepancy might be produced as a result of the development of interpersonal relationships in the experimental situation (e.g., a desire to please the experimenter on the part of the subject). The importance of this problem was highlighted in an important study by Hoenig and Reed (1966). They applied SD-I to four patients with severe monosymptomatic phobias of long duration. The effects of treatment were assessed in the usual way by the patients' verbal reports and reports from relatives. Using these criteria, two of the four patients indicated they had completely recovered from their phobia, one reported substantial improvement, and one slight improvement. Hoenig and Reed, however, also measured the GSR of each patient in three objective situations; the presentation of key words relating to the phobia; the presentation of the actual object of fear to which the patient had been desensitized; and visualization of the object of fear. The description of the results obtained with one patient shows clearly the problem of assessing "improvement":

"Patient 1 made, by conventional clinical criteria, a complete recovery. Each stage in her hierarchy was reached smoothly and efficiently. At the end of her course of therapy she not only reported that she had lost all fear of cats, but showed herself capable of fondling a large and ugly member of the species. Her psychogalvanic responses to the key word 'cat' showed a steady diminution. Similarly, her responses while imagining contacts with cats diminished noticeably, although with less consistency. By the end of the course she no longer showed responses to imaging, but reported spontaneously that she now found it difficult to imagine cats at all. As regards actual[14] stimuli, however, the PGR showed a different picture. By the end of the course the patient denied apprehension at the sight of a cat and even proudly patted it. But her psychogalvanic responses nevertheless still betrayed

gross disturbance" (Hoenig and Reed, 1966, p. 1282).

In another patient, however, the PGR record fully confirmed the patient's verbal report of complete recovery.[15] Hoenig and Reed comment that "the patient may report success out of gratitude, even temporarily succeed in deceiving himself about it, and may even manage to diminish his symptoms temporarily" (p. 1283). It is, of course, certainly true that the verbal report of the patient or his relatives and friends cannot be accepted at face value, and Hoenig and Reed's findings support the criticisms made above of many of the case studies where direct behavioral assessment of the strength of the phobia after treatment was not used as the criterion for evaluation of the patient's status. It would be wrong, however, to insist on complete concordance between verbal, physiological, and behavioral measures of fear before concluding that a significant improvement had taken place. We are undoubtedly dealing with a dimension of fear, indexed by several criteria, and it may well be the exception rather than the rule for a nonphobic normal person to show complete "normality" in all three indices in relation to objects which he is quite prepared to handle and toward which he manifests no obvious fear. There is here a fertile field for further investigation to establish what could be regarded as the "normal" range of fear responses in nonphobic subjects.

2. PROBLEMS IN THE USE OF SYSTEMATIC DESENSITIZATION

The question of the relative efficiency of SD-I as against SD-R has not thus far received any systematic attention, though it is clearly of the greatest importance. Wolpe, on the whole, has argued in favor of SD-I, though in his earlier work (Wolpe, 1958) he made considerable use of SD-R. Since this problem has been discussed in more detail in an earlier chapter it may merely be repeated here that SD-I certainly has economic advantages where a range of phobias exists, for each of which a hierarchy has to be constructed. There are examples on record, however, where SD-R apparently succeeded after failure with SD-I (e.g., Hain et al, 1966), and SD-R appears to

---

[14] By an "actual" stimulus it is clear from the table presented by Hoenig and Reed that they mean the presentation, in this case, of a live animal for the patient to handle.

[15] A study by Agras (1967), however, suggests that changes in PGR may *precede* changes in performance.

have been very successful with monosymptomatic phobias wherever it has been used. Again, systematic investigations seem to be called for.

We may also mention only briefly the more general problem concerning the several stages of systematic desensitization (training in relaxation—with or without the use of hypnosis; construction of hierarchies; proceeding through the hierarchies). The studies of Lazarus (1965) and Lang et al (1965) both suggest that relaxation may not be essential and that directed muscular (or other) activity toward the feared object may be equally successful. Badri (1967) has recently combined relaxation with overt verbalization around the feared object, thus in a sense obtaining the best of both worlds.

Wolpin and Pearsall (1965) have produced results suggesting that it might be possible to proceed much more rapidly through a hierarchy than is indicated by the cautious approach of Wolpe to this question. Wolpe has stressed the dangers of presenting stimuli that arouse more anxiety than the patient can tolerate and that may, as a result, produce an increase in the strength of the phobia, but the results of Wolpin and Pearsall at least suggest that this may not always be the case. A rather different aspect of SD-I was investigated by Ramsay et al (1966) who found that spaced practice in desensitization produced better results than in massed practice, and who suggested that therapy sessions should not exceed 25 minutes. Seager and Brown (1967) have suggested that the GSR may be used to monitor anxiety level during SD(I).

3. Prediction of Outcome

While the successful treatment of monosymptomatic phobias may be achieved rapidly and efficiently with relatively little expenditure of effort, it seems clear that the treatment of long-standing polysymptomatic phobias may turn out to be a time-consuming business. With this in mind, Gelder et al (1967) analyzed responses to the questionnaires given before treatment commenced to discover whether any particular responses predicted outcome better than others. Fourteen questions showing the highest negative correlation with favorable outcome were examined carefully and were found to be particularly useful in predicting the

outcome of desensitization therapy. Only one of the 16 patients given desensitization treatment in the third study was misclassified using a cutting score of seven, and only one of ten in the earlier series. The questions were clearly measures of the neuroticism factor and indicated a poor prognosis in regard to treatment for patients showing generally disturbed behavior in addition to the phobias present.

B. School Phobia[16]

The past ten years has witnessed a very rapid growth of interest in this problem, and the literature is now so extensive that separate treatment is warranted.

I. DEFINITIONS, INCIDENCE, MEASUREMENT

1. Definition

Superficially, the definition of school phobia seems quite straightforward. The term is usually used in connection with those children who refuse to attend school, the use of the term "phobia" indicating the assumption that this is because something about the school situation makes them afraid to attend. Yet the very simplicity of this definition obscures a number of important issues. In a sense, the truant child also refuses to attend school, yet, as we shall see, the dynamics of school phobia are very different from those of truanting, as indeed are the children involved. Second, the term tends to preempt the question of whether the child with school phobia is refusing to attend school as opposed to refusing to leave home, or whether both these possibilities are interacting. Third, the resolution of this problem is of crucial importance because of the need to decide whether treatment should be directed primarily toward returning the child to school, whether it should be directed primarily to resolving child/parent relationships in the home, or both. Are the disturbed home relationships which are commonly found in school phobia a cause or a result of the refusal to attend school?[17] Most of these questions will be resolved as the evidence is considered below.

---

[16] A comprehensive review of this topic will be found in Kahn and Nursten (1964). Quantitative data is not, however, presented.

[17] The question is similar to that previously discussed in relation to enuresis and stuttering.

2. INCIDENCE

The incidence of school phobia depends, as usual, to a great extent on the stringency of the criteria employed to define school phobia and on the facilities available for treatment. On the whole, psychotherapists have treated severe case of school phobia where other disturbances of behavior are usually present, whereas more recently there has been a tendency to identify as a mild case of school phobia any child who is absent without reasonable cause for more than a few days, on the assumption that immediate action may prevent the development of more intractable behavior. Thus, Weiss and Cain (1964) dealt with 16 cases of school phobia absent from school for 2–30 months and all showing neurotic or psychotic forms of behavior in addition to the school phobia. Kennedy (1965), on the other hand, treated a large number of school "phobics" who mostly had been absent from school for only a few days at the time of referral. Bearing these points in mind, it has generally been found that, in children's psychiatric clinics, the incidence of school phobia varies from 1% of a complete psychiatric sample over ten years (Chazan, 1962) to the slightly higher figure of 17/1000 (Eisenberg, 1958). Higher estimates for the incidence of school refusal in the general population have been given by Kahn and Nursten (1962), ranging up to as high as 8%. Whatever the true incidence of school refusal, there is no doubt that the problem exists to a significant degree and may require professional intervention if the child is to return to school.

3. DESCRIPTIVE CHARACTERISTICS OF SCHOOL PHOBICS

We shall discuss here the differential distinguishing features of school phobia and truancy; the general characteristics of school phobics; and the attempts to identify different types of school phobia.

(a) COMPARISON OF SCHOOL PHOBICS AND TRUANTS. There is little difficulty in distinguishing the school phobic child from the truant (Warren, 1948). The most comprehensive study is that of Hersov (1960a) who compared three groups of children (school refusal of greater than 2 months' duration; truancy record of greater than 2 months' duration; nonphobic nontruanting) on a 124-item schedule covering a wide range of traits and factors. The groups were matched rather inadequately on age, sex, and intelligence. Table 7.5 shows the main factors distinguishing the school

TABLE 7.5. *Factors Distinguishing School Phobic and Truanting Children*[a]

Category	School Refusal (n = 50)	Truancy (n = 50)
Absence of parents	Significantly uncommon	Not a factor
Absence of father after 5	Not a factor	Common
Maternal overprotection	Yes	No
Inconsistent home discipline	No	Yes
Eating disturbance	Yes	No
Enuresis	No	Yes
Abdominal pain, nausea	Yes	No
Sleep disturbance	Yes	No
Juvenile court appearance	No	Yes
Persistent lying	No	Yes
Wandering from home	No	Yes
Stealing	No	Yes
Diagnosis: anxiety reaction	Yes	No
Diagnosis: conduct disorder	No	Yes
History of family neurosis	Yes	No

Source: Hersov, 1960a.

[a] The significance was assessed by comparison with the incidence found in the normal control group.

phobic child from the truant. Clearly the groups are distinguished on behavioral and personality factors, with truancy being predictive of the classical psychopathic, delinquent pattern of behavior more generally, whereas the severe school phobic tends to be markedly neurotic.

(b) TYPES OF SCHOOL PHOBIA. The *general characteristics* of school phobics have been described by Kennedy (1965) as comprising:

(i) Morbid fears associated with school attendance (a vague dread of disaster).

(ii) Frequent somatic complaints (headaches, nausea, drowsiness).

(iii) Symbiotic relationship with mother, fear of separation, anxiety about many things (darkness, crowds, noises).

(iv) Conflict between parents and the school administration.

These characteristics have led many authors to argue that school phobia is indicative of neuroticism as a general characteristic of these children (Warren, 1948; Coolidge et al, 1957; Hersov, 1960a; Davidson, 1961; Chazan, 1962), with the presumption that these characteristics acting in a particular family relationship *produce* the school phobia, rather than the school phobia producing the disturbed family relationship.

The same authors have, however, also argued for two basic subtypes of school phobia. This suggestion was first put forward by Coolidge et al (1957), repeated by them on the basis of more extensive data (Waldfogel et al, 1957) and accepted by other workers (e.g., Kahn and Nursten, 1962). The differential characteristics of the subtypes has been spelled out most recently by Kennedy (1965), as shown in Table 7.6.

TABLE 7.6.   *Differential Characteristics of Two Types of School Phobia*

Type 1 (Neurotic)	Type 2 (Characterological)
1. The present illness is the first episode	1. Second, third, or fourth episode
2. Monday onset, following an illness the previous Thursday or Friday	2. Monday onset following minor illness not a prevalent antecedent
3. An acute onset	3. Incipient onset
4. Lower grades most prevalent	4. Upper grades most prevalent
5. Expressed concern about death	5. Death theme not present
6. Mother's physical health in question: actually ill or child thinks so	6. Health of mother not an issue
7. Good communication between parents	7. Poor communication between parents
8. Mother and father well adjusted in most areas	8. Mother shows neurotic behavior; father, a character disorder
9. Father competitive with mother in household management	9. Father shows little interest in household or children
10. Parents achieve understanding of dynamics easily	10. Parents very difficult to work with

Source: Kennedy, 1965.

A rather different set of subtypes (three in all) has been identified by Hersov (1960b) in terms of *family relationships*. He classified them in terms of the parental techniques for dealing with the child on the one hand, and the child's behavior at home and at school on the other, as shown in Table 7.7. In a rather similar analysis, Weiss and Cain (1964) identified two basic types: the overdependent child, with a clinging mother; and the overdependent child, with a rejecting mother.

These different classifications need not be regarded as contradictory, since they are dealing with two separate sets of factors: the basic personality characteristics of the child and the constellation of family relationships. They

TABLE 7.7. *School Phobias Classified in Terms of Family Relationships*

Person	Type 1	Type 2	Type 3
Mother	Over-indulgent	Over-controlling	Over-indulgent
Father	Passive	Passive	Firm
Child (at home)	Demanding	Obedient	Wilful
Child (at school)	Timid	Timid	Friendly

Source: Hersov, 1960b.

do, however, clearly indicate the importance of considering more than the problem of returning the child to school. As we shall see, the necessity for considering the total picture does not by any means support the necessity for a psychodynamic as opposed to a behavioral analysis. It is, however, a most interesting example of the necessity for behavior therapists to consider disorders in their social context (a point which will be considered in detail in a later chapter). Later on in this chapter, we shall also have occasion to refer to a most important qualification of the findings discussed above.

II. GENESIS AND MAINTENANCE OF SCHOOL PHOBIA

The basic question at issue is whether the child fears school or whether he is afraid of leaving home. We shall consider here the separation anxiety theory; the theory that there is a genuine fear of school and that the disturbance in family relationships results from this fear; and the theory that both factors can be implicated and explained in terms of learning theory.

1. THE SEPARATION-ANXIETY THEORY OF SCHOOL PHOBIA

The general psychodynamic theory has been that the school refusal is the result of a basically disturbed personality interacting with disturbed family relationships. Thus, Johnson et al (1941) argued that school phobia was produced by an unresolved mother/child dependency relationship which produced acute anxiety in the child and increased anxiety in the mother when the decisive break in home ties (going to school) became inevitable. The interaction, of course, is a two-way affair, with both mother *and* child showing separation anxiety. This basic viewpoint has been espoused in general terms by many workers in this field (Suttenfield, 1954;

Talbot, 1957; Waldfogel et al, 1957; Glaser, 1959; Coolidge, et al, 1960). There has, however, been some dispute as to whether the child does fear school or not. Eisenberg (1958) and Hersov (1960b) contended that there was rarely any evidence of real or even imagined fear of school and that separation-anxiety was the sole variable, but Glaser (1959) rejected this view. Waldfogel et al (1957), on the other hand, argued that a fear of school *was* present, but that this represented a form of *displacement* of anxiety from its real source (separation from the mother) to a source more able to be tolerated by the child (and which, of course, as a consequence actually abolished separation). The cause of the separation-anxiety itself was found in Freudian developmental theory, as exemplified in the standard psychoanalytic interpretations of school phobia put forward by Berryman (1959) and Sperling (1961).

2. THEORY OF THE GENUINENESS OF SCHOOL PHOBIA

The separation-anxiety theory seems to have won genuine acceptance even by behavior therapists (as we shall see). However, Leventhal and Sills (1964) rejected the theory altogether, arguing that, if it were true, it would be expected that school phobia would occur at a much earlier date than it usually does and that the child's independence of the mother *in other areas of behavior* is successfully achieved and maintained even in severe cases of school phobia. They put forward the theory that the potential school phobic is a child who has adopted, prior to attending school (or during early years at school), an unrealistic self-image of his achievement potential. If this self-image is destroyed by competition and actual performance at school relative to other children, the child may be unable to cope with the threat to his self-esteem and retreats by developing behaviors (nausea, etc.) which effectively enable him to justify to himself the need for avoiding school attendance. Among the parameters that are operating to produce school refusal, Leventhal and Sills implicate: objectively insecure overestimation of power of achievement; sensitivity to threats to this self-image; the use of "helplessness" to facilitate avoidance of the threat; moves to situations that enhance the self-image (e.g., if the school refusal persists long enough, the child may be placed in a class of younger children when he does return and thus can reestablish his "superiority"); and the child's use of the mother to maintain the self-image. In general, the theory of Leventhal and Sills provides an important point of contact with experimental work on the need for achievement and fear of failure, the research results of which have been largely ignored in relation to school phobia.

3. An Interaction Theory Based on Learning Principles

It can be argued that the parents (particularly the mother) serve as strongly reinforcing stimuli for the child in many ways during the preschool period. They provide a refuge to which the child can return whenever he is uncertain or frightened. Separation from the parent during the preschool period may lead then to increased fear which will mediate instrumental acts that return the child to the parent. These acts will then tend to be performed in any separation situations that induce anxiety. "Growing up," in one sense, consists essentially in gradually obtaining rewards while separated from the parents to the point at which "separation-situations" are at least as rewarding as "being-with-mother-at-home." Anyone who has carefully observed the behavior of his own children in separation-situations (such as attending kindergarten) will appreciate the validity of this argument. In some children, however, anxiety may become strongly attached to separation situations and this anxiety may be both generated and reinforced by the mother, who herself may feel undue anxiety about the safety of the child away from home (e.g., continually warning the child not to wander away or get lost). Hence, when compulsory attendance at school becomes necessary, the child may well have learned to fear separation from the mother in the ways described. Whether or not an intense fear of school develops will depend on the experiences to which the child is subjected at school, as well

as on the mother's reaction to any fears the child may manifest. If learned anxiety about separation is not too great, the child will gradually learn to achieve new rewards at school which will counteract the separation anxiety and he will discriminate the pattern of school (plus absence from home leading to reward) from the rewards obtained by staying at home to a degree sufficient to outweigh the initial anxiety resulting from separation. Clearly, maturational factors would be important here in producing rewards from school attendance (e.g., success in class and at sports). If the child is unlucky, however, the school situation may be insufficiently rewarding or may even constitute an anxiety-arousing situation itself (e.g., a change from a sympathetic to an unsympathetic teacher). Hence, the genesis of a school phobia may be complexly determined by one or more of the following factors: separation anxiety leading to overdependence on the home as a safe refuge; insufficient rewards or actual anxiety-arousing experiences at school; and possibly, of course, actual traumatic events at school (e.g., forced participation in strongly inhibited sexual exploratory activities). The learning theory approach does not deny the importance of mother-child relationships, in particular, in determining school phobia, but argues that this factor can readily be accounted for within a learning-theory framework. A similar account of the genesis of school phobia derived from an actual case history has recently been presented by Garvey and Hegrenes (1966), while Jarvis (1964) has pointed out that the problem may be aggravated by hostile reactions on the part of the school staff (who may fail to recognize the child's difficulties and fears). Eisenberg (1958) has stressed the importance of contradictory verbal and behavioral cues given by the parent.

It is evident that there is a good deal of common ground between the psychodynamic and the learning theory approach to the explanation of the genesis and maintenance of school phobia, with the usual distinction, however, relating to just where the basic source of the difficulty lies.

III. BEHAVIOR THERAPY APPLIED TO SCHOOL PHOBIA

The psychodynamic approach to the treatment of school phobia has, of course, laid most stress on the necessity to treat the parent/child relationship. Within this general agreement,

however, there has been an interesting divergence of views on two points. Some psychotherapists have argued for the desirability of
separating the child from the mother during
treatment, even to the extent of hospitalizing
the child (e.g., Warren, 1948), while others have
argued that the mother and the child should be
treated simultaneously. Second, and related to
this divergence, there has been disagreement as
to whether efforts should be made to get the
child back into school while treatment of the
mother/child relationship is being undertaken
or whether the child should be allowed to
remain out of school during treatment. Greenbaum (1964), for example, has stressed that
return to school may be undesirable during
treatment, whereas most of the psychodynamic
approaches have argued for the desirability of
an early return to school (Talbot, 1957;
Eisenberg, 1958; Berryman, 1959; Glaser, 1959).
They argue that the continued absence from
school has widespread effects of an undesirable
nature on the child's life, and that hospitalizing
the child or allowing it to remain away from
school suggests immediately to mother *and*
child that their worst fears about the seriousness
of the situation are fully justified. Most treatment techniques have therefore been based on
what Kennedy (1965) has called rapid treatment
procedures for returning the child to school.
Kennedy emphasized: the establishment of
good public relations; ignoring somatic complaints; forced school attendance; providing
the parents with specific strategies to follow;
and only briefly interviewing the child. Many of
these have, in fact, involved the use of SD-R,
either concentrating on the child (Kennedy,
1965), or on a "grand strategy in a power
struggle" (Leventhal et al, 1967) in which the
resources of the school and the family are
directed by the therapist to produce powerful
pressures on the child to return to school and to
prevent his playing off one party against
another. Garvey and Hegrenes (1966) give a
very clear account of the use of SD-R in a
particular study. Two special techniques may be
briefly mentioned. Lazarus et al (1965) made
use of classical and operant conditioning
procedures at different stages of treatment in a
case of school phobia, suggesting that the use of
reinforcers may be more effective in the later
stages of return to school. Patterson (1965)
utilized play sessions in which the child was
given nonsocial reinforcers for making appropriate nonphobic responses to structural situations relating to his phobia (the play situation

gradually approximating more and more the
feared school situations). In addition to this
variant of SD-I, the parents and teachers were
trained to reward appropriate parent-indepen-
dent behavior (e.g., playing alone outside the
house).

1. RESULTS OF BEHAVIOR THERAPY WITH SCHOOL PHOBICS

As we have pointed out, the psychodynamic
approach has often stressed measures to ensure
an early return to school and has, in effect,
employed the SD-R technique. These studies
will be considered in the next section. The most
substantial results utilizing SD-R techniques
alone is that of Kennedy (1965) who claimed
100% success with his rapid treatment procedure
and maintenance of this success on long-term
follow-up. It should be noted, however, that the
majority of Kennedy's cases were referred for
treatment within a few days of the appearance
of refusal to go to school. No doubt many of
these would not be regarded as school phobias
by many other workers; and no doubt also the
spontaneous remission rate in Kennedy's
sample would have been high it he had used
half his subjects as an untreated control group.
A striking case study of the success of SD-R
combined with "total push" therapy is provided
by Garvey and Hegrenes (1966) who obtained
return to school in a ten-year-old boy who had
been in psychotherapy for six months without
success. No return of refusal to go to school was
observed over a two-year follow-up period.
Lazarus et al (1965), utilizing SD-R and
operant reward techniques, also reported complete success with a ten-month follow-up.

2. COMPARATIVE AND CONTROL STUDIES OF TREATMENT

(a) RESULTS OF PSYCHOTHERAPY. Table 7.8
shows the results reported in four studies
which utilized psychotherapy alone for the
treatment of school phobia, using the criterion
of whether or not the child returned to school.
No emphasis was laid on a return to school, and
in two studies the children were hospitalized
while under treatment. Since all could be
regarded as severe or relatively severe cases, the
results are quite striking in relation to the
specified criterion.

(b) RESULTS OF PSYCHOTHERAPY COM-
BINED WITH PRESSURE TO RETURN TO
SCHOOL. The studies considered here com-
bined psychotherapy with strong pressure to

TABLE 7.8.   *Results of Psychotherapy in the Treatment of School Phobia*

Study	n	Age Range	Length of Phobia	Length of Treatment	Type of Treatment	Number Returned to School
Johnson et al (1941)	8	6–14	10 days–2 years	5 months–1 year +	Psychotherapy	7
Warren (1948)	8	9–14	Not stated	Not stated	Hospitalization + psychotherapy	5
Hersov (1960b)	8 42	7–9 10–16	} 2 months–2 years	6–12 months	Psychotherapy	34
Weiss & Cain (1964)	16	8–16	2–30 months	9 months	Hospitalization + psychotherapy	13

return to school. For example, Suttenfield (1954) even went so far as to threaten the child with court action to enforce a return. Table 7.9 shows results obtained in some representative studies. Again the results are impressive, though most of these studies are lacking in important information.

(c) RESULTS OF EMPHASIS ON A RETURN TO SCHOOL. Rodriguez et al (1959) reported on the results of short-term treatment with major emphasis on a return to school in 41 children (aged 5–13 years) whose absence from school was not greater than 6 months. They found that 71% were attending school regularly (within less than 4 months after treatment started in 75% of cases). Like several other investigators, however, they achieved a much higher success rate (89%) with children under 11 years than with children over 11 years (36%).

(d) SPONTANEOUS RECOVERY AND FOLLOW-UP. Virtually no evidence is available concerning the degree to which school phobia remits

TABLE 7.9.   *Results of Psychotherapy Combined with Pressure to Return to School in School Phobia*

Study	n	Age Range	Length of Phobia	Length of Treatment	Number Returned to School
Talbot (1957)	24	5–15	Not stated	2 months–2 years	20
Eisenberg (1958)	26	Not stated	Not stated	Not stated	21
Glaser (1959)	16 22	6–9 10+	} Not stated	5–10 + treatment sessions	36
Davidson (1961)	9 21	7–9 10+	} Not stated	Not stated	28
Chazan (1962)	33	5½–14	Not stated	2–5 months	29

"spontaneously." A study by Waldfogel et al (1959) is the only one relevant to this point. They followed 36 cases for six to 18 months after termination of treatment. The children were assessed on whether they were absent from school or not; their academic performance; and their classroom adjustment. In assessing their findings at follow-up, they were able to compare four groups: children given in-school or in-clinic therapy; a "spontaneous recovery" group (that is, children who returned to school before therapy could begin); and a no-treatment group. The results for the three variables assessed are shown in Table 7.10. While the treated groups largely maintained their improve-

ment, it is interesting to note that five children returned to school even before treatment commenced; and three out of 11 children receiving no treatment also remitted and were performing adequately at the time of follow-up. Waldfogel et al point out that the untreated group probably contained a higher percentage of severe cases than the treated groups. If the spontaneously remitting group is assumed to contain probably the least severe cases, then the combined figure of seven returned to school probably represents a reasonable estimate of the true spontaneous recovery rate, which works out at roughly 20%.

TABLE 7.10 *Status of 36 School Phobics 6–18 Months After Termination of Treatment*

Treatment	Symptom			Academic Performance			Classroom Adjustment		
	Absent	Recur-ring	Per-sistent	+ +	+	−	+	−	− −
In-school therapy	14	2	0	7	9	0	6	10	0
In-clinic therapy	4	0	0	1	3	0	2	2	0
Spontaneous recovery	4	1	0	2	3	0	0	5	0
No therapy	3	5	3	3	6	2	1	6	4

Source: Waldfogel et al, 1959.

Other follow-up studies also report very encouraging results. Kennedy reported continuing attendance at school with a long-term follow-up; Glaser (1959) stated that 36 out of 38 of his cases were still in school on 6-month and 24-month follow-up; and Rodriguez et al (1959) also reported satisfactory results with follow-up varying from 15–80 months. The longest follow-up to date is that of Coolidge et al (1964) who reported on 49 cases followed up for 10 years. While 47/49 children had returned to school, 50% still evidenced some phobic symptoms, 43% were performing below their estimated potential, and 34/49 were showing moderate or severe adjustment difficulties.

This brings us to the final problem to be considered. It will be recalled that school phobics have frequently been characterized as being severely disturbed children and the follow-up results of Coolidge et al (1964) would appear to lend further support to this contention. Warren (1960), in fact, argued that school phobia was prodromal of adult phobia. Nursten (1963), however, could find no significant personality differences between comparable groups of adults who had or had not suffered from school phobia. Thus, the question whether the family and child disturbance precede school phobia or are a result of the school phobia remains more open than it seemed. The results of Coolidge et al (1964) showing continued difficulty in personal and educational relationships on long-term follow-up could, of course, result from the serious effects any substantial interruption of schooling is likely to produce at critical age levels.

REFERENCES

Agras, W.A. Transfer during systematic desensitization therapy. *Behav. Res. Ther.*, 1967, **5**, 193–199.

Ashem, B. The treatment of a disaster phobia by systematic desensitization. *Behav. Res. Ther.*, 1963, **1**, 81–84.

Badri, M.B. A new technique for the systematic desensitization of pervasive anxiety and phobic reactions. *J. Psychol.*, 1967, **65**, 201–208.

Bentler, P.M. An infant's phobia treated with reciprocal inhibition therapy. *J. Child Psychol. Psychiat.*, 1962, **3**, 185–189.

Berryman, E. School phobia: management problems in private practice. *Psychol. Rep.*, 1959, **5**, 19–25.

Bregman, E.O. An attempt to modify the emotional attitudes of infants by the conditioned response technique. *J. genet. Psychol.*, 1934, **45**, 169–198.

Brough, D.I., Yorkston, N., & Stafford-Clark, D. A case of wasp phobia treated by systematic desensitization under light hypnosis. *Guy's Hospital Rep.*, 1965, **114**, 319–324.

Cautela, J.R. The application of learning theory "as a last resort" in the treatment of a case of anxiety neurosis. *J. clin. Psychol.*, 1965, **21**, 448–452.

Chazan, M. School phobia. *Brit. J. educ. Psychol.*, 1962, **32**, 209–217.

Clark, D.F. The treatment of monosymptomatic phobia by systematic desensitization. *Behav. Res. Ther.*, 1963, **1**, 63–68 (a).

Clark, D.F. The treatment of hysterical spasm and agoraphobia by behavior therapy. *Behav. Res. Ther.*, 1963, **1**, 245–250 (b).

Coolidge, J.C., Brodie, R.D., & Feeney, B. A ten-year follow-up study of sixty-six school-phobic children. *Amer. J. Orthopsychiat.*, 1964, **34**, 675–684.

Coolidge, J.C., Hahn, P.B., & Peck, A.L. School phobia: neurotic crisis or way of life. *Amer. J. Orthopsychiat.*, 1957, **27**, 296–306.

Coolidge, J.C., Miller, M.L., Tessman, E., & Waldfogel, S. School phobia in adolescence: a manifestation of severe character disturbance. *Amer. J. Orthopsychiat.*, 1960, **30**, 599–607.

Cowden, R.C. & Ford, L.I. Systematic desensitization with phobic schizophrenics. *Amer. J. Psychiat.*, 1962, **118**, 241–245.

Davidson, S. School phobia as a manifestation of family disturbance: its structure and treatment. *J. Child Psychol. Psychiat.*, 1961, **1**, 270–287.

Dixon, J.J., de Monchaux, C., & Sandler, J. Patterns of anxiety—the phobias. *Brit. J. med. Psychol.*, 1957, **30**, 34–40.

Eisenberg, L. School phobia—a study in the communication of anxieties. *Amer. J. Psychiat.*, 1958, **114**, 712–718.

English, H.B. Three cases of the conditioned fear response. *J. abnorm. soc. Psychol.*, 1929, **24**, 221–225.

Errera, P. Some historical aspects of the concept: phobia. *Psychiat. Quart.*, 1962, **36**, 325–336.

Errera, P. & Coleman, J.V. A long-term follow-up study of neurotic phobic patients in a psychiatric clinic. *J. nerv. ment. Dis.*, 1963, **136**, 267–271.

Freeman, H.L. & Kendrick, D.C. A case of cat phobia. *Brit. med. J.*, 1960, **2**, 497–502.

Freud, S. Analysis of a phobia in a five-year-old boy. In Strachey, J. (ed.). *The standard edition of the complete psychological works of Sigmund Freud*, Vol. X (pp. 5–149). London: Hogarth Press, 1955.

Friedman, D. A new technique for the systematic desensitization of phobic symptoms. *Behav. Res. Ther.*, 1966, **4**, 139–140 (a).

Friedman, D. Case history: treatment of a case of dog phobia in a deaf mute by behavior therapy. *Behav. Res. Ther.*, 1966, **4**, 141 (b).

Friedman, D.E.I. & Silverstone, J.T. Treatment of phobic patients by systematic desensitization. *Lancet*, 1967, **1**, 470–472.

Friedman, J.H. Short-term psychotherapy of "phobia of travel." *Amer. J. Psychother.*, 1950, **4**, 259–278.

Galibert, J. Subnarcose amphétaminée et psychotherapie des états d'angoisse. *Encéphale*, 1960, **4**, 332–366.

Galibert, J. L'angoisse, réflexe conditionné dans l'agoraphobie. *Evolut. psychiat.*, 1963, **28**, 137–147.

Garvey, W.P. & Hegrenes, J.R. Desensitization techniques in the treatment of school phobia. *Amer. J. Orthopsychiat.*, 1966, **36**, 147–152.

Geer, J.H. Phobia treated by reciprocal inhibition. *J. abnorm. soc. Psychol.*, 1964, **69**, 642–645.

Geer, J.H. The development of a scale to measure fear. *Behav. Res. Ther.*, 1965, **3**, 45–53.

Geer, J.H. Fear and autonomic arousal. *J. abnorm. Psychol.*, 1966, **71**, 253–255.

Gelder, M.G. & Marks, I.M. Severe agoraphobia: a controlled prospective trial of behavior therapy. *Brit. J. Psychiat.*, 1966, **112**, 309–319.

Gelder, M.G., Marks, I.M., & Wolff, H.H. Desensitization and psychotherapy in the treatment of phobic states: a controlled enquiry. *Brit. J. Psychiat.*, 1967, **113**, 53–73.

Glaser, K. School phobia and related conditions. *Pediatrics*, 1959, **23**, 371–383.

Greenbaum, R.S. Treatment of school phobias—theory and practice. *Amer. J. Psychother.*, 1964, **18**, 616–634.

Grossberg, J.M. & Wilson, H.K. A correlational comparison of the Wolpe-Lang fear survey schedule and Taylor Manifest Anxiety Scale. *Behav. Res. Ther.*, 1965, **3**, 125–128.

Hain, J.D., Butcher, R.H.G., & Stevenson, I. Systematic desensitization therapy: an analysis of results in twenty-seven patients. *Brit. J. Psychiat.*, 1966, **112**, 295–307.

Hersov, L.A. Persistent nonattendance at school. *J. Child Psychol. Psychiat.*, 1960, **1**, 130–136 (a).

Hersov, L.A. Refusal to go to school. *J. Child Psychol. Psychiat.*, 1960, **1**, 137–145 (b).

Hoenig, J. & Reed, G.F. The objective assessment of desensitization. *Brit. J. Psychiat.*, 1966, **112**, 1279–1283.

Holmes, F.B. An experimental investigation of a method of overcoming children's fears. *Child Developm.*, 1936, **7**, 6–30.

Jarvis, V. Countertransference in the management of school phobia. *Psychoanal. Quart.*, 1964, **33**, 411–419.

Jersild, A.T. & Holmes, F.B. Children's fears. *Child Develop. Monogr.*, 1935, p. 360 (a).

Jersild, A.T. & Holmes, F.B. Methods of overcoming children's fears. *J. Psychol.*, 1935, **1**, 75–104 (b).

Johnson, A.M., Falstein, E.J., Szurek, S.A., & Svendsen, M. School phobia. *Amer. J. Orthopsychiat.*, 1941, **11**, 702–711.

Jones, H.E. The conditioning of overt emotional responses. *J. educ. Psychol.*, 1931, **22**, 127–130.

Jones, M.C. The elimination of children's fears. *J. exp. Psychol.*, 1924, **7**, 383–390 (a).

Jones, M.C. A laboratory study of fear: the case of Peter. *J. genet. Psychol.*, 1924, **31**, 308–315 (b).

Kahn, J.H. & Nursten, J.P. School refusal: a comprehensive view of school phobia and other failures of school attendance. *Amer. J. Orthopsychiat.*, 1962, **32**, 707–718.

Kahn, J. & Nursten, J. *Unwillingly to school.* Oxford: Pergamon, 1964.

Kennedy, W.A. School phobia: rapid treatment of fifty cases. *J. abnorm. Psychol.*, 1965, **70**, 285–289.

Kraft, T. Treatment of the housebound housewife syndrome. *Psychother. Psychosom.*, 1967, **15**, 446–453.

Kraft, T. & Al-Issa, I. The application of learning theory to the treatment of traffic phobia. *Brit. J. Psychiat.*, 1965, **111**, 277–279 (a).

Kraft, T. & Al-Issa, I. Behavior therapy and the recall of traumatic experience—a case study. *Behav. Res. Ther.*, 1965, **3**, 55–58 (b).

Kraft, T. & Burnfield, A. Treatment of neurosis by behavior therapy. *London Hosp. Gaz.*, 1967, **70**, xii–xvi.

Kringlen, E. Obseesional neurotics: a long-term follow-up. *Brit. J. Psychiat.*, 1965, **111**, 709–722.

Kushner, M. Desensitization of a post-traumatic phobia. In Ullmann, L.P. & Krasner, L. (eds.). *Case studies in behavior modification.* New York: Holt, 1965, pp. 193–196.

Lang, P.J. & Lazovik, A.D. Experimental desensitization of a phobia. *J. abnorm. soc. Psychol.*, 1963, **66**, 519–525.

Lang, P.J., Lazovik, A.D., & Reynolds, D.J. Desensitization, suggestibility and pseudo-therapy. *J. abnorm. Psychol.*, 1965, **70**, 395–402.

Lanyon, R.I., & Manosevitz, M. Validity of self-reported fear. *Behav. Res. Ther.*, 1966, **4**, 259–263.

Lazarus, A.A. The elimination of children's phobias by deconditioning. *Med. Proc. South Africa*, 1959, **5**, 261–265.

Lazarus, A.A. Group therapy of phobic disorders by systematic desensitization. *J. abnorm. soc. Psychol.*, 1961, **63**, 504–510.

Lazarus, A.A. A preliminary report on the use of directed muscular activity in counter-conditioning. *Behav. Res. Ther.*, 1965, **2**, 301–303.

Lazarus, A.A. Broad-spectrum behavior therapy and the treatment of agoraphobia. *Behav. Res. Ther.*, 1966, **4**, 95–97.

Lazarus, A. & Abramovitz, A. The use of "emotive imagery" in the treatment of children's phobias. *J. ment. Sci.*, 1962, **108**, 191–195.

Lazarus, A.A., Davison, G.C. & Polefka, D.A. Classical and operant factors in the treatment of a school phobia. *J. abnorm. Psychol.*, 1965, **70**, 225–229.

Lazarus, A.A. & Rachman, S. The use of systematic desensitization in psychotherapy. *S. Afr. med. J.*, 1957, **31**, 934–937.

Lazovik, A.D. & Lang, P.J. A laboratory demonstration of systematic desensitization psychotherapy. *J. psychol. Stud.*, 1960, **11**, 238–247.

Leventhal, T. & Sills, M. Self-image in school phobia. *Amer. J. Orthopsychiat.*, 1964, **34**, 685–695.

Leventhal, T., Weinberger, G., Stander, R.J., & Stearns, R.P. Therapeutic strategies with school phobics. *Amer. J. Orthopsychiat.*, 1967, **37**, 64–70.

Little, J.C. & James, B. Abreaction of conditioned fear reaction after eighteen years. *Behav. Res. Ther.*, 1964, **2**, 59–63.

McLaughlin, F.L. & Millar, W.M. Employment of air-raid noises in psychotherapy. *Brit. Med. J.*, 1941, **2**, 158–159.

Mandler, G., Mandler, J.M., Kremen, I., & Sholiton, R.D. The response to threat: relations among verbal and physiological indices. *Psychol. Monogr.*, 1961, **75**, No. 9 (Whole No. 513) (pp. 22).

Manosevitz, M. & Lanyon, R.I. Fear survey schedule: a normative study. *Psychol. Rep.*, 1965, **17**, 699–703.

Marks, I.M. & Gelder, M.G. A controlled retrospective study of behavior therapy in phobic patients. *Brit. J. Psychiat.*, 1965, **111**, 561–573.

Meyer, V. The treatment of two phobic patients on the basis of learning principles. *J. abnorm. soc. Psychol.*, 1957, **55**, 261–266.

Meyer, V. & Gelder, M.G. Behavior therapy and phobic disorders. *Brit. J. Psychiat.*, 1963, **109**, 19–28.

Moss, F.A. Note on building likes and dislikes in children. *J. exp. Psychol.*, 1924, **7**, 475–478.

Murphy, I.C. Extinction of an incapacitating fear of earthworms. *J. clin. Psychol.*, 1964, **20**, 396–398.

Nursten, J.P. Projection in the later adjustment of school phobic children. *Smith College Studies in Social Work*, 1963, **32**, 210–224.

Patterson, G.R. A learning theory approach to the treatment of the school phobic child. In Ullman, L.P. & Krasner, L. (eds.). *Case studies in behavior modification.* New York: Holt, 1965, pp. 279–285.

Perinpanayagam, M.S. A monosymptomatic phobia relieved by behavior therapy. *Guy's Hosp. Rep.*, 1965, **114**, 329–332.

Rachman, S. Treatment of anxiety and phobic reactions by systematic desensitization psychotherapy. *J. abnorm. soc. Psychol.*, 1959, **58**, 259–263.

Rachman, S. & Costello, C.G. The aetiology and treatment of children's phobias: a review. *Amer. J. Psychiat.*, 1961, **118**, 97–105.

Ramsay, R.W., Barends, J., Breuker, J., & Kruseman, A. Massed versus spaced desensitization of fear. *Behav. Res. Ther.*, 1966, **4**, 205–207.

Rodriguez, A., Rodriguez, M., & Eisenberg, L. The outcome of school phobia: a follow-up study based on 41 cases. *Amer. J. Psychiat.*, 1959, **116**, 540–544.

Rubin, B.M., Katkin, E.S., Weiss, B.W., & Efran, J.S. Factor analysis of a Fear Survey Schedule. *Behav. Res. Ther.*, 1968, **6**, 65–75.

Scherer, M.W. & Nakamura, C.Y. A Fear Survey Schedule for children (FSS-FC): a factor analytic comparison with manifest anxiety (CMAS). *Behav. Res. Ther.*, 1968, **6**, 173–182.

Schwartz, L.A. Group psychotherapy in the war neuroses. *Amer. J. Psychiat.*, 1945, **101**, 498–500.

Seager, C.P. & Brown, B.H. An indicator of tension during reciprocal inhibition. *Brit. J. Psychiat.*, 1967, **113**, 1129–1132.

Shorvon, H.J. & Sargant, W. Excitatory abreaction: with special reference to its mechanism and the use of ether. *J. ment. Sci.*, 1947, **93**, 709–732.

Sim, M. & Houghton, H. Phobic anxiety and its treatment. *J. nerv. ment. Dis.*, 1966, **143**, 484–491.

Snaith, R.P. A clinical investigation of phobias: Part I. A critical examination of the existing literature. *Brit. J. Psychiat.*, 1968, **114**, 673–697.

Solyom, L. & Miller, S.B. Reciprocal inhibition by aversion relief of the treatment of phobias. *Behav. Res. Ther.*, 1967, **5**, 313–324.

Sperling, M. Analytic first aid in school phobias. *Psychoanal. Quart.*, 1961, **30**, 504–518.

Suttenfield, V. School phobia—a study of five cases. *Amer. J. Orthopsychiat.*, 1954, **24**, 368–380.

Talbot, M. Panic in school phobia. *Amer. J. Orthopsychiat.*, 1957, **27**, 286–295.

Terhune, W.B. Phobic syndrome: study of 86 patients with phobic reactions. *Arch. Neurol. Psychiat.*, 1949, **62**, 162–172.

Thorpe, J.G., Schmidt, E., Brown, P.T., & Castell, D. Aversion-relief therapy: a new method for general application. *Behav. Res. Ther.*, 1964, **2**, 71–82.

Waldfogel, S., Coolidge, J.C., & Hahn, P.B. The development, meaning and management of school phobia. *Amer. J. Orthopsychiat.*, 1957, **27**, 754–776.

Waldfogel, S., Tessman, E., & Hahn, P.B. A program for early intervention in school phobia. *Amer. J. Orthopsychiat.*, 1959, **29**, 321–332.

Walk, R.D. Self-ratings of fear in a fear-invoking situation. *J. abnorm. soc. Psychol.*, 1956, **52**, 171–178.

Walton, D. Strengthening of incompatible reactions and the treatment of a phobic state in a schizophrenic patient. In H.J. Eysenck (ed.). *Behavior therapy and the neuroses.* Oxford: Pergamon, 1960, pp. 170–180.

Walton, D. & Mather, M.D. The relevance of generalization techniques to the treatment of stammering and phobic symptoms. *Behav. Res. Ther.*, 1963, **1**, 121–125.

Warren, W. Acute neurotic breakdown in children with refusal to go to school. *Arch. Dis. Childh.*, 1948, **23**, 266–272.

Warren, W. Some relationships between the psychiatry of children and of adults. *J. ment. Sci.*, 1960, **106**, 815–826.

Watson, J.B. & Morgan, J.J.B. Emotional reactions and psychological experimentation. *Amer. J. Psychol.*, 1917, **23**, 163–174.

Watson, J.B. & Rayner, R. Conditioned emotional reactions. *J. exp. Psychol.*, 1920, **3**, 1–14.

Weinberg, N.H. & Zaslove, M. "Resistance" to systematic desensitization of phobias. *J. clin. Psychol.*, 1963, **19**, 179–181.

Weiss, M. & Cain, B. The residential treatment of children and adolescents with school phobia. *Amer. J. Orthopsychiat.*, 1964, **34**, 103–112.

Wilson, G.D. Social desirability and sex differences in expressed fear. *Behav. Res. Ther.*, 1967, **5**, 136–137.

Wilson, G.D. & Priest, H.F. The principal components of phobic stimuli. *J. clin. Psychol.*, 1968, **24**, 191.

Wolpe, J. Objective psychotherapy of the neuroses. *South African Med. J.*, 1952, **26**, 825–829.

Wolpe, J. Reciprocal inhibition as the main basis of psychotherapeutic effects. *Arch. Neurol. Psychiat.*, 1954, **72**, 205–226.

Wolpe, J. *Psychotherapy by reciprocal inhibition.* Stanford: Stanford Univer. Press, 1958.

Wolpe, J. The systematic desensitization treatment of neuroses. *J. nerv. ment. Dis.*, 1961, **132**, 189–203.

Wolpe, J. Isolation of a conditioning procedure as the crucial psychotherapeutic factor: a case study. *J. nerv. ment. Dis.*, 1962, **134**, 316–329.

Wolpe, J. & Lang, P.J. A fear survey schedule for use in behavior therapy. *Behav. Res. Ther.*, 1964, **2**, 27–30.

Wolpe, J. & Rachman, S. Psychoanalytic "evidence": a critique based on Freud's case of Little Hans. *J. nerv. ment. Dis.*, 1960, **130**, 135–148.

Wolpin, M. & Pearsall, L. Rapid deconditioning of a fear of snakes. *Behav. Res. Ther.*, 1965, **3**, 107–111.

Wolpin, M. & Raines, J. Visual imagery, expected roles and extinction as possible factors in reducing fear and avoidance behavior. *Behav. Res. Ther.*, 1966, **4**, 25–38.

Chapter 8

Obsessions and Compulsions

I. DEFINITIONS, INCIDENCE, MEASUREMENT

1. DEFINITIONS

THE TERM "obsession" is usually used by psychiatrists to refer to persistent, repetitive, and unwelcome trains of thought; the term "compulsion" to refer to impulsions to perform repetitive acts or rituals which may involve complex sequences of acts—or to the acts themselves. The use of these terms has raised a number of interesting and important questions that have been resolved to a considerable degree in recent years. We may profitably list these questions and then consider the evidence relating to them.

(i) Can obsessions (trains of thought) occur in the absence of compulsive behavior?

(ii) Can compulsive behavior (rituals) occur in the absence of obsessional thoughts?

(iii) Depending on the answers to (i) and (ii), do obsessional thoughts always precede and lead to (determine?) the occurrence of compulsive rituals?

(iv) Or are compulsive rituals merely the external manifestation of the internal thoughts? (If this were so, then the thoughts could be ignored for explanatory and treatment purposes and successful treatment of the ritualistic behavior by direct attack would presumably abolish the thoughts).

(v) Can valid distinctions be drawn between the obsessional/compulsive personality on the

one hand and obsessional/compulsive disorder on the other?

(vi) Is the person who suffers from an obsessional/compulsive disorder always found to have manifested obsessional and/or compulsive traits prior to his breakdown or can the disorder occur in persons without these personality traits? (That is, is an obsessional/compulsive personality *predictive* of obsessional/compulsive disorder?) Or is there such a thing as a "normal" obsessional and/or compulsive personality?

A good deal of research has been carried out in recent years in attempts to answer these questions.

2. THE MEASUREMENT OF OBSESSIONS AND COMPULSIONS

We shall here consider six aspects of obsessional and compulsive behavior: the relationship between obsessive thoughts and compulsive acts; the characteristics of obsessive/compulsive neurotic patients presenting for treatment; differential diagnosis; incidence; the possibility of a neurological etiology; and the question of whether a true obsessive/compulsive syndrome occurs in children.

(a) THE RELATIONSHIP BETWEEN OBSESSIONAL THOUGHTS AND COMPULSIVE ACTS. The most important study relating to many of the questions raised above is that by Sandler and Hazari (1960). They factor analyzed the results obtained on 40 items (including statements covering both thoughts and acts) of their questionnaire[1] given to 100 unselected neurotic

---

[1] See Chapter 7.

outpatients aged 16–54 and identified two rotated orthogonal factors. The first of these factors identified what they call the reactive-narcissistic obsessional character who is excessively orderly, neat, and overconscientious but whose traits appear to be well-integrated into the personality structure. The second factor was defined by traits indicative of the classically described obsessional neurotic, that is, "a person whose daily life is disturbed through the intrusion of unwanted thoughts and impulses into his conscious experience." Individuals characterized by these latter traits they label the "obsessional personality," and they consider that the traits may be present prior to neurotic breakdown. Three points should be noted about the Sandler/Hazari classification. First, their patients represented an unselected *neurotic* group; second, they did not relate their findings to diagnostic subclassifications within the group; and third, both factors included items referring to both thoughts *and* rituals. The importance of their findings lies in the suggestion that an "obsessional personality" may or may not be predictive of abnormality depending upon the kind of thoughts and behavior being manifested. There is, in fact, a nonneurotic type of personality. These results have been confirmed by Delay et al (1962).

(b) CHARACTERISTICS OF OBSESSIONAL PATIENTS. The patients of Sandler and Hazari (1960), as was pointed out earlier, were unselected neurotic outpatients and hence probably not particularly representative of the classical obsessive/compulsive inpatient. Ingram (1961a) and Pollitt (1960) have recently published, independently, very comprehensive studies of the natural history of severe classical cases of obsessive/compulsive neurosis. Pollitt examined 150 cases (of whom 69 were inpatients) and Ingram 89 inpatients. Ingram divided his patients into five subcategories (classical cases; phobic-ruminative states; doubtful schizophrenic; those with depressive features; and a miscellaneous—organic, etc.—group) to take account of previous suggestions in the literature. Both authors agreed that sex differences were unimportant; that high IQ and social status was the rule (probably accounting for the extremely socially crippling effects of the classical disorder as shown by Ingram's finding of high celibacy and low fertility rate); that onset was relatively early; and that five to ten years elapsed between onset and referral. They also claimed that precipitating factors were very various (pregnancy being a common precipitating factor in women, according to Ingram) and that the onset was usually insidious.

The question whether the classical obsessive/compulsive neurotic has an obsessional/compulsive personality prior to onset of the disorder has not been clearly answered. Sandler and Hazari (1960), as we have seen, argued that obsessional personality traits were not necessarily predictive of breakdown, but they were not dealing with the classical syndrome. Ingram (1961a) found that childhood symptoms (especially phobias and rituals) were very common and, in another study (Ingram, 1961b), claimed that there was a high correlation with prebreakdown obsessional personality traits. Pollitt (1960), on the other hand, found that 34% of his sample showed no obsessional traits prior to breakdown; and Rüdin (1953) reported similar figures. These three sets of findings are not necessarily contradictory, of course. We may accept that a high proportion (at least two-thirds) of patients manifesting the classical syndrome will demonstrate similar traits prior to breakdown, while still accepting the important distinction made by Sandler and Hazari.

(c) DIFFERENTIAL DIAGNOSIS. As we have seen in an earlier chapter, Eysenck (1947) described a dysthymic syndrome, comprising anxiety neurotics, depressives, and obsessional/compulsives. However, Ingram (1961a) carefully compared his obsessional neurotics with 100 unselected hysterics and 100 unselected anxiety neurotics and was able to demonstrate significant differences between the obsessionals and the anxiety neurotics on a number of characteristics (e.g., intelligence, neurotic symptoms in childhood, age of onset, and first admission). He did not, however, attempt discrimination on personality traits, which may be of more importance.

(d) INCIDENCE OF OBSESSIVE-COMPULSIVE NEUROSES. The incidence of obsessional and compulsive traits in unselected neurotic or psychotic groups is unknown. The incidence of the classical syndrome is, however, certainly very small. Michaels and Porter (1949) reported an incidence of only 0.2% in 1383 cases (but their sample was an Army sample and it has been pointed out that obsessionals may adjust to the orderly demands of army life rather better than they do to civilian life). Ross and Rice (1945) found only 7 classical cases in 3509 admissions. Pollitt (1960) found an incidence of 3% in 6230 cases and Judd (1965) an incidence of 1.2% in 1625 cases. Reviewing much of this material, Ingram (1961a) concludes that the incidence of classical cases is probably close to 1% of inpatient admissions.[2]

(e) NEUROLOGICAL FACTORS IN OBSESSIVE/COMPULSIVE DISORDERS. There has been some suggestion in the literature that severe obsessive/compulsive disorder may be correlated with EEG abnormality and hence possibly have a clear-cut neurological correlate. But early positive results (Pacella et al, 1944; Rockwell and Simons, 1947) were not confirmed by Ingram and McAdam (1960). In a careful comparison of large numbers of obsessional neurotics and nonobsessional neurotic controls, Grimshaw (1964) found a noticeably higher incidence of significant neurological disorders prior to breakdown in the obsessional patients. However, it seems likely that these kinds of abnormalities are uncorrelated with the presence of obsessional traits. In the Rockwell and Simons study, for example, the presence of abnormal EEG patterns was clearly correlated with the presence of other behavioral disorders (e.g., psychopathic behavior) much more likely to be causally related to the neurological abnormality than the obsessional symptoms.

(f) OBSESSIONAL AND COMPULSIVE BEHAVIOR IN CHILDREN. Judd (1965) has very thoroughly reviewed the literature on the unsettled question as to whether a classical obsessive/compulsive syndrome can occur in children. As he points out, ritualistic behavior appears as part of the normal developmental process in children. However, in a survey of 405 children under 12 years seen over a period of 6 years, 34 were found to have abnormal obsessive/compulsive symptoms, but only 5 of these appeared to be genuine classical cases. With respect to these 5 cases, however, he found a very striking uniform pattern of characteristics All of the children displayed the following characteristics: sudden onset; superior IQ; concomitant presence of compulsions *and* obsessions; severe disruption of adjustment to environment by symptoms; verbalized guilt feelings; rigid absolute moral code; active fantasy life; absence of psychosis. Four of the children showed: normal prebreakdown personality; family history of obsessive/compulsive symptoms; uneventful bowel training; identifiable precipitating event; transient phobic phenomena and excessive ambivalence toward parents, including strong overt aggression. None of the children showed any evidence of a

history of sexual trauma and, in general, the results in no way supported the classical Freudian account of the genesis of obsessive/compulsive neurosis.

The two principal conclusions to be drawn from this survey seem to be the following:

(i) That the classical obsessive-compulsive syndrome is very rare, both in children and adults, but does occur.

(ii) That a distinction must be drawn between the "normal" obsessive/compulsive traits which may be found in some persons and the obsessive/compulsive traits which approximate the classical syndrome and which may be predictive of future breakdown.

The question of whether obsessive thoughts precede and determine the occurrence of compulsive rituals has not been resolved. In this connection, we may note the important distinction drawn by Walton and Mather (1963) between new and long-standing obsessions and compulsions. They argue that ritualistic behavior of recent onset will be determined by the occurrence of anxiety responses (but do not necessarily identify this with obsessional thoughts) but that long-standing ritualistic behavior may have become relatively autonomous; and from this distinction they draw, as we shall see, important implications for treatment. The possibility must also be considered that *both* the obsessional thoughts and the ritualistic behavior are sequentially linked (the thoughts leading to the actions) but the sequence is triggered off by prior anxiety (conditioned fear).

II. GENESIS AND MAINTENANCE OF OBSESSIONS AND COMPULSIONS

We will consider here two recent formulations in behavioristic terms of the genesis and maintenance of obsessional forms of behavior. The first of these was put forward by Metzner (1963). He pointed out that there is experimental evidence that a conditioned instrumental avoidance response is likely to appear "spontaneously" in situations where severe conflict is set up. Thus, if a positive instrumental response is attached to a conditioned stimulus (with food as reinforcement) and a difficult discrimination is then set up so that the capacity to perform the positive CR breaks down, a conditioned instrumental avoidance response

---

[2] More recent figures by Kringlen (1965) suggest an incidence of 2.5% of all patients, and 4.3% of neurotics.

(paw-lifting, for example) may manifest itself. Metzner also relies heavily, in attempting to explain the *persistence* of obsessional behavior, on the notion of traumatic avoidance learning which (as we have seen in a previous chapter) may be partially irreversible. That is, obsessional behavior is regarded essentially as conditioned avoidance behavior which is maintained by the fact that it prevents reality testing by reducing anxiety and hence avoiding the appearance of the threatened disaster. Metzner also invokes as possible situations in which behavior can become fixated Farber's well-known experiment which showed that, if rats are trained to run through shock to food, the running behavior may be very hard to extinguish because of (1) double reinforcement —shock reduction and food (Farber, 1948); (2) situations where instrumental avoidance responses are unsuccessful (that is, lead to punishment) as in Maier's studies of fixation; and (3) situations involving the use of "free shock."

A rather different explanation has been put forward by Taylor (1963). Taylor argues that obsessive behavior fails to extinguish as a result of social criticism because the punishment (criticism) comes too late after the behavior to be effective. That is, the performance of the obsession produces immediate reinforcement, whereas the nonreinforcing social disapproval only comes later. Taylor's explanation is not, of course, incompatible with the notion of obsessive behavior as anxiety-reducing behavior; it merely adds to the explanation. However, Taylor goes on to develop his theory in an interesting way. He points out that social criticism of the obsessional behavior may itself produce what Taylor calls "guilt" and which he equates with conditioned autonomic reactions. This "anxiety" drive will, in turn, mediate avoidance behaviors, and Taylor argues that this sequence of events is the primary source of the internalization of obsessions. That is, instead of indulging in overt obsessional behavior, displacement will occur to internal obsessional behavior. An alternative explanation would, of course, account for obsessional thoughts on the basis of stimulus generalization.

The question of the relationship between obsessional thoughts and obsessional behaviors is a complex one, however. Wolpe (1958), for example, argued that a distinction must be made between anxiety-arousing obsessions and anxiety-reducing obsessions. Thus persistent thoughts about killing someone may lead to ritualistic behavior to prevent the patient from carrying out the act.

III. BEHAVIOR THERAPY APPLIED TO OBSESSIONS AND COMPULSIONS

1. BEHAVIOR THERAPY OF OBSESSIONS AND COMPULSIONS

The most important studies of the behavioral treatment of obsessive behaviors are those of Walton (1960) and Walton and Mather (1963; 1964).[3] Walton considered that obsessions, during the early stages of the disorder, represented examples of drive-reducing conditioned avoidance response, whereas in the later stages, they would achieve a considerable degree of "functional autonomy," by which he meant that they would now be evoked by a wide range of stimuli, in addition to the anxiety that originally produced them. From these considerations, he formulated two predictions. The first was that a direct attempt to remove the obsessional behavior in the early stages of the disorder would fail and that it was necessary to desensitize the patient to his anxiety-provoking stimuli. If this were successfully accomplished, the obsessional behavior would disappear, since there would be no anxiety to evoke it. On the other hand, in the case of long-standing obsessions, a direct attack on the obsessional behavior might be at least partially successful, since the behavior had become, to some extent, "divorced" from the anxiety that originally maintained it (however, removing the anxiety would not completely eliminate the obsessional behavior).

Working with a series of six obsessional patients, Walton and Mather (1963; 1964) examined these possibilities as systematically as possible, within the limitations of a clinical situation. The first two cases were acute cases of recent onset, and the method of treatment involved SD-R, using assertive training in social situations. In both cases the obsessional behavior disappeared. The first case could not be followed up; but the second was still free of his symptoms after one year.

In the next two cases, where the obsessional behavior was long standing, it was predicted that the successful diminution of the anxiety

---

[3] The 1964 paper of Walton and Mather is a much expanded version of Walton and Mather (1963b), with the addition of a new case.

mediating the obsessional behavior would leave the latter relatively unaffected for the reasons given earlier. In the first of these cases, SD-I was used to reduce anxiety over sexual matters which led to the obsessional behavior; in the second case, SD-R and SD-I were used to treat very severe claustrophobia and fear of being buried alive, which led to various ritualistic activities. In both cases, there was significant improvement in the anxiety but the obsessional behavior remained unchanged.

Walton and Mather then attempted to determine whether, in long-standing cases, it would be possible to reduce the obsessional behavior by a direct attack on it without concerning themselves with treatment of the conditioned anxiety responses which mediated the obsessional behavior. In their fifth case, Walton and Mather used SD-R, that is, hierarchies were constructed of the *stimuli* that currently evoked the ritualistic behavior and the patient was required to perform the ritual. The rationale of the procedure is not too clearly stated, since it is evident that the intention is still to reduce (by reciprocal inhibition) the anxiety evoked by these stimuli. However, an example will make the procedure clearer. The patient had an obsession for cleaning a door-knob. She was first required to touch the door handle after it had been cleaned with a cloth washed in hot water; then after it had been wiped with a hot, damp cloth; and so on up the hierarchy. The patient, in effect, is progressively being prevented from carrying out the ritual, while at the same time being progressively required to touch a knob which, in her eyes, is getting less and less clean. The results of these procedures, carried out over two months, were quite disappointing, only a small degree of improvement taking place. Walton and Mather concluded that, in long-standing obsessional cases, it is necessary to tackle both the conditioned autonomic drive state *and* the motor behavior simultaneously, and they attempted to do this with their sixth case. The details of their procedures are too complex to be reproduced here,[4] but the dual treatment was apparently successful only after a leucotomy had reduced the unconditioned autonomic level of responding so that the conditioned avoidance responses could be handled successfully by SD-I.

We have given this space to the studies of

Walton and Mather because they represent a very interesting example of behavior therapy of an experimental kind according in part with the definition given of behavior therapy in Chapter 1. In one sense, Walton and Mather could be said to have used standard techniques, but their endeavor does represent a genuine inter-action of technique with theory and as such merits very close attention.

Several other studies of the effects of behavior therapy on obsessions have been carried out; indeed, a striking feature of these studies is the variety of procedures that have been tried. Wolpe (1958), for example, used assertion therapy (in ways very similar to Walton and Mather); shock (for food imagining in a case of obsessional eating); and hypnosis plus counter-suggestion. Lazarus (1958), Bevan (1960), and Thorpe et al (1964) used aversion-relief therapy. The degree of success achieved in these studies is difficult to assess, but four other studies have produced fairly clear-cut results. Of these, perhaps the most interesting is that of Taylor (1963). He treated a female with a 30-year history of trichopilomania (pulling out of hairs on eyebrows).[5] In terms of Taylor's theory of obsessional behavior, the eyebrow plucking was immediately rewarding, whereas social disapproval came later. Taylor's method of treatment commenced by instructing the patient to inhibit the *first* movement in the chain of events leading to the plucking of a hair. She was instructed to consciously inhibit her hand from moving, while at the same time saying "No, stay where you are" or words to similar effect. A second stage involved the patient deliberately putting her hand to her brow until the impulse arose, when the hand would be removed. Taylor had expected that he would need to apply the first procedure to all of the links in the chain progressively, but in fact this did not prove necessary. It must be admitted that the results obtained by Taylor by this simple technique are astonishing—ten days' treatment produced total (bar two insignificant relapses) remission of a 30-year-old disfiguring habit, indexed after a three- and seven-month follow-up period by a perfect set of eyebrows. Taylor's treatment technique was based upon the fact that the patient could herself identify with complete accuracy the instant of the beginning of a compulsion to pluck and hence would be

---

[4] See Walton and Mather, 1964, pp. 137–148.

[5] Also termed "Trichotillomania." Greenberg and Sarner (1965) have presented an excellent review of the psychodynamic literature and the characteristics of a series of 19 cases.

the most efficient person to apply "counter-measures"; but it will certainly be puzzling to other behavior therapists (and to psychiatrists) that the patient was so readily able to carry out the counter-action.

A study by Weiner (1967), however, lends support to Taylor's finding that, in some instances at least, a simple solution to obsessional rituals may be found. A 15-year-old boy had recently developed a whole series of compulsive rituals, involving washing and dressing, reading and writing, and so on. The rituals were extensive and severe. Like Taylor, Weiner enlisted the cooperation of the boy and in effect applied desensitization in reverse. A list of five obsessional rituals was constructed by the experimenter and child together, and the reasons for which the behaviors were performed were listed also. For each of these "negative" reasons an alternative "positive" reason was constructed which could be satisfied by specified more limited courses of both *motor* and *verbal* actions. For example, it was found that after locking a drawer the child had to check three times that it had been locked because he was afraid he might be sent to Vietnam if he did not (negative reasons). The child was instructed to lock the drawer as usual, *check once deliberately* that it had been locked, assuring himself that this was to make sure it was secured against thieves (positive reason). Again, face washing was reduced from 15 to five minutes *and timed with a stop-watch*. Over eight weekly sessions, the patient was able to progressively alternate the rituals in this way. Not only did the ritualistic behavior gradually disappear, but there was a concomitant reduction of feelings of being dominated by unrealistic urges and a general diminution of anxiety. At a seven months' follow-up, the child was symptom free, the alternative rituals themselves had disappeared, and the parents reported that, as far as they were concerned, the child was normal. The possibility of spontaneous recovery cannot, of course, be ruled out, nor the effects of suggestion, but the essentially operant successive approximation technique in reverse certainly makes good sense as a possible approach to the changing of behaviors of this kind. This study represents a significant qualification of the conclusions of Walton and Mather (1964).

An important study by Meyer (1966) should be mentioned. It is generally considered that preventing the obsessional patient from performing his rituals will induce severe anxiety, just as forcing a phobic patient to stay in a feared situation will provoke panic, since in both instances the response or inhibition of response occurs in order to ward off a subjectively perceived threatened disaster. If the patient could be prevented from, as it were, leaving the threatening situation, and *nothing disastrous does happen*, the behavior should extinguish. Systematic desensitization is, of course, precisely designed to overcome this problem by *not* placing the patient directly in a situation he cannot handle and which may lead to a panic reaction and consequent strengthening of the fear. Its intent is to enable the patient *gradually* to handle the feared situation. Meyer, however, prevented his two patients from performing their obsessional rituals while at the same time making them perform actions *inconsistent* with the ritualistic activities. Thus, the patient with compulsive washing and cleaning was made to handle doorknobs, dustbins etc. without being given the opportunity of washing her hands or cleaning the objects. In other words, the patients were required to reality test for the belief that touching certain "unclean" objects would be followed by disastrous consequences such as contamination and illness or disease. Considerable success attended the use of this method with satisfactory long-term follow-up (14 months and two years).[6]

Haslam (1965) treated a 25-year-old girl with a phobia about broken glass which had led to obsessional rituals. The patient had previously received ECT, insulin, drugs, and leucotomy (indicating the severity of the disorder)[7] to no effect. Haslam successfully treated the phobia for glass by Watson's original desensitization technique, that is, the introduction by stages of broken glass objects in a feeding situation under strong hunger drive. The obsessions and compulsions disappeared simultaneously, and the patient was symptom free a year later.

Kushner and Sandler (1966) associated shock with visual imaging in a 48-year-old male with daily suicidal ruminations (classical aversive conditioning paradigm). Six specific suicidal images were available for treatment, and these

---

[6] The technique is essentially that of "flooding" or implosive therapy with the addition of active manipulation of the feared object (see Chapter 4).

[7] The patient had spent the last five years, all but four months, in a hospital with the disorder.

were treated in a total of 350 trials, using a partial reinforcement technique. A three-month follow-up indicated relative freedom from the suicidal ruminations in spite of the traumatic event of his brother's death.

We may conclude that a number of promising leads have been developed in recent years by behavior therapists in relation to the treatment of obsessive/compulsive behaviors. There appears to be a greater tendency to carry out genuine experimental studies of the single case

than we found with behavior therapy of the phobias.

2. COMPARATIVE AND CONTROL STUDIES OF TREATMENT

Rather surprisingly (by comparison with the phobias, for example), a good deal of information exists concerning the changes in status of obsessional/compulsive patients over long-term follow-up. Table 8.1 shows a selection of

TABLE 8.1. *Summary of Results of Treatment of Obsessive/Compulsive Patients*

Study	n	Follow-up Period	Percent Cured or Much Improved
Luff and Garrod (1935)	60	3 years (average)	52
Lewis (1936)	50	5+ years	50
Rudin (1953)	130	2–26 years	38
Müller (1953)	57	15–35 years	50
Pollitt (1957)	150	3–44 years	47
Hastings (1958)	23	6–12 years	44
Balslev-Olesen and Geert-Jorgensen (1959)	62	$\frac{1}{2}$– 8 years	66
Pollitt (1960)	101	(a) 1+ years	(i) 62 (leucotomized) (ii) 70 (nonleucotomized)
		(b) 4+ years	(i) 53 (leucotomized) (ii) 63 (nonleucotomized)
Ingram (1961a)	64	1–11 years	(i) 51 (leucotomized) (ii) 38 (nonleucotomized)
Grimshaw (1965)	100	$\frac{1}{2}$–14 years	64
Kringlen (1965)	91	13–20 years	25

the major studies from which data are available. It will be obvious that the prognosis for this disorder is the subject of some disagreement. With the exception of the leucotomized patients, the treatment involved in all of the studies was psychotherapy, usually of a relatively superficial kind. The results do, in fact, offer some suggestion that therapy might be of significant benefit to the obsessive-compulsive patient, since Kringlen's sample (which shows the poorest prognosis) is essentially an untreated control group. He reports that the mean duration of treatment for his cases was only two months and that more than 20% were in hospital for less than one month. The treatment given mostly involved ECT, drugs or supportive psychotherapy. Differences in sampling resulting in groups with different initial severity of disorder probably account for the differing

conclusions of various authors regarding the long-term prognosis in such cases.

Grimshaw's (1965) report is of particular interest, since he classified his patients according to the type of therapy that they had received. The results are shown in Table 8.2, where the patients are classified into those who recovered, were much improved or improved, as to symptoms on the one hand; and those who were unchanged on the other. Grimshaw (1965, p. 1055) concluded that "no elaborate type of therapy seems indicated in obsessional disorder. It will be noted that the group receiving no treatment showed as good a recovery rate as any of the others."

On the whole, it must be concluded that neither behavior therapy nor other kinds of therapy have thus far made any really impressive advances in the treatment of these disorders.

TABLE 8.2. *Result of Various Treatments on Obsessive/Compulsive Disorders*

Treatment	Effect on Symptoms	
	Recovered/Improved	Unchanged/Worse
ECT	16/31	15/31
Systematic psychotherapy	9/14	5/14
Supportive psychotherapy	24/36	12/36
Leucotomy	1/3	2/3
No treatment	10/16	6/16

IV. METHODOLOGICAL CONSIDERATIONS

Two major problems call for further intensive investigation before major advances can be expected in the behavioral treatment of obsessive/compulsive states.

1. MEASUREMENT OF OBSESSIVE AND COMPULSIVE BEHAVIOR

As was pointed out earlier, it is astonishing how little work has been carried out on the careful defining and quantifying of obsessional and compulsive behavior. It is unfortunate in this respect that the operant psychologists have not so far turned their attention to this area of behavior modification, since their approach, as we have seen, is characterized particularly by the initial establishment of stable base-rates of the behavior to be modified—and there can be no question but that this approach pays handsome dividends. Of course, the measurement of obsessional trains of thought may prove to be much more difficult than the measurement of ritualistic acts. But it is worth noticing in this respect that the combination of unusually high intelligence plus meticulousness makes the obsessional/compulsive patient the ideal self-observer—provided, of course, instructing him to observe and record his own behavior does not itself become a compulsion! Taylor (1963) has capitalized on these facts, but even Meyer's (1966) careful study did not produce more than the crudest estimates of frequency of compulsive checking, for example.

2. DURATION OF SYMPTOMS AND FORM OF TREATMENT

The study by Walton and Mather (1964) raises in acute form the question of the relationship between obsessions and compulsions in relation to treatment. Walton and Mather proceeded on the assumption that they were treating either the compulsive ritualistic behavior or the underlying anxiety that produced the ritualistic behavior. Aside from the question of whether a direct attack on the ritualistic behavior will be successful and, if so, under what circumstances, it is by no means clear whether Walton and Mather *were* treating the "anxiety." There may well be a triple sequence of events to be considered, namely, the conditioned fear drive, which produces the obsessional trains of thought, which in turn produces the ritualistic behavior. A much clearer delineation of the relationship between the fear, the obsession, and the compulsion is required, both theoretically and empirically. Elucidation of this problem would also throw light on the relationship between phobias and obsessions.

REFERENCES

Balslev-Olesen, T. & Geert-Jorgensen, E. The prognosis of obsessive-compulsive neurosis. *Acta psychiat. scand.*, 1959, **34**, 232–241.

Bevan, J.R. Learning theory applied to the treatment of a patient with obsessional ruminations. In Eysenck, H.J. (ed.). *Behavior therapy and the neuroses*. Oxford: Pergamon, 1960, pp. 165–169.

Delay, J., Pichot, P., & Perse, J. Personnalité obsessionelle et caractere dit obsessionel: étude clinique et psychométrique. *Rev. Psychol. appl.*, 1962, **12**, 233–262.

Eysenck, H.J. *Dimensions of personality*. London: Routledge & Kegan Paul, 1947.

Farber, I.E. Response fixation under anxiety and nonanxiety conditions. *J. exp. Psychol.*, 1948, **38**, 111–131.

Greenberg, H.R. & Sarner, C.A. Trichotillomania: symptom and syndrome. *Arch. gen. Psychiat.*, 1965, **12**, 482–489.

Grimshaw, L. Obsessional disorder and neurological illness. *J. Neurol. Neurosurg. Psychiat.*, 1964, **27**, 229–231.

Grimshaw, L. The outcome of obsessional disorder: a follow-up study of 100 cases. *Brit. J. Psychiat.*, 1965, **111**, 1051–1056.

Haslam, M.T. The treatment of an obsessional patient by reciprocal inhibition. *Behav. Res. Ther.*, 1965, **2**, 213–216.

Hastings, D.W. Follow-up results in psychiatric illness. *Amer. J. Psychiat.*, 1958, **114**, 1057–1066.

Ingram, I.M. Obsessional illness in mental hospital patients. *J. ment. Sci.*, 1961, **107**, 382–402 (a).

Ingram, I.M. The obsessional personality and obsessional illness. *Amer. J. Psychiat.*, 1961, **117**, 1016–1019 (b)

Ingram, I.M. & McAdam, W.A. The electroencephalogram, obsessional illness, and obsessional personality. *J. ment. Sci.*, 1960, **106**, 686–691.

Judd, L.L. Obsessive-compulsive neurosis in children. *Arch. gen. Psychiat.*, 1965, **12**, 136–143.

Kringlen, E. Obsessional neurotics: a long-term follow-up. *Brit. J. Psychiat.*, 1965, **111**, 709–722.

Kushner, M. & Sandler, J. Aversion therapy and the concept of punishment. *Behav. Res. Ther.*, 1966, **4**, 179–186.

Lazarus, A.A. New methods in psychotherapy: a case study. *S.Afr. med. J.*, 1958, **33**, 660–663.

Lewis, A.J. Problems of obsessional illness. *Proc. roy. Soc. Med.*, 1936, **29**, 325–336.

Luff, M.C. & Garrod, M. After-results of psychotherapy in 500 adult cases. *Brit. med. J.*, 1935, **2**, 54–59.

Metzner, R. Some experimental analogues of obsession. *Behav. Res. Ther.*, 1963, **1**, 231–236.

Meyer, V. Modification of expectations in cases with obsessional rituals. *Behav. Res. Ther.*, 1966, **4**, 273–280.

Michaels, J.J. & Porter, R.T. Psychiatric and social implication of contrasts between psychopathic personality and obsessive compulsion neurosis. *J. nerv. ment. Dis.*, 1949, **109**, 122–132.

Müller, C. Vorlaufige Mitteilung zur langen Katamnese der Zwangskranken. *Nervenartz*, 1953, **24**, 112–115.

Pacella, B.L., Polatin, P., & Nagler, S.H. Clinical and EEG studies in obsessive-compulsive states. *Amer. J. Psychiat.*, 1944, **100**, 830–838.

Pollitt, J.D. Natural history of obsessional states: a study of 150 cases. *Brit. med. J.*, 1957, **1**, 194–198.

Pollitt, J.D. Natural history studies in mental illness: a discussion based on a pilot study of obsessional states. *J. ment. Sci.*, 1960, **106**, 93–113.

Rockwell, F.V. & Simons, D.J. The electroencephalogram and personality organisation in the obsessive-compulsive reactions. *Arch. Neurol. Psychiat.*, 1947, **57**, 71–77.

Ross, D. & Rice, D. A case of obsessional state of unusual content. *J. ment. Sci.*, 1945, **91**, 495–498.

Rüdin, E. Ein Beitrag zur Frage der Zwangskrankheit, insbesondere ihrer hereditären Beziehungen. *Arch. Psychiat. Nervenkr.*, 1953, **191**, 14–54.

Sandler, J. & Hazari, A. The "obsessional": on the psychological classification of obsessional character traits and symptoms. *Brit. J. med. Psychol.*, 1960, **33**, 113–122.

Taylor, J.G. A behavioral interpretation of obsessive-compulsive neurosis. *Behav. Res. Ther.*, 1963, **1**, 237–244.

Thorpe, J.G., Schmidt, E., Brown, P.T., & Castell, D. Aversion-relief therapy: a new method for general application. *Behav. Res. Ther.*, 1964, **2**, 71–82.

Walton, D. The relevance of learning theory to the treatment of an obsessive-compulsive state. In Eysenck, H.J. (ed.). *Behavior Therapy and the Neuroses*. Oxford: Pergamon, 1960, pp. 153–164.

Walton, D. & Mather, M.D. The application of learning principles to the treatment of obsessive-compulsive states in the acute and chronic phases of illness. *Behav. Res. Ther.*, 1963, **1**, 163–174.

Walton, D. & Mather, M.D. The application of learning principles to the treatment of obsessive-compulsive states in the acute and chronic phases of illness. In Eysenck, H.J. (ed.). *Experiments in behavior therapy*. London: Pergamon, 1964, pp. 117–151.

Weiner, I.B. Behavior therapy in obsessive-compulsive neurosis: treatment of an adolescent boy. *Psychotherapy*, 1967, **4**, 27–29.

Wolpe, J. *Psychotherapy by reciprocal inhibition*. Stanford: Stanford Univer. Press, 1958.

Chapter 9

The "Hysterias"

THE TERM "hysterias" has been placed in quotation marks, since there is much dispute at the present time as to the utility of this classificatory term.[1] The studies of Breuer and Freud (1957), which appeared finally to introduce a scientific approach to the study of hysteria, did not in fact lead to any particular clarification of the issues involved in the use of the term, and indeed, as Forrest (1967) has recently pointed out, the theoretical literature on the topic has been surprisingly sparse over the last 50 years.

In this chapter, therefore, we shall first consider the problem of what might be meant by the use of terms such as "hysteria," "hysterical," and so forth; and then we shall discuss the application of behavior therapy techniques to specific disorders which at one time or another have been subsumed under those terms, without, however, preempting the question of whether these specific disorders can be regarded as being correlated with any particular type of personality structure.

I. DEFINITION AND MEASUREMENT OF "HYSTERIA"

1. MEANINGS OF THE TERM "HYSTERIA"

As Chodoff and Lyons (1958) point out, the term "hysteria" has been used in a number of different ways to refer to: the "hysterical personality"; conversion hysteria; anxiety hysteria; and a particular psychopathological pattern (including a particular psychosexual history). It has also, as they point out, been used as a term of opprobrium by psychiatrists for patients they find irritating and annoying (that is, who arouse hostility in the psychiatrist). The term "anxiety hysteria" was introduced by Freud to refer particularly to the neurotic patient with phobias and anxiety and need not be considered here. The most important problem appears to relate to the relationship between the "hysterical personality" and "conversion hysteria" and exactly parallels the problem, which was considered in a previous chapter, of the relationship between the "obsessional personality" and "obsessive-compulsive neurosis."

2. THE HYSTERICAL PERSONALITY AND CONVERSION HYSTERIA

There is a considerable measure of agreement that patients can be meaningfully classified as presenting a "hysterical personality" profile, though there is some difference of opinion as to whether subcategories of this syndrome exist. The main bone of contention has been whether patients demonstrating clear-cut conversion symptoms (such as hysterical blindness or deafness, anaesthesias, paralyses, and so on) will also manifest the hysterical personality syndrome; and whether conversion reactions themselves constitute a distinct syndrome or should be regarded as specific modes of reaction which can equally well arise in any psychiatric disorder.

---

[1] Veith (1965) has presented a comprehensive historical review of the concept of "hysteria" up to the end of the 19th century.

The general consensus of opinion now appears to be that no significant correlation exists between conversion hysteria and a hysterical personality structure. Thus, Chodoff and Lyons (1958) examined the personality structure of 17 patients with a clear-cut diagnosis of conversion hysteria and found that only three showed evidence of hysterical personality as they defined this term (see below). Lewis and Berman (1965) found 57 cases of clear-cut conversion hysteria in 16,000 discharges; 50% of these were also diagnosed as hysterical personality. They also found some evidence for a syndrome of classical symptoms in otherwise diversely presenting conversion hysterics, consisting of amnesia, fits, unexplained pain, vomiting, urinary retention, blindness, impotence, paralysis, and aphonia. A similar classical pattern in conversion hysteria was found by Ljungberg (1960) in a large-scale study. Considerable doubt as to the existence of a syndrome of conversion hysteria has been cast by other authors, however. It has been argued, for example, that conversion patients will also show a high incidence of depression, schizophrenia, and neurotic anxiety (Ziegler and Imboden, 1962) and careful follow-up studies of patients diagnosed as conversion hysteria show a remarkable incidence of subsequent organic basis for the symptoms, as well as a tendency for the diagnosis to change (Slater, 1961, 1965).[2]

Objective psychological studies have not, unfortunately, clarified this issue to any great degree. Eysenck's work has been described in detail in a previous chapter. But it is pertinent to note here particularly that he would appear not to make any clear distinction within his dimensional system between conversion hysteria and hysterical personality. In his original factor analytic study identifying the intro-version-extraversion dimension using psychiatric ratings on neurotic patients (Eysenck, 1947), he reported a correlation of -0.41 between "hysterical attitude" and the factor, while "hysterical conversion" correlated -0.63. This would appear to suggest a fairly strong relationship and, in a subsequent study reported in the same volume, he found very similar correlations with suggestibility for patients diagnosed either as "hysterical personality" or as "conversion hysteria." In another study (Eysenck, 1955), the selection of a criterion group of "hysterics" was

made on the basis that the psychiatric diagnosis should be "conversion hysteria" or hysteria (the latter term presumably referring to "hysterical personality" without conversion symptoms).

Turning now to the "hysterical personality," Forrest (1967) has argued that there are two rather different categories of patients subsumed under this term, though he admits that overlap occurs. First we have what might continue to be called the "hysterical personality." The characteristics of these patients have been well described by Chodoff and Lyons (1958) as follows:

(i) Egoism, vanity, egocentricity, self-centredness, indulgence.

(ii) Exhibitionism, dramatization, lying exaggeration, play acting, histrionic behavior, mendacity, pseudologia phantastica, dramatic self-display, center of attention, simulation.

(iii) Unbridled display of affects, labile affectivity, emotional capriciousness, deficient in emotional control, profusion of affects, emotions volatile and labile, excitability, inconsistency of reactions.

(iv) Emotional shallowness, affects fraudulent and shallow, go through the motions of feeling.

(v) Lasciviousness, sexualization of all non-sexual relations, obvious sexual behavior, coquetry, provocative.

(vi) Sexual frigidity, intense fear of sexuality, failure of sex impulse to develop toward natural goal, sexually immature, sexual apprehensiveness.

(vii) Demanding, dependent relationships.

Ziegler and his colleagues (Ziegler, Imboden and Meyer, 1960; Ziegler and Imboden, 1962; Ziegler, Imboden, and Rodgers, 1963) and Forrest (1967) have delineated a similar personality syndrome, but Forrest (1967) has also argued for a "hysterical psychopathic" syndrome which is characterized differentially from the hysterical personality by lower social class, tendency to develop addiction habits, frequent hospitalization and operations of an unnecessary kind, and complete failure to respond to any form of therapy or to cooperate in therapy. Forrest argues that the syndrome of "hysteria" developed by Guze and his colleagues (Gatfield and Guze, 1962; Guze and Perley, 1963) is essentially identical with his syndrome of the "hysterical psychopath."

[2] The existence of accompanying or preceding organic brain disorder in a high percentage of patients diagnosed as suffering from hysteria has been confirmed by Whitlock (1967).

In summary, the present position seems to be that most psychiatrists prefer to consider conversion hysteria as a separate classification from a more general personality disorder that may manifest itself in one of two overlapping forms: the hysterical personality or the hysterical psychopath.

In fact, behavior therapists have applied their techniques almost entirely to the study of conversion symptoms (or conversion reactions as they are alternatively called) and no work appears to have been carried out on the more general personality disorder.

In what follows, a quite arbitrary decision has been made to divide the disorders to be dealt with into two major categories: those involving diminished nonorganic[3] functioning and those involving heightened nonorganic functioning. Within these categories a distinction is also made between disorders of sensory and perceptual functioning on the one hand, and disorders of motor behavior on the other. Of course, some disorders appear to involve *both* sensory and motor functioning, and in these cases the disorder has been categorized according to whether the primary dysfunction is considered to be sensory or motor. It should be made clear, however, that the classification is heuristic only, and no particular significance should be attached to it in relation to either etiology or treatment.

II. DIMINISHED NONORGANIC SENSORY AND PERCEPTUAL FUNCTIONING

1. FUNCTIONAL BLINDNESS

The one case of functional blindness that has been investigated by behavioristic techniques has given rise to considerable controversy. Brady and Lind (1961) carried out a detailed experimental study of a male who had demonstrated apparent total hysterical blindness for more than two years, the condition being unaffected by various forms of psychiatric treatment. In the experiment, the patient was required to estimate a time interval of 18 seconds by pressing a key within 3 seconds of the end of the period. If the response was made correctly, a buzzer sounded to indicate success; if incorrect, the apparatus was reset to commence a new trial. Each session lasted one half

hour. The first six sessions constituted a base-rate situation. At the end of the sixth session, the patient's correct response rate had stabilized at about 50%. During the next 10 sessions, a light bulb (not visible to the patient) was illuminated at the 18-second point, remaining on for three seconds and serving as a visual cue for time interval by increasing the overall room illumination by a just perceptible amount for a person with normal vision. During these sessions, the patient's correct response rate declined significantly, since he tended to press the key prematurely and thus prevent the appearance of the light. In the following seven sessions, the light was turned on at full intensity and in a position where it could be seen by the patient. After a further initial fall, the correct response rate rose to 67%. The patient denied being able to see the light and attributed his success to feeling the heat from the lamp (an obviously incorrect explanation). During sessions 25 through 45, the intensity of the light was gradually diminished. After an initial improvement to 82% correct responses, the response rate suddenly dropped to 48% and the patient declared he could see the light. After this, the correct response rate rapidly improved (but only to about 70%). In the final group of sessions (45 through 63), the visual cues for pressing the key were made more complex by the introduction of a pattern of change to signal the end of an interval. In the final session the correct response rate was virtually 100%, and the patient could clinically see. On testing at seven-month follow-up after discharge, the patient was described as being gainfully employed as a switchboard operator, and as being able to read small print and identify geometrical patterns and small objects.

Some years later, however, Grosz and Zimmerman (1965) reported that the patient had failed to maintain either his employment or his sight and criticized Brady and Lind for failing to raise the issue of malingering as opposed to functional or hysterical blindness. Subsequently (Zimmerman and Grosz, 1966), they reported in detail on their own laboratory investigations of this patient. They carried out a series of five ingenious experiments over 132 sessions.

They set up a situation involving the presentation on each trial of three adjacent triangles, two inverted and one upright. The position of

---

[3] The term "nonorganic" is used here to indicate that the dysfunction cannot be correlated with physiological or other organic changes.

the triangles was randomly varied, and the only correct response was pressing the switch under the upright triangle. On control sessions (where no triangles were presented), the patient's performance should be determined by laws of chance; on experimental trials, an organically blind person's performance would also be determined by chance. Hence, it would be possible to conclude that this patient was functioning visually *if his correct response rate were higher or lower than that predicted on the basis of chance responding.*

To make the procedure clearer, the results of the first experiment are shown in Figure 1. In this experiment, the triangles were either present (E_1) or absent (C_1) and it can be seen that, during the experimental sessions, the patient was significantly "denying" the visual cue. But this nonchance denial could be accomplished only by making use of the visual cue, that is, by perceiving it. It will also be apparent that the correct response rate progressively diminished during the experimental trials, while the response latency became longer. As Zimmerman and Grosz put it, he was "seeing worse than a blind man," and they concluded that he was "denying vision" while functioning visually.[4]

In subsequent experiments, Zimmerman and

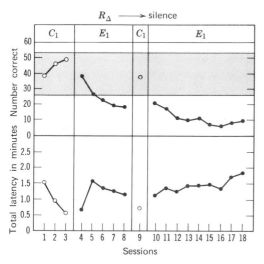

FIG. 1. Number of correct responses and cumulated buzzer to response latency in each session of Experiment 1. Shaded area covers region of chance values. Open circles and closed circles are values obtained in control (C_1) and experimental (E_1) sessions, respectively (Zimmerman and Grosz, 1966).

Grosz were able to show that the patient's behavior could be systematically manipulated by varying the conditions of the experiment. In particular, they showed that, when the patient was deviously informed of the task-behavior that would be expected of a genuinely blind person, his behavior on the task immediately changed in that direction.

There can be no question that the experiments of Zimmerman and Grosz (1966) represented a marked advance on the techniques used by Brady and Lind (1961). The former overcame the objection to the Brady and Lind study that temporal discrimination learning could have accounted for the majority of the results; made it possible to determine whether and under what conditions the patient was performing at the chance level expected of an organically blind person or, alternatively, was performing above or below chance expectations; and carefully examined the differential effects of the introduction of various kinds of information on the strategies being utilized by the patient.

Zimmerman and Grosz in effect raised the whole question of "genuine" hysterical blindness as against "conscious" malingering. This point was taken up by Brady (1966) in his comment on the Grosz/Zimmerman experiment, but the problem will be deferred for consideration at a later point.

Mention may be made here of a recent study by Meichenbaum (1966) who reported on a male patient who was unable to keep his eyes open. In the first stage of treatment, general training in bodily relaxation was given, using breathing exercises with the suggestion that his eyes would open as he exhaled. In the second stage, after the patient was discharged, residual difficulty in opening his eyes when awaking in the morning was treated rather similarly and, finally, he was given training in assertive behavior because his difficulties were to some extent regarded as arising from family relationships with his mother. At a three-month follow-up, the eye-closure difficulty had disappeared and his personal relationships had much improved.

2. FUNCTIONAL DEAFNESS

As in the case of functional blindness, the behavioristic approach to functional deafness has been almost entirely laboratory-based and not primarily with therapeutic intent. The

---

[4] A similar demonstration in a patient with unilateral functional blindness has recently been given by Miller (1968).

studies to which reference will be made were inspired by earlier investigations by Erickson (1938a) who described the very marked clinical changes occuring in normal subjects placed under profound hypnosis with induced hearing loss. In approximately two-thirds of his subjects, apparent total or partial deafness was achieved, this being indexed by alterations of auditory threshold and impairment of hearing in relation to various kinds of tests. In a second study, Erickson (1938b) carred out controlled experiments on two subjects from the previous study. He trained his subjects to produce a muscular CR (flexor muscles of the forearm) by pairing the sound of a buzzer with an electric shock to the hand while the subject was under deep hypnosis. When hypnotic deafness was then induced (by a sharp blow to the shoulder, the subjects being highly practiced), the CR to the buzzer disappeared, whereas it reappeared without further training if the hypnotic deafness were abolished. Various control studies showed that the results could not be attributed to simulation on the part of the subjects. Erickson also found that he could not *establish* a CR to sound in subjects who were hypnotically deaf.

Malmo, Davis, and Barza (1952) carried out experiments on a 19-year-old girl with total hysterical deafness. In their first experiment, they showed that a strong auditory stimulus elicited a startle response on the first presentation, but not on subsequent trials (as measured by muscle potentials recorded from forehead, right neck, right sternomastoid muscle, and left extensor and right extensor muscles of both arms). The initial startle response was accompanied by a strong emotional reaction, and the experience was described, not in auditory terms, but like being hit on the head. In a second experiment, an attempt was made to condition finger withdrawal, produced by shock, to a tone. This led to the interesting finding that muscle potential CRs were significantly more frequent than finger-withdrawal CRs in the deaf state, whereas the reverse was the case after hearing was recovered. This finding applied whether the trial was a nonreinforced (CS alone) or a reinforced (CS followed by US) one. In other words, conditioning did occur to the auditory stimulus, but during deafness it was primarily manifested by an involuntary rather than by a voluntary response. This evidence of conditioning is not incompatible with the findings of Erickson (1938b), since he did not measure EMG responses.

In a later study, Malmo, Boag, and Raginsky (1954) compared the results from their first experiment with those obtained in experiments that they carried out with two easily hypnotizable female subjects, and one patient with organically based middle ear deafness. An auditory stimulus of 700 cps was presented at 90 db above threshold under three conditions: "deaf" state; waking state; and under instructions to simulate deafness. They found that the hypnotized subjects behaved very similarly to the patient with hysterical deafness in showing elevated EMG reactions on the first presentation of the auditory stimulus followed by a sudden drop; whereas the organically deaf person, of course, showed no response whatever. They also found that there was a tendency in the hypnotized subjects to show the same sensory displacement as the functionally deaf patient, that is, to report a nonauditory stimulus at the time the auditory stimulus was presented. They speculated that inhibition of hearing may be produced by the emission of an incompatible motor response, such as subvocal speech (it was found that chin muscle activity increased in the deaf state).

It is clear that conditioning techniques, whether of the classical or operant kind, can be of particular value in relation to functional disorders of seeing and hearing. Barraclough (1966) has recently demonstrated a simple method of helping to determine whether hearing is present in possibly functionally deaf children, who are also lacking speech. He trained an apparently deaf (and speechless) child to choose that one of two tins which contained food by matching the sign on the tin with the sign on a card. When this was accomplished, the card was preceded by an appropriate number of sounds and gradually the child was required to choose on the basis of the number of sounds alone. This technique proved to be a useful way of showing that this child did have some degree of hearing and, in fact, demonstrated that the child could only do this successfully when the sounds were between 125 and 250 cps.

Finally, in connection with psychogenic deafness, mention should be made of an important study by Reed (1961). From a population of 3000 children, he identified 24 with psychogenic deafness. The children were categorized into two groups: those showing deafness for pure tones but not speech; and the reverse. He then examined personality characteristics of the two groups and found that the children psychiatrically diagnosed as predominantly "hysteric" showed deafness for pure tones but not speech in 13/14 cases; whereas children psychiatrically diagnosed as predominantly "anxiety state" showed deafness for speech in 9/12 cases. These results are particularly interesting because they appear to refute the view sometimes expressed that *all* forms of hysterical deafness represent a variety of the perceptual defense phenomenon (Kleinman, 1957; Kodman and Blanton, 1960). Reed attempts to relate his two types of functional deafness to Eysenck's neuroticism and extraversion dimensions. Although it is not entirely clear from his text, it appears that he relates pure-tone deafness to high extraversion, producing inattention in the audiometric testing situation; whereas deafness for speech (which manifests itself in social situations) may represent a defensive reaction against hearing the speech of others, which is regarded as threatening, and hence is related to high introversion *and* neuroticism.

3. FUNCTIONAL ANALGESIA, ASTEREOGNOSIS, AND ANAESTHESIA

Sears and Cohen (1933) reported a series of careful experimental studies of a 45-year-old female with three functional deficits in the left hand: analgesia to superficial and deep pain; astereognosis (inability to identify objects by manual examination without sight); and anaesthesia to superficial touch. Their technique essentially involved comparisons of reaction by the left hand with that by the right hand, which was normal except for numbness in the thumb.

The first experiment related to the analgesia. The effects of painful stimulation (algesimeter and shock) to the left and right hands were compared with respect to changes in the breathing reflex. The pre-post stimulation increase in the breathing reflex was significantly greater for both painful stimuli in the case of the normal hand as compared with the analgesic hand. The second experiment showed that, in relation to the astereognosis, two-point discrimination was severely reduced in the left hand and that, therefore, the disorder was not restricted to gross discrimination of objects. In the third experiment, relating to the anaesthesia for light touch, a CR could not be established to stroking the left hand with cotton wool, while using shock to the right hand as the US producing withdrawal. (No attempt was

made apparently to determine whether a CR to such an unsubstantial stimulus could be achieved in the normal right hand). However, a CR *was* established in the left hand when a sharp rap from a pencil was used as the CS and this generalized to the cotton as a higher order CS. It proved possible to demonstrate experimental extinction and relearning. It was also found that, as training proceeded, the patient began to perceive the touch of the cotton and the anaesthesia disappeared completely. It is impossible, however, to attribute the disappearance of the anaesthesia to the procedures used (they were not, of course, carried out with therapeutic intent), particularly in view of the fact that the astereognosis disappeared spontaneously during testing. As we shall see, however, it is not impossible to suppose that these conditioning procedures, may, under certain circumstances, raise perception of stimulation above threshold by the pairing of an initially unperceived (i.e., neutral) CS with an above-threshold US.

III. DIMINISHED NONORGANIC MOTOR FUNCTIONING

1. PARALYSIS OF MOTOR FUNCTION

Behavior therapists have thus far ignored the classical functional paralysis cases, even though there is no doubt that such patients provide unique opportunities for controlled experimental studies with possible therapeutic benefits. Hilgard and Marquis (1940) reported the results of an interesting experiment carried out on a schoolteacher with total paralysis of the left arm for six years following a car accident. Arm and hand were markedly atrophied from disuse, and anaesthesia was also present.[5] An attempt was first made to demonstrate sensitivity in the paralyzed hand by presenting shock as a *conditioned* stimulus to that hand while presenting shock as an *unconditioned* stimulus to the normal hand (that is, shock to the paralyzed hand would, if sensitivity were present, serve as a signal for an unconditioned response by the normal hand). There was little evidence of conditioning, but sensitivity gradually returned completely to the still paralyzed hand. The procedure was now reversed, with light shock to the normal hand serving as the

---

[5] The case is included here because paralysis persisted even after full sensitivity was restored. The degree to which paralysis and anaesthesia can exist

independently in conversion hysteria is an interesting, but little explored question.

CS, and strong shock to the paralyzed but sensitive hand as the US. It was found that conditioned withdrawal of the paralyzed hand did occur. Once this was achieved, it proved possible to reeducate the patient in voluntary control of the hand while physiotherapy helped strengthen the wasted muscles. At a two-year follow-up, recovery was still complete and there was no evidence of symptom substitution.

Apart from this interesting study, the only other example of a behavioristic approach appears to be that of Meichenbaum (1966),[6] whose patient complained that he was unable to walk. Treatment included the use of a tranquillizing drug with the suggestion that it would strengthen his legs; physical therapy; and a graded rewalking training program, with positive reinforcement for success and criticism (including the ridicule of other patients) for failure. Complete success with an eight-month follow-up was achieved, but it is impossible, of course, to determine which factors (if any) were responsible for the improvement.

2. WRITER'S CRAMP

The first serious behavioristic investigation of writer's cramp was carried out by Liversedge and Sylvester (1955). They analyzed the phenomenon very carefully and concluded that there were two triggering stimuli (which they regarded as CS) for the motor phenomena: tactual stimulation from the pen itself and tactual stimulation from the hand touching the writing surface. The motor disturbance also involved two components (which they regarded as CRs): a tremor of variable rate and magnitude and a spasm of the muscles of the hand, forearm, and upper arm involving excessive pressure of the thumb on the pen. In this early study, they treated the tremor and pressure components separately, but in each case using aversive shock which was produced by the maladaptive movements. The tremor was treated in two ways: by requiring the patient to insert a stylus into progressively smaller holes, and by requiring the patient to perform a stylus tracking task. In each case, failure to keep the stylus from touching the metal sides (of the hole or the track) resulted in shock. The excessive pen pressure was treated by providing shock if the pressure of the pen exceeded an arbitrarily set limit. Two patients were successfully treated in this way (with 3- and 4-month follow-up) while 4 other patients with writer's cramp of 3–10 years' duration markedly improved. A case of typist's cramp (which manifested itself by flexion of the fingers into the palm with great force) was similarly treated by shock to the palm (which produced involuntary extension) with apparently complete success.

These initial results were extremely encouraging since writer's cramp is notoriously intractable to treatment. In a later report, Sylvester and Liversedge (1960) treated[7] 39 cases by the methods described. Of these, 29 are described as successful as to outcome after relatively short (3–6 weeks) periods of treatment. There were 10 failures and five relapses. They accounted for their failures in terms of generalization of anxiety in long-standing cases and the unsuitability of the treatment for some cases. They produced cogent arguments in refutation of the contention that the recoveries were a result of a general therapy effect or placebo effects. Their general explanation of writer's cramp at this point involved conceptualizing writing as being controlled servomechanistically. In the development of writer's cramp, innervation of the protagonist muscles involved in writing is immediately followed by innervation of the antagonist muscles and, if this sequence occurs often enough, the antagonist innervation would become conditioned to proprioceptive feedback from innervation of the protagonist muscles (and, of course, probably generalize to the writing situation as a whole). The explanation given by Sylvester and Liversedge as to how the initial reciprocal innervation arises, however, is unconvincing, being couched in highly subjective terms. One possible explanation is that writing movements become aversive stimuli in some subjects and that therefore the antagonist innervation represents an escape response which reduces aversive stimulation and ultimately becomes an anticipatory avoidance response. This situation could perhaps arise in people whose writing skill is highly inefficient and who write frequently (hence the term, occupational cramp), the aversive stimulation thus being self-produced. The aversion treatment is intended then to produce inhibition of the antagonist response by making it less rewarding than the protagonist

---

[6] Wolpe's (1958) Case 14 (hysterical paralysis of right forearm) was successfully treated by repeated presentation of the precipitating event under hypnosis.

[7] They also provide a brief, but comprehensive review of the relatively sparse literature.

response. It also seems likely that, during the course of this treatment, the old protagonist writing response is reinstated in a more efficient form than was previously the case. Indeed, the success or failure of the treatment may well turn on just this point.[8]

Beech (1960) also reviewed the literature on writer's cramp and argued that the treatment techniques of Liversedge and Sylvester might in some circumstances do more harm than good. He postulated that, if writer's cramp is a response to *anxiety*, then the use of aversive techniques where the level of anxiety is high might lead to an *increase* in anxiety (the anxiety produced by shock summating with the anxiety already present in the writing situation) and thus *strengthen* rather than weaken the maladaptive response. Thus he suggested that, while the use of shock might be successful in patients with low anxiety, it would probably be preferable to use alternative methods with patients with high anxiety. The two alternative methods he suggested and utilized were massed practice and desensitization procedures (the latter to reduce the anxiety level). Massed practice involved the patient in reproducing the maladaptive finger movement as precisely as possible, but with weights attached to increase the rate of build-up of I_R. Beech gives several examples (mostly incomplete) of case studies where the Liversedge and Sylvester techniques failed to produce improvement and where the alternative techniques were more successful.

An important point of dispute here was whether or not patients suffering from writer's cramp tend to be neurotic and/or anxious or not. Liversedge and Sylvester argued that their patients were not neurotic and their anxiety was a result of the writer's cramp rather than the reverse; whereas Beech contended that many of his patients were neurotic and that the writer's cramp was a reaction to anxiety about writing (for whatever reason). The point remains in dispute. There seems no doubt, however, that the aversion techniques recommended by Sylvester and Liversedge will significantly improve an impressive percentage of patients suffering from this disorder. Bearing in mind the parallel we have drawn between the aversion methods of treating writer's cramp and

Goldiamond's aversion and retraining methods for treating stuttering, it would seem that further work on writer's cramp along the same lines might prove profitable. That is, the basic argument would be that writer's cramp arises as response to aversive stimulation produced by excessive and inefficient writing; that shock treatment abolishes the maladaptive "cramp" responses; and that the new writing responses produced in this situation need to be shaped toward a new normal writing style which will differ both from the cramp style and the original style of writing.[9]

3. HYSTERICAL APHONIA AND DYSPHONIA

Bangs and Freidinger (1949) treated a 13-year-old adolescent with functional aphonia of seven years' duration by reeducative speech therapy which was essentially a form of SD(R). The steps in treatment involved:

(i) Breathing and laryngeal exercises to restore tonicity of the speech muscles that had been affected by disuse.

(ii) Making of the easiest of the speech sounds (that is, those involving the least amount of muscular effort) namely,

$$\langle [m], [n], [z], [v] \rangle$$

(iii) Combining consonants with vowels.

(iv) Uttering individual words.

(v) Reading passages of prose.

This case is interesting as an example of a functional disorder producing physiological changes that compounded the disability. Progress in treatment was slow but steady, transference from the laboratory to real-life (ward, outside world) situations was obtained, and vocalization was maintained over a two-year follow-up. The treatment occupied $10\frac{1}{2}$ weeks. Similar techniques were used with an adult female with dysphonia of five years' duration (Bangs and Freindinger, 1950).[10] The patient made a good recovery which was maintained over a four-year follow-up. Given the severity of the disorder in both these cases, it is highly likely that the treatment techniques were directly responsible for the improvement.

A rather different approach was used by Gray, England and Mohoney (1965). They

---

[8] Compare Goldiamond's abolition of stuttering accompanied by the *instatement* (not *reinstatement*) of a new form of speech, which is then shaped toward normal speech.

[9] Crisp and Moldofsky (1965) produced significant improvement in six of their seven cases by

procedures which included general and specific relaxation training, supportive psychotherapy, and graded writing exercises.

[10] In this paper, the literature on hysterical dysphonia is reviewed.

treated a female with severe vocal nodules[11] impairing speech, not by a direct reeducative attack on the speech itself, but by the use of training in relaxation and desensitization (SD-I) of anxieties relating to the woman's children, husband, and "the other man," which were hypothesized to underly the condition. The treatment was successful, the vocal nodules disappearing completely and remaining absent over a six-week follow-up period. A theoretical interpretation of their case might be conceptualized in terms of high drive (conditioned anxiety) interfering with a skilled response, the inefficient response then producing the vocal nodules.

A study by Walton and Black (1959) relating to hysterical aphonia is important for several reasons, not least of which is the curious method of treatment applied. They argued that if the patient were given massed practice in trying to speak, the situation would lead to the accumulation of reactive inhibition in relation to the "not-being-able-to-speak" habit and hence this would extinguish through the generation of $_sI_R$ (not being able *not* to speak!). Periods of practice were prolonged if speech did not improve during a given session and shortened if it did. Leaving aside this curious theoretical reasoning, the study by Walton and Black is interesting because of the introduction into the practice situation of increasingly social stimulation in the form of other persons; and the use of reading situations (such as play-reading) which approximated real life more and more closely. By the end of treatment, the patient's voice had returned completely and the improvement was maintained over seven follow-up tests over nearly two years, in spite of severe traumatic experiences which the patient underwent. No symptom substitution was evident.

4. HYSTERICAL RETENTION OF URINE

Cooper (1965) attempted to apply conditioning theory to the study of a 60-year-old female, who developed inability to urinate, apparently as a defensive reaction against her husband's treatment of her. Cooper argued that, whenever the patient experienced involuntary retention of urine, the injection of carbochol would serve as a US for unconditioned urination (UR),[12] and found that on subsequent occasions the injection of sterile water would serve as a

CS producing involuntary urination. Subsequently, the mere sight of the syringe needle would produce the same effect. By higher-order conditioning, he predicted that eventually the increasing bladder tension (which had become associated with the *inhibition* of micturition) would now become associated with involuntary micturition and this indeed appeared to happen. The model used by Cooper is summarized in Figure 2. The patient was free of the disorder at a four-month follow-up.

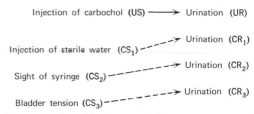

FIG. 2. Conditioning model for treatment of hysterical retention of urine (after Cooper, 1965).

Barnard et al (1966) treated a 27-year-old female with an exceptionally severe history of urinary retention with repeated catheterizations. Their treatment involved two stages. First, they argued that retention was a result of over-stimulation by the sympathetic division of the autonomic nervous system and consequent reciprocal inhibition of the parasympathetic division. To counter this situation, they used in effect the aversion-relief shock method of Thorpe et al (1964), giving increasing shock to the legs followed by sudden cessation and found that this produced urinary flow, which gradually came under voluntary control. Additionally, however, they argued that the urinary retention was only one aspect of a general learned tendency to be passive and nonassertive. Hence, they also used Wolpe's methods of training in assertiveness, initially associating shock termination with a gross assertive response and then refining, extending, and generalizing the assertive behavior by role-playing into real-life situations. The urinary retention was eliminated (follow-up 18 months) and the general adjustment of the patient markedly improved. This study represents a most interesting application of the proposition of Yates (1958) that, instead of symptoms plus underlying conflict, we are dealing with sequential combinations of behavior and that an attack at any or several points of the chain will influence the whole sequence of behavior.

---

[11] Operation to remove the nodules was followed by rapid regrowth.

[12] Injection of carbochol produces involuntary urination.

5. ANOREXIA NERVOSA

Since anorexia nervosa has attracted a good deal of *specific* attention from both the psychodynamic and behavioristic viewpoints, it will be considered in some detail.

(a) DEFINITION OF ANOREXIA NERVOSA. The disorder was first described, apparently independently, by Gull (1874) in England and by Lasegue (1873) in France.[13] The primary symptom, of course, is weight loss of a progressive and severe nature, following a refusal to eat. The classical accompanying symptoms have been clearly stated by Farquharson and Hyland (1938). It may be readily distinguished from Simmond's disease, which also results in wasting, and from hysterical abstention from food (Nicolle, 1939). Table 9.1 shows the main symptomatology for anorexia nervosa and Simmond's disease. Anorexia nervosa may be

TABLE 9.1. *Symptomatology of Anorexia Nervosa and Simmond's Disease*

Anorexia Nervosa	Simmond's Disease
Onset in adolescence	Found in older women
Neurotic personality	Normal personality
Phobia for eating	Physiological loss of appetite
No loss of sex function	Loss of sex function; organ atrophy
No glandular malfunction	Malfunction of thyroid gland
No intellectual impairment	Intellectual impairment
Restless activity	Apathy
Causation: psychological	Causation: destruction of pituitary anterior lobe
Insidious onset	Abrupt onset
Amenorrhea: early onset	Amenorrhea: late onset

Source: Farquharson and Hyland, 1938.

distinguished from hysterical abstention from food by several factors (e.g., the hysteric eats surreptitiously while parading her "noneating" whereas the anorexic tries to hide her genuine noneating). However, recent careful studies by Stunkard (1959), Crisp (1965), and Silverstone and Russell (1967) have demonstrated conclusively that gastric motility is not a significant factor in anorexia nervosa. Silverstone and Russell (1967) compared gastric motility in anorexics before and after high calorie treatment with activity in normal controls and could find no significant differences in either total gastric activity or Type II contractions (those lasting 20–60 seconds and produced by hunger following food deprivation).

(b) THE GENESIS OF ANOREXIA NERVOSA. The combination of symptoms such as amenorrhea, low basal metabolism, low blood sugar level, and restlessness have led to the theory that anorexia nervosa is a metabolic disorder of psychological origin (Farquharson and Hyland, 1938) or to a stress on primary ovarian failure resulting from the instability of sex gland activity at adolescence (Nicolle, 1939); but these theories have not met with wide acceptance, nor has any specific evidence been adduced in their favor. Its occurrence largely at adolescence has, however, led to a good deal of stress being laid on sexual problems.[14] Thus, Nicolle (1939) also stressed fears of sexual inadequacy (arising from the amenorrhea and plumpness which often *precedes* the refusal to eat) which led to dieting. Hallsten (1965) did not specifically stress the sexual aspect, but he also emphasized the fear of being fat leading to dieting which produced reinforcing weight loss. Disapproval of the weight loss by others then led to additional anxiety which was reduced by the technique (i.e., dieting) previously found successful in

---

[13] A recent valuable compendium of papers edited by Kaufman (1965) provides a historical account of the development of the etiological and treatment approaches to anorexia nervosa. It includes the original papers by Gull and Lasegue.

[14] Psychoanalytically-oriented theories have regarded the disorder as a pregnancy fantasy (Moulton, 1942; Waller et al, 1940).

reducing anxiety and hence a progressive diminution in food intake. The severity of anorexia nervosa is such, however, that additional factors must certainly be postulated and the possibility of some physiological dysfunction which interacts with the psychological factors cannot be ruled out.[15]

(c) TREATMENT OF ANOREXIA NERVOSA. Nearly all workers in this area have stressed the importance of hospitalization of the patient for two reasons: it removes the patient from the conditions in which the disorder is being manifested (primarily the family situation), and it enables the eating behavior of the patient to be brought under strict supervision. The most striking behavioristic study of the treatment of anorexia nervosa is that by Bachrach, Erwin, and Mohr (1965). Their patient was a 37-year-old female with a 20-year history of anorexia. Her weight on admission was 47 pounds and she was in serious danger of death. The treatment involved operant control of the contingencies following eating and noneating behavior. The patient was placed in a bare room and reinforcements (television, visits, etc.) were made in the first instance contingent on eating and later on weight gain. This treatment, which was strictly policed, was successful. The patient on discharge weighed 66 pounds and when last seen weighed 88 pounds, was well and in employment.[16]

The theoretical model for treatment is derived from Goldiamond's (1962) analysis of the methodology of free operant conditioning, the paradigm being as follows:

Controlling stimuli . . . . .SV
(state variables)

$S^D - S$ (discriminative)

SS^C (constant)

$\rightarrow R$ $S^r - S^o$
(response) (differential reinforcement)

Presentation of a discriminative stimulus (S^D), in the presence of other constant stimuli (SS^C) will produce a response (R). The consequences (S^r) and the state variables (SV—needs and deprivations) will determine whether the response (R) occurs again. The patient will thus learn that eating leads to positive (reinforcing) contingencies, whereas noneating leads to negative (aversive) contingencies. Since noneating has, prior to treatment, also led to aversive consequences (ridicule, criticism), it must be assumed that the critical difference during treatment lies in the experimental control of the *timing* of the sequences.

Leitenberg, Agras, and Thomson (1968) carried out a similar study with two cases of anorexia nervosa. Similar weight gains were obtained with an operant conditioning program, and the gains were maintained when the reinforcing stimuli were withdrawn temporarily in one patient. They present several possible explanations for this somewhat paradoxical result, but as has been pointed out several times, experimentally produced changes may ultimately come to be maintained by the normal positive contingencies associated with "normal" behavior.

The striking success obtained by Bachrach et al (1965), using operant conditioning techniques, was not, however, replicated by Hallsten (1965), who had no success in the case of a 12-year-old girl (it is possible, however, that he did not control the eating situation as firmly or successfully as Bachrach et al). When Hallsten utilized SD-I, however, to reduce the anxiety presumed to be motivating the anorexia, weight gain was rapid and eating patterns were still normal at a five-month follow-up. Hallsten admits that confounding of operant conditioning and desensitization procedures might have occurred, but ruled it out after careful examination of the results in relation to the treatments. His study is, however, clearly less well controlled than that of Bachrach et al. A study (Lang, 1965) also using SD-I (assertive training) produced unclear results, and it is very doubtful if this case is really one of anorexia nervosa of the classical kind.

Finally, a study by Lesser et al (1960) of anorexia nervosa in comparatively young children utilized forced feeding as the method of treatment. On a five-year follow-up, seven of 15 cases showed good social adjustment and six cases a fair social adjustment. Again, however, it is very doubtful whether these cases would properly qualify as classical examples of the disorder.

---

[15] Lundberg and Walinder (1967) have recently provided suggestive evidence of the presence of organic cerebral lesions in at least some cases.

[16] The reader is recommended to look at the striking preillness and pre- and posttreatment photographs of the patient reproduced in Bachrach et al (1965).

III. HEIGHTENED NONORGANIC SENSORY AND PERCEPTUAL FUNCTIONING

1. NEURODERMITITIS

Walton (1960b) treated a 20-year-old female with neurodermatitis which had been unsuccessfully treated by medical means for over two years. He argued that, while the skin condition was probably originally determined by physical causes, the fact that the girl (who complained of family neglect) had found it to be the one thing which produced the attention she craved led to its perpetuation by repeated scratching. Simply instructing the family and the fiance to withdraw attention from the complaint (while providing positive reinforcement of other kinds) led to complete disappearance of the skin condition over three months. The follow-up was four years, the complaint did not recur during this period, and no symptom substitution was in evidence.

2. HYPERESTHESIA OF TASTE AND TOUCH

Beyme (1964) reported on a patient with intolerance for certain tactual stimuli (touching sandpaper or other "gritty" objects, or "rough" objects such as jute, ticking, and so on). This intolerance was apparently a generalized reaction from the taste of acid stimuli in the mouth (apples, oranges) which itself arose following the removal of tartar from his teeth. The former disorder interfered with his employment. Treatment was by SD(I) with the added technique of using a reciprocally inhibiting substance (sugar) to counteract the acid taste experienced when imagining, for example, a slice of apple in the mouth. The treatment was completely successful over a one-year follow-up, and no symptom substitution was observed.

3. BRONCHIAL ASTHMA

The literature on bronchial asthma is, of course, enormous,[17] and behavior therapists have done no more than skirmish around the fringes of it. Some of the work has, however, been of considerable interest. We will pass over the question whether or not there is an "asthmatic personality" (Franks and Leigh, 1959; Leigh and Marley, 1956), since the search for such a personality constellation has been generally unfruitful (Freeman et al, 1964). Of more interest is the question whether asthma (whether or not a genuine allergic reaction to certain substances is present) can reasonably be conceptualized as, in part at least, a conditioned response, since both theoretical analyses and empirical studies have been directed toward this question. Of the theoretical analyses, two are of particular interest. After rejecting the classical conditioning model as a paradigm for the learning of conditioned asthmatic responses (since the model would predict easy extinction),[18] Turnbull (1962) derived his theoretical analysis of asthma as a conditioned response from an experiment by Brogden (1939). Brogden showed that if a bell (CS) is paired with shock (US) which produces leg flexion (UR and CR), and if the leg flexion is followed by reward (food), the CR will be maintained for longer periods of time in the absence of the US. Turnbull interpreted this experimental result in relation to asthma as follows.

"When a painful stimulus, such as shock, follows a conditioned stimulus, the conditioned stimulus becomes associated with the fear reaction elicited by the shock. After a number of trials the conditioned stimulus becomes a 'sign' of shock, and is able to elicit a portion of the fear reaction, *including variations in respiration*, prior to the occurrence of shock itself. This emotional reaction to the 'sign', a concomitant of which is respiratory fluctuation, could then serve to motivate the organism to try out various instrumental activities to avoid or escape shock. If an asthma-like pattern of respiration (i.e., quick inspiration and long expiration with greater than normal amplitude) happened to be performed, and if this led to avoidance or escape from a feared stimulus, then this breathing pattern would be more likely to appear the next time the 'sign' was presented" (Turnbull, 1962, p. 61, italics not in original).

Turnbull then applies this general theory (which is, of course, Mowrer's two-factor theory applied to a specific problem) in an ingenious way to account for the acquisition of conditioned asthmatic responses in infancy. Conditioned asthma, he argued, essentially

---

[17] A very thorough review of the psychological literature on allergic disorders (including bronchial asthma) will be found in Freeman et al (1964).

[18] Compare Lovibond's rejection of the classical conditioning model as an explanation for the treatment of enuresis by the Mowrer technique (*supra*, Chapter 5).

involves early learning of respiratory responses as escape or avoidance responses (which *follow* noxious stimulation initially, become attached to *conditioned* stimuli, and produce *reinforcement*—anxiety-reduction—and are hence strengthened). Discomfort leads to crying which produces mother and elimination of the discomfort. In time, the mother's absence may become a noxious stimulus leading to crying and subsequent appearance of the mother. If however, the mother does *not* appear, and the crying behavior is thus *not* reinforced, the anxiety will persist, the crying may be temporarily extinguished, and other similar responses (for example, respiratory ones) may occur. The same result may be produced if the crying is prohibited from direct expression by punishment. In either case, a conflict situation may be generated in which anxiety both motivates and inhibits crying. The child may then (by trial and error) learn a compromise response which *is* acceptable to the mother. These compromise (respiratory) responses may then be inadvertently shaped by the mother toward asthmatic responses (that is, the mother may fail to respond to each new type of response until it is shaped further to the point where the mother's concern is again aroused), and the process may be facilitated by such naturally occurring events as colds, bronchitis, etc. To explain the onset of asthma in adults, Turnbull invokes the phenomenon of instrumental act regression.[19]

It will be noted that Turnbull makes no reference to the existence of a genuine unconditioned allergic reaction;[20] but, in fact, Brogden's paradigm can be used to account for the genesis of asthmatic attacks to specific objects. Thus, if we regard a particular allergen as an unconditioned stimulus producing an unconditioned respiratory (or other) response, then if the asthmatic attack produces immediate attention of a reinforcing kind (which, of course, it usually does), the asthmatic attack may not only become attached to any neutral stimuli present at the time the allergen produces the UR but may become very resistant to extinction, in just the same way that Brogden's CR did.

Turnbull's explanatory model, is, of course, an oversimplification of the factors involved in the genesis of bronchial asthma. A much more complex model has been put forward more recently by Moore (1965) who has explicated particularly the role of mediating variables.

Moore also stresses the important role that is played by allergens as unconditioned noxious stimuli.

That conditioning does appear to play a significant role in bronchial asthma has been shown in studies by Dekker and Groen (1956) and Dekker, Pelser, and Groen (1957). Dekker and Groen (1956) stress the frequent relationship between the onset of asthma and a traumatic experience. In 12 subjects suffering from asthma, they recorded basic vital capacity first, since it is known that attacks of asthma reduce the vital capacity by 10% or more. They then introduced significant personal stimuli acknowledged by the subject to induce an attack and measured the change in vital capacity. This experiment was by no means conclusive, since six subjects showed no reaction to the presumed significant stimuli. However, three subjects showed a minor decrease in vital capacity, together with minor symptoms and signs; while three subjects showed a highly significant decrease in vital capacity and a typical asthmatic attack. In one subject, discussion of emotional difficulties had no effect, but introduction of a known significant stimulus did induce an attack. The second study (Dekker et al, 1957) attempted to condition an asthmatic attack directly in two subjects. Neutral stimuli (neutral solvent, oxygen, etc.) were paired with inhalation of nebulized allergens, to which the subjects were known to be highly sensitive. The allergic substance produced the expected result (progressive decrease in vital capacity to a significant degree), and conditioning occurred both to the postulated neutral stimuli and to the sight and feel of the glass tube. Further, an asthmatic attack occurred.

Turning to the treatment of asthma, we may first mention briefly studies by Walton (1960a) and Cooper (1964). Walton (1960a) treated a patient with asthma which appeared to be precipitated in social situations (in which the patient could not express felt hostility) by SD-I, using assertive training. A rapid favorable response was obtained, and the patient was symptom free at a follow-up of eight months. Cooper (1964), on the other hand, treated a case of bronchial asthma for which the precipitating situations appeared to be diffuse. He utilized relaxation training coupled with desensitization, beginning with relaxation alone

---

[19] See Yates (1962, Chapter 4).
[20] Freeman et al (1964) point out that this is a

common omission in psychological studies of asthma.

and then gradually introducing suggestions of anxiety and panic. Virtually complete remission of the asthmatic symptoms was maintained over a 16-month follow-up period.

The most important experimental/therapeutic study, however, is that by Moore (1965). She treated 12 patients who satisfied the following criteria: history of severe intermittent dyspnoea with relative freedom between attacks; X-ray findings not suggestive of emphysema; absence of cardiac lesions; reversible airways obstruction; not on steroids. Six of the patients were adults, and six were children. She utilized a balanced incomplete blocks design with three treatments: relaxation; relaxation combined with suggestion of improvement; and relaxation combined with reciprocal inhibition. The third treatment (SD-I) involved the construction of hierarchies related to an asthmatic attack, an allergic attack, and a psychological stress situation. The patients were used as their own controls in the experimental design, each patient being given two of the three possible treatments. Instead of using vital capacity change as the dependent variable, Moore used the maximum peak flow (MPF), together with a second derived measure, the percentage this performance represented of his optimal flow after removal of reversible airways obstruction by isoprenaline (%MPF). In addition, the patient's subjective report of change of state was measured, as indicated by the number of days on which attacks of wheezing occurred between the weekly sessions. Each treatment was given for one half hour per week for two months.

Figure 3 shows the change in MPF following each of the treatments. Relaxation combined with desensitization produced the most striking results and the curves suggest that the critical variable in producing significant improvement was the desensitization procedure. The same results were obtained for %MPF. Moore reports that the different treatments did not produce significant differences in number of reported attacks, that is, that the subjective and objective measures did not coincide. However, her results do suggest that a strong tendency in favor of desensitization was manifesting itself toward the end of treatment. All patients showed an improvement in subjective state during the first weeks of treatment, but the curves diverged sharply toward the end.[21] Moore concluded that desensitization is effective in producing a reduction in breathing difficulties in bronchial asthma.

All of these studies used SD-I to treat the patients involved, but, of course, where the reaction is fairly specific, the possibility of using SD-R will be obvious, though not without its dangers of further sensitizing the patient. These techniques have, in fact been used by allergists to some extent, though behavior therapists seem to be largely ignorant of this work. Thus, Herxheimer and Prior (1952) have described a method for testing bronchial sensitivity in asthma which can also be used for treatment by what he calls hyposensitization and which clearly is a straightforward form of SD-R.

> "When the patient had been accustomed to breathing with the spirometer and to recording a stable vital capacity, he received through the breathing circuit for an arbitrary short period the aerosolized allergen extract to which, according to his history or to his skin tests, he was suspected to be sensitive. If no attack occurred, the inhalation time for the next test was increased by 50% 3–7 days later. If a mild attack developed, the inhalation time of the next occasion was increased by 20–30%. If the attack was moderate or severe, the inhalation time was drastically reduced at the next sitting; this was repeated until either no attack or a mild attack was produced" (Herxheimer and Prior, 1952, p. 190).

Herxheimer applied the technique (which parallels Wolpe's systematic desensitization

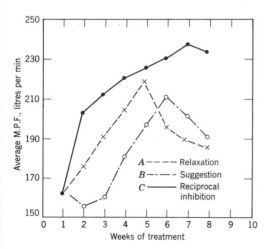

FIG. 3. Change in Mean Peak Flow under three conditions of treatment (Moore, 1965, Figure 2).

---

[21] See Moore (1965, Fig. 1, p. 261).

technique almost exactly, except that it involves "real" and not "imaginary" desensitization) to 72 patients with both monovalent[22] and polyvalent allergy. A fivefold increase in tolerance was showed by 27% of the patients, that is, they would tolerate without attack five times the shortest inhalation time that had formerly caused an attack. These patients remained symptom free also in spite of exposure to the allergen. A further 27% of the patients showed increased tolerance and relative freedom from attack. Herxheimer interprets his results very cautiously, but the results certainly seem promising. He gives illustrations of accidental hypersensitization by overexposure, and it could well be that his scaling of the steps in the procedure were too crude and hence produced resensitization in a number of cases. He also points out that failure of treatment may be produced by factors outside the control of the experimenter, such as exposure to a large dose of allergen in the natural environment, or by respiratory infection (on which Herxheimer lays great stress). The time interval between trials also appeared to be a critical variable. Herxheimer's paper is an outstanding example of the controlled experimental investigation and repays careful study.

In summary, there can be no doubt that some very interesting leads have been initiated in the study of conditioning and deconditioning factors in bronchial asthma. These leads would seems to offer far more promise than studies of the personality of the asthmatic. Further, it may very well turn out that studies using SD-R (following Herxheimer's approach) will prove to be more profitable than studies using SD-I.[23]

IV. HEIGHTENED NONORGANIC MOTOR FUNCTIONING

1. EXCESSIVE FREQUENCY OF MICTURITION

The possibility of conditioning the internal organs has been relatively neglected until recently by Western scientists, but has been intensively investigated by Russian physiological psychologists (Bykov, 1957). Recent studies in the West, for example, on conditioned inhibition of urine flow in animals (Dykman et al, 1962) and conditioned diuresis in man (Hofer and Hinkle, 1964) has confirmed the importance and validity of internal conditioning

and, of course, the work on enuresis, discussed earlier in Chapter 5, represents perhaps the most important application of these techniques so far on a large scale, though the experimental work on enuresis, as was pointed out, has not yet systematically investigated the internal processes directly as yet.

An early study by Jones (1956) represents a most ingenious approach to the not uncommon problem of excessive frequency of the urge to micturate, an abnormality that may have embarrassing social consequences. It is also an outstanding example of the method of the experimental investigation of the single case in behavior therapy.

Jones' patient was a 23-year-old woman who had been forced to give up a stage career as a dancer because of her symptom, which had become quite disabling. There was no evidence of any physical abnormality, psychotherapy and day hospital treatment over a short period (five weeks) produced no change in the disorder, and the patient had been advised to give up her stage career and take a secretarial job where toilet facilities would be readily available. This she was reluctant to do, and the possibility of treatment by conditioning techniques was therefore considered.

The experiment by Jones was based on the work of Bykov (1957) who introduced warm water into the bladder of human subjects, before whom were displayed on a manometer the resultant pressure changes. Apparently, Bykov's subjects acquired a conditioned "urge" to urinate at that pressure and this response was manifested even when the manometer reading was falsified by the experimenter in such a way that a reading was displayed which indicated the appropriate pressure level for the urge but when the true pressure level was, in fact, much lower. This response occurred even when bladder pressure was very low indeed and when the number was called out and not seen. This, of course, is an example of situational training and, as we have seen, there is no reason to doubt that the "urinary urge" does vary widely in normal subjects and that these differences are, in part at least, due to situational conditioning.

In his initial tests, Jones was able to demonstrate that the bladder responses of his patient were abnormal in a number of respects: the urge to urinate occurred at low bladder volumes

---

[22] The terms are equivalent to monosymptomatic and polysymptomatic.

[23] Studies of the effects of hypnosis on asthma have been reviewed by Edwards (1964).

and pressures, compared with normal control data; the detrusor muscle response to increased bladder pressures did not show the normal increase followed by adaptation, but rather tended to increase linearly; and the bladder musculature produced and maintained abnormally high pressures at low volumes.

The first stage in the treatment consisted in associating the experienced urge to micturate with the pressure level shown on the arbitrary scale of the manometer. The second, and critical stage, consisted in experimentally, without the patient's knowledge, producing a false, lower reading on the manometer while introducing the same amount of fluid into the bladder. Several trials resulted in the appearance of adaptive contractions and relaxations of the bladder wall and the elimination of the pressure and volume abnormalities at the onset of urgency. Subsequent training (which was not continued for very long) resulted in a marked improvement in the patient's ability to tolerate increased amounts of fluid in the bladder, although the bladder/pressure relationships were by no means entirely "normalized." "A week after the cessation of the laboratory treatment, her urinary frequency had practically disappeared and no other symptoms were evident in the setting of the day hospital" (Jones, 1956, p. 417). Thus, the treatment apparently abolished the abnormally intense urge to urinate at low bladder volumes and pressures; markedly improved the tone of the detrusor muscle activity; and partially modified the bladder/volume/pressure relationships. A 15-month follow-up indicated that these improvements had been maintained and the patient was free of symptoms.

Several points need to be noted about this treatment. First, it is apparent from the case report that the abnormal frequency of the urge to micturate was not present from birth, but commenced at the age of 17 and developed into a serious handicap over the next two years. Presumably, the etiology therefore involved conditioning to situational stimuli, but the mechanism of this is not elucidated[24] by Jones and remains obscure. In this connection, it should be noted that the urinary frequency was not the only abnormality from which the patient

suffered, since the disorder became attached to a fear of going outdoors or appearing on the stage.[25] Third, in spite of the complex nature of the patient's total disorder and lack of adequate knowledge of its etiology, it proved possible to treat the various aspects separately. Thus, the treatment of the urinary urge was carried out and completed before the treatment of the phobia of going outdoors. It is particularly interesting to note that the successful treatment of the urinary frequency did not affect her fear of going outside, even though the two phenomena appeared to be related.

2. SOMNAMBULISM[26]

Sleepwalking has attracted little attention thus far from behavior therapists, but two case studies have been carried out. Walton (1961) treated a somnambulist who attacked his wife during sleep each night, the attack being aborted by the wife awakening him.[27] Walton's theory was that this patient hated his domineering mother but was unable to express the hatred directly because of anxiety. During sleep, reduction in sympathetically-mediated anxiety allowed expression of the aggression indirectly against his wife. Walton therefore argued that training in assertive behavior against the mother would lead to disappearance of the somnambulism. After only one session of assertive training, the somnambulism was reported by Walton to have disappeared and to be still absent on follow-up two years later.

A rather different approach was used by Edmonds (1967) who treated a male somnambulist who had walked and talked in his sleep for seven years, two or three times per week, and had suffered severe injuries from falls. Aversion therapy was tried, utilizing shock to the arm whenever the patient initiated walking or talking in his sleep. The shock continued until the patient awoke or resumed sleeping (which he did do). However, the treatment was abandoned after 53 aversion trials had been given over a fortnight (44 for talking, the remainder for walking) without any apparent effect. When a midday sleep the patient invariably took was abolished and sedation with sodium amytal was given, the

---

[24] He considers it possible that her sexual history may be relevant.

[25] This aspect of her difficulties was treated simultaneously but independently by Jones, using Wolpe's technique of reciprocal inhibition.

[26] For an excellent review of the literature see Sours, Frumkin, and Indermill (1963); an equally thorough review of somniloquy has been published recently by Arkin (1966).

[27] Hostile behavior during a somnambulistic episode appears to be very rare.

somnambulism disappeared and was still absent on follow-up six months later, while talking occurred only one night per week on average.

It may be noted that both these patients were not typical somnambulists, in that actual offensive actions or self-injury are extremely rare.

3. OVEREATING RESULTING IN OBESITY

Very little work has been carried out by behavior therapists on the problem of obesity, but the condition is of considerable interest because of the very detailed and important analysis of the operant control of eating (and the factors which may produce and sustain excessive eating behavior) by Ferster et al (1962). Ferster points out that obesity involves a classical instance of the short-term reinforcing effects of over-eating becoming paramount over the longer-term aversive consequences. Furthermore, therapy in this area involves essentially the teaching of self-control, since eating behavior can become attached to so many environmental stimuli that external control is virtually impossible to sustain. The general aim of treatment therefore consists in attaching facts about the ultimate aversive consequences of over-eating to the eating behavior so that the latter becomes an aversive stimulus itself. Self-control procedures will then be reinforced because they reduce or terminate the aversive stimulus.

The critical point in Ferster's analysis, however, is his stress on the fact that it is simply not enough to *explain* to a passive patient the aversive consequences of over-eating. The patient must become an *active participant* in the process. Thus, the patient is in effect given an intensive course in the acquisition of knowledge about such factors as caloric values of food and so forth, while at the same time he is required to keep detailed records of food intake (analyzed *by the patient* into categories, etc.), of weight loss, and so on. He is also given explicit training in decreasing the range of stimuli for eating responses, in increasing the chain of responses which precede food ingestion, and by strengthening behaviors incompatible with food ingestion. All of this is based on the supposition that eating efficiently is a skilled activity which may have to be taught in a series of steps. It is difficult to convey briefly the richness of Ferster's analysis of eating behavior, but a close study of his paper will suggest rational and

meaningful programs for the development of self-control procedures. Ferster's paper unfortunately has thus far attracted little attention. Meyer and Crisp (1964), in their treatment of two cases of obesity, used aversive treatment (shock) for approach to "temptation" food while the patients were on a 1000 calorie diet and thus continuously hungry. Success was apparently achieved with one patient but not with the other. The analysis by Meyer and Crisp of the reasons for failure inadvertently points up the most telling arguments put forward by Ferster in his study.

V. METHODOLOGICAL PROBLEMS

The rather pessimistic conclusion that must be drawn from the above survey is that behavior therapists have scarcely begun to touch a wide range of abnormalities of behavior. It would be pointless to include in this chapter any evaluation of the effects of behavior therapy since, with the notable exceptions to which attention was drawn at various points, the material reviewed consists either of case studies of a seriously inadequate nature (and certainly not even beginning to approach satisfaction of the essential nature of behavior therapy as defined in Chapter 1) or laboratory experimental studies. The latter are, of course, of outstanding interest and importance, since the disorders we have been discussing lend themselves peculiarly well to the experimental approach. In this respect, the initial study of Brady and Lind (1961) and especially the later study of the same patient by Zimmerman and Grosz (1966) do meet the requirements of the systematic experimental study of the single case. The study of bronchial asthma by Moore (1965) falls into the category of studies that investigate processes systematically.

Because the studies of these various disorders is still in its infancy, behaviorally speaking, no extended review of methodological problems will be undertaken. Three points will, however, be briefly considered. First, the investigations by Brady and Lind (1961) and by Zimmerman and Grosz (1966) raise the very interesting problem of malingering as against hysterical dysfunction. Whether this is a pseudo-problem remains to be seen. Brady (1966), in a recent comment, has argued for a continuum of hysteria/malingering and believes that the patient in question was originally a "genuine" case of hysterical blindness which may subsequently have developed into malingering. The problem is a difficult one, since it is well known that hysterical disorders may involve in time a considerable degree of "secondary gain." In effect, this means simply that the patient learns to control his environment initially by means of the hysterical symptoms in a fairly general way but that, as a result of experiences consequent on the primary disability, he comes to utilize the disability to control many other aspects of his environment. Brady argues that conversion reactions are characterized by sudden onset, belle indifference, and non-exaggeration of the disability; whereas malingering is characterized by gradual onset, feigned concern, and exaggeration of the disability. We are, however, dealing with a continuum here and, instead of referring to malingering at all, it would probably be better to specify more closely the developmental sequence of the behaviors in question. In effect, this is precisely what Zimmerman and Grosz did. That a concentration on the experimental manipulation and control of the disability will pay very large dividends in the comprehension of the parameters of the disorder is undoubted. In fact, as has been pointed out, present lack of basic knowledge is deplorable and quite unnecessary. To illustrate with an example already referred to, the question whether functional paralysis is *invariably* accompanied by sensory anaesthesia is one which should surely be clearly answered by now. Yet no *objective* data on this question seem to be in existence.

The second example relates to Moore's finding in bronchial asthma of a lack of correlation between subjective and objective indices of change of state during treatment. This problem parallels the one we have already discussed in relation to indices of conditioned fear in relation to phobias. It may merely be repeated here that subjective reports are not to be equated with objective observations of behavior and that lack of direct observation of behavioral changes is always a serious deficiency.

Finally, reference should be made again to the importance of studies of hypnotically induced behavior and its possible importance for the understanding of hysterical phenomena. Recent years have witnessed very striking advances in the experimental investigation of phenomena found under hypnosis which are apparently similar to those found in hysterical states. The basic question at issue is whether phenomena attributed to heightened suggestibility in the hypnotic state can be produced to an equal degree in nonhypnotic states by the use of suggestion alone. As Barber (1967) has pointed out in a recent comprehensive review, most studies of hypnotically-induced behavior change have suffered from a failure to utilize a proper control group. In the majority of studies, the hypnotic group has not only been subjected to hypnosis, but also to heightened suggestibility whereas, when a control group has been used, it has not only not been subjected to hypnosis but also has not been subjected to suggestion. Hence, the results attributed to hypnosis plus suggestion might be the result of suggestion alone.[28] Thus, in any adequate study, four groups are required: hypnosis plus suggestion; hypnosis without suggestion; control waking group plus suggestion; control waking group without suggestion. Recent studies on hypnotic deafness (Barber and Calverley, 1964; Kline, Guze, and Haggerty, 1954), hypnotic blindness (Barber and Deeley, 1961), and hypnotic analgesia and anaesthesia (Barber and Hahn, 1962) showed that the phenomena attributed to the induction of hypnosis could be demonstrated equally well in the waking state with suggestion, providing the experimental and control groups were properly chosen. These results throw grave doubt on the interpretation placed on the earlier studies utilizing hypnosis (to which we have referred earlier) as well as other similar ones (Erickson, 1939; Pattie, 1935; Brown and Vogel, 1938; Dynes, 1932; Sears, 1932; Doupe, Miller, and Keller, 1939; West, Neill, and Hardy, 1952).[29]

The importance of these recent studies lies in the methodological suggestions arising out of them concerning the experimental investigation of the abnormal forms of behavior which we have considered in this chapter. Behavior therapists have scarcely begun to scratch the surface of experimental procedures for the systematic investigation of particular disorders.

---

[28] Barber (1967) also makes many other criticisms of these studies, particularly with respect to the biased selection of hypnotic and nonhypnotic groups.

[29] Shor (1967) has recently reviewed the literature on hypnotic analgesia and anaesthesia.

REFERENCES

Arkin, A.M. Sleep-talking: a review. *J. nerv. ment. Dis.*, 1966, **143**, 101–122.

Bachrach, A.J., Erwin, W.J., & Mohr, J.P. The control of eating behavior in an anorexic by operant conditioning techniques. In Ullmann, L.P. & Krasner, L. (eds.). *Case studies in behavior modification*. New York, Holt, 1965, pp. 153–163.

Bangs, J.L. & Freidinger, A. Diagnosis and treatment of a case of hysterical aphonia in a thirteen-year-old girl. *J. Speech Hearing Dis.*, 1949, **14**, 312–317.

Bangs, J.L. & Freidinger, A. A case of hysterical dysphonia in an adult. *J. Speech Hearing Dis.*, 1950, **15**, 316–323.

Barber, T.X. "Hypnotic" phenomena: a critique of experimental methods. In Gordon, J.E. (ed.). *Handbook of clinical and experimental hypnosis*. New York: Macmillan, 1967, pp. 444–480.

Barber, T.X. & Calverley, D.S. Experimental studies of "hypnotic" behavior: suggested deafness evaluated by delayed auditory feedback. *Brit. J. Psychol.*, 1964, **55**, 439–446.

Barber, T.X. & Deeley, D.C. Experimental evidence for a theory of hypnotic behavior: I. "Hypnotic color blindness" without "hypnosis." *Internat. J. clin. exp. Hypnosis*, 1961, **9**, 79–86.

Barber, T.X. & Hahn, K.W. Physiological and subjective responses to pain producing stimulation under hypnotically-suggested and waking-imagined "analgesia." *J. abnorm. soc. Psychol.*, 1962, **65**, 411–418.

Barnard, G.W., Flesher, C.K., & Steinbook, R.M. The treatment of urinary retention by aversive stimulus cessation and assertive training. *Behav. Res. Ther.*, 1966, **4**, 232–236.

Barraclough, B.M. A method of testing hearing based on operant conditioning. *Behav. Res. Ther.*, 1966, **4**, 237–238.

Beech, H.R. The symptomatic treatment of writer's cramp. In Eysenck, H.J. (ed.). *Behavior therapy and the neuroses*. Oxford: Pergamon, 1960, pp. 349–372.

Beyme, F. Hyperesthesia of taste and touch treated by reciprocal inhibition. *Behav. Res. Ther.*, 1964, **2**, 7–14.

Brady, J.P. Hysteria versus malingering: a response to Grosz and Zimmerman. *Behav. Res. Ther.*, 1966, **4**, 321–322.

Brady, J. & Lind, D.L. Experimental analysis of hysterical blindness. *Arch. gen. Psychiat.*, 1961, **4**, 331–339.

Breuer, J. & Freud, S. Studies on hysteria. In Strachey, J. (ed.). *Standard edition of the complete psychological works of Sigmund Freud* (Vol. II). London: Hogarth, 1957.

Brogden, W.J. Unconditioned stimulus substitution in the conditioning process. *Amer. J. Psychol.*, 1939, **52**, 46–55.

Brown, R.R. & Vogel, V.H. Psychophysiological reactions following painful stimuli under hypnotic analgesia contrasted with gas anesthesia and novocain block. *J. appl. Psychol.*, 1938, **22**, 408–420.

Bykov, K.M. *The cerebral cortex and the internal organs*. New York: Chemical Publ. Co., 1957.

Chodoff, P. & Lyons, H. Hysteria, the hysterical personality and "hysterical" conversion. *Amer. J. Psychiat.*, 1958, **114**, 734–740.

Cooper, A.J. A case of bronchial asthma treated by behavior therapy. *Behav. Res. Ther.*, 1964, **1**, 351–356.

Cooper, A.J. Conditioning therapy in hysterical retention of urine. *Brit. J. Psychiat.*, 1965, **111**, 575–577.

Crisp, A.H. Some aspects of the evolution, presentation and follow-up of anorexia nervosa. *Proc. roy. Soc. Med.*, 1965, **58**, 814–820.

Crisp, A.H. & Moldofsky, H. Psychosomatic study of writer s cramp. *Brit. J. Psychiat.*, 1965, **111**, 841–858.

Dekker, E. & Groen, J. Reproducible psychogenic attacks of asthma: a laboratory study. *J. psychosom. Res.*, 1956, **1**, 58–67.

Dekker, E., Pelser, H.E., & Groen, J. Conditioning as a cause of asthmatic attacks. *J. psychosom. Res.*, 1957, **2**, 97–108.

Doupe, J., Miller, W.R., & Keller, W.K. Vasomotor reactions in the hypnotic state. *J. Neurol. Psychiat.*, 1939, **2**, 97–102.

Dykman, R.A., Corson, S.A., Reese, W.G., & Seager, L.D. Inhibition of urine flow as a component of the conditional defense reaction. *Psychosom. Med.*, 1962, **24**, 177–186.

Dynes, J.B. An experimental study of hypnotic anaesthesia. *J. abnorm. soc. Psychol.*, 1932, **27**, 79–88.

Edmonds, C. Severe somnambulism: a case study. *J. clin. Psychol.*, 1967, **23**, 237–239.

Edwards, G. The hypnotic treatment of asthma. In Eysenck, H.J. (ed.). *Experiments in behavior therapy*. London: Pergamon, 1964, pp. 407–431.

Erickson, M.H. A study of clinical and experimental findings on hypnotic deafness: I. Clinical experimentation and findings. *J. gen. Psychol.*, 1938, **19**, 127–150 (a).

Erickson, M.H. A study of clinical and experimental findings on hypnotic deafness: II. Experimental findings with a conditioned response technique. *J. gen. Psychol.*, 1938, **19**, 151–167 (b).

Erickson, M.H. The induction of color blindness by a technique of hypnotic suggestion. *J. gen. Psychol.*, 1939, **20**, 61–89.

Eysenck, H.J. *Dimensions of personality*. London: Routledge & Kegan Paul, 1947.

Eysenck, H.J. Cortical inhibition, figural aftereffect, and theory of personality. *J. abnorm. soc. Psychol.*, 1955, **51**, 94–106.

Farquharson, R.F. & Hyland, H.H. Anorexia nervosa: a metabolic disorder of psychologic origin. *J. Amer. med. Assoc.*, 1938, **111**, 1085–1092.

Ferster, C.B., Nurnberger, J.I., & Levitt, E.E. The control of eating. *J. Mathetics*, 1962, **1**, 87–109.

Forrest, A.D. The differentiation of hysterical personality from hysterical psychopathy. *Brit. J. med. Psychol.*, 1967, **40**, 65–78.

Franks, C.M. & Leigh, D. The theoretical and experimental application of a conditioning model to a consideration of bronchial asthma in man. *J. psychosom. Res.*, 1959, **4**, 88–98.

Freeman, E.H. Feingold, B.F., Schlesinger, K., & Gorman, E.J. Psychological variables in allergic disorders: a review. *Psychosom. Med.*, 1964, **26**, 543–575.

Gatfield, P.D. & Guze, S.B. Prognosis and differential diagnosis of conversion reactions. *Dis. nerv. Syst.*, 1962, **23**, 623–631.

Goldiamond, I. Perception. In Bachrach, A.J. (ed.). *Experimental foundations of clinical psychology*. New York: Basic Books, 1962, pp. 280–340.

Gray, B.B., England, G., & Mohoney, J.L. Treatment of benign vocal nodules by reciprocal inhibition. *Behav. Res. Ther.*, 1965, **3**, 187–193.

Grosz, H.J. & Zimmerman, J. Experimental analysis of hysterical blindness: a follow-up report and new experimental data. *Arch. gen. Psychiat.*, 1965, **13**, 255–260.

Gull, W.W. Anorexia nervosa (apepsia hysterica, anorexia hysterica). *Trans. Clin. Soc. (London)*, 1874, **7**, 22–28.

Guze, S.B. & Perley, M.J. Observations on the natural history of hysteria. *Amer. J. Psychiat.*, 1963, **119**, 960–965.

Hallsten, E.A. Adolescent anorexia nervosa treated by desensitization. *Behav. Res. Ther.*, 1965, **3**, 87–91.

Herxheimer, H. & Prior, F.N. Further observations on induced asthma and bronchial hyposensitization. *Internat. Arch. Allergy & Appl. Immunol.*, 1952, **3**, 189–207.

Hilgard, E.R. & Marquis, D.G. *Conditioning and learning*. New York: Appleton-Century-Crofts, 1940.

Hofer, M.A. & Hinkle, L.E. Conditioned diuresis in man: effects of altered environment, subjective state, and conditioning experience. *Psychosom. Med.*, 1964, **26**, 108–124.

Jones, H.G. The application of conditioning and learning techniques to the treatment of a psychiatric patient. *J. abnorm. soc. Psychol.*, 1956, **52**, 414–420.

Kaufman, M.R. (ed.). *Evolution of psychosomatic concepts: anorexia nervosa: a paradigm*. London: Hogarth, 1965.

Kleinman, M.L. Psychogenic deafness and perceptual defence. *J. abnorm. soc. Psychol.*, 1957, **54**, 335–338.

Kline, M.V., Guze, H., & Haggerty, A.D. An experimental study of the nature of hypnotic deafness: effects of delayed speech feedback. *J. clin. exp. Hypnosis*, 1954, **2**, 145–156.

Kodman, F. & Blanton, R.L. Perceptual defence mechanisms and psychogenic deafness in children. *Percept. Mot. Skills*, 1960, **10**, 211–214.

Lang, P.J. Behavior therapy with a case of nervous anorexia. In Ullmann, L.P. & Krasner, L. (eds.). *Case studies in behavior modification*. New York, Holt, 1965, pp. 217–221.

Lasegue, E.C. On hysterical anorexia. *Arch. gen. Med.*, 1873, **2**, 265–266 and 367–369.

Leigh, D. & Marley, E. A psychiatric assessment of adult asthmatics: a statistical study. *J. psychosom. Res.*, 1956, **1**, 128–136.

Leitenberg, H., Agras, W.S., & Thomson, L.E. A sequential analysis of the effect of selective positive reinforcement in modifying anorexia nervosa. *Behav. Res. Ther.*, 1968, **6**, 211–218.

Lesser, L.L., Ashendon, B.J., Debuskey, M., & Eisenberg, L. Anorexia nervosa in children. *Amer. J. Orthopsychiat.*, 1960, **30**, 572–580.

Lewis, W.C. & Berman, M. Studies of conversion hysteria. *Arch. gen. Psychiat.*, 1965, **13**, 275–282.

Liversedge, L.A. & Sylvester, J.D. Conditioning techniques in the treatment of writer's cramp. *Lancet*, 1955, **2**, 1147–1149.

Ljungberg, L. Hysteria: a clinical prognostic and genetic study. *Acta psychiat. neurol. Scand.*, 1960, **32** (Suppl. No. 112).

Lundberg, D. & Walinder, J. Anorexia nervosa and signs of brain damage. *Internat. J. Neuropsychiat.*, 1967, **3**, 165–173.

Malmo, R.B., Boag, T.J., & Raginsky, B.B. Electromyographic study of hypnotic deafness. *J. clin. exp. Hypnosis*, 1954, **2**, 305–317.

Malmo, R.B., Davis, J.F., & Barza, S. Total hysterical deafness: an experimental case study. *J. Pers.*, 1952, **21**, 188–204.

Meichenbaum, D.H. Sequential strategies in two cases of hysteria. *Behav. Res. Ther.*, 1966, **4**, 89–94.

Meyer, V. & Crisp, A.H. Aversion therapy in two cases of obesity. *Behav. Res. Ther.*, 1964, **2**, 143–147.

Miller, E. A note on the visual performance of a subject with unilateral functional blindness. *Behav. Res. Ther.*, 1968, **6**, 115–116.

Moore, N. Behavior therapy in bronchial asthma: a controlled study. *J. psychosom. Res.*, 1965, **9**, 257–276.

Moulton, R. A psychosomatic study of anorexia nervosa including the use of vaginal smears. *Psychosom. Med.*, 1942, **4**, 62–74.

Nicolle, G. Prepsychotic anorexia. *Proc. roy. Soc. Med.*, 1939, **32**, 153–162.

Pattie, F.A. A report on attempts to produce uniocular blindness by hypnotic suggestions. *Brit. J. med. Psychol.*, 1935, **15**, 230–241.

Reed, G.F. Psychogenic deafness, perceptual defense, and personality variables in children. *J. abnorm. soc. Psychol.*, 1961, **63**, 663–665.

Sears, R.R. An experimental study of hypnotic anaesthesia. *J. exp. Psychol.*, 1932, **15**, 1–22.

Sears, R.R. & Cohen, L.H. Hysterical anaesthesia, analgesia and astereognosis. *Arch. Neurol. Psychiat.*, 1933, **29**, 260–271.

Shor, R.E. Physiological effects of painful stimulation during hypnotic analgesia. In Gordon, J.E. (ed.). *Handbook of clinical and experimental hypnosis*. New York: Macmillan, 1967, pp. 511–549.

Silverstone, J.T. & Russell, G.F.M. Gastric "hunger" contractions in anorexia nervosa. *Brit. J. Psychiat.*, 1967, **113**, 257–263.

Slater, E. The thirty-fifth Maudsley lecture: "hysteria 311." *J. ment. Sci.*, 1961, **107**, 359–381.

Slater, E. Diagnosis of hysteria. *Brit. med. J.*, 1965, **1**, 1395–1397.

Sours, J.A., Frumkin, P., & Indermill, R.R. Somnambulism. *Arch. gen. Psychiat.*, 1963, **9**, 400–413.

Stunkard, A.J. Obesity and the denial of hunger. *Psychosom. Med.*, 1959, **21**, 281–289.

Sylvester, J.D. & Liversedge, L.A. Conditioning and the occupational cramps. In Eysenck, H.J. (ed.). *Behavior therapy and the neuroses*. Oxford: Pergamon, 1960, pp. 334–348.

Thorpe, J.G., Schmidt, E., Brown, P.T., & Castell, D. Aversion-relief therapy: a new method for general application. *Behav. Res. Ther.*, 1964, **2**, 71–82.

Turnbull, J.W. Asthma conceived as a learned response. *J. psychosom. Res.*, 1962, **6**, 59–70.

Veith, I. *Hysteria: the history of a disease*. Chicago: Univer. Chicago Press, 1965.

Waller, J.V., Kaufman, M.R., & Deutsch, F. Anorexia nervosa: a psychosomatic entity. *Psychosom. Med.*, 1940, **2**, 3–16.

Walton, D. The application of learning theory to the treatment of a case of bronchial asthma. In Eysenck, H.J. (ed.). *Behavior therapy and the neuroses*. Oxford: Pergamon, 1960, pp. 188–189 (a).

Walton, D. The application of learning theory to the treatment of a case of neuro-dermatitis. In Eysenck, H.J. (ed.). *Behavior therapy and the neuroses*. Oxford: Pergamon, 1960, pp. 272–274 (b).

Walton, D. Application of learning theory to the treatment of a case of somnambulism. *J. clin. Psychol.*, 1961, **17**, 96–99.

Walton, D. & Black, D.A. The application of modern learning theory to the treatment of chronic hysterical aphonia. *J. psychosom. Res.*, 1959, **3**, 303–311.

West, L.J., Neill, K.C., & Hardy, J.D. Effects of hypnotic suggestions on pain perception and galvanic skin response. *Arch. Neurol. Psychiat.*, 1952, **68**, 549–560.

Whitlock, F.A. The aetiology of hysteria. *Acta psychiat. Scand.*, 1967, **43**, 144–162.

Wolpe, J. *Psychotherapy by reciprocal inhibition*. Stanford: Stanford Univer. Press, 1958.

Yates, A.J. Symptoms and symptom substitution. *Psychol. Rev.*, 1958, **65**, 371–374.

Yates, A.J. *Frustration and conflict*. New York: Wiley, 1962.

Ziegler, F.J. & Imboden, J.B. Contemporary conversion reactions: II. A conceptual model. *Arch. gen. Psychiat.*, 1962, **6**, 279–287.

Ziegler, F.J., Imboden, J.B., & Meyer, E. Contemporary conversion reactions: a clinical study. *Amer. J. Psychiat.*, 1960, **116**, 901–909.

Ziegler, F.J., Imboden, J.B., & Rodgers, D.A. Contemporary conversion reactions: III. Diagnostic considerations. *J. Amer. med. Assoc.*, 1963, **186**, 307–311.

Zimmerman, J. & Grosz, H.J. "Visual" performance of a functionally blind person. *Behav. Res. Ther.*, 1966, **4**, 119–134.

Chapter 10

Tics

Tics usually show a markedly fluctuating course in appearance and consistency; so also does psychiatric interest in the syndrome. Toward the end of the 19th century, a great deal of interest was shown in France in particular, culminating in the classic treatise of Meige and Feindel (1907), which, in so far as treatment was concerned, leaned heavily on the reeducative methods advocated by Brissaud. The rise of psychoanalysis, coupled with the notorious refractoriness of tics to almost any form of treatment, led to a rapid decline in interest on the part of psychiatrists, for whom tiqueurs vied with obsessionals in their unrewarding qualities as far as obtaining positive results was concerned. With but a few notable exceptions, serious study of tiqueurs between 1910 and 1950 was confined to psychoanalysts, who published detailed case histories and adumbrated complex theories about the nature of tics.[1]

In the last decade, however, there has been a considerable revival of interest in their study, both from an empirical and a theoretical point of view. From the empirical viewpoint, tics have the advantage of being readily observable and measurable as to frequency, intensity, and so on; so that the effects of applying particular techniques of treatment can be readily assessed. From the theoretical point of view, the objectivity of measurement makes it possible to test theories about tics more easily than is usually the case with behavior disorders. For these reasons, although tics are often regarded as a form of hysterical behavior, they are here treated separately.

I. DEFINITIONS, MEASUREMENT, INCIDENCE

1. Definition and Measurement of Tics

The definition of a tic given by Meige and Frindel has not been improved on:

"A tic is a coordinated purposive act, provoked in the first instance by some external cause or by an idea; repetition leads to its becoming habitual, and finally to its involuntary reproduction without cause and for no purpose, at the same time as its form, intensity and frequency are exaggerated; it thus assumes the character of a convulsive movement, inopportune and excessive; its execution is often preceded by an irresistible impulse, its suppression associated with malaise. The effect of distraction or of volitional effort is to diminish its activity; in sleep it disappears. It occurs in predisposed individuals who usually show other indications of mental instability" (Meige and Feindel, 1907, p. 260–261).

---

[1] The best-known studies by psychoanalysts on tics are those by Ferenczi (1921), Levy-Suhl (1937), Mahler and her colleagues (Mahler, 1944, 1949; Mahler and Rangell, 1943), and Gerard (1946). These studies are mentioned because, as will be seen later, this is one instance where some of the psychoanalytic theories are not too different from behavioristic formulations concerning the genesis of tics, though the deductions drawn as to treatment are very different.

The clarity and comprehensiveness of this definition, however, do not suffice, as Meige and Feindel were well aware, to make the operational or clinical definition of the presence or absence of a tic a matter of simplicity. Insofar as any tic involves motor movement, it must be differentiated from other movements which may have many of the characteristics of a tic, but which do not merit remedial action. Second, there are several classes of abnormal behaviors that must be differentiated from tics. Third, it should be differentiated from classes of movements which are often very difficult to distinguish behaviorally from tics, but which have a clearly organic origin and should be considered separately, even though this separation is not meant to imply that "organically based tics" cannot be behaviorally treated by the same methods.

The problems to be considered fall into three categories: differential diagnosis; types of tics; and measurements of "movement" in children and adults.

(a) DIFFERENTIAL DIAGNOSIS. Differential diagnosis of tics from other conditions is important because of the implications for treatment. Tic-like movements may occur in many organic conditions involving brain injury or physiological malfunction. In those cases, successful medical direct treatment of the disease-process will usually, though not always, result in disappearance of the tic-like behavior. (The analogy would be with the delusions and hallucinations found to accompany abnormal blood-sugar level; direct treatment of the latter will ameliorate the former.)

The principal *organic* conditions with which tics may be confused are spasms, choreas (Creak and Guttmann, 1935; Krauss, 1946), and cerebellar and cerebello - rubro - spinal tremor. Although the differential diagnosis may, in individual cases, be extremely difficult, the general differences are relatively easily specified. Table 10.1 incorporates the principal distinguishing signs, as elaborated by Meige and Feindel (1907), Wilson (1927), Williams (1932), and Hassin, Stenn, and Burstein (1930).

The principal *functional* conditions from which tics must be differentiated have included stereotyped acts (e.g., continuous rhythmic rocking, repetition of phrases, etc.) and such psychiatric conditions as compulsions and phobias, which often involve repetitive sequences of acts (Bender and Schilder, 1940, 1941; Hall, 1935; Mahler, 1944). The main distinction here lies in the nature of the compulsive acts or phobic inhibition of behavior, in that the phobias and compulsions usually involve much more extensive and complex sequences of behavior.

(b) TYPES OF TICS. Several attempts have been made to classify tics into various categories, but most of these are of little value. Thus, Meige and Feindel (1907, pp. 142–205) spent a good deal of time describing the various kinds of tics in terms of the musculature involved (face, eyes, neck, arms, etc.), but such a classification is probably irrelevant as far as treatment is concerned. A more important distinction may be that between clonic and tonic tics. Clonic tics are those where the movement or contraction is abrupt and short lived; whereas in tonic tics, the contractions are long lasting and more or less continuous. In the latter case, discrimination from athetoid or choreic movements becomes more difficult. From the theoretical and treatment viewpoint, as will be seen later, the most important factor about a tic may be its degree of complexity, which will determine in part the degree to which the subject can accurately reproduce the movement on a voluntary basis. Finally, it may be noted that only one clear-cut "tic-syndrome" has ever been described, and it is still uncertain whether it is organically based or not. This is the famous Gilles de la Tourette syndrome,[2] which is characterized by compulsive jerkings of the voluntary musculature of a widespread nature, but particularly affecting the face, neck, and extremities. The syndrome is differentiated from other complex tics, however, by the accompaniment of coprolalia (compulsive obscene utterances) and by echolalia (repetition of other persons' words and phrases) and, more rarely, echokinesis (repetition of other persons' actions). The condition is very rare, but its existence as an entity seems well established (Ascher, 1948).[3]

(c) THE METHODOLOGICAL PROBLEM OF MEASUREMENT. Careful observation of any individual will reveal the existence of stereotyped movements of which the individual is often completely unaware. The basic methodological problem, therefore, is that of deriving

---

[2] Also called maladie des tics; maladie des tics convulsifs; maladie des tics impulsifs; maladie des tics des dégénérés; Koordinierte Erinnerungskrampfe; mimische Krampf, myospasia impulsiva. In Mahler's (1949) distinction between tic syndrome and neurotic tic, the former term is equivalent to the Gilles de la Tourette syndrome.

[3] Kelman (1965) and Fernando (1967, 1968) have provided comprehensive reviews of the literature.

TABLE 10.1. *Differential Diagnosis of Tics from Organic Conditions Producing Tic-Like Movements*

Spasm	Tic	Chorea	Tremor
Not subject to voluntary control	Subject to voluntary control	Not subject to voluntary control	Not subject to voluntary control
No correlation with personality	Personality defect always present	No correlation with personality	No correlation with personality
Cannot be modified by external control (attention, distraction)	May be modified by external control (attention, distraction)	Cannot be modified by external control (attention, distraction)	Cannot be modified by external control (attention, distraction)
Abrupt, instantaneous	Brusque but slower	Still slower	Regular, increased by movement
Specific reflexes modified	Reflexes unimpaired	Reflexes often modified	Reflexes increased
Strength proportional to strength of stimulus	Not proportional to strength of stimulus	Not proportional to strength of stimulus	Not proportional to strength of stimulus
Continues during sleep	Disappears during sleep	Continues during sleep	Disappears during sleep
Muscle may atrophy	No muscular atrophy	Myasthenia, hypotonia	Myasthenia, hypotonia, or reverse
Painful/distressing	Painless	Sometimes painful	Painless
Purposeless	Purposeful	Purposeless	Purposeless
Cannot be reproduced voluntarily	Can be reproduced voluntarily	Cannot be reproduced voluntarily	Cannot be reproduced voluntarily
Cannot be inhibited	Inhibition increases tension level	Cannot be inhibited	Cannot be inhibited
Execution brings no tension reduction	Execution brings tension reduction	Execution brings no tension reduction	Execution brings no tension reduction
Etiology organic: peripheral irritation (lesion)	Etiology nonorganic	Hereditarily determined	Etiology organic: brain lesion or tumor

standard procedures for defining the presence of a tic, for which treatment would be desirable, as opposed to the presence of a movement which, while habitual, does not justify or require treatment. Mention should be made here of the *time-sampling* technique in which the individual is observed over standard time periods and every movement of a specified type is recorded. The methodological problems involved in the use of time-sampling techniques have been very thoroughly documented (Arrington, 1939, 1943), and the methods have been applied to the study of movements in children from preschool (Blatz and Ringland, 1935; Koch, 1935) through school (Seham and Boardman, 1934) to high school (Young, 1947), as well as with abnormal groups, such as psychotics (Jones, 1941). The observations have been made in a wide variety of situations, including free play, indoors and outdoors; controlled play with or without verbal restraint; regular teaching sessions; and under conditions which involved rest or the performance of distracting tasks; the taking of examinations; and subjection to severe stress (inhibition of micturition) (Blatz and Ringland, 1935; Koch, 1935; Seham and Boardman, 1934; Jones, 1941, 1943a, 1943b; Young, 1947). The movements observed have covered a very wide range indeed, mostly derived from the original classification of Olson (1929) into oral, nasal, hirsutal, irritational, manual, ocular, aural, genital, and facial. The measurement techniques have varied from the crude to the sophisticated, with more recent studies taking account of the necessity for training the observers carefully, for establishing within- and between-rater reliability, for establishing base-lines of movement frequency from which to estimate the influence of introducing new independent variables, and so forth. Of particular interest in this connection is the work of Sainsbury (1954a, 1954b) who correlated natural observational data with data obtained at leisure from film records and EMG records. Sainsbury (1954b) found that very short film records would produce highly reliable data and that EMG records correlated quite highly (0.83) with time-sampling techniques.

From the point of view of the definition of a tic, however, the methodological problems are of less significance than the clear-cut results that have been established on the basis of these studies. It has been clearly shown (e.g., Blatz and Ringland, 1935; Seham and Boardman, 1934), for example, that practically all children demonstrate one or more persisting movements

of a repetitive kind and that a high proportion (72 % in the Blatz and Ringland study) show two or more such movements. The existence of these movements may be reasonably attributed to the *instability of the developing nervous system* which leads to a failure of inhibition of excitatory nervous activity (Epstein, 1927). The gradual decline (but by no means the entire disappearance) of such movements with increasing age may likewise be attributed to increased maturation of the nervous system.

The two basic questions then become: first, are some tics simply the persistence of these involuntary movements in some children, resulting from defective development of inhibitory control; second, are some tics developed quite independently of increasing maturation of the nervous system and hence, in a sense, *qualitatively* different from repetitive movements of a "normal" kind?

There would appear to be two ways of approaching the problem of defining a tic in the light of the foregoing discussion. First, the presence of a tic as opposed to a persisting involuntary movement may be *empirically* determined by the systematic developmental study of tiqueurs with respect to questions such as whether the tic movements were present in embryonic form in childhood and, as such, indistinguishable from similar movements in children in whom these movements later disappeared. If this were the case, then the tics would simply be exaggerated forms of movements present in childhood and which had become very strong habits because of frequent repetition resulting from the failure of inhibitory processes. Second, it is possible that the definition of a tic may need to be made, not on an empirical basis (since the *form* of the tic may be indistinguishable from movements which are not regarded as tics), but on a *theoretical* basis. That is, either a movement which is present in the individual's repertoire may become fixated because of the intervention of a new independent variable not commonly experienced by most children (such as a highly traumatic event that may lead to the movement by chance and being capitalized on as an aggressive or defensive reaction in the threatening situation); or the insertion of a traumatic event into the life history may produce a completely *new* movement that serves the same purpose. The importance of the distinction is indicated by the problem of *preventive* treatment, that is, the possibility that, if a tic could be differentiated from a nontic movement in its embryonic stages, appropriate action might be taken to *prevent* its development. Clearly, if a tic, whatever its origin, ultimately becomes a strong habit, it will, like all strong habits, become extremely resistant to any form of modification.

In another sense, of course, the identification of a tic is made by the patient when he decides that the particular movement he manifests is socially embarrassing and he would like to be rid of it, but finds that he cannot abolish it himself, and hence presents himself for treatment. This is, of course, the usual way in which a tiqueur is identified at present.

This discussion of the methodological problems involved in the definition of a tic illustrates very clearly the difficulties arising in this respect. In terms of our earlier discussion of the essential characteristics of the behavior therapy approach, it is more important to achieve a clear and careful description of the *behavior* of the patient than to attempt to put a particular diagnostic label on him.

II. THE GENESIS AND MAINTENANCE OF TICS

Behavioristic approaches to developing theories of the genesis and maintenance of tics have been based largely on two models derived from general experimental psychology. On the one hand, theories have been derived from the work of Hull and his colleagues; on the other, from the work of Skinner and his colleagues (operant conditioning). In both approaches, however, the tic is regarded as a learned response.

1. A MODEL DERIVED FROM HULL

Early attempts were made to consider the tic as a conditioned response. Thus, Brain (1928) provides the paradigm of conjunctivitis as an unconditioned stimulus (US) producing the unconditioned response (UR) of blinking. Parental reactions and/or subjective thoughts will act as conditioned stimuli (CS) which becomes capable of evoking the UR as a conditioned response (CR) via classical conditioning. This model, however, has difficulty in accounting for the long-term persistence of the tic as a CR in the absence of the original US (conjunctivitis).

More recently, Yates (1958) conceptualized the tic as a drive-reducing conditioned avoidance response (CAR), originally evoked in a highly traumatic situation. In such a situation, intense fear may be aroused but *direct* escape from the situation may be impossible. Hence, a truncated movement of withdrawal or aggression may be the only possible response. If, however, the movement produces, or coincides with, the cessation of the fear-inducing stimulus, it will be strengthened by reinforcement. On subsequent occasions, through stimulus-generalization (including internal symbolization), conditioned fear (specific anxiety) may be aroused, which is then reduced by performance of the movement. In this way, the tic may ultimately come to be elicited by a wide variety of stimuli and achieve the status of a powerful habit.

It should be noted that no direct evidence has ever been provided for this theoretical formulation, but indirect evidence suggests it is not unreasonable. Solomon and Wynne (1954) have demonstrated that animals placed in a highly traumatic situation develop CARs which appear to reduce the anxiety associated with the original situation and which are highly resistant to extinction. The model also follows closely the original two-factor theory of Mowrer (1950) in which classically conditioned fear presents the individual with a problem that is resolved by the deliberate or random discovery of an instrumental response that reduces the fear.[4] In terms of Hullian learning theory, the reaction potential (sE_R) of the tic at a given moment may be conceptualized as a multiplicative function of the habit strength (sH_R) of the tic (determined mainly by the number of times it has previously been evoked) and the momentary drive strength of anxiety (D), which fluctuates from time to time. Since habit strength increases as a simple negatively accelerated positive growth function and eventually reaches asymptotic level, further performance of the tic cannot increase its habit strength beyond a given point.

It was pointed out earlier that psychoanalytic theorists have put forward theoretical models for the genesis of tics which resemble the model put forward above. Thus, while Ferenczi (1921) considered that tics represented the fixation of libido on single organs, he postulated that a tic might arise as the result of a traumatic event (not necessarily sexual in nature).[5] He wrote that ". . . an unexpectedly powerful trauma can

---

[4] See Chapter 2.

[5] The two other conditions giving rise to tics postulated by Ferenczi were: injury to a part of the body heavily charged with libido and injury to a part of the body closely linked with ego-integrity.

have the result in tic, as in traumatic neurosis, of an over-strong memory fixation on the attitude of the body at the moment of experience of the trauma, and that to such a degree as to provoke a perpetual or paroxysmatic reproduction of the attitude" (Ferenczi, 1921, p. 13). Similarly, Gerard (1946) conceptualized the tic as a response to a traumatic experience that inhibits the natural response, the traumatic experience being either punishment or loss of love due to restrictive training practices of the parents. Mahler (1944) also pointed out that the tic represented a defensive function of the neuromuscular system and stressed the failure to achieve inhibition of early motor activity (Mahler and Rangell, 1943).[6]

2. A Model Derived from Skinner

The operant conditioning model is readily derived from the basic principles governing the control of behavior, as described in Chapter 2. It would be argued that tics are generated and maintained by their consequences in just the same way that any other movements are. The contingencies which movements produce, either in the external environment or within the organism via internal feedback systems, are reinforcing and, therefore, strengthen and maintain the behavior. A precise model for the genesis and maintenance of tics, using operant principles, has not, however, been worked out yet.

III. BEHAVIOR THERAPY APPLIED TO TICS

In recent years, methods of treatment have been derived from both the Hullian and Skinnerian models.

1. Treatment Based on Hullian Learning Theory

According to the model proposed above, the tic may be conceptualized as a learned habit which has (in adults, at least) probably attained maximum habit strength (sH_R). In terms of the theory, it should be possible to extinguish this habit by building up a negative or incompatible habit of "not performing the tic." If the patient is given massed practice in the tic, then reactive inhibition (I_R) should build up rapidly. When I_R reaches a critical point, the patient will be forced to "rest" or not perform the tic. This fact by itself is, of course, trivial; however, the importance of the method lies in the further prediction that the dissipation of I_R during rest will be a reinforcing state of affairs for any responses performed by the subject during that period. The basic theory is that what will be reinforced during the rest period will be the response of not responding (i.e., of not being able to perform the tic). It should be noted carefully that this habit (sI_R) of "not responding" is not the *absence* of response, but rather an incompatible *positive* response.[7] The habit (sI_R) of not performing the tic will be associated with drive-reduction resulting from the dissipation of I_R and so will be reinforced. With repeated massed practice, therefore, a "negative" habit will be strengthened, incompatible with the positive habit of performing the tic. Furthermore, repeated voluntary evocation of the tic should *not* increase the strength of the positive habit, since it is already asymptotic and consequently not subject to strengthening by massed practice.

At any given moment, therefore, the effective reaction potential of the tic ($s\bar{E}_R$) i.e., the ability of the subject to perform the tic) will be a resultant of the forces in the equation:

$$s\bar{E}_R = (sH_R \times D) - (I_R + sI_R)$$

As sI_R increases, $s\bar{E}_R$ should diminish to a point at which the excitatory and inhibitory parts of the equation are equal. The positive response tendency of the tic will then be counterbalanced by the response tendency not to perform the tic and, behaviorally, extinction should be complete. During the learning process, of course, $s\bar{E}_R$ would be expected to fluctuate, since its momentary strength is affected by several unstable factors (e.g., variations in drive level) and any increase in drive may temporarily mask the effects of increasing sI_R (Yates, 1958).

The theoretical constructs of reactive and conditioned inhibition were derived largely from animal studies and some human studies involving massed and spaced practice in relation to the phenomenon of reminiscence. The optimum conditions of massed practice under which conditioned inhibition (sI_R) might be expected to grow most rapidly and effectively were, of course, unknown with respect to the

---

[6] The psychodynamic literature has been carefully reviewed by Weisman (1952).

[7] The analogy would be with the halting of a train by the "positive" force of friction when the engine is shut off.

extinction of tics. Yates' prolonged study of the effects of varying conditions of massed practice and rest with a single patient was therefore avowedly an *experimental* rather than a treatment study, and this was made plain to the patient involved who willingly accepted the experimenter's statement that no therapeutic benefits might be obtained. The subject was a female psychiatric patient, 25 years old, of high average intelligence, who was markedly neurotic and somewhat extraverted. She manifested four clear-cut tics, varying in complexity: a complex stomach-contraction/breathing tic; a nasal "explosion" (expiration) tic; a "throat-clearing" tic; and a bilateral eyeblink tic. These tics formed a related complex in so far as they appeared to have started following two very traumatic experiences about ten years earlier when the patient felt she was being suffocated while undergoing anesthesia. She reported being terrified that she was going to die and could not tolerate any object being placed over her face. The tics (which could occur independently) thus appeared to be CARs and to reduce anxiety, since the patient reported a need to perform the tics and relief following their performance.

The series of experiments carried out are reported in detail in Yates (1958). They involved varying combinations of massed practice and rest. Initially, the massed practice periods were of one minute's duration, followed by one minute's rest (the "standard procedure"). In any one session, each tic was practiced for five trials, and there were two sessions per day, one carried out under direct supervision of the experimenter, the other carried out by the patient alone at home. In later experiments, the massed practice periods were extended to 15 minutes and then one hour, followed by a prolonged rest period of several days to several weeks.[8] In all, some 315 experimental periods were utilized over a period of nine months.

The results of the experiments are shown in Figure 1, from which it can be seen that highly significant decrements in capacity to produce the tics voluntarily resulted. The patient also reported a significant decline in the involuntary occurrence of the tics in social situations, though no objective measures of this were available. The effect of the massed practice was most striking in relation to the relatively simple nasal tic and least striking in relation to the complex stomach tic.

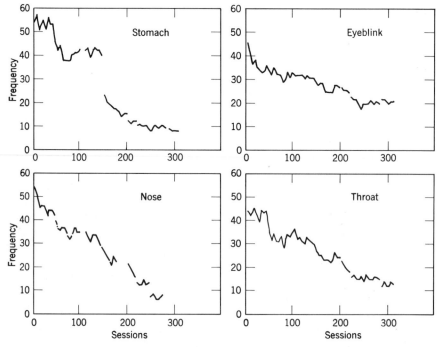

FIG. 1.   Change in frequency of voluntary evocation of four tics under massed practice (Yates, 1958).

[8] These prolonged periods of massed practice were not distressing to the patient since, after the first few minutes, most of the time was spent in involuntary rest pauses.

That the results obtained were in accordance with expectations from the theory is indicated by several factors: the shape of the curves suggests the obverse of a learning curve; a "negative" reminiscence effect was obtained following rest periods (i.e., a *decline* over rest of the capacity to produce the tics); and the failure to obtain a rise in frequency in the initial practice sessions (suggesting that, for this patient, sH_R was asymptotic).

Yates' study with this patient was continued by Jones (1960) who found no recovery of function on transfer of the patient from one experimenter to another; and who was able to reduce very markedly the capacity of the patient to reproduce the complex stomach contraction tic. Generalization to "real life" remained incomplete.

Several subsequent studies on other tiqueurs have offered fairly strong support for the validity of the theory and technique put forward by Yates. Thus, Rafi (1962) found a very significant decline in frequency of a head jerk and facial grimace in a patient subjected to 25 two-hour sessions of massed practice. The "standard procedure" of Yates (one minute massed practice periods) and slightly longer periods (five minutes) were, however, unsuccessful in reducing the rate of voluntary evocation of a foot-tapping tic in a second subject. (Both of these subjects were much older than Yates' patient.) The patient in whom no reduction of frequency with massed practice was obtained was slightly introverted; whereas Yates' patient was slightly extraverted and Rafi's other patient markedly so. In both of Rafi's patients, there was a significant decline in frequency of the involuntary movements, but they did not remit completely.

Two studies by Walton also obtained theory-congruent results. In the first study (Walton, 1961), a 12-year-old boy with multiple tics was given prolonged periods of massed practice in the major tic, and shorter periods of massed practice in the others. An interesting innovation of Walton's was the use of largactil to reduce drive-level and hence initiate involuntary rest pauses earlier; he also assumed that the drug would reduce tolerance for the buildup of reactive inhibition. A significant reduction in both voluntary and involuntary evocation of the tics was produced; and this improvement was maintained over a one-year follow-up period. In the second study (Walton, 1964) he subjected a second child (with three tics—nasal explosion, hiccoughing, and headshaking of 11 years' duration) to very prolonged periods of massed practice (half to $1\frac{1}{2}$ hours) over no less than 109 sessions, this time utilizing amylobarbitone as the drive-reducing drug. Again, there was a significant reduction in frequency of the tics over a five-month follow-up.

Lazarus (1960) also successfully used massed practice with a youth with severe mouth and head movements accompanying stuttering.

Finally, Clark (1966) has recently reported the successful application of massed practice to the compulsive obscene utterances found in Gilles de la Tourette's syndrome. One of his three cases withdrew from treatment (nevertheless, showing decrements in the predicted direction), but the other two cases have remained symptom free over a follow-up period of four years, have shown no signs of symptom substitution, and have improved generally in their social adjustment (not surprising, in view of the socially crippling nature of compulsive obscene utterances).

Thus, no less than seven studies provide partial or strong support for both the theory and the technique. In light of this, it is disappointing and disconcerting to find completely contradictory findings in a recent important study by Feldman and Werry (1966). They studied a 13-year-old boy with multiple tics of face, neck, and head of six years' duration. Of these tics, the head jerk was subjected to massed practice of periods of five minutes' duration (with a later attempt at periods of 15 minutes' duration). Not only did they not find any evidence of a decline in frequency of voluntary evocation following massed practice, but both voluntary and involuntary evocation increased very significantly and an old tic reappeared. The treatment was eventually abandoned. The changing frequency of *involuntary* tics at various stages of the study is shown in Figure 2.

The results obtained by Feldman and Werry are extremely puzzling in view of the positive results reported in the earlier studies. Feldman and Werry rightly reject any explanation in terms of the positive habit (sH_R) being non-asymptotic at the commencement of massed practice (and hence being strengthened by practice), since evocation frequency returned to the original level when massed practice was discontinued. Their preferred explanation is in terms of an increase in drive-level produced by the stress of the experimental method for this particular patient. This explanation they regard as accounting for the raising above threshold of an old, apparently extinguished, tic. They also

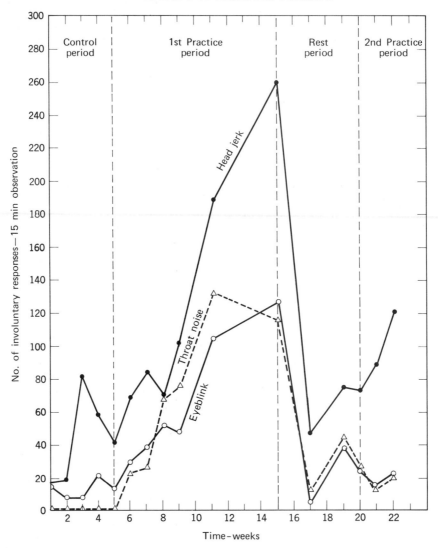

FIG. 2. Change in frequency of practiced and unpracticed tics in control and experimental periods (Feldman and Werry, 1966).

assume that, in the experimental situation, drive increased at a faster rate than reactive inhibition.

This explanation of the results does not seem to be adequate, though it is true the patient was described as obsessive and somewhat depressed, i.e., he was probably an introverted neurotic. The explanation may rather lie in the fact that the patient was introverted rather than extraverted and in methodological considerations relating to the ability of the patient to carry out the massed practice efficiently and to reproduce the tics accurately. These considerations will be discussed below.

In view of the positive results obtained in earlier studies, it is unfortunate that Feldman and Werry were unable to carry out further controlled experimental studies in an effort to pinpoint the reasons for failure. Thus, in terms of their drive theory, they could have made use of Walton's technique of administering drive-reducing drugs, or they could have increased the extraversion of the patient by the administration of drugs (thus altering the cortical excitation-inhibition balance). In the absence of such studies, it is unnecessary at present to conclude that massed practice is ineffective in reducing the evocation of tics or that the theory is necessarily wrong. Certainly, however, the Feldman and Werry study vividly points up the need for more controlled work in this area.

2. TREATMENT BASED ON OPERANT CONDITIONING

The only major study of the application of operant techniques to the modification of tics is that of Barrett (1962). She studied a 38-year-old male with multiple tics of 14 years' duration. Barrett made no attempt to record the frequency and amplitude of each separate tic but rather ingeniously recorded the overall occurrence of movement by special technical procedures. The patient was seated in a comfortable swivel-tilt armchair, to the back of which was attached a large U-shaped magnet which, via an induction coil, recorded the patient's most noticeable spasmodic movements, regardless of locus or amplitude. The recording was then transduced into a visible record on a cumulative response recorder.

The basic procedure followed by Barrett was to program her apparatus so that each recorded movement produced a contingent event of an aversive nature and to compare the effects of this with the effects of noncontingent events. The conditions compared were as follows.

(i) Each movement *turned off* otherwise continuous music in the headphones worn by the patient for 1.5 seconds (response-contingent elimination of reinforcing stimulus).

(ii) Each movement *initiated* a 1.5-second blast of 60 db white noise (response-contingent punishment or aversive stimulation).

(iii) Noncontingent presentation of continuous white noise (aversive stimulation) or music (reinforcing stimulation).

(iv) The patient attempted to inhibit movements himself using his customary devices.

Thus, the *cessation* of music or the *initiation* of white noise following a movement may be regarded as the contingent instatement of aversive stimulation, and the effects of these procedures was compared with control conditions involving attempted self-control or noncontingent aversive or nonaversive stimulation.

The operant or base-level of the frequency of movement (i.e., the rate produced in the absence of the above special procedures) varied from a minimal level of 64 movements per minute to a high of 116. Barrett found that continuous (noncontingent) noise did not change the base level; contingent noise reduced the rate to 40 movements per minute, as did noncontingent music. Contingent cessation of music was the most effective controller of movement rate, a reduction of 15–30 movements

per minute resulting (a drop of 40–50% in frequency). Self-control procedures by the patient reduced the movement rate to 50–60 times per minute. The reliability of the effects of contingent music was established as satisfactory by a retest after a two-month break.

Thus, Barrett demonstrated quite clearly that operant schedules of reinforcement or nonreinforcement will affect significantly the output of involuntary movements, just as has been shown equally clearly in studies of the control of normal speech and stuttering (Goldiamond, 1965). The only other reported use of operant procedures with tiqueurs is that by Rafi (1962). Using a buzzer as a contingent aversive stimulus, Rafi produced a significant reduction in evocation of foot tapping in the patient with whom massed practice had been unsuccessful.

3. TREATMENT OF SPASMODIC TORTICOLLIS

An interesting study of the application of behavior therapy to the treatment of spasmodic torticollis ("wry neck") has been reported by Brierley (1967). He devised a special simple headgear by means of which a mild shock occurred to the wrist if the patient turned his head to the side. The technique (a variant of which was reported by Meige and Feindel) appears to be an instance of Mowrer's passive avoidance (response-correlated) learning, since kinesthetic feedback from the turning movement could presumably serve as a CS for shock which would inhibit continuation of the movement. Both patients were reported to be symptom free about six months after cessation of treatment.

4. COMPARATIVE AND CONTROL STUDIES OF TREATMENT

Virtually all of the studies reviewed are seriously defective in the adequacy of follow-up data. Such data is of crucial importance in relation to the treatment of tics, since they are notoriously resistant to almost any form of treatment. Guttman and Creak (1940) followed up eight cases (aged 5–15 years on admission) for ten years. At least 50% of the cases were still displaying the tic behaviors, and the authors doubted the validity of the reported remission in the other cases, this being based on letters from the subjects and not on direct observation (these were untreated cases). Mahler and Luke (1946) presented follow-up data on ten cases aged 7–12 years on admission and treated by psychotherapy for periods varying from seven weeks to three years. On discharge from treatment, no cases could be regarded as "cured"; seven were "slightly" to "much" improved; and four were unimproved. Unfortunately, the follow-up data is not very satisfactorily presented, but Mahler and Luke conclude that there was ". . . no direct correlation between recovery from the tic syndrome and length or method of psychotherapy . . ." nor were ". . . thoroughness of treatment and good therapeutic results . . . in direct proportion, even when the syndrome was of short duration and the child was relatively young" (Mahler and Luke, 1946, p. 435). Somewhat better results were reported, however, by Paterson (1945) for 21 cases of spasmodic torticollis of apparently nonorganic origin. Thus the results reported by behavior therapists must be treated with extreme caution and should be regarded for the present as experimental studies of the control and manipulation of these forms of maladaptive behavior, rather than as therapeutic in intent or result.

Mention should also be made here of the recent discovery of the effectiveness of the drug haloperidol in the treatment of Gilles de la Tourette's syndrome. Early reports of success (Seignot, 1961; Challas and Brauer, 1963; Chapel, Brown, and Jenkins, 1964) have been fully confirmed by more recent studies (Stevens and Blachly, 1966; Connell et al, 1967; Lucas, 1967; Challas et al, 1967; Shapiro and Shapiro, 1968). The study of Stevens and Blachly (1966) is interesting because the use of operant conditioning techniques produced significant reduction of the abnormal behavior, but the improvement could not be generalized outside the experimental situation. The administration of 3 mg of haloperidol four times daily[9] abolished all aspects of the disorder and was accompanied by a truly remarkable improvement in personality functioning, the latter disturbance possibly being a secondary phenomenon. Administration of a placebo led to the return of the syndrome. The patient's improvement on the drug regimen was maintained at ten-month follow-up; other studies suggest it may be possible gradually to reduce the dosage. Stevens and Blachly provide a good discussion of the pharmacology of haloperidol and suggest that the syndrome may be a result of a metabolic disturbance which causes enzyme or neurotransmitter dysfunction of the central nervous system.

IV. METHODOLOGICAL PROBLEMS

Problems of methodology are of particular interest in relation to the study of tics and will therefore be considered here in some detail.

1. ESTABLISHMENT OF BASE RATES

Some of the early studies (e.g., Yates, 1958) failed to establish base rates for the *involuntary* rate of evocation of the tics from which to measure changes following treatment, relying instead on the subjective report of the patient. This deficiency was remedied in some subsequent studies (e.g., Feldman and Werry, 1966). Barrett (1962) also measured the base rate, but her study was essentially a laboratory experiment and hence no attempt was made to measure the involuntary rate "in real life." Clearly, it is desirable that base rates should be carefully established prior to the introduction of experimental conditions.

2. INTRASUBJECT CONTROL

In the study of Yates (1958) it would have been possible to apply one of the basic principles of behavior therapy, namely, the use of the subject as his own control, and thus provide a more rigorous test of the theory on which the method of massed practice was used. In other words, if one of the tics had not been subjected to massed practice, then spot checks on its frequency of voluntary evocation would have been expected to reveal little, if any, decline in rate because very little I_R would be generated by such spot checks. Stimulus generalization might be expected to produce some decline in the unpractised tic, but overall the prediction would be expected to be fulfilled if the theory were correct. Unfortunately, for a number of reasons, Yates did not utilize this essential control. This kind of internal control was, however, exercised in the study by Feldman and Werry (1966).

3. VOLUNTARY REPRODUCTION OF THE TICS

There is an interesting contrast between the massed-practice studies and the operant conditioning study of Barrett. In terms of the theory of reactive and conditioned inhibition, it would seem to be essential that the tics should be reproduced as accurately as possible. If this is

---

[9] This is a high dosage which may produce undesirable side effects. However, similar results have been produced with much lower doses in some patients.

not achieved by the subject, then slightly different groups of muscles will be involved in various reproductions of the tic and this will retard the growth of I_R and, consequently, of sI_R. Some evidence of the validity of this requirement is to be found in Yates' (1958) study where the most significant changes were produced in the relatively less complex tics. This could well have been one critical variable in the study of Feldman and Werry (1966) who found that, at the end of the early stages of the study, the patient "had not been practising the tic as instructed, often shortening the session by one or two minutes and sometimes omitting it entirely" (p. 113—the reference is to the sessions practiced on his own by the patient). As was pointed out earlier, Barrett (1962) did not attempt to modify *individual* movements in her patient but, instead, applied the contingencies to any movement or group of movements which activated the recorder sufficiently. Here research is obviously required within the operant framework to determine the relative efficacy of this technique as against attaching various contingencies to specific movements.

4. MEASURES OF DEPENDENT VARIABLES

Tics, of course, vary on a number of dimensions, including strength, frequency, and quality. Unfortunately, thus far, insufficient work has been carried out on techniques for objectively recording changes on these dimensions during treatment. Simple frequency counts are probably not adequate, since frequency could remain relatively stable while amplitude declines significantly, perhaps even to the point where the movements would no longer be perceived by an independent observer unaware of the nature of the subject's disorder.

5. TRANSFER FROM LABORATORY TO REAL LIFE

As we shall see in a later chapter, it has become apparent in recent years that one of the major problems of the behavior therapist relates to the transfer of results obtained in a laboratory to real-life situations. There are a number of aspects to this problem which may, however, be mentioned here. In so far as the maladaptive behavior is tied to *social* stimulus situations (probably the most common state of affairs), results produced in an impersonal laboratory situation are not very likely to

transfer very strongly outside the laboratory. Hence, the strictly laboratory-based studies must be regarded as a preliminary to the attempt to abolish the behavior outside. As Goldiamond (1965) has so clearly demonstrated in relation to stuttering,[10] this is *not* just a case of obtaining instances of stimulus generalization but may more often involve the instatement of entirely new forms of behavior, on the one hand, and the transfer (*not* through generalization) of laboratory-based stimulus control of this behavior to real-life-based stimulus control. As Goldiamond has also shown, this may involve training the subject to be his own experimenter.

In the case of tics treated by massed practice, Yates (1958) and Jones (1960) were well aware of the problem of extending conditioned inhibition to nonlaboratory real-life situations of a social nature in which the frequency of the involuntary tics tended to increase. One possible solution which occurred to these authors was to require the patient to indulge in massed practice in social situations as well as the laboratory and thus attach conditioned inhibition to these situations. Such a procedure was obviously impractical in view of the possible undesirable side-effects resulting from social embarrassment. An alternative solution, however, readily suggested itself. Since social situations by definition involved the presence of other people, then, instead of generalizing sI_R to *situations*, it could perhaps be generalized to *people*. Hence, a possible solution would be gradually to bring more and more people into the laboratory situation to observe the patient under conditions of massed practice, and to arrange for these observers gradually to behave in a more and more hostile fashion, thus increasingly approximating the real-life conditions in which the tic is exacerbated. In this way, sI_R would become attached to people. Unfortunately, neither Yates nor Jones reached the stage of carrying out these experiments.

6. PERSONALITY FACTORS AND THE USE OF DRUGS

Little attention has so far been paid to the possible significance of individual differences in personality structure in relation to the use of massed practice. Since inhibitory processes are being generated in opposition to excitatory processes, then individual differences in neuroticism and extraversion-introversion may be of

---

[10] See Chapter 6.

critical importance. A highly introverted neurotic (that is, a person with a combination of high autonomic drive and slow rate of buildup of reactive inhibition) may be a contra-indication to probable successful treatment. In such circumstances, the use of appropriate drugs which influence autonomic activity or alter the excitation-inhibition balance may be in order on an experimental basis. The studies of Walton (1961, 1964), in particular, point the way for future research. Unfortunately, little work has so far been carried out on the person-ality correlates of tiqueurs (Crown, 1953), and this study was not concerned with treatment.

7. METHODOLOGY OF MASSED PRACTICE

The necessity for accurate reproduction of the tic under massed practice conditions has already been pointed out. There is no doubt that much more experimentation will be necessary before any standard techniques are available. Thus, Yates (1958) tentatively concluded that the optimal conditions for the generation of conditioned inhibition were very prolonged periods of massed practice (possibly of the order of five to six hours, bearing in mind that the major part of such a period would be spent "not performing the tic") followed by very prolonged periods of rest (of the order of several weeks). Even though it is possible, on this basis, to criticize subsequent studies on the grounds that the periods of massed practice have been too short, it does *not* follow that prolonged massed practice followed by pro-longed rest should become a standard technique for the treatment of tiqueurs. As both Feldman and Werry (1966) and Rafi (1962) showed, some subjects are unable to tolerate much shorter periods of massed practice, though it may, of course, prove possible to increase tolerance for prolonged massed practice periods by the use of appropriate drugs.

8. METHODOLOGY OF OPERANT CONDITIONING

The study by Barrett (1962) was recognized by that author as being exploratory in nature and one particular point (fully recognized by Barrett) may be of special importance for future operant work. This relates to the importance of *partial reinforcement* techniques. Barrett used continuous rather than partial reinforcement methods, but it has been demonstrated repeat-edly[11] that the use of partial reinforcement techniques increases resistance to extinction—indeed, this factor may well account for the extreme tenacity of tics as motor habits.

In conclusion, it will be clear that the study of the application of theoretical and empirical knowledge derived from studies of learning and extinction has only begun to be applied to the control and modification of tics. The success or otherwise of the theories and methods thera-peutically, however, is of less importance than the fact that such studies are being carried out within a controlled experimental framework. Given greater methodological sophistication along the lines suggested above, there is every reason to anticipate a twofold reward: increase in basic knowledge of how fairly clear-cut and specific behavior may be modified and con-trolled with a feedback to general experimental psychology and, ultimately at least, a very real advance in the capacity of the abnormal experimental psychologist to significantly mod-ify, in real life, a peculiarly disabling form of maladaptive behavior.

REFERENCES

Arrington, R.E. Time-sampling studies of child behavior. *Psychol. Monogr.*, 1939, **51**, 1–193.

Arrington, R.E. Time sampling in studies of social behavior: a critical review of tech-niques and results. *Psychol. Bull.*, 1943, **40**, 81–124.

Ascher, E. Psychodynamic considerations in Gilles de la Tourette's disease (maladie des tics). *Amer. J. Psychiat.*, 1948, **105**, 267–276.

Barrett, B.H. Reduction in rate of multiple tics by free operant conditioning methods. *J. nerv. ment. Dis.*, 1962, **135**, 187–195.

Bender, L. & Schilder, P. Impulsions: a specific disorder of the behavior of children. *Arch. Neurol. Psychiat.*, 1940, **44**, 900–1008.

---

[11] See Chapters 2 and 5.

Bender, L. & Schilder, P. Mannerisms as organic motility syndrome (Paracortical disturbances). *Conf. Neurol.*, 1941, **3**, 321–330.

Blatz, W.E. & Ringland, M.C. The study of tics in preschool children. *U. Toronto Studies (Child Development Series No. 3)*. U. Toronto Press, 1935.

Brain, W.R. The treatment of tic (habit spasm). *Lancet*, 1928, **214**, 1295–1296.

Brierley, H. The treatment of hysterical spasmodic torticollis by behavior therapy. *Behav. Res. Ther.*, 1967, **5**, 139–142.

Challas, G. & Brauer, W. Tourette's disease: relief of symptoms with R1625. *Amer. J. Psychiat.*, 1963, **120**, 283–284.

Challas, G., Chapel, J.L., & Jenkins, R.L. Tourette's disease: control of symptoms and its clinical course. *Internat. J. Neuropsychiat.*, 1967, **3** (Suppl. 1), 95–109.

Chapel, J.L., Brown, N., & Jenkins, R.L. Tourette's disease: symptomatic relief with haloperidol. *Amer. J. Psychiat.*, 1964, **121**, 608–610.

Clark, D.F. Behavior therapy of Gilles de la Tourette's syndrome. *Brit. J. Psychiat.*, 1966, **112**, 771–778.

Connell, P.H., Corbett, J.A., Horne, D.J., & Matthews, A.M. Drug treatment of adolescent tiqueurs: a double blind trial of diazepam and haloperidol. *Brit. J. Psychiat.*, 1967, **113**, 375–381.

Creak, M. & Guttmann, E. Chorea, tics and compulsive utterances. *J. ment. Sci.*, 1935, **81**, 843–839.

Crown, S. An experimental inquiry into some aspects of the motor behavior and personality of tiqueurs. *J. ment. Sci.*, 1953, **99**, 84–91.

Epstein, J. Functional spasms in children, their physiologic pathology, and their relation to the neuroses in later life. *Amer. J. med. Sci.*, 1927, **173**, 380–385.

Feldman, R.B. & Werry, J.S. An unsuccessful sttempt to treat a tiqueur by massed practice. *Behav. Res. Ther.*, 1966, **4**, 111–117.

Ferenczi, S. Psycho-analytical observations on tic. *Internat. J. Psychoanal.*, 1921, **2**, 1–30.

Fernando, S.J. Gilles de la Tourette's syndrome: a report on four cases and a review of published case reports. *Brit. J. Psychiat.*, 1967, **113**, 607–617.

Fernando, S.J.M. Gilles de la Tourette's syndrome. *Brit. J. Psychiat.*, 1968, **114**, 123–125.

Gerard, M.W. The psychogenic tic in ego development. In Freud, A. et al (eds.). *Psychoanalytic study of the child* (Vol. 2). New York: Internat. Univer. Press, 1946, pp. 133–162.

Goldiamond, I. Stuttering and fluency as manipulatable operant response classes. In Krasner, L. & Ullmann, L.P. (eds.). *Research in behavior modification*. New York: Holt, 1965, pp. 106–156.

Guttmann, E. & Creak, M. A follow-up study of hyperkinetic children. *J. ment. Sci.*, 1940, **86**, 624–631.

Hall, M.B. Obsessive-compulsive states in childhood and their treatment. *Arch. Dis· Childh.*, 1935, **10**, 49–59.

Hassin, G.B., Stenn, A., & Burstein, H.J. Stereotyped acts or attitude tics? A case with a peculiar anomaly of gait. *J. nerv. ment. Dis.*, 1930, **71**, 27–32.

Jones, H.G. Continuation of Yates' treatment of a tiqueur. In Eysenck, H.J. (ed.). *Behavior therapy and the neuroses*. Oxford: Pergamon, 1960, pp. 250–258.

Jones, M.R. Measurement of spontaneous movements in adult psychotic patients by a time-sampling technique: a methodological study. *J. Psychol.*, 1941, **11**, 285–295.

Jones, M.R. Studies in "nervous" movements: I. The effect of mental arithmetic on the frequency and patterning of movements. *J. gen. Psychol.*, 1943, **29**, 47–62 (a).

Jones, M.R. Studies in "nervous" movements: II. The effect of inhibition of micturition on the frequency and patterning of movements. *J. gen. Psychol.*, 1943, **29**, 303–312 (b).

Kelman, D.H. Gilles de la Tourette's disease in children: a review of the literature. *J. Child Psychol. Psychiat.*, 1965, **6**, 219–226.

Koch, H.L. An analysis of certain forms of so-called "nervous habits" in young children. *J. genet. Psychol.*, 1935, **46**, 139–170.

Krauss, S. Post-choreic personality and neurosis. *J. ment. Sci.*, 1946, **92**, 75–95.

Lazarus, A.A. Objective psychotherapy in the treatment of dysphemia. *J. South African Logopedic Soc.*, 1960, **6**, 8–10.

Levy-Suhl, M. Resolution by psychoanalysis of motor disturbances in an adolescent. *Psychoanal. Quart.*, 1937, **6**, 336–345.

Lucas, A.R. Gilles de la Tourette's disease in children: treatment with haloperidol. *Amer. J. Psychiat.*, 1967, **124**, 147–149.

Mahler, M.S. Tics and impulsions in children: a study of motility. *Psychoanal. Quart.*, 1944, **17**, 430–444.

Mahler, M.S. A psychoanalytic evaluation of tic in psychopathology of children: symptomatic and tic syndrome. In Freud, A. et al (eds.). *Psychoanalytic study of the child.* New York: Internat. Univer. Press, 1949, pp. 3–4, 279–310.

Mahler, M.S. & Luke, J.A. Outcome of the tic syndrome. *J. nerv. ment. Dis.*, 1946, **103**, 433–445.

Mahler, M.S. & Rangell, L. A psychosomatic study of maladie des tics (Gilles de la Tourette's disease). *Psychiat. Quart.*, 1943, **17**, 579–603.

Meige, H. & Feindel, E. *Tics and their treatment.* London: Appleton, 1907.

Mowrer, O.H. *Learning theory and personality dynamics.* New York: Ronald, 1950.

Olson, W.C. *The measurement of nervous habits in normal children.* Minneapolis: Univer. Minnesota Press, 1929.

Patersor, M.T. Spasmodic torticollis: results of psychotherapy in 21 cases. *Lancet*, 1945, **2**, 566–559.

Rafi, A.A. Learning theory and the treatment of tics. *J. psychosom. Res.*, 1962, **6**, 71–76.

Sainsbury, P. The measurement and description of spontaneous movements before and after leucotomy. *J. ment. Sci.*, 1954, **100**, 732–741 (a).

Sainsbury, P. A method of measuring spontaneous movements by time-sampling motion pictures. *J. ment. Sci.*, 1954, **100**, 742–748 (b).

Seham, M. & Boardman, D.V. A study of motor automatisms. *Arch. Neurol. Psychiat.*, 1934, **32**, 154–173.

Seignot, J.N. Un cas de maladie des tics de Gilles de la Tourette guéri par le R1625. *Ann. médicopsychol.*, 1961, **119**, 578–579.

Shapiro, A.K. & Shapiro, E. Treatment of Gilles de la Tourette's syndrome with haloperidol. *Brit. J. Psychiat.*, 1968, **114**, 345–350.

Solomon, R.L. & Wynne, L.C. Traumatic avoidance learning: the principles of anxiety conservation and partial irreversibility. *Psychol. Rev.*, 1954, **61**, 353–385.

Stevens, J.R. & Blachly, P.H. Successful treatment of the maladie des tics. *Amer. J. Dis. Child.*, 1966, **112**, 541–545.

Walton, D. Experimental psychology and the treatment of a tiqueur. *J. Child Psychol. Psychiat.*, 1961, **2**, 148–155.

Walton, D. Massed practice and simultaneous reduction in drive level—further evidence of the efficacy of this approach to the treatment of tics. In Eysenck, H.J. (ed.). *Experiments in behavior therapy.* London: Pergamon, 1964, pp. 398–400.

Weisman, A.D. Nature and treatment of tics. *Arch. Neurol. Psychiat.*, 1952, **68**, 444–459.

Williams, T.A. Abnormal movements (tic), their nature and treatment, *Internat. J. Med. Surg.*, 1932, **45**, 23–26 and 101–103.

Wilson, S.A.K. The tics and allied conditions. *J. Neurol. Psychopathol.*, 1927, **8**, 93–103.

Yates, A.J. The application of learning theory to the treatment of tics. *J. abnorm. soc. Psychol.*, 1958, **56**, 175–182.

Young, F.M. The incidence of nervous habits observed in college students. *J. Pers.*, 1947, **15**, 309–320.

Chapter 11

Delinquency, Psychopathy, and Criminality

I. INTRODUCTION

THE LITERATURE on delinquency is enormous; the empirical facts overwhelming; the theories legion. The literature on psychopathy is sparser; the empirical facts fewer; the theories more clear cut. No attempt will be made to review the present position regarding delinquency, psychopathy, and criminality;[1] but some indication will be given of certain approaches to these topics. This will be followed by a more detailed examination of some relatively recent behavioristic formulations. Thus far, behavior therapists have paid relatively little attention to the development of therapeutic techniques but what little has appeared will be reviewed. The reader is therefore cautioned that, as in several other chapters of this book, a particularly selective approach is deliberately being adopted without any intention of denying the validity of alternative approaches, nor of denying the obvious fact that the various approaches may be complementary to each other.

The problem of the definition and incidence of delinquency has received a great deal of attention in recent years, as reflected, for example, in recent monographs by Sellin and Wolfgang (1964) and Lunden (1964). Here we may merely point out that the *legal* definition of delinquency need not (and usually does not) coincide with the *psychological* definition, while the *sociological* definition may differ yet again. As we shall see, the psychologist is mainly concerned with the question whether there is a "delinquent personality," a "psychopathic personality," or a "criminal personality"; and if so, what, if any, may be the relationship between the "personalities." The "incidence" of delinquency is almost a meaningless question, since the "incidence" will depend to such a large degree on the legal interpretation of what constitutes a "delinquent act" and this will differ markedly from one culture to another (Lunden, 1964).

The meaning of the term "psychopath" presents fewer difficulties, although some authors have attempted to distinguish various subgroups of psychopaths. Craft (1966), after reviewing the development of the concept, has stated that it is generally agreed that two primary features characterize the psychopath: a lack of emotional responsiveness in situations in which this would be called forth in normal persons, and an irresistible tendency to act on impulse. From these primary characteristics may be derived secondary characteristics:

---

[1] From the wealth of literature, mention should perhaps be made of the recent well-balanced review of delinquency research by various authors under the editorship of Quay (1965a); the reviews of the concept of psychopathic personality by Gurvitz (1951) and by Craft (1966); the bibliography of research on psychopathy by Hare and Hare (1967); and the excellent book on crime and personality by Eysenck (1964).

aggressiveness; lack of guilt following anti-social behavior; failure to be influenced by punishment or aversive consequences of anti-social behavior; and a lack of positive drive or motivation. An element of depravity or vicious-ness will usually be manifested in the behavior of the psychopath, but intelligence may vary from very high to low and psychotic behavior is uncommon. Reviews of the concept of psy-chopathy by Hare (1965a) and by Albert et al (1959) indicate essential agreement with the points made by Craft. The two principal sub-groups which have been distinguished are the *primary sociopath* of Cleckley (1950), which appears to be identical with the *general* descrip-tion of the psychopath given by Craft; and the *neurotic psychopath* (Aichhorn, 1935). These two subgroups have been alternatively named the *ideopathic* and the *symptomatic* psychopath. As we shall see, other formulations are also possible.

II. THEORIES OF DELINQUENCY AND PSYCHOPATHY

The principal theories of delinquency and psychopathy may be subsumed under the headings of biological, dynamic, sociological, and behavioral. Here we shall be mainly con-cerned with the behavioral theories of delin-quency and psychopathy, but examples may be provided of the alternative formulations first to provide a broader picture.

1. THE BIOLOGICAL APPROACH

This approach has been, in its extreme form, almost entirely confined to attempts to explain psychopathic and recidivist criminal behavior. The classical study is, of course, that by Lange (1931), and this approach has relied mainly on studies of the criminal record of identical twins reared apart. Lange studied 30 pairs of twins (13 identical, 17 fraternal), one of each pair being known to have been imprisoned. Lange found that, of the 13 identical twins, ten of the second of the twins had also been imprisoned, while this was true of only two of the second of the 17 fraternal twins. The discordant twin pairs in the identical twins were rather convincingly explained. This rather extreme approach has been replaced in recent years by a more sophisticated theory of "criminal personality" which is described below.

2. THE DYNAMIC APPROACH

This approach is well represented by the studies of Aichhorn (1935) and Lindner (1944) and argues essentially that delinquency and psychopathic behavior represent symptoms of underlying conflict. Probably the much earlier studies of Healy and Bronner (1926) have not been surpassed as illustrations of this approach. They made a very careful comparison of 105 pairs of delinquent and nondelinquent children *from the same family*, seeking to answer the question why only one child in the family became delinquent. Following a detailed com-parison of physical status, developmental history, personality characteristics, interests and activities, intrafamily situation, emotional ex-periences, and many other variables, they concluded that delinquency is *meaningful* for the individual indulging in antisocial behavior and is a symptom of internal disturbance which may reflect an attempt to escape from an unpleasant situation; an attempt to compensate for felt inadequacies; an attempt to gain recognition and status; an attempt to seek punishment; and so on. A person becomes delinquent through the interaction of unsatisfied inner drives with opportunities provided by the culture to indulge in substitute activities which offer at least partial satisfaction of these inner drives. Of course, by its very design, Healy and Bronner's study is unable to separate hereditary from environmental causes, but it cannot be denied that they at least recognized the com-plexity of forces which produced the end result of delinquent behavior in a way that the "crime is destiny" proponents did not.

3. THE SOCIOLOGICAL APPROACH

Many attempts have been made to provide sociological explanations for delinquent be-havior in particular. As representative of these, we may mention briefly one of the most interesting, the "subcultural" theory of Cohen (1956). Cohen argues that delinquent behavior may be treated as a form of learned behavior generated in, and representative of, a particular kind of culture. The principal characteristics of the delinquent subculture are that it is non-utilitarian, malicious, negativistic, versatile, hedonistic (short-run satisfactions predominate), and group autonomous. "The gang is a separate, distinct, and often irresistible focus of attraction, loyalty, and solidity" (Cohen, 1956, p. 31). Cohen rejects some of the earlier cultural-type explanations of delinquency (for example, that delinquency is a function of unorganized areas or of culturally heterogeneous areas). He puts forward a general theory of the rise of sub-cultures. Essentially, all behavior is problem solving and occurs within a particular cultural frame of reference. If a particular problem is insoluble within the given frame of reference, the latter may have to be changed, that is, the subject must cease to conform and may resist the pressures to conform. To do this success-fully, however, the individual needs the social support of other people with similar problems who are prepared to accept new, possibly unorthodox solutions. Maximum effectiveness is achieved when these nonconforming people band together to form a new subculture which will provide a new, stable frame of reference. The new reference group in its final form will, of course, represent a compromise between differ-ing viewpoints. Most important, the new subculture provides status for the individuals conforming to it. Furthermore, the cohesive-ness of the subculture will be strengthened in proportion to the degree to which it is subjected to outside pressures. In relation to delinquency, Cohen says that, in America at least, much of the delinquency problem arises from the fact that the majority frame of reference is derived from the influence of the Protestant ethic which prescribes "an obligation to strive, by dint of rational, ascetic, self-disciplined, and indepen-dent activity, to achieve in wordly affairs" (Cohen, 1956, p. 87). Achievement of the "moral" qualities is indicated by material success. The norms defining this ethic include: ambition as a virtue (and its lack as a sign of maladjustment); individual responsibility; praise for any outstanding activity; postponement of self-indulgence; forethought above taking a chance; extraversion as opposed to intro-version; lack of physical violence; constructive recreation; and (of course!) respect for property. The critical point in relation to achievement of this ethic lies in the fact that the whole of the American educational system is geared to providing the maximal opportunity for achiev-ing the ethic to the white, middle-class child. The negro and the working-class child start the race for achievement at a distinct disadvantage.[2]

"The delinquent subculture deals with these problems by providing criteria of status which these children can meet" (Cohen, 1956, p. 121). The essential mark of the delinquent subculture is the total rejection of middle-class standards

and the adoption of an alternative subculture which offers its members equal status com-pared with membership of culturally approved groups and which may also legitimize aggression.

Cohen's theory has been both criticized (e.g., Sykes and Matza, 1957) and extended (e.g., Cloward and Ohlin, 1960), the latter distinguishing three types—criminal, conflict, and retreatist—of delinquent subculture. Of course, as Cohen points out, the subcultural solution does not always involve delinquent behavior, a point strikingly illustrated in recent years by the development of various other subcultural solutions such as beatniks, hippies, etc. Cohen's formulation has, however, been perhaps the most influential of the sociological or cultural analyses of delinquency.

4. THE BEHAVIORAL APPROACH

In recent years important advances have been made in the formulation of a general theory for explaining individual differences in socialization which have significant implications for the understanding of those antisocial forms of behavior which are labeled delinquent, psycho-pathic, or criminal. A general outline of the theory will first be given, followed by a state-ment of some of the major predictions generated by the theory. The empirical evidence relating to the validity of these deductions will then be considered.

(a) THE GENERAL THEORY OF SOCIALIZ-ATION. The theory to be described can be attributed mainly to Eysenck (1957, 1964) though it has perhaps been most fully described by Trasler (1962). It is derived to a considerable extent from previous work by Mowrer (1950).

In the theory, a basic distinction is made between the learning of skilled forms of behavior, such as walking, and the learning of values. The former involves teaching, the latter training. In the former case, the teaching relates to the acquisition of behaviors, skill in which brings its own reward, and skill at which society usually approves. Hence the child is encouraged to practice and master these skills. In the latter case, however, society often seeks to protect itself by training the child to inhibit certain forms of behavior the practice of which (e.g., uncontrolled aggressive behavior) would be dangerous to other members of society.

---

[2] Cohen points out that the teachers of working-class children are predominantly middle class and hence set their standards as the norm without, however, providing as good an opportunity for meeting these standards.

Since the young child often experiences a strong drive to indulge in these behaviors, it becomes essential for society to train him to inhibit their expression.

Socialization essentially, therefore, involves training in conformity to certain rules of behavior laid down by society as essential to its own preservation, rules which often conflict with the child's natural urges. This training is basically mediated by the technique of passive avoidance training[3] in which conditioned fear (anxiety) is aroused by the initial approach to performance of the undesirable act, the conditioned fear then producing inhibition of the act as soon as it commences. Eventually, cognitive mediation may prevent the act from even getting started.

The basic training techniques to produce conditioned fear are those of physical punishment and withdrawal of parental approval. Internalization of the stimuli producing conditioned fear is essential, however, if socially-approved behavior is to be self-regulated and "conscience" developed (Eysenck, 1960). An important corollary is that the inhibition of antisocial tendencies is not controlled solely by the fear of immediate or future punishment, since clearly most adults do not behave antisocially even when there is no danger of detection. Trasler (1962), in particular, has stressed the importance of training in *generalized* inhibition of antisocial tendencies.

The most important contribution of this theory of socialization, however, has been its consideration of individual differences in degree of socialization and how these are produced. There are three factors to be considered here: that relating to personality differences; that relating to amount and kind of training; and that relating to differential cultural definitions of what constitutes antisocial behavior.

With respect to personality variables, Eysenck (1964) has argued that both neuroticism and introversion—extraversion may be crucial variables determining individual differences in degree of socialization involved in a particular individual. Since training in socialization involves the acquisition of conditioned fear responses, then it would follow from his theory that extraverts would be more difficult to socialize than introverts, and there is a good deal of evidence to support this view.[4] Neuroticism

(high autonomic lability) would, however, interact in a complex fashion with extraversion.

Second, degree of socialization would also depend on the amount of training given by the parents and other socializing agents. Thus, a child with a constitutional predisposition to develop extraverted patterns of behaviors and who is, therefore, basically hard to socialize might well turn out to be a thoroughly socialized person if subjected to a sufficiently severe and prolonged training in socialization during development; while, conversely, a child with a constitutional predisposition to develop introverted patterns of behavior, basically easy to socialize, might turn out to be undersocialized if provided with little or no training in socialization and might then readily acquire antisocial behaviors of particular kinds if exposed to a "delinquent subculture."

It should be particularly noted that the theory does not assert that there is any basic difficulty in learning instrumental responses in under-socialized persons—the psychopath, for example, is often a highly intelligent person who is skilled in deceiving his victims. The defect is asserted to be in the realm of emotional learning.

Trasler (1962) and others have drawn attention to the importance of social class differences in relation to this training in the development of "conscience." Thus, lower-class parents tend to rely more on physical punishment than on withdrawal of affection, whereas the reverse is the case with middle-class parents. The latter parents will also tend to train more in terms of *general* inhibition of antisocial behavior.

In summary, the theory states that degree of socialization is a function primarily of the interaction of the two basic variables of constitutional conditionability and amount and severity of social training and that socialization involves essentially the development of mediating conditioned fear responses which inhibit the tendency to perform antisocial acts. The interaction of these variables will produce a dimension of socialization which is very probably normally distributed in the general population.

(b) SOME IMPLICATIONS OF THE THEORY. We have assumed that there is a basic dimension of constitutionally determined capacity for socialization which is determined by the

---

[3] See Chapter 2.

[4] See Eysenck (1964, Chapter 6) for a review of the evidence.

capacity for acquiring conditioned fear responses. The degree to which behavior is actually socially acceptable, however, is a complex function of the interaction of this basic capacity with two other main factors: the amount and severity of socialization training and the degree of alternative socialization (or antisocialization, according to one's frame of reference) to which the individual is subjected. The pure form of failure of the socialization process would then be expected to be found in the *psychopath* because these individuals have a very poor constitutional capacity for socialization. The psychopath would therefore be expected to be highly neurotic and markedly extraverted; to be highly resistant to any socialization training, however severe (training in socialization would virtually be irrelevant); to be unaffected also by alternative subcultural influences; and to indulge in solitary forms of delinquency.

Any group of delinquents, however, would be a composite of the interaction of the basic factors listed above. Delinquent behavior would, on the one hand, be expected to result from poor constitutional capacity for socialization (high neuroticism and above-average extraversion) combined with only average or below-average training in socialization. Subcultural influences would be a relatively ineffective influence on these individuals who could be described as mild psychopaths. Other individuals with a similar constitutional incapacity for developing socialization would, however, be nondelinquent because they had been subjected to above-average training in socialization, but their adjustment would be relatively precarious. On the other hand, any group of delinquents would be expected to contain individuals with a satisfactory basic constitutional capacity for socialization (average or high neuroticism and above-average introversion) but who had been subjected to grossly inadequate socialization training procedures. If not subjected to subcultural delinquent influences, such individuals would be solitary delinquents but, if subjected to subcultural delinquent influences, would be expected to be members of delinquent groups.

The complexity of these interactions and particularly the fact that most investigations are made into the end-product make it extremely difficult to test the general theory relating extraversion - introversion to failure of socialization. Nevertheless, careful factor-analytic or experimental investigations should throw light on the problem. In addition, it would be expected, if the theory is correct, that delinquents in general would not be defective in learning activities unrelated to socialization processes. If pure forms could be isolated (as in the case of psychopaths), however, we would expect to find that there would be a significant failure to respond to the *threat* of punishment (as opposed to the effect of punishment itself), since the theory predicts that anticipation of punishment would not influence behavior.

With these considerations in mind, we may turn to a review of the empirical results of studies of personality and behavior in psychopathic delinquents and criminal samples.

(c) EMPIRICAL STUDIES. Turning first to *psychopaths*, we have predicted that this group would be highly neurotic and highly extraverted. Eysenck (1959) has provided some evidence that this is so. A group of 36 hospitalized psychopaths obtained a mean neuroticism score of 35.58 (σ10.91) which was one and one-half standard deviations above the mean (19.89) of a quota sample of 1800 (σ11.02); while the extraversion score of the psychopathic group (30.77; σ9.51) was nearly one standard deviation above that of the quota sample (24.91; σ9.71). Lykken (1957) found his two psychopathic groups to be significantly higher on the MMPI Pd-Scale than a group of controls; while similar results were obtained by Craddick (1962). In an interesting study of long-sentence chronic psychopathic American prisoners, Warburton (1965) found a significantly elevated score on Cattell's 16PF measure of extraversion.

Studies of the *conditionability* of psychopaths also lend support to the theory of a basic difficulty in socialization in terms of a failure to acquire conditioned fear responses. Essentially, these studies examine the autonomic responsivity of psychopaths as compared with nonpsychopaths. However, as Hare (1968a) has recently discussed at length, it is important to distinguish between resting level of autonomic activity, reactivity of the ANS to the introduction of a novel or threatening stimulus, and rate of return to original base-line when the novel or threatening stimulus is withdrawn, as well as the autonomic reaction to a primary aversive stimulus. The basic prediction relates to *reactivity of the ANS to a stimulus which is a sign of an approaching aversive stimulus*, the prediction being that psychopaths will show less reactivity than nonpsychopaths. A series of studies by Hare offers fairly strong support for this hypothesis. Hare (1965a) has postulated that "the gradient of avoidance tendencies is steeper and of lower height for the psychopath than for the normal person" (p. 16), and from this model he has deduced that psychopaths will show less generalization of avoidance responses, will be influenced by immediate punishment but not by the threat of punishment, and will show increased deficiency of learning as the onset of the punishing stimulus is more and more delayed.

In two studies, Hare (1965b, 1965d) presented his subjects with a series of 12 numbers presented sequentially in a memory drum apparatus. After a dry run to measure resting GSR activity, the subjects were told that severe shock[5] would be experienced to the eighth number in the series which was then repeated five times. Thus, by this technique, changes in GSR reactivity could be measured as a function of approach to the critical number, as well as recovery following shock.

In the first study, Hare (1965d) compared the GSR response of psychopathic prisoners, non-psychopathic prisoners, and student controls with results shown in Figure 1. The psychopathic prisoners showed a significantly lower GSR response to all numbers over all trials, a significantly lower GSR in the resting state, and a slower rate of increase in GSR response as the shock stimulus approached. The psychopaths were also less responsive to the shock

itself than the nonpsychopathic prisoners but did not differ from the controls. Hare concluded that:

"Relatively little fear is elicited in psychopathic persons in the interval prior to anticipated punishment" (Hare, 1965d, p. 445).

In his second study, Hare (1965b) obtained similar results with respect to the gradient of GSR response in "normal" subjects with high scores on the MMPI Pd-scale. Not unexpectedly, however, the overall responsiveness of the control and experimental groups in this study did not differ.

In a subsequent study, Hare (1965c) measured generalization of the GSR response to tones of 468 cps and 153 cps following conditioning to a tone of 1000 cps associated with shock, using a delayed conditioning procedure in which the CS was presented for seven seconds with the shock occurring at the offset of the CS and persisting for 200 msec. The subjects were psychopathic and nonpsychopathic prisoners and the results, shown in Figure 2, indicated that the psychopaths gave significantly fewer CR's during training and showed significantly less generalization to the tone more remote from the original CS.

In a different kind of experiment, Hare (1966) required the subject to choose between pressing a key which gave immediate shock and

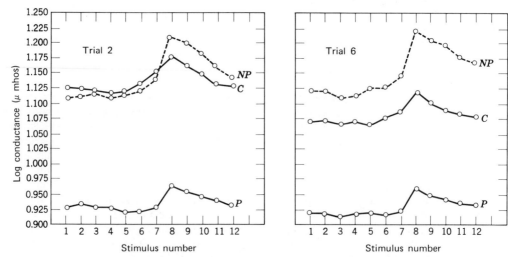

FIG. I.   Log conductance as a function of anticipated shock (shock at stimulus Number 8) (Hare, 1965d).

---

[5] The intensity of shock used for each individual was empirically determined as that level which he

was just able to tolerate (subjective report).

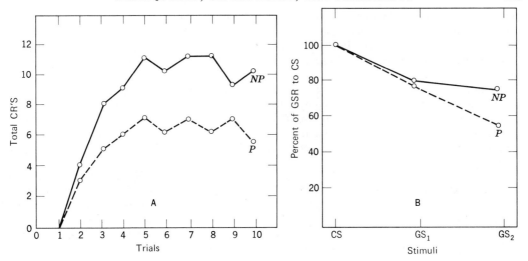

FIG. 2. Conditioning and generalization of a galvanic skin response by psycho-pathic subjects (*P*) and nonpsychopathic subjects (*NP*) (Hare, 1965c).

a key which gave a shock of similar intensity which was delayed for 10 seconds. The results are shown in Table 11.1 from which it is clear that the psychopathic subjects preferred de-layed to immediate shock. Furthermore, the tendency to prefer immediate over delayed shock increased over trials in the nonpsycho-pathic and student control groups, but not in the psychopathic group.

In all of these studies, a single measure of autonomic activity was utilized. In a more ambitious recent study, Hare (1968a) measured skin resistance, heart rate, digital vasoconstric-tion, and respiration rate of primary and secondary psychopathic, and of nonpsycho-pathic, prisoners in several conditions: the resting state; while blowing up a small balloon (to estimate maximal autonomic reactivity);

while listening to a series of 15 900 cps tones followed by a novel tone; and while solving a series of simple arithmetic problems. (Shock was not used in this study.) The study was methodologically much more sophisticated than the earlier ones, taking account, for example, of the possible effect on changes in autonomic activity of individual differences in the range of possible autonomic activity. In general, the results indicated lower levels of autonomic activity in the psychopathic group during the resting state but an absence of differences during the activity period. In another recent study, Hare (1968b) measured the detection threshold for electric shock to the forearm in psycho-pathic prisoners, using a psychophysical forced-choice procedure and a sophisticated technique for controlling the characteristics of the shock

TABLE 11.1. *Preference for Immediate Versus Delayed Shock in Psychopaths and Nonpsychopaths*

| | Group | | |
	Psychopathic Prisoners	Nonpsychopathic Prisoners	Student Controls
Mean trials on which immediate shock chosen	3.33	5.25	4.74
Percent immediate choices	55.50	87.50	78.90

Source: Hare, 1966.

administered. The results indicated a significantly higher threshold of detection for the psychopathic group. Although Hare is inclined to interpret this result in terms of a lowered level of conditioned fear, he points out that an alternative explanation would be possible in terms of a faster rate of growth of inhibition in a relatively monotonous situation in the psychopaths, a condition which would be expected in extraverted subjects in such a vigilance task.

The results obtained by Hare in his long series of studies are extremely interesting and provocative and will undoubtedly stimulate further research. As Hare himself has pointed out, however, several basic questions still remain unresolved.[6] Eysenck (1964), for example, has argued that psychopaths are *neurotic extraverts*. As such they should show high autonomic lability and a rapid growth of reactive inhibition. But Hare's studies do not support the notion of high autonomic lability, suggesting rather average or below-average reactivity. On the other hand, as Schachter and Latané (1964) point out, several studies have found higher autonomic lability in psychopaths, even though anxiety indices may be low (Lykken, 1957). Lykken, in fact, has suggested that there may be at least two types of psychopathy. Of course, as we have pointed out, autonomic reactivity may refer to responsivity in the resting state; responsivity to a conditioned stimulus preceding an aversive stimulus; responsivity to an unconditioned aversive or novel stimulus; or recovery time following response. It is tempting to argue that high neuroticism in psychopaths produces high autonomic reactivity to an unconditioned aversive stimulus (though Hare's results tend to argue against this), whereas the rapid growth of inhibition in a repetitive situation produces a smaller conditioned response to a conditioned aversive stimulus. Future research may throw further light on these problems.

What does appear to have been shown, however, is that psychopaths do not show any deficiency in an instrumental learning situation, as indeed one would expect. Thus, in the standard Taffel verbal conditioning situation, differences between psychopaths and non-psychopaths tend to be small or nonexistent (Bernard and Eisenman, 1967; Bryan and Kapche, 1967; Hetherington and Klinger, 1964;

Johns and Quay, 1962). Schachter and Latané (1964) found that psychopaths learned a mental maze task equally as well as nonpsychopaths, but both they and Hetherington and Klinger (1964) showed that punishment (shock or noncomplimentary remarks) had less effects in interfering with the ongoing skill in psychopaths. Persons and Bruning (1966) found that psychopaths improved faster and achieved a higher level of performance than nonpsychopaths in a simple drawing task.

In summary, only two clear conclusions appear to be justified: first, psychopaths do not appear to be defective in the acquisition of ordinary skills; second, psychopaths do appear to be less influenced by the threat of punishment, particularly when the punishment itself is to occur at some time (definite or indefinite) in the future. Both of these conclusions fit well with clinical impressions that the psychopath is often a very intelligent person who deceives his victims with great skill but who is defective in paying heed to (rather than being unable to assess) the delayed aversive consequences of his actions. As we have seen, suggestions have been made, both clinically and as a result of experimental results, that there are at least two subgroups of psychopathy (Lykken, 1957; Painting, 1961). In the case of the aggressive or explosive psychopath, of course, the possibility of brain injury must also be taken into account.

Turning now to *delinquency*, the model we have described would lead us to expect that factor analytic studies of the personality structure of unselected delinquents would lead to the discovery of several dimensions of delinquency since, as we have seen, delinquent behavior represents the end-result of the interaction of several factors. Of course, a clear-cut picture would be obtained only if the measures purporting to assess the different variables were relatively pure measures of the factors involved—and this is manifestly not the case. However, in spite of this difficulty, some very interesting and encouraging results have been obtained from factor analytic studies of the personality structures of delinquents.[7]

Hewitt and Jenkins (1946) rated 500 children referred to a child guidance clinic on 45 behavior traits and carried out a cluster analysis of the intercorrelations that identified three behavior syndromes: unsocialized aggressive, socialized delinquent, and overinhibited. While

---

[6] See Hare (1968a) for an excellent discussion of the complex issues involved.

[7] For a comprehensive review of this work, see Quay (1965b).

the children in this study were not representative of delinquents, a second study by Jenkins and Glickman (1947) identified the same three factors in an analysis of data obtained from 300 institutionalized male delinquents.

More recently, Quay and his colleagues have provided substantial evidence, based on factor analytic studies, suggesting the multidimensionality of delinquency. Quay (1964a) rated a group of 115 institutionalized adolescent delinquents on the frequency of occurrence of various behavior traits in case-history material. Factor analysis identified three factors which Quay labeled: unsocialized psychopathic, neurotic disturbed, and subcultural socialized. The rotated factor matrix is shown in Table 11.2. The results are very clear cut.

Several studies have tended to confirm the results obtained by Quay (1964a), using alternative sources of data. Thus, Peterson, Quay, and Cameron (1959) and Peterson, Quay, and Tiffany (1961) analyzed questionnaire responses of institutionalized delinquents and high school students. In the former study, factors of psychopathic delinquency, neurotic acting out, and history of family conflict were identified. In the latter the factors were labeled: psychopathic asocial, neurotic disturbed, and delinquent without personality maladjustment. Quay (1964b, 1966) factor-analyzed behavior ratings made on institutionalized male delinquents and identified three factors: psychopathy, neuroticism, and inadequacy-immaturity. Quay and Quay (1965) carried out a comparison of the factor structure of these behavior ratings in delinquent and nondelinquent groups, finding essentially the same factor structure in each and thus offering support for the position that there is a delinquent/nondelinquent (or socialization) continuum.

Other evidence supports the conclusion of Quay that there are at least three subgroups of delinquents. Thus, Quay and Blumen (1963) examined the court records of a large group of delinquents for the presence or absence of 13 delinquent acts. Factor analysis of the resulting correlations showed that four groups of acts could be identified: uncomplicated truancy, impulsivity and thrill-seeking delinquency, interpersonal aggression, and impersonal aggression. The suggestion is, of course, that the psychopathic delinquent will indulge in different kinds of offenses than the subcultural delinquent. Quay, Peterson, and Consalvi (1960) examined this problem and found that psychopathic delinquency was associated with: commitment for crimes against the person, recidivism, problem behavior while incarcerated, and longer institutionalization, but was unrelated to intelligence or anxiety. Neurotic delinquency, on the other hand, was related to anxiety, while the delinquent with a history of family conflict was found to be of lower intelligence. Randolph et al (1961) compared the "solitary" with the "social" delinquent and found the former to be higher on the MMPI Pd-Scale as well as being higher in general on the other subscales.

Thus, all of this work suggests that there may be three types of delinquents: the unsocialized psychopathic delinquent, the subcultural socialized delinquent, and the "acting-out" neurotic delinquent. Whether the latter should be considered a true delinquent is an open question. The distribution of these "types" would, of course, produce a great deal of overlap.

The establishment of a number of dimensions of delinquency makes interpretation of many studies of the characteristics of delinquents (not broken down into subgroups) difficult, and this

TABLE 11.2. *Factor Structure of Case-History Material in 115 Institutionalized Delinquents*

Factor 1—Subcultural Socialized		Factor 2—Unsocialized Psychopathic		Factor 3—Neurotic Disturbed	
Variable	Factor Loading	Variable	Factor Loading	Variable	Factor Loading
Bad companions	59	Assaultive	54	Shy	46
Seclusive	−38	Quarrelsome	43	Worries	67
Gang activities	58	Defies authority	47	Sensitive	70
Shy	−33	Irritable	61	Timid	59
Stays out late at night	48	Verbally aggressive	56	Anxious over own behavior	42
Accepted by delinquent subgroups	63	Feels persecuted	49	Praise or punishment ineffective	−31
Strong allegiance to selected peers	36	Praise or punishment ineffective	31		

Source: Quay, 1964a.

must be kept in mind in the following discussion of the personality and other characteristics of "delinquents."

The prediction of delinquency-proneness
from personality measures has been studied
extensively, notably in the famous study of
Glueck and Glueck (1950) who constructed
prediction tables based on traits that empirically
discriminated between known persistently delinquent and nondelinquent boys. However, the
validity of these signs would clearly be significantly reduced in attempts to predict future
delinquents from nondelinquents in children
who had not yet come to the attention of the
authorities. Four important studies by Dinitz
and his colleagues (Reckless, Dinitz, and Kay,
1957; Dinitz, Reckless, and Kay, 1958;
Scarpitti, Murray, Dinitz, and Reckless, 1960;
Dinitz, Scarpitti, and Reckless, 1962) have
thrown much light on this problem. First, they
showed that a group of sixth-grade boys judged
by their teachers to be potentially delinquent
scored significantly lower on the Socialization
Scale of the California Psychological Inventory
than did a similar group of boys judged to be
potentially law abiding. They also found that,
within the potentially delinquent group, a subgroup found to have already had police contact
were significantly lower on the Socialization
Scale than those who had not. A subsequent
follow-up study of the potentially delinquent
and nondelinquent boys indicated a very much
higher incidence of delinquent behavior in the
former group. Thus, degree of socialization
prior to the occurrence of delinquent behavior
does appear to be predictive of future delinquency, a finding well in line with our theoretical
model for at least one subgroup of delinquents.

Studies of personality structure as revealed by
MMPI patterns (Gough, Wenk, and Rozynko,
1965; Hathaway and Monachesi, 1957; Hathaway, Monachesi, and Young, 1960; Wirt and
Briggs, 1959) have shown a correlation between
scores on various scales of the test and delinquency proneness. Interpretation of the meaning
of the results of these studies is rendered uncertain because of the complex structure of the
scales, but they tend to indicate that delinquency
proneness is accompanied by high Pd scores and
possibly high neuroticism, again in line with
theoretical expectation.

Delinquents have been consistently discriminated from nondelinquents in terms of
two variables that appear to be related to extraversion; namely, time orientation and impulsivity. The belief that delinquents are more
present-oriented in time (that is, have little
future time perspective) has been verified by a
number of *experimental* studies of future time
orientation (Barndt and Johnson, 1955; Siegman, 1961; Davids, Kidder, and Reich, 1962;
Stein, Sarbin, and Kulik, 1968). The greater
impulsivity of delinquents has also been
demonstrated by means of objective tests, such
as the IES Arrow Dot test (Rankin and Wikoff,
1964) and other psychomotor tests (Kelly and
Veldman, 1964), while two large-scale factor-
analytic studies by Pierson and Kelly (1963a,
1963b) showed delinquents to be characterized
by low anxiety, high extraversion, and high
index of idiosyncrasy, as measured by questionnaire responses. The demonstration by Manne,
Kandel, and Rosenthal (1962) of a higher
performance than verbal IQ in delinquents fits
the same pattern of results, as do the numerous
studies of frequency of abnormal EEG patterns
in delinquents (Hodge, Walter, and Walter,
1953; Stafford-Clark, Pond, and Lovett-Doust,
1951).

Therefore, in spite of the heterogeneous
nature of the delinquent groups used in the
above studies, a fairly consistent pattern
appears to emerge of the delinquent as being
relatively unsocialized, extraverted, neurotic,
and impulsive. Future research will no doubt
take into account the necessity for separating
out subgroups of delinquents along the lines
indicated by the factor analytic studies but the
results appear to indicate that the group of
psychopathic, unsocialized delinquents may
form the largest subgroup, since their characteristics appear to show through all studies
most clearly.

Turning finally to the study of criminal
groups, it would be expected that the results of
personality studies would be most ambiguous in
unselected criminal groups, since such groups
would include some psychopaths (but not all
psychopaths are criminal, nor are all criminals
psychopaths), many individuals with normal
personalities, and so on. However, it would be
expected, perhaps, that recidivists would have
higher neuroticism and extraversion scores than
nonrecidivists. Table 11.3 shows the results of
some studies of the application of the MPI
scales to recidivists and nonrecidivists. While
the results are by no means unequivocal, they
suggest that recidivists are characterized by
higher neuroticism scores whereas the extraversion scale does not discriminate. Insignificant
correlations between recidivism and either
scale of the short form of the MPI were reported

TABLE 11.3. *MPI Scores of Recidivists and Nonrecidivists*

Group	N	Neuroticism		Extraversion		Source
		Mean	σ	Mean	σ	
Male recidivists	288	30.50	9.36	31.72	7.56	Bartholomew (1963)
Male recidivists	72	32.18	10.38	24.76	10.08	Bartholomew (1963)
Male recidivists	50	31.38	11.14	25.80	8.92	Bartholomew (1959)
Male recidivists	54	31.82	9.14	25.70	9.60	Bartholomew (1959)
Male recidivists	146	30.35	10.73	24.09	9.11	Eysenck (1959)
Male recidivists	61	25.30	7.40	28.06	12.62	Fitch (1962)
Male 1st offenders	50	24.86	11.82	21.42	10.20	Bartholomew (1959)
Male remand prisoners	114	29.73	11.15	24.95	9.35	Fitch (1962)
Male sentenced prisoners	165	26.74	11.69	24.43	7.67	Fitch (1962)
Male 1st offenders	55	26.08	8.03	24.12	9.80	Fitch (1962)
Female 1st offenders	159	28.64	11.22	28.04	8.52	Bartholomew (1963)
Normal Quota Sample	1800	19.89	11.02	24.91	9.71	Eysenck (1959)

by Little (1963) for 290 Borstal inmates. Marcus (1960) factor-analyzed 38 variables used to rate nearly 800 prisoners and identified two factors, one a social-class variable, the other an aggressive-outgoing pattern of life contrasted with a passive and seclusive pattern (the latter, of course, appears to be similar to the contrast noted earlier between the psychopathic and the nonpsychopathic delinquent). Clearly, studies of criminal populations will need to develop much more sophisticated techniques of analysis in future research.

The only clear conclusion to be drawn from this survey of personality structure and delinquency is that some promising leads have been developed in recent years relating to the multidimensionality of delinquent and criminal groups. At least, however, guidelines have been laid down for future research.

III. BEHAVIOR THERAPY FOR DELINQUENCY AND PSYCHOPATHY

It is generally considered that delinquents and psychopaths are resistant to psychotherapy, though recent disclaimers, based on careful empirical studies, have been entered (Persons, 1965, 1966; Persons and Pepinsky, 1966; Truax, Wargo, and Silber, 1966). Until very recently, however, behavior therapists had not even entered the lists, as may be seen rather strikingly from a symposium specifically held in 1965 to discuss the application of behavior therapy to the treatment of delinquency at which Jones (1965) and Gelder (1965) were reduced entirely to general theoretical observations, since they were unable, between them, to quote any instances of the attempted application of behavior therapy to either delinquency or psychopathy. Similarly, the earlier paper by Franks (1956) on recidivism, psychopathy, and delinquency could deal only with the general theoretical issues.

Within the last few years, however, the situation has gradually changed, and there are welcome signs of growing interest in the application of behavior therapy to delinquents and psychopaths. Nevertheless, only a tentative beginning has as yet been made. Before turning to these studies we may mention first an interesting study by Buehler, Patterson, and Furniss (1966) which demonstrates the influence of contingencies in developing and maintaining behaviors in delinquents and thus suggests very strongly the feasibility of applying operant conditioning techniques for remedial purposes. The basic hypothesis of Buehler was that the delinquent peer group provides reinforcement for deviant behaviors and aversive consequences for socially conforming behaviors. If this is so, then, of course, institutionalization of delinquents, unless very carefully handled, may actually strengthen delinquent behaviors, a consequence long suspected by observers of institutions (including, of course, prisons). Buehler developed observational techniques for studying the levels of communication (biochemical, motor movement, speech, and technology) among institutionalized girls in relation to deviant and socially conforming behavior and the type of reinforcement (positive or disinterest) received from the peer. The results indicated quite clearly that deviant behaviors were reinforced significantly more often than they were punished by peers and, furthermore, that the reinforcement was often at a nonverbal level. Socially conforming behaviors, on the other hand, were significantly more often punished than reinforced by peers. Buehler also demonstrated clearly that the institutional staff tended to reward and punish behaviors inconsistently and, indeed, tended to reinforce either deviant or conforming behavior indiscriminately in a girl they labeled "good"; while the behavior of girls labeled "bad" tended to be punished indiscriminately irrespective of whether it was deviant or conforming. Thus, on the one hand, it was difficult for some girls to receive reinforcement even if they conformed, while other girls tended to be praised even if their behavior was deviant.

Studies of the effect of operant conditioning procedures on the deviant and conforming behavior of individual delinquents are rare so far. Burchard and Tyler (1965), however, investigated a $13\frac{1}{2}$-year-old child with severe behavior problems who had been institutionalized and whose deviant behavior they considered was being maintained in part by the attention it attracted from the ward staff. The treatment involved isolation (time-out) on a nonemotional basis for behaviors labeled unacceptable, together with token rewards for acceptable behavior which was maintained over a defined period of time. The regimen was rigorously enforced over a period of five months and was accompanied by a significant decline in both the number and severity of the deviant behaviors.

An ingenious series of experiments by Walton (1963), while not directed toward the deviant psychopathic behavior itself, are important in suggesting modes of attack on the general problem of the distractibility and impulsiveness of the psychopath. Walton treated a severe reading defect in a psychopathic child of high intelligence by varying the conditions under which the remedial education was given. He was able to show that, by minimizing the rate of growth of reactive and conditioned inhibition while simultaneously increasing drive level by controlling the length of the teaching period, remarkable progress would be achieved in overcoming the reading difficulty. A similar technique could probably have been used to produce more general concentration and a decline in impulsivity. Wetzel (1966) succeeded in eliminating compulsive stealing in a ten-year-old boy over a period of three months by the use of operant conditioning techniques.

There have also been several recent studies of the application of operant conditioning techniques within the delinquent group situation. Burchard (1967) studied the effect of reinforcement for "social behavior" and punishment (time-out or seclusion accompanied by loss of token rewards) for "antisocial" behavior in 12 boys in a special intensive training unit. In one experiment, token reinforcement was provided for remaining seated in the workshop and completing specific tasks; and this was compared with the effects of punishment (time-out) for antisocial behavior. The results indicated that the behavior of delinquents could be controlled by manipulating behavior contingencies though really adequate control was not achieved in the punishment study.

The high degree of control that could be achieved in relation to antisocial behavior in delinquents was, however, clearly demonstrated in the study by Tyler and Brown (1967). They studied a group of 15 boys, aged 13–15, who were institutionalized for various offenses. The behavior selected for study was the occurrence of unacceptable responses (throwing balls, arguing, etc.) around a pool table in the recreation room. During the first phase (7 weeks) misbehavior was punished by time-out in isolation; during the second phase (13½ weeks) by verbal reprimand only; while, during the third phase (20 weeks), time-out in isolation was the punishment once more. The results, as shown in Figure 3, show quite clearly that time-out was effective in controlling the misbehavior, while verbal reprimand was not. The limitations of this important study are very well set out by the authors.

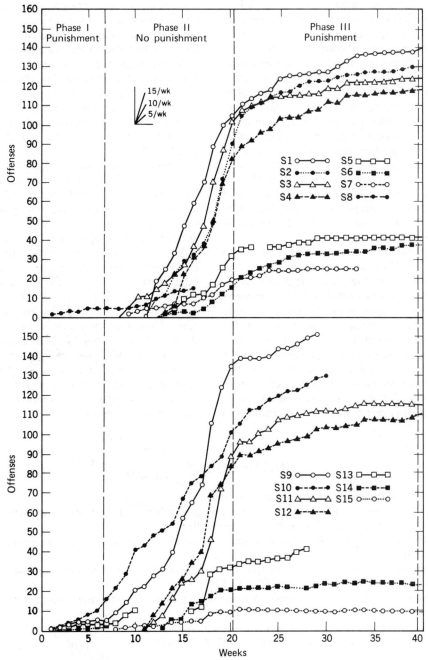

FIG. 3. Cumulative records of pool table offenses. Gaps in individual records indicate S was absent from cottage 7 or more days (Tyler and Brown, 1967).

A quite different and potentially powerful technique utilized by Clements and McKee (1968) made use of the Premack principle which states that if a high probability behavior is made contingent upon the occurrence of a lower probability behavior, the probability of evocation of the latter behavior will be increased. They negotiated "contracts" with prison inmates studying programmed educational materials in which increased output resulted in a choice between highly favored recreational activities. Subsequently, the subject was able, as it were, to negotiate a "contract" with himself, thus controlling his own behavior. Comparisons were made between work rate and accuracy under experimenter- and subject-controlled contractual arrangements with base rates without contingencies. A highly significant increase of work output was obtained under experimenter control, and this was maintained when the subject was allowed to contract with himself. This technique (which is really an elaborate form of operant conditioning) would appear to offer much promise in training prison inmates in more adequate social and useful behavior patterns.[8]

Finally, two studies by Schwitzgebel should be mentioned. In the first, Schwitzgebel and Kolb (1964) induced severe delinquents to come into the laboratory and record "free" interviews on tape. VI-VR schedules of reinforcement were used to reward socially conforming verbalizations, and the results of up to a year's treatment by this technique showed a significant decline in number of arrests and prison terms for this group compared with an untreated control group of delinquents. In the second study, Schwitzgebel (1967) used similar procedures to compare three groups of delinquents. The first group was given positive reinforcement for statements of concern about other people and for dependable and prompt arrival at the laboratory; the second group was given negative contingencies for hostile statements about people and positive reinforcement for socially acceptable nonverbal behaviors; while the third group served as a control, being seen twice only, once at the beginning and once at the end of the treatment of the experimental groups. An ingenious feature of this study was that the effects of treatment were assessed by having an independent judge rate the frequency of positive and negative statements by the delinquents before and after treatment in a natural, real-life setting, while the experimenter assessed nonverbal behavior. The results indicated that the group reinforced for on-time arrival did arrive significantly earlier as time went on compared with the other groups; that positive reinforcement for socially acceptable verbalizations increased their frequency; but that disapproval for hostile statements did not produce any significant change in their frequency. Social behavior in all groups showed little change.

Thus, while behavior therapists have thus far contributed little to the therapy of delinquents (and virtually nothing to the problem of psychopathy), what little has been done has been quite ingenious and thought-provoking. It seems likely that there will be many studies in the near future of the effects of controlling the environment of delinquents by manipulating contingencies for behavior as a member of the delinquent subculture. Changing the behavior of the psychopath will undoubtedly remain a major problem, however.

REFERENCES

Aichhorn, A. *Wayward youth*. New York: Viking, 1935.

Albert, R.S., Brigante, T.R., & Chase, M. The psychopathic personality: a content analysis of the concept. *J. gen. Psychol.*, 1959, **60**, 17–28.

Barndt, R.J. & Johnson, D.M. Time orientation in delinquents. *J. abnorm. soc. Psychol.*, 1955, **51**, 343–345.

Bartholomew, A.A. Extraversion-introversion and neuroticism in first offenders and recidivists. *Brit. J. Delinq.*, 1959, **10**, 120–129.

Bartholomew, A. Some comparative Australian data for the Maudsley Personality Inventory. *Aust. J. Psychol.*, 1963, **15**, 46–51.

Bernard, J.L. & Eisenman, R. Verbal conditioning in sociopaths with social and monetary reinforcement. *J. person. soc. Psychol.*, 1967, **6**, 203–206.

---

[8] For another example of the use of the Premack principle, see Chapter 17.

Bryan, J.H. & Kapche, R. Psychopathy and verbal conditioning. *J. abnorm. Psychol.*, 1967, **72**, 71–73.

Buehler, R.E., Patterson, G.R., & Furniss, J.M. The reinforcement of behavior in institutional settings. *Behav. Res. Ther.*, 1966, **4**, 157–167.

Burchard, J.D. Systematic socialization: a programmed environment for the habilitation of antisocial retardates. *Psychol. Rec.*, 1967, **17**, 461–476.

Burchard, J. & Tyler, V. The modification of delinquent behavior through operant conditioning. *Behav. Res. Ther.*, 1965, **2**, 245–250.

Cleckley, H. *The mask of sanity* (2nd ed.). St. Louis: C.V. Mosby, 1950.

Clements, C.B. & McKee, J.M. Programmed instruction for institutionalized offenders: contingency management and performance contracts. *Psychol. Rep.*, 1968, **22**, 957–964.

Cloward, R. & Ohlin, L. *Delinquency and opportunity*. Glencoe: Free Press, 1960.

Cohen, A.K. *Delinquent boys*. London: Routledge & Kegan Paul, 1956.

Craddick, R.A. Selection of psychopathic from nonpsychopathic prisoners within a Canadian prison. *Psychol. Rep.*, 1962, **10**, 495–499.

Craft, M. *Psychopathic disorders and their assessment*. London: Pergamon, 1966.

Davids, A., Kidder, C., & Reich, M. Time orientation in male and female juvenile delinquents. *J. abnorm. soc. Psychol.*, 1962, **64**, 239–240.

Dinitz, S., Reckless, W.C., & Kay, B. A self-gradient among potential delinquents. *J. crim. Law Criminol. police Sci.*, 1958, **49**, 230–233.

Dinitz, S., Scarpitti, F.R., & Reckless, W.C. Delinquency vulnerability: a cross group and longitudinal analysis. *Amer. Sociol. Rev.*, 1962, **27**, 515–517.

Eysenck, H.J. *The dynamics of anxiety and hysteria*. London: Routledge & Kegan Paul, 1957.

Eysenck, H.J. The differentiation between normal and various neurotic groups on the Maudsley Personality Inventory. *Brit. J. Psychol.*, 1959, **50**, 176–177.

Eysenck, H.J. The development of moral values in children: the contribution of learning theory. *Brit. J. educ. Psychol.*, 1960, **30**, 11–21.

Eysenck, H.J. *Crime and personality*. London: Routledge & Kegan Paul, 1964.

Fitch, J.H. Two personality variables and their distribution in a criminal population: an empirical study. *Brit. J. soc. clin. Psychol.*, 1962, **1**, 161–167.

Franks, C.M. Recidivism, psychopathy and delinquency. *Brit. J. Delinq.*, 1956, **6**, 192–201.

Gelder, M. Behavior and aversion therapy in the treatment of delinquency. II. Can behavior therapy contribute to the treatment of delinquency? *Brit. J. Criminol.*, 1965, **5**, 365–376.

Glueck, S. & Glueck, G. *Unraveling juvenile delinquency*. New York: Commonwealth Fund, 1950.

Gough, H.G., Wenk, E.A., & Rozynko, V.V. Parole outcome as predicted from the CPI, the MMPI, and a base expectancy table. *J. abnorm. Psychol.*, 1965, **70**, 432–441.

Gurvitz, M. Developments in the concept of psychopathic personality. *Brit. J. Delinq.*, 1951, **2**, 88–102.

Hare, R.D. A conflict and learning theory analysis of psychopathic behavior. *J. Res. in Crime and Delinq.*, 1965, **2**, 12–19 (a).

Hare, R.D. Psychopathy, fear arousal and anticipated pain. *Psychol. Rep.*, 1965, **16**, 499–502 (b).

Hare, R.D. Acquisition and generalization of a conditioned fear response in psychopathic and nonpsychopathic criminals. *J. Psychol.*, 1965, **59**, 367–370 (c).

Hare, R.D. Temporal gradient of fear arousal in psychopaths. *J. abnorm. Psychol.*, 1965, **70**, 442–445 (d).

Hare, R.D. Psychopathy and choice of immediate versus delayed punishment. *J. abnorm. Psychol.*, 1966, **71**, 25–29.

Hare, R.D. Psychopathy, autonomic functioning, and the orienting response. *J. abnorm. Psychol. Monogr. Suppl.*, 1968, **73** (No. 3, Part 2, pp. 1–24) (a).

Hare, R.D. Detection threshold for electric shock in psychopaths. *J. abnorm. Psychol.*, 1968, **73**, 268–272 (b).

Hare, R.D. & Hare, A.S. Psychopathic behavior: a bibliography. *Excerpta Criminologica*, 1967, **7**, 365–386.

Hathaway, S.R. & Monachesi, E.D. The personalities of delinquent boys. *J. crim. Law Criminol. police Sci.*, 1957, **48**, 149–163.

Hathaway, S.R., Monachesi, E.D., & Young, L.A. Delinquency rates and personality. *J. crim. Law Criminol. police Sci.*, 1960, **50**, 433–440.

Healy, W. & Bronner, A.L. *Delinquents and criminals: their making and unmaking*. New York: Macmillan, 1926.

Hetherington, E.M. & Klinger, E. Psychopathy and punishment. *J. abnorm. soc. Psychol.*, 1964, **69**, 113–115.

Hewitt, L.E. & Jenkins, R.L. *Fundamental patterns of maladjustment: the dynamics of their origin*. Springfield: State of Illinois, 1946.

Hodge, R.S., Walter, V.J., & Walter, W.G. Juvenile delinquency: an electrophysiological, psychological and social study. *Brit. J. Delinq.*, 1953, **3**, 155–172.

Jenkins, R.L. & Glickman, S. Patterns of personality organization among delinquents. *Nerv. Child*, 1947, **6**, 329–339.

Johns, J.H. & Quay, H.C. The effect of social reward on verbal conditioning in psychopathic and neurotic military offenders. *J. consult. Psychol.*, 1962, **26**, 217–220.

Jones, H.G. Behavior and aversion therapy in the treatment of delinquency: I. The techniques of behavior therapy and delinquent behavior. *Brit. J. Criminol.*, 1965, **5**, 355–365.

Kelly, F.J. & Veldman, D.J. Delinquency and school drop-out behavior as a function of impulsivity and nondominant values. *J. abnorm. soc. Psychol.*, 1964, **69**, 190–194.

Lange, J. *Crime as destiny*. London: Allen and Unwin, 1931.

Lindner, R.M. *Rebel without a cause*. New York: Grune and Stratton, 1944.

Little, A. Professor Eysenck's theory of crime: an empirical test on adolescent offenders. *Brit. J. Criminol.*, 1963, **4**, 152–163.

Lunden, W.A. *Statistics on delinquents and delinquency*. Springfield: C.C. Thomas, 1964.

Lykken, D.T. A study of anxiety in the sociopathic personality. *J. abnorm. soc. Psychol.*, 1957, **55**, 6–10.

Manne, S.H., Kandel, A., & Rosenthal, D. Differences between performance IQ and verbal IQ in a severely sociopathic population. *J. clin. Psychol.*, 1962, **18**, 73–77.

Marcus, B. A dimensional study of a prison population. *Brit. J. Criminol.*, 1960, **1**, 130–153.

Mowrer, O.H. *Learning theory and personality dynamics*. New York; Ronald, 1950.

Painting, D.H. The performance of psychopathic individuals under conditions of positive and negative partial reinforcement. *J. abnorm. soc. Psychol.*, 1961, **62**, 352–355.

Persons, R.W. Psychotherapy with sociopathic offenders: an empirical evaluation. *J. clin. Psychol.*, 1965, **21**, 204–207.

Persons, R.W. Psychological and behavioral change in delinquents following psychotherapy. *J. clin. Psychol.*, 1966, **22**, 337–340.

Persons, R.W. & Bruning, J.L. Instrumental learning with sociopaths: a test of clinical theory. *J. abnorm. Psychol.*, 1966, **71**, 165–168.

Persons, R.W. & Pepinsky, H.B. Convergence in psychotherapy with delinquent boys. *J. counsel. Psychol.*, 1966, **13**, 329–334.

Peterson, D.R., Quay, H.C., & Cameron, G.R. Personality and background factors in juvenile delinquency as inferred from questionnaire responses. *J. consult. Psychol.*, 1959, **23**, 395–399.

Peterson, D.R., Quay, H.C., & Tiffany, T.L. Personality factors related to juvenile delinquency. *Child Developm.*, 1961, **32**, 355–372.

Pierson, G.R. & Kelly, R.F. HSPQ norms on a state-wide delinquent population. *J. Psychol.*, 1963, **56**, 185–192 (a).

Pierson, G.R. & Kelly, R.F. Anxiety, extraversion, and personality idiosyncrasy in delinquency. *J. Psychol.*, 1963, **56**, 441–445 (b).

Quay, H.C. Dimensions of personality in delinquent boys as inferred from the factor analysis of case history data. *Child Developm.*, 1964, **35**, 479–484 (a).

Quay, H.C. Personality dimensions in delinquent males as inferred from the factor analysis of behavior ratings. *J. Res. Crime Delinq.*, 1964, **1**, 33–37 (b).

Quay, H.C. (ed.). *Juvenile delinquency: research and theory*. New York: Van Nostrand, 1965 (a).

Quay, H.C. Personality and delinquency. In Quay, H.C. (ed.). *Juvenile delinquency: research and theory*. New York: Van Nostrand, 1965, pp. 139–169 (b).

Quay, H.C. Personality dimensions in preadolescent delinquent boys. *Educ. Psychol. Measmt.*, 1966, **26**, 99–110.

Quay, H.C. & Blumen, L. Dimensions of delinquent behavior. *J. soc. Psychol.*, 1963, **61**, 273–277.

Quay, H.C., Peterson, D.R., & Consalvi, C. The interpretation of three personality factors in juvenile delinquency. *J. consult. Psychol.*, 1960, **24**, 555.

Quay, H.C. & Quay, L.C. Behavior problems in early adolescence. *Child Develop.*, 1965, **36**, 215–220.

Randolph, M.H., Richardson, H., & Johnson, R.C. A comparison of social and solitary male delinquents. *J. consult. Psychol.*, 1961, **25**, 293–295.

Rankin, R.J. & Wikoff, R.L. The IES Arrow Dot performance of delinquents and non-delinquents. *Percept. Motor Skills*, 1964, **18**, 207–210.

Reckless, W.C., Dinitz, S., & Kay, B. The self component in potential delinquency and potential nondelinquency. *Amer. sociol. Rev.*, 1957, **22**, 566–570.

Scarpitti, F.R., Murray, E., Dinitz, S., & Reckless, W.C. The "good" boy in a high delinquency area: four years later. *Amer. sociol. Rev.*, 1960, **25**, 555–558.

Schachter, S. & Latané, B. Crime, cognition, and the autonomic nervous system. In Levine, D. (ed.). *Nebraska symposium on motivation*. Lincoln: U. Nebraska Press, 1964, pp. 221–275.

Schwitzgebel, R.L. Short-term operant conditioning of adolescent offenders on socially relevant variables. *J. abnorm. Psychol.*, 1967, **72**, 134–142.

Schwitzgebel, R. & Kolb, D.A. Inducing behavior change in adolescent delinquents. *Behav. Res. Ther.*, 1964, **1**, 297–304.

Sellin, T. & Wolfgang, M.E. *The measurement of delinquency*. New York: Wiley, 1964.

Siegman, A.W. The relationship between future time perspective, time estimation, and impulse control in a group of young offenders and in a control group. *J. consult. Psychol.*, 1961, **25**, 470–475.

Stafford-Clark, D., Pond, D., & Lovett-Doust, J.W. The psychopath in prison: a preliminary report of a co-operative research. *Brit. J. Delinq.*, 1951, **2**, 117–129.

Stein, K.B., Sarbin, T.R., & Kulik, J.A. Future time perspective: its relation to the socialization process and the delinquent role. *J. consult. clin. Psychol.*, 1968, **32**, 257–264.

Sykes, G. & Matza, D. Techniques of neutralization. *Amer. sociol. Rev.*, 1957, **22**, 664–670.

Trasler, G. *The explanation of criminality*. London: Routledge & Kegan Paul, 1962.

Truax, C.B., Wargo, D.G., & Silber, L.D. Effects of group psychotherapy with high accurate empathy and nonpossessive warmth upon female institutionalized delinquents. *J. abnorm. Psychol.*, 1966, **71**, 267–274.

Tyler, V.O. & Brown, G.D. The use of swift, brief isolation as a group control device for institutionalized delinquents. *Behav. Res. Ther.*, 1967, **5**, 1–9.

Walton, D. The interaction effects of drive (D), reactive (I_R) and conditioned inhibition ($_sI_R$)—their application to the remedial treatment of an adolescent psychopath. *Behav. Res. Ther.*, 1963, **1**, 35–43.

Warburton, F.W. Observations on a sample of psychopathic American criminals. *Behav. Res. Ther.*, 1965, **3**, 129–135.

Wetzel, R. Use of behavioral techniques in a case of compulsive stealing. *J. consult. Psychol.*, 1966, **30**, 367–374.

Wirt, R.D. & Briggs, P.F. Personality and environmental factors in the development of delinquency. *Psychol. Monogr.*, 1959, **73** (Whole No. 485).

Chapter 12

Sexual Disorders

IT IS HARD to believe that most of the work carried out by behavior therapists in relation to disorders of sexual behavior has been accomplished since 1960.[1] In some ways, progress in this area has been greater than in almost any other, a great deal of attention having been paid to methodological problems, particularly to the development of objective methods of assessment. In this chapter, we shall concern ourselves with five main areas of interest: the assessment of sexual preferences; the genesis and maintenance of sexual disorders; treatment techniques; the assessment of changes following treatment; and behavior therapy as it has been applied to specific sexual disorders.

I. THE ASSESSMENT OF SEXUAL PREFERENCES

1. Introduction

It is not proposed here to review the wide range of approaches to the assessment of sexual preference or orientation. Information in relation to this has been sought in many ways, ranging from evidence derived from police records, through the individual's own report (or that of his family or friends), to the use of comprehensive questionnaires or interviews, such as those used by Kinsey. All of these approaches have yielded valuable information, but the emphasis here will be on certain techniques that have been constructed and used within the framework of the behavior therapy of sexual disorders.

2. Physiological Methods

The recent work of Masters and Johnson (1966), dealing with physiological changes that occur during various kinds of sexual activity, seems likely to lead eventually to substantial advances in the measurement of physiological concomitants of sexual behavior. However, within the field of behavior therapy, perhaps the most substantial work relating to the identification of sexual preferences is that carried out by Freund (1963b, 1965, 1967a, 1967b), using penile volumetry. The apparatus has been described by Freund et al (1965). Briefly, the technique consists of measuring changes in penis volume while the subject is observing colored slides of male or female nudes. Three age ranges are covered in the latest version of the test (Freund, 1965), roughly five to 12 years, thirteen to 16 years, and adult ages up to 40 years. The full details of the elaborate technique used by Freund need not concern us, but it may be noted that each slide is exposed for seven seconds, with genital volume being measured at the beginning and end of the exposure, and again seven seconds later.

The test is intended for diagnostic use as an objective indicator of sexual preferences, particularly where the subject may deny a particular preference. It has proved extremely promising in differentiating homosexual from heterosexual preference (Freund, 1963b). In a later study, Freund (1965) found that it discriminated with little overlap between normal

---

[1] Earlier reviews of the literature may be found in Rachman (1961) and Feldman (1966). The latter review is particularly useful for its critical attitude in relation to methodology.

heterosexuals and heterosexual pedophiles who had been convicted of sexual offenses against at least two girls under 13 years of age. In a recent validity study, Freund (1967a) used the test on normal heterosexuals; heterosexual and homosexual pedophiles; ephebopheliacs (homosexuals preferring adolescents); and androphiliacs (homosexuals preferring adults). In this study an attempt was also made to identify "pretenders," for example, pedophiliacs who claim to be heterosexual toward adults. The effects of deliberate attempted simulation have also been measured (Freund, 1963b).

The results obtained by Freund have been very encouraging but, clearly, independent replication is highly desirable. McConaghy (1967) carried out such a replication, using a modified version of Freund's technique. His method of measuring genital volume changes was simpler than that of Freund, and he used movie films instead of slides. All of the 11 male heterosexual subjects tested showed clear-cut preference for the films involving female activities as shown by penis volume changes, while 17 out of the 22 male homosexual subjects showed a definite preference for the films involving male activities.[2] Four of the homosexuals showed heterosexual preference and would have been misclassified on the basis of their response to the pictures alone; while one homosexual showed equality of preference. This study, therefore, offers quite strong support for the validity of the technique.

Bancroft et al (1966) criticized Freund's technique as cumbersome and likely to produce sexual arousal in itself. They developed a mercury strain-gauge which fitted around the shaft of the penis. It can be worn under the subject's clothing and is hardly noticed by the subject after initial adjustment. Its use is described in the case of a pedophiliac, but so far its validity has not been established by comparison with Freund's technique.

Solyom and Miller (1965) have reported the use of finger plethysmography with heterosexual and homosexual males, using pictures of nude male and female subjects as stimuli. They found that the homosexual subjects showed short latency, high amplitude, and long recovery times to nude male pictures as compared with female pictures; the normal control group, on the other hand, showed a similar pattern of preference for nude female over male pictures. Figure 1 shows the basic differences.

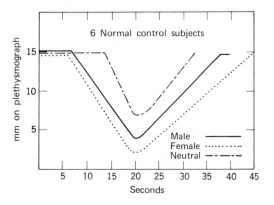

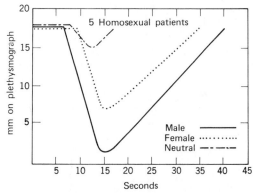

FIG. 1. Finger plethysmographic recordings of normal and homosexual male subjects to slides of nude males and females and to neutral pictures (Solyom and Miller, 1965).

An alternative technique, which has not actually so far been used by behavior therapists, has been reported by Hess et al (1965). They measured changes in pupil dilation while viewing slides of males and females (photographs and paintings) and showed that homosexual males showed greater response to the male than to the female figures, the reverse being the case for the heterosexual males. However, Scott et al (1967) were unable to replicate these differences in a study of normal males and females and of male homosexual and heterosexual prisoners. The utility of the technique therefore remains in doubt.

There seems every reason to suppose that these relatively simple physiological techniques can be used as objective indices of heterosexual as against homosexual preference and may also be used to verify abnormal inclinations toward children, possibly in advance of involvement with the law. A great deal more work, however, is required to examine the possibilities of faking.

---

[2] Although the films involved nude males or females engaged in various activities, they were not sexually provocative in order that the use to which they could be put would be as wide as possible.

Brown (1964), in particular, has pointed out that responses of this kind can be brought under some degree of voluntary control.

3. OPERANT CONDITIONING TECHNIQUES

Brown's (1964) concern with the possibility of voluntary control of plethysmographic responses led him to devise a new test, involving the use of pictures with primarily heterosexual, homosexual, or neutral content, but in which the subject was required to expose the picture by pulling a string which activated the shutter as often as possible in each one-minute trial. Using this technique, he demonstrated an apparent homosexual preference in a motor-cycle fetishist. His study was criticized on methodological grounds by Koenig (1965), but Brown (1965) effectively replied to these criticisms. It seems unlikely, however, that Brown's doubts need impede further research on the physiological techniques outlined above.

Other techniques which essentially involve the use of operant conditioning methods include those of MacCulloch et al (1965), who measured response latency to a conditioned stimulus; and Marks et al (1965) who used a simple but ingenious technique for identifying the strength of a fetish by means of a movement response under neutral and fantasy conditions. These methods will be described in more detail later.

4. THE SEMANTIC DIFFERENTIAL TECHNIQUE

Feldman et al (1966) have described the construction and validation of the sexual orientation test, which is constructed along similar lines to Osgood's semantic differential technique. Two concepts ("men are sexually to me . . ." and "women are sexually to me . . .") are used to which six adjectives with sexual implications (interesting, attractive, handsome (male) or beautiful (female), hot, pleasurable, exciting) are applied on a five-point rating scale. Standard patterns are constructed by comparing each scale position with each of the others (ten pairs in all). Although Feldman et al (1966) have used the test to measure the effects of treatment with known homosexuals, they have presented standardization data that show that the test

could be valuable for diagnostic purposes.[3] Thus, they found that the internal consistency of the responses of a group of known homosexuals was very high. The test-retest reliability was satisfactorily high on both homosexual and heterosexual measures. Both measures discriminated successfully between groups of unselected females, heterosexual males, and homosexual patients.[4] The scales also have the advantage of being unidimensional. This test is important because, as we shall see, changes accompanying treatment have been shown to be accompanied by predictable changes in attitudes toward sexual concepts related to the particular disorder being treated (Marks and Sartorius, 1968).

5. THE MEASUREMENT OF HETEROSEXUAL SOPHISTICATION

For purposes of initial assessment and assessment of change following treatment, adequate scales of normal heterosexual sophistication are clearly desirable. Bentler (1968a, 1968b) constructed sexual behavior scales for males and females which form a Guttman ordinal scale.[5] The scales consist of 21 items relating to sexual behavior. Remarkably consistent results for samples of males and females were obtained by Bentler who showed that the scales have exceptionally high internal consistency. The 21-item scale correlated 0.98 with a shorter 10-item scale. Validity was indicated by the fact that more sexually-experienced groups of males and females obtained higher scores. These scales should prove extremely useful both for basic research and for clinical work.

II. THE GENESIS AND MAINTENANCE OF SEXUAL DEVIATIONS

No attempt will be made to review the psychodynamic and psychoanalytic theories of sexual deviations, since this would present too large a task. However, psychodynamic theories about specific deviations will be presented below wherever appropriate.

---

[3] Vanasek et al (1968) have used this technique to examine the self-image of pedophiles.

[4] Phillips (1968) criticised the scoring technique of Feldman et al and has presented a revised scoring technique to overcome the objections which he raises.

[5] A Guttman ordinal scale is one in which a positive response to any item on the scale means that all items lower in the scale would be positively checked also.

1. THE ROLE OF LEARNING

It must be admitted at once that behavior therapists have shown little interest in formulating theories about the genesis and maintenance of sexual deviations. Hence, little time will be spent on this topic. Lukianowicz (1959) has emphasized the possible importance of such factors as parental rejection of a child who is of the "wrong" sex from their point of view, this state of affairs leading to confusion regarding sexual identification, to a precocious preoccupation with problems of masculinity and femininity, and to a rejection of the visible signs of sexual identity. He also stresses the effects of the deliberate creation by the parents of an opposite-sex role in the child by, for example, dressing him in the clothes of the opposite sex.[6] Favored status as a "little girl" is a general extension of cross-dressing and may lead to excessive contact with females by the male, while the opposite trend may occur in the case of the female child. Stevenson and Wolpe (1960) have implicated in addition the role of anxiety resulting from fear-inducing experiences with females in cases of homosexuality; for example, the rejection or punishment of sexual advances to females. The possible role of non-sexual factors such as the desire for companionship is also discussed by Wolpe and Stevenson and, of course, specific experiences (such as homosexual seduction in adolescence) cannot be neglected as factors leading to deviant behavior. The question of a constitutional predisposition, genetically determined, has been a matter of lively controversy, but hard evidence is still lacking.

2. SEXUAL DEVIATIONS AS CONDITIONED BEHAVIOR

The only serious attempt thus far to put forward a general behavioristic theory of the genesis of sexual deviations is that by McGuire et al (1965). The most interesting and crucial point made by these authors is the stress laid on the role of masturbation in producing deviant behavior, rather than sexual seduction experiences as such. They argue that ejaculation resulting from masturbation provides the critical reinforcing event for conditioning stimuli accompanying or preceding masturbation. Thus, sexual preference (for males as opposed

to females or for fetish objects or transvestism, etc.) may be arbitrarily determined by the particular early experiences to which the child is subjected in relation to masturbation, a phenomenon that is probably near-universal in young children. The general role that masturbation may thus play in the genesis of sexual deviations does not appear to have been recognized by psychodynamic psychologists. As McGuire et al (1965) point out, the theory has certain implications. For example, it makes no assumptions about innate sexual interests; it allows for the acquisition of any sexual deviation, according to particular circumstances.

Little evidence is available in support or refutation of this theory. Incidental clinical reports, however, suggest that it may well repay investigation. The history of the growth of sexual deviations in individual subjects is usually obscure, but Clark (1963a), for example, reported that a fetishist accidentally discovered the sexual pleasure associated with the handling of female garments at a stage when the patient's sex drive had not fixed completely on a full heterosexual object.

A direct attempt to test the hypothesis has recently been reported by Evans (1968). He predicted that, if the theory were correct, exhibitionists reporting normal (heterosexual) fantasying while masturbating would decondition more rapidly than exhibitionists whose masturbatory fantasies were related to their exhibitionistic behavior. He was able to form two groups of exhibitionists with an equally reported frequency of exhibitionistic behavior over the previous six months and who differed according to their characteristic masturbation fantasy. The treatment involved severe shock after a variable delay interval while viewing slides with phrases related to their exhibitionistic behavior. This procedure was carried out once a week for ten weeks, then once a fortnight for two months, then once a month during a two-year follow-up. Those subjects with normal masturbatory fantasy reported no further acting out or urges to do so after a median treatment period of four weeks (range: 3–5 weeks), whereas the subjects with exhibitionistic masturbatory fantasies achieved this status only after a median treatment period of 24 weeks (range: 4–24 weeks).[7]

---

[6] Lukianowicz is reviewing the literature on transvestism, but his remarks on learning factors are more generally applicable.

[7] The range of 4–24 weeks must represent an error, since the median is the midpoint of the range.

Rachman (1966) reported an interesting experiment which suggested that conditioning could play a significant role in the genesis of sexual deviations. Using three unmarried psychologists as subjects, he presented colored slides of a pair of black, knee-length woman's boots as the CS. The US consisted of colored slides of nude women, while the UR and CR were penis-volume changes. A CR was defined as five successive reactions above a given magnitude to the CS. An attempt was made to determine whether stimulus generalization would occur to slides of brown, short boots, high-heeled black shoes, and so on. Following extinction trials, a test for spontaneous recovery was given one week after the extinction trials terminated.

All three subjects achieved the conditioning criterion (in 30, 65, and 24 trials); and demonstrated extinction (in 19, 39, and 13 trials), spontaneous recovery, reextinction (in 14, 32, and 10 trials), and generalization. The whole procedure was successfully replicated (Rachman and Hodgson, 1968) with five naive subjects and with the addition of a control condition for possible pseudoconditioning. Further experiments along these lines, provided they do not violate ethical considerations, would clearly be extremely valuable.

It may be noted here that Rachman's studies were concerned with a possible model for the genesis of fetishism. More specific theories have also been advanced from time to time in relation to other specific sexual deviations, for example, masochism. These will be considered later.

III. BEHAVIORISTIC METHODS OF TREATMENT

The methods used by behavior therapists in the treatment of sexual deviations are of considerable interest and complexity. It will, therefore, be convenient to describe them in general rather than in the context of each particular disorder. They fall (with some overlap) into seven categories: classical aversive conditioning with drugs; classical aversive conditioning with shock; instrumental escape and avoidance conditioning with shock; aversion-relief therapy; positive training; systematic desensitization; and aversive imagery.

1. CLASSICAL AVERSIVE CONDITIONING WITH DRUGS

Early studies made considerable use of nausea-inducing drugs, by analogy with studies of aversive conditioning in alcoholism. The general technique (which was unpleasant and even traumatic in the extreme to the patient) has been described by Barker (1965).[8]

"The patient was treated in bed in a darkened room. A projector was mounted behind the head of his bed and a 48-inch screen erected at the foot. His physical condition was repeatedly checked and liberal fluids and daily injections of parentrovite were administered. . . . Aversion therapy was continued 2-hourly for 6 days and 6 nights, the principal agent being apomorphine. As soon as the injection took effect—the patient usually reporting a headache followed by nausea—a slide was projected on to the screen and the tape recording switched on.[9] Both were continued until he either vomited or became intensely nauseated . . . he received a total of 66 emetic trials, one every 2 hours, which consisted of: 53 intramuscular injections of apomorphine, one intramuscular injection of emetine hydrochloride, 5 oral doses of emetine hydrochloride in a glass of warm water, one dose of two dessertspoonfuls of mustard in a tumbler of warm water, 3 doses of two tablespoonfuls of salt in a tumbler of warm water, and 3 intramuscular injections of sterile water . . . the dose of apomorphine ranged between gr. 1/40 and gr. 1/8. Copious emesis lasting for 95 minutes followed the first injection of gr. 1/10 . . . vomiting invariably occurred in the earlier trials, but owing to drug tolerance it was either absent or replaced by headaches, nausea and giddiness in the later ones. . . . The stimulus was terminated as soon as the patient vomited or reported relief . . . the patient's physical condition remained excellent during the greater part of the treatment" (Barker, 1965, pp. 269–270).

In conditioning terminology, the US was the effect produced by the drug, the CS the color slides and tape recording, and the CR and UR the vomiting and nausea originally induced by the drug. The paradigm was supposedly classical aversive conditioning, since the US could not be escaped from or avoided by the

---

[8] The patient was a transvestite.
[9] The slides were colored transparencies of the

patient in female clothing; the recording was made by the patient and described his dressing up.

patient, being under the control of the experimenter (and not, of course, under the control of the patient once the drug had been injected or ingested). Variations on the technique relate to the US, where drugs such as pilocarpine and ephedrine (Cooper, 1963) have been used, and to the CS, where the patient has been required to *fantasy* actively to the slides (James, 1962); or to wear female clothing in the case of transvestism (Clark, 1963a, 1963b); or to perform the fetish (Cooper, 1963). Dexamphetamine has been used to facilitate conditioning (Barker, 1965). The need for booster treatments following initial success and the importance of partial reinforcement techniques have been stressed.

The problems (leaving aside ethical issues) involved in this form of treatment are obvious enough, and have been pointed out clearly by Barker (1965). The method is time consuming; the patient must be hospitalized and in optimal physical condition; a close vigil must be kept on the patient by a team of workers; the drugs used are variable in their action and tolerance to them rapidly develops; the treatment is exceptionally unpleasant for the patient (and, it may be added, for the therapist); and, in terms of the conditioning model used, the important timing relationships between US and CS are difficult, if not impossible, to achieve and maintain. Thus, systematic variation and control of the parameters involved are impossible. In the light of all these disadvantages, it is not surprising that alternative aversive techniques were sought.

2. CLASSICAL AVERSIVE CONDITIONING WITH SHOCK

With the exception of Raymond and O'Keefe (1965) who have continued to use the drug-aversion technique, the difficulties described above have led to the abandonment of this method and efforts have been concentrated on the use of aversive shock conditioning. Again, the technique has been described by Barker (1965).

"The electric grid was made from a 4 feet by 3 feet rubber mat with a corrugated upper aspect. Tinned copper wire, one-tenth of an inch thick, was stapled lengthwise in the grooves of this mat at approximately half-inch intervals . . . a manually operated G.P.O.

type generator . . . produced a current of approximately 100 volts a.c. when resistance of 10,000 ohms and upwards were introduced on to the grid surface. Two rapid turns of the generator handle were sufficient to give a sharp and unpleasant electric shock to the feet and ankles of persons standing on the grid. . . . Treatment sessions were administered every half hour, each session consisting of 5 trials with one minute's rest between each trial. A total of 400 trials was given over 6 days (average 65 to 75 per day). . . . The patient[10] utilized his own clothing, which was not interfered with in any way, except that slits were cut into the feet of his nylon hose to enable a metal conductor to be inserted into the soles of his black court shoes. He commenced dressing up at the beginning of each trial and continued until he received a signal to undress irrespective of the number of garments he was wearing at the time. This signal was either a shock from the electric grid or the sound of the buzzer which was introduced at random into half the 400 trials. The shock or buzzer recurred at regular intervals until he had completely undressed" (Barker, 1965, p. 272).

In conditioning terminology, the US was shock to the soles of the feet, the CS dressing up and undressing, the UR aversion to the shock, and the CR aversion to wearing the clothes (or to the sight of them, etc). Once again, it should be noted that the patient had no control over the shock and could not escape or avoid it.[11] The advantages of the shock aversion over the drug aversion treatment have been stated by Barker (1965) as follows: it is much simpler to operate; it can be administered by one person; it does not require hospitalization of the patient; it is far less unpleasant; it is safe and poses no health danger; the patient can dress and undress as part of the treatment; and the important timing relationships can be controlled to a much greater degree. Possible disadvantages are monotony and tolerance to shock, as well as anxiety occasioned by the use of shock. Only the latter appears to pose any possible significant problem (Thorpe and Schmidt, 1964).

It has since been shown that a simpler method of providing the shock stimulus (to the arm or leg rather than the soles of the feet) is equally effective (McGuire and Vallance, 1964); while there is now good evidence that the dressing

---

[10] The patient was again a transvestite.

[11] This statement is subject to qualification (see below).

and undressing procedure is unnecessary, since the shock may be associated with fantasy of the sexual deviation by the patient with equally good results (Barker, 1964; Mees, 1966).

3. Instrumental Escape and Avoidance Conditioning with Shock as the Aversive Stimulus

It will have been noted that, in the classical aversive (shock) conditioning situation described above (as well, possibly, in the classical aversive—drug—conditioning situation), the aversive stimulus is continued until the patient completes undressing (in the case of transvestism). The technique, therefore, in principle, could involve instrumental escape conditioning in that completion of the undressing results in cessation of the shock. The use of an instrumental avoidance paradigm for aversive conditioning with shock has been described by Feldman and MacCulloch (1965). After a very careful consideration of the literature relating to variables which are relevant to instrumental avoidance conditioning, they specified the following as critical if extinction of the aversive response was to be avoided: the interstimulus interval should be spaced and not massed; the US intensity need not exceed a certain level (since its effect was linear above a certain level); CS offset should coincide with onset of the avoidance response; the introduction of shock should be stepwise, not gradual; the CS should be clearly identifiable; partial reinforcement should be used; variable delay of reinforcement was desirable; the training situation should be variable to facilitate generalization outside the experimental situation; and the quantity of reinforcement (i.e., the level of shock) should be variable.

In their study, they initially used psychophysical procedures to identify for the individual patient attractive homosexual pictures, and established a level of shock regarded as unpleasant for the individual patient. The procedure involved two stages. Homosexual pictures were presented tachistoscopically, sometimes being followed by shock, sometimes not (partial reinforcement). The patient could *escape* the shock by turning off the picture; or he could *avoid* the shock altogether if he turned off the picture quickly enough (delay of reinforcement was also used). Because of the partial reinforcement technique used, the avoidance of shock was not completely under the control of the patient. In the second stage (simultaneously carried out with the first), as the shock ceased, a positive stimulus was presented (a slide of a female figure). Thus, cessation of shock was associated with relief from shock, and the relief from shock in turn was associated with heterosexual stimuli. The method therefore shades into the aversion-relief and positive conditioning techniques to be considered next.

4. The Aversion-Relief Technique

This method was introduced by Thorpe, Schmidt, Brown, and Castell (1964) as a relatively simple, standard technique which could be readily adapted for use with each individual patient, whatever the precise nature of his sexual deviation. The method involves the presentation of a series of words associated with the sexual deviation, accompanied by strong shock, and followed by cessation of shock accompanied by presentation of an "incompatible" word associated with the desired change (thus, a series of "homosexual" words with shock would be followed, immediately on cessation of shock by a "heterosexual" word). Both aversion and relief are involved, and the method shades into the positive conditioning techniques described below.

The method devised by Solyom and Miller (1965) in which the patient terminates a strong shock voluntarily and is immediately presented with a female slide is a variant of the aversive-relief technique; as is the procedure used by Clark (1965) where the patient is required to perceive and discriminate two types of stimuli (heterosexual and homosexual verbal and visual material) presented simultaneously before terminating (or not terminating) the shock.

5. Positive Training

In addition to (or in place of) attempting to render homosexual or other perverse stimuli aversive, it is possible to concentrate on strengthening the patient's response to normal heterosexual stimuli.[12] In the studies to be mentioned here, the positive conditioning was carried out at a different time from the aversive conditioning, rather than the two being directly linked together. Thus, Thorpe, Schmidt, and

---

[12] Ramsay and Van Velzen (1968) have suggested that the homosexual, for example, has a strong aversion for heterosexual relationships, rather than being merely neutrally inclined toward them.

Castell (1964) used aversion (shock) treatment with a homosexual patient. But they also (in different sessions) required the patient to masturbate while viewing the picture of a semi-nude female under varying conditions of illumination. James (1962) also used aversive (drug) treatment with a homosexual patient, but in addition, after the aversive treatment was completed, awakened the patient every two hours and played a tape-recording describing the value of heterosexual behavior, while "pin-ups" were also placed in his room. Srnec and Freund (1953) and Freund (1960) administered testosterone to their homosexual patients to increase heterosexual libido and then presented sexually-arousing films of nude or semi-nude women. In none of these studies, however, was the relative value of these alternative procedures assessed.

6. Systematic Desensitization

This method has been used in two main ways in the treatment of sexual disorders. First, it has been utilized to *directly* attack the presenting difficulty. Thus, Bond and Hutchison (1960) used SD(I) to reduce anxiety relating to situations which led to exposure in a patient who exhibited himself to females. Similarly, Brady (1966) used SD(I) (with brevital as a relaxing agent) to reduce anxiety relating to sexual intercourse in female patients suffering from dyspareunia. Haslam (1965), on the other hand, used a special form of SD(R) to reduce the discomfort associated with sexual intercourse in two female patients with dyspareunia.

Systematic desensitization has also been used to treat sexual disorders *indirectly*. Kraft (1967a), for example, treated a homosexual patient by desensitizing anxiety relating to normal sexual activity; Kraft (1967b) used SD(I) to reduce anxiety associated with heterosexual behavior in a patient presenting a number of "perversions" of a mild kind; Kraft and Al Issa (1967) a similar technique in a case of frigidity. Lazarus (1965) treated impotence by assertive training in *social* relations; while Stevenson and Wolpe (1960) treated two patients (a homosexual and a patient who committed offenses against children) by a similar method of assertive and social training.

7. The Aversive Imagery Technique

Two studies have utilized an aversive imagery technique with some novel features. Gold and Neufeld (1965) required a homosexual patient to visualize homosexual scenes and to place them in a setting involving danger. The patient then "rejected" the situation and was rewarded with verbal praise. He was also required to choose between situations involving an attractive (to him) man and a girl and required to choose the girl in preference to the man. Ideational cues were given indicating the "dangers" involved in choosing the man.

Kolvin (1967) treated a fetishist by requiring him to imagine vividly a story relating to his fetishism. When the imagined story reached its climax, an aversive image was introduced.

It may be concluded that a good deal of ingenuity and originality has been shown by behavior therapists in relation to the techniques used in the treatment of sexual disorders. Many methodological problems exist, of course, but a great deal has been learned in the course of the past ten years, and it may be confidently anticipated that new techniques and important advances in the present techniques will occur over the next ten years.

IV. ASSESSMENT OF CHANGES FOLLOWING TREATMENT

Attempts to assess changes in sexual orientation or behavior following treatment fall into two categories: those which assess changes in real-life behavior situations and those which make objective assessments, of a physiological or behavioral kind.

1. Real-Life Behavior

It must be admitted that many of the early (and some of the more recent) studies are seriously defective in their assessment of the results of the various methods of treatment described above. It is, of course, not easy to obtain reliable reports concerning the sexual behavior of discharged patients and, hence, in many reports a simple reliance on the patient's statement has been all that could be reported. Thus Barker et al (1961) and Blakemore et al (1963a) simply report absence of transvestism in treated patients, as do Bond and Evans (1967) in a case of fetishism. More detailed descriptive statements are made by Feldman and MacCulloch (1965) in their series of homosexuals, but the reliability of the patients' reports is essentially unknown. The criterion of "sexual adjustment" used by Lazarus (1963) in his series of frigid patients depended on answers given to three questions (Do you look forward to sexual intercourse? Do you nearly always reach an orgasm? Do you ever initiate sexual activity?). Brady (1966) used three criteria for deciding whether his frigid patients were "greatly improved" (thus terminating treatment), namely, that the patient enters freely into sexual relations; that no anxiety or pain is experienced during sexual intercourse; and that intercourse is reported to be pleasurable, with at least some orgasms.

Clearly, it is important that independent verification of the change in sexual orientation should be obtained wherever possible. Brady (1966) checked his patients' reports against reports from the husbands, as did Haslam (1965) in relation to satisfaction of both husband and wife in sexual relations. Raymond and O'Keefe (1965) checked with the wife of a homosexual in relation to his capacity for heterosexual relations. James (1962) claimed that his homosexual patient was completely heterosexual following treatment and noted that the change in sexual behavior was accompanied by a release of artistic activity which had previously been inhibited. Kraft (1967) noted that his homosexual patient had failed in attempts to win back his wife (who appeared to be highly neurotic and possibly frigid) but had subse-

quently formed sexually satisfactory heterosexual relations with other women. Kraft and Al Issa (1967) reported that a frigid patient had subsequently become pregnant (though, of course, frigid women are perfectly capable of conceiving children).

Subjective reports of the patient and his relatives and acquaintances would clearly be enhanced in value if more objective indices of change were available.[13] Fortunately, some very promising developments in this direction have occurred recently.

2. OBJECTIVE INDICES OF CHANGE IN SEXUAL BEHAVIOR

Three main objective indices have been devised to assess changes in sexual behavior and orientation following treatment: physiological measures; behavioral measures; and changes in objectively assessed attitudes.

(a) PHYSIOLOGICAL INDICES. Marks and Gelder (1967) plotted the changes in amplitude and latency of erections to stimuli associated with the perversions (fetishism and transvestism) in five patients treated with classical aversive (shock) conditioning. The results for one patient are shown in Figure 2. The erections

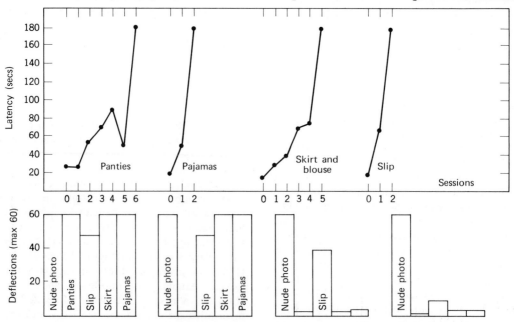

Erections after one minute exposure to stimulus

FIG. 2.   Changes in erection latency and amplitude in a transvestite at various stages of treatment (Marks and Gelder, 1967).

---

[13] Compare the problem of assessing change in phobic behavior by behavioral, verbal report, and   physiological indices, discussed in an earlier chapter.

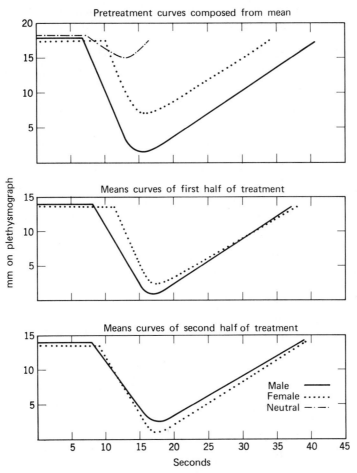

FIG. 3.   Changes in amplitude of plethysmographic response in five
homosexual patients (Solyom and Miller, 1965).

during performance and fantasying of the deviant behaviors ceased selectively as the treatment progressed. Similar results were found by Solyom and Miller (1965), using finger plethysmography involving measures of latency, amplitude, and recovery time. The results with respect to amplitude for five homosexual patients are shown in Figure 3. It will be noted that the treatment did not affect response amplitude to nude male pictures, but did produce significant change in response amplitude (in a "favorable" direction) to nude female pictures. MacCulloch et al (1965) measured changes in response latency to the CS (attractive male pictures) and changes in pulse rate in homosexuals during the course of treatment.

(b) BEHAVIORAL INDICES. Marks et al (1965) reported an ingenious simple procedure for measuring behavioral changes. They required their patient (a fetishist) to move a lever back and forth while (a) no fantasying of the fetish

was carried out; (b) the fetish was imagined and held; (c) the fetish was imagined and held and shock was received. They found that the rate of moving the lever increased above the neutral condition when the fetish was imagined or held but fell below the neutral condition when shock was introduced (the shock terminating whenever the rate fell below the neutral condition). The test was repeated after treatment with meaningful results in relation to changes which had occurred in behavior.

(c) ATTITUDE INDICES. Marks and Gelder (1967) measured changes in the rating of various concepts by making use of the semantic differential technique in which the patient made evaluative judgments of concepts before and after treatment. Some of these concepts related to the patient's deviant behavior directly and the change was expected to be in an unfavorable direction (e.g., rubber boots, high-heeled shoes, being kicked with boots—in the case of a fetishist with masochistic tendencies); others were of possible psychodynamic significance (women, my mother, my father, myself); others related to objects toward which a favorable change was expected (psychiatrists, sexual intercourse). The expected changes occurred.

Even more importantly, Marks and Gelder (1967) correlated the changes in clinical state with the changes in physiological responsiveness to specific stimuli and the changes in attitudes and were able to demonstrate important relationships between them. Thus, changes in reported fantasy correlated with erection changes; while attitude changes tended to precede the physiological changes.

These recently developed techniques hold great promise for the future assessment of the effects of treatment on sexual deviations and will undoubtedly be more widely applied in the future.

V. BEHAVIOR THERAPY OF SPECIFIC SEXUAL DISORDERS

A wide range of sexual disorders has been treated by behavior therapists.

1. FETISHISM[14]

Fetishism may be defined as "the tendency to be sexually attracted by some special part or peculiarity of the body or by some inanimate object" (Raymond, 1956, p. 854). In its perverse form (since undoubtedly mildly fetishistic behavior occurs in many normal males), it is relatively rare. It is one of the few specific sexual disorders to which Freud (1928), in his later years, devoted a complete paper. It is almost never observed in females and is not usually associated with homosexuality. According to Epstein (1960), the fetishist tends to be reserved and obsessional, to have sexual fears relating to body mutilation, to show strong maternal attachment, to manifest an early interest in sex, and to be sadistic. The object of the fetish can be almost anything, the connection apparently being fortuitous, the result of accidental association with ejaculation.[15] An occasional association with epilepsy has been noted (Davies and Morgenstein, 1960). Psychodynamic theories of fetishism are legion, Freud

(1928) regarding the fetish object as a substitute for the mother's penis which, as a child, the fetishist believed his mother to possess. The disorder is refractory to treatment, and Raymond (1956) could trace only three apparent therapeutic successes in the literature.

(a) CLASSICAL AVERSIVE CONDITIONING WITH DRUGS. Raymond (1956) treated a male patient with a long history of perambulator and handbag fetishes which were expressed by attacks on perambulators involving burning, scratching, or running into them. The case was a serious one because of the danger of injury to young babies and, therefore, perhaps justified the rigorous treatment. Apomorphine was used to induce neausea to pictures of handbags and perambulators, and the treatment was administered on a two-hourly basis, day and night, for a week, being repeated after an eight-day break until the patient was reduced to uncontrollable sobbing when fetish objects were offered to him. A booster treatment was given six months later. Nineteen months after discharge, the patient reported he was doing well, his wife confirmed this, and he had not been in trouble with the police. Ten years later, Raymond and O'Keefe (1965) reported the results of similar treatment given to a fetishist who masturbated to pin-up pictures. On a two-year follow-up, the fetish was not in evidence and the wife reported satisfactory sexual relations.

Similar positive findings were reported by Cooper (1963) in a case where the fetish consisted of masturbation while wearing women's clothing (this case could be regarded primarily as one of transvestism, though Cooper preferred to treat it as one of fetishism). A similar severe treatment regime was instituted with equal success on follow-up after 9 months. The only failure reported with this method of treatment related to a patient studied by Clark (1963a, 1963b). Initial success with a three-month follow-up was followed by complete relapse. Clark relates the failure to possible difficulties involved with this method of treatment in controlling CS-US timing, failure to carry out booster treatment, and failure to use partial reinforcement techniques. Clark's study was also criticized by Barker (1963) on the grounds that the patient was a transvestist and not a fetishist.

While the drug-aversion treatment appears

---

[14] The literature on fetishism was reviewed by Raymond (1956), and more thoroughly, by Epstein (1960). An excellent account of the development of psychoanalytic theory has been given by Gillespie (1964).

[15] Rachman's experiments which demonstrate the possibility of fetish behavior being a CR have been discussed earlier.

to work, then, the objections listed earlier to it as a technique have led to its virtual abandonment in favor of shock aversion treatment.

(b) CLASSICAL AVERSIVE CONDITIONING WITH SHOCK. McGuire and Vallance (1964) successfully used aversive shock conditioning with a patient who masturbated to a fantasy of being dressed in certain clothes (not women's) and of being bound. Barker (1964) pointed out the implication, since confirmed, that the association of shock with fantasy rather than overt behavior, had important treatment implications for both fetishism and transvestism. Shock-aversion treatment was also used by Kushner (1965) with a fetishist who masturbated while wearing female undergarments or watching pictures of scantily clad females. An interesting failure was reported by Thorpe and Schmidt (1964), the patient refusing to continue the treatment after the fourth session. Thorpe and Schmidt discovered later that this patient had a cancer phobia and was afraid the shocks would produce the disease.

Much the most important studies using shock, however, are the recent ones by Marks et al (1965) and Marks and Gelder (1967). The first study was particularly interesting in that the patient not only had a long-standing history of fetishism (shoes and boots) but was also a masochist who required his wife to stand on him and kick him as a prelude to sexual intercourse. The problem, of course, was that the use of shock might be inadvisable, since it might be pleasurable to a masochist. However, the treatment was proceeded with, shock being given to a fantasy of the fetish, and to the fantasy while the patient was also holding the fetish. Independent measures of change used were the operant conditioning procedure and the semantic differential ratings described earlier. The primary dependent variable was the latency of the fetish image, as indicated by a pencil tap. It was found that before treatment, imagining the fetish increased the lever pressing rate above the control rate, whereas shock reduced the rate below the control rate, thus producing shock avoidance. Treatment *suppressed* (but did not extinguish) the fetish image as measured by its latency and resulted in the rate of lever pressing being the same in neutral and imagining conditions. There was a significant change in the semantic differential ratings (in the direction of devaluation) of the concepts: rubber boots, high-heeled shoes, and being kicked with boots. The concepts of women, father, mother, and self were unchanged; whereas the concepts of sexual intercourse and psychiatrists moved in a favorable direction. The patient was able, following treatment, to have sexual intercourse with his wife without the need for fantasying the fetish and without the necessity to make masochistic demands. It should be noted that the masochism was not directly treated and that the attitude toward the fetish objects changed to neutral, not unfavorable, on the semantic differential.

In their later study, Marks and Gelder (1967) reported similar results in relation to two fetishists, where the treatment involved shock for both fantasying and performing the rituals associated with the fetish objects. In addition to the independent measures used in the earlier study, penile volume and latency changes were measured. Erections present during fantasy and performance of the fetish before treatment ceased *selectively* as each fetish was treated separately; and the images developed longer latencies and became indistinct. Masturbation fantasies diminished; normal sexual activity increased: no new sexual deviations appeared (that is, there was no evidence of symptom substitution); social relations improved; the attitude of the wives to the patients improved; and related deviations sometimes changed. Various emotional reactions (anger toward the therapist, irritability, tenseness, depression, and embarrassment at performing the fetish) were noted, but not considered in any way to contraindicate the treatment used.

As was pointed out earlier, the significance of these two studies lies primarily in the very careful correlation of the various indices of change (clinical, physiological, behavioral, and phenomenal) during the course of treatment. The subtlety of the changes and their relationship appeared to preclude artifacts or simulation.

In summary, then, the classical aversive conditioning technique with shock appears to provide real hope of being a rational method of treatment for fetishism.

(c) AVERSION-RELIEF THERAPY. Thorpe, Schmidt, Brown, and Castell (1964) introduced this technique, in which verbal stimuli relating to the sexual disorder are presented visually and accompanied by shock as the patient reads them aloud. The final word in each list, however, is a "sexually desirable" word (e.g., a heterosexual word if the patient is a homosexual). The "relief" (arising from shock-cessation) which immediately precedes the "good" word is supposed to give the "good" word secondary-reinforcing properties.

(d) OTHER TECHNIQUES. Bond and Evans (1967) applied a modified instrumental avoidance discrimination technique to two patients who stole female underwear. One of the patients masturbated while holding the underwear, while the other obtained sexual gratification from tearing the underwear up, without actually masturbating. In both cases, the treatment was apparently completely successful, with no further stealing incidents having occurred at the time of follow-up, several months later. Kolvin (1967) treated a fetishist with the habit of placing his hand under female clothing by means of his aversive imagery technique. The fetishistic behavior was still absent at an 11-month follow-up.

It may be concluded that the procedures described above have proved remarkably successful in dealing with a sexual disorder which has proved in the past to be exceptionally refractory to treatment. Furthermore, the most recent developments (Marks and Gelder, 1967) provide solid empirical grounds from which further advances in technique may be confidently expected in the near future.

2. TRANSVESTISM

Several of the cases treated as fetishists above could well have been regarded as transvestists and, indeed, differentiation between the two is often difficult and perhaps unnecessary with respect to treatment.

Lukianowicz (1959), in a comprehensive review of the literature, has pointed out that the term "transvestism" has been used to cover a number of different disorders.

"We use the term 'transvestism' for a sexual deviation characterized by: (a) a desire to wear the dress of the opposite sex, and (b) (less often) a wish to be looked upon, and to be socially accepted, as a member of this sex. The name 'trans-sexualism' is applied to those rare cases of transvestism, where, apart from both just mentioned tendencies, there exists: (c) a persistent morbid urge to undergo a 'conversion-operation', i.e., to have an anatomical 'change' of the inborn sex" (Lukianowicz, 1959, p. 37).

As in the case of fetishism, many theories have been propounded in attempts to account

for transvestite activity. The theory of genetically determined intersexuality has not so far received support from chromosomal analysis. Psychoanalytic theory postulates that fear of castration is denied through the creation of a phallic woman, based on a disturbed mother-child relationship, while adverse learning experiences producing a child with an opposite-sex role compulsion is often put forward as an explanation. No empirical evidence in support of either of these theories is available. The phenomenon of cross-dressing may vary from being confined to the home to risking prosecution by appearing in the streets. An interesting difference between fetishism and transvestism is found in the fact that, whereas fetishism is virtually confined to the male, cross-dressing is common in women (more so than in men) but is not regarded as abnormal unless accompanied by other behavioral and physical indications of abnormality. The degree of association between transvestism and homosexuality is uncertain. Fetishistic, narcissistic, exhibitionistic, and masochistic traits may be found accompanying transvestism.[16] The incidence of transvestism is, of course, unknown, since much of it is probably carried out only in private. Physical and surgical methods of treatment are of little use and there is no evidence for the efficacy of psychotherapy. In general, therefore, transvestism would appear to be as refractory a sexual disorder as fetishism.

(a) CLASSICAL AVERSIVE CONDITIONING WITH DRUGS. Barker et al (1961) reported a case in which the patient, a 22-year-old male who had cross-dressed for 14 years, wore female clothing three or four times per week.[17] This patient was subjected to the same severe regimen as the fetishist cases dealt with earlier. Dexamphetamine was given to facilitate aversive conditioning. At a three-month follow-up, the patient was apparently no longer cross-dressing, but the authors are understandably cautious in their evaluation of the result. In this case, the patient viewed slides of himself in female dress, but Glynn and Harper (1961) applied the same treatment to a long-standing transvestite who was required to be dressed in female clothing while undergoing the aversion treatment. The patient was apparently not indulging in transvestism at a seven-month follow-up.[18]

---

[16] Morgenstern et al (1965) reported their small sample to be characterized by high neuroticism, femininity, intelligence, anxiety, and suggestibility.

[17] A more detailed account of the same case will be found in Lavin et al (1961).

[18] The case treated without success by Davies and Morgenstern (1960) is not reported in sufficient detail for evaluation.

A brief report on apomorphine aversion treatment applied to 13 transvestists was given by Morgenstern et al (1965). Treatment was given three times a day for a total of 39 sessions and the patients were followed up at weekly, monthly, and then longer intervals for periods ranging from eight months to four years. Seven of the patients were assessed as "apparently cured" in that they were no longer cross-dressing, while the remaining six had had occasional relapses but were all rated as "much improved." Morgenstern et al (1965) particularly stressed the improved social relations which followed the cessation or reduction of the cross-dressing.

(b) CLASSICAL AVERSIVE CONDITIONING WITH SHOCK. As in the case of fetishism, aversive drug treatment was soon abandoned in favor of aversive shock treatment. Blakemore et al (1963a) reported the effects of such treatment on a male patient with a 29-year history of transvestism which started at the age of four. The patient dressed and undressed in female clothing while standing on a grill through which the shocks were given. A total of 400 trials was given over six days. The treatment appeared to have been successful on a six-month follow-up, with the exception of a single relapse while his wife was pregnant and sexual intercourse with her was impossible (Blakemore et al (1963b). Marks and Gelder (1967), using the more refined techniques described in the section dealing with fetishism, obtained similar results with three transvestists.

(c) AVERSION-RELIEF THERAPY. Thorpe, Schmidt, Brown, and Castell (1964) reported on the use of their technique in a transvestite patient while Clark (1965) used a modification of the aversion-relief method with a similar patient.

As in the case of fetishism, it would appear that classical aversion techniques using shock are quite promising, particularly in their more recent refined form, but much remains to be accomplished.

3. EXHIBITIONISM[19]

Little work has thus far been reported by behavior therapists in relation to this sexual deviation. However, Bond and Hutchison (1960) reported on a male, aged 25, who exposed himself before females. The case was a severe one, since the young man had already suffered nine prison sentences for offenses of this nature. A hierarchy of situations relating to anxiety experienced by the patient just before exposure took place was drawn up and the SD(I) technique used. After a total of 30 sessions, considerable improvement had been effected. The patient was now able to attend parties and walk through supermarkets without experiencing the anxiety preceding exposure. Two "relapses" took place, but these involved different behavior patterns from those previously experienced. No further relapses occurred during the following two months. Considering the severity of the case, as manifested by the frequency of exposure before treatment (often several times per day) and the time spent in prison, the improvement could probably reasonably be attributed to the effects of the treatment. A similar case was treated successfully by Wolpe (1958) by training in assertive behavior and desensitization of anxiety aroused by social situations. As we have seen earlier in this chapter, Evans (1968) successfully treated ten exhibitionists with instrumental escape conditioning, using shock as the aversive stimulus.

Kushner and Sandler (1966) treated a 32-year-old male exhibitionist of 26 years' duration with the aversive imagery technique (shock to the imagined urge to expose himself in an imagined situation). On 12-month follow-up, no repetition of the behavior had occurred.

4. HOMOSEXUALITY[20]

Marmor (1965b) has pointed out the importance of distinguishing between situationally-determined homosexual behavior in persons whose normal behavior is heterosexual and constitutionally-determined homosexual behavior in persons whose sexual orientation is homosexual as well as their actual behavior in (to them) normal situations. He defines the clinical homosexual as "one who is motivated, in adult life, by a definite preferential erotic attraction to members of the same sex and who usually (but not necessarily) engages in overt sexual relations with them" (Marmor, 1965b, p. 4). The problem of whether homosexuality of the second kind does involve a constitutional factor remains, in fact, an open one, since, despite the claims of Kallmann (1952), genetic factors remain obscure. (Pare, 1965.) Theories of the etiology of homosexuality, of course,

[19] The literature on exhibitionism, scopophilia, and voyeurism has been reviewed by Rosen (1964).

[20] For a recent well-balanced treatment of the problem of homosexuality, see Marmor (1965a).

range all the way from those embracing a completely acquired viewpoint to those stressing genetic and constitutional factors exclusively. Marmor (1965b) has pointed out that any theory accounting for the genesis of homosexuality in terms of early positive conditioning to objects of the same sex would, in view of the extreme hostility expressed by society to such behaviors, also have to develop learned inhibition of the normal heterosexual approach. This latter point is not necessarily valid, however, if the response to an object of the same sex is constitutionally determined, since there may simply be no attraction toward objects of the opposite sex and hence inhibition may not be necessary.

The studies which follow have mainly dealt with clear-cut, long-standing, confirmed homosexuals where the diagnosis is not in doubt.

(a) CLASSICAL AVERSIVE CONDITIONING COMBINED WITH POSITIVE TRAINING. Srnec and Freund (1953) describe early results obtained by using a combination of positive and aversive conditioning. The drug aversion technique was used with the addition of sexually arousing heterosexual films following the injection of testosterone to increase heterosexual libido. Ten out of 25 exclusively homosexual men became predominantly heterosexual; three ceased homosexual activity but did not become heterosexual; while 12 remained homosexually oriented. In a later paper, Freund (1960) reviewed the results of similar combined treatment in a series of 67 male homsexuals with a three-to-five-year follow-up. The results presented a more pessimistic picture than the one suggested by the earlier report. Only 12 of the patients showed a relatively long-term shift to heterosexual behavior and, even in these cases, the homosexual behavior tendency was still considered to be strong. Freund concluded that the "successful" patients had learned to perform heterosexual behavior without, however, receiving the normal gratification from the opposite sex and that the basic drive remained homosexual in orientation.[21]

In a single case study, James (1962), using similar techniques, claimed dramatic success with a male who had practised homosexuality for over 30 years and who was completely nonheterosexual. Following treatment, heterosexual behavior was indulged in for the first time with enjoyment.

A somewhat different approach was taken by Thorpe, Schmidt, and Castell (1964) who required their patient to masturbate while viewing pictures of semi-nude females. Aversion shock treatment was also used. Following treatment, the patient was able to resort to heterosexual fantasy while masturbating, but his behavior was still homosexual.

(b) INSTRUMENTAL AVOIDANCE AND ESCAPE TRAINING. The most careful studies so far carried out by behavior therapists in relation to homosexuality are those of Feldman and his colleagues (Feldman and MacCulloch, 1964, 1965; MacCulloch et al, 1965). Using the instrumental avoidance technique described earlier, they treated 16 homosexual patients. Thirty trials per treatment session were given for an average of 15 sessions. The results were analyzed very carefully in terms of several (fairly subjective) criteria over follow-up periods ranging from two to 14 months. It was very tentatively considered that ten of the patients could be regarded as "success" and six as "failures." The results were especially promising in the case of the younger patients. Further, not only did the "successes" become heterosexual in their behavior, but they showed no tendency to drift back to homosexual behavior as time from treatment termination increased. In part, this may have been a result of the use of follow-up and booster sessions. Objective data (such as response latencies to the CS during the course of treatment) showed meaningful changes (indicating learning) in those patients who were regarded as "successes" but not in those who were regarded as "failures." Feldman et al (1966) were able to show a significant decline in post-treatment measures of homosexual interest in the Sexual Orientation Test in homosexual males who have improved clinically. These changes did not take place if no clinical improvement occurred. Similarly, increases in heterosexual interest occurred in clinically improved male homosexuals. The changes were maintained on six- and 12-month follow-up.

(c) IDEATIONAL AVERSIVE TECHNIQUE. This method, which was described earlier, was used by Gold and Neufeld (1965) on a young homosexual. Ten formal treatment sessions were given, and the patient was followed up by seven interviews over 12 months. At that time, his behavior was reported to be entirely heterosexual.

(d) SYSTEMATIC DESENSITIZATION. Stevenson and Wolpe (1960) treated two male homo-

---

[21] Unfortunately, Freund's (1963a) book on homosexuality has not so far been translated into English.

sexuals indirectly by the use of assertive training in social situations. In each case follow-up over several years suggested significant improvement. A recent study by Kraft (1967a) presents an interesting example of the indirect treatment of an active homosexual who had, however, married but had been unable to achieve satisfactory relations with his wife and had separated from her. Kraft used SD(I) with brevital to reduce anxiety relating to sexual intercourse. Following treatment, the patient succeeded in forming satisfactory sexual relations with women, though not with his former wife who refused to return to him (she apparently had severe problems of her own).

In summary, the situation regarding behavior therapy for homosexuality is much less satisfactory than it is for fetishism or transvestism. This is not surprising in view of the complexity of this disorder. Only the future will tell whether behavior therapists will ultimately match in this area the progress made in other areas of sexual disturbance.

5. Pedophilia
(Sexual Offenses Against Children)

Pedophilia is such a serious offense that it is surprising that behavior therapists have not turned their attention to it, particularly since it is not as uncommon as some of the other sexual deviations to which a great deal of attention has been paid. Only one case appears to have been treated by behavior therapy, that of a male who manipulated the genitals of little girls. The treatment carried out by Stevenson and Wolpe (1960) was indirect, in that it was directed at the abnormal degree of servility toward, and dependence on, the father that was shown by the patient. Social and assertive responses were taught, and six and one half years after termination of treatment, the deviant sexual behavior had reportedly not returned. The details given of the treatment techniques are, however, sparse, and the patient's report as to improvement appears to have been accepted at its face-value.

6. Impotence and Premature Ejaculation

These problems may be considered together, since they may be reasonably regarded as falling along a continuum of sexual incompetence in normal sexual relationships.[22]

Treatment has been largely by the use of systematic desensitization techniques aimed at reducing the anxiety associated by the approach to sexual intercourse (Cooper, 1963; Kushner, 1965; Wolpe, 1958), though indirect treatment has also been attempted, usually by training the patient to be more asssertive in social relationships generally, and with females in particular (Lazarus, 1965; Wolpe, 1958). More direct training, by the use of SD(I), in sexual technique has also been used (Wolpe, 1958).

A more systematic study of two patients complaining of premature ejaculation during sexual intercourse has been reported by Kraft and Al-Issa (1968). A stimulus hierarchy of seven items relating to increasing degrees of sexual intimacy was constructed and SD(I) carried out with the use of brevital to assist in producing relaxation during training. Both patients were successful in achieving prolongation of sexual intercourse before ejaculation occurred (both patients were also given general instruction in sexual technique as they were apparently very inexperienced).

7. Frigidity and Dyspareunia

Brady (1966) has distinguished two types of frigidity in women. In the first type, sexual intercourse is indulged in but no pleasure is derived from it and orgasm is not achieved. In the second type, sexual approach by the male (even though sexual intercourse may not take place) evokes disgust and intercourse itself is regarded and experienced as painful.[23] The latter condition is usually referred to as dyspareunia, the disability being caused by a spasm of the perineal muscles and contraction of the adductors of the thighs, thus rendering intercourse impossible or painful. No organic disability is present, of course. Haslam (1965) has suggested that the spasm results from a conditioned fear response, the latter being experienced as a result of the attempted introduction of an object into the vagina (or presumably during first attempts at sexual intercourse) under stressful conditions. The condition becomes self-perpetuating, since the spasm itself renders intercourse painful, thus confirming the original fear.

(a) SYSTEMATIC DESENSITIZATION TREATMENT (SD-I). The use of SD(I) was first reported by Glynn and Harper (1961), but no details of the treatment were given.[24] Lazarus (1963)

---

[22] See Cooper (1968) for a review of the literature.
[23] Haslam (1965), however, defines dyspareunia

only in terms of its painful aspects and does not mention disgust.

described the use of SD(I) with 16 females, some of whom appeared to manifest dyspareunia, while others manifested a high degree of anxiety in relation to sexual intercourse. In all cases, the frigidity appeared to be a learned response, even though the circumstances under which the learning took place were very diverse. Lazarus also found that the patients varied markedly in personality and temperament— introverted patients tended to be anxious about sexual intercourse, whereas extraverted patients tended to complain of vaginismus. The treatment involved SD(I), using relaxation and anxiety hierarchies relating to increasing degrees of sexual intimacy. Nine of the 16 patients were regarded as "sexually adjusted" following a mean of 29 desensitization sessions, and success was achieved with every patient who received 15 or more training sessions. All of the successes were introverted patients. Four patients were followed up at 15 months and were reported as successfully adjusted. The criteria for success were, however, unsatisfactory, involving response to three questions[25] and, where possible, reports from the husbands.

Brady (1966) used SD(I) in conjunction with brevital to produce relaxation in five cases of severe dyspareunia. In four of the cases, the problem had persisted for nine months to nine years. The number of training sessions varied from ten to 14, and all four patients showed improvement (as measured by response to questions and husband reports) which was maintained at follow-ups of three to eight months. No evidence of symptom substitution was found. The fifth patient showed no tendency to improve and terminated treatment at the end of the fifth session.

A variation on the SD(I) approach to the treatment of frigidity has been reported by Kraft and Al-Issa (1967). Their patient, when first married, experienced sexual intercourse as revolting, so could be classed as a case of dyspareunia. However, Kraft and Al-Issa discovered that the patient showed anxiety in social situations in general, as well as in relation to sexual intercourse. Hence, their treatment was initially directed toward training in social relations generally, with sexual situations being introduced at a late stage of the treatment. A significant improvement in social relations with men was achieved and, on follow-up, the patient was married and expecting a child.[26] Madsen and Ullmann (1967) have described a variation on Lazarus' procedures, which involves the presence of the husband during treatment sessions of the wife. They also reject Lazarus' advice that abstinence from sexual relations should be advised during the early stages of treatment. Rather, the patient should be advised to indulge in sexual activities up to the point at which anxiety is about to be experienced. The danger of resensitization must be balanced against the possible gains from continuing at least some degree of sexual activity while treatment is proceeding.

(b) SYSTEMATIC DESENSITIZATION TREATMENT (SD-R). Desensitization treatment in the real-life sexual situation (SD-R) is probably impossible, but a very interesting alternative approach, which appears to be simple, rapid, and effective, has been reported by Haslam (1965). In two cases of dyspareunia involving spasm of the perineal muscles and contraction of the adductors of the thighs (but not, apparently, revulsion toward sexual intercourse), glass bougies of graded diameter were introduced into the vagina of the patient by the therapist and then withdrawn by the patient. At a later stage, the patient inserted and withdrew them herself. A successive approximation technique was used, with the size of the bougies being gradually increased until they approximated the diameter of an erect penis. In both cases, which were severe and long-standing, complete success was attained. In neither case had complete sexual intercourse been achieved prior to treatment but, following treatment, both patients were able to indulge in satisfactory sexual intercourse. Haslam noted, in agreement with the findings of Lazarus (1963), that the introverted patient improved at a faster rate than the extraverted patient. No evidence of symptom substitution was noted.

In summary, considerable success seems to have attended the behavior therapy of frigidity, a condition long considered to be refractory to treatment. Haslam's study appears to indicate that complete success may be achieved in certain cases by means of a relatively simple procedure.

8. MASOCHISM AND SADISM

The problem posed by masochism in relation to hedonistically-based theories of learning and

---

[24] Wolpe (1958) includes only one case of frigidity in the 88 cases listed in his book.

[25] See above, Section IV.

[26] The patient demonstrating Brady's first type of frigidity can, of course, conceive quite readily; in cases of dyspareunia, conception is much less likely since sexual intercourse may be impossible.

performance has been discussed by Sandler (1964) and Brown (J.S.) (1965). The paradox may be resolved by reference to the recent literature on punishment, reviewed in an earlier chapter,[27] where it was shown that, under certain special circumstances, punishment (or aversive stimulation) may become a discriminative cue for pleasurable events. The special conditions under which punishment may maintain or even strengthen behavior have been clearly stated by Sandler (1964). First, the punishing event should be introduced only after a response has been established by means of the usual reinforcing paradigm. Second, the punishment stimulus must be introduced gradually in such a way that the response is not completely inhibited by it during acquisition. Under these circumstances, the punishing stimulus may actually come to be sought or worked for by the subject, as a necessary precursor to pleasure.

The masochist patient who manifests other deviations as well presents a problem if the other deviations are treated by aversive techniques, since the use of shock treatment may, of course, become pleasurable to the patient and foster his masochism. However, Marks et al (1965) have presented evidence suggesting that this fear may be unfounded. They found that the pleasure experienced in masochism was restricted to a certain range of stimuli and that shock, for example, was perceived as equally aversive by these patients as by normal subjects. Of course, in certain patients, shock itself may have become a discriminative stimulus, in which case alternative techniques might have to be used, or shock itself turned into an aversive stimulus first.

Little empirical work has been reported by behavior therapists on either masochism or sadism, but Mees (1966) used painful shock in an attempt to modify sadistic fantasies in a male patient. Masturbation with sadistic fantasies was apparently replaced by masturbation with normal sexual fantasies in this patient. Davison (1968) succeeded in modifying sadistic fantasies indulged in during masturbation by a graduated training program in which masturbation was carried out by the subject to imaginal heterosexual stimuli.

9. Voyeurism

McConaghy (1964) reported a case in which the patient masturbated while following women.[28] Severe shock, given while the patient was sexually excited at the sight of women, was unsuccessful in changing the behavior. Wolpe (1958) treated interpersonal anxiety rather than voyeurism directly, but found that the latter disappeared as the former improved.

10. Pseudonecrophilia

Necrophilia (morbid sexual attraction to corpses) appears to be a very rare phenomenon, reported usually only in the more lurid textbooks of sexual psychopathology. However, Lazarus (1968) recently treated a case of pseudonecrophilia in which the patient indulged in masturbation while fantasying various sexual behaviors toward female corpses. There was no evidence of psychosis, and treatment was by way of systematic desensitization of the fear of normal sexual relations, with apparent success.

We may conclude that substantial advances have been made during the last ten years in relation to behavior therapy for sexual difficulties and deviations. The notorious refractoriness of sexual deviations to any form of treatment, however, demands extreme caution. Recent developments in correlating the changes that occur at various response levels (Marks et al, 1965; Marks and Gelder, 1967) provide grounds for optimism and certainly represent a notable advance over the earlier inadequate assessments of the results of treatment. The length of follow-up has generally been quite inadequate, though this is not necessarily a criticism that publication has been premature. The substitution of shock for drug aversion therapy is now virtually complete, and it may well be that alternatives to shock will be produced in the near future. Behavior therapists working in this field are now also well aware of the fact that, for example, homosexual behavior involves a great deal more than its sexual aspects and that, therefore, techniques will need to be developed for treating the entire social relations of such persons.

---

[27] See Chapter 2.

[28] This patient would probably better be considered as a fetishist.

REFERENCES

Bancroft, J.H.J., Jones, H.G., & Pullan, B.R. A simple transducer for measuring penile erection, with comments on its use in the treatment of sexual disorders. *Behav. Res. Ther.*, 1966, **4**, 239–241.

Barker, J.C. Aversion therapy of sexual perversions. *Brit. J. Psychiat.*, 1963, **109**, 696.

Barker, J.C. Electrical aversion therapy. *Brit. med. J.*, 1964, **1**, 436.

Barker, J.C. Behavior therapy for transvestism: a comparison of pharmacological and electrical aversion techniques. *Brit. J. Psychiat.*, 1965, **111**, 268–276.

Barker, J.C., Thorpe, J.G., Blakemore, C.B., Lavin, N.I., & Conway, C.G. Behavior therapy in a case of transvestism. *Lancet*, 1961, **1**, 510.

Bentler, P.M. Heterosexual behavior assessment: I. Males. *Behav. Res. Ther.*, 1968, **6**, 21–25 (a).

Bentler, P.M. Heterosexual behavior assessment: II. Females. *Behav. Res. Ther.*, 1968, **6**, 27–30 (b).

Blakemore, C.B., Thorpe, J.G., Barker, J.C., Conway, C.G., & Lavin, N.I. The application of faradic aversion conditioning in a case of transvestism. *Behav. Res. Ther.*, 1963, **1**, 29–34 (a).

Blakemore, C.B., Thorpe, J.G., Barker, J.C., Conway, C.G., & Lavin, N.I. Follow-up note to: the application of faradic aversion conditioning in a case of transvestism. *Behav. Res. Ther.*, 1963, **1**, 191 (b).

Bond, I.K. & Evans, D.R. Avoidance therapy: its use in two cases of underwear fetishism. *Canad. med. Assoc. J.*, 1967, **96**, 1160–1162.

Bond, I.K. & Hutchison, H.C. Application of reciprocal inhibition therapy to exhibitionism. *Canad. med. Assoc. J.*, 1960, **83**, 23–25.

Brady, J.P. Brevital-relaxation treatment of frigidity. *Behav. Res. Ther.*, 1966, **4**, 71–77.

Brown, P.T. On the differentiation of homo- or hetero-erotic interest in the male: an operant technique illustrated in a case of a motor-cycle fetishist. *Behav. Res. Ther.*, 1964, **2**, 31–35.

Brown, P.T. A reply to Koenig. *Behav. Res. Ther.*, 1965, **2**, 309–311.

Brown, J.S. A behavioral analysis of masochism. *J. exp. Res. Pers.*, 1965, **1**, 65–70.

Clark, D.F. Fetishism treated by negative conditioning. *Brit. J. Psychiat.*, 1963, **109**, 404–407 (a).

Clark, D.F. Treatment of fetishism by negative conditioning—a further note. *Brit. J. Psychiat.*, 1963, **109**, 695–696 (b).

Clark, D.F. A note on avoidance conditioning techniques in sexual disorder. *Behav. Res. Ther.*, 1965, **3**, 203–206.

Cooper, A.J. A case of fetishism and impotence treated by behavior therapy. *Brit. J. Psychiat.*, 1963, **109**, 649–652.

Cooper, A.J. A factual study of male potency disorders. *Brit. J. Psychiat.*, 1968, **114**, 719–731.

Davies, B.M. & Morgenstern, F.S. A case of cysticercosis, temporal lobe epilepsy, and transvestism. *J. Neurol. Neurosurg. Psychiat.*, 1960, **23**, 247–249.

Davison, G.C. Elimination of a sadistic fantasy by a client-controlled counter-conditioning technique: a case study. *J. abnorm. Psychol.*, 1968, **73**, 84–90.

Epstein, A.W. Fetishism: a study of its psychopathology with particular reference to a proposed disorder in brain mechanisms as an etiological factor. *J. nerv. ment. Dis.*, 1960, **130**, 107–119.

Evans, D.R. Masturbatory fantasy and sexual deviation. *Behav. Res. Ther.*, 1968, **6**, 17–19.

Feldman, M.P. Aversion therapy for sexual deviations: a critical review. *Psychol. Bull.*, 1966, **65**, 65–79.

Feldman, M.P. & MacCulloch, M.J. A systematic approach to the treatment of homosexuality by conditioned aversion: preliminary report. *Amer. J. Psychiat.*, 1964, **121**, 167–171.

Feldman, M.P. & MacCulloch, M.J. The application of anticipatory avoidance learning to the treatment of homosexuality. 1. Theory, technique, and preliminary results. *Behav. Res. Ther.*, 1965, **2**, 165–184.

Feldman, M.P., MacCulloch, M.J., Mellor, V., & Pinschof, J.M. The application of anticipatory avoidance learning to the treatment of homosexuality: III. The sexual orientation method. *Behav. Res. Ther.*, 1966, **4**, 289–299.

Freud, S. Fetishism. *Internat. J. Psychoanal.*, 1928, **9**, 161–166.

Freund, K. Some problems in the treatment of homosexuality. In Eysenck, H.J. (ed.). *Behavior therapy and the neuroses.* Oxford: Pergamon, 1960, pp. 312–326.

Freund, K. *Die Homosexualität beim Mann.* Leipzig: S. Hirzel Verlag, 1963 (a).

Freund, K. A laboratory method for diagnosing predominance of homo- or hetero-erotic interest in the male. *Behav. Res. Ther.*, 1963, **1**, 85–93 (b).

Freund, K. Diagnosing heterosexual pedophilia by means of a test for sexual interest. *Behav. Res. Ther.*, 1965, **3**, 229–234.

Freund, K. Diagnosing homo- or heterosexuality and erotic age-preference by means of a psychophysiological test. *Behav. Res. Ther.*, 1967, **5**, 209–228 (a).

Freund, K. Erotic preference in pedophilia. *Behav. Res. Ther.*, 1967, **5**, 339–348 (b).

Freund, K., Sedlacek, F., & Knob, K. A simple transducer for mechanical plethysmography of the male genital. *J. exp. Anal. Behav.*, 1965, **8**, 169–170.

Gillespie, W.H. The psychoanalytic theory of sexual deviation with special reference to fetishism. In Rosen, I. (ed.). *The pathology and treatment of sexual deviation.* London: Oxford Univer. Press, 1964, pp. 123–145.

Glynn, J.D. & Harper, P. Behavior therapy in a case of transvestism. *Lancet*, 1961, **1**, 619.

Gold, S. & Neufeld, I.L. A learning approach to the treatment of homosexuality. *Behav. Res. Ther.*, 1965, **2**, 201–204.

Haslam, M.T. The treatment of psychogenic dyspareunia by reciprocal inhibition. *Brit. J. Psychiat.*, 1965, **111**, 280–282.

Hess, E.H., Seltzer, A.L., & Shlien, J.M. Pupil response of hetero- and homosexual males to pictures of men and women: a pilot study. *J. abnorm. Psychol.*, 1965, **70**, 165–168.

James, B. Case of homosexuality treated by aversion therapy. *Brit. med. J.*, 1962, **1**, 768–770.

Kallmann, F.J. A comparative twin study on the genetic aspects of male homosexuality. *J. nerv. ment. Dis.*, 1952, **115**, 283–298.

Koenig, K.P. The differentiation of hetero- or homo-erotic interests in the male: some comments on articles by Brown and Freund. *Behav. Res. Ther.*, 1965, **2**, 305–307.

Kolvin, I. "Aversive imagery" treatment in adolescents. *Behav. Res. Ther.*, 1967, **5**, 245–248.

Kraft, T. A case of homosexuality treated by systematic desensitization. *Amer. J. Psychother.*, 1967, **21**, 815–821 (a).

Kraft, T. Behavior therapy and the treatment of sexual perversions. *Psychother. Psychosom.*, 1967, **15**, 351–357 (b).

Kraft, T. & Al-Issa, I. Behavior therapy and the treatment of frigidity. *Amer. J. Psychother.*, 1967, **21**, 116–120.

Kraft, T. & Al-Issa, I. The use of methohexitone sodium in the systematic desensitization of premature ejaculation. *Brit. J. Psychiat.*, 1968, **114**, 351–352.

Kushner, M. The reduction of a long-standing fetish by means of aversive conditioning. In Ullmann, L.P. & Krasner, L. (eds.). *Case studies in behavior modification.* New York: Wiley, 1965, pp. 239–242.

Kushner, M. & Sandler, J. Aversion therapy and the concept of punishment. *Behav. Res. Ther.*, 1966, **4**, 179–186.

Lavin, N.I., Thorpe, J.G., Barker, J.C., Blakemore, C.B., & Conway, C.G. Behavior therapy in a case of transvestism. *J. nerv. ment. Dis.*, 1961, **133**, 346–353.

Lazarus, A.A. The treatment of chronic frigidity by systematic desensitization. *J. nerv. ment. Dis.*, 1963, **136**, 272–278.

Lazarus, A.A. The treatment of a sexually inadequate man. In Ullmann, L.P. & Krasner, L. (eds.). *Case studies in behavior modification*. New York: Holt, 1965, pp. 243–245.

Lazarus, A.A. A case of pseudonecrophilia treated by behavior therapy. *J. clin. Psychol.*, 1968, **24**, 113–115.

Lukianowicz, N. Survey of various aspects of transvestism in the light of our present knowledge. *J. nerv. ment. Dis.*, 1959, **128**, 36–64.

McConaghy, N. A year's experience with non-verbal psychotherapy. *Med. J. Austr.*, 1964, **1**, 831–837.

McConaghy, N. Penile volume change to moving pictures of male and female nudes in heterosexual and homosexual males. *Behav. Res. Ther.*, 1967, **5**, 43–48.

MacCulloch, M.J., Feldman, M.P., & Pinshoff, J.M. The application of anticipatory avoidance learning to the treatment of homosexuality: II. Avoidance response latencies and pulse rate changes. *Behav. Res. Ther.*, 1965, **3**, 21–43.

McGuire, R.J., Carlisle, J.M., & Young, B.G. Sexual deviations as conditioned behavior: a hypothesis. *Behav. Res. Ther.*, 1965, **2**, 185–190.

McGuire, R.J. & Vallance, M. Aversion therapy by electric shock: a simple technique. *Brit. med. J.*, 1964, **1**, 151–153.

Madsen, C.H. & Ullmann, L.P. Innovations in the desensitization of frigidity. *Behav. Res. Ther.*, 1967, **5**, 67–68.

Marks, I.M. & Gelder, M.G. Transvestism and fetishism: clinical and psychological changes during faradic aversion. *Brit. J. Psychiat.*, 1967, **113**, 711–729.

Marks, I.M., Rachman, S., & Gelder, M.G. Methods for assessment of aversion treatment in fetishism with masochism. *Behav. Res. Ther.*, 1965, **3**, 253–258.

Marks, I.M. & Sartorius, N.H. A contribution to the measurement of sexual attitude: the semantic differential as a measure of sexual attitude in sexual deviations. *J. nerv. ment. Dis.*, 1968, **145**, 441–451.

Marmor, J. (ed.). *Sexual inversion: the multiple roots of homosexuality*. New York: Basic Books, 1965 (a).

Marmor, J. Introduction. In Marmor, J. (ed.). *Sexual inversion: the multiple roots of homosexuality*. New York: Basic Books, 1965, pp. 1–24 (b).

Masters, W.H. & Johnson, V.E. *Human sexual response*. Boston: Little, Brown, 1966.

Mees, H.L. Sadistic fantasies modified by aversive conditioning and substitution: a case study. *Behav. Res. Ther.*, 1966, **4**, 317–320.

Morgenstern, F.S., Pearce, J.F., & Rees, W.L. Predicting the outcome of behavior therapy by psychological tests. *Behav. Res. Ther.*, 1965, **2**, 191–200.

Pare, C.M.B. Etiology of homosexuality: genetic and chromosomal aspects. In Marmor, J. (ed.). *Sexual inversion: the multiple roots of homosexuality*. New York: Basic Books, 1965, pp. 70–80.

Phillips, J.P.N. A note on the scoring of the sexual orientation method. *Behav. Res. Ther.*, 1968, **6**, 121–123.

Rachman, S. Sexual disorders and behavior therapy. *Amer. J. Psychiat.*, 1961, **118**, 235–240.

Rachman, S. Sexual fetishism: an experimental analogue. *Psychol. Rec.*, 1966, **16**, 293–296.

Rachman, S. & Hodgson, R.J. Experimentally-induced "sexual fetishism": replication and development. *Psychol. Rec.*, 1968, **18**, 25–27.

Ramsay, R.W. & Van Velzen, V. Behavior therapy for sexual perversions. *Behav. Res. Ther.*, 1968, **6**, 233.

Raymond, M.J. Case of fetishism treated by aversion therapy. *Brit. med. J.*, 1956, **2**, 854–857.

Raymond, M. & O'Keefe, K. A case of pin-up fetishism treated by aversion conditioning. *Brit. J. Psychiat.*, 1965, **111**, 579–581.

Rosen, I. Exhibitionism, scopophilia and voyeurism. In Rosen, I. (ed.). *The pathology and treatment of sexual deviation*. London: Oxford Univer. Press, 1964, pp. 293–350.

Sandler, J. Masochism: an empirical analysis. *Psychol. Bull.*, 1964, **62**, 197–204.

Scott, T.R., Wells, W.H., Wood, D.Z., & Morgan, D.I. Pupillary response and sexual interest reexamined. *J. clin. Psychol.*, 1967, **23**, 433–438.

Solyom, L. & Miller, S. A differential conditioning procedure as the initial phase of the behavior therapy of homosexuality. *Behav. Res. Ther.*, 1965, **3,** 147–160.

Srnec, –. & Freund, K. Treatment of male homosexuality through conditioning. *Internat. J. Sexol.*, 1953, **7,** 92–93.

Stevenson, I. & Wolpe, J. Recovery from sexual deviations through overcoming non-sexual neurotic responses. *Amer. J. Psychiat.*, 1960, **116,** 737–742.

Thorpe, J.G. & Schmidt, E. Therapeutic failure in a case of aversion therapy. *Behav. Res. Ther.*, 1964, **1,** 293–296.

Thorpe, J.G., Schmidt, E., Brown, P.T., & Castell, D. Aversion-relief therapy: a new method for general application. *Behav. Res. Ther.*, 1964, **2,** 71–82.

Thorpe, J.G., Schmidt, E., & Castell, D. A comparison of positive and negative (aversive) conditioning in the treatment of homosexuality. *Behav. Res. Ther.*, 1964, **1,** 357–362.

Vanasek, F.J., Frisbie, L.V., & Dingman, H.F. Patterns of affective responses in two groups of pedophiles. *Psychol. Rep.*, 1968, **22,** 659–668.

Wolpe, J. *Psychotherapy by reciprocal inhibition.* Stanford: Stanford Univer. Press, 1958.

Chapter 13

The Psychoses: Children

I. DEFINITIONS, INCIDENCE, MEASUREMENT

THE PSYCHIATRIC LITERATURE on psychoses in childhood is so hopelessly confused that it can be meaningfully described only by a historical approach.[1] There has been considerable resistance to the notion that psychotic forms of behavior could occur in children, largely because of the powerful influence of Bleuler and Kraepelin in formulating the diagnosis of *dementia praecox*, but not that of *dementia praecocissima*. That is, while it was accepted that schizophrenia might occur during early adolescence, it was regarded as unlikely on theoretical grounds that it could arise during childhood. Children whose behavior was unusually peculiar were regarded as probably mental defectives with brain damage, and were dealt with accordingly by commitment to a mental deficiency institution.

1. DEVELOPMENT OF THE CONCEPT OF CHILDHOOD SCHIZOPHRENIA

In the first decade of this century, descriptions were given by De Sanctis, Weygandt, and Heller, among others, of children who showed early normal development, followed by sudden deterioration in behavior such that the child behaved like a grossly disturbed mental defective.

The first systematic study of such children was, however, reported by Potter (1933) who presented detailed case histories of six children aged four to 12 years on admission. The principal characteristics of these children were:

(i) Generalized retraction of interests from their environment.

(ii) Dereistic thinking, feeling, and acting.

(iii) Thought disorder (blocking, symbolization, mutism).

(iv) Defective emotional rapport.

(v) Diminution, rigidity, and distortion of affect.

(vi) A behavior change ranging from excitement to stupor.

All six children were diagnosed by Potter as schizophrenic; in four cases, of the catatonic type. Early development was stated to be mostly normal and uneventful with quite sudden deterioration. No evidence was found implicating constitutional factors; neurological examination was negative; there was no evidence of complications of pregnancy or birth trauma; and no evidence of postnatal illnesses of any significance. The family background was considered reasonably normal, considering the severity of the disorder (although Potter lays some emphasis on the importance of family psychodynamics). Potter considered that these children were suffering from a schizophrenic disorder which differed from schizo-

---

[1] The vast literature on childhood psychosis is illustrated by the two substantial bibliographies that have appeared (Goldfarb and Dorsen, 1956; Tilton et al, 1966). Four books have appeared (Bradley, 1941; Goldfarb, 1961; Rimland, 1964; and Wing, 1966). Substantial reviews have been published by Eisenberg, 1957a; Ekstein et al, 1958; and Rutter, 1967.

phrenia in adults only in its manifestations being modified by the incomplete maturation of the child (clearly, if the disorder developed before fluent verbalization had been achieved, it effects on behavior would be different).

During the next two decades, several important contributions were made which, however, produced a good deal of confusion. Bradley (1941, 1947) studied 14 children aged 7–13 diagnosed by him as childhood schizophrenia. They showed the following eight characteristics:

(i) Seclusiveness.
(ii) Irritability when seclusiveness is disturbed.
(iii) Daydreaming.
(iv) Bizarre behavior—posturing, repetitive purposeless motions, unintelligible language, irrelevant expression of emotion.
(v) Diminution of personal interests.
(vi) Regressive nature of personal interests.
(vii) Sensitivity to comment and criticism.
(viii) Physical inactivity.

The first two traits were found in all of the children and were regarded as pathognomonic; they were also found in five younger children (aged 3–4 years) diagnosed as schizophrenic.

However, Bradley disagreed with Potter on one important point. He claimed that the onset was not as unexpected as Potter had claimed and that abnormal developmental patterns were noted by most of the mothers during the first two years of life. Prognostic factors during this period included: diminished interest in the environment; failure to develop, or loss of, speech; feeding difficulties; and hyper- or hypo-motility patterns.

Despert (1938, 1947) also reported on children with acute onset following early normal development. She found evidence of hallucinatory behavior and paranoid traits, together with bizarre thinking, withdrawal, flattened affect, stereotyping, mannerisms, motor dissociations, speech peculiarities (in pitch, rhythm, and modulation), and peculiar reactions to sound (as, for example, ignoring loud sounds, while showing a startle reaction to soft sounds). The rapid fluctuations in symptomatology were emphasized by Despert.

The most influential worker during this period, however, was undoubtedly Bender (1947, 1955, 1956, 1960; Bender and Helme, 1953). Making use of Gesell's five maturation areas (homeostatic control, respiratory patterns, sleeping and waking patterns, muscular tone, and motor activity), Bender claimed that "every

patterned functioning field of behaviour" was disturbed in schizophrenic children. Thus they showed abnormalities of posture, balance, and speech (manifesting also the peculiar phenomenon of "whirling" which will be considered later); confusion of body-image, self-world perceptions, and reality testing; and social withdrawal (Bender and Helme, 1953). At different times, Bender stressed different aspects of the disabilities that she found in these children, but it is clear enough that, when she stressed, for example, difficulties in identifying the self and thereby relating to the rest of the world (Bender, 1947), she would regard this difficulty as derived from the developmental lag. Bender also stressed the *plasticity* of the nervous system of the schizophrenic child, which gave rise to both defects and islets of superior performance.

Like the earlier workers, Bender (1947) identified a distinct group of children in whom the disorder develops between the ages of three and four and one half years, preceded by apparently normal development. In a more recent publication, Bender (1964) characterizes these children as having a stormy childhood with a severe psychological precipitating cause. It is clear from Bender's description also that the children in this group do not have *retarded* speech (though the speech may be abnormal).

Mahler (1952; Mahler et al, 1949) has distinguished a form of symbiotic child psychosis which appears to be very similar to the concept of childhood schizophrenia in that it develops between two and one half to five years of age. Symbiotic child psychosis is distinguished by Mahler from late-onset benign psychosis in terms of the kind of defense mechanisms employed (psychotic in the former, neurotic in the latter). The *primary symptoms* of child psychosis are: panic reactions (rage or agitation); erotic aggressive responses; confusion of self and nonself; a failure to differentiate animate from inanimate objects; a spuriously-strong attachment to an adult chosen at random; and dereistic thinking, feeling, and acting. The *secondary symptoms* (which represent an attempt to handle the consequences which follow from the primary symptoms) include whirling; autistic behavior; the endowment of body parts with concentrated libido; the superficial mimicking of adult behavior; seclusiveness; temper tantrums; and islets of special skill. The *tertiary symptoms* are the neurotic defense mechanisms and include denial, fantasy, repression, and so on.

Finally, mention should be made here of Goldfarb (1961) who has attempted to distinguish between organic and nonorganic childhood schizophrenia. His work will be dealt with in more detail later.

2. DEVELOPMENT OF THE CONCEPT OF EARLY INFANTILE AUTISM

In 1943 Kanner described a syndrome which has since become famous as "early infantile autism." As described by Kanner and his colleague Eisenberg (Kanner, 1943, 1946, 1951, 1954; Eisenberg and Kanner, 1956), the major characteristics of the autistic child are the following:

(i) Inability to relate to people and situations ("aloneness").

(ii) Failure to use language for communicative purposes.

(iii) Obsessive maintenance of "sameness" in the environment.

(iv) Skill in fine motor movements.

(v) Very high cognitive potential as manifested by "islets" of performance.

The pathognomonic traits are the extreme self-isolation and the obsessive insistence on the preservation of sameness. The disorder is considered to be present from birth. While the child may please its parents by its apparent quietness during the first year of life, certain signs reveal the presence of the disorder to the percipient mother (for example, the "limpness" of the child when picked up and its complete lack of responsiveness to stimulation).

Kanner considered early infantile autism to be a very rare disorder and hence has rejected as spurious many claimed instances in the literature. However, several studies using Kanner's criteria quite rigorously, have confirmed his earlier results (Schain and Yannet, 1960).

Similar syndromes, formally regarded as equivalent to Kanner's early infantile autism (and distinct from childhood schizophrenia as outlined above), have been described by Bender (1947, 1964) who referred to "early autistic development"; Despert (1938, 1947; Despert and Sherwin, 1958); and Mahler (1952).

3. DIFFERENTIATION BETWEEN CHILDHOOD SCHIZOPHRENIA AND EARLY INFANTILE AUTISM

Rimland (1964) has most clearly described and summarized the differences supposed to distinguish childhood schizophrenia from early infantile autism. His comparisons are presented in Table 13.1.

TABLE 13.1. *Differential Characteristics of Childhood Schizophrenia and Early Infantile Autism*

Early Infantile Autism	Childhood Schizophrenia
Present from birth	Early development normal
Good health/appearance	Many ailments/frail appearance
EEG normal	EEG abnormal
No physical moulding	Physical moulding possible
No social interaction	Dependency on adult
Preservation of sameness	Variability
No hallucinations or delusions	Hallucinations/delusions
High level of motor skill	Motor skill poor/bizarre movements
Language disturbance (pronominal reversal, affirmation by repetition, delayed echolalia, metaphoric language, part-whole confusion)	Language development, but may be abnormal
Idiot-savant performance	No special skills
Unoriented, detached	Disorientated, confused
Not conditionable	Easily conditionable
Occurs in both of monozygotic twins	Does not occur in both of monozygotic twins
Stable, professional home background	Unstable home background
Low family incidence of psychosis	High family incidence of psychosis

Source: Based on Rimland (1964).

It is extremely doubtful whether all of the distinguishing characteristics listed by Rimland would hold up in carefully designed studies, but so confusing is the literature that any attempt at systematization is welcome.

In a rather different attempt to organize the data, Anthony (1958) also distinguished one group of children with early onset and a slow chronic course (Kanner's syndrome; Bender's first age group; Despert's no-onset group); and a second group of children with onset between three and five years of age, with an acute course leading to regression (Heller's[2] disease; De Sanctis and Weygandt dementias; Mahler's symbiotic psychosis; Bender's second age group; and Despert's acute onset type). The former is essentially the syndrome of early infantile autism; the latter the syndrome of childhood schizophrenia. It may be noted here that Bender (1964) has also distinguished a form of schizophrenia which develops between the ages of 11 and $13\frac{1}{2}$ years.

4. DEVELOPMENT OF THE CONCEPT OF INFANTILE PSYCHOSIS

The possibility cannot be discounted that the use of appropriate factor analytic techniques would demolish both of the above "dimensions" and replace them with quite different ones. For example, there may prove to be a general dimension of "psychoticism," together with a second factor of "autism," and all the children studied above may be placed within such a two-dimensional system. However, apart from an inadequate attempt by Goldfarb (1961), no sophisticated analysis of this kind has yet been carried out. In the meanwhile, however, some psychiatrists, disturbed at the mixture of description and interpretation which has characterized the use of the terms "childhood schizophrenia" and "early infantile autism," have preferred the term "schizophrenic syndrome in childhood" or "atypical development," and have attempted to reach some agreement concerning the basic characteristics of "childhood psychosis." The most notable of these attempts resulted in the formulation of the famous nine points of Creak (1951, 1961, 1963, 1964) and her working party colleagues. The nine characteristics are:

(i) Gross and sustained impairment of emotional relationships with people.

(ii) Apparent unawareness of own personal identity.

(iii) Pathological preoccupation with particular objects in a nonfunctional way.

(iv) Sustained resistance to change in the environment.

(v) Abnormal perceptual experience, including unusual responses to sensory stimuli.

(vi) Acute, excessive, and seemingly illogical anxiety.

(vii) Disordered speech.

(viii) Distortions in motility patterns (hypo- or hyper-kinesis; whirling).

(ix) General retardation with islets of normal or exceptional skill.

These criteria were derived by examining the literature and leaned heavily on several studies (e.g., Norman, 1954, 1955). They have been severely criticized in recent years, and there is now empirical evidence refuting the validity of some of the points. For example, Wolff and Chess (1965a), comparing direct observation of the child with information provided by the mother, could find no evidence to support the contention of a disturbance in body image.

5. THE PROBLEM OF DIFFERENTIAL DIAGNOSIS

There are several problems to be considered here. First, psychotic behavior may result from organic factors which are readily detectable if sought (Arajarvi and Alanen, 1964). Second, Goldfarb (1961) and Creak (1964) have distinguished within childhood schizophrenia (Goldfarb) or schizophrenic syndrome in childhood (Creak) a subgroup of presumed organic cases where the neurological deficit is *not* so readily specifiable but is inferred partly from behavior patterns and partly from tenuous neurological signs. The validity of the distinction is attested to by the fact that Goldfarb (1961) showed, using objective tests, that while some of these tests discriminated both organic *and* nonorganic schizophrenic children from normal controls, tests were also found which discriminated between the organic and nonorganic subjects within the schizophrenic group. Similarly, Creak (1964) found that some of the nine points discriminated organic from nonorganic schizophrenic children, whereas others did not. Table 13.2 shows the incidence for these two groups as well as for groups of organic children without psychotic traits and

---

[2] For a comprehensive account of Heller's disease, see Yakovlev et al (1948).

TABLE 13.2. *Percentage Occurrence of Creak's Nine Points in Four Groups of Children*

Group	N	Percentage Occurrence								
		1	2	3	4	5	6	7	8	9
1. Nonorganic schizophrenic	129	98	68	36	57	65	76	88	89	77
2. Organic schizophrenic	26	96	46	67	54	50	46	85	85	58
3. Organic without schizophrenia	34	44	29	18	24	15	24	53	47	35
4. Nonorganic and nonschizo- phrenic	24	66	21	25	25	29	63	58	63	50

Source: Creak (1964).

for nonorganic, nonschizophrenic children. The organic schizophrenics show more awareness of personal identity, more pathological pre-occupation with particular objects in a non-functional way, and more acute anxiety.

Third, a major diagnostic problem is the differentiation between the psychotic child and the disturbed nonpsychotic child. Early studies by Bender and Grugett (1956) suggested that a wide range of differences existed, and these findings have been confirmed more recently by Rutter and Lockyer (1967). The latter carefully matched for age, sex, and I.Q. 63 children with an "unequivocal" diagnosis of child psychosis, schizophrenic syndrome of childhood, or infantile autism with a number of disturbed children in whose case records no mention was made of "psychosis" or "psychotic traits." Of traits which occurred in more than 50% of the psychotic children, the following discriminated between the psychotic and disturbed non-psychotic children: autism; no speech at five years; abnormal preoccupations; resistance to change; other obsessional phenomena; stereotyped repetitive movements; short attention span; encopresis after four years. Additional traits mentioned by Bender and Helme (1953) as discriminatory include: abnormalities of posture and balance (including whirling); identity and orientation confusion.

The next problem arises from the fact that the psychotic child is often simply labeled as a disturbed mental defective. Potter (1933) first drew attention to this fact, but only Gillies (1965) appears to have investigated it systematically. She compared matched psychotics and defectives on verbal and nonverbal measures and found the groups not to be differentiable on a nonverbal measure, while a significant inferiority of the psychotics on a vocabulary test and social age as measured by the Vineland disappeared when the nonverbal psychotics were excluded. The psychotics, as would be expected, showed significantly greater variability in performance.

Mention may also be made of the problem of distinguishing between the psychotic child and the aphasic child. Kanner (1949) discussed this problem, and more recently it has been taken up by de Hirsch (1967). She points out that both "aphasoid" and psychotic children show perceptuomotor instability, figure-ground difficulties, and profound auditory inattention; while the language of both groups is characterized by a high auditory threshold for speech, inferior auditory discrimination, feedback distortions, echolalia, limitations in verbal output, and conceptual defects. However, the psychotic children are differentially characterized by a long auditory memory span, a lack of communicative intent in their auditory utterances (whereas gestures in aphasoid children have high meaningful content), the use of words as things, and "primary process distortion" (e.g., rejecting a letter of the alphabet because "it is not nice").

In some respects, the most vital problem concerns the relationship between childhood psychosis and autism. Kanner's use of the term "early infantile autism" appears to have pre-empted the term for that condition with the implication that autism is not characteristic of late-onset childhood schizophrenia. The danger of a premature false resolution of this question is shown by the increasing tendency to define a syndrome of "autism." Menolascino (1965) has investigated this question by, first, defining autistic behavior carefully (as involving extreme self-preoccupation, a highly personalized and stereotyped approach to inanimate objects, and unrelatedness to people); second, by detecting a group of children meeting these criteria of autistic behavior; and then by examining whether their homogeneity with respect to autism implied homogeneity with respect to formal diagnosis. Although he was able to assemble only 34 children who met the criteria out of 616 examined, he nevertheless found that eight different diagnostic categories were necessary; that only two children appeared to fit Kanner's criteria of early infantile autism; that some of the children did not appear to be psychotic at all; and that many had complex etiologies.

6. INCIDENCE

Given the extraordinary diagnostic confusion revealed by the above survey, it is clear that the incidence of any one of the variants of childhood psychosis is very difficult to determine. The only fact that appears to be established with certainty, whatever diagnostic category is considered, is the sex ratio of about four to one in favor of boys. Bender (1955) reported an incidence of childhood schizophrenia of 8% in 7000 cases seen over a period of 20 years. When only children less than six years of age were considered, the incidence was 12%. These figures are suspect, however, since they clearly refer to a special sample of patients seen at a clinic.

Fortunately, a very careful epidemiological study has been recently carried out by Lotter (1966). His work is a model of carefulness and thoroughness. It should be noted that he tried to establish the incidence of "autistic behavior" in a sample of 78,000 children by the distribution of a pretested questionnaire. Such was the quality of preparation that replies were received on 99% of the children. The technique then involved reducing the data so that a small number of possibly autistic children were picked out and subjected to intensive investigation, with careful cross-checking of information. The incidence of autistic behavior (or a pathological kind, of course) was estimated at 4.5 per 10,000 between the ages of eight and

ten years, with a ratio of 2.5/1 in favor of boys. For roughly two-thirds of the criterion group, the disorder was apparent virtually from birth on; for the remainder, early development was apparently normal, with regression. Thus, once more, the distinction between early and late onset is found.

7. CONCLUSION

In the absence of detailed factor-analytic studies, it is impossible to come to any firm conclusions concerning the dimensional structure of childhood psychosis. However, the most probable result that would be found would demand two factors which would cut across the usual diagnostic labels. One of the factors would be a general factor of "psychoticism", the other of "autism." These factors would most likely be orthogonal to each other (Figure 1). The important point to note, of course, is that, if this model were correct, the position of childhood schizophrenia and early infantile autism would be clear *but these syndromes would not exhaust the possibilities*. Thus it would be possible to be psychotic without being markedly autistic, and vice versa.

II. PSYCHIATRIC THEORIES OF THE ETIOLOGY OF CHILDHOOD PSYCHOSES

Three extreme positions have been taken up by psychiatrists in relation to the etiology of psychoses in childhood. Each will be considered in turn, together with supporting evidence, for and against.

1. GENETICALLY-DETERMINED CONSTITUTIONAL ABNORMALITY IN THE CHILD

The protagonists of this approach argue

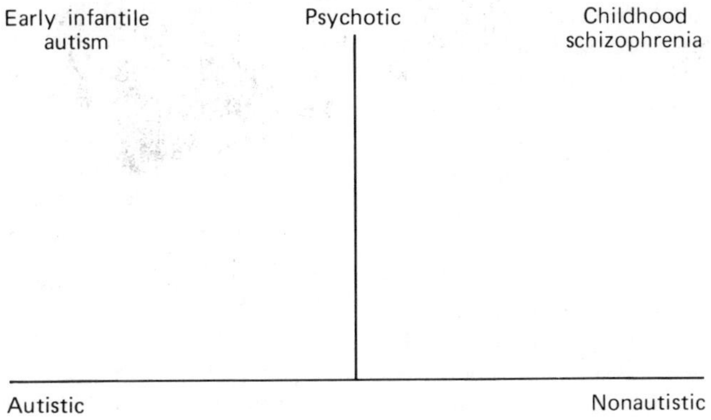

FIG. 1.   Orthogonal dimensions of childhood psychosis.

either that there is a history of family abnormality of a structure that suggests genetic transmission or, more broadly, that there is a biological "insufficiency" (presumably genetically determined) which produces "plasticity" of the nervous system.

(a) FAMILY HISTORY OF ABNORMALITIES. Leaving aside the study by Kallmann and Roth (1956) which dealt with "preadolescent schizophrenia," a distinction appears necessary between childhood schizophrenia and early infantile autism. Bender (1953) claimed that 40% of a sample of childhood schizophrenics studied by her had at least one parent with a definite or strongly suggestive diagnosis of schizophrenia; while 8% of the children had a sibling under treatment for schizophrenia. Her work has, however, been severely criticized by Pollack and Gittelmann (1964), and the estimates cannot be regarded as reliable or valid. In the case of early infantile autism, generally negative results have been obtained in the family history (e.g., Schain and Yannet (1960) found that no siblings of 50 autistic children had ever been diagnosed as autistic) and similar negative results were found in Rutter and Lockyer's (1967) mixed sample of psychotics.

(b) CYTOGENETICS OF THE CHILD. Book et al (1963) carried out cytogenetical analyses of long-term cell cultures *in vitro* derived from skin biopsies of ten severely regressed autistic children. No significant derivations from normal were found with respect to sex chromatin, chromosome numbers, and morphology. Of course, such investigations are worth pursuing in view of recent demonstrations of chromosome abnormalities in mongolism, and particularly in view of the sex incidence differential which suggests at least the possibility of a recessive gene transmitted through the mother.

(c) MATURATIONAL LAG. The clearest statement of Bender's theory concerning the etiology of childhood schizophrenia is to be found in the study by Bender and Helme (1953). Childhood schizophrenia is considered to be a disorder in the regulation of maturation of basic behavioral processes in childhood. It manifests itself in all areas of functioning. The "neurological hierarchy" and its control remain primitive (fetal) in nature. The plasticity which is characteristic of the constitution of the schizophrenic child enables both regression and precocity to occur, depending on environmental circumstances, so that "islets" of precocity are found. The overt behavior disturbances may be divided into the *primary* disturbances of

voluntary and autonomic functions and the *secondary* effects resulting from these disturbances, namely, anxiety and disturbance in self-perception and social relations. These disturbances and the resultant anxiety lead to three techniques of coping behavior: secondary neurotic habit patterns; precocious development in restricted areas; or regression to a torporous state.

The attempt by Bender and Helme (1953) to test this theory by comparing psychotic with disturbed children on a large number of traits supposedly relevant to the theory was completely illegitimate since, of course, the observed differences between the groups, purporting to test the theory, were hopelessly confounded by the fact that these variables had been used previously to diagnose the children and place them in the groups. Hence it is not surprising that the measures discriminated between groups. However, support for Bender's theory of widespread impairment in childhood schizophrenia has been provided by several independent studies. Berkowitz (1961), for example found very significant differences between psychotic and nonpsychotic, disturbed children on tests of motor performance, visual perception, memory, and lateral dominance, with the psychotic children inferior in nearly all of the tests. Simon and Gillies (1964) found that psychotic children were significantly retarded in height, weight, and bone age as compared with the norm; however, these results were not supported by the results obtained by Dutton (1964), Goldfarb (1961), or indeed Bender herself in relation to height.

2. NEUROLOGICAL ABNORMALITIES
PRODUCED BY PRE, PARA, OR
POSTNATAL TRAUMA

Rutter and Lockyer (1967) remark that, in 25% of the children studied by them, the existence of organic brain damage was considered a possibility. Here again, a distinction must be drawn between early infantile autism and childhood schizophrenia. In the former, Eisenberg and Kanner (1956) reiterated Kanner's original contention that no organic involvement could be pinpointed; and this conclusion was strongly supported by a very careful independent study by Schain and Yannet (1960) of 50 autistic children who satisfied Kanner's criteria for autism. Historical data were obtained from medical and social service records but, except for four doubtful cases, physical and neurological examination was within normal limits.

The situation is quite the opposite with childhood schizophrenia. Gittelmann and Birch (1967) found that CNS pathology was evident in 80% of 97 children diagnosed as childhood schizophrenia. Even more impressive was an important study by Taft and Goldfarb (1964). They compared three groups of children (schizophrenic, siblings of the schizophrenics, and normal controls) aged 6–11 years on 83 items relating to prenatal, natal, and postnatal complications of pregnancy possibly related to the production of minimal brain damage. The data used were derived from a neurologist's interview with the mother and hospital and physician records. The results indicated a very significant higher incidence of birth complications in the schizophrenic boys than in either their siblings or the controls. The results were in the same direction for schizophrenic girls but were of doubtful significance.

The two important methodological points to note about this study are the use of hospital records and the use of sibling controls. Since the ultimate diagnosis of childhood schizophrenia would be unknown at the time of birth, *the hospital records represent uncontaminated data* concerning neurological factors and thus render the evidence very weighty. Similar findings were obtained by Vorster (1960) in a less well-controlled study.

3. ACQUIRED ABNORMALITY IN CHILD PRODUCED BY FAMILY DYNAMICS

The constitutional-defect theories described above have been relatively unpopular compared with the dynamic theories put forward to account for psychotic behavior in childhood.

The most popular of these theories have implicated the personality of the unfortunate mother of these children. Thus, Reiser and Brown (1964) refer to the mother as fused and detached, and as overprotective; Garcia and Sarnis (1964) regard the disorder as arising as a result of maternal persecution; while, at the very least, the mother is regarded as abnormal (Tietze, 1949). Somewhat less extreme is Despert's (1951) view, based on prolonged observation of a single mother, that the autistic behavior is produced by rejection of the child by the mother. The abnormal maternal attitude results from conflict over sex leading to the child being regarded as illegitimate. Despert attempts to show that the same pattern of

rejection was developing in the mother's attitude toward her second child who was saved only by being removed from the mother's control.

Quite different is the view of Mahler (1952) who regards symbiotic psychosis as resulting from a failure on the part of the child to separate himself from initial dependence on the mother; a failure which may arise from constitutional inadequacy in the child or from the incompetence of an inadequate mother.

Both parents and, particularly, inadequate relations between them have been implicated by several workers (Despert, 1938, 1947; Boatman and Szurek, 1960; Szurek, 1956; Rank, 1949, 1955) while the father's role has been examined by Eisenberg (1957b) who found the "schizophrenogenic" father as common as the "schizophrenogenic" mother.

The empirical evidence, however, does not support these interpretations. While some evidence imputing abnormality in the parents has been found (Goldfarb et al, 1966; Singer and Wynne, 1963), two extensive and careful studies have failed to find any such correlation. Thus, Pitfield and Oppenheim (1964) administered the Oppenheim Attitude Inventory (covering ten child-rearing areas and very well standardized) to 100 mothers each of psychotic, mongol, and normal children, matched for age of mothers, family size, and sex and age of child in same ordinal position and social class. Factor analysis of the Inventory shows that it assesses two main attitudes: strictness of training and acceptance/rejection of the child by the mother. The study showed clearly that the mothers of the psychotic children were not markedly different from the other mothers. Indeed, they tended to be less strict with their children and to reject their children less— a remarkable finding, considering the stresses and strains to which they had been exposed. Similarly Creak and Ini (1960), after a very careful examination of the parents of 102 psychotic children, conclude drily that "this study hardly supports the view that parental personalities and child-rearing attitudes as seen in our sample are a principal cause of childhood psychosis." Goldfarb (1961) pointed out a difference between the families of organic and nonorganic schizophrenics. The families of the organic schizophrenic children were better integrated. He considered that organic schizophrenia produced some family disturbance; whereas severe family disturbance produced nonorganic schizophrenia.

This, however, is to beg the question. In general, it is equally likely that, where an organic basis for the disorder is suggested, the family will feel less guilty, but that where no organic basis can be found, the family will feel more guilty. In general, of course, attributing *causation* to family disturbance involves the same kind of faulty logic as is involved in the assessment of psychotherapy. In this case, the surprising thing is the stability and love for the children of many mothers in the face of the most extreme difficulties. This argument is, of course, rejected by the proponents of a psychodynamic explanation who argue that the adjustment" is skin-deep only and conceals severe pathology (e.g., Szurek, 1956).

4. THE ECLECTIC VIEWPOINT

Finally, it should be noted that Kanner (1949; Kanner and Eisenberg, 1955; Eisenberg and Kanner, 1956) and some others (e.g., Weiland and Rudnick, 1961) have adopted the position that probably both constitutional and environmental factors are significant, with the respective weights varying from child to child. Thus Kanner, while tending to reject biological theories and accept the "parental pathology" explanation, admits the difficulty of explaining how it is that such parents are able to bring up several normal children. On the other hand, he is unwilling to accept the possibility that the unusual behavior of the parents toward their autistic child is entirely produced in reaction to the child's bizarre behavior. These parents, he argues, were clearly abnormal before the birth of the child and may possibly be variants of autism themselves.

5. CONCLUSION

It would appear that direct evidence of genetic inheritance of psychosis in childhood has not yet been provided but that it is not impossible that it will be demonstrated in the future. On the other hand, the implication of neurological factors caused by paranatal difficulties seems a clearly suggested possibility.

III. PSYCHIATRIC TREATMENT OF CHILDHOOD PSYCHOSES

1. PSYCHODYNAMIC THERAPIES

The psychodynamic approach to the treatment of psychotic children has involved two main approaches which differ from each other in certain respects, but which are not necessarily contradictory. On the one hand, it has been argued that the therapist must enter into and accept fully the child's world so that gradually the child's basic fear of personal contact may be reduced (Despert, 1947; Rank, 1955; Alpert, 1964). On the other hand, the same authors have argued that the therapist must not only enter the child's world, but must do so in an active, directive manner, so as to produce stability of adult response. The *degree* of activity on the part of the therapist has varied from the very cautious approach of Betz (1947) to the firmness of Goldfarb (1965) and the very active interference (including continuous *prevention* of undesirable responses) of Weiland and Rudnick (1961). Other approaches have included those of Eickhoff (1952) who stresses the importance of providing bodily contact experiences; Mahler (1952) who has argued that the autistic child must be "coaxed into life" whereas the symbiotic child must be helped to reality test at his own pace; and Peck et al (1949) who have stressed the importance of group therapy for the parents, whereby they may be helped to realize that their apparently unique difficulties are not, after all, so uncommon.

2. RESULTS AND FOLLOW-UP STUDIES

It is generally recognized that the prognosis for psychotic children is very poor, and no claims have ever been made for the efficacy of psychodynamic forms of treatment in relation to this disorder. A good deal of information is now available concerning the natural history of psychosis in childhood, though unfortunately no adequate control studies have thus far been carried out for treated and untreated groups of psychotic children.

(a) DIAGNOSTIC STATUS ON FOLLOW-UP. Studies of the diagnostic status of psychotic children (whatever the subclassification might be) on follow-up have invariably resulted in pessimistic findings. Thus, Bender (1953) found no reason to change the initial diagnosis of schizophrenia in 89% of 143 cases of childhood schizophrenia followed up five to 15 years; and similar results have been reported by other workers (Annell, 1963; Arajarvi and Alanen, 1964; Darr and Worden, 1951; Reiser and Brown, 1964). Gittelman and Birch (1967) found a tendency for a substantial proportion of the children to be reclassified as brain-damaged, a tendency which has been confirmed by others.

(b) STATUS IN THE COMMUNITY. Mittler et al (1966) found that 75% of their psychotic children were hospitalized on follow-up after eight years; and similar results were found by Annell (1963) and Bender and Grugett (1956).

(c) SOCIAL ADJUSTMENT. The social adjustment of these children is, as may be expected, extremely poor. Of 63 autistic children followed up for from four to 20 years, Eisenberg (1956) found 46 with poor adjustment, a finding replicated for autistic children in other studies (Eisenberg and Kanner, 1956; Kanner and Eisenberg, 1955). Using Lotter's Behaviour Rating Scale, Mittler et al (1966) found that two-thirds of their psychotic children showed abnormal relationships with people.

(d) EDUCATIONAL ATTAINMENTS. Similar pessimistic results on follow-up have been reported for amount of schooling (Arajarvi and Alanen, 1964; Brown, 1963; Gittelman and Birch, 1967; Mittler et al, 1966; Reiser and Brown, 1964), for learning (Brown, 1963), and for intelligence level and progress in reading and arithmetic skills (Mittler et al, 1966).

3. THE EDUCABILITY OF PSYCHOTIC CHILDREN

The general validity of the above findings have been confirmed by the most careful follow-up study to date, that of Rutter et al (1967). Their follow-up results for 63 psychotic children reassessed after eight years are shown in Table 13.3. Rutter points out, however, that there are certain factors which militate against the psychotic child being given the opportunity of developing whatever capacity he has for improvement. The most significant of these is his very poor social adjustment which tends to lead to his exclusion from any normal school or from schools for retarded or even defective children. In spite of this very severe handicap, some of the psychotic children studied by Rutter made very substantial gains and the possibilities of educating these children have been clearly indicated in a number of important studies by Goldfarb and his colleagues. Thus, Goldfarb and Pollack (1964) utilized a special schooling program for psychotic children in a residential setting providing individualized attention and found remarkable improvement in both reading and arithmetic skills for organic and nonorganic schizophrenic children. Nearly all of the children had been considered ineducable at the commencement of training, yet all of the nonorganic and some of the organic children attained *normal* levels in reading and arithmetic over a period of three years. The amount of improvement was closely related to the length of time in training and to initial level of intelligence.

4. PROGNOSTIC FACTORS

Various prognostic factors have been considered to be related (favorably or unfavorably) to outcome in childhood psychosis, but most of these (stereotyped behavior, E.E.G. abnormality, level of anxiety, age of onset, occurrence of encephalitis, etc.) are of doubtful reliability. Depth and scope of withdrawal and failure to develop communicative speech by the age of five years are generally agreed to have grave prognostic implications (Brown, 1960;

TABLE 13.3. *Follow-up Status of 63 Psychotic Children*

Variable	Status
1. Administrative placement	44% in long-stay hospital
2. Overall social adjustment	48% very poor; 14% normal
3. Schooling	Less than 50% had 2 years regular schooling; 25% reading at 8-year + level
4. Type of treatment	No correlation with status
5. Autism	Improved, but still socially incompetent
6. Speech	50% without useful speech
7. Rituals and compulsions	Diminished in some
8. Delusions/hallucinations	Largely absent
9. Kinesis	Hyperactivity diminished
10. Epileptic fits	10 developed grand mal epilepsy
11. Anxiety and fears	Diminished

Source: Rutter et al, 1967.

Eisenberg, 1956; Rutter et al, 1967) but, as Rutter points out, this variable is very highly correlated with low intelligence or untestability when first seen. Rutter did find, however, that 25% of children lacking speech at age five did subsequently develop speech but that whether this happened depended almost entirely on level of assessed intelligence. Thus, only two out of 22 children with an initial I.Q. less than 60 and without speech at five years subsequently developed speech; whereas five out of eight children with an initial I.Q. greater than 60 and without speech at five years subsequently developed speech. Thus, the prognosis for a psychotic child depends largely on whether he is genuinely defective or whether he is functioning at a defective level but has a higher potential.

These results are important for two reasons. First, they suggest that the outlook for the psychotic child may be quite hopeful if, by whatever means, he can be helped to achieve speech. Second, they suggest that special educational or other training techniques may succeed in producing substantial development of abilities such as reading and arithmetic. In turn, of course, the development of language and these other basic abilities would lead to greater acceptance of the child into special classes and enable him to be placed within the school system. It is for this reason, if no other, that the special techniques developed in recent years by behavior therapists for manipulating the behavior of psychotic children are so important, particularly in so far as they relate to the development of language and social behavior in the psychotic child. To these we must now turn.

IV. THE BEHAVIORISTIC APPROACH TO CHILDHOOD PSYCHOSIS

1. The Objective Description of the Behavior of Psychotic Children

It is well known that the reliable and valid assessment of the abilities and behavior of psychotic children presents problems of considerable magnitude. In recent years, however, heroic efforts have been made to surmount these difficulties. On the one hand have been attempts to assess formally the level of performance of psychotic children on psychological tests; on the other hand, the behavior of the

children in a controlled environment has been more carefully examined.

(1) PERFORMANCE ON FORMAL TESTS. With respect to *physical measurements*, Goldfarb (1961) did not find any differences between schizophrenic and normal children in height; weight; sensory thresholds for vision, hearing, or touch; and color vision. The schizophrenic children were, however, significantly inferior on *neurological measurements* (double simultaneous stimulation, oculomotor functioning, muscle tone, etc.), thus supporting the suspicion referred to earlier of possible organic involvement. The incidence of neurological abnormalities was, however, greater in Goldfarb's "organic" group than in his "nonorganic" group of schizophrenic children. As far as more complex performances are concerned, it may prove useful to group them into those dealing with the input stage of the processing of information through the nervous system; those dealing with the output stage; and central processes. On the input side, it has been shown that the *perceptual performance* of psychotic children is generally inferior (Berkowitz, 1961; Goldfarb, 1961). In a particularly interesting study, Hoberman and Goldfarb (1963) showed that, while the pure tone threshold of schizophrenic children was not significantly different from that of normal controls, the speech reception threshold was significantly impaired. The defect would thus appear not to be at the receptor level, but rather at either the data-processing level[3] or at a cognitive level. On the output side, it has been shown that psychotics are significantly impaired in motor performance (Berkowitz, 1961; Goldfarb, 1961), in body stability, as measured by the whirling and Romberg tests (Rachman and Berger, 1964; Silver and Gabriel, 1964) and, of course, most severely, in language (De Hirsch, 1967; Tubbs, 1966; Wolff and Chess, 1965b). As far as central processes are concerned, formal intelligence tests reveal severe defective functioning (Goldfarb, 1961). Impairment of memory has been demonstrated (Berkowitz, 1961), as has more general defect in cognitive functioning (Friedman, 1961; Schulman, 1953). Farnham-Diggory (1966) has demonstrated impairment of present and future time perspective, but, by a series of ingenious experimental procedures, has cast serious doubt on the existence of any defect in self-image in psychotics.

(b) PERFORMANCE IN A CONTROLLED

---

[3] The distinction between receptor and data-processing levels will be elaborated in the next chapter.

ENVIRONMENT. The *spontaneous* behavior of the psychotic child in a controlled, but variable, environment has been investigated by O'Connor and his colleagues who studied the behavior of psychotic and severely subnormal children in a room containing various objects which acted as stimuli with different properties (O'Connor and Hermelin, 1964); and in a room which was empty but into which various stimuli (visual, auditory, manipulative, and social) were injected (Hermelin and O'Connor, 1963). The results serve as a useful corrective to psychiatric accounts of the behavior of psychotic children because it was found that these children were equally responsive to the environment as the subnormal controls; were not as preoccupied with objects as has been claimed; and did respond positively to social stimuli, such as the presence of an adult. They also, however, showed significantly more behavior which was not oriented towards external stimuli than did the subnormal controls. As Ferster (1961) pointed out, more studies of this kind are required to define the range of performances of which the psychotic child is capable, as well as to define his limitations.

2. BEHAVIORISTIC THEORIES OF CHILDHOOD PSYCHOSIS

Unfortunately, not a great deal has been accomplished so far regarding the formulation of theories of childhood psychosis from the behavioristic viewpoint. This, of course, is largely because most of the theory has been carried out by operant conditioning techniques where the utility of theory tends to be minimized and the task is to get on with the job of controlling behavior. However, four main theoretical approaches can be discerned.

(a) THE OPERANT REINFORCEMENT FRAMEWORK. Ferster (1961) has discussed at length the problem of how autistic behavior might be learned on the basis of operant principles. First, it is necessary to specify as carefully as possible the nature of the performance deficit. Ferster maintains that the behavior of the psychotic child is quantitatively, not qualitatively, different from that of the normal child, and is especially characterized by a minimal response rate which produces a low and narrow range of reinforcing stimuli. That is, behavior produces no contingencies, and since, in the operant paradigm, behavior is controlled by the contingencies it produces, development of more complex and

sophisticated forms of behavior becomes unlikely. The defect in speech is critical here, because the psychotic child uses only *mands* to obtain primary reinforcement and does not use *tacts* to obtain secondary reinforcement. As regards the *genesis of performance deficits*, Ferster points out that the parents may represent an important source of failure to provide the child with a steady stream of reinforcements, and he stresses the importance of failure of the child to develop conditioned and generalized reinforcers resulting from minimal response rate (a vicious circle thus being set up). He also points out that the process involves a two-way interaction between parent and child. Ferster's theory might appear, in fact, to be a translation into operant terms of Kanner's "refrigerator parent" concept. However, it should be noted that Ferster does not here consider the possibility of a constitutional defect as producing the initiation of the operant learning situation, although in a later paper (Ferster and DeMyer, 1962), the possible importance of physiological factors is explicitly mentioned.

Cowan et al (1965) have argued that slow learning in autistic children may arise from any or all of four factors: a deficit in biological capacity (Bender); a lack of experience (Ferster); a lack of positive motivation; or a strong negative motivation. In a most ingenious experiment, reminiscent of the Zimmerman and Grosz approach to hysterical blindness,[4] they were able to show that autistic children tended to perform significantly below chance level on a concept-formation test rather than at a chance level, thus implicating strong negative motivation or withdrawal. Thus, as Kanner has suggested, withdrawal may be the most important component of psychotic behavior, though these findings of Cowan et al (1965) do not necessarily conflict with Ferster's model, since strong negative motivation may be a relatively late *consequence* of a history of inadequate reinforcement, rather than the primary difficulty.

(b) THE APPROACH-AVOIDANCE CONFLICT FRAMEWORK. Phillips (1957) has argued that autistic children tend to be first-born males and learn over-assertiveness to the point of expecting too much from the environment. This predisposes him to failure, temper outbursts, and the general symptom complex associated with autism. It seems doubtful whether a theory of

---

[4] See Chapter 9.

this kind could hope to account for such a severe disorder.

(c) THE RECEPTOR-SHIFT FAILURE FRAME-WORK. It has been suggested that, in psychotic children, there has been a failure to shift from dependence on "contact" receptors (touch) to dependence on "distance" receptors (eye, ear) (Eickhoff, 1952; Schopler, 1965). In normal children, this shift take place abruptly at about six months and is critical with respect to future cognitive development. Failure to make the shift, it is argued, produces the apparent "blindness" and "deafness" (or visual and auditory imperception) so characteristic of the psychotic child. This theory is plausible but no satisfactory test of it has yet been performed.

(d) THE INFORMATION-PROCESSING FRAME-WORK. This is in many ways the most plausible of the theories put forward to account for the genesis of psychotic behavior. Basically, it argues that the primary defect in psychotic children relates not to the peripheral input or output sides, nor to the peripheral processes, but rather to the preliminary organization of adequately received information for trans-mission to the highest cortical centers.[5] The child, in effect, has great difficulty in sorting out and discriminating between items of input. A series of studies by (O'Connor and Hermelin, 1967; Hermelin and O'Connor, 1964, 1965) give some empirical support to this theory, as do others. It has already been mentioned that Hoberman and Goldfarb (1963) found a defect in speech reception but not pure tone thresholds. Metz (1967) showed that psychotic children preferred a high volume level of sound, while Tubbs (1966) found psychotic children signifi-cantly impaired on auditory decoding and encoding tasks (but not on visual decoding tasks) as measured by the Illinois Test of Psycholinguistic Abilities. Pronovost et al (1966) showed that psychotic children usually mis-understood verbal instructions *unless the instruction was accompanied by an appropriate nonverbal gesture.*

It seems likely, therefore, that the basic defect in psychotic children may lie at some stage in the processing of incoming information, which is higher than the sensory receptor level but lower than the cortical level. Such a theory would, of course, be in no way a contradiction of Ferster's (1961) model, since such a primary

deficit would lead to attempts to deal with it and hence operant conditioning would immedi-ately be involved.

V. BEHAVIOR THERAPY WITH PSYCHOTIC CHILDREN[6]

An impressively large number of therapeutic experiments has been carried out over the past few years. These may be divided into a number of categories.

1. ELIMINATION OF UNDESIRABLE BEHAVIORS

As will be seen later in the methodological section, a major problem in manipulating the behavior of psychotic children to produce positive changes stems from the fact that reinforcement contingencies, to be effective, must be programmed very carefully in relation to the child's behavior. The restlessness, dis-tractibility, and irritability of the psychotic child thus act as major factors militating against success. Hence, it has been found necessary, before positive training can proceed (as well as being important in its own right), to eliminate certain undesirable forms of behavior. Various methods have been employed to achieve this, and a selection of approaches is shown in Table 13.4. It has been demonstrated in these and in other studies that time-out (i.e., removal of the child to a side-room on his own until tantrumous behavior has ceased for a specified time) is a completely effective way of eliminating temper tantrums in both normal and psychotic children.[7]

Two studies require special mention, since they are of theoretical importance. Lovaas, Freitag, et al (1965a) attempted to control the self-destructive behavior (head and arm banging against sharp objects to the point of severe injury) of a 9-year-old schizophrenic female child. They showed that building up appropriate behavior to music diminished the occurrence and magnitude of the self-destructive behavior; likewise with building up bar-pressing behavior. In effect, they were training responses which were incompatible with the movements pro-ducing self-injurious behavior. They also showed that the self-injurious behavior would *increase* if followed by positive verbalizations by the experimenter; that ignoring the behavior

---

[5] As we shall see in the next chapter, similar theories have been put forward in relation to schizophrenia in adults. The theory will be elabor-ated more fully there.

[6] Leff (1968) has recently reviewed the literature.
[7] The reader may care to consider why time-out should be more effective under these conditions than when it is practiced by parents.

TABLE 13.4. *Elimination of Behaviors in Psychotic Children*

Study	Behavior	Technique
Blake and Moss, 1967	Continuous crying	Time-out
Jensen and Womack, 1967	Temper tantrums	Time-out
	Stereotyped behavior	Attention withdrawal
	Aggressive behavior	Light physical punishment
	Spitting, stepping on and hitting people	Not stated
Wetzel et al, 1966	Temper tantrums	Time-out
	Aggressive behavior	Attention withdrawal
Wolf et al, 1964	Temper tantrums	Time-out
	Bedtime problems	Room confinement
	Throwing spectacles	Time-out
	Throwing food, cutlery	Food-removal and time-out

did not reduce its incidence; and that with-drawal of reinforcement for a class of behavior associated with reduction of self-destructive behavior led to the reappearance of the self-destructive behavior. The latter finding is particularly interesting, since it suggests that the self-injurious behavior might have been triggered off by punishment of a different response.

Tate and Baroff (1966) also tried to extinguish self-injurious behavior in a nine-year-old blind boy. In a carefully designed experiment, they found that the average rate of self-injurious acts before experimentation was begun was 1.7 per minute. In the control condition, where self-injurious behavior was ignored, the rate increased to 6.6 per minute, while in the experimental condition, where self-injurious behavior was followed by withdrawal of body contact for three minutes (negative reinforce-ment), the rate dropped to 0.1 per minute. Following this pilot study, Tate and Baroff subjected the child to a 0.5 sec duration severe shock to the lower right leg following each act of self-injurious behavior. The shock was sometimes delayed, sometimes immediate, mak-ing it analogous to a partial reinforcement situation with respect to delay. This procedure resulted in apparent complete elimination of the self-injurious behavior over a period of 147 days. Three weeks later, there had been no recurrence of the behavior.

Thus, it appears that it is possible to eliminate these undesirable behaviors, often over a relatively short space of time. Risley and Wolf (1967) present much useful information con-cerning practical problems.

2. MANIPULATION OF NONSOCIAL BEHAVIOR IN A CONTROLLED ENVIRONMENT

In some of the earliest studies of the manipu-lation of the behavior of psychotic children, the emphasis was on discovering the extent to which the children could acquire repertoires of behavior if they were placed in controlled environments which could be systematically manipulated by the experimentsr. The pioneer-ing studies were those of Ferster and DeMyer (1961, 1962). The response studied was that of key-pressing, the reinforcers being both primary and secondary (coin dispenser; single and multiple column vendors dispensing coins and various kinds of food), a phonograph recording, a pinball machine, a color wheel, an organ, and so on. It was possible to develop various kinds of performances under these controlled con-ditions and to demonstrate discrimination and generalization. It was also found, for example, that initially, the children tended to manifest very restricted repertoires (e.g., a coin would be obtained by bar-pressing but would always be used to obtain candy). More complex forms of behavior could be developed, however; for example, by the use of the "matching to sample" technique in which the center of three windows with a figure displayed produced, if touched, a matching figure in one of the other two. If the second figure were also touched, reinforcement followed.

These two early studies demonstrated the possibilities inherent in a controlled environ-ment and inspired much of the subsequent work. More recently, Hingten and Coulter

(1967) have shown that autistic children can learn discrimination tasks of increasing difficulty on a fixed ratio (FR 10) schedule of reinforcement. The importance of these studies, of course, is that they demonstrate the basic ability of the psychotic child to learn complex tasks and thus help to justify the large expenditure of time spent in training him. They also give important clues as to the most effective techniques for training (Ferster, 1964).

3. TEACHING SPEECH TO PSYCHOTIC CHILDREN

Clearly the ability to both understand verbal requests of others and make such verbal requests oneself is the basis of understanding and of education. The language deficit of the psychotic child represents an enormous handicap to progress in other areas, such as social interaction. Hence, it is not surprising that a great deal of time has been spent on this problem by behavior therapists.

(a) NATURE OF THE PROBLEM. In a great many instances, the psychotic child either possesses no speech whatever (is mute) or utters sounds that are both peculiar and unintelligible. The initiation and shaping of speech, therefore, present a formidable problem. Lovaas (1966) has described the three kinds of discrimination required for speech. On the one hand, a non-verbal stimulus (objects, symbols, behavior) may require a verbal response (labeling or describing; texting; describing behavior of self or others). Second, a verbal stimulus (from oneself or others) may require a nonverbal response (following instructions, for example). Finally, a verbal stimulus may require a verbal response, as in conversation. Of course, there is a great deal more to learning communicative speech than this language training program which describes an ultimate aim, not how to achieve it. In the case of psychotic and, particularly, mute children, Schell et al (1967) have described the requirements for speech training. The child to be trained must have a functional capacity for speech, must be able to hear sounds, and must be able to receive reinforcement for making sounds. He must, before serious training can begin, also be able to look at and attend to the source of the speech sound (especially the mouth, of course); and, if mute, must have used his vocal apparatus to produce sounds prior to training; that is, there should be a history of crying and babbling in infancy leading to reinforcement. Absence of these conditions

does not absolutely preclude training but certainly makes it much more difficult.

(b) STAGES OF TRAINING. A number of fairly clear-cut stages in training may be discerned. Not all of these stages have always been used, of course, depending on the severity of the disorder. The *first stage* involves *measurement of the base-line of vocalization*, which may be carried out by direct observation where the disorder is very severe (Cook and Adams, 1966); or, where some language may be suspected, by the use of methods for classifying speech (Cunningham and Dixon, 1961). The *second stage* involves *the determination of effective reinforcers*. This is carried out on an empirical basis and may prove a difficult problem. Cook and Adams (1966), for example, found that each of their three children was most sensitive to different reinforcers; while Salzinger et al (1965) found candy *not* to be a reinforcer for their child.

As was pointed out earlier, training of psychotic children is often impeded by competing behavior. The *third stage*, however, may better be described in this context as *ensuring that the child is attending to the vocal stimuli and the reinforcers*. This problem was crudely solved by Lovaas, Berberich, et al (1966) by the device of holding the child between the experimenter's knees. Hewett (1965), however, has very successfully made use of a teaching booth. The teacher sits in one half of the booth, the child in the other, and they are separated by a partition with a shutter. The booth prevents the child from leaving the teaching situation and leaves the teacher free to present stimuli without distraction. The shutter has several advantages. When open, it helps to produce eye-contact and, therefore, attention to the experimenter's mouth; when closed, the darkness can serve as an aversive stimulus which motivates the child to perform to produce light and human contact via the opening of the shutter. Although the use of this booth may seem a rather harsh measure, the sheer difficulty of controlling the behavior of the psychotic child in the initial stages of training, and the beneficial results obtained by its use, would appear to justify it. During this stage, of course, competing behaviors, such as crying, may have to be eliminated (Blake and Moss, 1967).

The *fourth stage* is still preliminary to actual speech training and involves *training in eye-contact* (a form of social imitation, of course). As we have seen, the psychotic child may understand a gesture accompanying speech without understanding the speech itself, if produced alone. Hence, a most important adjunct in speech training is the position of the mouth and other facial expressions while enunciating sounds. Eye-contact training is important in this connection, as initially the child may look anywhere but at the experimenter's face (Hewett, 1965; Blake and Moss, 1967).

From this point on, the stages depend upon the aims of the experimenter, the rate at which the child develops, and so on. Thus, in some children, success has been achieved only in training in approximation to, and discrimination between, basic vowel sounds (Blake and Moss, 1967). Other children have proceeded beyond this stage to training in words and sentences (Hewett, 1965; Lovaas, Berberich, et al, 1966); in the use of prepositions and pronouns (Lovaas, 1966); and even in *spontaneous* speech (Lovaas, 1966; Jensen and Womack, 1967). A most important aim of the training, of course, is that the child should ultimately *generalize* newly acquired language beyond the situation in which it was learned, and many efforts have been made to do this (Blake and Moss, 1967; Hewett, 1965; Jensen and Womack, 1967; Risley and Wolf, 1967a; Salzinger et al, 1965).

It should be noted that Schell et al (1967) have presented some important variations on, and additions to, the above stages. They place a great deal of stress on prior training of the child in *guided* nonverbal sorting and discrimination tasks, following which verbal behavior is commenced by the experimenter and the child is taught to imitate by being taught the *movements* of speech (if necessary, by guided shaping of the mouth) rather than the sounds as such. Stress is also laid on the use of play activities to increase spontaneous vocalizations. The work of Schell et al illustrated very vividly the extreme complexity and difficulty of this work.

(c) SOME SPECIAL TECHNIQUES. Brief mention should also be made of one or two points relating to special techniques. Kerr et al (1965), and Risley and Wolf (1967a) have stressed the role of fading in and out of the experimenter's vocalizations. In some studies, reinforcement has been made contingent on the child's imitation of the experimenter's vocalizations (e.g. Lovaas, Berberich et al, 1966), whereas in other studies vocalization by the experimenter has itself been used as a reinforcer for vocalization by the child. The importance of supplementing vocalization by exaggerating the movements associated with speech has been confirmed by Lovaas, Berberich, et al (1966), being reminiscent of techniques used in teaching speech to deaf children. Mention has already been made of manual guidance of the child's movements related to speech (Schell et al, 1967). These variations serve to emphasize the essentially exploratory nature of much of the work so far on the training of speech.

(d) THE ROLE OF POSITIVE AND NEGATIVE REINFORCEMENT. This exploratory nature is indicated also by uncertainties concerning the precise role played by positive and negative reinforcers and by the lack of detailed knowledge of the importance of partial reinforcement schedules. Hewett (1965) used a *new reinforcer* for each new word taught. Jensen and Womack (1967) suggested that speech could be paired as a *secondary reinforcer* with food as a primary reinforcer, while Cook and Adams (1966) pointed out the *individuality of reinforcers* for each child. In relation to the use of negative reinforcers, *failure to vocalize* on the part of the child may be handled either by punishment—isolation and darkness in the teaching booth—(Hewett, 1965) or may be simply ignored (Lovaas, Berberich et al, 1966). The use of schedules of reinforcement has barely been touched on thus far, except for one significant study by Salzinger et al (1965). The reinforcement schedules and results obtained with a child of three and one half years without speech are shown in Table 13.5. They attempted to use different fixed ratio schedules simultaneously for sounds and words, but with little success.

(e) RESULTS AND CRITIQUE. Considering the extreme difficulty of the problem of teaching speech to psychotic children (given their general behavior characteristics), some quite remarkable results have been achieved. Hewett (1965), for example, dealing with a 4½-year-old child who not only had no speech but was highly distractible, succeeded in teaching the child a 32-word vocabulary over a period of six months. After passing through an echolalic phase, the child eventually developed a vocabulary of 150 words, at which time new words and phrases were being learned continuously. Similarly, Cook and Adams (1966) increased the vocabulary of a speech deficient child[8] from one to 76 clearly distinguishable words in 15 sessions. The child treated by Jensen and

[8] It is unclear whether the three children studied by Cook and Adams were psychotic or not.

TABLE 13.5. *Schedules of Reinforcement in Speech Training*

Sessions	Procedures	Results
1–2	All sounds reinforced (candy)	—
3–82	FR(1–1 to 37–1) for sounds	Emission of sounds increased
83–104	FR(1–1) for words; (37–1) for sounds	No success with words Sounds maintained
105–113	FR(1–1) for words; no rfct for sounds	Minimal success with words

Source: Salzinger et al, 1965.

Womack (1967) had made so little progress after 12 months' psychodynamic treatment that the ward staff was profoundly discouraged and sceptical of the possibilities of operant conditioning. After a ten-week operant therapy period, the improvement in the child's behavior (including the development of speech) was so striking that the effect on the ward staff was remarkable. Positive, but less significant, results were obtained by Blake and Moss (1967), by Kerr et al (1965), and by Risley and Wolf (1967b). The least significant results were obtained by Schell et al (1967), Wetzel et al (1966) and by Wolf et al (1964). It seems likely that these differential results were dependent on sophistication of techniques employed, rather than on initial severity of the speech disability, since almost all of the children were equally severely retarded in speech.

An interesting and important critique of this approach to speech training in psychotic children was made by Weiss and Born (1967). They trained a 7½-year-old child with minimal language (probably brain-damaged) to use sentences in specific situations but found that *it was unable to generalize the concepts underlying the use of words in new situations.* For example, the phrase "give me . . ." was never used outside of the specific situation in which it was taught. They suggested that discrimination learning techniques with reinforcement may elicit various forms of *speech behavior* in severely retarded children, but that this does not mean that they have acquired *language behavior*, which is conceptual in nature. In support of their reasoning, they quote Miller's (1965) argument that language acquisition in normal children does not follow the instrumental conditioning paradigm. The claim essentially is that the children are no more able to use language than a parrot which has been taught to emit intelligible (but not, to the parrot, meaningful) sounds.

The possible validity of this argument cannot be denied. However, Weiss and Born had been overtaken by facts even before their paper had been published. Hewett (1965) showed clearly that speech taught by operant techniques could be transferred to new situations. The point to note, however, is that *generalization itself may have to be taught.* That this can be done cannot be doubted. The problem to be solved is one of the teaching of *generalized imitation*, to which we now turn.

4. TRAINING IN GENERALIZED IMITATION

Clearly, if the psychotic child can be taught nonspecific imitative behavior, the teaching of specific items of behavior may thereby be expedited, thus short-circuiting to some extent what is often a painfully slow process. Metz (1965) first showed that training in imitiation may lead to repetition of behavior which is never reinforced, but the most impressive demonstration of this so far is the recent study by Hingten et al (1967). They pretested two mute autistic children for the extent to which 39 simple activities were imitated. The children were then isolated individually for three weeks and were subjected to six hours' training in imitation each day. Three types of imitative behavior were concentrated on—general use of the body (including the head, fingers, etc.); the use of objects (scissors, buttons, toys, etc.); and vocalizations. The positive reinforcements used were food, water, and release from physical restraint. They succeeded in training over 200 responses of the first two types; while an imitative vocabulary of 17 to 18 sounds and 11 to 18 words had been established at the end of the training period. Of these responses, however, *approximately* 25% *were imitated on the first presentation*, indicating that spontaneous generalization of imitation was occurring during training. On retesting on the original items, an improvement in score (of number of items imitated) occurred in one child from 13 to 36; and in the other from 13 to 37. After five further months of training, substantial progress beyond the imitative stage had been achieved— the children were printing letters of the alphabet, cutting out figures, naming pictures, and so on. As Hingten et al point out, this training, though time-consuming, forms a substantial basis on which more traditional techniques can build.

Similar encouraging results were reported by Lovaas et al (1967). They established, first, *generalized nonverbal imitative behavior*, using a wide variety of tasks (60 in all), progressing from simple to complex tasks (involving one-, two-, and three-way discriminations), with fading and prompting techniques, and continuous and partial reinforcement schedules. They showed that generalized imitation does occur. More importantly, they also showed that the imitative behavior can be extinguished if reinforcement is withheld, thus demonstrating the basic role of reinforcement at this stage of training. They also point out the important fact that some behaviors taught by these techniques are, once acquired, extremely resistant to extinction. Behavior such as swimming, once imitated, seems to be intrinsically reinforcing and to become "locked in." In the second stage of their experiments on generalized imitation, Lovaas et al (1967) showed that control of the imitated behavior could be gradually shifted, first from nonverbal to verbal control, and then from experimentation to subject self-control. The tasks studied here included personal hygiene, games played according to rules, appropriate sex-role behavior, drawing and printing, and nonverbal communication. A particularly striking illustration is given of the development of drawing by two children, to which the reader is referred.[9]

These studies indicate very substantial advances in training psychotic children and refute largely the criticisms of Weiss and Born (1967) that the children are merely being taught to be "mechanical robots." These studies also provide an important bridge between the highly specific training that is often necessary and the more complex forms of behavior which the child must acquire if it is to begin to take its place in society.

5. TRAINING IN COGNITIVE SKILLS

Not unexpectedly, there are few examples of attempted training of psychotic children in higher cognitive skills. However, Metz (1966) has reported training in the use of distance cues and progressively more complex matching tasks (identical, similar, and *classes* of objects); while Lovaas (1966) has presented a program of training in the more abstract aspects of language use (prepositions, etc.).

6. TRAINING IN SOCIAL SKILLS

The ultimate aim of all these efforts, of course, is to enable these children to take their place in society to as full an extent as is possible. Hence, training in social skills assumes the greatest importance. Thus far, such training has taken one of two forms.

(a) INTERACTION WITH ADULTS. Davison (1964), Metz (1966), and Wetzel et al (1966) have all reported successful shaping of behavior relating to interaction with adults. Of particular interest, however, are two studies by Lovaas and his colleagues. In the first (Lovaas, Schaeffer, and Simmons, 1965), a situation paralleling Miller's use of the black/white boxes with rats was used. Escape from shock (and subsequently avoidance of shock) could be effected by the child approaching an adult. In this way, it was hoped that the adult would become a reinforcing stimulus for approach behavior and thus that child/adult interaction would increase. Learning along predicted lines did occur and could be extinguished and re-established readily. Similarly, in a second experiment, the sight of the adult was associated with primary reinforcement (candy), the latter being contingent upon a bar-pressing response. The primary reward was then omitted, and it was found that the adult had taken on secondary reinforcing properties since the child would now press the bar to obtain a view of the adult.

The second experiment (Lovaas, Freitag, et al, 1966) is of special interest because the experimental procedure exactly paralleled the technique used by Zimmerman (1957) to obtain durable secondary reinforcement with rats and represents the first serious and successful use of

---

[9] Ney (1967) has obtained encouraging results in preliminary experiments which attempted to train general attitudes.

this method with abnormal persons.[10] Two adults were used in the experiment. In stage one, E_1, sitting some distance away from the child, said "good" and displayed a food reinforcer; while E_2 patted the child on the back. The child was rewarded if he went to E_1. Ninety trials were required to establish the discrimination of the secondary reinforcement. This procedure was followed by a similar series of trials, except that E_1 was not visible to the child; that is, the child did not know whether E_1 had food or not until he reached him. These steps parallel Zimmerman's procedure in which the rat runs to the goal box when the buzzer sounds, the door rises, and he receives food.

In the next stage, a partial reinforcement schedule was introduced, with a VR-20 schedule being attained over 1350 trials (just as the rat was eventually running on a VR-8 schedule). By the end of this part of the experiment, both children had been successfully trained to respond to the social stimulus (pat on the back by E_2) to obtain food; and their behavior was being maintained on a VR-20 schedule, that is, was durable.

It will be recalled that the critical second part of Zimmerman's experiment involved requiring the rat to press a lever to obtain the buzzer sound and raising of the gate, but that primary reinforcement was never provided for reaching the goal-box under these conditions. The bar-pressing, therefore, was being maintained entirely by a secondary reinforcer which, furthermore, was occurring itself on a partial reinforcement basis. Similarly, Lovaas, Freitag, et al (1966) now proceeded to require the child to press a bar to obtain the social secondary reinforcing stimulus (pat on the back). When the child then approached E_1, however, *he was always shown an empty hand*. Subsequently, the bar-pressing was maintained on a FR-20 schedule. The acquired reinforcement properties were maintained by presenting the social stimulus followed by food if the child did not press the bar for a specified interval of time. Attempts to extinguish the bar-pressing response following its establishment showed that it was highly, but not entirely, resistant to extinction.

This experiment is primarily of theoretical interest, of course, since it was extremely time-consuming; and it probably has no direct practical applications at present. It does, however, demonstrate, perhaps more clearly than any of the other studies of psychotic children, that the behavior of these children does follow the laws of operant conditioning.

(b) INTERACTION WITH OTHER CHILDREN. Psychotic children are characterized by a failure to indulge in social interaction with other children. Efforts have therefore been made to develop such co-operative behavior, with significant results. Hingten et al (1965) trained six psychotic children individually on an FR-15 schedule to operate a lever to obtain coins which could be used to operate vending machines to obtain food. The children were then paired on the basis of length of hospitalization and studied further in pairs. A nonverbal operant conditioning technique was used to shape co-operative behavior. First, any lever press by either child produced reinforcement. Then, to obtain coins, the children had to press the bar alternately. Next, they had to alternate on a new lever, before pressing the old lever would produce a coin. Finally, one child had to operate the new lever, followed by the other child operating the old lever, to produce reinforcement. This final stage was achieved in about 23 one-half-hour sessions. It was also found that both physical and verbal contact between the children increased during training. In a subsequent study (Hingten and Trost, 1966), cooperative behavior between two pairs of nonverbal children was shaped in stages by presenting reinforcement only if one child touched the other with his hand; then if either child touched the other with one hand *and* vocalized; then if both children touched each other while each vocalized; and finally, if one child touched the other with *both* hands and vocalized. These increasingly complex requirements were successfully established and maintained over a time interval. Similar encouraging results in training an autistic child in peer interaction and cooperative group play was reported by Jensen and Womack (1967). These essentially exploratory studies are of great importance in view of the characteristic "aloneness" of many psychotic nonverbal children.

7. A Case Study

The promise that is revealed by these studies may be illustrated by reference to an example of operant conditioning with a schizophrenic child which will certainly become a classic in the literature (Wolf et al, 1964, 1967). In this case,

---

[10] See Chapter 2 for a detailed account of Zimmerman's technique with rats.

the urgency of the real-life situation was very great, since the child in question was suffering from a serious eye-defect and his refusal to wear spectacles represented a real threat to his sight. The child was an exceptionally difficult one, manifesting severe temper tantrums (including head banging, face-slapping, hair-pulling and face-scratching), bedtime problems, eating problems, and the like, in addition to the primary problem. All of the secondary problems were treated with considerable success, and a successive approximation technique was used to obtain wearing of the spectacles. This involved the initial use of empty glass frames (to save on expenses!) to be carried around, then worn in positions successively approximating the correct position on the head, with glass being introduced into the frame at an appropriate time. At the conclusion of the initial treatment, the child was wearing the spectacles for 12 hours per day and had worn them for over 600 hours in all. In the later report, it was found that some reinstatement of the antisocial behaviors had taken place, but it is interesting to note that control was reestablished very rapidly on the second training occasion. Toilet training (both urination and defecation) was rapidly successful by reinforcement techniques, and the child was subsequently admitted to a special education class in a public school, where he learned to read.

IV. METHODOLOGICAL CONSIDERATIONS

The studies discussed above give rise to many interesting and important methodological problems which can be discussed here only briefly.

1. ESTABLISHMENT OF A CONTROLLED ENVIRONMENT

It is often desirable to study and control the psychotic child's behavior in an environment that is controlled, that is, one where the stimuli and responses can be objectively recorded. One such environment has been described in detail by Lovaas, Freitag, et al (1965b).

2. THE PROBLEM OF ATTENTION

The problem of obtaining *effective* stimuli has been discussed in detail by Blake and Moss (1967), Hewett (1965), and Schell et al (1967), among others. As has already been pointed out, while a free environment may be required for the purposes of measuring aspects of the child's behavior, the characteristic defect of attention may require the use of a very restricted environment for therapeutic training as, for example, in the case of Hewett's training booth.

3. PROBLEMS IN REINFORCEMENT PROCEDURES

Several aspects of reinforcement procedures need to be mentioned.

(a) ESTABLISHMENT OF BASE-LINES FROM WHICH TO MEASURE CHANGE IN BEHAVIOR. This important problem is receiving increasing attention. With respect to *speech training*, the base-line level of vocalization may be measured by direct observation, where emission of any sounds is very low (Cook and Adams, 1966) or by the use of special tests for categorizing vocalizations (Cunningham and Dixon, 1961; Pronovost, 1961). The base-line rate of *self-injurious behavior* has been measured by time-sampling procedures by Tate and Baroff (1966). Mobility and amount of *social behavior* before treatment have been measured by direct observation (Hermelin and O'Connor, 1963; Wetzel et al, 1966).

Two recent developments require special mention. Alpern (1967) has criticized the use of standardized tests with psychotic children, since they may lead to children being classified as "untestable" solely because all of the items exceed the ceiling of the psychotic child's abilities. Alpern argued that it was necessary to construct special scales for psychotic children and derived an Infant Items Passed (IIP) measure of 44 items from Cattell's Infant Scale. The areas covered by the IIP include motor, adaptive, verbal, and social up to a developmental level of one year with respect to normal children. The IIP was validated against the Vineland Social Maturity Scale and a skilled psychiatric rating. The test-retest reliability of the IIP over three days was 0.93, indicating considerable stability of performance. Preliminary results with this measure proved to be extremely encouraging, confirming that motor and adaptive development of psychotic children develops faster than verbal and social development. Confirmation was also found of the belief that the behavior level of the psychotic child is independent of its age. The test shows promise for use as a base-line from which to measure improvement, either spontaneously or as a result of therapy. Its major defect at present is its too-low ceiling, but this will no doubt be rectified.

A second test that shows considerable promise has been developed recently by Ruttenberg et al (1966) and has already been utilized by Wenar et al (1967). This *Behavior Rating Instrument for Autistic Children* (BRIAC) assesses degrees of Relationship (ranging from "no response to empathy); Communication (primitive affect to ideas); Mastery (stereotyping to creativity); Psychosexual Development (preoral to phallic); and Vocalization (nonverbal to use of sentences). Preliminary studies have shown high reliability. Additional scales (Social Skills; Perceptual, Motor, and Conceptual Levels) are in the process of development.

(b) ESTABLISHMENT OF EFFECTIVE REINFORCERS. It has already been pointed out that it is necessary to discover for each individual child the effective reinforcers which will maintain new forms of behavior. In some cases, this proves to be a very difficult task. Cook and Adams (1966), for example, found that candy and a puppet were effective reinforcers for one child; social attention for another; and candy, repetition of own sounds, and hand-clapping for a third. This problem has been discussed by Ferster and DeMyer (1961).

(c) SCHEDULING OF REINFORCEMENT. Not enough attention has been paid to this important problem. Ferster and DeMyer (1961) used FR, VI, and multiple FR/VI schedules; while Salzinger et al (1965) tried to use different FR schedules for two responses simultaneously, Ferster and DeMyer (1962) have stressed that, in shaping behavior by use of the successive approximation technique, a very fine balance has to be maintained. Thus, one response may be extinguished at the same time that a more sophisticated variant of it is being established. The danger is, of course, that the response-to-be-extinguished may be strengthened through generalization from the similar response being reinforced; and, contrariwise, the response being strengthened may be weakened by generalization from the response being extinguished.

The problem of obtaining durable secondary reinforcement has already been discussed in some detail and is clearly of the utmost importance. Mention should also be made of the use of prompting and fading techniques (Blake and Moss, 1967); of the possibility of punishing stimuli becoming cues for reinforcement (Lovaas, Freitag, et al, 1965a); and of the use of speech as a secondary reinforcer (Salzinger et al, 1965), all of which have been discussed earlier.

4. THE PROBLEM OF GENERALIZATION

As was pointed out earlier, it is, of course, desirable that improvements obtained by the use of operant procedures should not be confined to the specific situations in which improvement takes place. There are several aspects to this problem. First, specific training in generalization may be required (Blake and Moss, 1967; Hewett, 1965). Second, generalization may involve several stages, relating to the different kinds of control obtained. Thus, control may pass from nonverbal to verbal stimuli, while remaining essentially under the control of the experimenter. More important is the possibility of transferring control from the experimenter to the child so that the control is maintained in the absence of the experimenter. This training and achievement in self-control of behavior is, of course, the essence of normal, socialized behavior.

5. ANCILLARY AIDS

The training of psychotic children is a very time-consuming business. It is quite obvious, however, that the parents of psychotic children often come to exercise a considerable degree of control over the behavior of their children in the home, essentially by learning operant control techniques on a trial-and-error basis. There seems to be no reason why these parents should not be taught operant training principles so that they can apply them more systematically. Little has so far been accomplished in this direction, but there is definite evidence that it can be done (Jensen and Womack, 1967; Wetzel et al, 1966). The burden on the skilled experimenter may also be relieved to some extent by the training of ancillary workers (Davison, 1965) and, of course, instruction of ward stafff, doctors, etc. is often necessary if much of the results of experimental work is not to be undone by reinforcements (or the withholding of them) outside the experimental situation.

REFERENCES

Alpern, G.D. Measurement of "untestable" autistic children. *J. abnorm. Psychol.*, 1967, **72**, 476–486.

Alpert, A. Treatment of an autistic child. *J. Amer. Acad. Child Psychiat.*, 1964, **3**, 591–616.

Annell, A.L. The prognosis of psychotic syndromes in childhood: a follow-up study of 115 cases. *Acta Psychiat. Scand.*, 1963, **39**, 235–297.

Anthony, E.J. An experimental approach to the psychopathology of childhood: autism. *Brit. J. med. Psychol.*, 1958, **31**, 211–225.

Arajarvi, T. & Alanen, Y.O. Psychoses in childhood: I. A clinical, family, and follow-up study. *Acta psychiat. Scand.*, 1964, **40**, Suppl. 174 (pp. 6–32).

Bender, L. Childhood schizophrenia: clinical study of 100 schizophrenic children. *Amer. J. Orthopsychiat.*, 1947, **17**, 40–56.

Bender, L. Childhood schizophrenia. *Psychiat. Quart.*, 1953, **27**, 663–681.

Bender, L. Twenty years of clinical research in schizophrenic children with special reference to those under six years of age. In Caplan, G. (ed.). *Emotional problems of early childhood.* London: Tavistock, 1955, pp. 503–515.

Bender, L. Childhood schizophrenia: 2. Schizophrenia in childhood—its recognition, description and treatment. *Amer. J. Orthopsychiat.*, 1956, **26**, 499–506.

Bender, L. Diagnostic and therapeutic aspects of childhood schizophrenia. In Bowman, P.W. & Mautner, H.V. (eds.). *Mental retardation.* New York: Grune & Stratton, 1960, pp. 453–468.

Bender, L. A twenty-five year view of therapeutic results. In Hoch, P.H. & Zubin, J. (eds.). *The evaluation of psychiatric treatment.* New York: Grune & Stratton, 1964, pp. 129–142.

Bender, L. & Grugett, A.E. A study of certain epidemiological factors in a group of children with childhood schizophrenia. *Amer. J. Orthopsychiat.*, 1956, **26**, 131–143.

Bender, L. & Helme, W.H. A quantitative test of theory and diagnostic indicators of childhood schizophrenia. *Arch. Neurol. Psychiat.*, 1953, **70**, 413–427.

Berkowitz, P.H. Some psychophysical aspects of mental illness in children. *Genet. Psychol. Monogr.*, 1961, **63**, 103–148.

Betz, B.J. A study of tactics for resolving the autistic barrier in the psychotherapy of the schizophrenic personality. *Amer. J. Psychiat.*, 1947, **104**, 267–273.

Blake, P. & Moss, T. The development of socialization skills in an electively mute child. *Behav. Res. Ther.*, 1967, **5**, 349–356.

Boatman, M.J. & Szurek, S.A. A clinical study of childhood schizophrenia. In Jackson, D.D. (ed.). *The etiology of schizophrenia.* New York: Basic Books, 1960, pp. 389–440.

Book, J.A., Nichtern, S., & Gruenberg, E. Cytogenetical investigations in childhood schizophrenia. *Acta psychiat. Scand.*, 1963, **39**, 309–323.

Bradley, C. *Schizophrenia in childhood.* New York: Macmillan, 1941.

Bradley, C. Early evidence of psychoses in children. *J. Pediatrics*, 1947, **30**, 529–540.

Brown, J.L. Prognosis from presenting symptoms of preschool children with atypical development. *Amer. J. Orthopsychiat.*, 1960, **30**, 382–390.

Brown, J.L. Follow-up of children with atypical development (infantile psychosis). *Amer. J. Orthopsychiat.*, 1963, **33**, 855–861.

Cook, C. & Adams, H.E. Modification of verbal behavior in speech deficient children. *Behav. Res. Ther.*, 1966, **4**, 265–271.

Cowan, P.A., Hoddinott, B.A., & Wright, B.A. Compliance and resistance in the conditioning of autistic children: an exploratory study. *Child Developm.*, 1965, **36**, 913–923.

Creak, E.M. Psychoses in childhood. *J. ment. Sci.*, 1951, **97**, 545–554.

Creak, E.M. Schizophrenic syndrome in childhood: progress report of working party (April, 1961). *Cerebr. Palsy Bull.*, 1961, **3**, 501–504.

Creak, E.M. Childhood psychosis: a review of 100 cases. *Brit. J. Psychiat.*, 1963, **109**, 84–89.

Creak, E.M. Schizophrenic syndrome in childhood: further progress report of a working party (April, 1964). *Developm. Med. Child Neurol.*, 1964, **6**, 530–535.

Creak, E.M. & Ini, S. Families of psychotic children. *J. Child Psychol. Psychiat.*, 1960, **1**, 156–175.

Cunningham, M.A. & Dixon, C. A study of the language of an autistic child. *J. Child Psychol. Psychiat.*, 1961, **2**, 193–202.

Darr, G.C. & Worden, F.G. Case report twenty-eight years after an autistic disorder. *Amer. J. Orthopsychiat.*, 1951, **21**, 559–570.

Davison, G.C. A social learning therapy programme with an autistic child. *Behav. Res. Ther.*, 1964, **3**, 149–159.

Davison, G.C. The training of undergraduates as social reinforcers for autistic children. In Ullmann, L.P. & Krasner, L. (eds.). *Case studies in behavior modification.* New York, Holt, 1965, pp. 146–148.

De Hirsch, K. Differential diagnosis between aphasic and schizophrenic language in children. *J. Speech Hear. Dis.*, 1967, **32**, 3–10.

Despert, J.L. Schizophrenia in children. *Psychiat. Quart.*, 1938, **12**, 366–371.

Despert, J.L. Psychotherapy in child schizophrenia. *Amer. J. Psychiat.*, 1947, **104**, 36–43.

Despert, J.L. Some considerations relating to the genesis of autistic behavior in children. *Amer. J. Orthopsychiat.*, 1951, **21**, 335–350.

Despert, J.L. & Sherwin, A.C. Further examination of diagnostic criteria in schizophrenic illness and psychoses in infancy and early childhood. *Amer. J. Psychiat.*, 1958, **114**, 784–790.

Dutton, C. The growth pattern of psychotic boys. *Brit. J. Psychiat.*, 1964, **110**, 101–103.

Eickhoff, I.F.W. The etiology of schizophrenia in childhood. *J. ment. Sci.*, 1952, **98**, 229–234.

Eisenberg, L. The autistic child in adolescence. *Amer. J. Psychiat.*, 1956, **112**, 607–612.

Eisenberg, L. The course of childhood schizophrenia. *Arch. Neurol. Psychiat.*, 1957, **78**, 69–83 (a).

Eisenberg, L. The fathers of autistic children. *Amer. J. Orthopsychiat.*, 1957, **27**, 715–724 (b).

Eisenberg, L. & Kanner, L. Early infantile autism. *Amer. J. Orthopsychiat.*, 1956, **26**, 556–566.

Ekstein, R., Bryant, K., and Friedman, S.W. Childhood schizophrenia and allied conditions. In Bellak, L., & Benedict, P.K. (eds.). *Schizophrenia: a review of the syndrome.* New York: Logos Press, 1958, pp. 555–693.

Farnham-Diggory, S. Self, future, and time: a developmental study of the concepts of psychotic, brain-damaged, and normal children. *Soc. Res. Child Developm. Monogr.*, 1966, **31**, No. 103.

Ferster, C.B. Positive reinforcement and behavioral deficits of autistic children. *Child Develpm.*, 1961, **32**, 437–456.

Ferster, C.B. Psychotherapy by machine communication in disorders of communication. *Res. Publ. Ass. Res. Nerv. Ment. Dis.*, 1964, **12**, 317–333.

Ferster, C.B. & DeMyer, M. The development of performances in autistic children in an automatically controlled environment. *J. chron. Dis.*, 1961, **13**, 312–345.

Ferster, C.B. & DeMyer, M.K. A method for the experimental analysis of the behavior of autistic children. *Amer. J. Orthopsychiat.*, 1962, **32**, 89–98.

Friedman, G. Conceptual thinking in schizophrenic children. *Genet. Psychol. Monogr.*, 1961, **63**, 149–196.

Garcia, B. & Sarnis, M.A. Evaluation and treatment planning for autistic children. *Arch. gen. Psychiat.*, 1964, **10**, 530–541.

Gillies, S. Some abilities of psychotic children and subnormal controls. *J. ment. Defic. Res.*, 1965, **9**, 89–101.

Gittelman, M. & Birch, H.G. Childhood schizophrenia: intellect, neurologic status, perinatal risk, prognosis, and family pathology. *Arch. Gen. Psychiat.*, 1967, **17**, 16–25.

Goldfarb, W. *Childhood schizophrenia.* Cambridge: Harvard U.P., 1961.

Goldfarb, W. Corrective socialization: a rationale for the treatment of schizophrenic children. *Canad. Psychiat. Assoc. J.*, 1965, **10**, 481–496.

Goldfarb, W. & Dorsen, M.M. *Annotated bibliography of childhood schizophrenia and related disorders.* New York: Basic Books, 1956.

Goldfarb, W., Goldfarb, N., & Pollack, R.C. Treatment of childhood schizophrenia. *Arch. gen. Psychiat.*, 1966, **14**, 119–128.

Goldfarb, W. & Pollack, R.C. The childhood schizophrenic's response to schooling in a residential treatment center. In Hoch, P.H. & Zubin, J. (eds.). *The evaluation of psychiatric treatment.* New York: Grune & Stratton, 1964, pp. 221–246.

Hermelin, B. & O'Connor, N. The response and self-generated behavior of severely disturbed children and severely subnormal controls. *Brit. J. soc. clin. Psychol.*, 1963, **2**, 37–43.

Hermelin, B. & O'Connor, N. Crossmodal transfer in normal, subnormal, and autistic children. *Neuropsychologia*, 1964, **2**, 229–237.

Hermelin, B. & O'Connor, N. Visual imperception in psychotic children. *Brit. J. Psychol.*, 1965, **56**, 455–460.

Hewett, F.M. Teaching speech to an autistic child through operant conditioning. *Amer. J. Orthopsychiat.*, 1965, **35**, 927–936.

Hingten, J.N. & Coulter, S.K. Auditory control of operant behavior in mute autistic children. *Percept. Mot. Skills*, 1967, **25**, 561–565.

Hingten, J.N., Coulter, S.K., & Churchill, D.W. Intensive reinforcement of imitative behavior in mute autistic children. *Arch. gen. Psychiat.*, 1967, **17**, 36–43.

Hingten, J.N., Sanders, B.J., & DeMyer, M.K. Shaping cooperative responses in early childhood schizophrenics. In Ullmann, L.P. & Krasner, L. (eds.). *Case studies in behavior modification.* New York, Holt, 1965, pp. 130–138.

Hingten, J.N. & Trost, F.C. Shaping cooperative responses in early childhood schizophrenics: II. Reinforcement of mutual physical contact and vocal responses. In Ulrich, R., Stachnik, T., & Mabry, J. (eds.). *Control of human behavior.* Chicago: Scott Foresman, 1966, pp. 110–113.

Hoberman, S.E. & Goldfarb, W. Speech reception thresholds in schizophrenic children. *J. Speech Hear. Res.*, 1963, **6**, 101–106.

Jensen, G.D. & Womack, M.G. Operant conditioning techniques applied in the treatment of an autistic child. *Amer. J. Orthopsychiat.*, 1967, **37**, 30–34.

Kallman, F.J. & Roth, B. Genetic aspects of preadolescent schizophrenia. *Amer. J. Psychiat.*, 1956, **112**, 599–606.

Kanner, L. Autistic disturbances of affective contact. *Nerv. Child*, 1943, **2**, 217–250.

Kanner, L. Irrelevant and metaphorical language in early infantile autism. *Amer. J. Psychiat.*, 1946, **103**, 242–246.

Kanner, L. Problems of nosology and psychodynamics of early infantile autism. *Amer. J. Orthopsychiat.*, 1949, **19**, 416–426.

Kanner, L. The conception of wholes and parts in early infantile autism. *Amer. J. Psychiat.*, 1951, **108**, 23–26.

Kanner, L. To what extent is early infantile autism determined by constitutional inadequacies? *Res. Publ. Assoc. nerv. ment. Dis.*, 1954, **33**, 378–385.

Kanner, L. & Eisenberg, L. Notes on the follow-up studies of autistic children. In Hoch, P.H. & Zubin, J. (eds.). *Psychopathology of childhood.* New York: Grune & Stratton, 1955, pp. 227–239.

Kerr, N., Meyerson, L., & Michael, J. A procedure for shaping vocalizations in a mute child. In Ullmann, L.P. & Krasner, L. (eds.). *Case studies in behavior modification.* New York: Holt, 1965, pp. 366–370.

Leff, R. Behavior modification and the psychoses of childhood. *Psychol. Bull.*, 1968, **69**, 396–409.

Lotter, V. Epidemiology of autistic conditions in young children: I. Prevalence. *Social Psychiat.*, 1966, **1**, 124–137.

Lovaas, O.I. A program for the establishment of speech in psychotic children. In Wing, J.K. (ed.). *Early childhood autism.* London: Pergamon, 1966, pp. 115–144.

Lovaas, O.I., Berberich, J.P., Perloff, B.F., & Schaeffer, B. Acquisition of imitative speech by schizophrenic children. *Science*, 1966, **151**, 705–707.

Lovaas, O.I., Freitag, G., Gold, V.J., & Kassorla, I.C. Experimental studies in childhood schizophrenia: analysis of self-destructive behavior. *J. exp. Child Psychol.*, 1965, **2**, 67–84 (a).

Lovaas, O.I., Freitag, G., Gold, V.J., & Kassorla, I.C. Recording apparatus and procedure for observation of behaviors of children in free play settings. *J. exp. Child Psychol.*, 1965, **2**, 108–120 (b).

Lovaas, O.I., Freitag, G., Kinder, M.I., Rubenstein, B.D., Schaeffer, B., & Simmons, J.Q. Establishment of social reinforcers in two schizophrenic children on the basis of food. *J. exp. Child Psychol.*, 1966, **4**, 109–125.

Lovaas, O.I., Freitas, L., Nelson, K., & Whalen, C. The establishment of imitation and its use for the development of complex behavior in schizophrenic children. *Behav. Res. Ther.*, 1967, **5**, 171–181.

Lovaas, O.I., Schaeffer, B.M., & Simmons, J.Q. Building social behavior in autistic children by use of electric shock. *J. exp. Res. Pers.*, 1965, **1**, 99–109.

Mahler, M.S. On child psychoses and schizophrenia: autistic and symbiotic psychoses. In Eissler, R.S., Freud, A., Hartmann, H., & Kris, E. (eds.). *The psychoanalytic study of the child*. London: Imago Publ. Co., 1952 (Vol. VII, pp. 286–305).

Mahler, M., Ross, J.R., & De Fries, Z. Clinical studies in benign and malignant cases of childhood psychosis. *Amer. J. Orthopsychiat.*, 1949, **19**, 295–305.

Menolascino, F.J. Autistic reactions in early childhood: differential diagnostic considerations. *J. Child Psychol. Psychiat.*, 1965, **6**, 203 218.

Metz, J.R. Conditioning generalized imitation in autistic children. *J. exp. Child Psychol.*, 1965, **2**, 389–399.

Metz, J.R. Conditioning social and intellectual skills in autistic children. In Fisher, J. & Harris, R.E. (eds.). *Reinforcement theory in psychological treatment—a symposium*. California Mental Health Res. Monogr., No. 8, 1966 (pp. 40–49).

Metz, J.R. Stimulation level preferences of autistic children. *J. abnorm. Psychol.*, 1967, **72**, 529–535.

Miller, G.A. Some preliminaries to psycholinguistics. *Amer. Psychol.*, 1965, **20**, 15–20.

Mittler, P., Gillies, S., & Jukes, E. A follow-up report on a group of psychotic children. *J. ment. Defic. Res.*, 1966, **10**, 73–83.

Ney, P. Operant conditioning of schizophrenic children. *Canad. Psychiat. Assoc. J.*, 1967, **12**, 9–15.

Norman, E. Reality relationships of schizophrenic children. *Brit. J. med. Psychol.*, 1954, **27**, 126–141.

Norman, E. Affect and withdrawal in schizophrenic children. *Brit. J. med. Psychol.*, 1955, **28**, 1–18.

O'Connor, N. & Hermelin, B. Measures of distance and mobility in psychotic children and severely subnormal controls. *Brit. J. soc. clin. Psychol.*, 1964, **3**, 29–33.

O'Connor, N. & Hermelin, B. Auditory and visual memory in autistic and normal children. *J. ment. Defic. Res.*, 1967, **11**, 126–131.

Peck, H., Rabinovitch, R.D., & Cramer, J.B. A treatment program for parents of schizophrenic children. *Amer. J. Orthopsychiat.*, 1949, **19**, 592–598.

Phillips, E.L. Contributions to a learning theory account of childhood autisms. *J. Psychol.*, 1957, **43**, 117–125.

Pitfield, M. & Oppenheim, A.N. Child rearing attitudes of mothers of psychotic children. *J. Child Psychol., Psychiat.*, 1964, **5**, 51–57.

Pollack, M. & Gittelman, R.K. Siblings of childhood schizophrenics: a review. *Amer. J. Orthopsychiat.*, 1964, **34**, 868–874.

Potter, H.W. Schizophrenia in children. *Amer. J. Psychiat.*, 1933, **89**, 1253–1269.

Pronovost, W. The speech behavior and language comprehension of autistic children. *J. chronic Dis.*, 1961, **13**, 228–233.

Pronovost, W., Wakstein, M.P., & Wakstein, D.J. A longitudinal study of the speech behavior and language comprehension of fourteen children diagnosed atypical or autistic. *Except. Child.*, 1966, **33**, 19–26.

Rachman, S. & Berger, M. Whirling and postural control in schizophrenic children. *J. Child Psychol. Psychiat.*, 1963, **4**, 137–157.

Rank, B. Adaptation of the psychoanalytic technique for the treatment of young children with atypical development. *Amer. J. Orthopsychiat.*, 1949, **19**, 130–139.

Rank, B. Intensive study and treatment of preschool children who show marked personality deviations, or "atypical development," and their parents. In Caplan, G. (ed.). *Emotional problems of early childhood.* London: Tavistock, 1955, pp. 491–501.

Reiser, D.E. & Brown, J. Patterns of later development in children with infantile psychosis. *J. Amer. Acad. Child Psychiat.*, 1964, **3**, 650–667.

Rimland, B. *Infantile autism.* New York: Appleton-Century-Crofts, 1964.

Risley, T. & Wolf, M. Establishing functional speech in echolalic children. *Behav. Res. Ther.*, 1967, **5**, 73–88 (a).

Risley, T.R. & Wolf, M.M. Experimental manipulation of autistic behaviors and generalization into the home. In Bijou, S.W. & Baer, D.M. (eds.). *Child development: readings in experimental analysis.* New York: Appleton-Century-Crofts, 1967, pp. 184–194 (b).

Ruttenberg, B.A., Dratman, M.L., Fraknoi, J., & Wenar, C. An instrument for evaluating autistic children. *J. Amer. Acad. Child Psychiat.*, 1966, **5**, 453–478.

Rutter, M. Psychotic disorders in early childhood. In Coppen, A. & Walk, R.D. (eds.). *Recent developments in schizophrenia.* Ashford: Headley, 1968.

Rutter, M., Greenfeld, D., & Lockyer, L. A five- to fifteen-year follow-up study of infantile psychosis: II. Social and behavioral outcome. *Brit. J. Psychiat.*, 1967, **113**, 1183–1199.

Rutter, M. & Lockyer, L. A five- to fifteen-year follow-up study of infantile psychosis: I. Description of sample. *Brit. J. Psychiat.*, 1967, **113**, 1169–1182.

Salzinger, K., Feldman, R.S., Cowan, J.E., & Salzinger, S. Operant conditioning of verbal behavior of two young speech-deficient boys. In Krasner, L. & Ullman, L.P. (eds.). *Research in behavior modification.* New York: Holt, 1965, pp. 82–106.

Schain, R.J. & Yannet, H. Infantile autism: an analysis of 50 cases and a consideration of certain relevant neurophysiological concepts. *J. Pediat.*, 1960, **57**, 560–567.

Schell, R.E., Stark, J., & Giddan, J.J. Development of language behavior in an autistic child. *J. Speech Hear. Dis.*, 1967, **32**, 51–64.

Schopler, E. Early infantile autism and receptor processes. *Arch. gen. Psychiat.*, 1965, **13**, 327–335.

Schulman, I. Concept formation in the schizophrenic child. *J. clin. Psychol.*, 1953, **9**, 11–15.

Silver, A.A. & Gabriel, H.P. The association of schizophrenia in childhood with primitive postural responses and decreased muscle tone. *Develop. Med. Child Neurol.*, 1964, **6**, 495–497.

Simon, G.B. & Gillies, S.M. Some physical characteristics of a group of psychotic children. *Brit. J. Psychiat.*, 1964, **110**, 104–107.

Singer, M.T. & Wynne, L.C. Differentiating characteristics of parents of childhood schizophrenics, childhood neurotics, and young adult schizophrenics. *Amer. J. Psychiat.*, 1963, **120**, 234–243.

Szurek, S.A. Psychotic episodes and psychotic maldevelopment. *Amer. J. Orthopsychiat.*, 1956, **26**, 519–543.

Taft, L.T. & Goldfarb, W. Prenatal and perinatal factors in childhood schizophrenia. *Developm. Med. Child Neurol.*, 1964, **6**, 32–43.

Tate, B.G. & Baroff, G.S. Aversive control of self-injurious behavior in a psychotic boy. *Behav. Res. Ther.*, 1966, **4**, 281–287.

Tietze, T. A study of mothers of schizophrenic patients. *Psychiatry*, 1949, **12**, 55–65.

Tilton, J.R., DeMyer, M.K., & Loew, L.H. *Annotated bibliography on childhood schizophrenia, 1955–1964.* New York: Grune & Stratton, 1966.

Tubbs, V.K. Types of linguistic disability in psychotic children. *J. ment. Defic. Res.*, 1966, **10**, 230–240.

Vorster, D. An investigation into the part played by organic factors in childhood schizophrenia. *J. ment. Sci.*, 1960, **106**, 494–522.

Weiland, I.H. & Rudnick, R. Considerations of the development and treatment of autistic childhood psychosis. In Eissler, R.S., Freud, A., Hartmann, H., & Kris, M. (eds.). *Psychoanalytic study of the child* (Vol. 16). Internat. Univer. Press, 1961, pp. 549–563.

Weiss, H.H. & Born, B.B. Speech training or language acquisition? A distinction when speech training is taught by operant conditioning procedures. *Amer. J. Orthopsychiat.*, 1967, **37**, 49–55.

Wenar, C., Ruttenberg, B.A., Dratman, M.L., & Wolf, E.G. Changing autistic behavior: the effectiveness of three milieus. *Arch. gen. Psychiat.*, 1967, **17**, 26–35.

Wetzel, R.J., Baker, J., Roney, M., & Martin, M. Outpatient treatment of autistic behavior. *Behav. Res. Ther.*, 1966, **4**, 169–177.

Wing, J.K. (ed.). *Early childhood autism: clinical, educational and social aspects.* London: Pergamon, 1966.

Wolf, M., Risley, T., Johnston, M., Harris, F., & Allen, E. Application of operant conditioning procedures to the behavior problems of an autistic child: a follow-up and extension. *Behav. Res. Ther.*, 1967, **5**, 103–111.

Wolf, M., Risley, T., & Mees, H. Application of operant conditioning procedures to the behavior problems of an autistic child. *Behav. Res. Ther.*, 1964, **1**, 305–312.

Wolff, S. & Chess, S. A behavioral study of schizophrenic children. *Acta psychiat. Scand.*, 1965, **40**, 438–466 (a).

Wolff, S. & Chess, S. An analysis of the language of fourteen schizophrenic children. *J. Child Psychol. Psychiat.*, 1965, **6**, 29–41 (b).

Yakovlev, P.I., Weinberger, M., & Chipman, C. Heller's syndrome as a pattern of schizophrenic behavior disturbance in early childhood. *Amer. J. ment. Defic.*, 1948, **53**, 318–337.

Zimmerman, D.W. Durable secondary reinforcement: method and theory. *Psychol. Rev.*, 1957, **64**, 373–383.

Chapter 14

The Psychoses: Adults

For all practical purposes, this chapter on the psychoses will reduce to a consideration of the complex and almost certainly heterogeneous disorder known as schizophrenia. The amount of work carried out by psychologists in this area is so enormous that it will clearly be an impossible task to cover the topic completely. The reader should be forewarned that the organization and content of this chapter is highly selected and biased by the writer's present views about the essential nature of the disorder. At least, however, the approach here adopted may have some merit in that it is hoped that a reasonably consistent theoretical model will emerge. Fortunately, for nearly all of the aspects covered, excellent empirical reviews of the vast literature are available to serve as correctives to the account here presented.

The chapter will be divided into five main sections dealing with: diagnostic and classificatory problems; the empirical nature of the deficit in schizophrenia; theories of schizophrenic deficit; laboratory studies of the manipulation of the behavior of schizophrenics; and behavior therapy with schizophrenics. In many instances, it should be noted that the more general term "psychotic" may be used instead of the term "schizophrenic."

I. PROBLEMS OF DIAGNOSIS AND CLASSIFICATION

The use of the classical system of four types of schizophrenia (catatonic, hebephrenic, paranoid, and simple)[1] shows a surprising resistance

to extinction, even though, to a large extent, their usefulness has been outlived. Considerable controversy has arisen between psychologists addicted to factor analytic techniques as to the proper dimensions of the psychoses. These disputes resemble those relating to the number of factors required to describe the multidimensionality of normal personality structure and appear to reflect personal preferences as much as anything. As pointed out earlier in this book, what is important is not the number of dimensions preferred, but the theories that are erected to explain individual differences on these dimensions. The smaller the number of dimensions, the more readily theories are constructed. But whether theories erected on the basis of a small number of dimensions will prove more useful than those erected on the basis of a large number is a matter, not for polemics, but for empirical resolution.

1. Eysenck's Dimension of Psychoticism

Eysenck (1950, 1952a), in examining Kretschmer's notion of cyclothymia-schizothymia as a dimension of personality, gave a large battery of objective tests (including fluency, continuous addition, mirror-drawing, level of aspiration, expressive movements, perseveration, tapping, oscillation, etc.) to 100 normal controls, 50 schizophrenics, and 50 manic-depressives. Detailed analysis of the results suggested strongly, first, that a dimension of psychoticism exists, with a continuous distribution from normal through schizophrenic

---

[1] We ignore distinctions that have been made within these subcategories.

to manic-depressive; second, that this psychoticism dimension is orthogonal to the dimension of neuroticism (as shown by the fact that the tests which had previously been shown to discriminate neurotics from normals did not in this study discriminate psychotics from normals). Criterion analysis confirmed the factor of psychoticism, but no evidence was found for the postulated dimension of cyclothymia-schizothymia.

Eysenck (1952b, p. 217) has summarized the main empirical findings succinctly.

". . . psychotics are less fluent, perform poorly in continuous addition, perform poorly in mirror drawing, show slower oscillation on the reversal of perspective test, are slower in tracing with a stylus, are more undecided with respect to social attitudes, show poorer concentration, have a poorer memory, tend to make larger movements and to overestimate distances and scores, tend to read more slowly, to tap more slowly and to show levels of aspiration much less reality adapted."

The dimension of psychoticism and its independence from neuroticism were verified in a study by S.B.G. Eysenck (1956) which is of special interest in that she used both stable and unstable "normal" control groups. From a battery of 16 objective tests, six scores (relating to autonomic imbalance, motor control, etc.) were subjected to discriminant function analysis which indicated that two dimensions were required to describe the test differences between neurotics, psychotics, and normal controls. A misclassification of only 29% was obtained (21% if only the abnormal groups were compared), a very satisfying result when the unreliability of the diagnostic criterion is taken into account. A study by Eysenck (1955) also supported the necessity for two orthogonal dimensions.

The above studies largely (but not wholly) used objective, nonverbal response tests. Trouton and Maxwell (1956), on the other hand, carried out a large-scale study along lines similar to those used by Eysenck in his earlier studies of the neuroses. They factor analyzed the correlations between scores on a 45-item rating scale administered to 819 male inpatients aged 16–59. The first two of six factors extracted were identified as psychoticism and neuroticism and were orthogonal to each other.

Thus, the studies carried out by Eysenck and his colleagues appear to establish the existence of a general factor of psychoticism which is independent of the factor of neuroticism and which, like neuroticism, is a *dimension*; that is all shades of psychoticism are found.

2. SYNDROMES OF PSYCHOSIS

A quite different picture of the psychoses has been presented by other workers in the field. In these studies, a multidimensional system has resulted from the application of factor analytic techniques to symptoms as rated by observers. Among the earlier systematic explorers of the dimensionality of the psychoses was Wittenborn (e.g., Wittenborn et al, 1953),[2] who derived nine factors from his analyses, of which the most relevant are: manic state, depressed state, schizophrenic excitement, paranoid condition, and hebephrenic schizophrenia. As Eysenck (1960) has pointed out, however, Wittenborn's factors are not independent, the schizophrenic excitement and hebephrenic schizophrenia factors, for example, correlating to the extent of $+0.88$. Second-order analysis would clearly reduce the number of factors relating to psychotic behavior.

More recently, Lorr and his colleagues have carried out very detailed investigations and analyses of psychotic behavior as revealed by the correlations between rating scales. Lorr and O'Connor (1957) criticized the Trouton/Maxwell study severely and reanalyzed their data. Six syndromes which were not orthogonal reduced to two on further analysis: a bipolar factor contrasting schizophrenic reaction/belligerence with situational depression/hypochondriasis and a bipolar factor contrasting neurasthenia/depression with hyperirritability/hyperprojection.

In a long series of studies[3] using the Inpatient Multidimensional Psychiatric Scale (IMPS), Lorr and his colleagues identified ten syndromes which they labeled:

Excitement
Paranoid Projection
Hostile Belligerence
Perceptual Distortion

---

[2] Wittenborn, Guertin, Lorr, and others have published numerous papers which cannot be covered here. For a summary and critique of much of this work, see Eysenck (1960).

[3] See Lorr et al (1963) for a detailed summary of the earlier work; and Lorr (1966) for the more recent work.

Anxious Intropunitiveness
Retardation and Apathy
Motor Disturbances
Conceptual Disorganization
Disorientation
Grandiose Expansiveness

These factors were not orthogonal and were, in fact, reduced to seven by Lorr and O'Connor (1962). Second-order analysis resulted in three orthogonal factors:

Excitement/Hostility versus Retardation/
Apathy
Paranoid Projection
Schizophrenic Disorganization

These three second-order factors may combine to produce a third-order factor which Lorr calls schizophrenia.

In an interesting extension of their approach, Lorr et al (1963) have postulated six psychotic types:

Excited—grandiose
Excited—hostile
Retarded
Intropunitive
Hostile—paranoid
Disorganized

A ten-syndrome profile has been calculated for each of these psychotic types, with results for one analysis shown in Table 14.1. Canonical variance analysis of data such as these resulted in four dimensions of type differences.

As was pointed out earlier, the number and kind of dimensions obtained depends upon the kind of statistical analysis that is carried out and this, in turn, is determined in part by theoretical preconceptions. Hence, not too much should be made of the differences between Eysenck and Lorr. As we shall see in a moment, other classifications seem likely to play an even more significant role in future studies of the capabilities and defects of schizophrenics.

3. OTHER DIMENSIONAL SYSTEMS

In recent years, interest has grown in several quite different approaches to "types" of schizophrenia. Of these, the two most significant are probably the dimensions of *process* and

TABLE 14.1. *Syndrome Means for Six Patient Types*

IMPS Syndrome	Excited— Grandiose	Excited— Hostile	Retarded	Intro- punitive	Paranoid	Dis- organized
1. Excitement	6.86	6.35	4.21	4.40	4.82	4.86
2. Hostile belligerence	4.85	6.56	4.36	4.53	6.41	4.44
3. Paranoid projection	4.67	4.67	4.18	4.32	6.19	4.36
4. Grandiose expansiveness	6.18	4.85	4.43	4.53	4.61	4.54
5. Perceptual distortion	4.66	4.46	4.53	4.50	4.80	4.84
6. Anxious intro- punitiveness	4.48	4.34	4.69	6.42	4.61	4.38
7. Retardation and apathy	4.25	4.21	6.01	4.73	4.54	6.49
8. Disorien- tation	4.91	4.79	4.88	4.65	4.79	7.92
9. Motor disturbance	5.14	4.58	4.54	4.49	4.47	7.06
10. Conceptual disorgani- zation	5.68	5.06	4.52	4.26	4.47	6.44

Source: Lorr et al, 1963.

TABLE 14.2. *Characteristics of Process and Reactive Schizophrenics*

Process	Reactive
Inadequate, shut-in, withdrawn, prepsychotic personality	Relatively normal prepsychotic personality
Slow, insidious development of psychosis	Acute onset of psychosis
Relative absence of precipitating factors	Identifiable precipitating factors
Dull, rigid or inappropriate affect	Strong emotionality or tension

Source: Becker, 1956.

reactive schizophrenia, on the one hand, and of *good premorbid* and *poor premorbid* on the other. The relationship between these two classificatory systems and the acute/chronic and paranoid/nonparanoid distinctions remains to be determined.

(a) THE PROCESS-REACTIVE DISTINCTION. This distinction essentially deals with a presumed relationship between prepsychotic peronality organization and outcome of the disorder. The major characteristics of process and reactive schizophrenics are shown in Table 14.2. The process schizophrenic is characterized by a gradual development of the disorder within the framework of a long history of personal inadequacy in social relations, of withdrawnness, and of "queerness." There is no clear point at which the disorder commences, hospitalization being merely the apparently inevitable result of a long process of deterioration. The reactive schizophrenic, on the other hand, is characterized by a relatively normal prepsychotic personality structure and development, breakdown occurring within the framework of a severe traumatic episode. The prognosis, treated or untreated, for the process schizophrenic is very poor; for the reactive, much more hopeful.

It is unnecessary to pursue here the many studies to which this distinction has given rise, as the literature has been carefully reviewed by Higgins (1964) and by Herron (1962). It is strange that the relationship between process and reactive schizophrenia, on the one hand, and early infantile autism and childhood schizophrenia, on the other, does not appear to have been noted. In the light of the evidence reviewed in the previous chapter, however, it seems unlikely that early infantile autism leads to process schizophrenia in adulthood or that

childhood schizophrenia leads to reactive schizophrenia, though the possibility cannot be confidently discounted at present.

(b) THE GOOD-PREMORBID/POOR-PREMORBID DISTINCTION. Phillips (1953) developed a Scale of Premorbid Status which provides estimates of prepsychotic recent sexual adjustment; developmental aspects of sexual life during adolescence; social aspects of recent sexual life; development of personal social relations; and recent premorbid adjustment in personal relations. Basically, the scales assess social competence (including sexual adjustment). Farina and Webb (1956) have shown that the distinction between a good and a poor premorbid history is related to success in rehabilitation of schizophrenics. In an extension of this early work, Zigler and Phillips (1960) developed a scale for measuring the social maturity of individual patients in six areas of development (age, intelligence, education, occupation, employment history, and marital status. A further complementary formulation by Phillips and Zigler (1961) has related level of maturation to a dimension of action as opposed to thought.

(c) THE PARANOID/NONPARANOID DISTINCTION. There is now a good deal of evidence that suggests that paranoid schizophrenics differ in important respects from nonparanoid (catatonic, hebephrenic and simple) schizophrenics. The comprehensive and carefully designed experiment of Payne and Hewlett (1960) lends strong support to this distinction.

(d) A POSSIBLE RESOLUTION OF THE PROBLEM. In addition to the three distinctions discussed above, the acute/chronic distinction has remained active in the literature. The relationship between these four dimensions has been examined in a study by Johannsen et al

(1963). They classified 52 schizophrenics several times according to the above distinctions in relation to performance on a repetitive double alternation problem. The results indicated that the acute/chronic, process/reactive, and good/poor premorbid dimensions correlated highly together (that is, they appeared to be measuring much the same aspects of behavior), whereas the paranoid/nonparanoid dimension appeared to be quite independent. As would be expected, it was also found that the paranoid psychotic performed better on the double alternation task than did the nonparanoid psychotics. The other distinctions did not result in differential performance on this task.

No firm or absolutely clear-cut conclusions can be drawn from this brief survey of some recent dimensional approaches to schizophrenia. As in the case of childhood psychoses, however, it is quite possible that the dimensional question may turn out to be of importance with respect to treatment possibilities and success, though, as we shall see, thus far the behavior therapists have tended to ignore such distinctions. Obviously, since most of the conditioning and learning treatment approaches to schizophrenia assume that the psychotic is conditionable and can learn (however slowly and painfully), it would be important to know if some schizophrenic patients were genuinely nonconditionable. Unfortunately, most of the empirical studies to be considered below cannot be clearly interpreted in relation to the dimensions that have been discussed.

II. PSYCHOLOGICAL DEFICIT IN SCHIZOPHRENIA

The range of behaviors which have been found or alleged to be deviant in schizophrenia is very wide indeed. However, as the present author has pointed out (Yates, 1966a), interpretation of these findings in relation to theory construction is extremely difficult, since the obtained results more often provide no clue to the factors underlying the deficit. It has been argued that a given deficit may result from a failure at any one of at least four levels of data-processing. Thus, failure may occur at the *receptor level*, either through failure of the stimulus complex to impinge on the receptors or through distortion of the stimulus complex

at this level. A second level at which failure may occur involves what the writer has termed the *data-processing level*, which involves the initial organization of incoming stimuli (including the screening out of some stimuli) for subsequent presentation to higher cortical levels. The data-processing level is tentatively placed in the subcortex. The third level of analysis refers to the *higher cortical or mediational levels*, at which the organized (or disorganized) incoming information is tied in with the "apperceptive mass" of previous learning and associative structures to produce decision-points. The final level involves the *executive level*, at which the decision-processes are translated into a complex of responses. Now, the important point to note, of course, is that it has very often been assumed that the primary deficit in schizophrenia lies at the cortical or mediational level, as manifested, for example, in the thought disorder which is alleged to be a major characteristic of schizophrenia. However, it is at least possible that *the highest cortical processes are basically unimpaired in schizophrenia, but are prevented from functioning efficiently by failures at the lower levels.* Clearly, if this should turn out to be the case, there would be important implications for both the understanding and treatment of schizophrenia.

It will be impossible to review here the vast literature on psychological deficit in schizophrenia, and the reader is referred to the many excellent reviews of recent investigations that now exist.[4] The following selection has been made with particular reference to the theories of schizophrenic deficit that follow in the next section. It should be remembered in each case, however, that the locus of the deficit has usually not been determined.

1. SENSATION AND PERCEPTION

(a) PSYCHOPHYSICAL TASKS. Huston (1934) found no impairment of tactual thresholds in schizophrenia. The *reported* threshold for pain was found to be higher in schizophrenics by Hall and Stride (1954). Studies of cortical flicker frequency (CFF) thresholds have produced conflicting results. Irvine (1954) and McDonough (1960) found no differences between schizophrenics and normals; but more recent studies by King (1962a) and Johannsen, Friedman, and Liccione (1964) produced

---

[4] Of particular value in this connection are the reviews by Buss and Lang, 1965; Lang and Buss, 1965; Payne, 1960; Silverman, 1964; and Johannsen, 1964. The recent review by Yates (1966a) updates some of these reviews.

conflicting results. Cooper (1960), using three psychophysical measures (Galton bar, Sander parallelogram, and Kunnapas squares) found chronic (process) schizophrenics to be significantly less accurate and more variable than hospitalized controls. With these tasks, she achieved very powerful discrimination.

(b) PERCEPTUAL TASKS. Many studies of shape and size constancy maintenance have been carried out with schizophrenics. The most recent work rather strongly suggests that chronic (process) schizophrenics show reduced (under) constancy—that is, the perceived size approximates the retinal size of the object more than it does in nonschizophrenics under the same test conditions (Boardman et al, 1964; Hamilton, 1963; Kidd, 1964; Weckowicz, 1964); whereas paranoid and acute schizophrenics show increased (over) constancy (Raush, 1952; Hamilton, 1963; Hartman, 1962; Weckowicz, 1964). In relation to time estimation, it has been recently shown that schizophrenics overestimate both short (King, 1962b; Wright et al, 1962) and long (Orme, 1962) time intervals.

Thus, there is some suggestion that receptor processes may be distorted in schizophrenia, but the evidence is quite equivocal since it is not possible to determine which or how many of the levels specified above are involved in producing the deviant response or, indeed, whether it is the response level itself that is involved.

2. PSYCHOMOTOR PERFORMANCE

It has long been known that the performance of schizophrenics on relatively simple psychomotor tasks is defective (Yates, 1960). That this is not because of simple defective reflex circuits was early shown by Huston's (1935) demonstration that the patellar reflex was not impaired in schizophrenia.

(a) REACTION TIME. The earlier studies of RT were comprehensively reviewed by Yates (1960). These investigations, mainly carried out by Shakow and his colleagues,[5] showed that chronic schizophrenics are significantly slower than all other psychiatric groups (including acute schizophrenics); that they show more inter and intravariability than normal subjects; and that short preparatory intervals (PI) with the irregular procedure lead to longer RTs than is the case with the regular procedure (the

well-known crossover effect in RT)[6] (Rodnick and Shakow, 1940; Tizard and Venables, 1956). More recent work has extended these findings, showing, for example, that a preceding preparatory interval (PPI) shorter than or equal to the succeeding PI speeds up RT, compared with a PPI longer than the succeeding PI (Zahn et al, 1963). It may be noted in passing that Shakow (1962) rejects the notion of a peripheral defect in relation to these results.

(b) OTHER PSYCHOMOTOR TASKS. Schizophrenics have been shown to be impaired on many other simple psychomotor tasks, including cancellation, tapping, mirror-drawing, manual and finger dexterity, and fluency (Yates, 1960). Of particular interest in this connection is the deficit found on continuous performance tasks of a very simple kind. The "curve-of-work" decrement, first noticed by Kraepelin, has been verified in many studies (e.g., Mailloux and Newburger, 1941). Schizophrenics of the nonparanoid variety are, in effect, characterized by extreme slowness of psychological functioning (motor speed) (Babcock, 1930, 1933), a finding amply sustained by the more recent investigation of Payne and Hewlett (1960).

3. LEARNING

The results of studies relating to the learning capacity of schizophrenics are confusing. Thus, in relation to conditionability, O'Connor and Rawnsley (1959) and Howe (1958) found little difference between schizophrenics and controls, whereas Spence and Taylor (1953) and Taylor and Spence (1954) claimed to have demonstrated that schizophrenics condition more readily than other psychiatric groups. That schizophrenics learn is undoubted, but it appears that they learn more slowly than nonpsychotics (King, 1954; Huston and Shakow, 1948, 1949).[7] It has also been alleged that schizophrenics, under certain conditions, show a flattened generalization curve (Garmezy, 1952; Mednick, 1955). All in all, the results of studies of learning in schizophrenics are unclear.

4. MOTIVATION

The relationship between the motivational state of the schizophrenic, the reinforcement (positive or negative) that is offered for acquiring or performing (or learning to acquire or

---

[5] See Shakow (1962, 1963) for excellent summaries of later work.

[6] For a description of the meaning of these terms, see Yates (1960).

[7] See Franks (1960) and Jones (1960) for reviews of the literature up to that time.

perform) a particular response, is extremely complex. The question of the effect of reinforcement on learning and performance will be deferred to a later section. Here the question to be considered is whether schizophrenics show heightened, lowered, or normal states of motivation (whether innate or acquired), as indicated by measures of habitual levels of activity and reactivity (basal skin resistance; cardiovascular system and respiration; muscle activity). The extensive body of empirical evidence has been very thoroughly reviewed by Lang and Buss (1965). They conclude:

"The picture of schizophrenic deficit that emerges from these findings is remarkably consistent across a number of very different response systems. Latency and/or amplitude of psychomotor, vestibular, cardiovascular, sweat gland, and cortical EEG responses are reduced, relative to normal subjects. In at least three of the above systems and in verbal association, excessive intraindividual variability of response has also proved to be pathognomonic of schizophrenic disorder. In addition, the levels of cardiovascular activity and muscular tension are unusually high among these patients. All these behaviors —reduced responsivity, deterioration of associational or psychomotor control, and high somatic tension—are positively related to increased withdrawal or clinically judged exacerbation of the illness. They are more marked for chronic and process schizophrenics than for acute and reactive patients. These relationships do not appear to hold for relatively intact paranoids, and perhaps not for early schizophrenics (recent, first admissions)" (Lang and Buss, 1965, p. 95).

Thus, process schizophrenics are found to demonstrate *reduced* overt activity but may be in a state of *high arousal*, and the hypothesis of reduced levels of motivation seems not to be supported by the most recent careful studies (Venables, 1963a, 1963b, 1963c; Venables and Wing, 1962).

5. COGNITIVE BEHAVIOR

The cognitive behavior of schizophrenics has been exhaustively reviewed by Payne (1960), and we shall here confine our attention to some recent work in this area.

(a) CONCEPT FORMATION AND OVER-INCLUSION. After reviewing the literature on these topics, Payne (1960) concluded that schizophrenics are *not* abnormally concrete, nor

are they unable to form new concepts; that they may have difficulty in adhering to new concepts, when required to employ them over a period of time; that some do tend to form unusual and eccentric concepts; and that some do tend to be overinclusive. It has since been amply demonstrated that schizophrenics *can* form the *same kind* of concepts as normals (Carson, 1962; Hall, 1962; Kew, 1963; Whitman, 1963). Overinclusiveness has been extensively investigated by Payne and his colleagues and related particularly to paranoid schizophrenia (Payne, 1962; Payne and Hewlett, 1960; Payne et al, 1963, 1964; Payne and Friedlander, 1962).

(b) MEDIATION PROCESSES. A major study on mediation processes in schizophrenics has been reported by Moran, Mefferd, and Kimble (1964). In this very carefully controlled study, 79 pairs of normal subjects and schizophrenics, matched for age, education, and vocabulary, were tested individually on four successive days on equivalent lists of 125 words each under free-association instructions. Responses were scored for synonym, contrast, coordinate, superordinate, subordinate, functional, multiword, blank, and distant categories, as well as for average RT, reproduction failure, and commonality. These variables, together with age, education, and vocabulary, were factor-analyzed for each day separately, by normal and schizophrenic subjects. The same three independent idiodynamic factors were obtained in both the normal and the schizophrenic groups, and remained stable across days. The factors were defined in terms of tendencies to produce: *concrete* (functional) responses; *conceptual* (synonym—superordinate) responses; and *speed orientation* (contrast—coordinate) responses. The implication of these results was clear: *schizophrenics and normals share a common associative structure*. Studies by Lang and Luoto (1962) and Spence and Lair (1964) on learning in schizophrenics support this interpretation.

Finally, a methodologically sophisticated study by Williams (1964) on syllogistic reasoning in schizophrenics did not detect any impairment in this ability, confirming earlier results with a similar task obtained by Gottesman and Chapman (1960).

(c) LANGUAGE. That the language of schizophrenics is peculiar is a well-attested fact, both experimentally (Mabry, 1964; Mattsson, 1964; Richman, 1964) and clinically. But this motor response could, of course, as was pointed out earlier, be a result of failure at an earlier processing stage.

6. TENTATIVE CONCLUSION

The above brief survey does not resolve the question of the primary locus of the deficit in schizophrenia. It has generally been assumed that schizophrenics suffer from a defect in thinking (thought-disorder). Thus, Cameron, after giving examples of *language* disturbance, continues:

> "It is hardly necessary to repeat that such language distortions involve the patient's thinking along with his talking" (Cameron, 1963, p. 611).

It is quite clear, however, that the inference from language disturbance to thinking disturbance is not logically demanded. As Williams has put it:

> "It seems reasonable to suppose that, if speech is to be ordered, then thought must be ordered. It does not follow logically, however, that if speech is disordered, then thought is disordered" (Williams, 1964, p. 59).

If a breakdown occurs at one of the earlier processing levels, then the efficiency of all subsequent levels will be impaired (an analogy may be drawn with a motorcar engine which will only function adequately with an adequate supply of fuel and if other relevant systems are working).

The importance of the above survey of some recent empirical findings lies in the apparent demonstration that, *under appropriate conditions*, the higher level processes may function adequately in schizophrenics and that, therefore, the deficit may lie at one of the earlier stages in the chain of events which result in abnormal forms of behavior. The possibility that this might be the case has led to several theoretical formulations in recent years which may produce an empirical reorientation.

III. AN INFORMATION-PROCESSING THEORY OF SCHIZOPHRENIC DEFICIT[8]

1. THE THEORY

The basic argument to be advanced here is that the fundamental deficit in schizophrenia is related to difficulties experienced at the data-processing level, that is, at the point at which incoming information must be initially organized for orderly sequential presentation to the highest levels of organization. The evidence on which this argument is based is derived mainly from recent studies by Chapman and McGhie, though the present theoretical formulation differs somewhat from theirs, which describes the fundamental defect in schizophrenia as an inability to process incoming information efficiently. In one study, Chapman and McGhie (1962) showed that tasks not involving distraction could be performed by schizophrenics equally as well as by normals; but when attention had to be selective, especially when competing sensory channels were involved, performance tended to deteriorate. Moreover, the capacity for temporal integration, especially in the *perception* of speech, breaks down in schizophrenia (Chapman and McGhie, 1963). Schizophrenics are unable to screen out irrelevant incoming sensory data, with the result that the short-term memory system is over-loaded (Chapman and McGhie, 1964). In a crucial experiment, they showed that schizophrenics are able to repeat sentences of low redundancy equally as well as normals, but they do not improve to the same extent as normals when redundancy is increased, i.e., the redundant words of normal speech are, in fact, distractors for schizophrenics (Lawson, McGhie, and Chapman, 1964). This latter finding has been independently replicated by Nidorf (1964). Clinical data vividly supporting their position has been reported (McGhie and Chapman, 1961), and the theory has been summarized together with more recent results (McGhie, Chapman, and Lawson, 1964).

The Chapman/McGhie theory may, however, be modified and extended along the following lines. According to Broadbent's filter theory, there is a limit to the amount of information that can be processed in a given unit of time (Broadbent, 1958). While the primary processing channel is thus occupied, other relevant incoming information must be temporarily stored in the short-term memory system. The present theory holds that the *primary deficit in schizophrenia consists in the abnormally slow rate at which information in the primary channel is processed*. But if this hypothesis is correct, then it follows inevitably that, since by definition the short-term memory system can retain information for a limited time only, *the amount of stored information lost per unit of time will be*

---

[8] What follows is reprinted (with minor changes) from Yates (1966b), by kind permission of the publishers.

much greater than in normals. Hence, only a fragmentary part of the relevant incoming stimulation will be successfully processed. A further corollary is that, *if the subject is under continuous pressure to respond*, the highest cortical processes will be adversely affected and ultimately the efficiency of the response processes will deteriorate, with the appearance of language disturbance and other indices of "thought disorder."

Several points about this formulation should be noted. First, it differs from the theory of Chapman and McGhie largely in that they stress the importance of the overloading of the short-term memory system with *irrelevant* stimulation which is not screened out. This part of their theory may be unnecessary, however. It is here argued that the basic difficulty is an inability to process *relevant* information which is, for the schizophrenic, often presented at a rate faster than his primary processing channel can handle. Second, the present theory stresses the importance of pressure to respond.

Several lines of evidence suggest the plausibility of this theory. Thus, Harwood and Naylor (1963) showed that psychotics (mainly schizophrenics) took significantly longer than nonpsychotics to perceive a single unit in a perceptual task and also took longer to perceive multiple units. They concluded that their results demonstrated "a reduced rate of integration in basic perceptual assimilation which thereby deprives higher mental processes of an adequate supply of material to manipulate" (Harwood and Naylor, 1963, p. 35)—a conclusion exactly in line with the present formulation. Payne and Hewlett (1960) used the Nufferno Level and Speed Tests with carefully chosen groups of normals, neurotics, and schizophrenics. These tests make use of the Thurstone letter series problems. In the power form of the test (where speed is irrelevant and achievement solely a function of level of ability), the schizophrenics were not differentiated from the other groups. However, in the speed versions of the test (where level of ability is unimportant), they found schizophrenics to be significantly slower than normals or neurotics. In a factor analysis of their data, Payne and Hewlett obtained a clear-cut factor of "retardation" (or slowness of psychological function)

and commented that "the striking feature of this factor is that it is measured by all the speed tests, regardless of their content" (Payne and Hewlett, 1960, p. 102).

Another line of evidence, stemming from the work of Inglis and his colleagues, suggests a method of testing the present theory more directly. In a series of studies (e.g., MacKay and Inglis, 1963), they have presented evidence which strongly supports the validity of Broadbent's filter theory and which suggests that normal aging produces progressive deficit in short-term memory, a decline which is accentuated by memory deficit.[9] The technique used is that of dichotic stimulation where pairs of stimuli (in this case, digits) are presented simultaneously to each ear. Inglis has shown conclusively that the memory defect is related to a difficulty in reproducing the second set of digits (in this situation, digits presented to one ear tend to be reproduced as a group followed by the digits from the other ear). Now, the dichotic stimulation technique used by Inglis exactly parallels the two systems postulated as involved in the schizophrenic deficit, namely, the primary processing system and the short-term memory system. It is here suggested that the dichotic technique, using paired sets of digits as stimuli, provides a means of testing the hypothesis outlined above. As far as the author can discover, this particular technique has not been utilized with schizophrenics. Recent studies by McGhie, Chapman, and Lawson (1965a; 1965b) did *not* use it in this way; the review of the literature by Buss and Lang (1965) and Lang and Buss (1965) mentions both the technique of dichotic stimulation and the phenomenon of short-term memory, but does not arrive at the formulation presented in this paper. As Inglis has pointed out, the technique has the very great advantage that the rate of presentation can be very readily controlled by the experimenter. Hence, it would be predicted, first, that a presentation rate could be discovered at which the performance of schizophrenics would not be inferior to that of normal subjects but that, second, a fairly precise breakdown point for schizophrenics could be discovered at which the presentation rate became fast enough to impose too great a burden, thus leading to a decline in efficiency of reproduction of the second set of

---

[9] An interesting tangential piece of evidence is the demonstration by Lynn (1962) that aging is associated with an increase in psychoticism, a finding which would be expected if the present theory is

correct. Increased psychoticism with age would be distinguished from schizophrenia mainly in terms of the time of onset and duration of the defect in the short-term memory system.

items from the short-term memory system. Chapman and McGhie explicitly mention as one of the consequences of their theory the implication that, if material is presented at a sufficiently slow rate, the processing defect should be overcome.

2. CORRELATIVE EVIDENCE

There is a good deal of indirect supporting evidence for the theory outlined above which may be briefly summarized without going into detail. This evidence also suggests some further extensions of the theory. Thus, it may be argued that the social withdrawal characteristic of schizophrenia, manifested in its most extreme form as catatonia, is a protective mechanism against excessive stimulation. That this may well be so is indicated in studies by McReynolds (1963) and Sidle, Acker, and McReynolds (1963), indicating that schizophrenics inhibit the input of novel stimulation, a finding in line with Russian work on the role of protective inhibition in schizophrenia (Lynn, 1963). Furthermore, as we have seen, it has been demonstrated that withdrawn schizophrenics, contrary to common opinion, tend to be in a state of *high* arousal, accompanied by a narrowing of the field of attention (Venables, 1963b; Venables and Wing, 1962).

Evidence from neurophysiological studies have led to formulations similar to the theory outlined here. Thus, Belmont, Birch, Klein, and Pollack (1964) refer to "primary defects in central nervous system organization"; Venables (1963a, 1963c) to defects in the "cortical regulatory system"; Snyder, Rosenthal, and Taylor (1961) to defects in the reticular activating or limbic systems.

Strictly psychological studies have also led to similar formulations. Thus, Moran et al (1964) refer to temporary inaccessibility of essentially normal structures; Shakow (1962; 1963) to a failure in the scanning process; Payne et al (1963) to a defect in the screening mechanism; and Pishkin et al (1962) to a deterioration in channel capacity.

Usdansky and Chapman (1960) have evoked schizophrenic-like responses from normals under increased rates of stimulus presentation. On a more basic level, Stilson and Kopell (1964) have demonstrated a raised visual threshold for shapes in the presence of visual noise (random dots), while Shagass and Schwartz (1963) have demonstrated a diminished recovery rate of cortical evoked potentials in schizophrenia.

All of this evidence is compatible with a theory of a slowness of processing of data in the primary channel with consequent loss of information from the short-term memory system.

3. OTHER THEORIES OF SCHIZOPHRENIA

No attempt will be made to relate the present theory in detail to other current psychological theories of schizophrenic deficit. However, several alternative formulations will be mentioned briefly. Silverman (1964) has utilized the theoretical system of the Menninger Clinic workers, particularly the concepts of *scanning control* and *field-articulation* which were originally developed to explain perceptual phenomena. Silverman relates extensive scanning and field-articulation responsiveness to the paranoid subtype, while minimal scanning and undifferentiated field-articulation responsiveness characterize the other schizophrenic subcategories, and he has formulated the concept of an ideational gating mechanism which serves to protect the organism. Utilizing these constructs, Silverman has skilfully coordinated a mass of experimental data relating particularly to perceptual phenomena in schizophrenia. Although he explicitly mentions Broadbent's filter theory, Silverman's formulation differs from the present one in two important ways. First, he appears to place the defect at a cortical rather than a subcortical level; second, he considers the schizophrenic as actively screening out or attending to stimulation whereas the present theory (and that of Chapman and McGhie) regard the schizophrenic primarily as being passively overwhelmed with stimulation which he cannot handle. The active screening out of stimulation would be regarded by the present theory as a secondary effect derived from the primary defect, i.e., as an ultimate protective mechanism in the face of an intolerable persisting situation.

Silverman's theory, in fact, is essentially a cognitive variant of the defensive-mechanism theories of schizophrenia. These theories relate deficit in concept-formation and similar tasks to the *threatening content* of the material (e.g., Brodsky, 1963; Lewinsohn and Riggs, 1962; Pishkin and Blanchard, 1963) and ultimately to traumatic experiences in childhood, with special emphasis being laid on the mother-child relationship. Again, the present theory would regard these defective relationships, if they exist, as derivative from the primary difficulty in processing material efficiently. This basic difficulty, which is regarded as being present from birth and probably genetically determined, would naturally be expected to manifest itself initially in mother-child relationships, since these are the earliest form of social interaction experienced by the child. In this connection, it is relevant to note the recent studies by Albee and his colleagues. They obtained childhood intelligence records of adult schizophrenics and claimed to have shown that the childhood and adult IQs were not different (Albee, Lane, Corcoran and Werneke, 1963); that, even as children, the schizophrenics-to-be had lower IQs than the normative averages of children in their own class (Albee, Lane, and Reuter, 1964); that they had lower IQs than their siblings as children (Lane and Albee, 1964); and that deterioration was evident *during* childhood (Lane and Albee, 1963). They concluded that the adult schizophrenic had been subjected to progressive intellectual deterioration during childhood and that the deficit was complete before adult breakdown. While their evidence must be viewed cautiously (since the dangers of comparing scores on different tests administered many years apart are obvious), the overall results did suggest a basic difficulty which is manifested from an early age.[10]

Chapman, Chapman, and Miller (1964) have formulated a theory of the verbal behavior of schizophrenics based on their extensive experimental studies over many years. It may be noted in passing that they found that "the kinds of errors that were hypothesized to be features of schizophrenic disorder were also found in normal control subjects, although in reduced number" (Chapman et al, 1964, p. 50). Their theory states that "schizophrenics' misinterpretation of the meanings of words arise in part from mediation of overt responses to words by their strongest meaning responses with a relative neglect of their weaker meaning responses, while the interpretation of words by normal persons reflects the use of the weaker as well as the stronger meaning responses" (Chapman et al, 1964, p. 53), and they have produced cogent evidence in support of this theory.

Chapman's theory does not seem to be incompatible with the present formulation. Thus, one prediction made by Chapman is that in verbal tasks in which the contextual cues are weak, schizophrenics will fail to use these cues and will instead interpret words in accordance with the meaning responses to the words which are strongest when the words are encountered out of context. Furthermore, he concludes from the results of one of his experiments that "schizophrenics tended more than the normal *S*s to narrow their interpretation of the conceptual classes to that one interpretation mediated by the strongest normal meaning response" (Chapman et al, 1964, p. 68). These results would follow directly from the present theory of a deficit in short-term memory, since contextual cues would be the ones most likely to be stored in the short-term memory system when the subject is bombarded with more stimulation than he can handle. Hence, responses would tend to be made on the basis of commonest association, that is, given his basic slowness of processing, the schizophrenic would be forced to concentrate on (i.e., pass first through the primary processing channel) the essential features of the incoming material and ignore the more subtle features. This interpretation fits well with the finding mentioned earlier that schizophrenics did not differ significantly from normals in handling verbal material of low redundancy, though this would be expected to hold only where the material is being processed by the schizophrenic at his own rate. It is interesting to note that Donahoe, Curtin, and Lipton (1961), in the context of a verbal learning experiment, stressed that "experimental situations in which the *S* controls the time of presentation of the critical stimuli are of particular benefit to schizophrenics" (Donahoe et al, 1961, p. 558).

Nor does the present theory appear to be in any way incompatible with the formulation in terms of a deficit in set by Shakow (1962; 1963). Bannister's (1960, 1962a, 1962b, 1963, 1965) serial invalidation hypothesis states that the condition of schizophrenic thought disorder is the end product of the repeated experience of invalidation of construing, which he argues eventually leads to a looseness of expectations as to whether one event will or will not be likely to lead to a subsequent event.

It is not possible here to examine in detail the formulations made by learning and motivation theorists in relation to schizophrenic thought disorder, except to say that it is not intended in any way to deny or minimize the importance

---

[10] In a recent note, Lane and Albee (1968) have concluded that some of their earlier findings may not be valid.

of learning or motivational factors. However, these factors are considered to come into play in relation to attempts to deal with the *results* of the basic disturbance.

IV. LABORATORY STUDIES OF THE MANIPULATION OF THE BEHAVIOR OF SCHIZOPHRENICS

Since most of the therapeutic efforts with schizophrenics to be reviewed in the next section have utilized various reinforcement contingencies, it is of considerable importance and interest to look at laboratory studies which have examined the effects found under laboratory conditions when particular responses lead to particular contingencies. Several issues have been brought to the fore as a result of these studies. First, what is the relative importance of punishment for incorrect responses as compared with reward (reinforcement) for correct responses? Second, what are the relative merits of social punishments and rewards, as compared with nonsocial, in changing behavior? Third, must punishing and rewarding contingencies be closely tied to responses in order to facilitate change in behavior or will the same effects be produced by *general* praise or punishment? The latter question can be rephrased in terms of the informational value of the contingent stimuli. In seeking answers to these questions, we shall look at several different kinds of experimental design.

1. Contingent but Nonavoidable Rewards and Punishments

Three kinds of studies may be considered here.

First, a whole series of studies, usually carried out with chronic schizophrenics, has shown that these patients do acquire new response patterns *when positive reinforcement is contingent upon the emission of a novel response.* In the following studies, the response required has usually been nonverbal in nature and the reinforcement is also nonverbal, hence no direct interaction between subject and experimenter is required. Thus King et al (1957) and Bullock (1960) provided positive reinforcement for discrimination between two knobs to be pulled out but, even for such a simple task, only 60% of psychotic patients were found to be testable (Bullock and Brunt, 1959), similar difficulties being encountered by Lindsley (1960). It has

been shown, however, that improved learning and performance can be obtained by the appropriate use of schedules of reinforcement (Lindsley and Skinner, 1954). Thus, Hutchinson and Azrin (1961) used fixed ratio schedules of reinforcement, ranging from FR-1 to FR-25 for lever-pulling, with cigarettes or candy as the reinforcers, and found that the higher FR schedules led to higher response rates. Peters and Jenkins (1954) stressed the importance of strong motivation and achieved this by a combination of food deprivation and subacute insulin injections. Mednick and Lindsley (1958) pointed up some of the difficulties inherent in this work and claimed that operant rates correlated with ward behavior ratings, provided the two measures compared were taken close in time together.

Another set of studies has examined *the effect of positive verbal reinforcements on verbal learning and performance tasks.* The use of the Taffel procedure (or variations of it) has produced somewhat conflicting results. Thus, Bryan and Lichtenstein (1964) failed in attempts to condition socially desirable speech; and Cohen and Cohen (1960) did not obtain verbal conditioning (first and third pronoun use) in schizophrenics, using verbal reinforcement. Similarly, Slechta et al (1963) were unable to replicate an earlier preliminary study by Krasner (1958b). In these studies, verbal reinforcement was provided for use of a class of nouns during story telling. Normals conditioned well in the Slechta et al study, but schizophrenics conditioned very poorly indeed; and similar results were reported by Ebner (1965). However, a very carefully designed study by Beech and Adler (1963) resulted in possibly the most strongly positive results so far found. Furthermore, schizophrenics conditioned successfully, even when the troublesome confounding variable of "awareness" was allowed for.

Conflicting results were also reported in two studies which attempted to train schizophrenics to give common associations on the Kent-Rosanoff Word Association Test. Sommer et al (1962) provided positive verbal or nonverbal reinforcers for common associations (praise or cigarettes) but, even when the subjects were told in advance that common associations would be reinforced, very little conditioning occurred in the schizophrenic group as compared with a group of alcoholics who conditioned very well. On the other hand, Ullmann et al (1964) found that schizophrenics gave fewer common associations than did a control group under base-line (neutral) conditions, but gave significantly more when reinforcement was introduced. It should be noted that this kind of experimentation involves peculiarly difficult problems, since clearly no reinforcement will occur unless the subject emits *some* common associations. General information beforehand that common associations will be reinforced may not be helpful in this regard, in view of the difficulty schizophrenics experience in maintaining a set.

All of these studies involved the presence or absence of a positive reinforcer for emitting a particular response. Failure to emit an appropriate response did not produce specific punishment but the absence of reward. Whether absence of reward in such a situation represents a form of punishment is an open question, but in general it seems to be now generally agreed that schizophrenics do not respond to positive reinforcers in the same manner as normal subjects.

Studies in which the effects of rewards and punishments are compared fall into two broad categories. On the one hand, rewards and punishments may be manipulated simultaneously, that is, a correct response elicits a reward, an incorrect response elicits punishment, within a given trial. Alternatively, the same response may be rewarded on one occasion and punished on another in the same subject (or, of course, matched groups may be used, one group being rewarded, the other punished, for performance on the same task). Other variations are, of course, possible. In the first category fall studies such as those by Buss and his colleagues (Buss and Buss, 1956; Buss et al, 1954, 1956) who found that verbal censure following an incorrect response facilitated learning more than verbal praise following a correct response. As an example of the second category, Johannsen (1962) compared chronic paranoid and nonparanoid groups of schizophrenics with hospitalized normal controls on a letter-cancellation task under conditions of punishment (verbal criticism), reward (verbal praise), and no contingency, each subject serving as his own control. The effects of the reward and neutral conditions were similar and both were inferior to the effects of punishment in all three groups. A study by Losen (1961) was of particular interest in that he used partial reinforcement (0/50/100%) techniques in a comparison of censure and neutral conditions and found that schizophrenics showed greater improvement than the controls under the censure condition, while partial reinforcement produced better results in the Arithmetic Reasoning Test than did continuous reinforcement. Olson (1958) also found that negative reinforcement increased performance, but to a lesser extent than positive reinforcement.

The picture in relation to nonavoidable rewards and punishments is therefore confusing and unclear. In part, no doubt, this is related to the fact that patient samples are not always comparable across studies and that subclassification is probably of significance. It also seems likely, however, that a good deal of difficulty arises from a failure to distinguish within positive and negative reinforcement the degree to which "knowledge of results" is provided by the contingent stimulus.

2. CONTINGENT NOXIOUS STIMULATION

The essential feature of the experiments to be described here is that, on the one hand, the subject may *escape* the noxious stimulation which a previous response or failure to respond produces, either by speeding up the previously inadequate response, or by producing a new response, or by terminating a response, depending on the experimental situation. On the other hand, the subject may learn to *avoid* the noxious stimulus (i.e., prevent its appearance), either by performing or ceasing to perform a particular response within a given time limit.

(a) ESCAPE TRAINING. Pascal and Swensen (1952), using a disjunctive RT test, presented the stimulus in conjunction with a noxious stimulus (intense white noise), the latter terminating when the correct response was made. The appropriate control condition is, of course, the presentation of the stimulus without the noxious white noise. Under the control condition, Pascal and Swensen found that the schizophrenics were inferior to the normal controls; whereas, under the experimental condition, the schizophrenics improved to the extent that they were no longer distinguishable from the controls. Very similar results were reported (using shock as the noxious stimulus terminated by the correct response) by Cohen (1956) and Rosenbaum et al (1957), while Lang (1959) replicated the results of Pascal and Swensen with white noise. Cavanaugh (1958) was also able to report similar results with white noise as the noxious stimulus, but this time in connection with performance on a concept formation task.

Thus, there is strong evidence that a contingent aversive stimulus which can be terminated by an appropriate response will facilitate the emission of that response compared with a control condition. It would seem likely that a similar technique could be used to *eliminate* as well as facilitate responses.

(b) AVOIDANCE TRAINING. Even more important than the finding that responses can be facilitated by aversive stimulation is the demonstration that schizophrenics will learn to emit responses faster, provided they prevent the appearance of a noxious stimulus which will otherwise occur. Thus, Cavanaugh et al (1960), using a disjunctive RT task, provided verbal censure or nonverbal censure (a 300 cps tone) if the reaction time occurred too slowly. A control condition was also used in which slow responding produced no contingency. Using matched groups of chronic male schizophrenics, one group to each condition, they found that verbal censure under these conditions led to improved performance.

3. GENERALIZATION OF THE EFFECTS OF REWARDS AND PUNISHMENTS

The question of whether the use of positive and negative reinforcers for responses made in one situation transfer to new situations is a relatively neglected topic in relation to schizophrenia. However, Long (1961) compared acute and chronic schizophrenics on two tasks involving similar motor skills where praise, censure, or neutral conditions were in force for the first task, and the effect of these was measured in relation to performance on the second task under neutral conditions. For the acute schizophrenics, the censure condition produced more positive transfer to the second task than did the praise or neutral conditions, but these differences were not found for the chronic schizophrenics.

Only a small selection of the reinforcement experiments carried out with schizophrenics has been reviewed here.[11] The overall evidence suggests that contingent aversive stimulation is more effective than contingent positive stimulation in changing the behavior of the schizophrenic and that it is particularly effective when, in addition to being aversive, it provides information about the incorrect and correct responses required.

4. THE REINFORCEMENT OF VERBAL BEHAVIOR IN QUASI-THERAPEUTIC SITUATIONS

The demonstration that verbal behavior can be controlled and manipulated by varying its contingencies (Krasner, 1958a, 1965; Salzinger, 1959) has led to the suggestion that the classical therapeutic situation, even where it is supposedly nondirective, involves essentially an interaction between the therapist and the client in which the client's verbal behavior is shaped by the therapist toward goals of which the latter approves by the differential provision of positive and negative reinforcements for various kinds of verbal responses.[12] The reinforcements may be either verbal or nonverbal (facial expression, etc.). As a result, attempts have been made to set up experimental situations which resemble the therapy interview and to demonstrate whether or not the client's verbal behavior can be so influenced.

(a) THE INTERVIEW SITUATION. A series of studies by Salzinger and his colleagues show clearly both the difficulties and possibilities of research of this kind. Salzinger and Pisoni (1958) divided 36 schizophrenics into experimental and control groups and subjected both to a standard interview situation lasting 30 minutes. For both groups the first 10 minutes of the interview served as a baseline, during which the rate of emission of the dependent response was measured, This response was arbitrarily defined as "any statement describing or evaluating the state (other than intellectual or physiological) of the patient by himself." During the second ten minutes of the interview, subjects in the experimental group were reinforced (verbal agreement by the experimenter) for emitting the appropriate responses, whereas subjects in the control group were not. In the final ten minutes, conditions reverted to those pertaining to the first ten minutes. It was found that the groups were comparable as to base-line emission of appropriate responses; that the experimental group emitted significantly more appropriate responses during the reinforcement period than it had during the baseline period; that it emitted more than the control group during the reinforcement period; and that it emitted more during the extinction

---

[11] See particularly Buss and Lang (1965), Johannsen (1964), Lang and Buss (1965), and Silverman (1963) for more comprehensive reviews of the literature.

[12] The possibility that the client may simultaneously shape the therapist's verbal behavior cannot be neglected, of course.

period. Salzinger and Pisoni (1961) were unable to replicate this result, however, but a careful analysis of the data suggested that conditioning did not occur unless the subject emitted sufficient responses to receive a minimum of six reinforcements. Thus, the failure to replicate could be a result of the fact that in the second experiment the subjects did not verbalize sufficiently. In a further experiment, Salzinger and Pisoni (1961) verified this interpretation by arranging for each subject to receive a specified number of reinforcements. When the subjects were divided into those receiving more than ten, and those receiving less than eight reinforcements, the former group showed clear evidence of conditioning, whereas the latter did not. An indirect verification of this hypothesis was presented by Salzinger and Portnoy (1964) who failed to establish conditioning of self-referring statements in a group of chronic schizophrenics. The verbal output of these patients was, however, very low, so that the median number of reinforcements received was only 4.3. Salzinger et al (1964) divided 35 schizophrenics[13] into three groups. One group received reinforcement (light flash) for every self-referred affect statement during a period when they were asked to talk continuously; the second group received the same reinforcement for speech in general on a 30-second fixed-interval schedule; while, for the third (control) group there were no contingencies. The results indicated that conditioning took place.

Finally, mention may be made here of a methodologically sophisticated study by Ullmann et al (1965). One of the major problems in this kind of research lies in controlling the stimulus-situation so that an equal opportunity will be afforded for responses of various kinds to be emitted. In an ingenious design, Ullmann et al used a structured interview situation in which six areas of enquiry were covered during the interview. Within each of these areas, an equal number of questions relating to "health" and "sickness" were paired. After a base-line measurement had been taken, verbal reinforcement was given for either "healthy" or "sick" answers, and the percentage change in "sick talk" from base-line period to last five minutes of the experimental period were measured. It was found that the group reinforced for "healthy talk" decreased in

percentage of "sick talk" and that the group reinforced for "sick talk" increased in percentage of "sick talk."

Thus, it does seem as if the verbal behavior of the schizophrenic in a quasi-therapy interview situation can be successfully directed along certain lines by appropriate manipulation of the reinforcement contingencies. This conclusion is, of course, buttressed by a vast amount of experimental work carried out in similar situations with normal subjects.

(b) THE GROUP-THERAPY SITUATION. Little research has been carried out thus far on the part played by reinforcement in relation to verbal interaction in a group therapy situation. Dinoff, Horner, Kurpiewski, and Timmons (1960) classified the verbalizations during group therapy of chronic male schizophrenics into five categories and found that differential reinforcement significantly affected verbal output. However, in both this and a subsequent study (Dinoff, Horner, Kurpiewski, Rickard, and Timmons, 1960), the results were transient and did not carry over from the training session to a test session without reinforcement. Ullmann et al (1961), however, did find that a group provided with positive personal reinforcement during group therapy showed a significant rise on a Group Therapy Scale (as rated by a psychiatrist) compared with two other groups not given the positive reinforcement.

V. BEHAVIOR THERAPY WITH SCHIZOPHRENICS[14]

The studies to be reviewed here do not fall into any clear-cut categories. In some cases, the experimental work was carried out primarily to demonstrate that operant conditioning techniques could be successfully utilized to modify the behavior of severely chronic psychotic patients or, indeed, to reinstate behavior which the patient had once had but had not manifested for many years. In other instances, the aim was to show that much of the day-to-day behavior of institutionalized psychotics is acquired behavior resulting from unprogramed reinforcement techniques unwittingly used by ward attendants and that it, too, could be modified by appropriate techniques. Some work has also been reported on the trainability of psychotic patients in sheltered workshops. The arrangement of the

---

[13] They excluded 53 subjects (who did not talk enough) from the study on the basis of the earlier results.

[14] See Lindsley (1956) for a description of the early studies in behavior modification experiments with schizophrenics.

materials to be discussed here is, therefore, somewhat arbitrary.

1. Reinstatement of Speech in Mute Psychotic Patients

In a remarkable experiment, Isaacs et al (1960) applied operant conditioning techniques to reinstate verbal behavior in two mute catatonic males who had not emitted verbal responses for over 14 years. Clearly, the major presenting problem in such cases would appear to be the fact that reinforcers cannot be presented unless *some* verbal behavior is emitted. The solution to the problem lay in the use of the successive approximation technique, commencing with a nonvocal bit of behavior. The first step involved using several primary reinforcers (e.g., candy) and discovering, by trial and error, which one (if any) would evoke a response. In the case of one patient, it was found that candy evoked a following eye movement. Once this response had been established, the patient was then required to make a slightly different movement to obtain the reinforcement, the program being designed in such a way that each successive movement approximated more and more the movements involved in the production of sounds. Then sounds (of whatever nature) were demanded, and these were then gradually shaped to approximate meaningful sounds and then speech. The first patient was treated on an individual basis, the second in a group therapy situation. Considering the severity and long-standing nature of the mutism, the program, although protracted and painfully slow, achieved remarkable success. Of particular interest was the fact that reinstatement of minimal vocal behavior, by the use of the successive approximation technique, *led to the spontaneous reinstatement of other verbal behaviors not directly treated*. There is, of course, no suggestion that mute catatonic patients are *physically* unable to speak, or indeed that they are unaware of what is going on around them.[15] Rather, they appear to suffer from a massive degree of inhibition. Any break through the inhibition, therefore, represents a major advance and may lead to spontaneous reinstatement of whole areas of behavior. In one of the patients, the verbal behavior reinstated generalized to persons other than the experimenters, provided, for example, ward personnel were instructed not to respond (as they were accustomed to do) to nonvocal requests by the patient. The second patient, however, did not show any generalization to the ward and never reached the stage of voluntarily initiating conversations or even verbal requests.

An experimental demonstration of this kind is impressive enough in itself as an example of the power of operant conditioning in the most severe cases. It becomes doubly so when the findings are then replicated by independent workers. Confirmation of the validity of these techniques was forthcoming a few years later in a study by Sherman (1965). He applied three techniques (shaping, reinforced imitation of nonverbal behaviors which generalized to verbal behaviors, and fading) to three schizophrenics hospitalized for from 20 to 45 years, and with 16 to 43 years' history of mutism. Sherman also demonstrated that the behaviors under study could be systematically manipulated by changing the reinforcement contingencies. The first of these patients built up a repertoire of 30 words over 122 sessions and retained them for six months; the second patient reached the stage of using sentences five and six words long; while the third was able, after training, to name scores of objects and use simple sentences. Generalization to a second experimenter was achieved, both within the training situation and on the ward. However, as in the earlier study, there was little generalization to other ward personnel. Spontaneous reinstatement of other verbal responses was also found.

Four points should be noted about these studies. First, it is not surprising that generalization to other persons was slight, given the history of mutism; but this is not to say that these patients could not have been taught such generalization, had the experiment continued. Second, Sherman's study, as well as the earlier one, suggests the importance of using nonvocal imitation procedures as preliminary steps towards shaping vocalization. The complete absence of any vocal behavior on the part of the patient does not make the case hopeless. Third, Sherman used a 100% versus 0% reinforcement schedule in shaping up the behavior. It is evident that the use of partial reinforcement techniques might be a powerful tool in building up resistance to extinction of the reinstated behaviors. Fourth, although verbal requests to imitate verbal behavior by the experimenter may produce no effect in the early

---

[15] Venables' finding of high activation states in chronic schizophrenics, coupled with inhibition of overt action, discussed earlier, supports this contention.

stages of training, such requests may become effective once some vocal behavior has been elicited.

A recent experiment by Wilson and Walters (1966) examined the relative importance of reinforcement and a model on the reinstatement of verbal behavior in 12 near mute schizophrenics. Three groups were formed and presented with slides which they were asked to talk about, their verbal productivity being recorded. In one group, a model was provided (the experimenter first talking about the slides) together with reinforcement; in the second group, the model only was provided; while in the third group, neither model nor reinforcement was provided. Sixteen sessions were given to each group, with base-line measurements of verbal productivity being recorded in the first, eighth, and last two sessions for all groups. The results clearly indicated that the reinforcement variable plus model condition produced significantly greater verbal productivity in the later sessions than the model condition alone. However, there was again no generalization from the experimental situation to the ward; indeed, if anything, the subjects of the experiment were less talkative than they had been before on the ward.

These experiments, therefore, serve primarily as demonstrations for the efficacy of operant conditioning techniques in manipulating the behavior of chronic psychotics under controlled conditions. However, in principle, as has been pointed out, the problem of generalization outside the initial experimental situation should not be insoluble.

2. THE CONTROL OF PSYCHOTIC SPEECH

There is good reason to suppose that much of the ward behavior of psychotic patients is maintained by reinforcement received for it from ward personnel. Several examples will be given later, but the maintenance of psychotic speech in this way is one of the more striking examples. Ayllon and Haughton (1964) measured the base-line frequency of psychotic and normal speech in a female schizophrenic and found the two categories occurred with about equal frequency. They then showed that the proportions could be systematically varied by appropriate procedures. The reinforcing variable in this case appeared clearly to be attention to the psychotic speech by the ward staff. This

attention, which takes the form of a brief vocal acknowledgment of the patient by the staff member is usually indulged in by the latter as the easiest way of dealing with the patient. In a second study, Ayllon and Haughton (1964) also showed that nonpsychotic verbal behavior about somatic ailments (which almost certainly had no basis in physical fact) could be eliminated by the use of similar procedures. Furthermore, the shaping of such behaviors by ward personnel is probably inadvertently carried out on a partial reinforcement basis; thus making the behaviors highly resistant to extinction.

A study by Rickard et al (1960) also showed clearly how such behaviors may be manipulated by reinforcement contingencies. The patient was a 60-year-old male with delusional speech. Base-line assessment showed that only two minutes out of a 45-minute session were occupied by rational speech. After training sessions in which rational speech was reinforced by nodding and smiling, while delusional speech was punished by being ignored, the amount of rational speech had increased to 30 minutes out of a 45-minute session. In this case, however, the subsequent use of partial reinforcement procedures resulted in an increase in delusional speech. In a further experiment six months later, positive results were again obtained. Two years later, a follow-up study was conducted (Rickard and Dinoff, 1962). Two 30-minute sessions were used, with periods of alternating "maximal" and "minimal" reinforcement.[16] The patient produced 93% rational speech during periods of minimal reinforcement and 100% rational speech during periods of maximal reinforcement.

These studies demonstrate that psychotic speech can be manipulated by the reaction of the listener; and it seems a reasonable inference that in an institutional setting such speech may well be strengthened by the behavior of the ward staff.

3. THE CONTROL OF PARANOID BEHAVIOR

A major problem in the application of behavior modification techniques to psychotic states lies in the accurate delineation and conceptualization of the behaviors to be modified, which are often difficult to specify. This is so particularly in relation to paranoid behavior. Two recent studies depart somewhat

---

[16] Maximal reinforcement involved the interruption of delusional reinforcement; minimal reinforcement encouragement by E on a random basis with respect to speech output.

from the usual procedures of operant conditioning which have dominated behavior therapy techniques in the psychoses and, in doind so, suggest novel ways of approaching the problem. Of particular interest is a study by Davison (1966) dealing with difficulties experienced by a truck driver who was diagnosed as a "paranoid schizophrenic" or "paranoid state." The "paranoid delusional system" was defined by Davison as consisting of a preoccupation with "pressure points" which were experienced over the right eye during stress (for example, if he lost his way while driving his truck in an unfamiliar area) and were interpreted by the patient as messages emanating from a spirit helping him to make decisions. Treatment in this case involved a number of steps involving both differential relaxation training and cognitive restructuring. First, he was shown that similar pressures could arise from muscular tension by instructing him in the production of severe forearm tension. Then, he was shown how the tension could be relaxed by voluntary control. Cognitive restructuring was attempted by an appeal to the subject's interest in philosophical matters, for example, by explaining to him that "unusual" phenomena (such as pressure points in unexpected places) are interpreted by the layman by appeal to mystical events. He was then trained in deep muscular relaxation and differential relaxation and in how to eliminate pressure points wherever they might arise. The techniques were apparently successful, and the patient was much improved on six-week follow-up.

Cognitive restructuring was also used by Wickramasekera (1967) in his study of a female admitted for the fifth time with persecutory delusional ideas and auditory hallucinations. The patient felt she was being accused of making improper sexual responses toward her six-year-old son and other females. Wickramasekera reasoned that anxiety had become attached to mature sexual responses and that this had led to regression toward less socially adaptive undifferentiated responses of a polymorphous perverse kind which previous psychodynamic therapy had reinforced by the attention given them by the therapist. The aims of therapy in this experiment were to teach the patient to think more clearly about her problems by helping her to label her experiences, and to induce her to indulge in more adaptive motor behavior toward her husband and son. The delusional ideas about her son were treated by reducing the fear of approaching her son (for

fear of sexually assaulting him) by encouraging direct interaction in which such an attack obviously could not take place; while the difficulty with her husband (resistance to sexual relationships when initiated by the husband) was treated as a problem in discrimination. It is interesting to note that the patient was required to keep a detailed record of her actions in a notebook, a procedure not dissimilar from that described in an earlier chapter in relation to the control of eating behavior. It is also interesting to note that in Wickramasekera's study, the emphasis was on active behavior by the patient, while the emphasis in Davison's study was on relaxation; in each case, the procedure being accompanied by cognitive discrimination training.

Kennedy (1964) obtained some success in treating three severe paranoid patients by strongly reinforcing with verbal approval behavior and verbalizations which were nonparanoid while strongly disapproving paranoid statements. While none of these studies (especially that by Kennedy) were well controlled, they all offer interesting suggestions for approaching the very difficult problems involved in applying behavior therapy techniques to ideas of reference and delusions.

4. THE CONTROL OF WARD BEHAVIOR OF PSYCHOTICS

Among the most interesting applications of behavior modification techniques in relation to the psychoses are those studies which attempt to modify ward behavior. Apart from their theoretical interest, these investigations are important because they show clearly that much of the ward behavior of psychotics is maintained by natural reinforcement contingencies provided by ward staff. These studies indicate that much of this behavior can be readily eliminated by relatively simple techniques which can be taught to the ward staff.

Casual observations that ward behavior may be strengthened and maintained by staff actions were reported by Ayllon (1965) and Ayllon and Haughton (1962, 1964), among others. An explicit study of the problem has recently been reported by Gelfand et al (1967). They observed (by the use of time-sampling techniques) the behavior of six chronic severely psychotic males for 55 hours and rated their behavior for its social appropriateness. The responses to these behaviors of nurses, nursing assistants, and other patients were also assessed and classified as positive or negative attention or as ignoring the patient's behavior. It was found that 61% of appropriate behavior was rewarded, 5% punished, and 34% ignored; whereas 26% of inappropriate behavior was rewarded, 8% punished, and 66% ignored. Interesting differences were found between the reactions of the nurses and the nursing assistants. The nurses tended to reward indiscriminately, whereas the nursing assistants tended to reward inappropriate behavior, for example, by coaxing (attending to) patients who refused to go to the dining room.

In considering the studies of the control of ward behavior, it will be convenient to consider separately those which deal with the manipulation of single patients on an experimental basis and those which deal with groups of patients.

(a) INDIVIDUAL STUDIES. Ayllon and Michael (1959) provided the earliest detailed reports on the application of operant conditioning procedures to the control of ward behavior in psychotic patients. In one case, excessive and annoying visits by a patient to the ward office were eliminated by the simple procedure of complete withdrawal of attention by the office staff, the visits being thus reduced from 16 per day to two over seven weeks. In a second patient, psychotic speech was reduced from 90% of total talk to 50% over 13 weeks, again by withdrawal of attention from the psychotic speech. An unsuccessful attempt was made to eliminate violent behavior in a third patient by rewarding a response (sitting on the floor) incompatible with violence. The fourth patient was treated in a distinctly novel way. She refused to eat unless spoon fed. It was, however, noticed that she was extremely concerned to keep her clothing neat and clean. Spoon feeding was therefore continued, but the nurse was instructed to become careless and allow food to spill onto the patient's dress. Over eight weeks of treatment, spoon feeding was completely discontinued and the patient fed herself. Ayllon and Michael comment that "although nothing was done to deal directly with her claims that the food was poisoned, these statements dropped out of her repertoire as she began to eat on her own" (p. 332). In the final case reported, magazine hoarding was significantly reduced in a patient by flooding him with magazines (stimulus satiation).[17]

Ayllon (1963) reported in detail the case of a chronic schizophrenic in whom three types of behavior were eliminated. This patient weighed 250 pounds and stole food, as well as hoarding towels and clothing (the latter by wearing excessive clothing which added to her already grotesque appearance). The food stealing was eliminated in two weeks by food deprivation for stealing and was absent on a one-year follow-up. The hoarding of towels was eliminated by the satiation technique referred to above. The excessive weight and clothes-hoarding were tackled simultaneously by making food reinforcement dependent on meeting a weight criterion. Over 14 weeks' treatment, the towel hoarding disappeared, the patient's weight returned to normal, and she was taken home for a weekend by her parents for the first time in nine years.

In a later study, Ayllon (1965) successfully eliminated refusal to eat in a female psychotic who had not eaten for 16 years unless accompanied by her nurse to the dining room and partially fed there. The treatment involved cessation of the practice of accompanying the patient to the dining room or of helping the patient with her tray, feeding, and so on. Because of the length of time the patient had "needed" help, strong objections were raised to the institution of this treatment, yet it was completely successful with no untoward side effects and with some side benefits (e.g., the reinstatement of some speech). In a second case, Ayllon treated a female psychotic who never left the dining room after her meal unless prompted to do so by the nurse. Prompting was dropped, and the patient reinforced with candy if she left the room before at least one other patient. Within five weeks, the patient was never the last to leave the room.

Similar successes have been reported with individual patients (Milby et al, 1967; Agras, 1967; Gericke, 1965). Gericke's description of the case of Susan is of considerable interest in demonstrating the importance of identifying stimuli which are contingently reinforcing. Susan had sat seclusively in a corner by herself for months, the token system used in the hospital having influenced her but little. However,

"The nursing staff noticed that milk was the only nourishment she would take and that she would dress only in white or light-

---

[17] These five cases were selected by Ayllon and Michael from a total of 19 treated in similar ways.

coloured clothing. The nurse assigned to her mentioned this preference, and we decided to use white clothing as a positive reinforcer for acceptable behavior. When Susan's white dress was taken away from her, and institution dark olive-drab clothing substituted, she reacted for the first time in the course of her current hospitalization: she tore the institution dress, sat on her bed and refused to dress. The nurses left her and waited to see what would happen next. After about two hours Susan called the nurse and asked for a needle and thread to fix the dress that she had ripped. The nurse complied and immediately gave her a white scarf to wear with her dark dress.

The resulting change in Susan's behavior was dramatic. After she had mended the clothing, she asked for odd jobs in the kitchen. Each time she completed a task, she received a token and some of her white clothing back. During the next few days she earned the right to get all her clothing back. She added white ice cream and mashed potatoes to her diet, after being satiated by increasing portions of milk daily. The next goal of the staff was to condition her to wearing dark clothing and to eating foods that were not white.

During discussions between the charge nurse and Susan, it emerged very clearly that the colour white was an irrationally powerful control stimulus for Susan. She associated white with purity, goodness, and the worth of life. Black and dark colours symbolised the devil, sin, and everything undesirable. She felt that God had punished her by giving her black hair and that she would have to bear this burden. Her first reaction to the milk satiation program was to gorge herself with milk. After a few days the nurse began to charge extra tokens for extra glasses of milk but not for other food. Since Susan, until then, had not earned sufficient tokens to stay with the program, one of two things was expected to happen. She would either have to work more and interact more with patients (a behavior that was, of course, sought for her) or she would have to choose other foods that would cost her no tokens. The second alternative happened. Susan began to eat bacon and toast for breakfast. Although Susan's troubles were not over, some com-

munication had been established between this withdrawn girl and the nursing staff" (Gericke, 1965, p. 8).

(b) GROUP STUDIES. The encouraging results of these early studies has led to large-scale attempts to provide a more controlled environment for psychotic patients by setting up special wards. On these wards, the patients must work to obtain reinforcing events, the aim being, of course, to improve initially by these means their personal hygiene and move on from there to more complex behaviors in possible preparation for a return to society. The original and best-known of these "controlled environments" is that established by Ayllon at the Anna State Hospital in Illinois, but others have since been developed, as for example by Schaeffer at the Patton State Hospital, California, and by Atthowe at the VA Hospital, Palo Alto.[18] These controlled environments serve both as experimental laboratories and as places where individual problems can be tackled on an experimental basis.

Before turning to the work of Ayllon and of Schaeffer, mention may be made of a study by Mertens and Fuller (1963) which dealt with the reinstatement of shaving behavior in a large group of very severely regressed psychotic males (the neglected backward patients) who had been hospitalized for a mean of 32 years. A very carefully validated scale to assess the efficiency of shaving was developed first. Three groups of patients were then formed. The first group was given specific reinforcement (candy, etc.) for correct shaving responses; the first control group was given only general reinforcement; while the second control group was given only the usual hospital care. Shaving ability was assessed before and after 51 days of training, and it was found that only the experimental group showed improvement that remained stable. These results are distinctly encouraging, considering the extremely deteriorated state of the patients.

Ayllon and Haughton (1962) have applied operant conditioning procedures to controlling the mealtime behavior of schizophrenic patients. In the first experiment, involving 32 female patients (seven of whom presented severe feeding problems), all of the usual methods (coaxing, reminding, exhorting, spoon or tube feeding, etc.) were discontinued and the nurses

---

[18] Krasner (1968) has recently reviewed much of the work on "token economy" programs in the

U.S.A.; while Krasner and Atthowe (1968) have compiled a bibliography of the work going on.

were kept away from the patients at mealtimes to prevent social reinforcers (attention, etc.) being given. Entry to the dining room (and, therefore, feeding) was made contingent upon arrival within a given time limit after the announcement of mealtime. This time limit was originally 30 minutes and was progressively reduced to five minutes. It was shown that the patients without eating problems adjusted successfully to the more stringent time limits with a slight fall off in percentage of meals eaten when the time limit was five minutes; and that the patients who were eating problems improved in percentage of meals eaten when the time limit was made more stringent, though at all time limits they ate fewer meals than the other patients.

The procedures were taken a stage further in a second experiment in which the same patients (plus six new ones with feeding problems) were required now to drop a penny into a collection box to gain entry to the dining room. During this period, only five minutes was allowed for access. Verbal encouragement and direct verbal instructions were used to shape the behavior. All patients learned to deposit coins to gain access to the dining room. In the final experiment, the patients were required to cooperate in pairs to gain entry to the dining room. To obtain the pennies to gain entrance, two patients had to press buttons simultaneously. All patients learned the social response, and verbalization between patients increased spontaneously.

Several points should be noted about these experiments. First, none of the patients, some of whom went for long periods without food in the first part of the experiment, suffered any medical handicaps as a result of the treatment. Second, the eating behavior of schizophrenics can be controlled solely by food as a reinforcer. The persuasion techniques so often used in chronic wards are unnecessary and strengthen the undesirable behaviors. Third, severe psychotic patients can learn to make social responses to obtain reinforcers. Fourth, this new social behavior may reinstate verbal behavior.[19]

Ayllon and Haughton refer to the effect of the results of their studies on the hospital staff as follows.

"The results of this experiment were very surprising to the staff. Because virtually all of the patients were regarded as chronic, and 'out of reality contact', it seemed useless to expect them to be aware of each other. Because many patients exhibited hallucinations, e.g., gesticulating and talking incessantly in the absence of a visible audience, it seemed unreasonable to the staff to expect these patients to interrupt their psychotic symptoms in time to engage in the social response demanded in this experiment. Finally, the experiment was regarded as so stressful for the patients that a 'wave' of eating problems, particularly among those with a long history of such behavior, was anticipated. None of these apprehensions was supported by our results" (Aylion and Haughton, 1962, p. 349).

In a more recent series of studies, Ayllon and Azrin (1965) have carried these techniques to a much more advanced stage. Six experiments were carried out with a stable ward population of 43 to 45 females (mostly schizophrenics, but also including some defectives). The patients worked for tokens which could be exchanged for primary (or, at least, more significant) reinforcers, namely, privacy (selection of particular room for sleeping, personal chair, etc.); leave from the ward (walk in hospital grounds, trip to town, etc.); social interaction with staff (private audience with ward psychologist or social worker); devotional opportunities; recreational opportunities (movie on ward, exclusive use of radio, etc.); shopping items (food, toilet requisites, clothing, etc.). Each type of reinforcer cost a specified number of tokens.

In the first experiment, involving eight of the best-adjusted patients, four main types of jobs off the ward were made available. For example, the job of dietary worker involved helping to serve meals for 85 patients and clean the tables afterwards. The job was done for six hours daily, and 70 tokens were awarded after job-completion. Each job in this experiment led to an equal number of tokens. The patient could choose his job, and the experiment examined whether the patient would shift from a preferred job for which no tokens were given to a nonpreferred job for which tokens were given, as indicated by verbal instructions issued before the job was chosen. It was found that tokens controlled job choice in that seven out of the eight patients shifted to the nonpreferred but rewarded job. The second experiment, using the

---

[19] It is interesting to speculate whether Isaacs et al (1960) would have done better to reinstate *social* behavior first in their mute catatonics, rather than attempting to reinstate the vocal behavior directly.

same patients, showed that these patients would not work on a preferred job if the tokens were given on a noncontingent basis (that is, before work commenced). Even the preferred jobs, therefore, were apparently not intrinsically reinforcing.

It is unnecessary to report the details of the remaining four experiments except to say that they involved similar studies relating to on-ward behavior. These studies provide a model for the controlled analysis and manipulation of the behavior of psychotic patients in quasi real-life situations and show clearly that secondary reinforcers can significantly control behavior.

Schaeffer (1966) has also described the use of operant conditioning procedures in a mental hospital, and Schaeffer and Martin (1966) have reported the results of an experiment designed to reduce apathy in hospitalized schizophrenic patients. Two groups of patients were formed, matched on degree of apathy.[20] The experimental group was reinforced (usually by tokens, occasionally by primary reinforcement) for personal hygiene responses, social interaction, and adequate work performance; while the control group received normal ward reinforcement. Base-line data relating to apathy were collected for ten days, and the experimental procedures were then followed for three months, with base-line data being measured twice during the reinforcement period. It was found that the single-code entries, which defined the measure of apathy, declined significantly in the experimental group but not in the control group, and that these changes were also reflected in psychiatrists' ratings. Similar encouraging results have recently been reported by Atthowe and Krasner (1968).

In general, therefore, it certainly appears to have been convincingly demonstrated that quite complex behavior (including *social* behavior) can be manipulated by reinforcement contingencies. Of course, immense problems remain because, even if the patient's behavior on the ward improves significantly and comes under the control of "normal reinforcing events," the problem of the transition from hospital ward to real life outside the hospital remains. The basic requirements for this to occur would clearly be the provision of intermediate wards approximating real-life conditions more closely, and

probably the training of the relatives of the patient so that inadvertent reinforcing of the largely extinguished abnormal behavior did not reinstate it. However, Schaeffer and Martin (1966) make the point that much of the re-training of psychotic patients by behavioral techniques are likely to be more helpful in producing adjustment outside the hospital precisely because they involve nonverbal activities. A patient who is largely nonverbal may still be able to cope with life outside the hospital, even if with difficulty. But a patient who cannot carry out the multitude of small nonverbal tasks required in everyday life is at a very serious disadvantage indeed.

5. THE TRAINABILITY OF PSYCHOTIC PATIENTS

Much less work appears to have been done with respect to the trainability of schizophrenics as compared with mental defectives.[21] Early studies by O'Connor et al (1956) and others showed that chronic schizophrenics could reach normal levels on simple tasks (in this case, button sorting) but that they took much longer. Thorpe (1962) examined the effects of incentives on the work performance of chronic schizophrenics and could not reproduce earlier results which suggested incentives were a significant factor in improved performance. Lerner (1963) demonstrated the importance of social interactive processes, while Wadsworth, Wells, and Scott (1962a, 1962b) found that constant checking of work was essential if improvement was to be maintained. Wadsworth, Scott, and Wells (1962) have demonstrated the economic viability of a sheltered workshop for schizophrenics. All in all, it must be concluded that this represents a relatively unexplored area.

6. COMPARATIVE STUDIES OF THERAPY

A dearth of studies exists which compare behavior therapy techniques with alternative approaches in the area of psychotic behavior. In the classic study of King et al (1960), four groups of 12 chronic severe schizophrenics were formed and matched on severity of illness and length of hospitalization. The first group was given what was called operant interpersonal therapy. This involved procedures similar to those used by Ayllon and his colleagues, namely,

---

[20] The method of measuring apathy will be described below, in the section on methodology.

[21] Occupational therapy is, of course, very com-

monly used with psychotics, but not usually with a view to ultimate employment. It is not, therefore, job oriented.

training in simple operant behavior, followed by training in simple and complex problem solving, and finally in co-operative problem solving. The second group constituted a verbal therapy control group, with initial individual therapy leading to group therapy. The third group was a recreational control group, and the fourth group a no-treatment control group. Subjects in the three "activity" groups were seen three times per week for $3\frac{1}{2}$ months. Pre-post treatment changes in ratings of various kinds constituted the dependent variables and included scores on psychiatric rating scales, ward behavior rating scales, amount of vocalization, and a clinical improvement scale.

On all four measures, the operant-interpersonal technique was found to produce the most significant changes, with the recreational therapy producing better results than the individual and group therapy. These differences were maintained over a six-month follow-up period. Various other indices (such as expressed wish to leave the ward and be discharged) were found to be related to change in scores. Taken in conjunction with all of the evidence previously presented, this study would appear to indicate a tendency for the operant conditioning techniques to be superior to verbal psychotherapy with respect to both the verbal and nonverbal behavior of psychotic patients. Certainly, the results compare favorably with results from "total push therapy" (Tourney et al, 1960).

The only other comparative study that needs to be mentioned was carried out by Hamilton and Salmon (1962) who compared occupational therapy with workshop therapy or no treatment in chronic schizophrenics. In addition, comparisons were made relating to flat rate versus piecework payments for work done and relating to individual versus group work. Changes in performance on various measures of intelligence and personality were also measured. It was found that the most significant changes were produced in the workshop therapy group, relating especially to social competence, clinical state, accuracy of estimation, reaction time, and so on. Within the workshop training itself, productivity was most affected by flat-rate payments when the patient was working on his own.

VI. METHODOLOGICAL CONSIDERATIONS

Two problems only will be discussed here briefly.

1. ASSESSMENT OF BASE-LINE FROM WHICH TO MEASURE CHANGE

As Ayllon and Azrin (1965) pointed out, the operant conditioning technique is imposed upon a patient who, though he may be extremely deteriorated, will still usually indulge in some forms of behavior. It is important, therefore, to know the base-line rate of any particular response or complex of responses to be altered. In this connection, mention should be made of several studies that have investigated this problem. Hunter et al (1962) developed a set of scales to measure various aspects of chronic schizophrenic behavior on the ward so that the effects on ward behavior of introduced variables could be reliably measured. The procedure involved the time-sampling of behavior in four categories:

(i) Location—position on ward (which was divided into 14 geographical areas).

(ii) Position—against wall, etc. (6 categories).

(iii) Posture—sitting, standing, etc. (6 categories).

(iv) Activity—social, parasocial, etc. (5 categories).

For 100 deteriorated chronic schizophrenics, the results obtained are shown in Table 14.3. While the position category seems to be insufficiently defined, the scales would be valuable for assessing pre-post treatment changes in ward behavior in deteriorated schizophrenics.

A somewhat similar approach has more recently been adopted by Schaeffer and Martin (1966). They recorded three types of behavior:

(i) Those which are "mutually exclusive" (walking, running, standing, etc.).

(ii) Those which are "concomitant" (group activity, smoking, etc.).

(iii) Those which are "idiosyncratic" (rocking, pacing, etc.).

A fixed number of observations are made for each patient per day. While the system can, of course, be used to measure patient activity directly, Schaeffer and Martin developed with it a measure of "apathy," which was defined as the degree to which a patient indulged in only one type of behavior at the time of observation.

These two studies are singled out because, as we found in the case of psychotic children, it seems likely that very simple measures of activity will be required in relation to behavior therapy of psychotic adults. Of course, more sophisticated measures have been used, as was

TABLE 14.3. *Ward Behavior of 100 Chronic Schizophrenics*

Percent Total Frequencies in Each Category

Position		Posture		Activities	
Against wall	46.0	Sitting	61.1	Null behavior	44.0
Against corner	4.6	Standing	17.2	Sleeping	10.0
Facing wall	0.8	Lying	6.7	Social (interaction)	2.7
Facing corner	0.3	Walking	13.1	Parasocial	15.4
Looking out window	1.4	Sitting on floor	1.1	Functional nonsocial	9.2
				Nonfunctional pathological	18.7
None of above	45.4	Lying on floor	0.3		
No recording	1.5	No recording	0.7		

Source: Hunter et al, 1962.

the case in the study of King et al (1960); and alternative techniques are readily available, such as the measures used by Ayllon and Azrin (1965), namely, the number of tokens earned in a given period. Finally, mention should be made of the development by Nathan et al (1964). This is a complex but ingenious technique for automatically recording many aspects of the patient's behavior during interview or therapy while simultaneously manipulating the extent to which the patient sees the therapist through a one-way screen, depending upon the patient's responses.

Reference should also be made to Davison's (1966) operational definition of a paranoid state and to Lindsley's (1960) definition and measurement of psychotic behavior as fruitful examples of base-line measurements.

2. ELICITATION AND CONTROL OF THE RESPONSE TO BE MANIPULATED

Holz et al (1963) trained four psychotic patients to pull a lever (R_1) under reinforcement conditions which progressed from FR-1 to FR-10 and then to a VR schedule, following which the response was extinguished by non-reinforcement. However, during some extinction periods, an alternative response (R_2) was made available to the patients, whereas in other extinction periods, no alternative response was available. It was found that R_1 was much more readily suppressed during extinction if an alternative response was available. This result suggests, of course, that some of the behaviors studied in the experiments reviewed in this chapter might have been eliminated quicker if alternative responses were available. Indeed,

some of the experiments could be interpreted within such a framework. Thus, in Ayllon's studies of the control of dining-room behavior, it could be argued that the provision of alternative responses (putting coins into slots, working for coins) facilitated the effects of the primary reinforcer by helping to extinguish previous attention-getting responses faster.

As was pointed out earlier, reinforcement procedures will obviously be ineffective if the response to be reinforced does not occur. An experimental study by Ayllon and Azrin (1964) not only demonstrated this, but gave some useful clues as to how to proceed in such circumstances. In the first experiment, they tried to induce a group of schizophrenics to pick up their eating utensils on entering the dining room by offering conditional reinforcement in the form of a food bonus whenever the utensils were picked up. The experiment was a failure because only three of the 18 patients ever picked up utensils. The addition of verbal instructions, coupled with the additional reinforcement if they were picked up, resulted in a very significant increase in the percentage of patients picking up the utensils.

Simple though this experiment may be, the interesting point to note is that the addition of verbal instructions was by no means uniformly successful. In a second experiment, Ayllon and Azrin (1964) utilized verbal instructions only, but provided an aversive consequence for failure to follow the instructions. The aversive consequence involved delayed access to the food counter. Verbal instructions alone were found to be only partly effective, but addition of the aversive consequence produced complete compliance with the request.

Ayllon and Azrin (1968) have recently investigated the problem of nonutilization of reinforcements earned. They noted that, not infrequently, the patient did not "cash in" his tokens for reinforcers (walks, attending music sessions and movies) which had previously been shown to be reinforcers for him. They showed that utilization of these reinforcers (which could be regarded as a form of responding) could be significantly increased by means of "forced sampling." Thus, if a walk were announced, participation in the activity increased significantly if all patients were required to assemble for the walk, even though payment of a token was a prerequisite for participation in the walk itself.

VII. CONCLUSION

There can be no doubt that the therapeutic work reported here has opened a new and potentially fruitful chapter in the history of attempts to help psychotic patients to readjust to society. It is true, of course, that for many of these patients, not too much can be hoped for. Nevertheless, it does appear feasible to at least improve the behavior of even the most regressed and deteriorated psychotics by the application of relatively simple techniques. It would be foolish indeed to expect too much of these methods but, in an area where thus far only the use of drugs appears to have had any significant effect on behavior, the outlook is now more promising for significant advances.

REFERENCES

Agras, W.S. Behavior therapy in the management of chronic schizophrenia. *Amer. J. Psychiat.*, 1967, **124**, 240–243.

Albee, G.W., Lane, E.A., Corcoran, C., & Werneke, A. Childhood and intercurrent intellectual performance of adult schizophrenics. *J. consult. Psychol.*, 1963, **27**, 364–366.

Albee, G.W., Lane, E.A., & Reuter, J.M. Childhood intelligence of future schizophrenics and neighbourhood peers. *J. consult. Psychol.*, 1964, **28**, 141–144.

Atthowe, J.M. & Krasner, L. Preliminary report on the application of contingent reinforcement procedures (token economy) on a "chronic" psychiatric ward. *J. abnorm. Psychol.*, 1968, **73**, 37–43.

Ayllon, T. Intensive treatment of psychotic behavior by stimulus satiation and food reinforcement. *Behav. Res. Ther.*, 1963, **1**, 53–61.

Ayllon, T. Some behavioral problems associated with eating in chronic schizophrenic patients. In Ullmann, L.P. & Krasner, L. (eds.). *Case studies in behavior modification.* New York: Holt, 1965, pp. 73–77.

Ayllon, T. & Azrin, N.H. Reinforcement and instructions with mental patients. *J. exp. Anal. Behav.*, 1964, **7**, 327–331.

Ayllon, T. & Azrin, N. The measurement and reinforcement of behavior of psychotics. *J. exp. Anal. Behav.*, 1965, **8**, 357–383.

Ayllon, T. & Azrin, N.H. Reinforcer sampling: a technique for increasing the behavior of mental patients. *J. appl. Behav. Res.*, 1968, **1**, 13–20.

Ayllon, T. & Haughton, E. Control of the behavior of schizophrenic patients by food. *J. exp. Anal. Behav.*, 1962, **5**, 343–352.

Ayllon, T. & Haughton, E. Modification of symptomatic verbal behavior of mental patients. *Behav. Res. Ther.*, 1964, **2**, 87–97.

Ayllon, T. & Michael, J. The psychiatric nurse as a behavioral engineer. *J. exper. Anal. Behav.*, 1959, **2**, 323–334.

Babcock, H. An experiment in the measurement of mental deterioration. *Arch. Psychol.*, 1930, **18** (Whole No. 117).

Babcock, H. *Dementia praecox, a psychological study.* New York: Science Press, 1933.

Bannister, D. Conceptual structure in thought-disordered schizophrenics. *J. ment. Sci.*, 1960, **106**, 1230–1249.

Bannister, D. Personal construct theory: a summary and experimental paradigm. *Acta Psychol.*, 1962, **20**, 104–120 (a).

Bannister, D. The nature and measurement of schizophrenic thought disorder. *J. ment. Sci.*, 1962, **108**, 825–842 (b).

Bannister, D. The genesis of schizophrenic thought disorder: a serial invalidation hypothesis. *Brit. J. Psychiat.*, 1963, **109**, 680–686.

Bannister, D. The genesis of schizophrenic thought disorder: retest of the serial invalidation hypothesis. *Brit. J. Psychiat.*, 1965, **111**, 377–382.

Becker, W.C. A genetic approach to the interpretation and evaluation of the process-reactive distinction. *J. abnorm. soc. Psychol.*, 1956, **47**, 489–496.

Beech, H.R. & Adler, F. Some aspects of verbal conditioning in psychiatric patients. *Behav. Res. Ther.*, 1963, **1**, 273–282.

Belmont, I., Birch, H.G., Klein, D.V., & Pollack, M. Perceptual evidence of CNS dysfunction in schizophrenia. *Arch. gen. Psychiat.*, 1964, **10**, 395–408.

Boardman, W.K., Goldstone, S., Reiner, M.L., & Himmel, S. Constancy of absolute judgments of size by normals and schizophrenics. *J. abnorm. soc. Psychol.*, 1964, **68**, 346–349.

Broadbent, D.E. *Perception and communication*. Oxford: Pergamon, 1958.

Brodsky, M. Interpersonal stimuli as interference in a sorting task. *J. Pers.*, 1963, **31**, 517–533.

Bryan, J.H. & Lichtenstein, E. Failure to verbally condition socially desirable speech. *Psychol. Rep.*, 1964, **14**, 141–142.

Bullock, D.H. Performance of psychiatric patients in a brief operant discrimination test. *Psychol. Rec.*, 1960, **10**, 83–93.

Bullock, D.H. & Brunt, M.Y. The testability of psychiatric patients in an operant conditioning situation. *Psychol. Rec.*, 1959, **9**, 165–170.

Buss, A.H., Braden, W., Orgel, A., & Buss, E.H. Acquisition and extinction with different verbal reinforcement combinations. *J. exp. Psychol.*, 1956, **52**, 280–295.

Buss, A.H. & Buss, E.H. The effect of verbal reinforcement combinations on conceptual learning. *J. exp. Psychol.*, 1956, **52**, 283–287.

Buss, A.H. & Lang, P.J. Psychological deficit in schizophrenia: I. Affect, reinforcement, and concept attainment. *J. abnorm. Psychol.*, 1965, **70**, 2–24.

Buss, A.H., Wiener, M., & Buss, E.H. Stimulus generalization as a function of verbal reinforcement combinations. *J. exp. Psychol.*, 1954, **48**, 433–436.

Cameron, N. *Personality development and psychopathology*. Boston: Houghton Mifflin, 1963.

Carson, R.C. Proverb interpretation in acutely schizophrenic patients. *J. nerv. ment. Dis.*, 1962, **135**, 556–564.

Cavanaugh, D.K. Improvement in the performance of schizophrenics on concept formation tasks as a function of motivational change. *J. abnorm. soc. Psychol.*, 1958, **57**, 8–12.

Cavanaugh, D., Cohen, W., & Lang, P.J. The effect of "social censure" and "social approval" on the psychomotor performance of schizophrenics. *J. abnorm. soc. Psychol.*, 1960, **60**, 213–218.

Chapman, J. & McGhie, A. A comparative study of disordered attention in schizophrenia. *J. ment. Sci.*, 1962, **108**, 487–500.

Chapman, J. & McGhie, A. An approach to the psychotherapy of cognitive dysfunction. *Brit. J. med. Psychol.*, 1963, **36**, 253–260.

Chapman, J. & McGhie, A. Echopraxia in schizophrenia. *Brit. J. Psychiat.*, 1964, **110**, 365–374.

Chapman, L.J., Chapman, J.P., & Miller, G.A. A theory of verbal behavior in schizophrenia. In Maher, B.A. (ed.). *Progress in experimental personality research* (Vol. I, pp. 49–77). New York: Academic Press, 1964.

Cohen, B.D. Motivation and performance in schizophrenia. *J. abnorm. soc. Psychol.*, 1956, **52**, 186–190.

Cohen, E. & Cohen, B.D. Verbal reinforcement in schizophrenia. *J. abnorm. soc. Psychol.*, 1960, **6**, 443–446.

Cooper, R. Objective measures of perception in schizophrenics and normals. *J. consult. Psychol.*, 1960, **24**, 209–214.

Davison, G.C. Differential relaxation and cognitive restructuring in therapy with a "paranoid schizophrenic" or "paranoid state." *Proc. 74th Ann. Conv. APA.*, Washington, D.C., 1966, pp. 177–178.

Dinoff, M., Horner, R.F., Kurpiewski, B.S., Rickard, R.C., & Timmons, E.O. Conditioning verbal behavior of a psychiatric population in a group therapy-like situation. *J. clin. Psychol.*, 1960, **16**, 371–372.

Dinoff, M., Horner, R.F., Kurpiewski, B.S., & Timmons, E.O. Conditioning verbal behavior of schizophrenics in a group therapy-like situation. *J. clin. Psychol.*, 1960, **16**, 367–370.

Donahoe, J.W., Curtin, M.E., & Lipton, L. Interference effects with schizophrenic subjects in the acquisition and retention of verbal material. *J. abnorm. soc. Psychol.*, 1961, **62**, 553–558.

Ebner, E. Verbal conditioning in schizophrenia as a function of degree of social interaction. *J. Pers. soc. Psychol.*, 1965, **1**, 528–532.

Eysenck, H.J. Cyclothymia and schizothymia as a dimension of personality: I. Historical review. *J. Pers.*, 1950, **19**, 123–152.

Eysenck, H.J. Schizothymia-cyclothymia as a dimension of personality: II. Experimental. *J. Pers.*, 1952, **20**, 345–384 (a).

Eysenck, H.J. *The scientific study of personality.* London: Routledge and Kegan Paul, 1952 (b).

Eysenck, H.J. Psychiatric diagnosis as a psychological and statistical problem. *Psychol. Rep.*, 1955, **1**, 3–17.

Eysenck, H.J. Classification and the problem of diagnosis. In Eysenck, H.J. (ed.). *Handbook of abnormal psychology.* London: Pitman, 1960, pp. 1–31.

Eysenck, S.B.G. Neurosis and psychosis: an experimental analysis. *J. ment. Sci.*, 1956, **102**, 517–529.

Farina, A. & Webb, W.W. Premorbid adjustment and subsequent discharge. *J. nerv. ment. Dis.*, 1956, **124**, 612–613.

Franks, C.M. Conditioning and abnormal behavior. In Eysenck, H.J. (ed.). *Handbook of abnormal psychology.* London: Pitman, 1960, pp. 457–487.

Garmezy, N. Stimulus differentiation by schizophrenic and normal subjects under conditions of reward and punishment. *J. Pers.*, 1952, **20**, 253–276.

Gelfand, D.M., Gelfand, S., & Dobson, W.R. Unprogramed reinforcement of patients' behavior in a mental hospital. *Behav. Res. Ther.*, 1967, **5**, 201–207.

Gericke, O.L. Practical use of operant conditioning procedures in a mental hospital. *Psychiat. Studies & Projects*, 1965, **3**, 2–10.

Gottesman, L. & Chapman, L.J. Syllogistic reasoning errors in schizophrenia. *J. consult. Psychol.*, 1960, **24**, 250–255.

Hall, G.C. Conceptual attainment in schizophrenics and nonpsychotics as a function of task structure. *J. Psychol.*, 1962, **53**, 3–13.

Hall, K.R.L. & Stride, E. The varying response to pain in psychiatric disorders: a study in abnormal psychology. *Brit. J. med. Psychol.*, 1954, **27**, 48–60.

Hamilton, V. Size constancy and cue responsiveness in psychosis. *Brit. J. Psychol.*, 1963, **54**, 25–39.

Hamilton, V. & Salmon, P. Psychological changes in chronic schizophrenics following differential activity programs. *J. ment. Sci.*, 1962, **108**, 505-520.

Hartman, A.M. The apparent size of after-images in delusional and nondelusional schizophrenics. *Amer. J. Psychol.*, 1962, **75**, 587–595.

Harwood, E. & Naylor, G.F.K. Nature and extent of basic cognitive deterioration in a sample of institutionalized mental patients. *Austr. J. Psychol.*, 1963, **15**, 29–36.

Herron, W.G. The process-reactive classification of schizophrenia. *Psychol. Bull.*, 1962, **59**, 329–343.

Higgins, J. The concept of process-reactive schizophrenia: criteria and related research. *J. nerv. ment. Dis.*, 1964, **138**, 9–25.

Holz, W.C., Azrin, N.H., & Ayllon, T. Elimination of behavior of mental patients by response-produced extinction. *J. exp. Anal. Behav.*, 1963, **6**, 407–412.

Howe, E.S. GSR conditioning in anxiety states, normals, and chronic functional schizo-phrenic subjects. *J. abnorm. soc. Psychol.*, 1958, **56**, 183–189.

Hunter, M., Schooler, C., & Spohn, H.E. The measurement of characteristic patterns of ward behavior in chronic schizophrenics. *J. consult. Psychol.*, 1962, **26**, 69–73.

Huston, P.E. Sensory threshold to direct current stimulation in schizophrenic and normal subjects. *Arch. Neurol. Psychiat.*, 1934, **31**, 590–596.

Huston, P.E. The reflex time of the patellar tendon reflex in normal and schizophrenic subjects. *J. gen. Psychol.*, 1935, **13**, 3–41.

Huston, P.E. & Shakow, D. Learning in schizophrenia: I. Pursuit learning. *J. Pers.*, 1948, **17**, 52–74.

Huston, P.E. & Shakow, D. Learning capacity in schizophrenia. *Amer. J. Psychiat.*, 1949, **105**, 881–888.

Hutchinson, R.R. & Azrin, N.H. Conditioning of mental hospital patients to fixed-ratio schedules of reinforcement. *J. exp. Anal. Behav.*, 1961, **4**, 87–95.

Irvine, R. Critical flicker frequency for paretics and schizophrenics. *J. abnorm. soc. Psychol.*, 1954, **49**, 87–88.

Isaacs, W., Thomas, J., & Goldiamond, I. Application of operant conditioning to re-instate verbal behavior in psychotics. *J. Speech Hearing Dis.*, 1960, **25**, 8–12.

Johannsen, W.J. Effect of reward and punishment on motor learning by chronic schizophrenics and normals. *J. clin. Psychol.*, 1962, **18**, 204–207.

Johannsen, W.J. Motivation in schizophrenic performance: a review. *Psychol. Rep.*, 1964, **15**, 839–870 (Monogr. Suppl., 6–V15).

Johannsen, W.J., Friedman, S.H., Leitschuh, T.H., & Ammons, H. A study of certain schizophrenic dimensions and their relationship to double alternation. *J. consult. Psychol.*, 1963, **27**, 375–382.

Johannsen, W.J., Friedman, S.H., & Liccione, J.V. Visual perception as a function of chronicity in schizophrenia. *Brit. J. Psychiat.*, 1964, **110**, 561–570.

Jones, H.G. Learning and abnormal behavior. In Eysenck, H.J. (ed.). *Handbook of abnormal psychology*. London: Pitman, 1960, pp. 488–528.

Kennedy, T. Treatment of chronic schizophrenia by behavior therapy: case reports. *Behav. Res. Ther.*, 1964, **2**, 1–6.

Kew, J.K. A comparison of thought processes in various nosological groups. *J. clin. Psychol.*, 1963, **19**, 162–166.

Kidd, A.H. Monocular distance perception in schizophrenia. *J. abnorm. soc. Psychol.*, 1964, **68**, 100–103.

King, G.F., Armitage, S., & Tilton, J. A therapeutic approach to schizophrenics of extreme pathology. *J. abnorm. soc. Psychol.*, 1960, **61**, 276–286.

King, G.F., Merrell, D., Lovinger, E., & Denny, M. Operant motor behavior in acute schizophrenics. *J. Personality*, 1957, **25**, 317–326.

King, H.E. *Psychomotor aspects of mental disease*. Cambridge: Harvard Univer. Press, 1954.

King, H.E. Two-flash and flicker-fusion thresholds for normal and schizophrenic subjects. *Percept. Mot. Skills*, 1962, **14**, 517–518 (a).

King, H.E. Anticipatory behavior: temporal matching by normal and psychotic subjects. *J. Psychol.*, 1962, **53**, 425–440 (b).

Krasner, L. Studies of the conditioning of verbal behavior. *Psychol. Bull.*, 1958, **55**, 148–170 (a).

Krasner, L. A technique for investigating the relationship between the behavior cues of the examiner and the verbal behavior of the patient. *J. consult. Psychol.*, 1958, **22**, 364–366 (b).

Krasner, L. Verbal conditioning and psychotherapy. In Krasner, L. & Ullmann, L.P. (eds.). *Research in behavior modification*. New York: Holt, 1965, pp. 211–228.

Krasner, L. Assessment of token economy programs in psychiatric hospitals. *Ciba Foundation symposium: the role of learning in psychotherapy*. London: Churchill, 1968 (in press).

Krasner, L. & Atthowe, J. *Token economy bibliography* (unpublished paper, 1968).

Lane, E.A. & Albee, G.W. Childhood intellectual development of adult schizophrenics. *J. abnorm. soc. Psychol.*, 1963, **67**, 186–189.

Lane, E.A. & Albee, G.W. Early childhood intellectual differences between schizophrenic adults and their siblings. *J. abnorm. soc. Psychol.*, 1964, **68**, 193–195.

Lane, E.A. & Albee, G.W. On childhood intellectual decline of adult schizophrenics: a reassessment of an earlier study. *J. abnorm. Psychol.*, 1968, **73**, 174–177.

Lang, P.J. The effect of aversive stimuli on reaction time in schizophrenia. *J. abnorm. soc. Psychol.*, 1959, **59**, 263–268.

Lang, P.J. & Buss, A.H. Psychological deficit in schizophrenia: II. Interference and activation. *J. abnorm. Psychol.*, 1965, **70**, 77–106.

Lang, P.J. & Luoto, K. Mediation and associative facilitation in neurotic, psychotic, and normal subjects. *J. abnorm. soc. Psychol.*, 1962, **64**, 113–120.

Lawson, J.S., McGhie, A., & Chapman, J. Perception of speech in schizophrenia. *Brit. J. Psychiat.*, 1964, **110**, 375–380.

Lerner, M.J. Responsiveness of chronic schizophrenics to the social behavior of others in a meaningful task situation. *J. abnorm. soc. Psychol.*, 1963, **67**, 295–299.

Lewinsohn, P.M. & Riggs, A. The effect of content upon the thinking of acute and chronic schizophrenics. *J. abnorm. soc. Psychol.*, 1962, **65**, 206–207.

Lindsley, O.R. Characteristics of the behavior of chronic psychotics as revealed by free-operant conditioning methods. *Dis. nerv. Syst. Monogr. Suppl.*, 1960, **21**, 66–78.

Lindsley, O.R. Operant conditioning methods applied to research in chronic schizophrenia. *Psychiat. Res. Rep.*, 1956, **5**, 118–139.

Lindsley, O.R. & Skinner, B.F. A method for the experimental analysis of the behavior of psychotic patients. *Amer. Psychol.*, 1954, **9**, 419–420.

Long, R.C. Praise and censure as motivating variables in the motor behavior and learning of schizophrenia. *J. abnorm. soc. Psychol.*, 1961, **63**, 283–288.

Lorr, M. (ed.). *Explorations in typing psychotics.* Oxford: Pergamon, 1966.

Lorr, M., Klett, C.J., & McNair, D.M. *Syndromes of Psychosis.* Oxford: Pergamon, 1963.

Lorr, M. & O'Connor, J.P. The relation between neurosis and psychosis: a reanalysis. *J. ment. Sci.*, 1957, **103**, 375–380.

Lorr, M. & O'Connor, J.P. Psychotic symptom patterns in a behavior inventory. *Educ. Psychol. Measmt.*, 1962, **22**, 139–146.

Losen, S.M. The differential effect of censure on the problem solving behavior of schizophrenics and normal subjects. *J. Pers.*, 1961, **29**, 258–272.

Lynn, R. Aging and expressive movements: an interpretation of aging in terms of Eysenck's construct of psychoticism. *J. genet. Psychol.*, 1962, **100**, 77–84.

Lynn, R. Russian theory and research on schizophrenia. *Psychol. Bull.*, 1963, **60**, 486–498.

McDonough, J.M. Critical flicker frequency and the spiral aftereffect with process and reactive schizophrenics. *J. consult. Psychol.*, 1960, **24**, 150–155.

McGhie, A. & Chapman, J. Disorders of attention and perception in early schizophrenia. *Brit. J. med. Psychol.*, 1961, **34**, 103–116.

McGhie, A., Chapman, J., & Lawson, J.S. Disturbances in selective attention in schizophrenia. *Proc. roy. soc. med.*, 1964, **57**, 419–422.

McGhie, A., Chapman, J. & Lawson, J.S. The effect of distraction on schizophrenic performance: (1) Perception and immediate memory. *Brit. J. Psychiat.*, 1965, **111**, 383–390 (a).

McGhie, A., Chapman, J., & Lawson, J.S. The effect of distraction on schizophrenic performance: (2) Psychomotor ability. *Brit. J. Psychiat.*, 1965, **111**, 391–398 (b).

MacKay, H.A. & Inglis, J. The effect of age on a short-term auditory process. *Gerontol.*, 1963, **8**, 193–200.

McReynolds, P. Reactions to novel and familiar stimuli as a function of schizophrenic withdrawal. *Percept. Mot. Skills*, 1963, **16**, 847–850.

Mabry, M. Language characteristics of scattered and nonscattered schizophrenics compared with normals. *J. Psychol.*, 1964, **57**, 29–40.

Mailloux, N.M. & Newburger, M. The work curves of psychotic individuals. *J. abnorm. soc. Psychol.*, 1941, **36**, 110–114.

Mattsson, P.O. The Stein Sentence Construction Test and cognitive disturbance: a cross-validational study. *J. clin. Psychol.*, 1964, **20**, 368–369.

Mednick, M.T. & Lindsley, O.R. Some clinical correlates of operant behavior. *J. abnorm. soc. Psychol.*, 1958, **57**, 13–16.

Mednick, S.A. Distortions in the gradient of stimulus generalization related to cortical brain damage and schizophrenia. *J. abnorm. soc. Psychol.*, 1955, **51**, 536–542.

Mertens, G.C. & Fuller, G.B. Conditioning of molar behavior in "regressed" psychotics: I. An objective measure of personal habit training with "regressed" psychotics. *J. clin. Psychol.*, 1963, **19**, 333–337.

Milby, J.B., Stenmark, D.E., & Horner, R.F. Modification of locomotive behavior in a severely disturbed psychotic. *Percept. Mot. Skills*, 1967, **25**, 359–360.

Moran, L.J., Mefferd, R.B., & Kimble, J.P. Idiodynamic sets in word association. *Psychol. Monogr.*, 1964, **78** (Whole No. 579) (pp. 22).

Nathan, P.E., Schneller, P., & Lindsley, O.R. Direct measurement of communication during psychiatric admission interviews. *Behav. Res. Ther.*, 1964, **2**, 49–57.

Nidorf, L.J. The role of meaningfulness in the serial learning of schizophrenia. *J. clin. Psychol.*, 1964, **20**, 92.

O'Connor, N., Heron, A., & Carstairs, G.M. Work performance of chronic schizophrenics. *Occup. Psychol.*, 1956, **30**, 153–164.

O'Connor, N. & Rawnsley, K. Two types of conditioning in psychotics and normals. *J. abnorm. soc. Psychol.*, 1959, **58**, 157–161.

Olson, G.W. Failure and subsequent performance of schizophrenics. *J. abnorm. soc. Psychol.*, 1958, **57**, 310–314.

Orme, J.E. Time estimation and personality. *J. ment. Sci.*, 1962, **108**, 213–216.

Pascal, C. & Swensen, G. Learning in mentally ill patients under unusual motivation. *J. Pers.*, 1952, **21**, 240–249.

Payne, R.W. Cognitive abnormalities. In Eysenck, H.J. (ed.). *Handbook of abnormal psychology*. London: Pitman, 1960, pp. 193–261.

Payne, R.W. An object classification test as a measure of overinclusive thinking in schizophrenic patients. *Brit. J. soc. clin. Psychol.*, 1962, **1**, 213–221.

Payne, R.W., Ancevich, S.S., & Laverty, S.G. Overinclusive thinking in symptom-free schizophrenics. *Canad. Psychiat. Assoc. J.*, 1963, **8**, 225–234.

Payne, R.W., Caird, W.K., & Laverty, S.G. Overinclusive thinking and delusions in schizophrenic patients. *J. abnorm. soc. Psychol.*, 1964, **68**, 562–566.

Payne, R.W. & Friedlander, D. A short battery of simple tests for measuring overinclusive thinking. *J. ment. Sci.*, 1962, **108**, 362–367.

Payne, R.W. & Hewlett, J.H.G. Thought disorder in psychotic patients. In Eysenck, H.J. (ed.). *Experiments in personality* (Vol. II, pp. 3–104). London: Routledge and Kegan Paul, 1960.

Peters, H.N. & Jenkins, R.L. Improvement of chronic schizophrenic patients with guided problem-solving, motivated by hunger. *Psychiat. Quart. Suppl.*, 1954, **28**, 84–101.

Phillips, L. Case history data and prognosis in schizophrenia. *J. nerv. ment. Dis.*, 1953, **117**, 515–525.

Phillips, L. & Zigler, E. The action-thought parameter and vicariousness in normal and pathological behaviors. *J. abnorm. soc. Psychol.*, 1961, **63**, 137–146.

Pishkin, V. & Blanchard, R.J. Stimulus and social cues in concept identification of schizophrenics and normals. *J. abnorm. soc. Psychol.*, 1963, **67**, 454–463.

Pishkin, V., Smith, T.E., & Leibowitz, H.W. The influence of symbolic stimulus value on perceived size in chronic schizophrenia. *J. consult. Psychol.*, 1962, **26**, 323–330.

Raush, H.L. Perceptual constancy in schizophrenia. *J. pers.*, 1952, **21**, 176–187.

Richman, J. Symbolic distortion in the vocabulary definitions of schizophrenics. *J. gen. Psychol.*, 1964, **71**, 1–8.

Rickard, H.C., Digman, P.J., & Horner, R.F. Verbal manipulation in a psychotherapeutic relationship. *J. clin. Psychol.*, 1960, **16**, 364–367.

Rickard, H.C. & Dinoff, M. A follow-up note on "verbal manipulation in a psychotherapeutic relationship." *Psychol. Rep.*, 1962, **11**, 506.

Rodnick, E. & Shakow, D. Set in the schizophrenic as measured by a composite reaction-time index. *Amer. J. Psychiat.*, 1940, **97**, 214–225.

Rosenbaum, G., Mackavey, W.R., & Grisell, J.L. Effects of biological and social motivation on schizophrenic reaction time. *J. abnorm. soc. Psychol.*, 1957, **54**, 364–368.

Salzinger, K. Experimental manipulation of verbal behavior: a review. *J. gen. Psychol.*, 1959, **61**, 65–94.

Salzinger, K. & Pisoni, S. Reinforcement of affect responses of schizophrenics during the clinical interview. *J. abnorm. soc. Psychol.*, 1958, **57**, 84–90.

Salzinger, K. & Pisoni, S. Some parameters of the conditioning of verbal affect responses in schizophrenic subjects. *J. abnorm. soc. Psychol.*, 1961, **63**, 511–516.

Salzinger, K. & Portnoy, S. Verbal conditioning in interviews: application to chronic schizophrenics and relationship to prognosis for acute schizophrenics. *J. psychiat. Res.*, 1964, **2**, 1–9.

Salzinger, K., Portnoy, S., & Feldman, R.S. Experimental manipulation of continuous speech in schizophrenic patients. *J. abnorm. soc. Psychol.*, 1964, **68**, 508–516.

Schaefer, H.H. Investigations on operant conditioning procedures in a mental hospital. In Fisher, J. & Harris, R.E. (eds.). *Reinforcement theory in psychological treatment— a symposium.* California Mental Health Res. Monogr., No. 8, 1966, pp. 25–39.

Schaefer, H.H. & Martin, P.L. Behavioral therapy for "apathy" of hospitalized schizophrenics. *Psychol. Rep.*, 1966, **19**, 1147–1158.

Shagass, C. & Schwartz, M. Psychiatric correlates of evoked cerebral cortical potentials. *Amer. J. Psychiat.*, 1963, **119**, 1055–1061.

Shakow, D. Segmental set: a theory of the formal psychological deficit in schizophrenia. *Arch. gen. Psychiat.*, 1962, **6**, 1–17.

Shakow, D. Psychological deficit in schizophrenia. *Behav. Sci.*, 1963, **8**, 275–305.

Sherman, J.A. Use of reinforcement and imitation to reinstate verbal behavior in mute psychotics. *J. abnorm. Psychol.*, 1965, **70**, 155–164.

Sidle, A., Acker, M., & McReynolds, P. "Stimulus-seeking" behavior in schizophrenics and nonschizophrenics. *Percept. Mot. Skills*, 1963, **17**, 811–816.

Silverman, J. Psychological deficit reduction in schizophrenia through response-contingent noxious reinforcement. *Psychol. Rep.*, 1963, **13**, 187–210 (Monogr. Suppl., 2–V13).

Silverman, J. The problem of attention in research and theory in schizophrenia. *Psychol. Rev.*, 1964, **71**, 352–379.

Slechta, J., Gwynn, W., & Peoples, C. Verbal conditioning of schizophrenics and normals in a situation resembling psychotherapy. *J. consult. Psychol.*, 1963, **27**, 223–227.

Snyder, S., Rosenthal, D., & Taylor, I.A. Perceptual closure in schizophrenia. *J. abnorm. soc. Psychol.*, 1961, **63**, 131–136.

Sommer, R., Witney, G., & Osmond, H. Teaching common associations to schizophrenics. *J. abnorm. soc. Psychol.*, 1962, **65**, 58–61.

Spence, J.A. & Lair, C.V. Associative interference in the verbal learning performance of schizophrenics and normals. *J. abnorm. soc. Psychol.*, 1964, **68**, 204–209.

Spence, K.W. & Taylor, J.A. The relation of conditioned response strength to anxiety in normal, neurotic, and psychotic subjects. *J. exp. Psychol.*, 1953, **45**, 265–277.

Stilson, D.W. & Kopell, B.S. The recognition of visual signals in the presence of visual noise by psychiatric patients. *J. nerv. ment. Dis.*, 1964, **139**, 209–221.

Taylor, J.A. & Spence, K.W. Conditioning level in the behavior disorders. *J. abnorm. soc. Psychol.*, 1954, **49**, 497–502.

Thorpe, J.G. The response of chronic female schizophrenics to monetary incentives. *Brit. J. soc. clin. Psychol.*, 1962, **1**, 192–198.

Tizard, J. & Venables, P.H. Reaction—time responses by schizophrenics, mental defectives, and normal adults. *Amer. J. Psychiat.*, 1956, **112**, 803–807.

Tourney, G., Senf, R., Dunham, H.W., Glen, R.S., & Gottlieb, J.S. The effect of re-socialization techniques on chronic schizophrenic patients. *Amer. J. Psychiat.*, 1960, **116**, 993–1000.

Trouton, D.S. & Maxwell, A.E. The relation between neurosis and psychosis: an analysis of symptoms and past history of 819 psychotics and neurotics. *J. ment. Sci.*, 1956, **102**, 1–21.

Ullmann, L.P., Forsman, R.G., Kenny, J.W., McInnis, T.L., Unikel, I.P., & Zeisset, R.M. Selective reinforcement of schizophrenics' interview responses. *Behav. Res. Ther.*, 1965, **2**, 205–212.

Ullman, L.P., Krasner, L., & Collins, B.J. Modification of behavior through verbal conditioning: effects in group therapy. *J. abnorm. soc. Psychol.*, 1961, **62**, 128–132.

Ullmann, L.P., Krasner, L., & Edinger, R.L. Verbal conditioning of common associations in long-term schizophrenic patients. *Behav. Res. Ther.*, 1964, **2**, 15–18.

Usdansky, G. & Chapman, L.J. Schizophrenic-like responses in normal subjects under time pressure. *J. abnorm. soc. Psychol.*, 1960, **60**, 143–146.

Venables, P.H. Changes due to noise in the threshold of fusion of paired light flashes in schizophrenics and normals. *Brit. J. soc. clin. Psychol.*, 1963, **2**, 94–99 (a).

Venables, P.H. Selectivity of attention, withdrawal, and cortical activation. *Arch. gen. Psychiat.*, 1963, **9**, 74–78 (b).

Venables, P.H. The relationship between level of skin potential and fusion of paired light flashes in schizophrenic and normal subjects. *J. psychiat. Res.*, 1963, **1**, 279–287 (c).

Venables, P.H. & Wing, J.K. Level of arousal and the subclassification of schizophrenia. *Arch. gen. Psychiat.*, 1962, **7**, 114–119.

Wadsworth, W.V., Scott, R.F., & Wells, B.W.P. The employability of chronic schizo-phrenics. *J. ment. Sci.*, 1962, **108**, 300–303.

Wadsworth, W.V., Wells, B.W.P., & Scott, R.F. A comparative study of the fatiguability of a group of chronic schizophrenics and a group of hospitalized nonpsychotic depressives. *J. ment. Sci.*, 1962, **108**, 304–308 (a).

Wadsworth, W.V., Wells, B.W.P., & Scott, R.F. A comparative study of chronic schizo-phrenics and normal subjects on a work task involving sequential operations. *J. ment. Sci.*, 1962, **108**, 309–316 (b).

Weckowicz, T.E. Shape constancy in schizophrenic patients. *J. abnorm. soc. Psychol.*, 1964, **68**, 177–183.

Whitman, J.R. Learning from social and nonsocial cues in schizophrenia. *J. gen. Psychol.*, 1963, **68**, 307–315.

Wickramasekera, I. The use of some learning theory derived techniques in the treatment of a case of paranoid schizophrenia. *Psychotherapy*, 1967, **4**, 22–26.

Williams, E.B. Deductive reasoning in schizophrenia. *J. abnorm. soc. Psychol.*, 1964, **69**, 47–61.

Wilson, F.S. & Walters, R.H. Modification of speech output of near-mute schizophrenics through social learning procedures. *Behav. Res. Ther.*, 1966, **4**, 59–67.

Wittenborn, J.R., Holzberg, J.D., & Simon, B. Symptom correlates for descriptive diagnosis. *Genet. Psychol. Monogr.*, 1953, **47**, 237–301.

Wright, D.J., Goldstone, W., & Boardman, W.K. Time judgment and schizophrenia: step interval as a relevant contextual factor. *J. Psychol.*, 1962, **54**, 33–38.

Yates, A.J. Abnormalities of psychomotor functions. In Eysenck, H.J. (ed.). *Handbook of abnormal psychology*. London: Pitman, 1960, pp. 32–61.

Yates, A.J. Psychological deficit. *Ann. Rev. Psychol.*, 1966, **17**, 111–144 (a).

Yates, A.J. Data-processing levels and thought disorder in schizophrenia. *Austr. J. Psychol.*, 1966, **18**, 103–117 (b).

Zahn, T.P., Rosenthal, D., & Shakow, D. Effects of irregular preparatory intervals on reaction time in schizophrenia. *J. abnorm. soc. Psychol.*, 1963, **67**, 44–52.

Zigler, E. & Phillips, L. Social effectiveness and symptomatic behaviors. *J. abnorm. soc. Psychol.*, 1960, **61**, 231–238.

Chapter 15

Alcoholism and Drug Addiction

A. Alcoholism[1]

I. DEFINITION AND INCIDENCE

1. DEFINITION OF ALCOHOLISM

ALTHOUGH THE EXISTENCE of alcoholism as a major problem is not in doubt, little agreement has been reached concerning an adequate and acceptable definition of the disorder. Thus, the World Health Organization Expert Committee on Mental Health (Alcoholism) (1951) defined the population of alcoholics as "those excessive drinkers whose dependence upon alcohol has attained such a degree that it shows a noticeable mental disturbance or an interference with their bodily and mental health, their interpersonal relations and their smooth social and economic functioning; or shows the prodromal signs of such developments." Jellinek (1960, p. 35), on the other hand, defines alcoholism as "any use of alcoholic beverages that causes any damage to the individual or society or both." Jellinck, however, does not regard alcoholism as a single entity (and therefore as having possibly a single etiology) but distinguishes five main categories.

(i) "*Alpha alcoholism* represents a *purely* psychological *continual* dependence or reliance upon the effect of alcohol to relieve bodily or emotional pain" but it "*does not lead to 'loss of control' or 'inability to abstain'*" (Jellinek, 1960, p. 36; italics in original).

(ii) "*Beta alcoholism* is that species of alcoholism in which such alcoholic complications as polyneuropathy, gastritis and cirrhosis of the liver may occur without either physical or psychological dependence upon alcohol" (Jellinek, 1960, p. 37).

(iii) "*Gamma alcoholism* means that species of alcoholism in which (1) acquired increased tissue tolerance to alcohol, (2) adaptive cell metabolism, (3) withdrawal symptoms and 'craving', i.e., physical dependence, and (4) loss of control are involved" (Jellinek, 1960, p. 37).

(iv) "*Delta alcoholism* shows the first three characteristics of gamma alcoholism as well as a less marked form of the fourth characteristic—that is, instead of loss of control there is inability to abstain" (Jellinek, 1960, p. 38).

(v) *Epsilon alcoholism* refers to periodic bouts of alcoholism.

Jellinek rejects alpha and beta alcoholism as diseases, since he regards alpha alcoholism as a symptom of an underlying disturbance while, in the case of beta alcoholism, the physiological changes involved are a *result* of the excessive drinking which itself does not indicate any causal physical or psychological pathology. He

---

[1] Brief reviews of the present status of alcoholism research in the psychiatric literature are presented by Zwerling and Rosenbaum (1959) and by Mayer-Gross et al (1960). The most comprehensive review of etiological factors is that by Jellinek (1960), while Voegtlin and Lemere (1942) have reviewed the results of various methods of treatment. Three reviews by Franks (1958, 1963, 1966) deal with psychological approaches to alcoholism, while Popham and Schmidt (1962) give an excellent account of a decade of research (1950–1960) in one country (Canada).

is inclined to regard gamma and delta alcoholism as diseases because the physiological changes themselves come to increase the "necessity" for alcoholic intake (it should be noted carefully that the *initial* drinking may not be precipitated by physiological abnormalities). He reserves judgment on epsilon alcoholism. Jellinek's classification is, of course, a descriptive one, though its acceptance would certainly require a multidimensional etiological system rather than a unidimensional one.

2. INCIDENCE OF ALCOHOLISM

The difficulties involved in assessing the incidence of alcoholism have been carefully pointed out by Mayer-Gross et al (1960) and illustrated more recently by Lipscombe (1966); it will be sufficient to indicate here the undoubted gravity of the problem. Thus Keller and Efron (1955) estimated that in 1953 the rate in the United States was about 4400 per 100,000 adults (with a ratio of about 6 males to one female), giving a total of almost five million.[2] According to Mayer-Gross et al (1960), alcoholic illnesses totalled 18% of all male admissions to the University Psychiatric Clinic, Burghölzli (Switzerland) during the years 1946–1950, roughly 11% being for chronic alcoholism. Of course, wide variations in these figures occur according to the location of the survey (e.g., rural versus urban) and other factors (Zax et al, 1967). Opinions also vary as to whether alcoholism is increasing (when population changes are allowed for) or decreasing. The seriousness of the problem (which affects not only the alcoholic himself, but at the very least his wife, children, and employer as well) is not to be doubted.

II. ETIOLOGICAL THEORIES

Attempts to account for the onset and maintenance of alcoholism have proceeded at all levels of analysis, from biochemical to psychological. The following brief descriptions will serve to orient the reader to the various theories. It will be clear, however, from our earlier discussion of the multidimensional determination of human behavior that the theories need not be mutually exclusive, although the proponents of a particular theory tend to write as if they were.

1. PHYSIOLOGICAL FORMULATIONS

The most important of the physiological formulations are the *nutritional deficiency* theories proposed by Mardones (1951) and Williams (1947, 1959). In essence, these theories assert that in some individuals there is a genetically determined failure to utilize one or more of the basic nutritional elements and that this failure creates a craving for the "missing" elements which, as it happens, can be satisfied by the continual ingestion of alcohol. It is usually assumed that the deficiency is present *prior* to the development of alcoholic drinking patterns, although it is regarded as possible that the deficiency is initially *produced* by excessive alcohol consumption. Within this framework, then, the "need" for alcohol is akin to the "need" for sugar intake when the blood-sugar level reaches abnormally low levels or the need for water when there is excessive thirst. Nutritional deficiency as a *causative* factor in the precipitation of drinking can hardly be said to have been satisfactorily demonstrated, and such experimental evidence as there is in support of it is open to alternative interpretations.

Closely akin to the nutritional deficiency theories is the *endocrinological theory* of Smith (1949) and others. Smith postulated a primary metabolic disturbance associated with adrenal cortex and pituitary functioning which were disturbed by alcohol ingestion. This disturbance in turn led to a craving for alcohol. Smith's theory has been criticized mainly on the grounds that the physiological changes observed are most likely a consequence of alcohol ingestion and not a cause of it.

Physiological theories, then, postulate a basic disturbance of body chemistry which leads to a deficiency state which is temporarily ameliorated by the ingestion of alcohol. The alcohol may exacerbate the deficiency state, thus setting up a vicious circle—deficiency—alcohol intake—increased deficiency—alcohol intake . . . etc.

2. PSYCHOANALYTIC AND PSYCHODYNAMIC FORMULATIONS

Feldman (1956, p. 82) has argued that "the basic concept in the psychotherapy of the alcoholic patient is the idea that alcoholism is a symptom of an underlying emotional disturbance," and this view represents the position

---

[2] A more conservative estimate by Bailey et al (1965) puts the rate at 1900 per 100,000 with a ratio of 3.6 males to every female.

of the psychoanalyst and psychodynamic psychologist accurately. As far as psycho-analytical formulations are concerned, alcoholism has proved to be in much the same category as the obsessional neuroses in resisting interpretation and treatment and, compared with other neurotic abnormalities, not a great deal has been written about it. Stress is usually laid on the use of alcohol as an adult substitute for the infantile soothing effects of milk in that it temporarily produces a feeling of soothing well-being which also reduces hostile feelings.

It is interesting to note, however, that not all psychodynamicists reject "symptomatic" treatment of alcoholism on the grounds that the underlying "conflict" or disturbance must be attacked. Thus, Kant (1944b) argues that:

"conditioning against alcohol is a symptomatic treatment. It does not eliminate the underlying causes of maladjustment. What it does is to frustrate a pseudo-adjustment by the inadequate means of alcohol. The patient is forced to face reality without the help of alcohol, he is prevented from withdrawing and escaping into intoxication. What will be the result? Several psychotherapists actually see a danger in treating the symptoms without adjustment of the underlying personality disorder. . . . Theoretically, this might be a possibility, but it is a purely hypothetical assumption not substantiated by experience. On the contrary, it is a fact that most alcoholics are, for all practical purposes, well adjusted so long as they do not drink; and those who are not, nevertheless get along better during sober periods. The histories given by wives of alcoholic husbands are nearly identical and absolutely characteristic: during periods of abstinence the alcoholic was a wonderful husband, father, and provider" (Kant, 1944b, pp. 372–373).

Finally, Tiebout (1951) draws interesting parallels between alcoholism and fever, on the one hand, and cancer on the other. In searching for the cause of an illness, the presence of fever may be ignored, but if the fever becomes dangerously high, then it may become imperative to take steps to reduce it by whatever means are available. Cancer may result from the presence of an irritative substance, but once the cancer has taken a firm hold, removal of the irritative substance will not effect a cure of the cancer, which may need to be attacked directly. Tiebout concludes that "alcoholism is a symptom which has become a disease" and

supports the use of "symptomatic" therapy (while not denying the value of psychotherapy). As we have pointed out before, there are dangers in drawing analogies between medical and behavioral problems, but Tiebout's examples have the merit of demonstrating the dangers of too readily assuming the validity of the symptom substitution viewpoint.

3. SOCIOLOGICAL FORMULATIONS

That cultural influences exercise a significant effect in determining the incidence of alcoholism, when availability of alcohol is held constant, is not to be doubted, in spite of the formidable methodological problems involved. Without going into the evidence, it may be stated that there are widely different incidences in different countries and in different areas within the same country (related to ethnic groups and religious teachings, in part). In general, the sociological findings support the approach based on learning theory, in that they suggest that the incidence of alcoholism is partly a function of the degree to which it is available to reduce tensions produced by the conditions of life in a particular society.

4. LEARNING THEORY FORMULATIONS

That a considerable learned component is involved in alcoholism can hardly be denied. Unfortunately, little progress has been made in spelling out the details in terms of learning theory except in the rather general sense that alcohol serves as a drive-reducing agent and hence strengthens all of the behaviors preceding it. As a drive-reducing agent, alcohol may work in two main ways, which are not mutually exclusive. First, it may reduce the physiological deficit state referred to above and, in this sense, it would be directly comparable with the rewarding effects of food or water in animal experiments. Second, it may serve to reduce anxiety responses and their attendant stimulation (Kepner, 1964; Kingham, 1958). In this latter respect there is clearly an analogy with the sociological formulations, individual anxiety patterns being substituted for social ones. Instrumental or operant conditioning would be involved, since the person in a state of anxiety or physiological deprivation would perhaps try several methods of reducing the drive level until he hit upon alcohol. It is conceivable that *both* drives must be present for alcohol to become the dominant or preferred method of reducing the drive.

Conger (1956) has provided laboratory evidence in relation to this formulation in studies with rats, although, as we have seen, there is a formidable body of evidence relating to fear or anxiety as a learned drive motivating instrumental behavior which ultimately succeeds in reducing the drive and hence is reinforced. Since alcoholism obviously results in a good deal of suffering and pain for the individual, Conger invokes other important principles of learning to account for the persistence of alcoholic addiction. He points out that the *immediately* reinforcing effects of alcohol are likely to predominate over the more remote non-reinforcing effects of social punishment; and that the anxiety-reducing effects of alcohol may well be stronger than the anxiety-inducing effects of anticipated punishment (alcohol itself would, of course, have the effect of at least temporarily reducing the latter). More direct evidence of the effect of immediate reward over delayed punishment in alcoholics has been provided by Vogel-Sprott and Banks (1965) who found that a rewarded response was suppressed significantly more often in non-alcoholics than in alcoholics when the rewarded response was accompanied or followed by shock.

5. PERSONALITY AS AN ETIOLOGICAL FACTOR

A great deal of futile endeavor has been directed to a search for a common underlying personality structure in alcoholics. For example, groups of alcoholics have been subjected to a variety of psychological tests, personality and otherwise, in the hope of finding a constellation of traits characteristic of alcoholics. Aside from the fact that such studies inevitably confound personality characteristics present in the individual before he became an alcoholic with changes in the characteristics (or the development of new traits) as a result of addiction to alcohol, it will be clear, in terms of our earlier discussion of the nature of personality and its development, that it is most unlikely that any basic constellation will be found. Thus, it is possible that a high degree of conditionability would favorably predispose an individual to the development of alcoholic addiction compared with a low degree of conditionability. However, if the former individual also receives a strict upbringing in which alcohol is strictly forbidden, whereas the latter receives a lax upbringing in which alcohol may even be pressed upon him, the result may be an equal degree of alcoholism. A particular degree of alcoholism

will therefore result from the interaction of a number of factors, each of which may contribute in widely varying degrees to produce the same end-result. This is not, of course, to deny the existence of a basic set of factors in the etiology of alcoholism but merely to point out that the alcoholic-nonalcoholic group comparison method is not likely to throw any light on these factors.

A much more adequate methodology is to be found in a number of recent important studies by Vogel which show clearly the value of working systematically within a dimensional framework, the empirically testable implications of which may be clearly stated. Using Eysenck's theory of introversion-extraversion, Vogel (1959) first derived several predictions regarding *the relationship between alcohol and introversion-extraversion in nonalcoholic subjects.* In terms of the theory, since alcohol is a depressant, its effects will be:

(i) To retard the formation and facilitate the extinction of conditioned responses.

(ii) To shift performance in the extraverted direction on tasks such as physical persistence, accuracy in speed tests, and so on; and to decrease systolic blood pressure and stressed pulse rate.

It also follows that introverts should have a higher threshold for intoxication and that the performance shift in the extraverted direction will be smaller for introverts than for extraverts under the influence of alcohol (provided ceiling effects do not obscure the effect).

Predictions may also be made concerning *the relationship between alcoholism and extraversion-introversion.* Thus, compared with extraverted alcoholics, introverted alcoholics will:

(i) Acquire conditioned responses more quickly and extinguish them more slowly.

(ii) Respond better to conditioned response therapy and relapse less often.

(iii) Benefit less from an organization like Alcoholics Anonymous.

(iv) Report fewer blackout phenomena and be less likely to enter Jellinek's prodromal stage.

(v) Be more often solitary drinkers.

(vi) Be steady rather than explosive drinkers.

Finally, since long-term alcoholism is likely to lead to progressive brain damage, which itself increases degree of extraversion, there should be a positive correlation between length of addiction and degree of extraversion.

It should be noted carefully that Vogel makes no assumptions about whether alcoholics as a group are more or less introverted than a control group of nonalcoholics, which is an empirical question. The *position* of an alcoholic on the extraversion-introversion dimension, however, has clear implications of a practical nature for the etiology and treatment, as well as for the social behavior, of the alcoholic.

In four subsequent studies, Vogel (1960, 1961a, 1961b, 1961c) has explored some of the predictions outlined above. Her conditioning procedure utilized the GSR as the unconditioned and conditioned response, a loud tone as the unconditioned stimulus, and nonsense syllables embedded in neutral stimuli as the conditioned stimuli. She demonstrated that introverted alcoholics and nonalcoholics established the conditioned response more readily than extraverted alcoholics and nonalcoholics, and took longer to extinguish. This was so even when degree of neuroticism was controlled. Furthermore, ten of the 81 subjects used (nine alcoholics and one nonalcoholic) failed to condition in the time allowed and all of these had high extraversion scores, in line with theoretical expectation.

Vogel also examined in these studies the relationship between conditioning and drinking patterns in alcoholics. She found that introversion was significantly associated with a steady drinking pattern, solitary drinking, and a longer interval between the first and subsequent blackouts. The information about drinking habits was, however, obtained by questionnaire investigation from the alcoholics themselves, and its validity is uncertain. The relationship between solitary drinking, blackouts, and conditioning was not confirmed in a second study.

Vogel obtained two other results of importance: first, that alcoholics tend to be more neurotic than a control sample of nonalcoholics; second, that their introversion pattern of scores is not different from that found in a normal population. As Vogel points out, this fact may be of great importance in relation to the conditioned response therapy of alcoholism, the success or failure of which may largely depend on the ease with which the patient forms conditioned responses.[3]

There is, therefore, some evidence that individual differences in personality structure may be predictive of the development of differential patterns of behavior in the development of alcoholism.

6. CONCLUSION

The above brief review merely confirms the conclusion arrived at by almost every practical and research worker in the problem of alcoholism: that it is one of the most intractable and difficult of all behavior problems and that any apparently successful new treatment must be viewed with extreme caution. In light of this, the conditioned aversion treatment of alcoholism deserves serious (albeit sceptical) consideration, since any genuine increase in success ratio with this technique (even if not completely permanent) would represent an important advance over or, at least, a supplement to other methods of treatment.

III. BEHAVIOR THERAPY AND ALCOHOLISM

1. HISTORICAL DEVELOPMENT OF CONDITIONING TECHNIQUES

The earliest reported deliberate attempt at conditioned reflex treatment of alcoholism appears to be that of Kantorovich (1929) who used electric shock as the unconditioned stimulus and claimed that 14 out of 17 subjects remained sober for one to several months following treatment. The first to use an emetic drug (apomorphine) appears to have been Markovnikov (1934) whose technique was described in a French journal by Ichok (1934) as follows.

"L'alcoolique qui recoit Occ.3 d'une solution d'apomorphine à 1 p.100 est mis, quelques minutes après, en présence d'une boisson alcoolique. Comme l'injection entraîne une forte envie de vomir, il sera nécessaire d'offrir, en ce moment, de l'alcool au malade, qui, quelques instants après, le rejettera. Ainsi, il sera aisé d'associer, dans l'esprit du malade, les deux faits, liés l'un à l'autre, à savoir: le vomissement inévitable, après l'ingestion de l'alcool"[4] (p. 1745).

---

[3] Smart (1965) found that deteriorated alcoholics obtained higher extraversion scores than non-deteriorated alcoholics (where deterioration was measured by VIQ-PIQ difference scores on the WAIS), a result in line with Vogel's position.

[4] "Several minutes after receiving O.3 cc of apomorphine in a 1 part per hundred solution, the alcoholic is given an alcoholic drink. At the moment the injection produces severe nausea, alcohol is offered to the patient who will vomit a few seconds later. Thus, an association will readily be formed in the mind of the patient between the ingestion of alcohol and subsequent unavoidable vomiting."

The technique was quickly taken up, not only by other workers in Russia but also in many other countries, such as Germany (e.g., Galant, 1936) and the United Kingdom (e.g., Dent, 1934).

Since then, a great many studies have been published by enthusiastic workers, an examination of which shows that many of them had little or no knowledge of the facts or methodology of conditioning studies.

2. PRINCIPAL TECHNIQUES

Most of the techniques used in behavior therapy with alcoholics parallel (and indeed formed the inspiration for) those already described in the treatment of sexual disorders. It will not be necessary, therefore, to describe them in any great detail.

(a) CLASSICAL AVERSIVE CONDITIONING WITH DRUGS. The basic technique used by Voegtlin and his colleagues has been described in detail by Voegtlin (1940) and by Lemere, Voegtlin, Broz, O'Hollaren, and Tupper (1942a). A verbal description of the treatment is first given to the patient, following which he drinks two 10-ounce glasses of warm saline solution containing one and one half grains of oral emetine and one gram of sodium chloride to 20 ounces of water. He is then given an injection of six minims of a 40 cc sterile acqueous solution containing 3.25 grams of emetine hydrochloride (to produce diaphoresis) and one and one half grains of ephedrine sulphate (for support). Immediately before vomiting occurs, he is given a 4-ounce glass of whiskey (to produce gastric irritation), which he is required to smell, taste, swill round in the mouth, and then swallow. The patient is then given a 10-ounce glass of warm water with 2 ounces of whiskey in it. If vomiting has still not occurred, he is given another straight whiskey. Following vomiting, a glass of near beer containing tartar emetic is given to prolong nausea. Subsequent treatments involve an increase in the dose of injected emetine, an increase in the length of treatment time, and a widening of the range of spirits used.

These details have been provided to indicate the severity of the treatment regimen used by Voegtlin, which was undoubtedly much harsher than those used in later studies and in the drug aversion treatment of sexual disorders. Since Voegtlin's studies have been severely criticized

by subsequent workers who appear not to have studied the original sources and to have relied on second-hand reports, it is worth pointing out that Voegtlin and his colleagues were exceptionally well aware of the problems involved in this form of treatment. Voegtlin, Lemere, and Broz (1940), for example, provide a detailed discussion of the problems involved in the use of apomorphine, pointing out its short-term effect, the narcosis that it produces which could interfere with conditioning, and its possible dangerous side-effects. They discuss the importance of conditioning the patient to aversion to a range of spirits, and the problem of timing relationships.[5] In the later series of patients, they preferred the use of emetine to apomorphine (Lemere and Voegtlin, 1950).

Voegtlin's technique was taken up by other workers, who used it in a modified form. Thus, Shadel (1944) gives a detailed account of the importance he attached to "ancillary" details, such as pretreatment interviews, institutional care during treatment, and so on. A more important modification was that of Kant (1944a) who argued that the patient should not be allowed to ingest the alcohol, since this would be likely to retard conditioning. The conditioned aversion, he argued, should be developed to the sight, taste, and smell of alcohol, but not the swallowing of it. When the conditioned aversion is established, Kant encourages the patient to drink at the point at which vomiting is imminent, thus preventing (it is hoped) alcohol from remaining in the stomach. Kant also terminated his sessions (unlike Voegtlin) before nausea ended to prevent reduction in the potency of the conditioned response. Thimann (1949a) has also described a modification of Voegtlin's procedure, involving the use of benzedrine sulphate, strychnine sulphate, and emetine as the aversive drugs.

More recently, Raymond (1964) has suggested that vomiting is not an essential part of the treatment (nausea being sufficient), but has continued to use apomorphine, in spite of its disadvantages. Raymond also introduced an operant procedure in which, following the establishment of aversive conditioning, the patient is given a placebo injection and is presented with a choice of beverages, including both alcohol and soft drinks. If the latter are chosen (which, according to Raymond, is invariably the case), the choice is reinforced by the failure of vomiting or nausea to occur and

---

[5] See also the very clear discussion of the timing of CS-US relationships in Voegtlin (1947, p. 809).

the turning of the session into a "positive" training session.

Finally, an important innovation has been described by Miller et al (1960), which involves the use of Voegtlin's technique in a group setting, the unpleasant details of which need not be detailed here.[6]

(b) CLASSICAL AVERSIVE CONDITIONING WITH SHOCK. This technique does not appear to have been used in the treatment of alcoholism.

(c) CLASSICAL AVERSIVE CONDITIONING WITH PARALYSIS. Unpleasant as the Voegtlin technique might be, an even severer form of aversive conditioning has been developed by Sanderson et al (1963), the rationale of which has been subsequently experimentally verified more generally by Campbell et al (1964). The aversive stimulus in this technique involves the total paralysis of the respiratory system (producing, of course, total cessation of breathing) of the patient by the injection of 20 mg of succinylcholine chloride dyhydrate. The paralysis and cessation of breathing lasts for 60 to 90 seconds and, while it does not produce any harmful after-effects, a state of extreme terror is induced in the patient, who is rendered quite helpless and may be convinced he is going to die. The technique was described by Sanderson et al (1963) as follows.

"After the subject was connected with the polygraph, he was allowed to settle down so that a constant baseline of physiological function was established. Once this had appeared he was given a bottle containing a few drops of his favorite beverage and told to grasp it, look at it, put it to his nose and sniff it, then put it to his lips and taste it, and then hand it back to the experimenter. This was repeated five times at intervals of about a minute; this routine usually took about 10 or 15 secs. After five trials, 20 mg. of succinylcholine was injected into the drip and the drip was then turned full on. As soon as the drug entered the blood stream, there was a characteristic change of GSR. This was signaled to the experimenter in the room who at once handed the bottle to the subject and at just the moment when the bottle was about to be put to the subject's lips, the full effect of the drug took hold. The experimenter then held the bottle to the subject's lips and put a few drops of the drink into his mouth. As soon as any signs of regular breathing appeared the bottle was taken away" (Sanderson et al, 1963, p. 263–264).

The technique undoubtedly has the advantage of enabling timing relationships to be controlled with a considerable degree of accuracy, and there can be no doubt about the aversiveness of the unconditioned stimulus.

(d) INSTRUMENTAL ESCAPE CONDITIONING WITH SHOCK. Blake (1965) presented shocks of increasing intensity to the forearm contiguously with the sipping of the patient's favorite drink. The shock could be terminated by spitting out the drink, rather than swallowing it. A partial reinforcement technique was used, with rejection of the alcohol taking place to a green light signal on nonreinforced trials.

(e) INSTRUMENTAL AVOIDANCE CONDITIONING WITH SHOCK. MacCulloch et al (1966) used the same technique as they applied to the treatment of homosexuality. The stimuli varied from a range of photographs of beer and spirits to the sight of the actual bottles, the visual stimulation being accompanied by a tape recording inviting the patient to have a drink (the stimuli were under the control of the experimenter who could make the visual objects visible or invisible for specified periods of time). A relief stimulus was incorporated into the procedure. The patient could avoid shock if he turned off the conditioned stimulus within eight seconds of its presentation. If he did so, the relief stimulus was immediately presented. Response latencies to the CS were measured, as well as pulse rates during conditioning.

(f) AVERSIVE IMAGERY TECHNIQUE. Although he called it a verbal aversion technique, Anant's (1966, 1967a, 1967b) procedure is very similar to that used by Gold and Neufeld with sexual disorders, reported in an earlier chapter. The patient is required to imagine various situations involving drinking and is then asked to imagine various unpleasant consequences which involve social shame and degradation. This procedure is preceded by relaxation training involving deep breathing and exhaling.

(g) RELAXATION-AVERSION TECHNIQUE. This technique, devised by Blake (1965), differs from his aversion technique (described above) only in that the aversion training is preceded by training in progressive relaxation. It may be noted that the relaxation training is followed by "motivation training" which involves self-analysis of the problem of drinking in the patient.

---

[6] Group techniques of this kind were first carried out in Germany and France.

(h) BROAD-SPECTRUM THERAPY. Lazarus (1965) has stressed the need for applying behavior therapy techniques to more than just the question of stopping the drinking of the patient. He stresses the need to improve the patient's physical state, to improve social relations, to eliminate concomitant anxiety responses by desensitization, assertive training, behavior rehearsal, and hypnosis, and to enlist the cooperation of wife and relatives. It would not, of course, be true to say that earlier workers had neglected these problems. But the stress laid by Lazarus on the need to investigate and treat all of the behavior problems of the alcoholic is a timely one in this area particularly.

3. THE RESULTS OF BEHAVIOR THERAPY

Consideration of the results obtained ·with behavior therapy in relation to alcoholism will be made with reference to the techniques described in the previous section.

(a) CLASSICAL AVERSIVE CONDITIONING WITH DRUGS. There can be no doubt that the studies of Voegtlin and his colleagues, ranging over a period of more than ten years, represent one of the most monumental applications of behavior therapy yet undertaken. The early studies (Voegtlin, 1940; Voegtlin et al, 1942; Lemere, Voegtlin, Broz, O'Hollaren, and Tupper, 1942b) reported initial follow-up

studies on fairly large numbers. By 1950, however, Voegtlin and Broz (1949) were able to report the results from over 3000 cases, with results as shown in Figure 1 for 2323 cases. It should be noted that a very strict criterion for abstinence was used. "Abstinence" was defined as "total abstinence" and excluded from this category were (i) those cases subsequently successfully reconditioned by further treatment who were abstinent at the time of the survey; and (ii) those who had relapsed from total abstinence but were only moderate drinkers (i.e., were no longer alcoholic). The results, as shown in Figure 1, indicate that the overall abstinence rate was 44.8%, with the rate falling to 25–30% at the end of ten years. One year later, Lemere and Voegtlin (1950) reported similar findings for a sample increased to over 4000 patients. Voegtlin and Broz (1949) further report that even relapsed patients treated by their technique enjoyed some period of abstinence before relapsing. Thus, of 868 relapsed subjects, 640 were abstinent for at least 3–6 months, and 276 for over 12 months. It should be realized that the figures given include those patients treated during the development of the technique.

An important study by Voegtlin et al (1941) investigated the effects of reconditioning following original treatment over a period of one year.

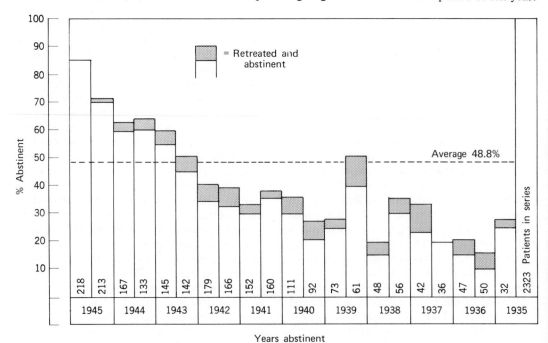

FIG. 1. Percentage abstinence rates by six-month intervals over a ten-year follow-up period (Voegtlin and Broz, 1949).

A total of 197 patients was divided into sub-groups which were given from one to four reconditioning treatments at 30, 60, then every 90 days following the original treatment. The results clearly indicated the value of periodic reconditioning for maintaining abstinence. A control group not offered the reconditioning therapy showed a higher relapse rate than any of the experimental groups.

Edlin et al (1945) reported results on 100 cases (mostly men) with an average addiction period of 12½ years. They claimed that 55% of patients treated privately remained abstinent for 5–15 months, but that this was so with only 15% of subjects treated in a general hospital. Unfortunately, the description of their technique is poor, and it seems likely that they did not exercise nearly such careful experimental control as did Voegtlin.

Thimann (1949b) reported on results obtained with 282 patients aged 17–64, of which results were available for 245. He claimed that 125 were still total abstainers after 1–3 years, with 58 having abstained for more than 5 years. He further asserted that his abstainers included many who would be very poor long-term bets (e.g., bartenders).

An important qualification to these results was provided in a study by Quinn and Henbest (1967). They found that ten patients given a course of apomorphine aversion therapy (at two-hourly intervals for 72 hours) to the sight, smell, and taste of whisky had apparently developed a persistent aversion to this particular liquor. However, the degree of *generalized* aversion to other spirits and drinks varied widely. Three patients had avoided whisky for from four to eight years following treatment. They were now drinking stout or beer, but not to excess, and showed significant improvement in general adjustment and marital relations. Three patients had also avoided whisky for long periods of time following treatment, but were drinking other spirits excessively; while the remaining four patients avoided whisky but were drinking beer or wine excessively. Quinn and Henbest speculate that the seven patients still drinking to excess were doing so to reduce a primary drive and that the avoidance of whisky was a reinforcing state of affairs.

Results similar to those obtained by Voegtlin and his colleagues have been reported from other workers. Negative results have, of course, been noted, but Franks (1958) has effectively pointed out the obvious methodological deficiencies in most of these studies.

In their study of group aversion, Miller et al (1960) used the Voegtlin procedure over ten successive days, 20 patients being tested in groups of four. All patients acquired the conditioned aversion reaction. In an eight-month follow-up of ten of these patients, five were still totally abstinent, three were abstinent except for brief temporary relapses, and two had relapsed completely. The authors conclude that there is no doubt that conditioning can be established in a group situation, but the long-term effects remain uncertain.

(b) CLASSICAL AVERSIVE CONDITIONING WITH SHOCK. As was pointed out earlier, this technique does not appear to have been used in the treatment of alcoholism.

(c) CLASSICAL AVERSIVE CONDITIONING WITH PARALYSIS. This technique was applied by Sanderson et al (1963) to 12 alcoholics. They regarded their results as only suggestive, but they provide illustrations of subsequent behavior outside the hospital situation that suggest that the conditioning which undoubtedly occurred generalized outside the test situation. On follow-up, six out of 12 patients were known not to be drinking, three were drinking, and three could not be traced. The length of follow-up was not stated.

The cautious interpretation of their results by Sanderson et al (1963) was thoroughly justified. Holzinger et al (1967) replicated as closely as possible this study under the direct guidance of one of the authors of the original study, applying the technique to 23 alcoholics with an average of ten years of problem drinking. Seventeen out of 21 patients contacted at follow-up of four months on average were drinking, and over 33% had been rehospitalized for alcoholism during the follow-up period. Similar disappointing results were obtained by Farrar et al (1968). Of twelve patients treated by this technique, only two out of nine located on 12-month follow-up were totally abstinent, and one of these felt that the effects of the "cure" were worse than the alcoholism.

Two studies utilizing control groups also threw serious doubt on the validity of the results of the original experiment as far as "real-life" effects are concerned. Madill et al (1966) subjected three groups of matched alcoholics to identical experimental procedures up to the point of injection of succinylcholine. One group was then injected with the drug and liquor presented during paralysis; the second group received the injection but without liquor presentation during paralysis; and the third group was presented with liquor but received no injection. While ratings of degree and speed of onset of induced fear significantly discriminated the two drug-injected groups from the non-injected group, only minor differences in subsequent drinking patterns were found on follow-up. In a rather similar experiment, Clancy et al (1967) injected the drug into one group of alcoholics; a saline placebo into a second group; and compared results obtained with these two groups with two control groups, one of which was given the customary hospital treatments for alcoholism (individual, group, or drug therapies), the other group consisting of patients who refused treatment. At a one-year follow-up assessment, 88% of the succinyl-choline-treated group had been abstinent for at least three months, compared with 70% of the placebo group, 66% of the hospital treatment group, and 45% of the nontreatment group. The difference between the succinylcholine and placebo groups was not significant.

These results are difficult to explain, since not only were these studies careful replications as far as technique was concerned, but there was no doubt that exactly the same objective results were obtained in the experimental situation; while the subjective reports of intense fear (and its link to the sight, taste, and smell of alcohol) were also obtained. The problems raised by these studies have been very thoroughly discussed by Madill et al (1967) and by Laverty (1966).

(d) INSTRUMENTAL ESCAPE CONDITIONING WITH SHOCK. Blake (1967) reported on the results of this method of treatment with 20 males and five females. Four outcome categories were used: abstinent (no drinking at all); improved (social drinking only); relapsed (drinking at pretreatment level); and others (opted out of treatment, etc.). Follow-up was carried out at six and 12 months after treatment. At six months, 48% of the patients were abstinent and 12% improved; at 12 months, 23% were abstinent and 27% improved.

(e) INSTRUMENTAL AVOIDANCE CONDITION-ING WITH SHOCK. A salutary shower of cold water was administered to the increasing optimism engendered by earlier reports of the effects of shock treatment by MacCulloch et al (1966). They reported complete failure with four alcoholics over ten to 46 sessions. They were, however, able to point out some striking differences between the behavior of these

patients during training and the homosexual patients with whom the instrumental avoidance-relief technique had been so encouraging. The alcoholic patients, during aversive conditioning, showed variable response latencies to the conditioned stimuli and slow and irregular learning of the avoidance response. Furthermore, none showed evidence of pulse rate conditioning. This record of therapeutic failure does not, of course, necessarily condemn the technique as useless for alcoholism. The patient sample may have been unique in its characteristics, and MacCulloch et al may simply have been unfortunate in picking four patients in succession who were essentially nonconditionable or, at least, in whom stable conditioning could not be achieved. Certainly their study offers suggestive evidence relating to factors which may militate against successful avoidance conditioning.

(f) AVERSIVE IMAGERY TECHNIQUE. Anant (1967a) reported that 25 alcoholics (all except one, male) who completed his aversive imagery program had abstained from alcohol for follow-up periods ranging from eight to 15 months. Eleven of these patients were treated on an individual basis, whereas the remaining 15[7] were seen in four groups. A much less optimistic account was given in a later paper, however (Anant, 1967b), where it was stated that, of the 15 patients who were treated on a group basis, only three were still sober on follow-up six to 23 months later. Since Anant gives no details of how follow-up status was assessed, his results must be regarded with due caution. Much less optimistic results using a similar technique have recently been reported by Ashem and Donner (1968).

(g) RELAXATION - AVERSION TECHNIQUE. Blake (1965) reported that 54% of 37 alcoholics treated by this technique were abstinent at six months' follow-up, while a further 8% were improved; on follow-up at 12 months, 46% were rated as abstinent and 13% as improved. The criteria for abstinence and improvement were the same as those used by Blake (1967) to assess the results of aversion conditioning alone.

(h) BROAD-SPECTRUM THERAPY. Although Lazarus (1965) has reported a single case study using what, in effect, is a simultaneous attack on a number of aspects of the behavior of alcoholics, no systematic studies have so far been reported,[8] though McBrearty et al (1968) have described a program of treatment along these lines.

---

[7] Twenty-six patients were treated in all, but one dropped out before completion of treatment.

[8] Kraft and Al-Issa (1967) treated social diffi-

culties in an alcoholic by SD(I) and reported that alcoholic activity reduced to "normal" as social difficulties diminished.

4. Comparative Results

Alcoholism is notoriously refractory to any form of treatment, but perhaps not so refractory as is commonly supposed. Kendall and Staton (1965) followed up 62 untreated alcoholics for a mean of 6.7 years and found only one person to be abstinent. The effect of minimal first-aid management was investigated by Vallance (1965) who followed up over two years 68 alcoholic admissions to the psychiatric department of a general hospital. While 25% of the sample were "improved," less than 5% were abstinent. Thus, it seems that the "spontaneous remission" rate in the absence of specific forms of treatment is very low indeed.

Drugs have, of course, been used on a wide scale, with antabuse perhaps being the most preferred (Mann et al, 1952). The use of disulfiram was investigated by Davies et al (1956) who found that 36% of 50 alcoholics treated with this drug were abstinent for most of the two-year follow-up period. More recently, d-lysergic acid diethylamide (LSD) has been used, with some glowing reports of its efficacy in reducing drinking frequency in alcoholics (e.g., Chwelos et al, 1959). These studies were reviewed and severely criticized for their methodological inadequacies, however, by Smart and Storm (1964). In a very carefully controlled study, using LSD, ephedrine control, and no-drug control groups, Smart et al (1966) could not find any significant effect for either drug over the control group on six-month follow-up. All three groups showed a significant gain in abstinence over the six-month period.

The effects of group therapy on alcoholism were investigated by Glatt (1961) who reported that one-third of 94 alcoholics treated in this way had "recovered" at the end of a two-year follow-up period; while a further one-third had "improved" during the same period.

Only two studies enable comparisons to be made between different kinds of behavior therapy. Blake (1967) compared the results of the two techniques (instrumental escape from shock training, preceded or not preceded by relaxation training) used by him, with results shown in Table 15.1, using the criteria discussed earlier. None of the differences in outcome were significant.

Pemberton (1967) compared outcome in 50 female and 50 male alcoholics followed up for periods ranging from 8 to 24 months after discharge, the mean follow-up period being 18 months. Within the male and female groups, two subgroups were formed. One subgroup was subjected to "intensive" treatment, using Blake's instrumental escape conditioning technique or by uncovering psychotherapy, using as an abreative agent carbon dioxide or LSD, or a combination of both. The other subgroup received supportive psychotherapy, sometimes with appropriate drug therapy or antabuse as an adjunct. In the female group, 10 out of 24 and, in the male group, 10 out of 23 patients subjected to "intensive" treatment were categorized as successful cases; whereas none out of 22 females, but eight out of 20 males subjected to "routine" treatment were categorized as successful cases. It is unfortunate that the conditioned aversion treatment results were confounded by the use of drugs and uncovering psychotherapy.

These results and those reviewed earlier suggest the cautious conclusion that the advantages found for shock treatment over drug treatment in the case of sexual disorders may not be present in the case of alcoholism,

TABLE 15.1.   *Comparative Results with Relaxation-Aversion and Aversion-Only Therapy in Alcoholism*

| Status on Follow-Up | Technique | | | |
| | Relaxation-Aversion | | Aversion only | |
	6 Months	12 Months	6 Months	12 Months
Abstinent	54% } 62%	46% } 59%	48% } 60%	23% } 50%
Improved	8%	13%	12%	27%
Relapsed	27%	30%	20%	27%
Other	11%	11%	20%	23%

Source: Blake, 1967, Tables 1–4.

and that, indeed, the reverse may be the case. Certainly, it seems that the results obtained by Voegtlin and his colleagues have been cavalierly dismissed in favor of the use of shock treatment although, quite recently, Raymond (1964) has obtained striking results over a three-year follow-up period with the use of a modified Voegtlin technique.

IV. METHODOLOGICAL PROBLEMS

We will discuss here factors associated with success and failure of conditioned aversive training; criteria for the assessment of results; and transfer from laboratory to real-life.

1. FACTORS ASSOCIATED WITH SUCCESS AND FAILURE

From time to time, so many contraindications to conditioned aversion treatment with drugs have been indicated that one is tempted to surmise that if they were all taken seriously, there would be no patients left for treatment. Since the drug aversion treatment at the present time still looks more promising than the shock aversion treatment, it is necessary to consider at least some of these contraindications carefully. Taking *physical* factors first, reservations about instituting drug-aversive conditioning may be indicated where there is a history of cardio-vascular-renal disturbance, active lung tuberculosis, active peptic ulcer, cirrhosis of the liver, angina, myocarditis, coronary disease, hernia, or bowel or lung hemorrhage (Thimann, 1949b; Lemere et al, 1942a). With respect to *personality and intellectual factors*, Thimann (1949b) considered that dull subjects and psychopaths (including those with a serious record of crime while sober) were relatively poor prospects. These factors may be related to extraversion, which Smart (1965) showed increased with alcoholic deterioration and which presumably would retard conditioning rate. Lemere et al (1942) agreed with Thimann's reservations and added uncooperative subjects, the psychotic, and the mentally deteriorated alcoholics. Voegtlin and Broz (1949) considered the neurotic patient was a poor prospect. *Social factors* were implicated by Lemere et al (1942) and by Edlin et al (1945) who both considered that the treatment had a better chance of success with private hospital than with public

hospital patients, a distinction that appeared to reduce to the ability of the patient to pay, which in turn apparently reflected the degree of motivation of the patient. Finally, Thimann (1949b) considered that a poor prognosis was indicated when an alcoholic presenting for treatment was also a drug addict.

What factors then make for successful treatment? Voegtlin and Broz (1949) considered that being older, being married, being able to pay, coming from a rural area, and having a previous period of abstinence were all favorable indicators. Lemere et al (1942) summed up the "ideal patient" as follows.

". . . the type of patient best suited for the conditioned reflex treatment of chronic alcoholism is the essentially normal, stable person who has gradually developed the habit until it has gotten the best of him, and now he wants help in breaking this habit and is willing and anxious to stop drinking for good . . . it is surprising how often (in these cases) a neurosis disappears when alcoholism is eliminated from the picture" (Lemere et al, 1942, p. 91).

With respect to shock aversion treatment, MacCulloch et al (1966), as was pointed out earlier, found that irregularity and slowness in forming the conditioned avoidance response, coupled with failure to develop a conditioned pulse rate, were present in their four failures. However, as they had no successes to report with alcoholics, the prognostic value of these indicators remain to be demonstrated. Pemberton (1967) found his successes were associated with introversion and neuroticism.

2. CRITERIA FOR THE ASSESSMENT OF RESULTS

Voegtlin and Lemere (1942) reviewed the literature through 1940 relating to the treatment of alcoholism. In evaluating the results of their own treatment at a later date, they pointed out (Lemere and Voegtlin, 1950) that they had been able to find only three papers using other methods of treatment (ranging from vitamins to psychoanalysis) which could be said to meet satisfactorily the minimal requirements of methodological adequacy, even though the requirements they laid down were not particularly rigorous.[9] They included the demand

---

[9] A recent review (Hill and Blane, 1967) of 49 American and Canadian studies dealing with psycho-

therapy of alcoholics was, if anything, even more severely critical of their methodological inadequacies.

for information as to: number and type of patients treated; a follow-up period of at least one year; a statement as to the length of time the patients remained abstinent after treatment; and use of a criterion of total abstinence as the indicator of successful therapy.

Voegtlin and his colleagues made the most painstaking efforts to follow up their own cases by means of personal contact, even where long distances were involved. Thus, in their review of 3125 admissions over a $10\frac{1}{2}$-year period, Voegtlin and Broz (1949) write:

"Individual data were secured by personal contact in all instances except those patients living east of the Mississippi River. In the latter cases, written replies known to be reliable were accepted. Unless current and accurate information was to be had, the patient was counted as unknown" (Voegtlin and Broz, 1949, p. 580).

Furthermore, a criterion of complete abstinence was used to establish success rate.

"The overall abstinence for the entire series of cases was found to be 44.8 per cent, for 1,042 of the 2,323 cases treated during the previous ten and a half years were found to be abstinent at the end of 1945. In addition, 92 patients of this group who relapsed and within a short time were treated a second time remained sober. If these latter patients are considered as successful cases, the percentage of abstinence is 48.8 per cent. Not a few patients were treated a third or even a fourth time. Such cases were counted as relapsed even though they happened to be abstinent on the closing date of the survey" (Voegtlin and Broz, 1949, p. 581).

Certainly, none of the more recent studies by behavior therapists even begin to match the meticulous care in the collection and analysis of follow-up data shown by Voegtlin and his colleagues.

3. TRANSFER FROM LABORATORY TO REAL LIFE

The fragile nature of changes produced under laboratory conditions in relation to alcoholism is, of course, well known. Nevertheless, the discrepancy between the encouraging results

obtained with apneic paralysis by Sanderson et al (1963) and the subsequent results obtained by Holzinger et al (1967) and others raises once again the problem of transferring laboratory results to real life. Although Farrar et al (1968) point out that the only evidence that conditioning occurred is the verbal report of the patient, there seems little reason to doubt that it did. Farrar et al also point to the well-known difficulty of obtaining generalization of autonomic conditioning and of its ready extinction. Once again, we are faced with the fact, unpalatable though it may be, that laboratory control of behavior will not be maintained outside the laboratory unless specific steps are taken to widen the control of environmental contingencies. This problem will be considered in detail in a later chapter, but here it may be pointed out that extra-laboratory familiar contingencies that are uncontrolled may prove more powerful in determining behavior once the patient is released than the recently-induced, relatively weak laboratory-induced contingencies.

B. Drug Addiction

In spite of the enormous increase in publicity given to drug addiction in recent years, there has been a deplorable lack of hard facts relating to incidence, outcome, and the effects of various methods of treatment. Into this confusion, behavior therapists have scarcely begun to penetrate and no attempt therefore will be made to provide a comprehensive survey of the present position.[10]

I. INTRODUCTION

The principal drugs of interest are the opiates (heroin and morphine), the barbiturates, the amphetamines, marihuana, the hallucinogens (including, of course, the notorious LSD drug), and various odd addictions which crop up from time to time, such as lighter fluid sniffing (Ackerly and Gibson, 1964). The problems of determining the incidence of usage of these drugs are formidable indeed and have been graphically described by Chein et al (1964). Heroin is a narcotic which is relatively infrequently used (compared, for example, with

---

[10] The most valuable sources of information at the time of writing are to be found in Wilner and Kassebaum (1965) and O'Donnell and Ball (1966). The United Nations Bulletin on Narcotics provides

regular reviews of various aspects of drug addiction throughout the world. A recent study of drug addiction in a single country (Czechoslovakia) will be found in Vondracek et al (1968).

the barbiturates), but even here, Winick (1965) experienced the greatest difficulty in determining its epidemiology in the United States, in spite of the resources expended on just this problem by the Federal Bureau of Narcotics. After a very careful analysis of the records kept by the Bureau, he concluded that, at the end of 1962, there were about 60,000 users of heroin in the United States, with about 7000 new users being detected each year. The incidence was highest in younger age groups and, contrary to the popular stereotype of the life-long "hooked" addict, it appears that the average length of usage of the drugs is less than ten years, with many users giving up the drug during their thirties and forties. Men outnumber women by four to one, and the problem tends to be concentrated in large cities, and especially in slum areas. Many of the more lurid accounts of heroin, both with respect to its effects and to the question of how addiction commences, have been shown to be untrue. The two basic problems arising from the use of heroin are the difficulties experienced by heroin users in obtaining regular supplies (and paying for them) on the one hand, and the very severe effects of deprivation of the drug (as long as regular supplies are available, the effects of heroin may be so slight that addicts of many years' standing may be undetectable except by special tests). Barbiturate and hallucinogen addiction is probably much more common than opiate addiction, but hard data are even more lacking than in the case of heroin and morphine, since the barbiturates and hallucinogens are regarded much more tolerantly than the opiates, even though the behavioral effects of the former may be more dangerous.

The etiology of drug usage is virtually unknown. Isbell (1965) has discussed the pharmacology, physiology, and biochemistry of drug addiction and has pointed out that psychological explanations fall into three categories—the psychobiologic, the psychoanalytic, and the pharmacodynamic.

The pharmacodynamic viewpoint essentially reduces to a conditioning model, in which use of the drug (however precipitated initially) reduces anxiety. Wikler (1965), in trying to account for relapses, has put this point of view as follows.

"Relapse may be attributed at least in part to two factors operating during previous episodes of addiction: (1) classical conditioning of physical dependence through repeated temporal contiguities between a specific environment and the occurrence of morphine-abstinence phenomena; and (2) reinforcement of instrumental activity (morphine acquisitory behavior) through repeated reduction by the drug of such abstinence phenomena as developed during intervals between doses" (Wikler, 1965, pp. 88–89).

Wikler's theory utilizes Mowrer's original two-factor model for learning in which classical aversive conditioning is reduced by instrumental behavior which reduces the aversive state. No direct evidence as to the validity of this theory in relation to addiction is available, but Wikler (1965) has reviewed his own investigations and those of others on the "morphine abstinence syndrome" in rats, the results of which appear to make the theory at least a plausible one.

The stress in Wikler's theory, it should be noted, is not primarily on the reduction in anxiety, but rather on the reduction in a physiological state which is produced by the drugs. This physiological state may take a number of forms, one of which might be an excessive intolerance of physical discomfort. Martin and Inglis (1965) have produced suggestive evidence that drug addiction may, in some cases, represent a form of self-therapy to increase an abnormally low tolerance for painful stimuli. They applied Hardy's cold-pressor test (immersion of the hand in water at 5° centigrade for as long as possible) to female addicts (not on the drug at time of test) and nonaddicts who were in prison, and found that the addicted group was very significantly less tolerant of the painful situation than the nonaddicted group. The addicts could hold their hand in the water for an average period of only 1.22 minutes compared with an average of 6.74 minutes for the nonaddicts. There was no evidence that the pain intolerance was the *result* of addiction and none but trivial correlations were found with any personality variables.

Similar formidable difficulties are found in relation to attempts to follow up drug addicts. Thus, Knight and Prout (1951) followed up 75 patients admitted to hospital over a period of 20 years, the follow-up period ranging from one to 21 years. There were 34 morphine addicts in the group; 24 were addicted to barbiturates and 17 to heroin, codeine, and demerol, with average duration of the use of drugs being $6\frac{1}{2}$ years. They found that 36% of the patients had benefited from treatment, and that 15 had been abstinent for periods varying from one to 15 years. More recently, Retterstöl and Sund (1965) carried out a very careful follow-up of 122 drug abusers, of whom 62 were addicted and 60 habituated[11] (mostly to barbiturates). The follow-up period varied from one to ten years, with 52 patients being followed up after a period exceeding five years. On follow-up (personal interview), 14 of the 62 addicted patients were abstinent compared with 26 of the 60 habituated patients. Only three of the latter had become addicted during this period.

The problems involved in follow-up studies have been carefully discussed by O'Donnell (1965) who was severely critical of the 11 studies he reviewed. The results obtained, however, do not appear to contradict the opinion expressed earlier that there is quite a high rate of "spontaneous remission."

As was pointed out earlier, this brief review is not intended to provide a comprehensive picture of the drug-addiction situation but rather to show that serious research has only just begun.

II. BEHAVIOR THERAPY FOR DRUG ADDICTION

Behavior therapists have thus far only engaged in preliminary skirmishes with the problem of drug addiction and only four studies have been found that relate to it. Raymond (1964) used his modified apomorphine technique with a woman addicted to self-injections of physeptone for six years with apparent success (the patient was free of the drug two and one half years after treatment ended). A similar technique was used by Liberman (1968) in treating two cases of morphine addiction. Initial success was achieved in both cases; one subsequently relapsed, but the other was still not taking the drug one year after the end of treatment. A most interesting study was reported by Wolpe (1965). He pointed out that shock-aversion treatment is usually directed toward stimulation arising externally to the subject whereas, particularly in the case of drugs, the craving may arise "internally." Hence, he treated a physician addicted to demerol (pethidine) by means of a portable shock apparatus. The physician administered shocks to himself whenever the craving for the drug arose or whenever it was precipitated by external stimulation, such as administering the drug to a patient. Complete abstention for three months occurred. During the final part of the abstention period, the shock was discontinued and the patient was able to resist the craving without it. Under a series of anxiety-provoking situations, relapse occurred, but Wolpe makes the interesting suggestion that this occurred, not because of inherent flaws in the technique, but because, during the nonshock period of abstinence, the craving was gradually reinstated by the repeated anxiety-evoking experiences. The use of regular booster treatments (self-administered) on a partial reinforcement basis might well have prevented reinstatement of the craving. It is possible that this represents an instance of spontaneous recovery following extinction, the recovered response then gradually increasing in strength from its lowest value to full strength.

Lesser (1967) used an aversion-relief technique, involving verbal conditioning, with a college student indulging to a moderate degree in the use of morphine (but not an addict). After training in deep relaxation and social assertiveness, the patient was required to visualize five steps in the injection of morphine. These were associated with a severe continuous shock until the patient said "stop" (two of the steps involved actually picking up objects associated with injections). Continuous followed by partial reinforcement procedures were used. The treatment was apparently successful, with the patient reporting "great improvement" on follow-up at seven and at ten months.

There can be no doubt that the next few years will see the development of research and therapy in the area of drug addiction to a very significant degree.

REFERENCES

Ackerly, W.C. & Gibson, G. Lighter fluid "sniffing." *Amer. J. Psychiat.*, 1964, **120,** 1056–1061.

Anant, S.S. The treatment of alcoholics by a verbal aversion technique: a case report. *Manas*, 1966, **13,** 79–86.

---

[11] The term "habituated" is used in an unusual sense in this study, referring to "slight usage" of a drug, as opposed to addiction to it.

Anant, S.S. A note on the treatment of alcoholics by a verbal aversion technique. *Canad. Psychol.*, 1967, **8**, 19–22 (a).

Anant, S.S. Treatment of alcoholics and drug addicts by verbal aversion technique. *Paper read at the 7th Internat. Congress of Psychotherapy, Wiesbaden,* 1967 (b).

Ashem, B. & Donner, L. Covert sensitization with alcoholics: a controlled replication. *Behav. Res. Ther.*, 1968, **6**, 7–12.

Bailey, M.B., Hamberman, P.W., & Alksne, H. The epidemiology of alcoholism in an urban residential area. *Quart. J. Stud. Alcohol.*, 1965, **26**, 19–40.

Blake, B.G. The application of behavior therapy to the treatment of alcoholism. *Behav. Res. Ther.*, 1965, **3**, 75–85.

Blake, B.G. A follow-up of alcoholics treated by behavior therapy. *Behav. Res. Ther.*, 1967, **5**, 89–94.

Campbell, D., Sanderson, R.E., & Laverty, S.G. Characteristics of a conditioned response in human subjects during extinction trials following a single traumatic conditioning trial. *J. abnorm. soc. Psychol.*, 1964, **68**, 627–639.

Chein, I., Gerard, D.L., Lee, R.S., Rosenfeld, E., & Wilner, D.M. *Narcotics, delinquency, and social policy: the road to H.* London: Tavistock, 1964.

Chwelos, N., Blewett, D.B., Smith, C.M., & Hoffer, A. Use of d-lysergic acid diethylamide in the treatment of alcoholism. *Quart. J. Stud. Alcohol,* 1959, **20**, 577–590.

Clancy, J., Vanderhoff, E., & Campbell, P. Evaluation of an aversive technique as a treatment for alcoholism: controlled trial with succinylcholine-induced apnea. *Quart. J. Stud. Alcohol.*, 1967, **28**, 476–485.

Conger, J.J. Reinforcement theory and the dynamics of alcoholism. *Quart. J. Stud. Alcohol.*, 1956, **17**, 296–305.

Davies, D.L., Sheppard, M., & Myers, E. The two-year prognosis of fifty alcohol addicts after treatment in hospital. *Quart. J. Stud. Alcohol,* 1956, **17**, 485–502.

Dent, J.Y. Apomorphine in the treatment of anxiety states with special reference to alcoholism. *Brit. J. Ineb.*, 1934, **43**, 65–69.

Edlin, J.V., Johnson, R.H., Hletko, P., & Heilbrunn, G. The conditioned aversion treatment in chronic alcoholism (preliminary report of 100 cases). *Amer. J. Psychiat.*, 1945, **101**, 806–809.

Farrar, C.H., Powell, B.J., & Martin, L.K. Punishment of alcohol consumption by apneic paralysis. *Behav. Res. Ther.*, 1968, **6**, 13–16.

Feldman, D.J. The treatment of chronic alcoholism: a survey of current methods. *Ann. intern. Med.*, 1956, **44**, 78–87.

Franks, C.M. Alcohol, alcoholics and conditioning: a review of the literature and some theoretical considerations. *J. ment. Sci.*, 1958, **104**, 14–33.

Franks, C.M. Behavior therapy, the principles of conditioning, and the treatment of the alcoholic. *Quart. J. Stud. Alcohol.*, 1963, **24**, 511–529.

Franks, C.M. Conditioning and conditioned aversion therapies in the treatment of the alcoholic. *Internat. J. Addict.*, 1966, **1**, 61–98.

Galant, J.S. Uber die Apomorphinbehandlung der Alkoholiker. *Psychiat.-neurol. Wschr.*, 1936, **38**, 85–89.

Glatt, M.M. Treatment results in an English mental hospital alcoholic unit. *Acta psychiat. Scand.*, 1961, **37**, 143–168.

Hill, M.J. & Blane, H.T. Evaluation of psychotherapy with alcoholics: a critical review. *Quart. J. Stud. Alcohol,* 1967, **28**, 76–104.

Holzinger, R., Mortimer, R., & Van Dusen, W. Aversion conditioning treatment of alcoholism. *Amer. J. Psychiat.*, 1967, **124**, 246–247.

Ichok, G. Les réflexes conditionnels et le traitement de l'alcoolique. *Prog. Med.*, 1934, **45**, 1742–1745.

Isbell, H. Perspectives in research on opiate addiction. In Wilner, D.M. & Kassebaum, G.G. (eds.). *Narcotics.* New York: McGraw-Hill, 1965, pp. 36–50.

Jellinek, E.M. *The disease concept of alcoholism.* New Haven: Hillhouse Press, 1960.

Kant, F. Further modifications in the technique of conditioned-reflex treatment of alcohol addiction. *Quart. J. Stud. Alcohol.*, 1944, **5**, 228–232 (a).

Kant, F. The conditioned-reflex treatment in the light of our knowledge of alcohol addiction. *Quart. J. Stud. Alcohol.*, 1944, **5**, 371–377 (b).

Kantorovich, N.V. [An attempt at associative reflex therapy in alcoholism.] *Nov. reflex. fiziol. nerv. syst.*, 1929, **3**, 436–447 (Psychol. Abstracts, 1930, No. 4282).

Keller, M. & Efron, V. The prevalence of alcoholism. *Quart. J. Stud. Alcohol.*, 1955, **16**, 619–644.

Kendall, R.E. & Staton, M.C. The fate of untreated alcoholics. *Quart. J. Stud. Alcohol.*, 1965, **26**, 685–686.

Kepner, E. Application of learning theory to the etiology and treatment of alcoholism. *Quart. J. Stud. Alcohol.*, 1964, **25**, 279–291.

Kingham R.J. Alcoholism and the reinforcement theory of learning. *Quart. J. Stud. Alcohol.*, 1958, **19**, 320–330.

Knight, R.G. & Prout, C.T. A study of results in hospital treatment of drug addictions. *Amer. J. Psychiat.*, 1951, **108**, 303–308.

Kraft, T. & Al-Issa, I. Alcoholism treated by desensitization: a case report. *Behav. Res. Ther.*, 1967, **5**, 69–70.

Laverty, S.G. Aversion therapies in the treatment of alcoholism. *Psychosom. Med.*, 1966, **28**, 651–666.

Lazarus, A.A. Towards the understanding and effective treatment of alcoholism. *South African med. J.*, 1965, **39**, 736–741.

Lemere, F. & Voegtlin, W.L. An evaluation of the aversion treatment of alcoholism. *Quart. J. Stud. Alcohol.*, 1950, **11**, 199–204.

Lemere, F., Voegtlin, W.L., Broz, W.R., & O'Hollaren, P. Conditioned reflex treatment of chronic alcoholism: V. Type of patient suitable for this treatment. *Northwest Med. (Seattle)*, 1942, **41**, 88–91.

Lemere, F., Voegtlin, W.L., Broz, W.R., O'Hollaren, P., & Tupper, W.E. Conditioned reflex treatment of chronic alcoholism: VII. Technic. *Dis. nerv. Syst.*, 1942, **3**, 243–247 (a).

Lemere, F., Voegtlin, W.L., Broz, W.R., O'Hollaren, P., & Tupper, W.E. The conditioned reflex treatment of chronic alcoholism: VIII. A review of six years' experience with this treatment of 1,526 patients. *J. Amer. med. Assoc.*, 1942, **120**, 269–270 (b).

Lesser, E. Behavior therapy with a narcotics user: a case report. *Behav. Res. Ther.*, 1967, **5**, 251–252.

Liberman, R. Aversive conditioning of drug addicts: a pilot study. *Behav. Res. Ther.*, 1968, **6**, 229–231.

Lipscombe, W.R. Survey measurements of the prevalence of alcoholism. *Arch. gen. Psychiat.*, 1966, **15**, 455–461.

McBrearty, J.F., Dichter, M., Garfield, Z., & Heath, G. A behaviorally oriented treatment program for alcoholism. *Psychol. Rep.*, 1968, **22**, 287–298.

MacCulloch, M.J., Feldman, M.P., Orford, J.F. & MacCulloch, M.L. Anticipatory avoidance learning in the treatment of alcoholism: a record of therapeutic failure. *Behav. Res. Ther.*, 1966, **4**, 187–196.

Madill, M.F., Campbell, D., Laverty, S.G., Sanderson, R.E., & Vanderwater, S.L. Aversion treatment of alcoholics by succinylcholine-induced apneic paralysis. *Quart. J. Stud. Alcohol.*, 1966, **27**, 483–509.

Mann, N.M., Conway, E.J., Gottesfeld, B.H., & Lasser, L.M. Co-ordinated approach to antabuse therapy. *J. Amer. med. Assoc.*, 1952, **149**, 40–46.

Mardones, R.J. On the relationship between deficiency of B vitamins and alcohol intake in rats. *Quart. J. Stud. Alcohol.*, 1951, **12**, 563–575.

Markovnikov, A. [Le traitement de l'alcoolisme au moyen de la suggestion et de la formation d'un réflexe conditionnel, provoqué par une gorgée de spiriteu.] *Sovet. vrach. Gaz.*, 1934, **10**, 807–808 (quoted in Ichok, 1934).

Martin, J.E. & Inglis, J. Pain tolerance and narcotic addiction. *Brit. J. soc. clin. Psychol.*, 1965, **4**, 224–229.

Mayer-Gross, W., Slater, E., & Roth, M. *Clinical psychiatry* (rev. 2nd ed.). Baltimore: Williams and Wilkins, 1960.

Miller, E.C., Dvorak, B.A., & Turner, D.W. A method of creating aversion to alcohol by reflex conditioning in a group setting. *Quart. J. Stud. Alcohol.*, 1960, **21**, 424–431.

O'Donnell, J.A. The relapse rate in narcotic addiction: a critique of follow-up studies. In Wilner, D.M. & Kassebaum, G.C. (eds.). *Narcotics*. New York: McGraw-Hill, 1965, pp. 226–248.

O'Donnell, J.A. & Ball, J.C. (eds.). *Narcotic addiction*. New York: Harper, 1966.

Pemberton, D.A. A comparison of the outcome of treatment in female and male alcoholics. *Brit. J. Psychiat.*, 1967, **113**, 367–373.

Popham, R.E. & Schmidt, W. *A decade of alcoholism research* (Brookside Monograph No. 3). Toronto: Univer. Toronto Press, 1962.

Quinn, J.T. & Henbest, R. Partial failure of generalization in alcoholics following aversion therapy. *Quart. J. Stud. Alcohol.*, 1967, **28**, 70–75.

Raymond, M.J. The treatment of addiction by aversion conditioning with apomorphine. *Behav. Res. Ther.*, 1964, **1**, 287–291.

Retterstöl, N. & Sund, A. *Drug addiction and habituation*. Kristiansand: Universitetsforlaget, 1965.

Sanderson, R.E., Campbell, D., & Laverty, S.G. An investigation of a new aversive conditioning treatment for alcoholism. *Quart. J. Stud. Alcohol.*, 1963, **24**, 261–275.

Shadel, C.A. Aversion treatment of alcohol addiction. *Quart. J. Stud. Alcohol.*, 1944, **5**, 216–228.

Smart, R.G. The relationships between intellectual deterioration, extraversion, and neuroticism among chronic alcoholics. *J. clin. Psychol.*, 1965, **21**, 27–29.

Smart, R.G. & Storm, T. The efficacy of LSD in the treatment of alcoholism. *Quart. J. Stud. Alcohol.*, 1964, **25**, 333–338.

Smart, R.G., Storm, T., Baker, E.F.W., & Solursh, L. A controlled study of lysergide in the treatment of alcoholism: I. The effects on drinking behavior. *Quart. J. Stud. Alcohol.*, 1966, **27**, 469–482.

Smith, J.J. A medical approach to problem drinking. *Quart. J. Stud. Alcohol.*, 1949, **10**, 251–257.

Thimann, J. Conditioned reflex treatment of alcoholism: I. Its rationale and technic. *New Eng. J. Med.*, 1949, **241**, 368–370 (a).

Thimann, J. Conditioned reflex treatment of alcoholism: II. The risks of its application, its indications, contraindications and psychotherapeutic aspects. *New Eng. J. Med.*, 1949, **241**, 406–410 (b).

Tiebout, H.M. The role of psychiatry in the field of alcoholism, with comment on the concept of alcoholism as symptom and as disease. *Quart. J. Stud. Alcohol.*, 1951, **12**, 52–57.

Vallance, M. Alcoholism: a two-year follow-up study. *Brit. J. Psychiat.*, 1965, **111**, 348–356.

Voegtlin, W.L. The treatment of alcoholism by establishing a conditioned reflex. *Amer. J. med. Sci.*, 1940, **199**, 802–810.

Voegtlin, W.L. Conditioned reflex therapy of chronic alcoholism: ten years' experience with the method. *Rocky Mountain med. J.*, 1947, **44**, 807–811.

Voegtlin, W.L. & Broz, W.R. The conditioned reflex treatment of chronic alcoholism: X. An analysis of 3125 admissions over a period of ten and a half years. *Ann. inter. Med.*, 1949, **30**, 580–597.

Voegtlin, W.L. & Lemere, F. The treatment of alcohol addiction: a review of the literature. *Quart. J. Stud. Alcohol.*, 1942, **2**, 717–803.

Voegtlin, W.L., Lemere, F., & Broz, W.R. Conditioned reflex therapy of alcoholic addiction: III. An evaluation of present results in the light of previous experiences with this method. *Quart. J. Stud. Alcohol.*, 1940, **1**, 501–516.

Voegtlin, W.L., Lemere, F., Broz, W.R., & O'Hollaren, P. Conditioned reflex therapy of chronic alcoholism: IV. A preliminary report on the value of reinforcement. *Quart. J. Stud. Alcohol.*, 1941, **2**, 505–511.

Voegtlin, W.L., Lemere, F., Broz, W.R., & O'Hollaren, P. Conditioned reflex therapy of alcoholic addiction: VI. Follow-up report of 1042 cases. *Amer. J. med. Sci.*, 1942, **203**, 525–528.

Vogel, M.D. Alcohol, alcoholism, and introversion-extraversion. *Canad. J. Psychol.*, 1959, **13**, 76–83.

Vogel, M.D. The relation of personality factors to GSR conditioning of alcoholics: an exploratory study. *Canad. J. Psychol.*, 1960, **14**, 275–280.

Vogel, M.D. The relationship of personality factors to drinking patterns of alcoholics. *Quart. J. Stud. Alcohol.*, 1961, **22**, 394–399 (a).

Vogel, M.D. The relationship of GSR conditioning to drinking patterns of alcoholics. *Quart. J. Stud. Alcohol.*, 1961, **22**, 401–410 (b).

Vogel, M.D. GSR conditioning and personality factors in alcoholics and normals. *J. abnorm. soc. Psychol.*, 1961, **63**, 417–421 (c).

Vogel-Sprott, M.D., & Banks, R.K. The effect of delayed punishment on an immediately rewarded response in alcoholics and nonalcoholics. *Behav. Res. Ther.*, 1965, **3**, 69–73.

Vondracek, V., Prokupek, J., Fischer, R., & Ahrenbergova, M. Recent patterns of addiction in Czechoslovakia. *Brit. J. Psychiat.*, 1968, **114**, 285–292.

Wikler, A. Conditioning factors in opiate addiction and relapse. In Wilner, D.M. and Kassebaum, G.G. (eds.). *Narcotics*. New York: McGraw-Hill, 1965, pp. 85–100.

Williams, R.J. The etiology of alcoholism: a working hypothesis involving the interplay of hereditary and environmental factors. *Quart. J. Stud. Alcohol.*, 1947, **7**, 567–589.

Williams, R.J. *Alcoholism: The nutritional approach.* Austin: Univer. Texas Press, 1959.

Wilner, D.M. & Kassebaum, G.G. (eds.). *Narcotics.* New York: McGraw-Hill, 1965.

Winick, C. Epidemiology of narcotics use. In Wilner, D.M. & Kassebaum, G.G. (eds.). *Narcotics.* New York: McGraw-Hill, 1965, pp. 3–18.

Wolpe, J. Conditioned inhibition of craving in drug addiction: a pilot experiment. *Behav. Res. Ther.*, 1965, **2**, 285–288.

World Health Organization. Expert Committee on Mental Health (*Alcoholism*): Report on the Second Session, 1951, pp. 15–20.

Zax, M., Gardner, E.A., & Hart, W.T. A survey of the prevalence of alcoholism in Monroe County, N.Y., 1961. *Quart. J. Stud. Alcohol.*, 1967, **28**, 316–327.

Zwerling, I. & Rosenbaum, M. Alcoholic addiction and personality. In Arieti, S. (ed.). *American handbook of psychiatry* (Vol. I, Chap. 31, pp. 623–644). New York: Basic Books, 1959.

Chapter 16

Mental Deficiency

IT WOULD NOT be an exaggeration to say that a revolution has occurred over the past ten years in the approach to and understanding of mental deficiency; so much so that a good deal of what will be reported in this chapter is not to be found in even recent textbooks on the subject.[1] It would, of course, be quite impossible as well as unnecessary to provide a complete review of all aspects of the problem. In this chapter, therefore, the reader is forewarned that a particular line of argument is being advanced, namely, that the pessimistic views, which have been so widely and for so long entertained regarding the ineducability of the mental defective, are unwarranted. The problem of mental deficiency is a classic instance of the immense harm that can be done when the medical model is inappropriately applied.[2] In this chapter, a great deal of stress will be laid on the importance of the use of operant procedures, both to *define* the nature of the deficits in mental defectives and to develop systematic techniques for *overcoming* the deficits. No apology is made for continuing to use the terms "mental deficiency" and "mental defective" in preference to "exceptional child," "retarded child," and so forth. The former terms are quite clear in their everyday connotations and, even if ambiguous when looked

at more closely, are less so than the terms which are tending to replace them.

I. DEFINITION, MEASUREMENT, INCIDENCE

1. THE MAGNITUDE OF THE PROBLEM

Both the magnitude and nature of the problem of mental deficiency may be illustrated by reference to some objective data. At the end of 1954, there were approximately 61,000 *institutionalized* mental defectives in Great Britain, of whom some 5000 were on licence; and there were approximately 77,000 *non-institutionalized* mental defectives who were under supervision at home or with guardians by the local health authorities (O'Connor and Tizard, 1956, p. 30). Let us suppose that we define as mentally defective any person whose I.Q. falls more than two standard deviations below the mean of a specified intelligence test (that is, has an I.Q. of 70 or less on a test with a mean of 100 and S.D. of 15). Then, assuming a normal distribution of intelligence on the test, we would expect, in Great Britain, with a population of 50 million, that roughly one million persons (if we include all age levels) would be mentally defective by definition. Of course, it is well known that the above premises

---

[1] Of the many modern textbooks of mental deficiency, three are outstanding. The American viewpoint is represented by Ellis (1963b); the British approach by Clarke and Clarke (1965). The biologically oriented book of Penrose (1963) remains unrivalled in the areas it covers. The even more recent *International Review of Research in Mental Retardation* provides definitive overviews of recent

research trends. Articles from the first two volumes (1966) will be referred to where appropriate.

[2] It is not intended to imply that the medical model is wholly inapplicable in this area (the elucidation of the genetics of mongolism and the unraveling of the problem of phenylketonuria are examples of its appropriate application).

are open to serious objections (which will be detailed later). Even allowing for this, however, it is clear that the total of 137,000 people certified as mentally defective would represent not much more than 10% of the group that falls more than two standard deviations below the mean. This fact is an encouraging rather than a discouraging one, of course, for it means that a very large proportion of those people who are of low intelligence do not come to the attention of the certifying authorities; in other words, that they manage to make a sufficiently satisfactory social adjustment to keep out of trouble. This fact alone suggests, first, that intelligence alone is an inadequate criterion on which to base a decision to institutionalize a person on the grounds of mental deficiency and, second, that perhaps some institutionalized defectives may have been incarcerated on grounds other than level of intelligence.

That the latter suspicion is, in fact, true was clearly demonstrated in a study carried out in England. Table 16.1 shows the frequency distributions of the I.Q.'s of 104 consecutive male admissions to a large mental deficiency hospital (excluding imbeciles and physically handicapped patients). It will be noted that, on all but one of the tests, the mean I.Q. is higher than the arbitrary cutting point of I.Q. 70, which is often used as a criterion. A very similar result was obtained in a subsequent survey of 100 admissions to the same hospital, using this time the Wechsler-Bellevue Verbal Scale, the mean I.Q. being 69.38 (S.D. 10.07).

Why do some persons with relatively high intelligence find themselves institutionalized in a mental deficiency hospital, whereas other persons of relatively low intelligence never come to be institutionalized? The answer, in England at least, is unfortunately not simply to be found in the conclusion that the criterion for institutionalization is one of *social competence* rather than *intelligence level* per se. At the time of the surveys reported above, the only person with legal powers to certify a person as mentally defective and order his institutionalization was a medical officer of health. But these conscientious and hard-working persons more often than not made their assessments on the basis of intelligence tests which they themselves administered, often with a deplorable lack of knowledge of problems of administration, scoring, and interpretation. The tests were often given under grossly unfavorable conditions of administration (sometimes, of course, no psychometric assessment was made at all), while the person being examined was grossly emotionally disturbed. Even worse, however, was the undesirable fact that admission to a mental deficiency hospital was often a matter of sheer "luck" (or "bad luck," according to the point of view). As O'Connor (1965a) recently put it:

"Until recently the birth of an illegitimate child to a woman in recept of relief was sufficient for her to be certified and made the responsibility of the Board of Control. Even the child itself might be certified. It has sometimes been suggested that magistrates

TABLE 16.1. *Frequency Distributions of I.Q.s on Five Intelligence Tests—not corrected for S.D. Differences* (*n* = 104)

I.Q.	Kohs	Matrices	Binet Vocabulary	Porteus I.Q.	Cattell
Median I.Q.	75.36	72.33	71.10	85.69	65.10
Mean I.Q.	75.41	74.55	71.38	82.56	63.78
S.D. of I.Q.s	17.00	12.73	14.89	22.00	14.07
120+	1	0	2	3	0
110–119	2	1	0	11	0
100–109	5	2	2	4	3
90–99	13	12	5	18	1
80–89	23	16	11	29	4
70–79	20	33	40	13	22
60–69	15	28	23	8	43
50–59	19	10	18	10	15
Less than 50	6	2	3	8	16

Source: O'Connor and Tizard, 1956, p. 48.

have used certification as a means of securing for an unwanted child, conditions which they have judged better than those of children's homes. In other cases, backwardness at school which may or may not have been due to innate lack of ability has been offered as evidence of backwardness which, when combined with a legal offence, may result in permanent hospitalization instead of a jail sentence" (O'Connor, 1965, p. 32–33).

Even more disturbing, however, than the capricious nature of commital to a mental deficiency institution is O'Connor's reference to "permanent hospitalization" for, unhappily, once committed, it is extraordinarily difficult for the person concerned to regain his liberty. This undesirable fact arises, in England, from the very structure of the mental deficiency services which are based on the concept of *hospitalization*, that is, treating mental deficiency as essentially a *medical* problem. As O'Connor and Tizard (1956) point out, nearly half of all institutionalized defectives in England are confined in a few very large hospitals (four with populations exceeding 2000; three with populations between 1500 and 2000; and eight with populations between 1000 and 1500). The famous Wood report of 1929 put the matter quite clearly and unequivocally:

> "An institution which takes all grades and types is economical because the high grade patients do the work, and make everything necessary, not only for themselves, but also for the lower grade. In an institution taking only lower grades the whole of the work has to be done by paid staff; in one taking only higher grades the output is greater than is required for the institution itself, and there is difficulty in disposing of it" (Board of Education and Board of Control, 1929).

In other words, the higher the grade of the institutionalized person, the more reluctant the hospital is to release him because of his value as a source of unpaid labor. Hence the not infrequent cases (usually reported by vigilant Civil Liberties Committees) in English newspapers of patients who have absconded from the hospital and supported themselves successfully in the community for months or even years, only to be eventually recaptured and returned to the institution, in spite of having demonstrated their ability to fend for themselves in society. As recently as 1966, a leading article in *Lancet* pointed out that secretaries, engineers, finance officers, senior nursing officers, and even chaplains in English mental deficiency institutions are paid according to the number of beds in the hospital. Thus "the harder a matron or chief male nurse works to rehabilitate patients, the more they undermine their own salaries" (*Lancet*, 1966, **1**, 532–533).

All of this evidence[3] indicates that the question of the assessment of mental deficiency needs to be considered very carefully as a *social* problem, as indeed the title of O'Connor and Tizard's (1956) book so aptly suggests.

2. THE ASSESSMENT OF MENTAL DEFICIENCY

Doll (1941) has postulated six criteria that must be satisfied before a diagnosis of mental deficiency can be seriously considered. The person must show *social incompetence* which is due to *mental subnormality* that has been *developmentally arrested*, which *obtains at maturity*, which is of *constitutional origin*, and which is *essentially incurable*. It will be noted that Doll's criteria imply that the social incompetence is the *result* of the intellectual defect, but this is clearly a position difficult to sustain in the light of our earlier discussion. It is, in fact, now generally held that the basic criterion for institutionalization is the degree of social incompetence displayed. Whether or not a socially incompetent person is committed to a mental hospital or to a mental deficiency hospital may, however, depend on his intellectual level as well as on other factors such as age (as in cases of senile dementia), the presumed cause of the social incompetence, and so on.

The most tenable position would appear to be one which regards the intellectual and social competence factors as separate dimensions that are, however, correlated with each other in a complex fashion. Thus, persons at the extreme low end of the intelligence dimension will inevitably be socially incompetent but, as the intelligence level increases, the correlation with social competence will become significantly less than perfect. In practice, this means that intelligence level alone may validly be used as a criterion of mental deficiency if the test results indicate idiot or imbecile level, but that social

---

[3] Based mainly on the epoch-making book of O'Connor and Tizard (1956). Unfortunately, there is little reason to believe that the position in England has changed much in the succeeding 12 years (Clarke and Clarke, 1965).

competence will become the main criterion in cases where the intelligence level shades into dull normal. Indeed, as we shall see later, it will be wise to take into account social competence even at the imbecile levels of intelligence.

In spite of the importance of the social competence criterion, it is worthwhile considering the intelligence criterion by itself, both on practical and theoretical grounds. The classification of mental defectives may be considered briefly from two points of view: the *types* and *levels* of intellectual subnormality.

(a) TYPES OF INTELLECTUAL SUBNORMALITY. A distinction has usually been made between primary (endogenous) and secondary (exogenous) amentia. As was pointed out earlier, if intelligence is normally distributed in the population[4] and, further, if this normal distribution is produced (like height and weight) by the random shuffling of large numbers of small genes, then a given proportion of mentally defective persons will result as "normal" biological variants, in the same way that a given proportion of exceptionally intelligent persons will be produced. Thus, these cases may truly be said to be genetically determined (the argument does not, of course, deny the influence of interaction between this innate capacity for intellectual activity and the richness of the environment in producing the final performance level of the individual). One would not expect to find any special factors at work in persons whose low intelligence is determined in this way. This argument is supported by the fact that only about 6% of the mothers or fathers of mental defectives are themselves defective and that mental defectives who marry tend to have children who are brighter than themselves (the well-known phenomenon of regression toward the mean).

Superimposed on this normal biological variation, however, are those special cases of mental deficiency that arise from the operation of special genetic inheritance. The classical example now, of course, is the finding of 47 chromosomes in mongol mental defectives, where the precise number of the trisomy has been demonstrated.

The normal curve of the distribution of intelligence can, further, be demonstrated (if sufficiently large samples are tested) to be distorted at the lower end by a hump, indicating the presence of more low intelligence persons than would be expected in terms of a normal distribution. The hump is produced by those cases of exogenous (secondary) amentia, where the low intelligence results from the operation of special environmental factors such as prenatal deficiencies, birth injuries, glandular dysfunctions, and early encephalitis or meningitis. In effect, individuals who are mentally defective as a result of the operation of these factors are persons who would otherwise have been distributed throughout the range of intelligence levels but who have been reduced to the same level because of the operation of these special factors. Such exogenous cases of mental defect are rarer than is commonly supposed (possibly not more than 8% of all defectives) and certainly almost never result from a child being "dropped on its head" as parents commonly suppose.

(b) LEVELS OF INTELLECTUAL SUBNORMALITY. Mental defectives have commonly been classified into three categories according to intelligence level as measured by a test having a mean of 100 and standard deviation of 15. The lowest level is that of the *idiot* with an I.Q. less than 30; the *imbecile* is the person with an I.Q. between 30 and 50; and the *moron* is the person with I.Q. between 50 and 70. The moron is often now termed a high-grade mental defective, this category of course shading imperceptibly into the intellectually dull (I.Q. between 70 and 85) and the dull-normal (I.Q. between 85 and 90). The terms idiot and imbecile have virtually disappeared from the American literature, the term "severely and profoundly retarded" being preferred, if only for aesthetic reasons.

(c) THE SOCIAL COMPETENCE CRITERION. At all but the very lowest levels of intelligence, the concept of social competence has come to be of primary significance in determining the disposal of the intellectually defective person. This approach was pioneered by Doll in the United States and by Tredgold in England. Instead of determining the "pure" level of intelligence by means of formal intelligence tests, the individual's capacity for looking after himself in basic social activities is measured. One of the best known examples of such a test is the Vineland Social Maturity Scale. It is important to note, however, that an assessment of this kind can be as unfair to a particular

---

[4] It should be noted that the normal distribution of intelligence is a *theoretical* construct, the validity of which is *not* proved by the normal distributions

achieved with a "good" intelligence test, which is constructed deliberately so as to produce a normal distribution in accordance with the theory.

individual as sole reliance on an intelligence test score. Clearly, a severely disadvantaged child of normal intelligence may appear socially incompetent because of lack of training in his early years.

Hence, it is now generally agreed that the assessment of the child who is apparently mentally defective must involve an assessment both of his fundamental intellectual capacity, determined as far as possible by tests that are uncontaminated by cultural factors, and of his social competence. There can be no justification whatever for institutionalizing a person of low intelligence because of that fact alone nor, of course, should social incompetence alone lead to a diagnosis of mental deficiency in a person whose intelligence level on culture-fair tests is relatively high.

In recent years, however, the whole notion of assessing the status of mentally defective persons by the means outlined above has come under heavy fire and, in the United States in particular, a completely different approach to the question has been gaining ground rapidly. Although this movement is still in its infancy, the implications of the approach are so important and revolutionary that a special section of this chapter must be devoted to it.

II. THE OPERATIONAL DEFINITION OF DEFICIT IN MENTAL DEFICIENCY

The psychometric approach which had dominated the field of investigation of mental deficiency for more than 50 years has rapidly given way over the past ten years to two new approaches. On the one hand, careful laboratory-based experimental investigations have been instituted into all aspects of the behavior of mental defectives, making use of the standard controlled procedures of the experimental laboratory and drawing on all of the resources, empirical procedures, methodology, and theory which have resulted from the tradition of experimental investigation. Even more recently, however, within this general framework an important special approach has developed, largely as a result of the growing interest of psychologists in mental deficiency, working within the operant conditioning framework.

1. LABORATORY ANALYSIS OF FUNCTIONING IN MENTAL DEFECTIVES

It would be impossible to review here the very large body of empirical knowledge that has resulted from the application of the methods of experimental psychology to the study of performance in mental defectives. Such a review is, in any event, unnecessary because a large number of highly competent and very comprehensive reviews have appeared within the last five years. A selection of these reviews is listed in Table 16.2 for the interested reader. It will be noted that the coverage is virtually complete, extending from the study of sensory and perceptual processes through short-term retention, learning and discrimination, mediating processes and learning sets, up to long-term retention, speech and communication, problem-solving and conceptual processes, academic skills, and personality. This body of knowledge is gradually building up a comprehensive picture of the precise nature of the deficits (and assets) of mental defectives as compared with intellectually normal persons and with other abnormal groups. Even so, there are still large gaps in the body of knowledge; for example, not nearly enough is known even now concerning the conditionability of mental defectives, and many of the reviews listed bemoan the serious lack of hard data.

2. THE USE OF OPERANT TECHNIQUES IN DIAGNOSIS AND ASSESSMENT

There are two aspects of the use of operant techniques that are of special interest in relation to mental deficiency. First, the use of standard psychometric techniques has been criticized on the grounds that this approach does not enable the precise nature of the deficits to be pinpointed with accuracy and is particularly likely to lead to reification (Barrett and Lindsley, 1962). Second, and of even more significance, the use of operant techniques has led to the conclusion that it may be even more important to modify the techniques themselves rather than to concern oneself with modifying the child.

The empirical and theoretical underpinnings of operant techniques in relation to mental deficiency have been worked out in some detail in recent years (Lindsley, 1964; Bijou, 1965, 1966; Denny, 1966). Bijou (1966), for example, has concerned himself with the problem of explaining how retarded development may be produced. He accepts, of course, the obvious fact that the defective may suffer from abnormal anatomical structure and that his physiological functioning may be abnormal but, from the *psychological* viewpoint, the importance of such

TABLE 16.2. *Reviews of Studies of Functioning of Mental Defectives in Various Areas*

Behavior Analyzed	Review
Sensory processes	Kodman (1963)
Perceptual processes	Spivack (1963)
Verbal, perceptual-motor, and classical conditioning	Lipman (1963)
Conditioning	Astrup et al (1967)
Motor skills	Malpass (1963)
Short-term retention	Spitz (1966)
Learning and performance	Denny (1964)
Learning	O'Connor (1965b), Ross (1966)
Discrimination learning	Stevenson (1963)
Learning sets and transfer of learning	Kaufman and Prehm (1966)
Learning and transfer of mediating responses	Shepp and Turrisi (1966)
Long-term retention	Belmont (1966)
Speech and thought	O'Connor and Hermelin (1963)
Language and communication	Spradlin (1963)
Problem-solving and conceptual processes	Rosenberg (1963), Blount (1968)
Academic skills	Quay (1963)
Personality	Zigler (1966)

defects lies in the fact that they may produce certain contingencies, such as isolation, which will in turn produce an inadequate reinforcement history. Thus, the existence of anatomical and physiological defects should not in itself be accepted as a sufficient cause for mental retardation. Even more important, in Bijou's view, is the objective delineation of the degree of inadequacy of reinforcement and discrimination histories, of the significance of contingent aversive stimulation histories, and of the significance of a history of the reinforcement of aversive behavior.

This general orientation resulted in the setting up of specially developed laboratories for the controlled investigation of the behavior of mentally defective children (e.g., Orlando et al, 1960). The details of these laboratories need not concern us here, since they were similar to those devised for the study of the behavior of autistic children.[5] A description will be given, however, of some of the ingenious experimental procedures that have been devised in these settings, as examples of the development of this approach in recent years. Barrett and Lindsley (1962), for example, used a task involving two lights (C_1 and C_2), each of which was activated (M_1 and M_2) by a manipulandum (a lever). The association C_1M_1 was reinforced

on a FR-10 schedule, whereas associations C_1M_2, C_2M_1, and C_2M_2 were not reinforced. By this simple means, Barrett and Lindsley were able to investigate the acquisition of response differentiation, stimulus discrimination, and motivational level. Thus, *response differentiation*, was acquired if, after training, the association C_1M_1 exceeded C_1M_2; *stimulus discrimination* if C_1M_1 exceeded C_2M_1; and both *response differentiation and stimulus discrimination* if C_1M_1 exceeded C_2M_2. The *general motivational level* could be assessed by the total number of responses per session. The system could also, however, be used to measure and analyze inefficiencies in performance. Thus, a high rate of C_2M_2 accompanied by a reduction in rate of C_1M_2 and C_2M_1 would indicate *overgeneralization*. Analysis of the performance of 25 institutionalized defectives produced some interesting results. Not only was there a wider range of performance shown than would have been anticipated from formal intelligence test results, but highly individualized *response patterns* were found if the testing program were continued for long enough. Examples of individual patterns were: initial rapid learning, followed by a slow loss of stimulus discrimination; abrupt intrasession loss of response

---

[5] See Chapter 13.

differentiation; initial overgeneralization; response stereotypy; long-term, highly variable acquisition; and abnormally low response rates. Barrett and Lindsley stress particularly that these individual response patterns may manifest themselves only with prolonged testing—hence, they would not be likely to be detected by ordinary psychometric procedures. It should be noted that the technique does, of course, produce more general results as well. For example, response differentiation was always acquired more rapidly than stimulus discrimination in those defectives who reached an optimal performance level.

Denny (1966) has described the use of a simple but ingenious piece of apparatus that allows investigation of a wide range of performance at different levels of complexity. The Multiple Differential Response and Feedback Apparatus (MUDRAFA) enables concepts of space, color, time delay, and so on to be both investigated and taught. Essentially, the apparatus consists of a panel with a hollow cross cut into it, along the arms of which a lever can be moved vertically and horizontally. In addition, however, the lever can be also moved in such a way that it can disappear behind the panel or can move toward or away from the subject. Thus, a wide range of concepts from concrete to abstract (such as the notion of "behind," "in front of," "toward," and "away from") can be investigated *without the necessity for verbal explanation* by the experimenter. When it is realized that much of the behavior of defectives is apparently inefficient because of the failure to develop concepts of space and time (i.e., *mediating* concepts, whether verbal or not), the value of such a technique can scarcely be overestimated.

A good deal of work has also now been accomplished in the investigation of mental defectives placed on multiple-schedule contingencies in a controlled situation (Bijou and Orlando, 1961; Ellis et al, 1960; Orlando, 1961). Orlando (1965) has more recently investigated in considerable detail the problems involved in obtaining stable base-line multiple-schedule performances in mental defectives—an essential preliminary to attempts to systematically modify and control the behavior. The target that Orlando set himself was adequate performance on a multiple VR-25 extinction schedule with two-minute periods of S^D and S^Δ

alternating regularly.[6] Base-line criteria are more than 50 responses per minute when S^D is present; less than 10% of the S^D rate when S^Δ is present; and average S^D onset latency less than 10 seconds. Attainment of the schedule is, of course, achieved by the use of successive approximation techniques. Orlando's results with 16 retarded subjects confirm the finding of Barrett and Lindsley of wide individual differences in performance.

One of the most important contributions within the operant framework relates to the assumption that defective performance should never be taken to indicate inability of the subject to acquire the particular response pattern in question. Rather, *failure on the part of the mental defective in a particular task should be taken as an indication that the experimenter has failed to analyze the task sufficiently, precisely, and discriminatively.* The general validity of this assumption is shown by a recent outstanding study by Sidman and Stoddard (1966). They constructed an automated laboratory for assessing visual discrimination skills. The apparatus has general applicability, of course, for work with both children and adults, but seems likely to prove particularly useful for work with mentally defective and psychotic patients. The apparatus basically consists of a panel divided into nine equal squares in rows and columns of three. Onto each square, a figure can be projected simultaneously while the relative brightness of each square can be independently varied. Each square on the panel is actually a key which, when pressed, records the response-occurrence automatically. At the same time, a reinforcement is presented or omitted according to the correctness or incorrectness of the response.

Sidman and Stoddard set themselves the task of determining whether they could train profoundly defective persons to discriminate between a circle and an ellipse and, if so, whether progressively finer discriminations could be achieved. The *real* problem, however, was to demonstrate whether progressive refinements of the stages of programming the experimental procedures would produce learning where none apparently existed. In effect, the method of successive approximations was used with the basic question being: what *structure* of successive approximations would have to be instituted to produce high-level discrimination?

---

[6] S^D designates a stimulus, the response to which will be followed by reinforcement (on a VR

schedule); S^Δ a stimulus, the response to which will be followed by nonreinforcement.

The details of the series of studies carried out by Sidman and Stoddard are too complex to report here, but the general procedure may be indicated. In the case of one very severe defective, the initial task set the subject was to press the one key that was lit, the others being dark.[7] Then he was required to press the key that was lighted and had a shape on it. Following this, the other keys gradually increased in brightness on successive trials so that the discrimination was gradually made more difficult. Then a circle was introduced on one of the keys accompanied by a very flat ellipse on all of the others. At first, the ellipses were practically invisible on a dark ground, then the brightness of the ground was gradually increased, the ellipses being "faded in." In the final stage, all keys were equally brightly illuminated, the only basis for discrimination being the one shape that was not an ellipse. Once this discrimination had been achieved, the fineness of the visual discrimination required could be increased.

Two important points should be noted about these procedures. First, a "backup" procedure was used in which, when an error was made, the subject was taken back to a previous success point and he proceeded from there. Sidman and Stoddard found that this procedure frequently resulted in an increase in errors at the earlier success point. Instead, however, of assuming that the subject had reached the limit of his discrimination capacity, *they asked themselves what was wrong with the programming procedures* that was producing difficulty in the subject's learning. This led them to examine the program rather than the patient, for example, to introduce a series of smaller (or sometimes, larger) number of stages at this particular point (they found it necessary at one point to fade in brightness changes and stimulus changes successively rather than simultaneously).[8]

Two further advances in this area will be mentioned. Friedlander et al (1967) have devised a Playtest apparatus for use with severely retarded (vegetative) mental defectives. This consists of a panel with two large transparent knobs protruding from it. If one knob is pressed (this action requiring only gross manipulation) a single, short auditory sound (a chime) is produced, while if the other is pressed, a continuous auditory sound (organ-scales) is produced which continues for as long

as the knob is pressed. No reinforcement other than the sounds is provided. Using this simple technique with very profoundly retarded subjects, Friedlander et al (1967) were able to show that independent measures of response frequency and duration produced significantly more information than if the more usual frequency response only had been used. Although the two children differed markedly in *frequency* of responding, a mean *duration/response proportion* measure was the same for both children. The experimental situation used by Friedlander et al, while yielding objective response measures, is of particular interest because it represents a fairly natural testing situation, as compared with that used by the other writers discussed here. It showed, incidentally, that the amount and variety of responding that can be obtained from children as severely retarded as this is much greater than had formerly been supposed.

Finally, Hollis (1965a, 1965b) has described a laboratory set-up for examining objectively the behavior in free space of defective children and the influence on that behavior of the introduction of social and nonsocial stimuli.

No attempt will be made here to review the empirical work that has been carried out within the operant framework, since much of it is still in the preliminary stages and no firm conclusions can be drawn as yet. The interested reader is referred, for examples of this work, to studies on operant differentiation and discrimination by Barrett (1965); on the relative importance of social and nonsocial stimuli as reinforcers by Hollis (1965a, 1965b), and by Stevenson and his colleagues (Stevenson and Cruse, 1961; Stevenson and Fahel, 1961; Stevenson and Knights, 1962); on the significance of delay in reward, as a determinant of behavior, by Schoelkopf and Orlando (1965); and on behavior under FR and FI schedules of reinforcement (Spradlin et al, 1965). Much of this work has been reviewed by Spradlin and Girardeau (1966).

III. BEHAVIOR THERAPY WITH MENTAL DEFECTIVES

The history of remedial work with mental defectives is long and dedicated. Here, however, we shall consider three areas only: the modifiability of the behavior of severely and

---

[7] The position of the lighted key varied, of course, from trial to trial.

[8] For a recent extension of this work, see Sidman and Stoddard (1967).

profoundly retarded persons; the educability of high-grade defectives; and the trainability and employability of both low-grade and high-grade defectives. The emphasis will be, as usual, on experimental studies.

1. MODIFIABILITY OF THE BEHAVIOR OF SEVERELY RETARDED PERSONS

A wide range of studies has been carried out in recent years which parallels much of the work reported earlier in relation to the psychoses.[9]

(a) CONDITIONABILITY OF VEGETATIVE AND EXTREMELY LOW-GRADE DEFECTIVES. Attempts to modify the behavior of vegetative human organisms are relatively rare, but their interest is not entirely theoretical. Fuller (1949) described the successful conditioning and extinction of an arm-raising response in a non-ambulatory vegetative 18-year-old male, using as reinforcement a sugar-milk solution fed through a tube. It was noted that anticipatory mouth opening appeared and that *selective reinforcement* had to be used (that is, the patient would respond only for the reinforcement indicated above and showed negative behavior when other reinforcers were tried). Similar findings and difficulties have been reported more recently by Rice and McDaniel (1966) and by Rice et al (1967). More optimistic findings were reported in the study by Friedlander et al (1967), previously discussed, but perhaps the most interesting report thus far, dealing with patients at this level, is that of Whitney and Barnard (1966). Their report indicates yet again that certain behaviors may persist because of inadvertent reinforcement by ward personnel, even though in this case the patient was a 15-year-old girl who, as assessed by the Gesell Developmental Scales, was functioning at no better than a 7-month-old level. At the beginning of the study, the patient could not (or would not!) sit unsupported, grasp, release, or bring objects to her mouth. She was extremely destructive in relation to anything placed within her reach and would toss food about at random. Careful observation suggested that her potential level of performance was significantly higher than her actual level. She was first taught to spoon-feed herself by the use of successive approximation techniques, with food reinforcement for appropriate responses and withdrawal

of food reinforcement for inappropriate responses (such as knocking over food). Striking success was achieved over a short period of time, but this behavior rapidly extinguished when the experimenter abruptly withdrew and normal ward procedures (involving, as they did, reinforcement by attention to her antisocial behaviors) were reinstated. Reinstitution of the experimental procedures, however, resulted in rapid reinstatement of the new forms of behavior. A second withdrawal by the experimenter, but this time by a fading procedure rather than abruptly, resulted in retention of the improved behavior. Cup-holding was then successfully achieved by the use of similar techniques while, eventually, this patient was trained to sit at a table for meals with other patients. Some success with toilet training was also achieved. While there is no doubt about the severity of defect in this patient, there also seems to be no doubt that the extremely low level of behavior before training was partly at least a function of the reinforcing contingencies that it produced from the ward personnel in the form of special attention.[10]

(b) TOILET TRAINING OF LOW-GRADE DEFECTIVES. A great deal of work has been accomplished in relation to this problem which is, of course, of major significance in institutionalized patients. Clearly, if severely defective patients can be successfully trained in this area of performance, a great deal of time would be freed for other work; and, of course, incontinence on such a scale poses a major health hazard in patients who are often highly susceptible to infection.

Most of the work to be considered has been derived from the theoretical model proposed by Ellis (1963a) which was outlined in an earlier chapter[11] and which involves *situational* training, that is, teaching the person to eliminate at the right time in the right place. Ellis proposed a detailed regimen for the toilet training of mental defectives, and this has been closely followed in many studies. More recently, Giles and Wolf (1966) have expanded Ellis' suggestions, giving a detailed account of the procedures they used with five severe mental defectives. They stress the need for the establishment of base-lines from which to measure improvement and the importance of discovering individually effective reinforcers.

---

[9] See Chapters 13 and 14.

[10] Similar dramatic results with operant procedures in eating problems in a severely defective

adolescent have been reported by Zeiler and Jervey (1968).

[11] See Chapter 5.

A detailed account of the studies need not be provided here, but the results claimed certainly seem to justify the time spent. Thus, Giles and Wolf (1966) reported that, at the end of eight weeks of training, all five of their severe defectives were eliminating (in relation to both urination and defecation) consistently in the toilet. Positive results have also been reported by Baumeister and Klosowski (1965), Bensberg et al (1965), Kimbrell et al (1967), Marshall (1966)[12] and Miron (1966).

Two studies, however, merit special attention because of their methodological interest. Dayan (1964) treated 25 severe mental defectives (I.Q. 30 or below) by placing them on the toilet every two hours, with verbal praise as the reward for elimination and withdrawal of attention as the consequence of failure to eliminate. He used two criteria against which to measure the effectiveness of the training procedure. The number of pounds of soiled linen treated by the laundry of the institution per month dropped over the five-month treatment period from an average of 1200 pounds per week to 600 pounds, the average for the institution as a whole. A cost saving of the order of $1000 per annum was thus effected. He also compared the changes in the treatment group with changes in a comparable untreated control group over the same period and, as would be expected, found a very significant difference. Hundziak et al (1965) divided a group of severely retarded boys into three treatment groups. The experimental group received operant reward training with the reinforcers being candy, a light, and a tone. A second group received conventional treatment (verbal reward and scolding for soiling), while a third formed an untreated control group. Training was instituted for seven hours per day for five days each week and continued for the relatively short period of 27 days. A further innovation by Hundziak et al was that the post-training assessment was made by observers who did not know to which of the three groups each child belonged. Hundziak et al found that the operant group showed a significant increase in the use of toilet facilities for both urination and defecation, the untreated control group for urination only, and the conventionally treated group for neither.

Thus, there is good evidence that toilet training can be accomplished with severe mental defectives by the use of operant conditioning procedures.

(c) CONTROL OF BEHAVIOR ON THE WARD. In the light of results discussed in an earlier chapter on the control of undesirable or disruptive ward activities in psychotic patients, it would be anticipated that the use of similar techniques would be successful in controlling the ward behavior of mental defectives. A remarkable instance of this was provided in a study by Hamilton et al (1967) who treated various disruptive behaviors in five female patients of very low intelligence by a time-out procedure. Thus, in one patient, head and back banging of a frequency of several thousand responses in a six-hour period and of a severity that produced marked self-injury was reduced to zero in five weeks. Other behaviors similarly successfully treated included continuous breaking of windows with the head, undressing repeatedly, and assaultive behavior against other patients. Once again, it appeared that most of these behaviors were being maintained by the attention they evoked from ward personnel.[13] No evidence was found of the development of new forms of undesirable behavior.

Another remarkable study was recently reported by Henriksen and Doughty (1967) who attempted to eliminate five types of undesirable mealtime behaviors (eating too fast; eating with the hands; stealing food from other patient's trays; hitting other patients at the meal table; and throwing food-trays or spilling food deliberately) in four patients who exhibited these to an extreme degree. The procedure involved isolating the four patients at a table and stationing two aides there, each at a corner of the table. The aim of the aides was to interrupt the undesirable behaviors as soon as they began and *before* they were completed, together with an expression of verbal and facial disapproval and a positive response if a proper eating response was made. The training period lasted for 13 weeks and was total, that is, was carried out at each meal seven days a week. An interesting feature of the procedure involved the gradual fading out of the aides as training progressed by gradually increasing their physical distance from the table and by the return of the children to the normal dining room situation.

---

[12] Marshall (1966) found that reduction of number of bowel movements into the child's pants was accompanied by a significant *increase* in number of bowel movements per se, indicating that the former effect was not due to anal retention.

[13] The reader is reminded that attention here can include verbal or physical punishment as well as positive responses.

The results were striking. Before treatment, the number of recorded misbehaviors per week for the four subjects was 350, 265, 150, and 125, respectively; at the end of treatment, the frequencies were 50, 25, 10, and 20, respectively.

Finally, Wiesen and Watson (1967) eliminated continuous attention-seeking behavior in a six-year-old severely retarded child (of a kind to seriously interfere with the attendant's duties to other children). Two procedures were used. Time-out was instituted for interference with adults (which was extended if soiling occurred during the period, the soiling also being followed by delay in cleaning up and the use of colder water for cleaning up). At the same time, positive reinforcement was provided for social interaction with other children. The interesting point about this latter procedure is that the reinforcement (candy) was provided by the child who was interacted with, this child being rewarded for its action at a later date. The training extended over 21 days and was very successful. The operant level of interference with adults was reduced to zero, and toilet accidents were virtually eliminated. Of course, it was not intended that interaction with adults should be reduced to zero but, in such a severe case, this might well be an essential first step, with a normal level of social interaction with adults being subsequently reinstated.

(d) TRAINING IN SELF-CARE BEHAVIOR. Considerable success has also attended efforts to train mental defectives in self-care activities. Mazik and Macnamara (1967) placed eight such children (who were severely disturbed and destructive) of very low intelligence (I.Q. 29 or below) in a separate ward and applied operant conditioning techniques to specific target areas. The children were trained, for example, to put on their trousers, essentially by a successive approximation technique "in reverse." The program was so successful that the children were able to remain in the training institution although all, before training, had been candidates for deenrollment. Minge and Ball (1967) used a similar approach with six even more retarded girls who were not toilet trained and who did not dress themselves. They were given graded training (successive approximation technique) in 11 simple activities over a 60-day training period involving two 15-minute sessions per day. The activities trained in this way included response to commands (look at me,

come here, sit down, stand up), followed by training in self-care activities such as taking dress off, taking pants off, putting on socks, dress, and pants. The results indicated significant gains in ability to perform these activities compared with a control group given no training. Similar results have been reported by Girardeau and Spradlin (1964) and by Bensberg et al (1965).[14]

2. THE EDUCABILITY OF HIGH-GRADE DEFECTIVES

The use of programmed instruction techniques to teach the basic skills of reading, writing, spelling, and arithmetic is exciting rapidly increasing interest in the field of mental deficiency, though much of the work has not yet been published.[15] We will consider here several studies which are of special interest.

The procedures and problems involved in developing instructional materials and their use with mental defectives have been outlined by Bijou et al (1966) in a review of three years of work. A special classroom was set up with the goal of achieving self-pacing of their development by the children by initially shaping scholastic attitude by the use of reinforcers. As we have seen so frequently, Bijou and his colleagues found it necessary to train their subjects first in general classroom behavior, with positive reinforcement (in the form of tokens as secondary reinforcers, since verbal praise proved ineffective) for "acceptable" classroom behaviors and time-out in an annex (if verbal warning failed) for "unacceptable" classroom behaviors. Instructional materials were developed for reading, writing, and arithmetic, based on three criteria: that they be suitable for individual use; that they involve graduated increase in difficulty; and that the level of work presented to the child at any given moment be geared to his current level of achievement. Certain basic principles were followed in running the classroom: positive reinforcement to be preferred over punishment by verbal reproof or time-out; reinforcements to be immediate so that they would be clearly associated with the behavior being rewarded; continuous reinforcement to be provided at first, with a gradual shift to partial reinforcement (in practice, this means that the child is required to complete larger and larger segments

---

[14] For an interesting discussion of these studies, see Hollis and Gorton (1967) or Watson (1967).

[15] Greene (1966) has exhaustively reviewed the unpublished as well as the published work.

of scholastic behavior before being reinforced); reinforcements to be given in association with other neutral stimuli so that the latter would take on the properties of conditioned reinforcers; and successive approximations of the desired behavior to be required, so that learning proceeded in small steps. Over the three-year period covered by the report, 27 boys and girls with a mean I.Q. of 63 have entered the program which is regarded as being still in its early stages.[16]

The work of Hewett et al (1967) is derived from that of Bijou and his colleagues and involves a teaching-machine approach together with individual teacher instruction in a reading program for brain-damaged, retarded, disturbed children. A five-part standard lesson has been developed for the learning of individual words with the provision of an errorless training sequence for those children who are unable to profit from the standard sequence. The errorless training program is, of course, analogous to the procedures used by Sidman and Stoddard (1966) described earlier in relation to visual discrimination training. Otherwise the procedures used are similar to those of Bijou et al. Again, this report is a preliminary one, but the results appear to be very promising, considering the severity of the defect in these children.

However, two substantial studies have been completed recently. In the first, Blackman and Capobianco (1965) developed an automated instructional device to present reading and arithmetic materials. In the reading program, 20 units (comprising 218 subprograms, of which 55 were used) were constructed, covering 311 words; while in the arithmetic program, a set of 54 subprograms has been used, beginning with form discrimination and leading to simple division and basic fractions. The program was applied to half of 36 institutionalized retardates, the other half serving as a control group taught by traditional methods. No difference was found between the two groups on the reading or arithmetic programs except for a special test in arithmetic on which the experimental group was superior.

Malpass et al (1964) divided 66 educable retarded children into three groups matched for sex, CA, MA, programmed words known, standardized reading test score, and other relevant variables. A list of 100 basic words was selected (46 nouns, 10 adjectives, 9 verbs, 4 conjunctions, 2 prepositions, 1 article), of which 72 were used for teaching purposes, the remaining 28 being used for test purposes. The first group of children was exposed to a semi-automated multiple-choice teaching machine employing 3000 card frames divided into 40 lessons, each lesson being repeated once. The second group was exposed to a fully-automated typewriter-keyboard machine with an identical program. The third group was taught by conventional classroom techniques. The evaluation measures consisted of pre-post training changes in the recognition and spelling of both programmed and unprogrammed words and in performance on the Word Recognition section of the Gates Primary Reading Test. The results of the experiment are shown in Table 16.3 and indicate a clear superiority for the programmed learning techniques over conventional instructional methods in the acquisition and retention of the programmed words. Similar, but less striking, results are evident for acquisition and retention of the unprogrammed words. Comparable results were also found with respect to ability to spell the words. Malpass et al reported, however, that *individual* teaching techniques produced results equal to those obtained by the programmed learning techniques. In effect, therefore, the programming of the material appears to produce the same effect as that which can be achieved by a skilled teacher giving individual instruction, as might indeed be expected in this field of teaching. However, the advantage of the teaching machine program, once developed, lies in the economy of resources effected.

Mention may also be made here of a study by Penney and McCann (1962) who attempted to train *originality* in mental defectives. They utilized the Maltzman technique in which a word-association test is given once and then repeated several times with instructions that the subject produce a new association to each word on each trial. Following training, a test list is given and scored for unusualness of responses. Penney and McCann divided their 18 subjects into an experimental group which was given the training and a control group which was pre and posttested, but not trained. They found no difference between the experimental and control groups on the criterion measure, but the experimental group did score more highly on an Unusual Uses test of originality following

---

[16] A related study by Birnbrauer et al (1965) demonstrated clearly the wide range of individual differences in responsiveness to the presence or absence of a token economy in the classroom.

TABLE 16.3. *Effectiveness of Three Teaching Techniques on Reading Scores*[a]

Materials	Teaching Method		
	Multiple Choice	Keyboard	Classroom
1. Programmed Words (n = 72)			
Preinstruction score	10.2	14.3	13.4
Postinstruction score (gain)	30.7 (20.5)	42.4 (28.1)	17.1 (3.7)
Retention score (60 days)	28.4 (18.2)	36.0 (21.6)	19.2 (5.8)
2. Nonprogrammed Words (n − 28)			
Preinstruction score	2.6	3.0	3.3
Postinstruction score (gain)	5.1 (2.5)	7.8 (4.8)	4.3 (1.0)
Retention score (60 days)	5.1 (2.5)	8.2 (5.2)	5.7 (2.4)

Source: Malpass et al, 1964.

[a] Score: number of words correct.

training. The results were therefore equivocal, possibly because only three training trials were given, compared with five used by Maltzmann.

All of these techniques are still in their infancy, of course, but the initial results show distinct promise and will undoubtedly be developed significantly in the next few years.

3. THE TRAINABILITY AND EMPLOYABILITY OF DEFECTIVES

For many years, it was considered by medical authorities that only a small proportion of institutionalized mental defectives were capable of being trained to the point at which they would be both employable in the community and able to support themselves independently while so employed. Yet this belief was clearly at variance with the known fact that the great majority of defectives were never institutionalized. It was also at variance with the empirical facts. A great deal of evidence was available to show that a substantial proportion of mental defectives could be released to the community and maintain themselves successfully in it.[17] The justly famous studies of Baller (1936) and Charles (1953) may be used as illustrations of the "natural history" of noninstitutionalized mental defectives. Baller followed up 206 children from special opportunity classes, comparing their subsequent history with that of

an equal number of controls matched for age, sex, and nationality by pairs. The mean I.Q. of the defectives at first testing was 60.50 (males) and 59.00 (females), but all had I.Q.'s below 70 on the Stanford-Binet. The mean age on this first follow-up was about 25 years. Baller found that 33 of the defective children had gone on to complete eight grades of school, while three had attended high school. Only 12 (less than 7%) were in mental deficiency institutions, only one was in a mental hospital, and only two were in prison or a reformatory. As might be expected, the defective group did break the law more frequently (or at least were more frequently caught!) than the controls and they had a less stable history of employment. But 27% of them were wholly self-supporting. Baller concluded that his results indicated a much more favorable prognosis for defectives living in the community than was commonly supposed, particularly as the follow-up assessment was made during the depression period when unemployment was widespread.

Nearly 20 years later, Charles (1953) traced 127 of the original 206, their mean age now being about 42 years, and saw no reason to question the optimistic conclusions of Baller. He also found that the mean I.Q. of the children of these defectives was 95 with a range from 50 to 138.[18] An even more recent follow-up, now covering

---

[17] The evidence has been reviewed in great detail by Windle (1962); a briefer summary may be found in Tizard (1965).

[18] This estimate is probably somewhat inflated, since probably Charles traced on the whole the more successful of the subjects.

30 years (Baller et al, 1967), confirms further the earlier results.

There have also been specific cases reported in the literature of very low intelligence level defectives who have supported themselves successfully with little help. One such striking case was reported by Butterfield (1961) of a mongol with an assessed Binet I.Q. of only 28 who supported his mother for many years, even after she had had a heart attack, doing all of the shopping, house-cleaning, and so on with more than average efficiency. He could also read and write to some degree.

These findings raised the question of whether institutionalized defectives who, as we have seen, often had a relatively high I.Q. could be trained to take their place in the community rather than remain institutionalized for the whole of their lives. The series of investigations of this problem to be reported here have not only not received the recognition they deserve but unfortunately appear not to have produced the changes which should have followed upon their publication. The studies, carried out by O'Connor, Tizard, Clarke and Clarke, Loos, and others are of great importance for a number of reasons. They specify precisely the reasons for the previous failures in attempts to train defectives; state clearly the factors that influence the degree of trainability; spell out in detail the factors that must be controlled if training is to succeed; and specify the factors that influence success and failure when the trained defective is sent out to work in the community.

(a) CRITIQUE OF HOSPITAL WORKSHOP TRAINING. In the large mental deficiency hospitals, such training as is available includes carpentry, book-binding, envelope-making, box-making, tin-smithing, tailoring, upholstering and mattress-making, printing, needlework, painting, building, wood-chopping and bundling, and shoe-repairing.[19] In a devastating critique of the situation obtaining in mental deficiency institutions, Tizard and O'Connor (1952) listed the limitations of these facilities.

(i) The work available was designed to keep the defectives occupied rather than to train them for employment outside the institution.

(ii) The training methods and equipment used were usually hopelessly out of date and thus bore no relation to the methods currently in use

in industry, nor to the requirements of industry.

(iii) There was no contact with outside firms which were naturally reluctant to let contracts for work.

(iv) Monetary incentives were largely absent or, where present, pitifully inadequate.

(v) No attention was paid to the specialized training which was needed by the workshop supervisors for coping with the special problems of these patients.

(vi) If the defective was released on license to the community and obtained employment, he would usually find himself under a supervisor who had no training in coping with the special problems of the defective.

(b) FACTORS INFLUENCING THE TRAIN-ABILITY OF MENTAL DEFECTIVES. A series of studies which need not be detailed here showed that among the factors that needed to be taken into account in studies of the trainability of defectives were: the level of I.Q. in relation to job requirements (with special attention to special abilities and limitations of defectives); the degree of emotional stability of the defective; the role of incentives; the nature of supervision during training and employment; the quality of the training; and an analysis of the type and range of jobs suitable for defectives to engage in. It became clear that a series of empirical investigations was required to study these factors. The investigations that were carried out covered three areas: the type of defective trained (imbeciles and high-grade defectives); the place of study (the laboratory, the workshop, and the community); and the influence of certain important factors (incentives, supervision, competition, and encouragement). It is not possible to cover all of this work here. Attention will therefore be directed to some of the most important studies.[20]

(c) WORKSHOP STUDIES. About 1950, O'Connor and Tizard (1956) established two experimental workshops for the training (with a view to subsequent employment on license) of high-grade adolescent and adult defectives. Three basic principles were followed in relation to the organization of the workshops.

(i) The work taught should be similar to that carried out in industry. The jobs chosen involved the filing of rough edges from molded plastic objects and the folding and glueing of cardboard boxes.

---

[19] Of course, in any one hospital workshop, only a small selection of these activities would be available.

[20] See O'Connor and Tizard (1956) for a comprehensive review of their work.

(ii) The work performed should be paid for at trade-union piecerates (that is, on the basis of number of items completed). It should be noted that contracts were obtained from industrial firms, and the completed work had to pass the usual inspection procedures of the firm.

(iii) A normal $36\frac{1}{2}$-hour week should be worked. The patients, in other words, were required to work a five-day week from 8:30 to 12:00 and 1:30 to 4:30.

As would be expected, some troubles were encountered. For example, the initial group of patients had to be selected very carefully (it was found that more disturbed patients could be introduced later when a group feeling had been built up) and the initial suspicions of the patients had to be overcome; a stable routine of work took some eight months to achieve.

Over the first two years, 194 patients passed through the workshop, some of whom attended for only a short while. Of the 60 who were tried on license, 36 succeeded on their first trial outside the workshop; five were unsuccessful in their initial placement, but subsequently succeeded; and 19 were unsuccessful while on license. Thus, the preliminary results were quite encouraging.

This early experience indicated quite clearly the importance, not merely of training high-grade mental defectives in meaningful tasks if they were to be successfully released into the community, but highlighted also the important role sympathetic and adequate supervision played during the training period. A series of studies was therefore carried out relating to the role of supervision (Tizard, 1953) and incentives (Clarke and Hermelin, 1955), the latter being based on earlier studies of a laboratory kind on the role of incentives in the performance of imbeciles (Gordon, O'Connor, and Tizard, 1954; Walton and Begg, 1955). In the study on types of supervision (Tizard, 1953), 36 high-grade defectives were subjected to three types of supervision (strict, laissez-faire, and friendly) over a period of 12 weeks, while performing the same kind of work described earlier. Three supervisors were used, each one rotating between the different kinds of supervision. The reaction to supervision was assessed by time-sampling procedures applied each day to industriousness and talkativeness, as measured on a 3-point scale. It was found that there was no difference between the strict and friendly types of supervision, and that both were superior to laissez-faire. The brightest patients benefited most from strict supervision. This study also clearly revealed the need for well-trained supervisors, for good rapport between the supervisor and the patients, and for clear and simple communication between supervisor and patient.

These studies were followed by one of the most remarkable investigations ever carried out in the field of mental deficiency research. (Loos and Tizard, 1955; Clarke and Hermelin, 1955.) Six imbeciles aged 18–23 with I.Q.'s ranging from 22 to 42 were selected as among the least competent of the hospital patients. They were trained in an industrial task which involved folding and glueing boxes, nine separate movements (which had to be performed in the correct order) being required. After 11 weeks of training, the output of these very low-grade patients (which had to be passed at commercial standards) was superior to that of high-grade defectives working at the same task. Nevertheless, efforts were made to improve the output still further by the provision of special incentives and by making progress on one part of the task (folding) contingent on completion of the other part of the task (glueing). Thus, instead of the folders completing their work and stockpiling it, each folder worked with a gluer who could not proceed with his work unless a supply of folded boxes was maintained.

The further details of this experiment need not concern us here, but the final outcome, as described by Clarke and Hermelin (1955), is of absorbing interest and importance.

> "For the last two and a half years, these six imbeciles have been employed as cardboard-box-folders in a small experimental workshop, where their work and behavior have been carefully observed. On the average, their output of cardboard boxes has been 30,000–40,000 per 35-hour week, but on occasion—e.g., when a special order had to be fulfilled rapidly—they have reached 60,000–70,000 . . . during the whole of this period, sickness has been very rare . . . supervision is minimal, since they work reliably and consistently . . . indeed, one weekend, in the absence of the supervisor, all six imbeciles became bored, gained access to the closed workshop, and worked all morning without any supervision at all" (Clarke and Hermelin, 1955).

All of this work had to pass normal factory inspection. Subsequently, they were also trained in other tasks of a more complex nature (using a guillotine to cut insulated wire to exact lengths; using a soldering iron to solder four differently colored wires to the correct terminals of an 8-pin television plug; and assembling a bicycle pump, using a particular sequence of nine separate movements). Clarke and Hermelin also pointed out that while the *initial* level of the imbeciles on these tasks was unquestionably below average, the initial level was not predictive of the *final* level which could be achieved. In the final analysis, the only significant difference in performance was the time taken to do the job, not the quality of the job.

(d) EMPLOYABILITY IN THE COMMUNITY. Tizard and O'Connor (1950a, 1950b) reviewed the earlier studies of the employability of high-grade mental defectives in the community, but naturally their own results in the workshop studies encouraged them to investigate the possibility of placing trained defectives in outside jobs (O'Connor and Tizard, 1956). In one study, high-grade defectives were sent out on license to work in plastic factories after initial training. In one factory 82% of the defectives were successful; but in another only 44% succeeded. Analysis showed that failure was most likely to occur in the early months of employment and that it was produced partly by sheer physical problems (susceptibility to illness) and partly related to the quality of the supervision afforded on the job. If, however, the critical early period was overcome, then the work record was actually superior to non-institutionalized "normal" workers performing the same tasks. Similar results were found in a second study of the employability of defectives on a building site where the failure rate varied from twice to only half that of normal laborers on the site, eventually settling down to two-thirds that of the normal employees.

In summarizing all of this work, O'Connor and Tizard state that "at least two-thirds and probably four-fifths of those who might on I.Q.

score be classed as feeble-minded can live in financial and social independence under present economic circumstances" (O'Connor and Tizard, 1956, p. 130). This conclusion, however, is valid only if the important factors studied by O'Connor and Tizard and their colleagues are taken into account. These may be summed up as follows.

(i) Adequate training facilities must be provided, directly related to industrial conditions of employment.

(ii) The instructors and supervisors of the training program must themselves be highly trained.

(iii) When initially placed in employment, the factory supervisor must be trained to awareness of the special problems of defectives.

(iv) In the early stages of training and, later, of employment, considerable perseverance on the part of the supervisors and trainers is necessary.

(v) Adequate and relevant incentives must be provided, both during training and in employment.

It does not appear that the implications of this outstanding series of laboratory, workshop, and employment studies have yet been fully grasped, even though similar striking results have been reported (e.g., Neuhaus, 1967). It is obvious that the policy of building large, expensive (in terms of capital cost) mental deficiency hospitals should be abandoned as soon as possible. They should be replaced by small specialized hospitals for dealing with the very low-grade defective patients. For all other mentally defective patients, the money saved in this way should be put into the construction of large well-equipped workshops and the training and provision of skilled supervisors and trainers. When this is done, a "new deal" will indeed have been achieved in the field of mental deficiency.

REFERENCES

Astrup, C., Sersen, E.A., & Wortis, J. Conditional reflex studies in mental retardation: a review. *Amer. J. ment. Defic.*, 1967, **71**, 513–530.

Baller, W.R. A study of the present social status of a group of adults who, when they were in elementary schools, were classified as mentally deficient. *Genet. Psychol. Monogr.*, 1936, **18**, 165–244.

Baller, W.R., Charles, D.C., & Miller, E.L. Mid-life attainment of the mentally retarded: a longitudinal study. *Genet. Psychol. Monogr.*, 1967, **75**, 235–329.

Barrett, B.H. Acquisition of operant differentiation and discrimination in institutionalized retarded children. *Amer. J. Orthopsychiat.*, 1965, **35**, 862–885.

Barrett, B.H. & Lindsley, O.R. Deficits in acquisition of operant discrimination and differentiation shown by institutionalized retarded children. *Amer. J. ment. Def.*, 1962, **67**, 424–436.

Baumeister, A. & Klosowski, R. An attempt to group toilet train severely retarded patients. *Ment. Retard.*, 1965, **3**, 24–26.

Belmont, J.M. Long-term memory in mental retardation. *Internat. Rev. Res. ment. Retard.*, 1966, **1**, 219–255.

Bensberg, G.J., Colwell, C.N., & Cassel, R.H. Teaching the profoundly retarded self-help activities by behavior shaping techniques. *Amer. J. ment. Def.*, 1965, **69**, 674–679.

Bijou, S.W. Experimental studies of child behavior, normal and deviant. In Krasner, L. & Ullmann, L.P. (eds.). *Research in behavior modification.* New York: Holt, 1965, pp. 56–81.

Bijou, S.W. A functional analysis of retarded development. *Internat. Rev. Res. Ment. Retard.*, 1966, **1**, 1–19.

Bijou, S.W., Birnbrauer, J.S., Kidder, J.D., & Tague, C. Programmed instruction as an approach to teaching of reading, writing and arithmetic in retarded children. *Psychol. Rec.*, 1966, **16**, 505–522.

Bijou, S.W. & Orlando, R. Rapid development of multiple-schedule performances with retarded children. *J. exp. Anal. Behav.*, 1961, **4**, 7–16.

Birnbrauer, J.S., Wolf, M.M., Kidder, J.D., & Tague, C.E. Classroom behavior of retarded pupils with token reinforcement. *J. exp. Child Psychol.*, 1965, **2**, 219–235.

Blackman, L.S. & Capobianco, R.J. An evaluation of programmed instruction with the mentally retarded utilizing teaching machines. *Amer. J. ment. Defic.*, 1965, **70**, 262–269.

Blount, W.R. Concept usage research with the mentally retarded. *Psychol. Bull.*, 1968, **69**, 281–294.

Board of Education and Board of Control. *Report of the mental deficiency committee* (*Wood report*). London: H.M. Stationery Office, 1929.

Butterfield, E.C. A provocative case of over-achievement by a mongoloid. *Amer. J. ment. Defic.*, 1961, **66**, 444–448.

Charles, D.C. Abilities and accomplishments of persons earlier judged to be mentally defective. *Genet. Psychol. Monogr.*, 1953, **47**, 3–71.

Clarke, A.D.B. & Hermelin, B. Adult imbeciles: their abilities and trainability. *Lancet*, 1955, **2**, 337–339.

Clarke, A.M. & Clarke, A.D.B. (eds.). *Mental deficiency: the changing outlook* (2nd ed.). London: Methuen, 1965.

Dayan, M. Toilet training retarded children in a state residential institution. *Ment. Retard.*, 1964, **2**, 116–117.

Denny, M.R. Research in learning and performance. In Stevens, H.A. & Heber, R. (eds.). *Mental retardation.* Chicago: Univer. Chicago Press, 1964, pp. 100–142.

Denny, M.R. A theoretical analysis and its application to training the mentally retarded. *Internat. Rev. Res. ment. Retard.*, 1966, **2**, 1–27.

Doll, E.A. The essentials of an inclusive concept of mental deficiency. *Amer. J. ment. Defic.*, 1941, **46**, 214–219.

Ellis, N.R. Toilet training the severely defective patient: an S-R reinforcement analysis. *Amer. J. ment. Def.*, 1963, **68**, 98–103 (a).

Ellis, N.R. (ed.). *Handbook of mental deficiency.* New York: McGraw-Hill, 1963 (b).

Ellis, N.R., Barnett, C.D., & Pryer, M.W. Operant behavior in mental defectives: exploratory studies. *J. exp. anal. Behav.*, 1960, **3**, 63–69.

Friedlander, B.Z., McCarthy, J.J., & Soforenko, A.Z. Automated psychological evaluation with severely retarded institutionalized infants. *Amer. J. ment. Def.*, 1967, **71**, 909–919.

Fuller, P.R. Operant conditioning of a vegetative human organism. *Amer. J. Psychol.*, 1949, **62**, 587–590.

Giles, D.K. & Wolf, M.M. Toilet training institutionalized severe retardates: an application of operant behavior modification techniques. *Amer. J. ment. Defic.*, 1966, **70**, 766–780.

Girardeau, F.L. & Spradlin, J.E. Token rewards on a cottage program. *Ment. Retard.*, 1964, **2**, 345–351.

Gordon, S., O'Connor, N., & Tizard, J. Some effects of incentives on the performance of imbeciles. *Brit. J. Psychol.*, 1954, **45**, 277–287.

Greene, Frances M. Programmed instruction techniques for the mentally retarded. *Internat. Rev. Res. ment. Retard.*, 1966, **2**, 209–239.

Hamilton, J., Stephens, L., & Allen, P. Controlling aggressive and destructive behavior in severely retarded institutionalized residents. *Amer. J. ment. Def.*, 1967, **71**, 852–856.

Henriksen, K. & Doughty, R. Decelerating undesired mealtime behavior in a group of profoundly retarded boys. *Amer. J. ment. Def.*, 1967, **72**, 40–44.

Hewett, F.M., Mayhew, D., & Rabb, E. An experimental reading program for neurologically impaired, mentally retarded, and severely emotionally disturbed children. *Amer. J. Orthopsychiat.*, 1967, **37**, 35–48.

Hollis, J.H. The effects of social and nonsocial stimuli on the behavior of profoundly retarded children: Part 1. *Amer. J. ment. Defic.*, 1965, **69**, 755–771 (a).

Hollis, J.H. The effects of social and nonsocial stimuli on the behavior of profoundly retarded children: Part 2. *Amer. J. ment. Defic.*, 1965, **69**, 772–789 (b).

Hollis, J.H. & Gorton, C.E. Training severely and profoundly developmentally retarded children. *Ment. Retard.*, 1967, **5**, 20–24.

Hundziak, M., Maurer, R.A., & Watson, L.S. Operant conditioning in toilet training of severely mentally retarded boys. *Amer. J. ment. Def.*, 1965, **70**, 120–124.

Kaufman, M.E. & Prehm, H.J. A review of research on learning sets and transfer of training in mental defectives. *Internat. Rev. Res. ment. Retard.*, 1966, **2**, 123–149.

Kimbrell, D.L., Luckey, R.E., Barbuto, P.F., & Love, J.G. Operation dry pants: an intensive habit-training program for severely and profoundly retarded. *Mental Retardation*, 1967, **5**, 32–36.

Kodman, F. Sensory processes and mental deficiency. In Ellis, N.R. (ed.). *Handbook of mental deficiency*. New York: McGraw-Hill, 1963, pp. 463–479.

Lindsley, O.R. Direct measurement and prosthesis of retarded behavior. *J. educ.*, 1964, **147**, 62–81.

Lipman, R.S. Learning: verbal, perceptual-motor, and classical conditioning. In Ellis, N.R. (ed.). *Handbook of mental deficiency*. New York: McGraw-Hill, 1963, pp. 391–423.

Loos, F.M. & Tizard, J. The employability of adult imbeciles in a hospital workshop. *Amer. J. ment. Def.*, 1955, **59**, 395–403.

Malpass, L.F. Motor skills in mental deficiency. In Ellis, N.R. (ed.). *Handbook of mental deficiency*. New York: McGraw-Hill, 1963, pp. 602–631.

Malpass, L.F., Gilmore, A.S., Hardy, M.W., & Williams, C.F. Automated instruction for retarded children. *Amer. J. ment. Defic.*, 1964, **69**, 405–412.

Marshall, G.R. Toilet training of an autistic eight-year-old through conditioning therapy: a case report. *Behav. Res. Ther.*, 1966, **4**, 242–245.

Mazik, K. & Macnamara, R. Operant conditioning at the training school. *Training School Bull.*, 1967, **63**, 153–158.

Minge, M.R. & Ball, T.S. Teaching of self-help skills to profoundly retarded patients. *Amer. J. ment. Def.*, 1967, **71**, 864–868.

Miron, N.B. Behavior shaping and group nursing with severely retarded patients. In Fisher, J. & Harris, R.E. (eds.). *Reinforcement theory in psychological treatment— a symposium*. California Mental Health Res. Monogr., No. 8, 1966, pp. 1–14.

Neuhaus, E.C. Training the mentally retarded for competitive employment. *Except. Child.*, 1967, **33**, 625–628.

O'Connor, N. The prevalence of mental defect. In Clarke, A.M. & Clarke, A.D.B. (eds.). *Mental deficiency: the changing outlook* (2nd ed.). London: Methuen, 1965, pp. 23–43 (a).

O'Connor, N. Learning and mental defect. In Clarke, A.M. & Clarke, A.D.B. (eds.). *Mental deficiency: the changing outlook* (2nd ed.). London: Methuen, 1965, pp. 188–213 (b).

O'Connor, N. & Hermelin, B. *Speech and thought in severe subnormality*. London: Pergamon, 1963.

O'Connor, N. & Tizard, J. *The social problem of mental deficiency*. London: Pergamon, 1956.

Orlando, R. Component behaviors in free operant temporal discrimination, *Amer. J. ment. Def.*, 1961, **65**, 615–619.

Orlando, R. Shaping multiple schedule performances in retardates: establishment of baselines by systematic and special procedures. *J. exp. Child Psychol.*, 1965, **2**, 135–153.

Orlando, R., Bijou, S.W., Tyler, R.M., & Marshall, A.D. A laboratory for the experimental analysis of developmentally retarded children. *Psychol. Rep.*, 1960, **7**, 261–267.

Penney, R.K. & McCann, B. Application of originality training to the mentally retarded. *Psychol. Rep.*, 1962, **11**, 347–351.

Penrose, L.S. *Biology of mental defect* (2nd ed.). New York: Grune and Stratton, 1963.

Quay, L.C. Academic skills. In Ellis, N.R. (ed.). *Handbook of mental deficiency*. New York: McGraw-Hill, 1963, pp. 664–690.

Rice, H.K. & McDaniel, M.W. Operant behavior in vegetative patients. *Psychol. Rec.*, 1966, **16**, 279–281.

Rice, H.K., McDaniel, M.W., Stallings, V.D., & Gatz, M.J. Operant behavior in vegetative patients: II. *Psychol. Rec.*, 1967, **17**, 449–460.

Rosenberg, S. Problem-solving and conceptual behavior. In Ellis, N.R. (ed.). *Handbook of mental deficiency*. New York: McGraw-Hill, 1963, pp. 439–462.

Ross, L.E. Classical conditioning and discrimination learning research with the mentally retarded. *Internat. Rev. Res. ment. Retard.*, 1966, **1**, 21–54.

Schoelkopf, A.M. & Orlando, R. Delayed vs. immediate reinforcement in simultaneous discrimination problems with mentally retarded children. *Psychol. Rec.*, 1965, **15**, 15–23.

Shepp, B.E. & Turrisi, F.D. Learning and transfer of mediating responses in discriminative learning. *Internat. Rev. Res. ment. Retard.*, 1966, **2**, 86–121.

Sidman, M. & Stoddard, L.T. Programming perception and learning for retarded children. *Internat. Rev. Res. ment. Retard.*, 1966, **2**, 151–208.

Sidman, M. & Stoddard, L.T. The effectiveness of fading in programming a simultaneous form discrimination for retarded children. *J. exp. Anal. Behav.*, 1967, **10**, 3–15.

Spitz, H.H. The role of input organization in the learning and memory of mental retardates. *Internat. Rev. Res. ment. Retard.*, 1966, **2**, 29–56.

Spivack, G. Perceptual processes. In Ellis, N.R. (ed.). *Handbook of mental deficiency*. New York: McGraw-Hill, 1963, pp. 480–511.

Spradlin, J.E. Language and communication of mental defectives. In Ellis, N.R. (ed.). *Handbook of mental deficiency*. New York: McGraw-Hill, 1963, pp. 512–555.

Spradlin, J.E. & Girardeau, F.L. The behavior of moderately and severely retarded persons. *Internat. Rev. Res. Ment. Retard.*, 1966, **1**, 257–298.

Spradlin, J.E., Girardeau, F.L., & Corte, E. Fixed ratio and fixed interval behavior of severely and profoundly retarded subjects. *J. exp. Child. Psychol.*, 1965, **2**, 340–353.

Stevenson, H.W. Discrimination learning. In Ellis, N.R. (ed.). *Handbook of mental deficiency*. New York: McGraw-Hill, 1963, pp. 424–438.

Stevenson, H.W. & Cruse, D.B. The effectiveness of social reinforcement with normal and feebleminded children. *J. Pers.*, 1961, **29**, 124–135.

Stevenson, H.W. & Fahel, L.S. The effect of social reinforcement of institutionalized and noninstitutionalized normal and feebleminded children. *J. Pers.*, 1961, **29**, 136–147.

Stevenson, H.W. & Knights, R.M. The effectiveness of social reinforcement after brief and extended institutionalization. *Amer. J. ment. Def.*, 1962, **66**, 589–594.

Tizard, J. The effects of different types of supervision on the behavior of mental defectives in a sheltered workshop. *Amer. J. ment. Defic.*, 1953, **58**, 143–161.

Tizard, J. Longitudinal and follow-up studies. In Clarke, A.M. & Clarke, A.D.B. (eds.). *Mental deficiency: the changing outlook* (2nd ed.). London: Methuen, 1965, pp. 482–509.

Tizard, J. & O'Connor, N. The employability of high-grade mental defectives: I. *Amer. J. ment. Def.*, 1950, **54**, 563–576 (a).

Tizard, J. & O'Connor, N. The employability of high-grade mental defectives: II. *Amer. J. ment. Def.*, 1950, **55**, 144–157 (b).

Tizard, J. & O'Connor, N. The occupational adaptation of high-grade mental defectives. *Lancet*, 1952, **2**, 620–623.

Walton, D. & Begg, T.L. Adult imbeciles. *Lancet*, 1955, **2**, 616–617.

Watson, L.S. Application of operant conditioning techniques to institutionalized severely and profoundly retarded children. *Mental Retardation Abstracts*, 1967, **4**, 1–18.

Whitney, L.R. & Barnard, K.E. Implications of operant learning theory for nursing care of the retarded child. *Ment. Retard.*, 1966, **4**, 26–29.

Wiesen, A.E. & Watson, E. Elimination of attention seeking behavior in a retarded child. *Amer. J. ment. Defic.*, 1967, **72**, 50–52.

Windle, C. Prognosis of mental subnormals. *Amer. J. ment. Defic. Monogr. Suppl.*, 1962, **66**, 1–180.

Zeiler, M.D. & Jervey, S.S. Development of behavior: self-feeding. *J. consult. clin. Psychol.*, 1968, **32**, 164–168.

Zigler, E. Research on personality structure in the retardate. *Internat. Rev. Res. ment. Retard.*, 1966, **1**, 77–108.

Chapter 17

"Normal" Disorders of "Normal" People

THE GENERAL ORIENTATION of this book is that behavior therapy is concerned with the experimental modification and control of *behavior disorders*. In an earlier chapter, an attempt was made to distinguish between those disturbances of behavior which are characteristic of persons usually termed "neurotic" and which result from the interaction between high "neuroticism" and low stress. Behavior disorders in such persons tend to be polysymptomatic. It was also pointed out, however, that, under appropriate conditions, "normal" persons (that is, persons low on "neuroticism") may develop behavior disorders also, these usually being specific or monosymptomatic. The occurrence of severe monosymptomatic disorders in "normal" persons has generally been dealt with in earlier chapters. However, there are three other broad classes of "difficulty" which may occur in basically nonneurotic persons. On the one hand, normal adults may display various forms of behavior that are not necessarily regarded as abnormal by society or indeed by the individual himself. Nevertheless, the individual manifesting these behaviors may feel uncomfortable about them and may wish to be rid of them. Such behavior may come to the attention of the behavior therapist because the person concerned may have found it difficult or impossible to rid himself of the behavior in question by his own efforts or may have succeeded temporarily and then relapsed. A classic example of such behavior is excessive smoking where many people have become

concerned about the alleged causal connection between smoking and cancer (as well as other diseases).

A second class of such behaviors relates to "normal" developmental difficulties in childhood. Among the other "normal" difficulties of development we may include temper tantrums; operant crying; hyperactivity; elective mutism; head bumping; and a wide range of interpersonal difficulties, such as sibling rivalry, excessive dependency, disruptive behavior in groups, and so on. Of course, in all of these kinds of behavior, a very wide range of disturbance may be observed and undoubtedly in some instances, the behavior may rightly be considered to be "abnormal."

A third class of such behaviors is also developmental in nature but refers to educational problems such as backwardness in elementary skills such as reading and writing. These difficulties are often inextricably entangled with interpersonal difficulties, since educational retardation may, for example, result from hyperactivity which produces lack of attention and concentration. Hence, before the reading or writing difficulty can be tackled, it may be necessary to eliminate or control other behaviors.

In this chapter, therefore, we shall first of all consider examples of adult behaviors (smoking, gambling, insomnia, and overeating) that behavior therapists have attempted to modify by experimental means; then consider the modification of undesirable behaviors in children;

and finally consider techniques that have been used in remedial education. It should be noted that it is not intended to try and cover here all of the behaviors that behavior therapists have attempted to modify in "normal" adults and children, and that attention will be restricted to the use of behavior therapy techniques. In the latter case, no slight is, of course, intended toward the long history of remedial education by more conventional means, many of which employ the same techniques in a perhaps less systematic fashion.

I. BEHAVIOR MODIFICATION WITH NORMAL ADULTS

1. SMOKING[1]

Eysenck (1965) has provided a methodologically oriented account of smoking and health which is extremely thought-provoking. He has pointed out that while a *correlation* between smoking and lung cancer has been demonstrated beyond doubt, the demonstration of a *causal connection* (in the sense that smoking causes lung cancer through the action of some substance contained in the smoke of cigarettes) is not yet certainly established.

An alternative formulation would be that smoking is not a specific causative agent in lung cancer but rather that there exists a relatively homogeneous group of people who have certain characteristics in common, including heavy smoking and a tendency to develop lung cancer (as well as other diseases). The argument that there may be a genetic factor which predisposes to both smoking and lung cancer was first advanced by Fisher (1950). Eysenck has expanded this suggestion by postulating a correlation between smoking and extraversion, since the extravert seeks stimulation to combat the accumulation of reactive inhibition and nicotine may be regarded as a stimulant drug. In two comprehensive studies (Eysenck et al, 1960; Eysenck, 1963) the correlation was confirmed, whereas no correlation was found between smoking and neuroticism (as defined in Eysenck's terms). The correlation with extraversion was confirmed independently in a study by Schubert (1965) who argued that smoking represents an arousal-seeking form of behavior.

The validity of these findings still remains in some doubt, since many American studies have claimed to demonstrate a relationship between "neuroticism" and smoking (Matarazzo and Saslow, 1960). If Eysenck's claim should receive further support in future studies, then there might well be important implications for the behavior therapy techniques used in attempts to modify smoking behavior.

(a) BEHAVIOR THERAPY. Interesting though they are, the above formulations have no direct bearing at present on the question of modification of smoking behavior, except in as far as extraversion may affect conditionability. We may consider behavior therapy for smoking in terms of techniques used and results obtained.

There have, of course, been many attempts of a nonbehavioristic kind to modify smoking habits, ranging from traditional psychotherapy and hypnosis through hortatory public health campaigns in the United States (Greenberg, 1964) and the United Kingdom (Cartwright et al, 1960) to supportive counseling (Koenig and Masters, 1965) and such simple methods as requiring the smoker to keep a tally of the number of cigarettes smoked (Koenig and Masters, 1965; Pyke et al, 1966). The latter method (which is analogous to part of the techniques used to control overeating) has been utilized by behavior therapists in conjunction with other methods. Koenig and Masters (1965) made use of *classical aversive conditioning* (shock) in which severe shock was presented while the subject was performing one of the 18 responses delineated by Koenig and Masters as being involved in the process of lighting and smoking a cigarette. The point in the sequence at which the shock was applied was varied on each trial so that in effect a partial reinforcement technique was used. Shock was also used by McGuire and Vallance (1964) and by Powell and Azrin (1968). A form of *instrumental aversive escape conditioning* was used by Wilde (1964) who developed a special form of apparatus in which an unpleasant mixture of cigarette smoke and hot air was blown into the face of the smoker while he was smoking a cigarette. The smoker tolerated the situation as long as possible while smoking, and the aversive stimulus was terminated when he could no longer stand it and stubbed out his cigarette. At this point, he was rewarded by a blast of fresh air (mixed with menthol on 50% of the trials), so that the technique also involved *aversion-relief conditioning*. An improved version of this apparatus has been developed by Franks et al (1966). A rather different technique within the same general framework was used by Greene

---

[1] Eysenck (1965), Matarazzo and Saslow (1960), and Pflaum (1965) have reviewed the psychological literature.

(1964). The subject sat in a booth and listened to music while smoking, the situation being disguised as a task of music appreciation. Each time the subject drew on the cigarette, its glow activated a relay which produced aversive white noise (masking the music) until the puff was completed.

Various forms of systematic desensitization (SD-I) have also been used. On the assumption that smoking was a response to anxiety, Koenig and Masters (1965) required their subjects to visualize smoking scenes while in a relaxed state, the scenes being ranked from least to most productive of smoking behavior, and a similar technique was used by Pyke et al (1966). Kraft and Al-Issa (1967), on the other hand, working from the same assumption, used SD-I to reduce anxiety in relation to social situations in which smoking was likely to occur.

Somewhat unexpectedly, only two studies have used *massed practice* in an attempt to produce satiation and conditioned inhibition: Resnick (1968), who brought his smokers up to smoking four packs of cigarettes a day within two days of the commencement of treatment, and Keutzer (1968).

Covert sensitization was utilized by Tooley and Pratt (1967). They required their smokers to imagine lighting and smoking, and this led to nausea in various social situations. A technique which could be regarded as a variant of this procedure was used by Janis and Mann (1965) and by Mann (1967). In their studies, the subject was required to role-play an interview with a doctor, falling into five stages involving unfavorable results of medical tests. In a control condition, the subject listened to a similar interview, but did not role-play. In Mann's (1967) later study, an attempt was made to distinguish between the effects of inducing fear and shame by role playing. It is possible to regard the role-playing situation as a form of sensitization in real life, the counterpart of SD-R.

Tooley and Pratt (1967), who used covert sensitization, regarded this as only the preliminary step in their treatment procedure. The subsequent stages are of very considerable interest. The first involves what they called *contingency management* which is based on the Premack principle that the more probable response will serve as a reinforcer for the less probable. Thus, low probability thoughts incompatible with smoking (e.g., that parental

smoking will have a bad influence on the children) are reinforced by high probability events (e.g., drinking coffee) and the smoker contracts not to indulge in the high probability behavior until he has thought of at least one low probability event. The final stage of treatment involves what Tooley and Pratt called *contractual management* in which the smoker contracts not to indulge in smoking in a specific situation which produces reinforcement from another person (e.g., not smoking at the breakfast table). These nonsmoking contracts can then gradually be extended. The importance of these two procedures lies in the fact that they represent another example of the need for the institution of *environmental control* of smoking (Nolan, 1968). We have already seen the importance of this in relation to mental deficiency and the psychoses in particular. Clearly, the initiation of the smoking sequence becomes attached to so many environmental stimuli that laboratory control of smoking is unlikely (however successful) to maintain control over smoking behavior outside the laboratory. The Tooley and Pratt techniques therefore represent an important extension of technique to produce and increase control of smoking behavior in the real environment.

It must be admitted that the results of all of these approaches within the framework of behavior therapy techniques have not thus far been very impressive at all. Thus, Wilde (1964), who reported encouraging results with seven smokers (using his aversive smoke-generating apparatus) later reported (Wilde, 1965) that all five of his "successes" had relapsed, and the more favorable results reported by Franks et al (1966) with the same technique must therefore be treated with great caution until adequate follow-up data are available. Greene (1964) reported an *increase* in smoking following operant aversive conditioning and attributed this to positive conditioning resulting from certain features of the procedure used. Koenig and Masters (1965) compared SD(I) with classical aversive conditioning (shock) and supportive counseling and found no difference in the effect of the three treatments, although all three were followed by a reduction in smoking behavior. They did, however, find a significant difference between *therapists*, an effect which was no longer present on six-month follow-up. Pyke et al (1966) found that "enriched" SD(I)[2]

---

[2] The smokers utilizing SD(I) also attended group sessions for discussion, information dissemination, and feedback, as well as keeping a daily tally of cigarette consumption.

produced a greater decline in smoking during treatment than merely keeping a daily tally or receiving no treatment; but the difference had vanished on four-month follow-up. Furthermore, some of the smokers who significantly reduced their smoking during treatment were smoking *more* on follow-up. It is, therefore, interesting to note that perhaps the most promising successes were those achieved by Janis and Mann (1965) and by Tooley and Pratt (1967), though the latter study involved treatment of only two persons, who were not only husband and wife but were well-known to the experimenters. Nevertheless, it does seem likely that the technique of combining individual treatment with systematic manipulation of the smoker's real environment by means of contractual arrangements will be an essential part of any successful program for the control of smoking behavior. The motivational difficulties experienced by Gutmann and Marston (1967) in their program for *controlling* smoking (rather than trying to *eliminate* it altogether) highlight this point.

The most substantial study of behavior therapy techniques in relation to smoking has been reported recently by Keutzer (1968), using relatively large numbers of subjects in a design that compared the effects of "coverant" control,[3] breath-holding (a particular form of covert sensitization), massed practice, placebo tablet, and no treatment. All four treatment conditions (including placebo) produced better results than no treatment but did not differ among each other. Furthermore, no significant relationships were found between improvement and various personality measures. The care with which Keutzer's study was carried out suggests that thus far behavior therapy has little to offer in this field.

2. GAMBLING

Chronic gambling usually results in severe social consequences for the unfortunate family of the gambler. It is not surprising, therefore, that the limited attempts so far made by behavior therapists to deal with this disorder have attracted a great deal of attention. Barker and Miller (1966a, 1966b) reported on the effects of classical aversive conditioning, with shock as the unconditioned stimulus, in two cases of gambling. In the first case, the subject had gambled continuously for 12 years on one-armed bandits. His entire weekly salary was spent on this pursuit, and he was financially supported by his wife. He was required to gamble continuously on the machine for three hours at a time while receiving during this period a minimum of 150 severe 70-volt shocks to the forearm. The shocks were programmed to occur at random in relation to the sequence of movements required. During a total of 12 hours of treatment, he received a total of 672 shocks, resulting in pronounced retraction of the left forearm. The subject became increasingly reluctant to continue the treatment but persisted to the end of the 12 hours. At a two-month follow-up, he had not resumed his gambling habit. In the second case (again, a male who spent all of his salary gambling on the races), a slightly different technique was used. Color films were made of his behavior, both in the betting shop and at home with his wife and family; additionally, tape recordings were made of the sounds of activity in the betting shop and of his wife describing the effects of his gambling on the family, particularly in so far as it affected the children's welfare. The patient was hospitalized and received over 450 shocks to the wrist while watching the betting shop film and listening to the betting shop tape recording (over a period of ten days). He also watched the film and listened to the tape recording of his wife under conditions of no-shock. This patient also had not resumed his gambling behavior two months after treatment.[4]

A recent study by Goorney (1968) has, extended this method of treatment. In this case there was a 13-year history of periodic gambling, each episode lasting up to six months. Goorney made a careful analysis of the sequence of behaviors involved in this subject's gambling activities, dividing them into several stages (selecting and recording bets from the morning newspapers; thinking about the selected names, races, odds, and possible winnings before the races began; listening to the race results on the radio; and watching the races subsequently on television). All of these stages related, of course, to a single day's gambling activity, and Goorney provided shocks to the upper arms during ten-minute sessions carried out during the various sessions. The treatment lasted nine days in all, involving 45 sessions and a total of 675

---

[3] The term *"coverant" control* is identical in meaning with the term *contingency management* as used by Tooley and Pratt (1967).

[4] Barker and Miller (1968) have recently provided fuller details of their studies and added results on several new cases.

shocks. The patient reported increasing reluctance to think about racing or make selections from the newspaper. He was followed up for more than 12 months and appeared to manifest no interest in gambling or racing in general. Both he and his wife reported a significant improvement in sexual and social relationships. Goorney makes the point that it is important to treat the maladaptive behavior in all its possible forms (both overt and covert) and at all stages of its manifestation. He discusses and rejects alternative explanations of the results.[5]

The follow-up in these cases is relatively short, of course, and relapse may be a very probable outcome. In view of the social consequences of persistent gambling on this scale, however, the procedures described above can certainly be justified. It would, of course, be interesting and important to know the status of these subjects at the present time.

3. Overeating

We have already referred to the problem of obesity produced by overeating in relation to psychiatric patients.[6] Ferster's procedures have been adopted and extended for use with normal overeating problems by Stuart (1967) who deals with both operant and respondent behavior and has introduced also the use of covert sensitization. Stuart's procedures, in fact, represent another example of the detailed control of the environment to which we have already referred. As in Ferster's model, however, the ultimate aim is to train the subject to control his own environment. Stuart provides a detailed step-by-step procedure for each of several weeks of treatment, including (in sequential order): interruption of the meal for short, fixed periods of time; restriction of food to one place (the kitchen) in the house; the divorcing of eating from other activities; the use of pauses between each mouthful; engaging in alternative high probability behaviors at eating times; and the use of covert sensitization techniques. In addition, detailed food consumption and weight records are to be kept, as recommended by Ferster, although, as we have seen in the case of smoking, these kinds of records, by themselves, do not appear to be very effective. Stuart reports the results of using these techniques with eight female patients over a 12-month treatment period. All subjects lost a substantial amount of weight, ranging from 26–47 lbs over 16–41 sessions.[7]

The use of covert sensitization in the treatment of overeating has also been reported by Cautela (1966). His patient's weight dropped from 200 to 134 pounds at the end of treatment. Kennedy and Foreyt (1968) reported a weight loss of 30 pounds over 22 weeks in a patient weighing 322 pounds at the start of treatment. They paired an extremely unpleasant odor with the smell of favorite foods. In neither of these studies was there any adequate control of possibly confounding variables.

4. Insomnia

Insomnia appears to be a label describing the persistence of behaviors which are incompatible with sleep. This was strikingly illustrated in a study by Geer and Katkin (1966). A 29-year-old female, with no other obvious signs of abnormality, had suffered from insomnia for 12 months. Analysis showed that three persistent themes prevented her from sleeping: ruminations over a broken engagement; ruminations over her future (whether, for example, she should return to nursing); and ruminations over her inability to sleep. The subject was trained in relaxation, but SD-I could not be applied in the usual way because, since the subject experienced no anxiety before going to bed or when anticipating sleep, no fear hierarchy could be constructed. Instead, she was instructed to visualize going to bed, ruminating, and then relaxing. At the end of 14 sessions of treatment, the subject reported that she no longer had difficulty in going to sleep. An eight-month follow-up indicated that the improvement had been maintained, although occasionally she stayed awake for two to three hours. She was, however, quite satisfied with her new-found ability to go to sleep normally on most nights.

5. Social Anxiety (Stage Fright)

If social competence is an acquired skill, failure to acquire such an essential skill to the degree required for "comfortable" operation in modern society may produce social anxiety which, in turn, is reduced by the avoidance of social situations or, in situations where social intercourse cannot be avoided, produces incompetent social behavior. It is, of course,

---

[5] Seager et al (1966) have reported the use of an instrumental escape conditioning technique for gambling, but provide no details of results.

[6] See Chapter 9.

[7] Mendelson (1966) has discussed the psychological aspects of obesity.

obvious that social competence is a continuum and that most people vary in the degree of competence they will exhibit in various social situations. There would also be marked inter-individual differences in general social competence.

One particular form of social incompetence which is quite common in nonneurotic individuals relates to the ability to interact with others in a public situation, and a fairly extreme form of this relates to public-speaking situations in which even normally socially competent individuals may be severely affected. The phenomenon of "stage-fright" has been highlighted by the remarkable study of Paul (1966) which has justly become celebrated. The relevance of Paul's study to the evaluation of behavior therapy by comparison with alternative methods of treatment will be considered in a later chapter.[8] Here, we are concerned with the technique used and results obtained by Paul.

From a pool of 710 students who completed a pretreatment battery of tests (the Anxiety Differential, the IPAT Anxiety Scale Questionnaire, the Pittsburgh Social Extraversion-Introversion and Emotionality Scales, the Interpersonal Anxiety Scales from the S-R Inventory of Anxiousness, and a short form of the Personal Report of Confidence as a Speaker), Paul selected a group of 96 subjects manifesting strong to severe anxiety of relatively long (two to 20 years) duration. Before allocation to treatment groups, all of the subjects underwent a stress-condition assignment in which they were required to give a four-minute speech before a panel of observers who assessed the degree of anxiety shown during the speech on a check list that referred to behavioral (that is, observed, not inferred) manifestations of anxiety. In addition, just prior to the speech, indices of palmar sweat and pulse rate were obtained, and the Anxiety Differential was administered. The subjects were then allocated randomly to one of five treatment groups.

(i) *Modified systematic desensitization* ($n = 15$). Subjects in this group essentially received individual SD(I) training, using hierarchies relating directly to speaking in or to a group.

(ii) *Insight-oriented psychotherapy* ($n = 15$). Subjects in this group received traditional nonspecific individual therapy aimed at increasing insight into adjustment problems.

(iii) *Attention-placebo* ($n = 15$). Subjects in this group were required to perform a vigilance task while under the influence of what they supposed was a "fast-acting tranquillizer drug" to inhibit anxiety engendered by the task but which was, in fact, a placebo preparation. While they were performing the task, the "therapist" gave them a good deal of nonspecific attention and support. This group was essentially a control for possible effects of expectation of relief, attention, warmth, and interest of the "therapist," suggestion and "faith."

(iv) *No-treatment classroom control* ($n = 29$). Subjects in this group received no "treatment" other than that which might have resulted from having to make two classroom speeches subsequent to the initial testing with brief contact with the investigator, including a promise of future treatment.

(v) *No-contact classroom control* ($n = 22$). Subjects in this group were not contacted at all during the period between pre and post-assessment measures.

The three treatment groups were treated by five experienced psychotherapists who were trained specially in the SD-I and attention-placebo procedures and who each utilized all three techniques. Five sessions of treatment were carried out with each subject over a six-week period. At the end of the treatment period, a posttreatment stress speech was again required of all groups except the no-contact classroom control group, the same measures being taken again. Six weeks later, a first follow-up assessment of changes in the original test battery was carried out on all five groups. Two years later a most painstaking effort was made to contact all of the subjects (except for a small group of the untreated controls who had been used for another purpose in the meantime). All of the treated subjects were contacted and information obtained, while 70% of the contacted controls returned data (Paul, 1967).

The reader must be referred to Paul's original studies (1966, 1967) for full details of the results obtained. At the end of treatment (as measured by the stress test) and on the first follow-up (FU_1), a clear superiority for systematic desensitization procedures was found over all the other procedures. The effects of insight-oriented therapy and attention-placebo therapy did not differ, but both of these procedures were superior to the two no-treatment control groups. These differences were maintained on the second follow-up assessment (FU_2) carried out two years later.

---

[8] See Chapter 18.

The results for both FU_1 and FU_2 for various measures are shown in Figure 1. In addition, Paul very carefully investigated the possibility of symptom substitution by the use of specially-designed questionnaires and could find no evidence whatever for it. On the contrary, there was a tendency for the results to generalize to other aspects of social behavior in a beneficial way. Nor was there any evidence of relapse.

In another study, organized along very similar lines, Paul and Shannon (1966) com-

pared the effects on anxiety of a combination of group SD-I and intensive group discussion with reeducative goals with the effects of individual SD-I, insight - oriented therapy, attention-placebo, and no contact control conditions.[9] In addition to measuring changes on the test battery used in the earlier studies, Paul and Shannon evaluated the comparative effectiveness of these various treatments in relation to grade point average (GPA) changes in examinations, a variable which might be expected to be

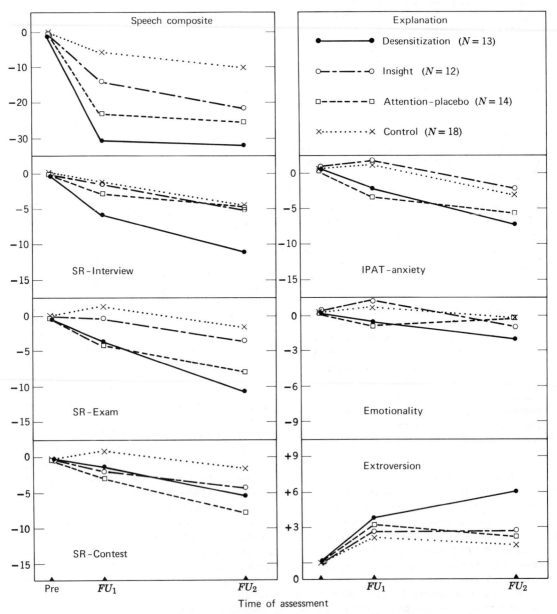

FIG. I. Mean change from pretreatment to six-week follow-up (FU_1) and two-year follow-up (FU_2) for Ss retained at FU_2 (Paul, 1967).

affected significantly by changes in anxiety. They found that the untreated control group showed a decline in GPA over the time-span (two semesters) of the experiment, whereas the group desensitization subjects showed an increase in GPA. No difference was found, however, between the effects of individual desensitization and combined group desensitization/therapy. Nevertheless, Paul and Shannon considered that the combined technique had certain advantages over the individual technique, apart from the saving in time.

"One factor which may add additional benefit over individual desensitization derives from the construction of hierarchies through group discussion. Not only may discrimination learning occur as in individual programs, but a reduction in anxiety as subjects become aware of the similarity between themselves and other group members. . . . The group setting also provides an ideal opportunity for persons debilitated by social anxiety to practice deficient skills after a degree of anxiety reduction has been attained. Initially, the group treatment appeared to increase immediate feelings of awkwardness. However, after a few sessions, the groups pulled together . . . typically left the clinic together, and reported socializing between sessions" (Paul and Shannon, 1966, p. 134).

It could, in fact, be argued that, instead of sequentially training in social skills, first in the laboratory, and then extending this training into real social situations, Paul and Shannon are telescoping the two stages together. Alternatively, the group desensitization/therapy procedure could be described as a combination of SD(I) and SD(R) procedures.

Not many other examples of the application of behavior therapy techniques to social anxiety in normal persons appear to have been reported thus far, though no doubt Paul's work will stimulate much research in the near future. Kondas (1967), however, studied the comparative effects of four treatment methods on examination anxiety in children and students. He compared the effects of relaxation training, relaxation training followed by SD(I), presentation of anxiety hierarchy items without relaxation, and no treatment in 23 children aged 11–15 years. The dependent variables were a general measure of fears (the FSS score) and a specific measure of examination anxiety (palmar sweat activity recorded under actual examination conditions). Both relaxation training alone and relaxation training followed by SD(I) produced significantly greater changes than the other two conditions, but on a five-month follow-up, only the SD(I) group maintained the initial improvement. A similar study with psychology students (omitting the condition in which anxiety hierarchy items were presented without relaxation) resulted in significant changes only in the SD(I) treatment condition. Katahn et al (1966) have reported similar favorable changes to those obtained by Paul and Shannon in a group of highly test-anxious subjects, using a combination of SD(I) and group counseling. Katahn (1967) achieved moderate success with the combined method with a basketball player whose anxiety prior to games, practice, or anything to do with basketball produced vomiting and interfered seriously with his basically high level of competence in this game. An interesting feature of this study was that Katahn was apparently able to train the player to reciprocally inhibit the anxiety by practicing experiencing the sensations he felt when he was playing well. Cohen (1965) and White et al (1968) have also reported the successful use of SD(I) in cases of social anxiety whenever interaction with a group of people was required.

Finally, the particularly interesting study of Gibbs (1965) should be mentioned. The subject was seriously troubled by excessive blushing in social situations (a response mediated by the sympathetic division of the autonomic nervous system). Gibbs postulated that the blushing was a learned response to anxiety and, although he does not explicitly say so, it could be argued that the subject's tendency to withdraw from social situations effectively served to reduce anxiety. Treatment involved training in assertiveness behavior which, according to Gibbs, would be mediated through the parasympathetic division of the ANS. Considerable improvement in reducing the amount of blushing, together with improved social competence, was claimed by Gibbs; the improvement being maintained over a follow-up period of six months.

We may conclude that significant advances have been made in the behavior therapy of social incompetence in recent years. Essentially, socially anxious persons are being trained in a complex, high-level skill which they have either failed to acquire to an adequate degree or which has been interfered with by nonreinforcing

---

[9] These latter groups were the same as those used by Paul (1966) in the earlier study.

experiences, the result in either case being a high degree of anxiety in social situations, leading to a tendency to avoid such situations whenever possible.

6. Nightmares

Geer and Silverman (1967) treated a 22-year-old male with a recurring nightmare while falling asleep of being threatened by a shadowy figure. The nightmare had occurred three to five times a week for over 15 years. Apart from the nightmare, there was no evidence of abnormality. Direct treatment of the nightmare by visualizing various stages of it while relaxing was successful when the subject told himself in addition, "It's only a dream," whenever the visualization produced anxiety (as it did). The treatment was successful over seven sessions, the nightmare being absent (and normal dreams occurring) on 18-month follow-up. In this case, there was no apparent anxiety about the dream content outside the specific situation in which the nightmare occurred. In a second case, however, studied by Silverman and Geer (1968), a 19-year-old otherwise normal girl not only experienced a recurrent nightmare (of four years' duration) relating to fear of falling off bridges, but also had a real, extreme fear of crossing bridges. Here treatment was directed at the real fear, using SD-I procedures, with success over seven sessions, the subject being able to cross bridges while under observation. The nightmare disappeared at the same time without direct treatment, and both fear and nightmare were absent on six-month follow-up. In neither case was symptom substitution or other abnormal behavior or difficulty observed or reported.

II. BEHAVIOR MODIFICATION WITH CHILDREN

Behavior therapy techniques are being applied with increasing frequency in a wide variety of situations relating to childhood. There is no doubt that a good many of the developmental problems that arise in children are inadvertently produced by parental (and peer) reinforcement schedules. There seems also to be no doubt that in very many instances these maladaptive behaviors can be abolished by relatively simple procedures, provided these are carefully and systematically applied. There also seems to be no doubt that, in many instances, educational progress in the classroom is hindered to a serious

extent by competing learned behaviors of a disruptive nature. Finally, there is now good evidence that the acquisition of basic skills in the classroom can be accelerated by the appropriate use of operant training techniques in backward children where no disruption by competing activities is present. In what follows, we shall be presenting a selection of developmental problems essentially as illustrations of what can be achieved. Four problem areas will be considered: common developmental problems encountered by parents and others, social difficulties in the home, social difficulties in group situations outside the home, and the application of behavior modification techniques in remedial education. There is, of course, considerable overlap between the last three areas.

1. Some Common Developmental Problems

(a) temper tantrums. Williams (1959), in one of the simplest and shortest behavior therapy studies on record, eliminated tantrum behavior in a 21-month-old child who had been given much special attention when seriously ill and who subsequently indulged in a severe temper tantrum at bedtime unless one parent stayed with him until he fell asleep. The treatment was simple in the extreme—the child's temper tantrum was simply ignored and the door of his room left closed. On the first occasion, the child cried for 45 minutes before going to sleep; on subsequent occasions the crying behavior followed a standard extinction curve, extinction being completed over ten trials. The behavior was inadvertently reinstated shortly afterwards by a visiting relative but was readily extinguished a second time by the use of the same procedures over nine sessions. No abnormal side-effects of the procedure were noted and at three and three-quarter years of age on follow-up the child was described as friendly, expressive, and outgoing; in fact, as perfectly normal.

The question arises, of course, as to why the parents were unable to extinguish the behavior themselves. The answer probably lies in the strength and length of the crying on the first occasion of treatment, namely, 45 minutes. It is highly unlikely that many parents can steel themselves sufficiently to continue to ignore their own child when he cries for that length of time at that age. But, of course, if it is true that the behavior is being maintained by parental attention, then it follows that the longer the parents delay in going in to the child, the more reinforcing will be their eventual appearance. In other words, it would be better not to try at all to extinguish the behavior by attention-withdrawal than to try and fail. Hence, simple as the procedure is in principle, it may be necessary for it to be carried out by a psychologist not emotionally involved with the child.

It may be noted that Williams' study has often been quoted as the paradigm for the time-out procedure which, as we have seen, has been successfully used in extinguishing tantrum behavior, even in psychotic children. This is unfortunate, since a critical aspect of these studies appears to be the readmission of the child so treated to the social situation once the tantrum has ceased. Furthermore, the time-out procedure appeared to be successful only if the social situation from which the child was excluded had positive reinforcing properties. Hence, Williams's procedure (especially with such a young child) appears better conceptualized as a straightforward case of experimental extinction through withdrawal of reinforcement.

That the treatment of temper tantrums may usually turn out to be much more complicated was demonstrated in an important study by Patterson and Brodsky (1966) who treated a five-year-old boy who manifested severe temper tantrums among several other behavior disturbances. In this case, attendance at kindergarten appeared to be stimulus which signified deprivation (separation from the mother). The anxiety generated by this deprivation state produced the tantrum behavior which had two consequences: terminating the aversive state (by delaying the departure of the mother) and maintaining the positive social reinforcers of attention by the kindergarten staff and the mother. The treatment instituted by Patterson and Brodsky involved physical restraint of the child until the temper tantrum subsided; treatment of the separation anxiety by doll play; increasing the number and range of positive reinforcements in the kindergarten situation by rewarding the child and his peers for interaction; and training the parents to avoid reinforcing the negativistic behavior *outside* the kindergarten situation. The tantrums were eliminated over a period of ten days and were still absent on a three-month follow-up; the negativism and isolated behaviors were also eliminated and, as a consequence, social interaction between the child and his peers increased. Thus, Patterson

and Brodsky stress the importance of manipulating the total environment of the child, so that improvements within the kindergarten situation (the immediately precipitating stimulus) will be maintained outside; they stress also the importance of training parents, teachers, and peers of the child so that positive reinforcement for adaptive behaviors incompatible with the tantrum behavior will be forthcoming.

(b) OPERANT CRYING. In a remarkable experiment, Etzel and Gewirtz (1967) modified operant crying in two babies, aged six weeks and 20 weeks. There was good reason to suppose that the crying was being strengthened and maintained by the nursing staff. They first measured the base-rate emission of smiles, cries, fusses, and frowns in one baby; and smiles, number of eye-contacts, and cries in the other. In a specially devised and ingenious experimental situation, they then reinforced (by the experimenter's smiling face) responses other than cries, while removing reinforcement for crying. Very significant changes were achieved, the link to the experimental procedures being verified by temporarily reversing the contingencies and reinstating the crying behavior. The importance of this study lies in its suggestion that operant crying may be acquired at a very early age indeed and may then be maintained by the attention that it attracts.

Hart et al (1964) studied the behavior of two four-year-old kindergarten boys who cried frequently in situations that would not normally produce crying in boys of their sturdy physique. Once again, there was reason to suppose that the crying was maintained by the attention it attracted. After establishing base-rates for the behavior (defining crying as a response that could be heard at least 50 feet away and lasted for five seconds or more), they arranged with the kindergarten teacher to withdraw all attention from the crying behavior but to reward by attention any appropriate noncrying behavior to the harmless falls, scrapes, pulls, or pushes which usually produced the crying. The crying behavior was eliminated and, in this study also, the link to the procedures was established by reinstatement of the crying when the contingencies were temporarily reversed. An interesting side observation was the sudden disappearance of the crying during reinstatement in one of the children. It was noted in this case that the teachers were attending, not to the crying, but to its precursors (screwing-up of the face, etc.). The explanation is an *ad hoc* one, but not unreasonable, and illustrates again the significance of timing in reinforcement procedures. It suggests also the difficulty of programming these contingencies under "real-life conditions."

(c) HEAD-BUMPING. This is a common activity indulged in by young children at night and is so harmless that treatment is quite unnecessary. However, it is perhaps another matter when indulged in for periods of up to five minutes at a time in a ten-year-old girl, as was the case in the girl seen by Mogel and Schiff (1967). The behavior was not dangerous, since the child placed her hands on a table and bumped her head on her hands. Mogel and Schiff asked the child to demonstrate the head bumping with a view to treating it by means of massed practice. However, after demonstrating it for only two minutes, the child stopped in embarrassment. She was told she would have to perform in this way on future visits. The behavior had not occurred again over a follow-up period of two years. This must represent the shortest treatment on record (two minutes), and the authors rightly point up the possible importance of cognitive factors in a case such as this. Certainly, the possibility that this child might have been subjected to prolonged periods of massed practice should give every behavior therapist addicted to such a technique much food for thought. This is also one of the few studies pointing up the fact that attention may not invariably be the positively reinforcing contingency that most behavior therapists assume it to be and that its negative properties should also be investigated.

(d) THUMBSUCKING.[10] This common phenomenon (Traisman and Traisman, 1958) has proved a happy hunting ground for psychodynamic therapists, whose speculations appear to have no basis in fact. Palermo (1956) trenchantly criticized medical, dental, and psychodynamic formulations and attempted to account for the genesis and maintenance of thumbsucking in terms of learning theory. Hunger contractions in the newborn child are followed closely in time by the child being put to the nipple which results both in sucking and feeding, followed by saliva flow and drive reduction. Subsequently, hunger contractions lead to thumbsucking which produces saliva flow and drive reduction. Palermo points out that the use of thumbsucking as a substitute activity for nipple sucking arises from the fact that, in the young child, the fingers are frequently

in contact with the mouth and that the initial connection is therefore very likely. Of course, it is arguable also that, alternatively, the child has a need to suck for a given length of time each day and that, if sufficient sucking at the nipple is not obtained, sucking of the thumb will become more likely. Baer (1962) has provided direct empirical evidence that rate of thumbsucking can be controlled by withdrawing positively reinforcing stimuli during periods of nonthumbsucking.

Davidson et al (1967) have provided some empirical evidence against the psychodynamic interpretation of thumbsucking. They showed that thumbsucking children did not differ significantly from nonthumbsucking children on various personality (including projective) measures. They also showed that there was no significant incidence of new symptoms in children whose thumbsucking was arrested by means of a palatal crib as compared with untreated thumbsucking children over a follow-up period of 12 months.

With respect to various methods of treatment for thumbsucking, mention should be made of an important experimental study by Haryett et al (1967). They divided 66 thumbsucking children into six treatment groups: control (no treatment); psychological treatment only; use of a palatal arch only; use of the arch with associated psychological treatment; use of a palatal crib only; and use of a palatal crib with associated psychological treatment. In the case of the mechanical devices, psychological treatment involved explanation of the purpose of using the arch or crib. The results of the various treatments over 12 months were very clear. All children using the palatal crib (with or without explanation) desisted from the habit within three weeks; whereas only six of the children in the other four groups desisted and took much longer to do so. More than 50% of the children given psychological treatment only developed new mannerisms compared with only one-third of the crib-treated children and none of the children treated with the crib and an explanation of its use. The mannerisms were quite trivial. Furthermore, associated habits diminished much more in those children who stopped thumbsucking than in those who did not. There was no evidence of differential personality changes in the groups. Three minor disadvantages associated with the use of the crib were increased irritability, some speech difficulty

---

[10] Davidson (in press) has reviewed the large literature on this topic.

(especially lisping), and some eating difficulty (food lodging in the appliance). However, these problems were transitory in nearly all the children.

The question whether thumbsucking produces malformation of the teeth and other oral structures is a controversial one, but the weight of evidence now suggests that persistent thumbsucking may produce such changes, depending on the precise form of sucking (Haryett et al, 1967; Davidson, 1968). Hence, the demonstration by Haryett et al (1967) that use of the crib method (particularly if supported by explanation of its use to the child) definitely eliminates thumbsucking and produces no symptom substitution or other important side effects becomes of considerable significance in relation to a disorder that is otherwise quite trivial.

(e) REFUSAL TO EAT. Feeding difficulties in normal children are nearly always produced by parents who believe that the child should finish whatever is put before him; who fail to realize that children can fail to eat for several meals in succession without suffering any harm; and who fail to take account of the widely fluctuating food intake needs of children at different stages of development. It may truly be said, therefore, that in nearly all cases of feeding difficulties in children (unless there are physiological factors involved, of course), it is the parents who need reeducating rather than the child. Occasionally the battle between parents and child may become so complicated that intervention is necessary. One such case was reported by White (1959). In this instance, special factors had led to a serious situation in which the child refused to eat unless the father was present. The death of the father precipitated a serious crisis, which was treated by the psychologist taking over the role of the father and gradually training the child to eat independently of his presence, essentially by using the method of successive approximation.

(f) EXCESSIVE SCRATCHING. Allen and Harris (1966) reported an unusual case in which a five-year-old child scratched her head, nose, cheeks, chin, and one arm and leg so severely that large sores and scabs disfigured her body. There was no medical basis for the scratching, but the physical effects had become so severe that mechanical restraint had been suggested. Careful observation showed that although the father physically punished the child, her relationships with him were good, but that the mother's relationships with the child were very poor. Although she did not physically punish the child, they were in a constant state of friction and the mother was quite excessively severe and critical with her. The interesting feature of the treatment related to the observations that the mother almost never rewarded the child for positive behaviors (such as not scratching). In other words, if the child "behaved" herself she was ignored; only if she misbehaved or scratched herself did she receive attention (even though it took the form of criticism) from the mother. The mother was therefore trained to not only ignore the scratching altogether (which she found very difficult to do) but to reward nonscratching periods and other positive behaviors. Although setbacks were experienced in this program (because of the mother's difficulty in giving social approval), the treatment was completely successful, as manifested by the complete disappearance of the sores and scabs and their absence on four-month follow-up. It is interesting to note that it proved quite feasible to reward nonscratching behaviors on a continuous reinforcement basis followed by the introduction of partial reinforcement. Eventually there was a switch from primary to social reinforcers and a gradual tapering off of the reinforcers until verbal reinforcement alone sufficed.

No doubt similar techniques could be applied to the modification of many other childhood behaviors. It is clear, however, that in many instances specific training of the parents is required and that the institution of new schedules of reinforcement is often very difficult for parents who have been acting according to undesirable schedules for a long time. The techniques are not nearly so simple in practice as they may seem.

2. SOCIAL DIFFICULTIES IN THE HOME

Essentially here we are dealing with social relationships between parent and child on the one hand and between children of the same family on the other.

(a) EXCESSIVE VERBAL DEMANDS. Parents often tend *not* to reward "good" behavior (if the child is playing quietly and happily, the mother will heave a sigh of relief and get on with the housework); try to ignore the initial attempt of the child to obtain attention for as long as possible, and respond only when the child's demand for attention reaches such a pitch that it can no longer be ignored. Thus, in effect, the parent is failing to reinforce the very behavior which pleases him most, while reinforcing the very behavior he would really like to eliminate. Of course, the pattern is not usually by any means consistent, that is, a partial reinforcement schedule is in operation, which renders the behavior highly resistant to extinction. Since such problems do not usually result in an appeal for help, behavior therapists have not thus far had many opportunities to attempt to modify the behavior of the child by training the parents. However, several interesting studies do exist. In one such case, a 20-month-old child called his parents persistently whenever he awoke in the morning until one or other parent went into him (Pumroy and Pumroy, 1967). The problem to be solved was how to train the child not to call out to the parents before eight o'clock. Base-line observation over three days indicated that the child would call out up to 100 times if the parents did not go to him until eight o'clock.[11] On the fourth day, it was arranged that a small lamp would light up at the child's bedside at eight o'clock, at which time the parents also went in and told the child it was "time to get up." On subsequent days, the parents went in to the first call that was made after the lamp lit up at eight o'clock, but not before. Over 68 days of training, the number of calls before eight o'clock diminished from an average of 100 calls to between zero and 20. Thus, the early calling behavior was not eliminated, but it was significantly reduced.

(b) REBELLIOUS BEHAVIOR. The treatment of rebellious, disobedient behavior in normal children has been described by Boardman (1962), Straughan (1964) and Russo (1964). Essentially, it involves training the parents in applying both positive and negative contingencies appropriately and consistently, a procedure fraught with difficulties and setbacks in the case of older children, since an exacerbation of the behavior frequently results initially. In such circumstances, parents are likely to retreat and need a great deal of support. A detailed example of the procedures involved in training the parents to modify these kinds of behavior may be found in Wahler et al (1965). Their technique involves bringing the mother and child into a playroom and first observing their interaction very carefully. A record is made of the child's deviant behaviors and of the mother's reaction to it and her ways of handling it. Careful observation is also made of

behaviors of the child that are incompatible with the deviant behaviors. The mother is then trained not to reinforce the deviant behaviors and to reinforce incompatible behaviors by using a system of cues to signal to the mother when she should indulge in appropriate reinforcing and nonreinforcing behaviors. Reversal of reinforcement contingencies again serves as a check that the behavior is under the control of the specified maternal responses. The behavior of three children with various deviant behaviors (bullying the mother, dependency on the mother, and negativism) was significantly modified by these procedures.

(c) SIBLING RIVALRY. Competition between siblings sometimes reaches worrying levels, and the mother may need help in coping with it. O'Leary et al (1967) studied the behavior of a six-year-old, possibly brain-damaged boy and his three-year-old brother who fought constantly in a basement where a high noise level was required before the mother's attention would be attracted from above. First, the base-line levels of three kinds of interaction (verbal or physical aggression, cooperative play, and solitary behavior) were measured (with satisfactory reliability for two observers). Then the experimenters provided primary reinforcers (candy) on a partial reinforcement schedule for cooperative behaviors, following which tokens were substituted for the primary reinforcers (the tokens could, of course, be exchanged later for primary reinforcers). After testing the link by reversing the contingencies, the mother was trained in the procedure, time-out for certain behaviors also being used. The results were highly successful.

Thus, there is some evidence that the social behavior of children can be significantly modified by the introduction of reinforcement schedules and that parents can be trained to identify and reinforce "desirable" behaviors and to cease reinforcing "undesirable" behaviors. Again, there appears to be almost unlimited scope for the application of behavior therapy techniques.

3. SOCIAL DIFFICULTIES OUTSIDE THE HOME

Disorders of social behavior in normal children appear to fall into two broad categories, which may well form the extreme ends of a normal distribution. At one end, we have

---

[11] It is interesting to note that the calling-out showed no apparent extinction tendency under these conditions (cf. Williams, 1959, above).

isolate behavior and, at the other, excessive interference with other children.

(a) ISOLATE BEHAVIOR. Allen et al (1964) applied operant conditioning techniques to a four-year-old kindergarten child who spent most of her time in solitary activity and with adult teachers rather than with other children. Her behavior rapidly changed to increased interaction with the other children when attention from the teacher was made contingent on such interaction. In this case, also, reversal of the contingency was shown to reinstate the undesirable orientation of the child. This study is a very clear example of how isolate behavior can actually be strengthened by the very procedures that are supposed to reduce it, namely, the concern and attention of the teacher to a child behaving in this fashion. The other point to note is that it is apparently quite easy to fade out the teacher attention for peer interaction, since the reinforcers provided by interaction with other children take over control of the behavior.

Clement and Milne (1967) chose 11 boys aged 8–9 years who were of average intelligence but who were socially withdrawn, lacking in spontaneity, maladjusted, yet able to attend school regularly.[12] They very carefully assessed the behavior of these children while in playroom activity together in small groups. For three of the children, token rewards were provided on a VR/VI schedule for social approach to each other, the therapist being present. A second group of three of the children were placed in the same situation but given only verbal reinforcement by the therapist for social interaction. The third group of four boys was left alone for the play period. Fourteen treatment or control sessions were given, one per week. In addition to changes in social interaction, assessments were made in relation to report card grades in school; anxiety level (as measured by the Children's Manifest Anxiety Scale); adjustment as measured by a Q-sort completed by the mother; and number of problem behaviors.

The principal results of the experiment are shown in Figure 2 in relation to social interactive behavior in the playroom situation. The token reinforcement group showed greater change than the verbal reinforcement group, and the verbal group more than the control. The token group showed an increase in social approach behavior and a decrease in discrete problem behavior. There were no changes in any groups in report card grades, anxiety or adjustment, the changes therefore being fairly specific. An important point to note is that the changes reported by the mothers appeared to overestimate the degree of improvement as compared with the objective measures. Whatever

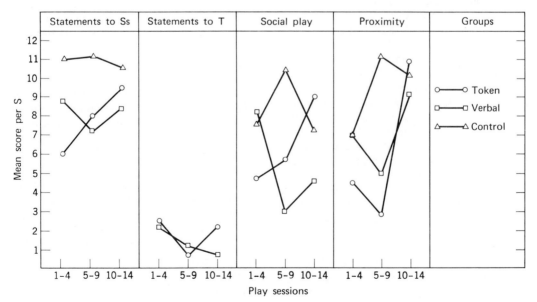

FIG. 2. Frequency of measures of social interaction as a function of token, verbal, or no reinforcement (Clement and Milne, 1967).

[12] The 11 boys were chosen by various procedures from a sample of over 2700 children.

the reason for this (desire to please the experimenters, etc.), this result suggests caution in accepting estimates of improvement provided by the mother unless these can be checked against direct objective assessment of the child's behavior.

(b) ELECTIVE MUTISM. This problem seems first to have been described in the German literature[13] but has recently received a good deal of attention in America and England (Salfield, 1950; Morris, 1953; Browne et al, 1963; Pustrom and Speers, 1964; Elson et al, 1965). The defining characteristic is the use of fully developed, normal speech toward some persons, with absolute silence in the presence of others. It is readily distinguishable from mental deficiency or psychosis, usually appears between three and five years of age, and is highly resistant to treatment. The children always show great timidity in social situations. Only one follow-up study appears to have been carried out. Elson et al (1965) studied four girls aged 7–10 years when first seen and followed them up for six months to five years. They had been treated by uncovering and supportive psychotherapy (in so far as this was possible). All of the children showed marked improvement and were attending school better than 90% of the time. None had been hospitalized during the follow-up period; none had required psychiatric treatment. There was no evidence of depression, excessive anxiety, sleep disturbance, defects in orientation, hallucinations, or sociopathic behavior. Interpersonal relations in the home were good and peer relations outside the house were improved, though still impaired. If these four cases were typical of elective mutism, then the long-term outlook is very good.

Reed (1963) found only four cases of elective mutism in 2000 successive referrals to a child guidance clinic and these four did not conform to the patterns reported by Salfield (1950) and Morris (1953). Reed distinguished (tentatively, no doubt, on the basis of four cases) two clinical types of elective mutism. On the one hand, mutism might be learned as an attention-getting device; on the other hand, as a fear-reducing response. The former would show little anxiety, the latter would be very tense and watchful.

Reed suggested that operant conditioning procedures might be used to eliminate mutism that was attention getting, but presented no results of his own. However, Brison (1966) succeeded in eliminating mutism in a kindergarten child by moving him into a new class and arranging for the mutism to be ignored. Nonverbal behavior that might achieve results normally achieved by talking was also ignored. The child soon began to talk in a whisper (which was reinforced by social approval) and was soon talking normally.

The study by Reid et al (1967) appears to deal with Reed's other category of elective mutism. In this case, a child of six years would talk only in the family circle and not even then when a stranger was present. Psychotherapy was impossible because the child would not talk to strangers. Reid et al decided to eliminate the child's fear of strangers by the use of SD-R.[14] In the first stage, the mother was alone with the child and fed him breakfast in small portions, receipt of each portion being dependent on the child asking for it. Then the first experimenter (E_1) gradually insinuated himself into the room and approached the child. The child became more verbal at this point but did not talk to E_1. Eventually, however, E_1 was able to substitute for the mother in feeding the child while maintaining the verbal behavior. Gradually the situation was turned into a social situation, with E_2 and E_3 taking part, as well as other children. It may be noted that no less than seven stages were introduced in a single day.

(c) REGRESSED CRAWLING. Harris et al (1964) studied a three-year-old child who spent most of her time off her feet in kindergarten and at home whenever strangers were present—possibly an early indicator of elective mutism. Treatment was by the usual procedure of withdrawing all reinforcement for off-feet behavior while providing immediate attention for on-feet behavior. In two weeks the child's behavior was indistinguishable from that of the other kindergarten children in relation to locomotor behavior although social behavior was still not engaged in. It was shown that the off-feet behavior could be reinstated and reextinguished by reversing the contingencies.

Thus, there seems little doubt that isolate behavior in young children may be maintained by its attention-getting results and may be readily eliminated by withdrawal of the attention. Since isolate behavior on the part of

---

[13] See Pustrom and Speers (1964) or Elson et al (1965) for the main German references.

[14] The procedure could readily be described in terms of operant conditioning, with food as the reinforcer.

young children almost invariably results in an increase in attention in natural conditions, the implications for therapy are obvious.

(d) HYPERACTIVITY. Restlessness and excessive mobility are often associated with the presence of neurological abnormalities. It is of particular interest to note that such behavior in brain-injured children can be significantly controlled by simple operant procedures. Several studies will be mentioned here that actually deal with hyperactive behavior in brain-injured children, but the principles are, of course, applicable to hyperactive children in general.

Pihl (1967) carried out a series of experiments with a seven-year-old brain-damaged boy whose hyperactivity was aggravated by the various drugs being used to control his seizures. The child was requested to sit in a specially-wired chair for 45 minutes in each session. After measuring the base-line activity for three sessions, Pihl arranged for remaining seated in the chair to activate a light which flashed each second. For each uninterrupted period of 25 seconds, the child was awarded a point on a digital counter, the points (tokens) being exchangeable for primary reinforcers (money and home privileges) after the session. The amount of time spent sitting in the chair increased from 7–15 minutes under baseline conditions to 42–45 minutes in the experimental situation after eight sessions. In the next session, Pihl successfully trained the child to discriminate (sitting when a pilot light was on; standing when it was off). More importantly, he was able to extend the procedure to the boy's home successfully, teaching him to remain seated for meals, for example. An interesting side-effect of the procedure was that it became possible to assess the child's intelligence reliably and validly. Whereas previously his hyperactivity had interfered with testing so severely that his performance was apparently at defective level, now his intelligence was assessed as average. This very simple operant procedure used by Pihl, therefore, could have very important implications for the assessment of hyperactive children, apart from its utility for training purposes.

Allen et al (1967) were able to control the behavior of a normal hyperactive kindergarten child by providing social reinforcement only if the child persisted in a single activity for a period exceeding one minute. The hyperactive behavior was reduced by 50% by this simple technique. Reversal of the contingencies temporarily reinstated the hyperactivity. Positive results in training hyperactive children have also been reported by Patterson (1965) Patterson et al (1965), and Doubros and Daniels (1966).

(e) SOCIAL INTERACTION WITH PEERS. The control of aggressive behavior in a nursery school class was carefully studied by Brown and Elliott (1965). Using scales developed by Walters et al (1957), they established base rates for physical and verbal aggression in a class of 27 three- to four-year-old male children, using two observers. In the first treatment period (lasting two weeks) the teachers were instructed to ignore aggressive behavior and reward quiet and cooperative behavior, ratings of aggressive behavior being taken during the second period. Three weeks after the end of the first treatment period, follow-up ratings were made, the teachers having reverted to their usual control techniques during the intervening period. Thus, a measure of the durability of the first treatment effect was obtained. Two weeks later, a second treatment period of two weeks' duration was instituted (the procedures being identical with those of the first treatment period).

The results of the study are shown in Table 17.1. There was a significant decline in both physical and verbal aggression from pre-treatment to selective reinforcement conditions. The decline in verbal aggression was maintained on follow-up, even though "natural" contingencies had been reinstated, but this was not the case with physical aggression that showed full "recovery." The second training period reduced the level of verbal aggression still further while the physical aggression fell to its previous level.

Scott et al (1967) were able to exercise a similar degree of control over aggressive behavior in a four-year-old boy showing a high frequency of unprovoked aggression toward his peers, the aggression being maintained apparently by the resulting attention from both peers and teachers. They were able to increase or decrease the aggressive behavior by varying its consequences in the usual way.

It may be noted that Patterson and Fagot (1967) have provided experimental evidence indicating that deviant behavior of this kind seems to occur in boys at least who have become selectively responsive to social reinforcers. Thus, for example, if the child, through its mode of upbringing, has become primarily responsive only to reinforcers dispensed by the mother, it may fail to acquire social behaviors ordinarily learned in socializing interactions with peers (of

TABLE 17.1. *Changes in Physical and Verbal Aggression* (*Average Daily Number of Responses*)

Condition	Physical Aggression	Verbal Aggression	Total Aggression
Pretreatment	41.2	22.8	64.0
First treatment	26.0	17.4	43.4
Follow-up	37.8	13.8	51.6
Second treatment	21.0	4.6	25.6

Source: Brown and Elliott, 1965.

both sexes) and with men. They showed that children experimentally exposed to reinforcement from only one of three sources (mother, father, or peer) would display more deviant behaviors than children exposed to reinforcement from all three sources. Thus, therapy for aggressive behavior toward peers may be more successful if the social reinforcement history of the child is known.

4. REMEDIAL EDUCATION

We have already seen, in the chapter on mental deficiency, that increasing use is being made of operant conditioning techniques for remedial education purposes with promising results. Similar approaches are, of course, being instituted with increasing frequency to deal with educational problems of nonretarded children. These studies may be considered fairly briefly, since the general principles involved will by now be quite familiar to the reader.

(a) CONTROLLING DISRUPTIVE CLASSROOM BEHAVIOR. In many instances, backwardness in educational subjects results, not from intellectual inability per se, but from behavior in the classroom which is incompatible with scholastic progress. Such behavior not only retards the child who manifests the behavior but may seriously interfere with the teacher's control of the class and reduce the amount of time he can spend in teaching. Thus, several studies have attempted to show that these disruptive behaviors can be brought under operant control and, indeed, that they may be maintained by the amount of attention that they attract (Zimmerman and Zimmerman, 1962; Patterson, 1965; Valett, 1966; O'Leary and

Becker, 1967; Carlson et al, 1968; Hall et al, 1968).[15] An impressive example of the difficulties involved in this work is provided in a recent study by Becker et al (1967) who selected ten target children to be worked on by five teachers. Following base-line observation of both the disruptive behaviors of the child *and* of the classroom techniques used by the teachers in attempts to control these behaviors, the teachers were carefully instructed in the reinforcement procedures to be followed. Although over a nine-week period of reinforcement there was a drop in deviant behavior from 62% to 29%, Becker at al show very clearly the difficulties some of the teachers experienced in maintaining consistency.[16]

(b) CONTROLLING ORIENTATION IN THE CLASSROOM. Even though the child's behavior may not be overtly disruptive, his learning may be severely affected if he is unable to orient himself consistently toward the teacher. Quay et al (1966, 1967) showed that visual orientation could be brought under control very rapidly, even in hyperactive, aggressive children. Even more importantly, they showed that it could be accomplished in a group setting. Five children (aged six to nine years) sat in a circle around the teacher in a special class. The experimenter sat behind the childen and observed them randomly in serial order. If the child observed attended to the teacher for ten seconds without interruption during the period of observation, a small light on the child's desk flashed and earned him points which could be subsequently exchanged for candy. The procedure involved a VR schedule of reinforcement, since only one child was observed at a time. The experiment

[15] Ross (1967) provides an excellent overview of the principles involved. See also Haring and Phillips (1962).

[16] Thomas et al (1968) have shown that the incidence of disruptive behavior in a well-controlled classroom may increase significantly if approving teacher behavior is withdrawn.

involved three stages; first, 45 sessions in which light flashes and candy were used as reinforcers; then 30 sessions in which social reinforcement only was used (the light was not used but the children were observed and their scores announced at the end of each session); and, finally, 30 extinction sessions in which no reinforcement was given. The mean number of orienting responses increased significantly during the token reinforcement sessions; decreased, then increased (but not to the first level) during the social reinforcement period; and decreased significantly but not to the original baseline level during the extinction period.

(c) A REMEDIAL READING CLASSROOM. The problem of the "disabled reader" (Money, 1966) is one which has concerned educators for many years. Recently, however, operant conditioning principles have been utilized in attempts to teach reading to backward children, or to teach children to read at an earlier age than is commonly found by the usual techniques. The operant principles involved in teaching reading have been described by Goldiamond and Dyrud (1966), and the most comprehensive attempt to apply these principles so far is that of Staats and his colleagues.[17]

Staats and Staats (1962) described the acquisition of speech in operant conditioning terms and raised the question why reading is apparently more difficult to acquire than speaking. They pointed out that speech is characterized by gradual acquisition over a number of years; that primary reinforcement is usually given by the delighted parents for the earliest manifestations of speech; and that the reinforcement is both strong and immediate. Thus, all of the conditions are present in terms of reinforcement procedures which make for rapid and efficient learning. In the case of reading, however, training tends to be instituted suddenly and intensively in situations that may be strongly aversive (starting school, for example); that reading is usually taught in a group situation precluding the use of immediate, relevant, individual reinforcement; and that, therefore, only general reinforcers may be provided. Staats and Staats might well also have pointed out that, in relation to speech, the child is provided with models for speech by anyone who talks to him, whereas no such models can be presented for reading in natural situations.

As Staats and Staats (1962) point out, reading involves *texting* (to use Skinner's terminology), that is, a verbal response which is controlled by a visually presented verbal stimulus. The problem in teaching reading, therefore, becomes one of analyzing this situation in such a way that the critical steps can be provided for the child in small enough increments for progress to be assured so that positive reinforcement will be continuously received. Furthermore, texting may be only the final stage in the complex process of learning to read, being preceded by picture and word matching.

As a result of these considerations, Staats et al (1962) constructed a special reading laboratory.[18] The child was seated in front of a large panel containing plexiglass windows in which letter, word, sentence, or picture stimuli appeared. Three stages in training were involved: picture matching-to-sample; word matching-to-sample; and texting, the latter involving modeling, since the child was required to say the word appearing in a window after the experimenter had said it. A correct matching response, whether nonverbal in the early stages or verbal in the later stages, produced reinforcement. The child could choose either an immediate primary reinforcer from a Universal Feeder cabinet (in which case, the exact reinforcer received would not be known until after the choice was made) or could accumulate tokens (marbles) in one of several jars on top of which were located primary reinforcers (toys, etc.) chosen earlier by the child from a selection of toys and for which varying numbers of tokens were required (the child could work for more than one toy at a time). In this early study with six four-year-old children, Staats et al (1962) compared the effects of using only social reinforcement (verbal approval) with token reinforcement and examined also the effects of discontinuing token reinforcements on persistence at the matching and texting behaviors. In the texting stage, single words were used first, followed by phrases and sentences in which the single words were embedded. Progress was tested by presentation of the individual words for recognition and repetition without prompting at the beginning of each session. The results of this experiment indicated that the children would continue working at the tasks for much longer periods of time when token reinforcers were used than when social approval only was

---

[17] For comprehensive accounts of this work, see Staats (1965, 1968b).

[18] It is interesting to note that the laboratory set-up appears to have been progressively de-automated since these early studies (Staats, 1968a).

used, and that rapid learning occurred (which was maintained) with token reinforcement. Three of the children acquired 16–17 words by this technique over eight 45-minute sessions.

In a later experiment, Staats, Minke, et al (1964) described a more sophisticated procedure for training children in a phonetic alphabet reading program, involving vowel sounds followed by consonant/vowel sounds, using the matching-to-sample technique. With three four-year-old children, they found that there was wide variability in the ability of the children to achieve *anticipatory* matching as opposed to *echoic* matching (that is, saying the sounds before, as opposed to after, the experimenter). Subsequently, Staats, Finley, et al (1964) examined the effects of training in a similar task under alternating schedules of reinforcement. The four training conditions they compared were: continuous reinforcement (CRF) versus no reinforcement (EXT); multiple CRF versus variable rates (mult. CRF/VR2-5); multiple CRF versus variable interval (mult. CRF/VI 2 mins); and multiple VR versus multiple VI. They found that CRF produced a higher acquisition rate than EXT; VR was superior to CRF; VI was better than CRF in the early stages of training, but this was reversed in the later stages; and that there was no difference between VR and VI schedules (the latter finding was, however, considered to be an artifact). Since only one child was involved in each of these comparisons, these results were, of course, only illustrative of the possibilities of the techniques. The experiments did, however, suggest that variable reinforcement schedules were successful in delaying satiation for the various reinforcers being worked for, an important source of difficulty in this kind of work with very young children.

The wider applications of these techniques have been shown in several further studies. Staats and Butterfield (1965) demonstrated their value in the treatment of nonreading in a culturally-deprived juvenile delinquent. Staats et al (1967) showed that establishing a token reinforcement economy could have very striking effects in motivating subjects who could already read to improve their reading significantly; while even more remarkable results have recently been obtained by Wolf et al (1968) with a similar system. They set up an after-school remedial education class for low-achieving

fifth and sixth grade children, making available materials in various areas, including reading. They investigated the effects on number of units completed of introducing and withdrawing a token system and found that the token reinforcement system did indeed influence significantly the number of units completed. The remedial group was compared over a period of one year of treatment with a control group not so treated. On the Stanford Achievement Test, the remedial group gained $1\frac{1}{2}$ years, the control group only half a year. Similarly, the remedial group showed a gain of 1.1 grade points compared with a gain of only 0.2 grade points for the control group.[19] Similarly, Whitlock (1966) has shown that the token reinforcement system can be used in individual cases of reading retardation to produce very rapid gains indeed.

Essentially, what Staats and his colleagues have tried to do is to provide learning conditions for reading that parallel those for the acquisition of speech, as was described earlier. This involves breaking down the stages in reading into smaller sections, providing immediate reinforcement under partial reinforcement conditions, and ensuring the use of relevant reinforcers. This latter point seems to be particularly important. Apparently, many young children simply will not work for any length of time for social reinforcement in the reading situation. This finding has clear implications for current *group* methods of teaching reading where the reinforcement (if any) tends to be general.

Two other studies may be mentioned here. McKerracher (1967) treated an 11-year-old boy of average intelligence whose reading age was only eight years. Three months' treatment using conventional remedial techniques produced a reading gain of only one month. For the next three months, an operant conditioning procedure was used in which correctly read words (then sentences, phrases, etc.) lit a panel of bulbs successively, primary reinforcement being provided after every sixth bulb was lit (the procedure thus involved an FR-6 schedule). For every word missed, a loud buzzer (aversive stimulus) was sounded. A gain of four months in reading age was achieved. In the final three months of training, the aversive contingency was dropped. A gain of nine months in reading age was achieved. Thus, over the nine-month training period, involving a total of $17\frac{1}{2}$ hours of

---

[19] Clark et al (1968) have shown, with appropriate controls, that similar techniques may be success-

fully used to improve the educational standing of school dropouts.

treatment, a gain of 14 months in reading age was achieved, nearly all of which occurred during the operant training conditions. While appropriate controls for motivational effects were not instituted, it seems unlikely that such factors could account for these results.

Finally, Ancevich and Payne (1961) investigated severe reading retardation in a young boy of average intelligence. Experimental investigation suggested that the disability arose from a visual perceptual defect involving the recognition of words as opposed to letters and that this was compounded by his peculiar method of writing. Following special training in normal methods of writing, a significant amelioration of the perceptual defect occurred.

REFERENCES

Allen, K.E. & Harris, F.R. Elimination of a child's excessive scratching by training the mother in reinforcement procedures. *Behav. Res. Ther.*, 1966, **4**, 79–84.

Allen, K.E., Hart, B., Buell, J.S., Harris, F.R., & Wolf, M.M. Effects of social reinforcement on isolate behavior of a nursery school child. *Child Develop.*, 1964, **35**, 511–518.

Allen, K.E., Henke, L.B., Harris, F.R., Baer, D.M., & Reynolds, N.J. Control of hyperactivity by social reinforcement of attending behavior. *J. educ. Psychol.*, 1967, **58**, 231–237.

Ancevich, S.S. & Payne, R.W. The investigation and treatment of a reading disability in a child of normal intelligence. *J. clin. Psychol.*, 1961, **17**, 416–420.

Baer, D.M. Laboratory control of thumbsucking in three young children by withdrawal and re-presentation of positive reinforcement. *J. exper. Anal. Behav.*, 1962, **5**, 525–528.

Barker, J.C. & Miller, M.E. Aversion therapy for compulsive gambling. *Lancet*, 1966, **1**, 491–492 (a).

Barker, J.C. & Miller, M.E. Aversion therapy for compulsive gambling .*Brit. med. J.*, 1966, **2**, 115 (b).

Barker, J.C. & Miller, M.E. Aversion therapy for compulsive gambling. *J. nerv. ment. Dis.*, 1968, **146**, 285–302.

Becker, W.C., Madsen, C.H., Arnold, C.R., & Thomas, D.R. The contingent use of teacher attention and praise in reducing classroom behavior problems. *J. spec. Educ.*, 1967, **1**, 287–307.

Boardman, W.K. Rusty: a brief behavior disorder. *J. consult. Psychol.*, 1962, **26**, 293–297.

Brison, D.W. A nontalking child in kindergarten: an application of behavior therapy. *J. School Psychol.*, 1966, **4**, 65–69.

Brown, P. & Elliott, R. The control of aggression in a nursery school class. *J. exp. Child Psychol.*, 1965, **2**, 103–107.

Browne, E., Wilson, V., & Laybourne, P.C. Diagnosis and treatment of elective mutism in children. *J. Amer. Acad. Child Psychiat.*, 1963, **2**, 605–617.

Carlson, C.S., Arnold, C.R., Becker, W.C., & Madsen, C.H. The elimination of tantrum behavior of a child in an elementary classroom. *Behav. Res. Ther.*, 1968, **6**, 117–119.

Cartwright, A., Martin, F.M., & Thompson, V.G. Efficacy of an antismoking campaign. *Lancet*, 1960, **1**, 327–329.

Cautela, J.R. Treatment of compulsive behavior by covert sensitization. *Psychol. Rec.*, 1966, **16**, 33–41.

Clark, M., Lachowitz, J., & Wolf, M. A pilot basic education program for school dropouts incorporating a token reinforcement system. *Behav. Res. Ther.*, 1968, **6**, 183–188.

Clement, P.W. & Milne, D.C. Group play therapy and tangible reinforcers used to modify the behavior of 8-year-old boys. *Behav. Res. Ther.*, 1967, **5**, 301–312.

Cohen, B.B. The desensitization of social anxiety: a case study. *Penn. Psychiat. Quart.*, 1965, **5**, 31–36.

Davidson, P.O. Thumbsucking. In Costello, G.C. (ed.). *Symptoms of psychopathology*. New York: Wiley (in press).

Davidson, P.O., Haryett, R.D., Sandilands, M., & Hansen, F.C. Thumbsucking: habit or symptom: *J. Dent. Child.*, 1967, **33**, 252–259.

Doubros, S.G. & Daniels, G.J. An experimental approach to the reduction of overactive behavior. *Behav. Res. Ther.*, 1966, **4**, 251–258.

Elson, A., Pearson, C., Jones, C.D., & Schumacher, E. Follow-up study of childhood elective mutism. *Arch. gen. Psychiat.*, 1965, **13**, 182–187.

Etzel, B.C. & Gewirtz, J.L. Experimental modification of caretaker maintained high-rate operant crying in a 6- and a 20-week-old infant (infans tyrannotearus): extinction of crying with reinforcement of eye contact and smiling. *J. exp. Child Psychol.*, 1967, **5**, 303–317.

Eysenck, H.J. Smoking, personality, and psychosomatic disorders. *J. psychosom. Res.*, 1963, **7**, 107–130.

Eysenck, H.J. *Smoking, health and personality.* London: Weidenfeld and Nicolson, 1965.

Eysenck, H.J., Tarrant, M., & England, L. Smoking and personality. *Brit. med. J.*, 1960, **1**, 1456–1460.

Fisher, R.A. *Smoking—the cancer controversy.* Edinburgh: Oliver and Boyd, 1950.

Franks, C.M., Fried, R., & Ashem, B. An improved apparatus for the aversive conditioning of cigarette smokers. *Behav. Res. Ther.*, 1966, **4**, 301–308.

Geer, J.H. & Katkin, E.S. Treatment of insomnia using a variant of systematic desensitization: a case report. *J. abnorm. Psychol.*, 1966, **71**, 161–164.

Geer, J.H. & Silverman, I. Treatment of a recurrent nightmare by behavior modification procedures. *J. abnorm. Psychol.*, 1967, **72**, 188–190.

Gibbs, D.N. Reciprocal inhibition therapy of a case of symptomatic erythema. *Behav. Res. Ther.*, 1965, **2**, 261–266.

Goldiamond, I. & Dyrud, J.E. Reading as operant behavior. In Money, J. (ed.). *The disabled reader: education of the dyslexic child.* Baltimore: Johns Hopkins Press, 1966, pp. 93–115.

Goorney, A.B. Treatment of a compulsive horse race gambler by aversion therapy. *Brit. J. Psychiat.*, 1968, **114**, 329–333.

Greenberg, D.S. Tobacco: after publicity surge, Surgeon General's report seems to have little enduring effect. *Science*, 1964, **145**, 1021–1022.

Greene, R.J. Modification of smoking behavior by free operant conditioning methods. *Psychol. Rec.*, 1964, **14**, 171–178.

Gutmann, M. & Marston, A. Problems of S's motivation in a behavioral program for reduction of cigarette smoking. *Psychol. Rep.*, 1967, **20**, 1107–1114.

Hall, R.V., Lund, D., & Jackson, D. Effects of teacher attention on study behavior. *J. appl. Behav. Anal.*, 1968, **1**, 1–12.

Haring, N.G. & Phillips, E.L. *Educating emotionally disturbed children.* New York: McGraw-Hill, 1962.

Harris, F.R., Johnstone, M.K., Kelley, C.S., & Wolf, M.M. Effects of positive social reinforcement on regressed crawling of a nursery school child. *J. educ. Psychol.*, 1964, **55**, 35–41.

Hart, B.M., Allen, K.E., Buell, J.S., Harris, F.R., & Wolf, M.M. Effects of social reinforcement on operant crying. *J. exp. Child Psychol.*, 1964, **1**, 145–153.

Haryett, R.D., Hansen, F.C., Davidson, P.O., & Sandilands, M.L. Chronic thumbsucking: the psychological effects and the relative effectiveness of various methods of treatment. *Amer. J. Orthodont.*, 1967, **53**, 569–585.

Janis, I.L. & Mann, L. Effectiveness of emotional role-playing in modifying smoking habits and attitudes. *J. exp. Res. Pers.*, 1965, **1**, 84–90.

Katahn, M. Systematic desensitization and counseling for anxiety in a college basketball player. *J. spec. Educ.*, 1967, **1**, 309–314.

Katahn, M., Strenger, S., & Cherry, N. Group counselling and behavior therapy with test-anxious college students. *J. consult. Psychol.*, 1966, **30**, 544–549.

Kennedy, W.A. & Foreyt, J.P. Control of eating behavior in an obese patient by avoidance conditioning. *Psychol. Rep.*, 1968, **22**, 571–576.

Keutzer, C.S. Behavior modification of smoking: the experimental investigation of diverse techniques. *Behav. Res. Ther.*, 1968, **6**, 137–157.

Koenig, K.P. & Masters, J. Experimental treatment of habitual smoking. *Behav. Res. Ther.*, 1965, **3**, 235–244.

Kondas, O. Reducation of examination anxiety and "stage-fright" by group desensitization and relaxation. *Behav. Res. Ther.*, 1967, **5**, 275–281.

Kraft, T. & Al-Issa, I. Desensitization and reduction in cigarette consumption. *J. Psychol.*, 1967, **67**, 323–329.

McGuire, R.J. & Vallance, M. Aversion therapy by electric shock: a simple technique. *Brit. med. J.*, 1964, **1**, 151–153.

McKerracher, D.W. Alteration of reading difficulties by a simple operant conditioning technique. *J. child Psychol. Psychiat.*, 1967, **8**, 51–56.

Mann, L. The effects of emotional role playing on desire to modify smoking habits. *J. exp. soc. Psychol.*, 1967, **3**, 334–348.

Matarazzo, J.D. & Saslow, G. Psychological and related characteristics of smokers and nonsmokers. *Psychol. Bull.*, 1960, **57**, 493–513.

Mendelson, M. Psychological aspects of obesity. *Internat. J. Psychiat.*, 1966, **2**, 599–612.

Mogel, S. & Schiff, W. "Extinction" of a head-bumping symptom of eight years' duration in two minutes: a case report. *Behav. Res. Ther.*, 1967, **5**, 131–132.

Money, J. (ed.). *The disabled reader: education of the dyslexic child*. Baltimore: Johns Hopkins Press, 1966.

Morris, J.V. Cases of elective mutism. *Amer. J. ment. Defic.*, 1953, **57**, 661–668.

Nolan, J.D. Self-control procedures in the modification of smoking behavior. *J. consult. clin. Psychol.*, 1968, **32**, 92–93.

O'Leary, K.D. & Becker, W.C. Behavior modification of an adjustment class: a token reinforcement program. *Except. Children*, 1967, **33**, 637–642.

O'Leary, K.D., O'Leary, S., & Becker, W.C. Modification of a deviant sibling interaction pattern in the home. *Behav. Res. Ther.*, 1967, **5**, 113–120.

Palermo, D.S. Thumbsucking: a learned response. *Pediatrics*, 1956, **17**, 392–399.

Patterson, G.R. An application of conditioning techniques to the control of a hyperactive child. In Ullmann, L.P. & Krasner, L. (eds.). *Case studies in behavior modification*. New York: Holt, 1965, pp. 370–375.

Patterson, G.R. & Brodsky, G. A behavior modification programme for a child with multiple problem behaviors. *J. Child Psychol. Psychiat.*, 1966, **7**, 277–295.

Patterson, G.R. & Fagot, B.I. Selective responsiveness to social reinforcers and deviant behavior in children. *Psychol. Rec.*, 1967, **17**, 369–378.

Patterson, G.R., Jones, R., Whittier, J., & Wright, M.A. A behavior modification technique for the hyperactive child. *Behav. Res. Ther.*, 1965, **2**, 217–226.

Paul, G.L. *Insight versus desensitization in psychotherapy: an experiment in anxiety reduction*. Stanford: Stanford Univer. Press, 1966.

Paul, G.L. Insight versus desensitization in psychotherapy two years after termination. *J. consult. Psychol.*, 1967, **31**, 333–348.

Paul, G.L. & Shannon, D.T. Treatment of anxiety through systematic desensitization in therapy groups. *J. abnorm. Psychol.*, 1966, **71**, 124–135.

Pflaum, J. Smoking behavior: a critical review of research. *J. appl. behav. Sci.*, 1965, **1**, 195–209.

Pihl, R.O. Conditioning procedures with hyperactive children. *Neurology*, 1967, **17**, 421–423.

Powell, J. & Azrin, N. The effects of shock as a punisher for cigarette smoking. *J. appl. behav. Anal.*, 1968, **1**, 63–71.

Pumroy, D.K. & Pumroy, S.S. A case study in discrimination learning. *J. genet. Psychol.*, 1967, **110**, 87–89.

Pustrom, E. & Speers, R.W. Elective mutism in children. *J. Amer. Acad. Child Psychiat.*, 1964, **3**, 287–297.

Pyke, S., Agnew, N.McK., & Kopperud, J. Modification of an overlearned maladaptive response through a relearning programme: a pilot study on smoking. *Behav. Res. Ther.*, 1966, **4**, 196–203.

Quay, H.C., Sprague, R.L., Werry, J.S., & McQueen, M.M. Conditioning visual orientation of conduct problem children in the classroom. *J. exp. Child Psychol.*, 1967, **5**, 512–517.

Quay, H.C., Werry, J.S., McQueen, M.M., & Sprague, R.L. Remediation of the conduct problem child in the special class setting. *Except. Child.*, 1966, **32**, 509–515.

Reed, G.F. Elective mutism in children: a reappraisal. *J. Child Psychol. Psychiat.*, 1963, **4**, 99–107.

Reid, J.B., Hawkins, L., Keutzer, C., McNeal, S.A., Phelps, R.E., Reid, K.M., & Mees, H.L. A marathon behavior modification of a selectively mute child. *J. child Psychol. Psychiat.*, 1967, **8**, 27–30.

Resnick, J.H. The control of smoking behavior by stimulus satiation. *Behav. Res. Ther.*, 1968, **6**, 113–114.

Ross, A.O. The application of behavior principles in therapeutic education. *J. spec. Educ.*, 1967, **1**, 275–285.

Russo, S. Adaptations in behavioral therapy with children. *Behav. Res. Ther.*, 1964, **2**, 43–47.

Salfield, D.J. Observations on elective mutism in children. *J. ment. Sci.*, 1950, **96**, 1024–1032.

Schubert, D.S. Arousal seeking as a central factor in tobacco smoking among college students. *Internat. J. soc. Psychiat.*, 1965, **11**, 221–225.

Scott, P.M., Burton, R.V., & Yarrow, M.R. Social reinforcement under natural conditions. *Child Developm.*, 1967, **38**, 53–63.

Seager, C.P., Pokorny, M.R., & Black, D. Aversion therapy for compulsive gambling. *Lancet*, 1966, **1**, 546.

Silverman, I. & Geer, J.H. The elimination of a recurrent nightmare by desensitization of a related phobia. *Behav. Res. Ther.*, 1968, **6**, 109–111.

Staats, A.W. A case in, and a strategy for, the extension of learning principles to problems of human behavior. In Krasner, L. & Ullman, L.P. (eds.). *Research in behavior modification*. New York: Holt, 1965, pp. 27–55.

Staats, A.W. A general apparatus for the investigation of complex learning in children. *Behav. Res. Ther.*, 1968, **6**, 45–50 (a).

Staats, A.W. *Learning, language and cognition*. New York: Holt, 1968 (a).

Staats, A.W. & Butterfield, W.H. Treatment of nonreading in a culturally-deprived juvenile delinquent: an application of reinforcement principles. *Child Developm.*, 1965, **36**, 925–942.

Staats, A.W., Finley, J.R., Minke, K.A., & Wolf, M.M. Reinforcement variables in the control of unit reading responses. *J. exp. Anal. Behav.*, 1964, **7**, 139–149.

Staats, A.W., Minke, K.A., Finley, J.R., Wolf, M., & Brooks, L.O. A reinforcer system and experimental procedure for the laboratory study of reading acquisition. *Child Develop.*, 1964, **35**, 209–231.

Staats, A.W., Minke, K.A., Goodwin, W., & Landeen, J. Cognitive behavior modification: "motivated learning" reading treatment with sub-professional therapy-technicians. *Behav. Res. Ther.*, 1967, **5**, 283–299.

Staats, A.W. & Staats, C.K. A comparison of the development of speech and reading behavior with implications for research. *Child Develop.*, 1962, **33**, 831–846.

Staats, A.W., Staats, C.K., Schutz, R.E., & Wolf, M. The conditioning of textual responses using "extrinsic" reinforcers. *J. exp. Anal. Behav.*, 1962, **5**, 33–40.

Straughan, J.H. Treatment with child and mother in the playroom. *Behav. Res. Ther.*, 1964, **2**, 37–41.

Stuart, R.B. Behavioral control of overeating. *Behav. Res. Ther.*, 1967, **5**, 357–365.

Thomas, D.R., Becker, W.C., & Armstrong, M. Production and elimination of disruptive classroom behavior by systematically varying teacher's behavior. *J. appl. Behav. Anal.*, 1968, **1**, 35–45.

Tooley, J.T. & Pratt, S. An experimental procedure for the extinction of smoking behavior. *Psychol. Rec.*, 1967, **17**, 209–218.

Traisman, A.S. & Traisman, H.S. Thumb and fingersucking: a study of 2650 infants and children. *J. Pediatrics*, 1958, **52,** 566–572.

Valett, R.E. A social reinforcement technique for the classroom management of behavior disorders. *Except. Child*, 1966, **33,** 185–189.

Wahler, R.G., Winkel, G.H., Peterson, R.F., & Morrison, D.C. Mothers as behavior therapists for their own children. *Behav. Res. Ther.*, 1965, **3,** 113–124.

Walters, J.C., Pearce, D., & Dahms, L. Affectional and aggressive behavior of preschool children. *Child Developm.*, 1957, **28,** 15–26.

White, J.G. The use of learning theory in the psychological treatment of children. *J. clin. Psychol.*, 1959, **15,** 227–229.

White, J.G., Caldbeck-Meenan, J., & McAllister, H. The desensitization of phobic anxiety and its physiological concommitants. *Papers in Psychol.*, 1968, **2.**

Whitlock, S.C. Note on reading acquisition: an extension of laboratory principles. *J. exp. Child Psychol.*, 1966, **3,** 83–85.

Wilde, G.J.S. Behavior therapy for addicted cigarette smokers: a preliminary investigation. *Behav. Res. Ther.*, 1964, **2,** 107–109.

Wilde, G.J.S. Correspondence. *Behav. Res. Ther.*, 1965, **2,** 313.

Williams, C.D. The elimination of tantrum behavior by extinction procedures: case report. *J. abnorm. soc. Psychol.*, 1959, **59,** 269.

Wolf, M.M., Giles, D.K., & Hall, R.V. Experiments with token reinforcement in a remedial classroom. *Behav. Res. Ther.*, 1968, **6,** 51–64.

Zimmerman, E.H. & Zimmerman, J. The alteration of behavior in a special classroom situation. *J. exp. Anal. Behav.*, 1962, **5,** 59–60.

Part III

Critical Evaluation

Chapter 18

Assessment of Results

IN PREVIOUS CHAPTERS dealing with specific abnormalities of behavior an attempt has been made to indicate the efficacy of behavior therapy as compared with either alternative methods of therapeutic intervention or with no therapy. In some instances, the "natural history" of the disorder, where known, has been utilized for comparative purposes. For reasons which will become apparent, *it is not intended in this chapter to provide any overall assessment of the comparative "success" of behavior therapy by comparison with the more traditional approaches.* Rather, the basic problem for consideration is a methodological one, namely, the problem of *how* behavior therapy should be assessed. Attention will first be directed toward the methodology of outcome research in both psychotherapy and behavior therapy in relation to group studies; and reasons will be given why these approaches are unsatisfactory in so far as they have been applied to the assessment of the efficacy of behavior therapy. Attention will then be directed toward experimental studies that bear on the problem. Consideration will next be given to a quite different approach that will be shown to represent the appropriate technique for validating the behavior therapy approach. Finally, the important questions of relapse and spontaneous recovery will be discussed.

I. METHODOLOGY OF OUTCOME RESEARCH IN GROUP STUDIES

As we have already seen, Eysenck (1952) pointed up the methodological fallacy ("*post*

hoc, ergo propter hoc") of assuming that changes following the administtation of psychotherapy were caused by the psychotherapy. Since then, a great deal of water has flowed under the bridge and research sophistication in this area has increased significantly in theory, if not so satisfactorily in fact.

1. THE BASIC PARADIGM

Meehl (1955) pointed out that the absolute minimum requirements for outcome research in therapy[1] are: the use of control and experimental groups; the use of pre and posttherapy evaluation procedures; and an adequate follow-up period. Of course, as Meehl recognized, these three requirements conceal a host of difficult problems which will be discussed in the following sections. At that point of time, however, his search of the literature revealed almost no studies that met even these minimal requirements, however defective they might be in the finer points of control.

2. THE SELECTION OF GROUPS

The selection of comparable "treatment" and "no-treatment control" groups has attracted a great deal of attention, since Eysenck (1952) drew attention to the common failure to use control groups. It has been further discussed by Eysenck (1960) himself. Particularly thorough discussions of the problem, as well as some empirical studies relating to it, may be found in recent publications by Goldstein and his

---

[1] In what follows, the reader should remember that the reference is always to *group* comparative studies.

colleagues (Goldstein and Dean, 1966; Goldstein et al, 1966). No extended discussion of the matter need therefore be provided here, but a few of the more important points may be mentioned. The use of the term "control groups" itself has largely been abandoned as misleading, since it is quite clear that it is almost impossible to obtain an "untreated" control group. Patients allocated to an "untreated" control group, for example, may, on being placed in the group, obtain all kinds of uncontrolled treatment from doctors, relatives, friends, or quacks. In any event, such a group will clearly differ from a group of patients with the same disorder who have not requested treatment. Hence, such a "control" group should more properly be called a "nonspecific treatment group."

A second problem relates to the methods by which the specific and nonspecific treatment groups are formed. Eysenck (1960) has pointed out that random allocation to either group of patients from a pool may not achieve the desired aim of making the groups comparable on all variables except that of specific treatment. Goldstein and Dean (1966) have distinguished between "within-sample matching" and "between-sample matching." In the former case, pairs of patients are matched on one or more relevant variables; and then one of each pair is randomly assigned to one of the treatments, the other to the other treatment. In the latter case, the treatment groups are formed first and then matched pairs are formed in relation to one or more relevant variables. A third alternative in forming groups is to use the "invited remedial treatment method" (Campbell and Stanley, 1963). In this instance, treatment and control samples are drawn from a sample of potential patients for treatment. Of course, these relatively simple two-group designs are tending to be replaced by multiple control groups. As Eysenck (1960) has pointed out, special control groups may be necessary to estimate the effect of the many possible confounding variables. It might be pointed out here that a further possible design is to compare several groups of patients with the same disorder in relation to the effects of more than one technique of behavior therapy, without using nonspecific or psychotherapy control groups at all; or the "crossover" design may be used in which the group initially given nonspecific treatment is eventually given the specific treatment.

3. CONFOUNDING VARIABLES

Many other problems that arise in outcome research have been discussed in detail by Goldstein and Dean (1966). Of these, one of the most important has been artpicularly stressed by Campbell and Stanley (1963) and refers to the problem of regression. This is really a subcategory of the placebo effect which, as we have seen, refers to the production of changes that are not the result of the specific treatment employed, but of uncontrolled factors. The regression effect refers to the fact that patients selected for treatment will usually enter treatment at a point at which the severity of the disorder is at its maximum. Hence, in a very real sense, there is no change that can occur except improvement. Thus, an improvement that would be very likely to occur anyway shortly after entering treatment is likely to be attributed to the treatment itself. Closely related to this problem is the possible interaction between pretreatment assessments and the treatment itself, an interaction which may also affect the nonspecific treatment control group. Mention should also be made of the often-neglected factor of therapist expectations. Clearly, if the therapist also makes the assessments of change, considerable bias may be involved. Pretreatment assessment and assessment of change during and after treatment should always be made, therefore, by independent assessors as well.

A point of special importance to which little attention has thus far been paid relates to the fact that the wrong dependent variables may be measured. As we have seen, Hoenig and Reed (1966) in relation to phobias, and Marks and Gelder (1967) in relation to fetishes, found that differential change occurred during treatment. If only a single dependent variable is measured, important effects may be missed. We now turn to a consideration of the dependent variables.

4. THE DEPENDENT VARIABLES

Eysenck (1960) has listed the *sources of information* that may be utilized to assess outcome. These include: introspective reports by the patient; the use of ratings; the use of objective measures, including personality tests; the use of physiological measures; and social action effects. Another important source lies in specific changes predicted on the basis of some theory (that is, the use of experimental investigations). The *types of information* may be divided into two main categories: *intrapersonal* and *interpersonal*. With respect to the former, measurements may be made of changes in the main symptom or disability, in related symptoms, and in broader areas of adjustment such as level of anxiety, depression, obsessions, and degree of depersonalization. With respect to the latter, work adjustment, leisure activities, sexual adjustment, family relationships, and relationships with other people may be assessed. Finally, with respect to *time of information*, the above assessments may be made before treatment is begun, during the course of treatment, at the termination of treatment, and at several points in time during follow-up.

To summarize, the consensus of opinion in relation to the assessment of outcome in therapy seems to be that a satisfactory study should meet the following requirements.

(i) Experimental and control (specific and nonspecific treatment) groups should be chosen that are matched carefully on all relevant variables.

(ii) Several sources of information should be drawn on to measure the results of treatment, including both specific and general behavior being assessed.

(iii) Measures should be taken before, during, and at the end of treatment, and for an adequate period of time following the termination of treatment.

We shall now consider how far those studies, which have had as their primary aim the assessment of the validity of behavior therapy, have succeeded in meeting these criteria.

II. GROUP STUDIES OF THE VALIDITY OF BEHAVIOR THERAPY

1. STUDIES NOT USING CONTROL GROUPS

Wolpe (1958, 1961, 1964) has published three assessments of the efficacy of his techniques of behavior therapy. In the first (Wolpe, 1958), he brought together the results of three groups of patients totaling 210 subjects in all. The sole criterion for inclusion in the survey was that the patient be designated "neurotic" (the majority of the patients being polysymptomatic). Exclusions comprised three groups of patients: psychotics, psychopaths, and those for whom a reasonable trial of Wolpe's techniques was not

available. This latter category was not, unfortunately, further defined, and neither the numbers nor characteristics of any of the three groups are given. Change in status was evaluated by two means. First, the five criteria of Knight were used: symptomatic improvement (the most important for Wolpe); increased productiveness; improved adjustment and pleasure in sex; improved interpersonal relations; and ability to handle ordinary conflicts and stresses in everyday life. Second, changes in score on the Willoughby questionnaire were assessed. Each characteristic was rated on a five-point scale (apparently cured; much improved; moderately improved; slightly improved; unimproved). Conventional diagnostic categories were used to classify the patients, the majority being "anxiety states" (135 out of 210). The entire range of treatment techniques described by Wolpe in his book were used. For the last series of 88 patients reported, 57 had 40 interviews or less, the mean duration of treatment being approximately ten months.

On the rating scales, analysis of the results indicated that 82 patients (39%) were "apparently cured"; 106 patients (50.5%) were "much improved"; 15 patients (7.2%) were "moderately" or "slightly" improved; and 7 (3.3%) were "unimproved." Forty-five of the patients who were "apparently cured" or "much improved" (representing only 24% of these groups) were followed up for two to seven years after the termination of treatment; only one had "relapsed" and this followed a traumatic event.

It will be clear that Wolpe's study does not meet even the minimal criteria set out earlier in this chapter. In fairness to Wolpe, however, it should be pointed out that he was well aware of the deficiencies of this pioneering effort. It should also be noted that more objective evidence was available relating to the validity of the changes claimed. For 13 "apparently cured" patients, the mean Willoughby score changed from 45.5 before treatment to 12.2 at the end of treatment; whereas the Willoughby score for 21 "much improved" patients changed only from 44.8 to 25.6.[2]

In two subsequent papers, Wolpe (1961, 1964) reported essentially similar results, using comparable techniques of assessment, for samples of patients that appear to have been drawn from the main series reported earlier

---

[2] The Willoughby questionnaire was not routinely given to all patients; hence data were available

relating to change scores for only a small proportion of the groups.

(Wolpe, 1958). In the most recent study (Wolpe, 1964), a comparison was made between the results obtained with "simple" as opposed to "complex" neuroses (the distinction is essentially the same as that made in this book between monosymptomatic and polysymptomatic disorders, though Wolpe would regard both types of patients as neurotic). Wolpe found that the "complex" neuroses took much longer to treat successfully than the "simple" neuroses.

Hussain (1963) claimed a recovery rate of 95% in a series of 105 patients which included 50 "anxiety states" and which was similar in composition to those reported by Wolpe. The follow-up period was six months to two years. Although Hussain claimed to use Wolpe's techniques, a virtual disclaimer that this was so was entered by Wolpe, who pointed out in a footnote to the paper that "Hussain's method is distinctly different from the desensitization technique" (Hussain, 1963, p. 56). Hussain's criteria were direct observation of the patient, comments from relatives, patient's own report, and reports of social adjustment. No quantitative data were presented apart from the statement of the "recovery rate."

Lazarus (1963) reported on a series of 126 cases of "generalized neurotic disturbance." He excluded the following categories of patients from consideration: those receiving less than six sessions of treatment; those in which therapy was unavoidably terminated (due to death, etc.); those under 15 years of age; those with monosymptomatic disorders; and psychotics. Lazarus took up a suggestion from Wolpe (1958) that *intensity* of the behavior disorder should be assessed and, instead of using the standard diagnostic categories, he utilized measures of "pervasive anxiety," "generalized anxiety," "phobic reaction," and so on; an individual patient could receive a rating on all of these categories, though it is not clear whether, in fact, each of them did. Four main criteria of change were used: Willoughby score; MPI N and E scores; Bernreuter score; and a five-point rating scale, ranging from "deteriorated" to "recovered completely." A very wide range of treatments was used, including SD-I, behavior rehearsal, anxiety-relief, instrumental avoidance conditioning, massed practice, drugs, etc. No attempt was made to evaluate these treatments separately. Lazarus claimed a "significant improvement" rate of 61.9% (19% "completely recovered," 42.9% "markedly improved").

Follow-up data were presented for 20 patients, the mean follow-up time being just over two years. Only one relapse was found. The average number of treatment sessions was 14 (ranging from 11 to 16).

Lazarus investigated the possible factors prognostic of failure and reported that this was more likely in patients with high Willoughby and neuroticism scores, and with high scores on introversion. Put another way, patients diagnosed as "pervasive anxiety" and "panic" tended not to respond as well to treatment.

Lazarus' study is, of course, open to the same objections as those of Wolpe and Hussain in failing to meet the minimal criteria for evaluation of results.

One further study may be mentioned here. McGuire and Vallance (1964) reported the results of classical aversive conditioning with shock in a series of 39 cases (including 10 smokers, 7 alcoholics, 14 sex perverts, and 8 other patients of diverse kinds). The sole criterion of change appears to have been the self-report of the patient on a five-point rating scale, ranging from "discontinued treatment" to "symptom removed." It was claimed that 69% of the patients showed at least some "improvement," but no follow-up data were presented.

Even if one accepts the validity of the group-design paradigm, all of these studies fail to satisfy the most elementary criteria for assessment of validity. No control groups were used; the criteria for change were inadequate and very general for the most part; and follow-up data were inadequate or nonexistent. It may be noted also that no attempt was made in these studies to obtain direct observation of changes in real-life situations (e.g., by measuring the strength of a phobia during exposure to the phobic situation).

2. STUDIES USING CONTROL GROUPS

Here we shall consider studies in which groups treated by behavior therapy techniques are compared with groups treated by other techniques, and studies in which different methods of behavior therapy are compared.

(a) BEHAVIOR THERAPY COMPARED WITH OTHER THERAPIES. Three *retrospective* studies that have tried to evaluate behavior therapy against other therapies may be dealt with briefly, as they are now only of historical interest and are open to serious objections. Cooper et al (1965)[3] compared 77 patients given

---

[3] The results of an earlier study by Cooper (1963) were incorporated in the later study.

at least five sessions of behavior therapy with 55 patients given other forms of therapy. The behavior therapy patients included 29 with agoraphobia, 12 with other (mainly mono-symptomatic) phobias, 10 with obsessive rituals, 13 with writer's cramp, and 13 with other disorders (tics, stuttering, etc.). As far as possible, each behavior therapy patient was matched with an "other therapy" patient on sex and type of symptom, and then for age, and duration and severity of symptoms. Information about symptoms and activities before and after treatment was extracted from the case-notes and assessed clindly by two independent[4] judges on a five-point symptom-severity scale and on a general scale relating to work, home, sexual, and social adjustment immediately before the start of treatment; at the end of treatment; and one month and one year after the end of treatment. Excluded from the samples were cases of enuresis, encopresis, and school phobia. The behavior therapy treatments included reciprocal inhibition, desensitization, relaxation, and so on (for the phobias, SD-I and SD-R were used). The control treatments included individual and group supportive interviews, intensive psychotherapy (10 cases), drugs, and tranquillizers. The analysis of the results suggested that behavior therapy was superior for specific phobias at the end of treatment (but the difference had vanished at one-year follow-up); but was very poor for writer's cramp and obsessional ruminations. Behavior therapy in this study took on average twice as long as the conventional therapies. The overall "improvement rate" was assessed at 61% (much improved: 29%) at the end of treatment, dropping to 55% (much improved: 27%) at one-year follow-up, compared with "improvement rates" for the control group of 44% (22%) at the end of treatment, and 51% (24%) at one-year follow-up. The cases treated were considered to be severer than those in Wolpe's samples. Cooper et al concluded that "behavior therapy was useful in patients with circumscribed phobias, and is worth further application in other conditions in which anxiety is manifest in relatively specific situations" (Cooper et al, 1965, p. 1225). A similar retrospective study by Marks and Gelder (1965), dealing only with phobias, utilized improved techniques and arrived at broadly similar conclusions, but need not be considered further

here, since later studies by these workers also incorporated these improvements.

Several *prospective* studies have been carried out which, methodologically, represent a very significant advance on any of the studies discussed so far. In the first of these, Gelder and Marks (1966) allocated 20 severe agoraphobics randomly to one of two treatment groups. Prior to treatment, the experimental and control groups were shown not to differ with respect to a large number of possibly confounding variables, including: age at treatment and symptom onset; type, duration, and severity of symptom; degree of general anxiety; score on a checklist of phobic symptoms; intelligence, neuroticism, and extraversion; ratings of family adjustment; other social relationships; work and leisure activities; sexual relations; and self-satisfaction. The particular interest of the study lies, however, in the measurements that were made in relation to outcome. Assessments were made on a symptom rating scale and on a social adjustment scale. These scales were completed by the therapists, the patients, and an independent medical assessor every two weeks during treatment and every three weeks during follow-up. In addition, symptom and social adjustment ratings were completed by assessors before treatment began; two months later; at the end of treatment; and six and 12 months after termination of treatment. Finally, a symptom checklist and checklists of phobias and social anxieties, as well as a self-adjustment scale and the MPI, were completed by the patients at the beginning and end of treatment, and at six- and 12-month follow-up. The behavior therapy treatment involved SD-R (graded retraining) and SD-I, while the control group received therapy interviews. Treatment for each group was given three times weekly for three-quarters of an hour.

In yet a further prospective study, Gelder et al (1967) applied much the same research model to a comparison of three groups of phobics. One group was treated by SD(I); the second by group psychotherapy; the third by individual psychotherapy. The groups, which had 16 patients in each, were carefully matched on age, sex, duration of illness, and other variables (similar to those in the earlier study), although matching in this instance was by no means entirely successful, especially with respect to

---

[4] This claim is difficult to follow, since one of the "independent" judges was Gelder, 31 of whose

patients from another study were included in Cooper's sample.

duration of illness which was much longer in the patients given group therapy. Behavior therapy sessions occurred once per week for one hour over nine months on average; group therapy one and one half hours per week for 18 months; and individual therapy one hour per week for one year. Behavior therapy was carried out by five psychiatrists, four of whom had no previous experience of behavior therapy, though this did not worry Gelder et al who apparently considered that SD-I was so simple to apply that it could be carried out by novices. The assessments were similar to those in the earlier study, but with a very interesting addition in relation to the follow-up data, which were collected by a psychiatric social worker who interviewed the patient (she was not aware of which kind of therapy the patient had received) and at least one relative or close friend.

We are not primarily concerned with assessing the inferiority or superiority of behavior therapy in this chapter, but it may be noted that, in the Gelder et al study, behavior therapy produced significantly better results in relation to the main phobia during treatment (as assessed by both patient and combined therapist ratings); at 18 months after the beginning of treatment, these differences were no longer significant (but this was due to slow, regular improvement in the other groups rather than relapse on the part of the behavior therapy group). On a final rating, 9/16 behavior therapy patients were rated "much improved" as compared with 2/16 for group therapy, and 3/10 for individual therapy.

The major improvements of these studies over the earlier ones relate to the use of independent assessors, the wide range of measurements used, and the detailed follow-up. It will be noted that there is still an almost complete reliance on subjective reports from the patient and ratings from others, with an absence of in vivo testing for the strength of phobia.

Lazarus (1966) allocated 75 successive patients at random to one of three types of treatment: behavior rehearsal, direct advice, and reflection-interpretation therapy. These treatments (for the purpose of the study) were not necessarily applied to the major area of disturbance, but to specific interpersonal problems that arose in the course of treatment. Each patient was given a maximum of four 30-minute sessions over a period of one month. The criterion of change was "objective evidence of adaptive behavior"

arrived at by any of several procedures (subjective report, observation of behavior, etc.), and Lazarus claimed that such evidence of change was found in 92% of the patients treated by behavior rehearsal, but in only 32% of patients treated by psychotherapy, and in only 44% of patients given advice.

Finally, mention should be made of the two studies by Paul (1966, 1967) and the study by Kondas (1967) which used group designs. Since their models were described in detail in the previous chapter,[5] they need not be repeated here. Paul's studies, of course, represent the most sophisticated investigations thus far within the group-comparison paradigm, being distinguished by the use of multiple control groups, very careful matching of groups, and very careful assessment of change, including the use of objective tests and physiological measures made in the actual anxiety-inducing situation. Paul's studies, in fact, possibly represent the ultimate in this kind of design.

(b) CROSS-OVER DESIGNS. In this design, the control group which is not initially given behavior therapy is provided with it subsequently. The model may be illustrated by the study of Lazarus (1966) who used the following paradigm.

Behavior therapy in phase 2 was applied to those patients in the "advice" and "psychotherapy" groups who had not responded to these treatments. Of 27 such patients, "there was evidence of learning in 22 (81%)" (Lazarus, 1966, p. 212). A similar design was employed by Paul and Shannon (1966) and by Gelder and Marks (1968). The latter study is of particular interest. They took seven patients from the study of Gelder et al (1967) who had not improved under the group psychotherapy situation at the end of that treatment and who were still unimproved six months later, and they treated them with behavior therapy (SD-I and graduated tasks). Five were agoraphobics and two had circumscribed phobias. At the end of four months of behavior therapy, the main phobias had decreased significantly though there was little change in anxiety, depression, social adjustment, and other general characteristics. A six-month follow-up by the psychiatric social worker showed that the three patients rated "much improved" at the end of treatment had retained and even improved their status; of the four patients showing lesser improvement at the end of treatment, two retained their improved

[5] See Chapter 17.

Group	Treatment	
	Phase 1	Phase 2
Experimental	Behavior therapy	—
Control 1	Advice only	Behavior therapy
Control 2	Psychotherapy	Behavior therapy

status, and two partially (but not completely) relapsed. Gelder and Marks noted that these patients made gains in four months of behavior therapy that were equivalent to the gains made in nine months of treatment by the original group of patients given behavior therapy. They suggested that the group therapy that had apparently failed may nevertheless have relieved widespread other difficulties, thus "clearing the way" for behavior therapy in relation to their main symptoms.

The methodological problem inherent in cross-over studies of this kind relates to the lack of control data (unless a nonspecific treatment control group is used, which was not the case in any of these studies) for possible changes resulting from the earlier treatment condition, but that are slow to appear. In part, however, this difficulty was overcome in the Gelder and Marks study by allowing a period of time without specific treatment to elapse between the end of the group therapy treatment condition and the commencement of the behavior therapy treatment condition. The fact that no significant improvement occurred either during group therapy or the "wait" period strengthens the conclusion that the subsequent change could be attributed to the behavior therapy techniques.

(c) BETWEEN BEHAVIOR THERAPY TREATMENT DESIGNS. Thus far, little work has been reported in which comparisons have been made between matched groups subjected to alternative techniques of behavior therapy. Rachman (1965) has very thoroughly reviewed the advantages and disadvantages of aversion therapy using drugs on the one hand and electric shock on the other. In a retrospective study, Schmidt et al (1965) reported results on 42 patients subjected to one of three types of behavior therapy, classified in terms of positive or negative reinforcement techniques: positive reinforcement techniques only (relaxation training, reciprocal inhibition); negative reinforcement techniques only (all forms of aversive conditioning); and

a combination of positive and negative reinforcement techniques (aversion-relief, electric shock plus behavioral retraining, etc.). The combination of positive and negative reinforcement techniques appeared to produce the best results though it should be noted that very few patients were given the other treatments.

Several other studies may be mentioned briefly. Johnson and Sechrest (1968) compared the effects of SD(I) with training in relaxation only on anxiety in test situations. Using examination scores before and after therapy as the major dependent variable, they found that SD(I) was superior to relaxation alone, the latter not differing from the effects of no treatment. Wagner and Cauthen (1968) obtained results suggesting that SD(I) and operant conditioning procedures (using E as a positive reinforcer) were equally effective in reducing fear of snakes. However, the numbers of subjects involved in the study were far too small to justify definite conclusions. Garfield et al (1967) found little difference in the effectiveness of SD(I) alone as compared with SD(I) plus SD(R) in a study of phobic reactions to snakes. In a carefully designed study, Zeisset (1968) compared the effects of SD(I) with progressive relaxation-plus-application training (RPA),[6] also utilizing two control conditions (attention-control and no-treatment control). The dependent variable (interview anxiety) was assessed before and after treatment in neurotic and functionally psychotic patients. No difference was found between SD(I) and RPA, both of which were superior to the control conditions in reducing interview anxiety.

(d) THE CO-TWIN CONTROL DESIGN. Lazarus (1964) reported an unusual method involving three pairs of identical twins. In one pair, both twins suffered from agoraphobia and social anxiety; in a second pair, from claustrophobia; and in a third pair, from general anxiety. In each pair, one twin was treated by SD(I) and SD(R) while the other twin was not

---

[6] Application training is really a form of SD(R), the relaxation response being practiced while the subject is actively moving about.

treated until after treatment of the first twin had proceeded for some time. Reasonable objective evidence was available relating to change of behavior (e.g., one treated twin travelled abroad by plane, an activity impossible before treatment). In the first two pairs, the treated patients improved significantly: the twins did not until they were treated, when significant improvement took place. In the case of the third pair, the treated twin improved significantly, but the other patient refused treatment and showed no change.

3. EXPERIMENTAL LABORATORY STUDIES

It is, of course, extremely difficult to carry out the kind of group studies which have been discussed above under properly controlled conditions. The general validity of behavior therapy techniques may, however, be established by carefully controlled laboratory experiments. In many ways, this kind of validity is more important than success "in the field," just as in the natural sciences the essential validity of a technique or process may be established in the laboratory even though its realization in practical conditions may prove to be extremely difficult. If basic validity has been established in the laboratory, then one may be reasonably sure that continued efforts to establish controlled changes in real-life conditions are worth pursuing.

We have already discussed in some detail in an earlier chapter the work of Lang and his colleagues in relation to phobias. After establishing that Wolpe's systematic desensitization procedures apparently did reduce intense fear of snakes in otherwise normal subjects (Lazovik and Lang, 1960), it was shown in a second study that repeated exposure to the feared situation without use of the desensitization procedure did not reduce the fear and that, of the steps used in desensitization therapy (relaxation, hypnosis, construction of hierarchies, and desensitization), desensitization was the principal *effective* variable in producing change (Lang and Lazovik, 1963). Finally, Lang et al (1965) compared the effectiveness of three treatment procedures in reducing phobic behavior. The experimental group was subjected to systematic desensitization therapy, including all four stages listed above; a "pseudo-therapy" group was subjected to relaxation, hypnosis, hierarchy building, and discussion of fears in general, but was not given desensitization training; a "non-specific treatment" group was given no therapy.

Real-life tests of the strength of the snake phobia were made, and the results indicated that the nonspecific treatment and pseudotherapy groups did not differ from each other in amount of change, while both changed significantly less than the behavior therapy group. They concluded that changes in the strength of phobic behavior were a function neither of suggestion nor of a therapeutic relationship and that hypnosis, relaxation, and hierarchy building are not a sufficient cause of change when desensitization is used in conjunction with them, though they may be a necessary concomitant of desensitization therapy.

An important paper by Wolpe (1963) deserves mention here. Wolpe noted that the number of presentations required to progress from one level of an anxiety hierarchy during desensitization varied greatly between patients; furthermore, as the patients moved from "easy" to "difficult" items, some progressed at increasingly faster rates even though the items were becoming more difficult, whereas others made slower and slower progress. These considerations led Wolpe to distinguish three kinds of phobias in which a *quantitative* estimate of the strength of the phobic stimulus could be estimated.

(i) Proximation phobias (anxiety increases as the phobic stimulus is approached).

(ii) Claustrophobias (anxiety increases as freedom of movement in space decreases).

(iii) Remoteness phobias (anxiety increases as a safe stimulus—object, location, or person—becomes increasingly distant).

A fourth point related to phobias in which anxiety increases as a function of the number of phobic objects. Wolpe plotted graphically the cumulative number of presentations required to overcome (i.e., reduce anxiety to zero) particular hierarchies related to each of the four types of phobia, with results as shown in Figure 1. It will be seen that characteristically positively or negatively accelerated curves were obtained, the particular curve form being a function of the type of phobia under treatment. Since the same patient could produce positive and negative curves if different kinds of phobia were desensitized, the curves appear to reflect phobia differences rather than personality differences.

This study by Wolpe represents a significant contribution to the experimental investigation of the validity of behavior therapy. As Wolpe points out, it also "affords a method for predicting, in certain cases, how much more treatment is likely to be needed when desensitization has gone on for long enough to provide data from which to derive a mathematical function" (Wolpe, 1963, p. 1067).

4. CRITICAL COMMENTS

Let us return to Eysenck's (1952) critique of the alleged efficacy of psychotherapy. To recapitulate, Eysenck argued that the effectiveness of psychotherapy could be established only by the utilization of appropriate control groups so that the effects of "spontaneous recovery" (that is, of course, changes produced by un-

controlled factors not part of the treatment being used) could be assessed. Now let us reconsider (as an exemplar of the group studies reviewed above) the study by Gelder et al (1967), which involved essentially three steps.

(i) The formation of three groups of phobic patients, matched on as many relevant, possibly confounding variables, as possible.

(ii) The administration to each group of one of three treatments (behavior therapy, individual psychotherapy, or group psychotherapy).

(iii) The assessment of comparative changes (improved, unimproved, or worse) in these

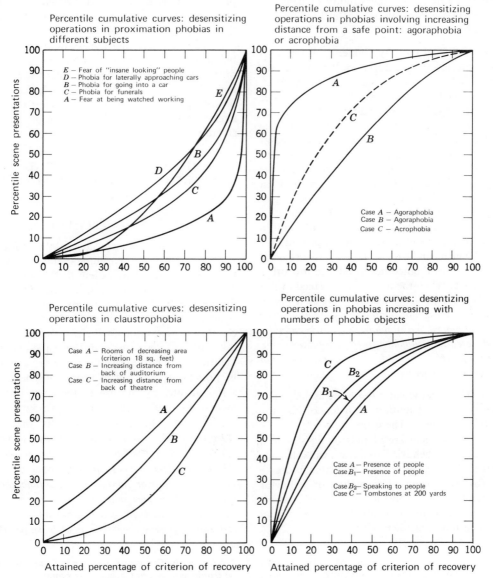

FIG. 1. Desensitization curves for four hierarchies in case of car phobia (Wolpe, 1963).

three groups during treatment, at the end of treatment, and at the end of various follow-up periods.

The model used appears to meet Eysenck's criteria for outcome research as far as is humanly possible in practical circumstances. It may seem odd, therefore, to argue that, valuable as the results of this and other similar studies may be for certain purposes, *the study reveals a fundamental misconception of the essential nature of behavior therapy and is, strictly speaking, irrelevant to the assessment of the validity of behavior therapy.*

The principle objections to be raised against attempts to determine the validity of behavior therapy by means of studies of this kind may be summarized as follows.

(i) The model used by Gelder et al (1967) is based on several assumptions which are not stated by them, but are plainly obvious. First, it is assumed that there is a standard disorder from which some people suffer with the result that comparable clinical groups may be formed.[7] Second, it is assumed that, to one of these groups, a standard method of behavior therapy (systematic desensitization—with its stages of relaxation training, with or without hypnosis; construction of hierarchies; and progression through the hierarchies) may be applied.[8] Third, that the technique will result in an outcome (improved, not improved, or worse) which can be quantitatively assessed and compared with outcomes produced by other techniques. When the model is described in this way, however, *it is immediately apparent that it is simply a version of the medical model in which a patient placed in a standard diagnostic category is subjected to a standard form of treatment as a result of which he either recovers, does not change, or gets worse.*

(ii) The model violates the basic assumptions underlying the definition of behavior therapy given in Chapter 1. These are:

(a) That there are at present no standard techniques of behavior therapy available, nor are there likely to be in the foreseeable future.

(b) That each abnormality of behavior represents a new problem, so that each patient must be considered as a subject of experimental investigation in his own right.

It is not, of course, denied that behavior therapy may be investigated at different levels of complexity and in different conditions. To imagine, however, that at the present time meaningful validity studies of the group comparison kind can be carried out to assess the validity of behavior therapy in the clinical situation is merely to practice self-deception. Thus, far too little is known at present about systematic desensitization itself to apply it in a routine fashion and then to arrive at conclusions as to the validity of behavior therapy from an examination of the results obtained. The technique itself is essentially unvalidated at present, nor is there enough known about the necessity for each of its component parts and their relative importance.

It is argued here that the essential validity of behavior therapy depends upon considerations other than group-comparison designs which, as has been pointed out, merely reflect the persisting influence of the inappropriate and irrelevant medical model. To these other considerations we now turn.

III. THE EXPERIMENTAL INVESTIGATION OF THE SINGLE CASE

1. GENERAL PRINCIPLES

We have already[9] considered the position adopted by Shapiro in arguing that it is possible to treat the individual patient as the subject of controlled experimental research in a rigorous fashion, and those arguments need not be repeated here. As was pointed out in that chapter, it was but a small step from Shapiro's position to argue that, if the patient's disabilities could be described in this way, it should be possible to attempt to change his behavior systematically by the use of the same experimental approach applied to the study of the single case. The position here is that *the essential validity of behavior therapy is determined by the experimental operations to which the individual patient is subjected, that is, that the validity of behavior therapy is not a function of whether he improves, deteriorates, or remains the same in relation to some arbitrary external criterion; but rather whether it can be shown that*

---

[7] The fact that the disorder may take various forms (monosymptomatic versus polysymptomatic, etc.) and appear in varying degrees of severity does not, of course, negate this point.

[8] Again, the fact that variations in technique may be employed does not negate this point.

[9] See Chapter 1.

changes in his behavior are lawfully related to the experimental operations which were intended to produce them.

This position needs to be spelled out in more detail so that it will not be misunderstood. First, it is not intended to imply that "improvement" in the patient's disabilities is not of great interest to the behavior therapist. However, in determining the validity of behavior therapy, the "cure" of the patient is not the primary consideration. So limited is current knowledge about human behavior in a scientific sense that it will be many decades before scientific psychology achieves the position physics established in the 19th century. If this is so, then it is futile and self-deceptive to suppose that there will be *any* standard techniques of treatment in behavior therapy for a long time to come. Indeed, any behavior therapy technique that claimed complete success would *ipso facto* have to be viewed with the gravest suspicion on these grounds alone. All that can be required of any experimental clinical study is that, as far as possible, the results of the experimental operations can be meaningful related to the operations themselves.

If this should seem to be a harsh prescription when so many patients await and seek treatment, then one can only refer to other examples where such a position is accepted without question. In the case of cancer, for example, no one queries the necessity of the painstaking research which is carried out, even though much of the research may have no immediate implications for treatment. Furthermore, it is quite plain that the needs of current patients for treatment must be balanced against the equal necessity to ensure that current treatments are evaluated and improved while being applied so that future patients may benefit from advances in knowledge that may only result from the current patients being treated on a controlled, experimental basis.

Unfortunately, in psychology, there has always been an impatience to discover and apply standard treatment techniques which may, in the long run, actually retard progress. An example from the writer's own work may illustrate the points being made. The application of massed practice to the treatment of tics on an experimental basis (Yates, 1958) which was derived from particular theoretical considerations[10] resulted in a dramatic reduction in the frequency with which the tics could be produced. *The validity of this technique was not dependent upon whether or not the patient "recovered"; the validity was essentially an "internal" validity, that is, the demonstration that predictions made from the theory as to how behavior would change under certain conditions were, in fact, fulfilled.* Furthermore, it would be quite wrong to draw the conclusion from this study that a standard technique (massed practice) should be routinely applied to all future patients presenting with tics. The best that could be hoped for would be that *the results of this study could serve as a rational starting point for the next patient with tics. But this next patient would himself then become the subject of a further controlled experiment, the validity of which would be determined in the same way.* To relate the validity of the behavior therapy approach in this instance to the answer to the question whether the patient was "cured" is to misconceive the nature of behavior therapy completely. Indeed, it could be said with considerable justification that *the controlled investigation of the single case is the only unique feature of behavior therapy that distinguishes it from other kinds of therapy.* If this unique feature is abandoned (and, as we have seen, there is a strong tendency in this direction now), then behavior therapy will rapidly approximate more and more to the standard medical model, with catastrophic effects.

2. METHODOLOGICAL PROBLEMS

It is unfortunate that methodological problems associated with *nomothetic* (quantitative) single-case investigations have so far attracted little attention from the statisticians although, as Dukes (1965) showed, there is a respectable list of such investigations in both general experimental and abnormal experimental psychology. As Dukes pointed out, while experimental psychologists have in general looked askance at $n = 1$ experiments as far as *subjects* are concerned, they have usually failed to realize that the $n = 1$ statistical inference problem applies equally as much to *experimenters = 1* and to *situations = 1*. Only recently has serious attention been directed towards the problem of experimenter = 1 (Rosenthal, 1966) while the problem of situations = 1 might not exist for all the attention paid to it. Dukes (1965) points out (and gives examples of) some of the situations in which $n = 1$ experiments might be

---

[10] See Chapter 10 for the details.

justified or, indeed, necessary: when individual variations in the function under study are negligible; when data obtained from one subject have point-for-point congruence with data obtained from dependable collateral sources; when data from one subject clearly contradict a widely-held theory; when examples of the function under study are rare (e.g., multiple personality studies and unilateral color blindness); and when the project is extremely time-consuming.

However, the use of nomothetic single case studies has received considerable support from several sources in recent years. Chassan (1960, 1961)[11] has both criticized the "extensive" design for its methodological inadequacies and put forward a strong case for the advantages of single-case studies. Thus he states:

"It is hard to understand why the intensive individual approach has been so completely neglected in formal clinical research. One must conclude that the reason for this failure probably results from a general misunderstanding, or at best a haziness, about the inferential possibilities of the much maligned 'individual case'. It is certainly not as generally recognized as it ought to be that *the intensive statistical study of a single case can provide more meaningful and statistically significant information than, say, only endpoint observations extended over a relatively large number of patients*" (Chassan, 1960, p. 178; italics in original).

Chassan goes on to point out that:

"*From the point of view of statistical inference per se the intensive single case study can be considered as providing data sampled from a statistical distribution or population defined by the set of particular parameters or characteristics of the patient under study*" (Chassan, 1960, p. 179; italics in original).

In relation to the "extensive model," Chassan points out that there are formidable difficulties in the way of obtaining homogeneous samples of patients against which to evaluate by group comparison the relative efficacy of several treatments. If such homogeneity is attained, then paradoxically it becomes impossible to generalize the results from the samples used; whereas if the samples are allowed to vary along several dimensions (even though matched on

them), it becomes very difficult to relate differential changes (or, indeed, any changes) to the variables in question. A similar viewpoint has been advanced by Edgington (1966, 1967) who comments:

"The belief that you cannot statistically generalize to a population of individuals on the basis of measurements from only one subject is certainly correct. However, it is also correct that you cannot statistically generalize to a population from which you have not taken a random sample, and this fact rules out statistical generalization to a population (at least to a population of some importance) for initially all psychological experiments, those with large samples or small" (Edgington, 1967, p. 195).

In one sense, the major difficulty with the "extensive" design is that it makes it very difficult to produce meaningful statements in relation to individual subjects in so far as it is important to relate change in the individual to any or all of the variables in question. Chassan (1960, 1961) and Edgington (1966, 1967) have pointed out that this prime aim in clinical research may be meaningfully realized by use of the "intensive" design. Thus, Chassan (1961) states that the "intensive" model capitalizes on variability within a given subject of the characteristics under study. Changes in state can be systematically related to patient characteristics. Furthermore, each subject serves as his own control; and important factors (age, sex, genetic endowment, etc.), which are rarely satisfactorily controlled in "extensive" designs, are held constant.

The problem of *generalization* of results obtained from single-case studies is also considered by Chassan and by Edgington. The solution involves two possible procedures. First, predictions may be made onto other patients whose characteristics are judged to be similar to those of the previous patient tested; second, the hypotheses in question may be tested by choosing the next patient so that he varies in only one of the characteristics under study.

Finally, of course, mention should be made of the methodology of operant conditioning which is essentially based on the single-case study paradigm. Sidman (1960) has spelled this position out in considerable detail, and statistical

---

[11] Chassan (1967) has expanded his earlier discussions into more formal consideration of the "intensive design."

designs for assessing the results of research using operant conditioning methodology have been provided by Revusky (1967) and Browning (1967).

Thus, a respectable body of opinion now exists that argues for the validity of the quantitative study of the single case, and Chassan (1967) has recently provided a detailed account of possible models.[12] The methodological problems involved in such research should not, of course, be minimized, but it may be anticipated that more attention will be devoted to them in the future by experts in research design.

3. METHODS OF CONTROL IN SINGLE-CASE STUDIES

Attention may be drawn to some important points in relation to the evaluation of the significance of change in single-case studies. The writer's study of the application of learning theory to the treatment of tics (Yates, 1958) may be used occasionally as an example. First, it may be noted that the *natural history* of the disorder, both as generally known and in relation to the particular patient in question, may be legitimately utilized for control purposes. Thus, there is ample evidence relating to the refractoriness to change of some disorders, notably obsessions and compulsions. If, therefore, a dramatic and lasting change is produced by the application of a special therapeutic technique, then the change may cautiously, but with some confidence, be attributed to the technique. This would not, of course, absolve the experimenter in any way from considering possible alternative explanations of the change. Second, operant conditioning methodology has made particular use of the base line/change/reversal-to-baseline paradigm. Here, the particular response in question is first evoked repeatedly in a standard situation until a stable base-rate of response is established under a specified contingency. (It may be noted that very prolonged observation may be necessary before stabilization occurs; and, of course, in some cases, stabilization may include variability in behavior, provided this is nonrandom in nature.) Once the base-line of performance has been established, a new contingency may be introduced (or the original contingency withdrawn without a new one being introduced) and performance continued until a new stable rate is

achieved. The efficacy of the new contingency may then be established by restoring the original condition and determining whether performance reverts to its original level. In previous chapters, we have seen many examples of the use of this technique, which raises an interesting problem that has not been sufficiently considered in operant methodology. In a sense, if it is argued that performance will be identical provided the contingencies are identical, then it is also being argued that stable (i.e., irreversible) change does not occur. In most clinical therapeutic endeavors, however, the aim is usually to produce permanent change. However, it can be argued that learning can be defined out of the situation in that the behavior will remain stable in its changed form only if the contingencies remain stable. This is an important point that impinges upon the earlier discussion as to whether the aim should be to apply a treatment, the results of which can be discretely categorized as improvement, no change, or worse. As we saw in the chapter on mental deficiency, the operant conditioners take up the position that, if an experimental operation fails to produce change in the patient, the basic assumption to be followed is that *the fault lies in the experimental technique and not in the patient.*

Another important source for assessing the validity of change relates to the use of theory. Thus, if the theory makes anticommonsense predictions and these are confirmed, the validity of the techniques used is suggested. Thus, in the experiment on tics, the use of Hull's constructs of I_R and sI_R led to the prediction that if, instead of trying not to perform the tic, the patient was required to perform it continuously under massed practice, the frequency of its voluntary evocation would decline, even though common sense says that "practice makes perfect." It should be noted, of course, that the critical prediction here was that sI_R would produce a permanent decrement (since temporary decrement due to I_R—fatigue—would have been merely a trivial finding).

Another technique that could prove very valuable would be to hold one response as an untreated control for comparison with the effects of treatment on the others. Thus, in the study on tics, instead of all four tics being subjected to massed practice, one tic could have been held as an untreated control in this way. Of course, merely measuring the frequency of

---

[12] The reader may also be referred to two books by Maxwell (1958, 1961) which deal with experimental design problems in this kind of research.

the untreated tic at regular intervals might produce some increment of $_sI_R$, and some generalization of inhibition from the treated tics to the untreated tic might take place. If, in spite of this, a significant difference in frequency of evocation (allowing for base-rate differences) occurred, the validity of treatment would be strengthened.

In conclusion, we see that the experimental study of the single case proceeds by progressive modification of hypotheses in the light of the relationship of the empirical results to the deduction made from the theories used and the specific hypotheses formulated. It is not intended to deny that *ultimately* some standard techniques may be derived that can be used in a relatively routine fashion, at least at the commencement of an investigation. Even in the one instance where this desirable state of affairs may appear to have already been achieved in behavior therapy (the use of conditioning techniques in the treatment of enuresis), a salutory warning has been given. As was pointed out in the chapter dealing with enuresis, the premature acceptance of both Mowrer's theoretical rationale and the empirical treatment derived from it led to the treatment being widely used without being questioned for over 20 years until the theory was called into question, an alternative theory proposed, and a modified method of treatment derived from it. This particular "case study" should serve as a paradigm for behavior therapists.

IV. THE PROBLEM OF RELAPSE AND SPONTANEOUS RECOVERY

As we have seen, "spontaneous" recovery or remission in "untreated" abnormalities of behavior is not uncommon. At the same time, some abnormalities of behavior are apparently very resistant to treatment and relapse following treatment is not uncommon. How is the paradox to be explained?

In two papers, Eysenck (1963a, 1963b) has suggested an ingenious solution to the paradox. He divides what he calls the "neurotic disorders" into two major classes: those involving classically conditioned sympathetic reactions (anxieties, phobias, etc.) and those involving reactivity of the parasympathetic division of the autonomic nervous system (alcoholism, psychopathy, etc.). Taking the phenomenon of "spontaneous" recovery first, he argues that, in

neurotic disorders of the first kind, a percentage of "spontaneous" remission without formal treatment would be expected since the conditioned fear response would extinguish unless the unconditioned stimulus that produced the initial learned fear were to occur regularly.[13] This would represent a straightforward case of extinction. However, if, in such a situation, the patient were to acquire an instrumental avoidance response that not only prevented "reality testing" but also reduced the conditioned anxiety or fear, then extinction would not occur. In the case of neurotic disorders of the second kind, however, extinction of the abnormal response pattern would not be expected to occur "spontaneously" because the occurrence of the parasympathetic response would produce *immediate* reward which would offset any possible punishing effect of a *delayed* aversive stimulus, as in the case of alcoholism, drug addiction, or psychopathic behavior.

Turning now to relapse following treatment, Eysenck argues that treatment of the first kind of disorders involves essentially the use of positive reinforcement techniques, thus strengthening incompatible parasympathetic activity. Since parasympathetic activity produces immediate reward, these incompatible "normal" behaviors would be highly resistant to extinction for the same reason that the "abnormal" parasympathetic responses in, for example, psychopathic persons, are resistant to extinction. Hence, relapse following treatment would be expected to be rare in disorders of the first type. In disorders of the second type, however, relapse following treatment would be common. In these disorders, the preferred treatment technique involves the use of aversive stimuli in which the reward/punishment sequence is reversed or at least the punishment is made coterminous with the reward. Since, however, aversive techniques usually do not involve overlearning, the balance between "abnormal" and "normal" response strengths will be very finely balanced. Oscillation of response strength will then lead in time to the reappearance of the "abnormal" response with consequent immediate reward while, at the same time, the "normal" response will tend to extinguish. Eysenck points out that the probability of relapse following treatment may be reduced by the use of partial reinforcement techniques, overlearning, and "booster" training sessions in follow-up.

---

[13] Just as conditioned salivation in the dog extinguishes unless primary reinforcement is presented regularly.

Eysenck included such disorders as enuresis in his second category of parasympathetic responses, but it will be clear that, in fact, enuresis should be regarded as a failure to acquire certain patterns of response rather than the acquisition of abnormal responses. Rachman (1963) has argued that a quite different set of factors may be operative in producing "spontaneous" *improvement* in skill deficiencies such as enuresis, namely, what he calls "latent learning." By this, he means that uncontrolled factors may be operative at a "subliminal" level over long periods of time which, by summation, may eventually exceed threshold and produce observable improvement. Stevenson (1961) has provided a series of case histories in which improvement could be traced to real-life experiences of the patient, that is, in which the behavior was changed by the operation of environmental factors such as change in job situation, family attitudes, and so on. Many of these factors could also be present in "spontaneous" remissions in Eysenck's first type of neurotic disorder.

Thus, it is possible that "spontaneous recovery" and "posttreatment relapse" are different faces of the same coin and can be accounted for in terms of a single explanatory model. At the very least, these ingenious suggestions will warrant careful further investigation.

REFERENCES

Browning, R.M. A same-subject design for simultaneous comparison of three reinforcement contingencies. *Behav. Res. Ther.*, 1967, **5**, 237–243.

Campbell, D.T. & Stanley, J.C. Experimental designs for research on teaching. In Gage, N.L. (ed.). *Handbook of research on teaching*. Chicago: Rand McNally, 1963, pp. 171–246.

Chassan, J.B. Statistical inference and the single case in clinical design. *Psychiatry*, 1960, **23**, 173–184.

Chassan, J.B. Stochastic models of the single case as the basis of clinical research design. *Behav. Sci.*, 1961, **6**, 42–50.

Chassan, J.B. *Research design in clinical psychology and psychiatry*. New York: Appleton-Century-Crofts, 1967.

Cooper, J.E. A study of behavior therapy in thirty psychiatric patients. *Lancet*, 1963, **1**, 411–415.

Cooper, J.E., Gelder, M.G., & Marks, I.M. Results of behavior therapy in 77 psychiatric patients. *Brit. med. J.*, 1965, **1**, 1222–1225.

Dukes, W.F. $N=1$. *Psychol. Bull.*, 1965, **64**, 74–79.

Edgington, E.S. Statistical inference and nonrandom samples. *Psychol. Bull.*, 1966, **66**, 485–487.

Edgington, E.S. Statistical inference from $N=1$ experiments. *J. Psychol.*, 1967, **65**, 195–199.

Eysenck, H.J. The effects of psychotherapy: an evaluation. *J. consult. Psychol.*, 1952, **16**, 319–324.

Eysenck, H.J. Behavior therapy, spontaneous remissions and transference in neurotics. *Amer. J. Psychiat.*, 1963, **119**, 867–871 (a).

Eysenck, H.J. Behavior therapy, extinction and relapse in neurosis. *Brit. J. Psychiat.*, 1963, **109**, 12–18 (b).

Eysenck, H.J. The effects of psychotherapy. In Eysenck, H.J. (ed.). *Handbook of abnormal psychology*. London: Pitman, 1960, pp. 697–725.

Garfield, Z.H., Darwin, P.L., Singer, B.A., & McBrearty, J.F. Effect of "in vivo" training on experimental desensitization of a phobia. *Psychol. Rep.*, 1967, **20**, 515–519.

Gelder, M.G. & Marks, I.M. Severe agoraphobia: a controlled prospective trial of behavior therapy. *Brit. J. Psychiat.*, 1966, **112**, 309–319.

Gelder, M.G. & Marks, I.M. Desensitization and phobias: a cross-over study. *Brit. J. Psychiat.*, 1968, **114**, 323–328.

Gelder, M.G., Marks, I.M., & Wolff, H.H. Desensitization and psychotherapy in the treatment of phobic states: a controlled inquiry. *Brit. J. Psychiat.*, 1967, **113**, 53–73.

Goldstein, A.P. & Dean, S.J. (eds.). *The investigation of psychotherapy*. New York: Wiley, 1966.

Goldstein, A.P., Heller, K., & Sechrest, L.B. *Psychotherapy and the psychology of behavior change*. New York: Wiley, 1966.

Hoenig, J. & Reed, G.F. The objective assessment of desensitization. *Brit. J. Psychiat.*, 1966, **112**, 1279–1283.

Hussain, A. Behavior therapy in 105 cases. In Wolpe, J., Salter, A., & Reyna, L.J. (eds.). *The conditioning therapies: the challenge in psychotherapy*. New York: Holt, 1963, pp. 54–61.

Johnson, S.M. & Sechrest, L. Comparison of desensitization and progressive relaxation in treating test anxiety. *J. consult. clin. Psychol.*, 1968, **32**, 280–286.

Kondas, O. Reduction of examination anxiety and "stage-fright" by group desensitization and relaxation. *Behav. Res. Ther.*, 1967, **5**, 275–281.

Lang, P.J. & Lazovik, A.D. Experimental desensitization of a phobia. *J. abnorm. soc. Psychol.*, 1963, **66**, 519–525.

Lang, P.J., Lazovik, A.D., & Reynolds, D.J. Desensitization, suggestibility and pseudo-therapy. *J. abnorm. Psychol.*, 1965, **70**, 395–402.

Lazarus, A.A. The results of behavior therapy in 126 cases of severe neurosis. *Behav. Res. Ther.*, 1963, **1**, 69–79.

Lazarus, A.A. Behavior therapy with identical twins. *Behav. Res. Ther.*, 1964, **1**, 313–319.

Lazarus, A.A. Behavior rehearsal vs. nondirective therapy vs. advice in effecting behavior change. *Behav. Res. Ther.*, 1966, **4**, 209–212.

Lazovik, A.D. & Lang, P.J. A laboratory demonstration of systematic desensitization psychotherapy. *J. psychol. Stud.*, 1960, **11**, 238–247.

McGuire, R.J. & Vallance, M. Aversion therapy by electric shock: a simple technique. *Brit. med. J.*, 1964, **1**, 151–153.

Marks, I.M. & Gelder, M.G. A controlled retrospective study of behavior therapy in phobic patients. *Brit. J. Psychiat.*, 1965, **111**, 561–573.

Marks, I.M. & Gelder, M.G. Transvestism and fetishism: clinical and psychological changes during faradic aversion. *Brit. J. Psychiat.*, 1967, **113**, 711–729.

Maxwell, A.E. *Experimental design in psychology and the medical sciences*. London: Methuen, 1958.

Maxwell, A.E. *Analysing qualitative data*. London: Methuen, 1961.

Meehl, P.E. Psychotherapy. *Ann. Rev. Psychol.*, 1955, **6**, 357–378.

Paul, G.L. *Insight versus desensitization in psychotherapy: an experiment in anxiety reduction*. Stanford: Stanford U.P., 1966.

Paul, G.L. Insight versus desensitization in psychotherapy two years after termination. *J. consult. Psychol.*, 1967, **31**, 333–348.

Paul, G.L. & Shannon, D.T. Treatment of anxiety through systematic desensitization in therapy groups. *J. abnorm. Psychol.*, 1966, **71**, 124–135.

Rachman, S. Spontaneous remission and latent learning. *Behav. Res. Ther.*, 1963, **1**, 133–137.

Rachman, S. Aversion therapy: chemical or electrical? *Behav. Res. Ther.*, 1965, **2**, 289–299.

Revusky, S.H. Some statistical treatments compatible with individual organism methodology. *J. exp. Anal. Behav.*, 1967, **10**, 319–330.

Rosenthal, R. *Experimenter effects in behavioral research*. New York: Appleton-Century-Crofts, 1966.

Schmidt, E., Castell, D., & Brown, D. A retrospective study of 42 cases of behavior therapy. *Behav. Res. Ther.*, 1965, **3**, 9–19.

Sidman, M. *Tactics of scientific research*. New York: Basic Books, 1960.

Stevenson, I. Processes of "spontaneous" recovery from the psychoneuroses. *Amer. J. Psychiat.*, 1961, **117**, 1057–1064.

Wagner, M.K. & Cauthen, N.R. A comparison of reciprocal inhibition and operant conditioning in the systematic desensitization of a fear of snakes. *Behav. Res. Ther.*, 1968, **6,** 225–227.

Wolpe, J. *Psychotherapy by reciprocal inhibition.* Stanford: Stanford Univer. Press, 1958.

Wolpe, J. The systematic desensitization treatment of neuroses. *J. nerv. ment. Dis.*, 1961, **132,** 189–203.

Wolpe, J. Quantitative relationships in the systematic desensitization of phobias. *Amer. J. Psychiat.*, 1963, **119,** 1062–1068.

Wolpe, J. Behavior therapy in complex neurotic states. *Brit. J. Psychiat.*, 1964, **110,** 28–34.

Yates, A.J. The application of learning theory to the treatment of tics. *J. abnorm. soc. Psychol.*, 1958, **56,** 175–182.

Zeisset, R.M. Desensitization and relaxation in the modification of psychiatric patients' interview behavior. *J. abnorm. Psychol.*, 1968, **73,** 18–24.

Chapter 19

Critiques

It is well known that new approaches in psychology usually generate a wave of enthusiasm which is rapidly followed by a wave of criticism. Precisely this has happened in relation to behavior therapy over the past few years. It will be the purpose of this chapter to consider in some detail these criticisms. In addition, however, the present author has some grave misgivings on his own behalf about what he regards as serious misconceptions within the behavior therapy movement and certain trends which, if not checked, may spell disaster for the whole concept of behavior therapy within a relatively short period of time. The rise of behavior therapy also appears to have sharpened, though it did not, of course generate, the ethical dilemma inherent in all forms of therapy. This problem will also be examined.

We shall consider first the similarities and differences in general between behavior therapy and psychotherapy and then look at some more specific criticisms that have been made about behavior therapy by psychodynamic and cognitively-oriented psychologists. We shall then consider some criticisms that have been made within the behavior therapy movement, including our own criticisms; and finally consider the ethics of behavior therapy.

I. SIMILARITIES AND DIFFERENCES BETWEEN BEHAVIOR THERAPY AND PSYCHOTHERAPY

A most curious and intriguing situation has grown over the past few years concerning the relationship between behavior therapy and psychotherapy. Four quite distinct positions

have been established. First, some behavior therapists and psychotherapists insist that behavior therapy and psychotherapy reflect fundamentally different and irreconcilable positions in relation to the theory of the genesis and maintenance of abnormalities of behavior and in relation to the appropriate treatment techniques. Second, others insist that there are both similarities and differences, so that the two approaches are complementary rather than antagonistic. Thirdly, some psychodynamic psychologists argue that behavior therapy (both theory and technique) can be reduced to psychotherapy. Fourth, some behavior therapists argue that psychotherapy (both theory and technique) can be reduced to behavior therapy. It will be apparent that not all of these positions can be equally correct. Each will be examined in turn.

1. THAT THERE ARE FUNDAMENTAL DIFFERENCES WHICH ARE IRRECONCILABLE

In a generally well-balanced and sympathetic review of the differences between behavior therapy and psychotherapy (as represented especially by Rogerian nondirective therapy), Barrett-Lennard (1965) identified seven principal sources of difference which are summarized in Table 19.1. He concluded his review with the statement that:

> "In their view of man's nature, and the aims and methods of modifying his behavior, the two types of system presented stand too far apart for present reconciliation" (Barrett-Lennard, 1965, p. 32).

TABLE 19.1. *Differences Between Behavior Therapy and Psychotherapy From the Standpoint of the Psychotherapist: I. Barrett-Lennard*

Behavior Therapy	Psychotherapy
1. Mechanistic - associationist view of personality	1. Person viewed as organized, dynamic whole
2. Multiple secondary-drives motivate S to tension-reducing behavior	2. Specific motives stem from basic pervasive growth and actualizing tendency
3. Behavior change results from cumulative effects of specific positive and negative reinforcements	3. Change involves shifts in balance, organization, and functional unity of a complex whole
4. Do not use concept of self or ego	4. Self is a pivotal concept
5. Seeks to control specific maladaptive habits or internal mediators of these	5. Seeks to help the person gain greater access to his own internal experience, especially self-awareness
6. Control based on positive and negative contingencies	6. Control based on empathic, non-directive relationship between therapist and patient
7. Little concern with values	7. Much concern with values

Source: Barrett-Lennard, 1965.

Barrett-Lennard, of course, was writing from the Rogerian viewpoint, and his conclusion would certainly be supported by Rogers himself (Rogers and Skinner, 1956). A similar viewpoint, which is expressed in a much more hostile fashion, is taken by Murray (1963). He contrasted what he called the *biotropic* approach with the *sociotropic* approach on ten points of difference which are shown in Table 19.2. Several comments need to be made about Murray's alleged differences. His first point (that behavior therapists place a relatively greater reliance on classical Pavlovian conditioning whereas psychotherapists place relatively greater reliance on operant, or instrumental, learning) will come as something of a surprise to readers of the earlier chapters of this book, as well as to Rogerian and psychoanalytic psychotherapists, since it appears to place the latter within the Skinnerian operant conditioning framework. As we have seen, a great deal of behavior therapy has made use of the operant conditioning paradigm which has certainly been regarded as typical of behavior therapy by others of its critics. Much the same comment may be made about Murray's second distinction (nonverbal as against verbal techniques). As we have seen, the manipulation of verbal behavior has become a major part of

behavior therapy. The reader may care to examine for himself the remaining contrasting points of Murray along similar lines. We may also note the use of pejorative terms by Murray, such as "naive behaviorist tradition," in relation to behavior therapy, together with a stress on the "subtle means of influencing behavior" of psychotherapy.

Murray was by no means the first to indulge in such language, however, since even earlier, Eysenck (1959) had produced his own list of ten contrasting characteristics of behavior therapy and psychotherapy, reproduced in Table 19.3. Thus, Eysenck argues that behavior therapy is "based on consistent, properly formulated theory leading to testable deductions" whereas psychotherapy is "based on inconsistent theory never properly formulated in postulate form."

For reasons that will become clear shortly, it is not proposed here to attempt to synthesize these three attempts to show that behavior therapy and psychotherapy are irreconcilable. As Barrett-Lennard and Eysenck, in particular, have shown, it is certainly true that there are significant differences in philosophy, theory, and technique in the two approaches; but, in this writer's view, all three authors miss the essential feature of behavior therapy in their eagerness to find contrast.

TABLE 19.2. *Differences Between Behavior Therapy and Psychotherapy*
from the Standpoint of Psychotherapy:
II. Murray

Behavior Therapy	Psychotherapy
1. Relatively greater reliance on classical Pavlovian conditioning	1. More emphasis placed on operant, or instrumental, learning
2. Direct transposition of laboratory hardware into clinic, e.g., P.G.R. conditioning, bar pressing apparatus	2. Translation of laboratory findings into verbal and expressive techniques
3. More use of reinforcement based on physiological drives, e.g., electric shock, candy bars, erotic pictures	3. Social reinforcement and acquired drives more important, e.g., approval, empathy, interest, understanding, respect, life goals of individuals
4. Primary stimulus generalization and discrimination central to psychopathology and therapy, e.g. trains, buses, cars in phobias	4. Secondary, or mediated, generalization and discrimination of most importance, e.g., verbal symbols, feelings
5. Restriction of interest to overt muscular responses and peripheral autonomic reactions in naive behaviorist tradition	5. Recognition of important, although difficult to measure, cognitive processes such as thinking, fantasy, and dreams (which on the physiological level would be central brain mechanisms)
6. Transference is not part of treatment —"Personal relations are not essential"	6. The therapeutic relationship is seen as the key learning experience in all forms of therapy
7. Causal factors in neurosis are seen as primarily genetic, physiological, and medical	7. Cultural variables play a great role in determining disturbance, e.g., social class, family relations, and social learning
8. Affinity for the directive-organ school of psychiatry	8. Affinity for the analytic-psychological school of psychiatry
9. Techniques deemed of most importance include hypnosis, suggestion, progressive relaxation, drugs, and overt manipulation	9. Point to techniques such as insight, labeling, permissiveness, and other subtle means of influencing behavior
10. Learning theory presented as an alternative to traditional psychotherapy	10. Adopt a strategy of first reinterpreting and then extending and modifying traditional therapy

Source: Murray, 1963.

2. THAT THERE ARE BOTH SIMILARITIES AND DIFFERENCES WHICH MAKE THE TWO APPROACHES COMPLEMENTARY

From time to time, behavior therapists and psychotherapists have worked fairly closely together in dealing with patients. The degree of contact thus engendered appears to have resulted in a mutual interaction that has softened the antagonism apparent in the views discussed above, with a consequent modification of extreme views. Thus, while not denying that there are important differences in the two approaches, some authors have tended to stress the similarities and have been led to argue that, instead of being alternative ways of conceptualizing and treating disorders of behavior, the approaches are rather *complementary* to each other and hence can live in harmony rather than conflict (Bergin, 1966; Crisp, 1966; Meyer and Crisp, 1966). Most typical of this attitude, perhaps, are Marks and Gelder (1966) who attempted to specify in some detail these alleged similarities and differences, as shown in Table 19.4. Once again, however, it should be noted that Marks and Gelder have missed completely the essential distinguishing mark of behavior therapy.

3. That Behavior Therapy Can be Reduced, Either Wholly or Partly, to Psychotherapy

Occasional attempts have been made to demonstrate that behavior therapy is not what it claims to be either in relation to theory or to practice. The argument takes two forms, both of which are exemplified by the study of Weitzman (1967). On the one hand, it is argued that the

TABLE 19.3. *Differences Between Behavior Therapy and Psychotherapy from the Standpoint of Behavior Therapy: Eysenck*

Behavior Therapy	Psychotherapy
1. Based on consistent, properly formulated theory leading to testable deductions	1. Based on inconsistent theory never properly formulated in postulate form
2. Derived from experimental studies specifically designed to test basic theory and deductions made therefrom	2. Derived from clinical observations made without necessary control, observations, or experiments
3. Considers symptoms as unadaptive conditioned responses	3. Considers symptoms the visible upshot of unconscious causes ("complexes")
4. Regards symptoms as evidence of faulty learning	4. Regards symptoms as evidence *of repression*
5. Believes that symptomatology is determined by individual differences in conditionability and autonomic lability, as well as accidental environmental circumstances	5. Believes that symptomatology is determined by defense mechanisms
6. All treatment of neurotic disorders is concerned with habits existing at *present*; their historical development is largely irrelevant	6. All treatment of neurotic disorders must be *historically* based
7. Cures are established by treating the symptom itself, i.e., by extinguishing unadaptive CRs and establishing desirable CRs	7. Cures are achieved by handling the underlying (unconscious) dynamics, not by treating the symptom itself
8. Interpretation, even if not completely subjective and erroneous, is irrelevant	8. Interpretation of symptoms, dreams, acts, etc. is an important element of treatment
9. Symptomatic treatment leads to permanent recovery provided autonomic as well as skeletal surplus CRs are extinguished	9. Symptomatic treatment leads to the elaboration of new symptoms
10. Personal relations are not essential for cures of neurotic disorder, although they may be useful in certain circumstances	10. Transference relations are essential for cures of neurotic disorders

Source: Eysenck, 1959.

TABLE 19.4. *Similarities and Differences Between Behavior Therapy and Psychotherapy*

Common to Both

1. Placebo ⎫
2. Patient expectations ⎬ Nonspecific
3. Suggestion ⎭

1. Encouragement, advice, reassurance ⎫
2. Environmental manipulation ⎪
3. Pointing out current sources of stress ⎬ More specific
4. Pointing out repetitive patterns of behavior ⎭

Specific to Behavior Therapy[a]	Specific to Psychotherapy[a]
1. Emphasis on direct symptom modification	1. Pointing out unrecognized feelings
2. Use of a hierarchy in practical retraining	2. Understanding relationship with therapist
3. Use of a hierarchy in fantasy retraining	3. Encouraging expression of feeling about therapist
4. Aversion techniques	4. Relating present behavior to past patterns
5. Positive conditioning	5. Interpreting fantasy and dream material
6. Negative practice	6. Pointing out symbolic meanings
7. Other special techniques	7. Attempting modification of present personality

Source: Marks and Gelder, 1966.

[a] The juxtaposed points are not regarded as antagonistic.

theoretical structure on which behavior therapy is allegedly based can be readily translated into psychodynamic terms. On the other hand, it is argued that the results of behavior therapy are produced, not by the techniques used by behavior therapists, but rather by other factors unrecognized by behavior therapists.

In order to sustain this thesis, Weitzman is compelled to argue that "the evidence of the practical effectiveness of behavior therapy while not conclusive, is indeed impressive" (Weitzman, 1967, p. 301). Weitzman is virtually forced to this conclusion (which is hotly denied by other critics of behavior therapy), since he wishes to show that these "impressive" results are really produced by psychotherapy and not behavior therapy techniques; and, of course, it would be somewhat embarrassing to his argument if the results of behavior therapy were insignificant, since this would indict psychotherapy.

Weitzman goes on to argue that, of all the behavior therapy techniques, only systematic desensitization has been shown to be effective, a statement which will surprise both behavior therapists and their critics. But, he goes on, it is clear that systematic desensitization affects "the total psychological matrix." He reports the preliminary results of a number of ingenious and interesting experiments which, in his view:

". . . suggest that the use of intensity gradients and other means of controlling anxiety arousal may be unnecessary for desensitization and call into question a crucial procedural and theoretical emphasis in systematic desensitization" (Weitzman, 1967, p. 312).

In other words:

". . . the effects of behavior therapy (systematic desensitization) can be understood in terms of principles derived from analytic theories" (Weitzman, 1967, p. 313).

Similar reinterpretations of behavior therapy have been attempted by other psychodynamic psychologists, but with quite a different purpose sometimes in view. Thus, Crisp (1966) and Coates (1964) have argued that in behavior therapy the changes that are produced are the result of the establishment between behavior therapist and patient of a transference relationship—which is, of course, the very essence of psychotherapy. This produces an interesting paradox since Coates (1964), for example, quotes with obvious approval from Glover's (1959a) critique of Wolpe's book the following passage:

". . . laboratory-minded normal psychologists are, with outstanding exceptions . . . inevitably poor clinicians (largely because they neglect the factor of mental suffering) and notoriously inept and unapt in psychotherapy . . ." (Glover, 1959, p. 74).

Indeed, Glover asserts roundly that the results obtained with systematic desensitization are produced by nothing other than the time-honored processes of suggestion and laying on of hands. Thus, on the one hand, it is asserted that behavior therapists are "notoriously inept and unapt" in psychology; but that, on the other hand, these "inept and unapt" psychologists achieve results which are "indeed impressive" by establishing, without training or even conscious awareness, successful transference relationships with their patients. It would seem to follow either that behavior therapists are not "inept and unapt" (in which case Glover is wrong) or that psychotherapy is not a skilled activity. Fortunately, most behavior therapists have not concerned themselves with the resolution of this difficult problem.

It might be noted here that the attribution of successes in behavior therapy to "suggestion," "hypnosis," or "laying on of hands" has usually been advanced without any evidence of the validity of the contention being offered. Cautela (1966) has had no difficulty in showing essential differences between behavior therapy techniques and the techniques used in hypnotherapy.

4. That Psychotherapy can be Reduced to Behavior Therapy

Here also the argument has been put forward in two parts. On the one hand, it has been claimed that the theoretical structure of psychotherapy can be translated into behavioristic terms; on the other, that any success that is achieved by psychotherapy is really because of inadvertently practiced forms of behavior therapy (particularly, of course, systematic desensitization). Thus, Dollard and Miller (1950), as we have seen, attempted to translate psychoanalytic theory into learning theory terminology. More recently, Kanfer (1961) has tried to explain the psychotherapy process in learning theory terminology and Brady (1967) has tried to perform the same task with respect to "insight" which is, of course, the very core of change in psychotherapy. Similarly, Wolpe (1958) has argued that psychotherapists make (inefficient) use of procedures such as systematic desensitization during psychotherapy and that it is these procedures which produce any beneficial changes that may take place. At a more specific level, Eysenck (1963) has tried to account for the transference phenomenon in terms of the therapist as a conditioned stimulus producing drive reduction.

5. Conclusion— The "Paradigm Clash"

The curious situation described above in which behavior therapists and psychotherapists are busily trying to define each other out of existence is by no means uncommon in the history of science, although it is highly probable that awareness of this fact would not make any difference in such a charged conflict. A well-known monograph by Kuhn (1962) introduced the term "paradigm clash" to describe the kinds of conflict which have been delineated clearly in a recent note by Katahn and Koplin (1968).

"In these controversies, each of the antagonists describes his opponent's position in the most extreme form in order to formulate telling counterarguments. At the same time, each insists that the other's criticisms are based upon inadequate understanding of one's preferred theoretical framework as well as a lack of knowledge concerning the relevant supporting data" (Katahn and Koplin, 1968, p. 147).

In a very real sense, therefore, the "clashes" described above are futile exercises that will ultimately have no significant effect. Behavior therapists and psychotherapists will go on doing what they have been doing with the final outcome being in no way determined by these disputes.

One further point needs to be made, however, in connection with the supposed similarities and differences between behavior therapy and psychotherapy, since it appears to have been consistently missed. It is the present writer's contention that, at a fundamental level, behavior therapy has only one critical distinguishing mark of uniqueness which really does separate it from other forms of therapy. This is, of course, *the stress on the experimental investigation of the single case*. This point will be developed in more detail later in this chapter and is mentioned here only because of its total neglect by the protagonists whose arguments have been described above.

II. SPECIFIC CRITICISMS OF BEHAVIOR THERAPY

Kiesler (1966), in a very thought-provoking paper, criticized both behavior therapy and psychotherapy severely, summarizing his conclusions as follows.

". . . the basic deficiencies in prevailing theoretical formulations are that they perpetuate and do not attack the Uniformity Myths described in the previous section[1]; do not explicitly deal with the problem of confounding variables; and do not specify the network of independent, dependent, and confounding variables in sufficient enough detail to permit researchers to solve sampling and other methodological problems" (Kiesler, 1966, p. 125).

Of course, the Uniformity Myths referred to by Kiesler are relevant in relation to behavior therapy only in so far as the behavior therapist continues to be bound by the medical model which, unfortunately, continues to be the case very frequently. His point about the specification of dependent, independent, and confounding variables is, of course, well taken. If behavior therapy is conceived of as the application of the experimental method to the single case, sampling and other methodological problems become quite different from those considered by Kiesler who is thinking, of course, in terms of the medical model. We may pass over the controversy between Glover (1959a, 1959b) and Wolpe (1959) and turn to the most substantial critique of behavior therapy thus far published, that of Breger and McGaugh (1965). Although Katahn

and Koplin's (1968) point about "paradigm clash" was made specifically in reference to the controversy generated by the critique of Breger and McGaugh, this critique contains many specific criticisms about behavior therapy that need to be considered.

Before doing so, however, it is worth drawing attention to one serious misconception contained in the Breger/McGaugh critique of a more general kind. They distinguish:

". . . three different positions, all of which are associated with the behaviorism or 'learning-theory' label. These are: (a) Dollard and Miller (1950) as represented in their book, (b) the Wolpe/Eysenck position as represented in Wolpe's work (1958; Wolpe et. al., 1964) and in the volume edited by Eysenck (1960), and (c) the Skinnerian position as seen in Krasner (1961) and the work that appears in the *Journal of the Experimental Analysis of Behavior*" (Breger and McGaugh, 1965, p. 338).

This is so seriously misleading a statement as to indicate profound ignorance of the history of the development of behavior therapy in England, South Africa, and America.[2] First, Dollard and Miller could not possibly be regarded as behavior therapists in any meaningful sense of that term, for what they did was to translate Freudian theory into learning theory terms and then apply the theory in the clinic. But Dollard and Miller's clinical procedures were, in fact, indistinguishable from the classical procedures of psychotherapy. At no point did they attempt to apply the experimental method to the individual patient. Second, the linking of Wolpe with Eysenck is grossly misleading. As was shown in Chapter 1, behavior therapy developed in England relatively independently of Wolpe's work in South Africa (the reverse is even more strongly true). Furthermore, while encouraged by Eysenck, behavior therapy at the Maudsley (again, as was shown in Chapter 1) developed within the Clinical-Teaching section at the Maudsley Hospital and was largely influenced by the ideas of Shapiro on the experimental investigation of the single case. Finally, it should be noted that, at least up to 1960, Wolpe, if he should be linked with anyone, should be linked with Dollard and Miller since, like Dollard and Miller, Wolpe formulated a general

---

[1] The Uniformity Myths referred to are: the patient uniformity myth, the therapist uniformity myth, the spontaneous remission myth, and the

myth that present theoretical formulations provide adequate research paradigms.

[2] See Chapter 1.

theory that involved the construction of a conceptual neuro-physiological model from which deductions as to treatment were made. But, again like Dollard and Miller, *Wolpe did not, in his earlier work, carry out controlled experiments on his patients but rather used a series of techniques that involved many uncontrolled variables* and was analogous to the clinical work of Dollard and Miller. It must be stated frankly that the earlier work of Wolpe was completely different from that carried out by the English behavior therapists.[3] Thus, to talk of a Wolpe-Eysenck "position" is factually incorrect. Only confusion can result from a failure to realise that developments in England and South Africa followed quite distinct paths up to about 1960.

Turning now to the specific criticisms of behavior therapy, these may be grouped into four main categories: that behavior therapists falsely claim that their approach is more "scientifically-based" than other therapeutic approaches; that behavior therapy is based on a number of faulty (if not false) assumptions; that the conception of neurosis advanced by behavior therapists is faulty; and that the claim that behavior therapy produces a higher "cure" rate than other forms of therapy is not borne out by an examination of those claims. We shall look at each of these areas of criticism in turn. In doing so, it should be made clear that it is not intended to attempt to offer an unqualified "defense" of behavior therapy, nor to deny the value of Breger and McGaugh's review. It is not only natural, but essential, that behavior therapy should be submitted to searching criticism, and the fact that some of the criticisms of Breger and McGaugh do seem to be based on misunderstandings and misconceptions should not be allowed to obscure the value of much of what they say.

1. THE CLAIM TO SCIENTIFIC RESPECTABILITY

Breger and McGaugh argue essentially that the claim to scientific respectability (as compared with traditional psychotherapy) is spurious, being based on analogy rather than fact. Thus:

"The claim to scientific respectability rests on the misleading use of terms such as stimulus, response, and conditioning, which have become associated with some of the

methods of science because of their place in experimental psychology. But this implied association rests on the use of the same *words* and not on the use of the same *methods*" (Breger and McGaugh, 1965, p. 340, italics in original).

They particularly object to the use of the terms "stimulus" and "response" by behavior therapists, as if they were being used with the same rigor as in experimental psychology. After giving an example of a "stimulus" (imagination of a scene) and "response" (relaxation) from systematic desensitization procedures, they state that "the use of the terms stimulus and response are only remotely allegorical to the traditional use of these terms in psychology" (Breger and McGaugh, 1965, p. 340).

Second, they argue that the claim by behavior therapists that their techniques are based on the application of "modern learning theory" is misleading because there is no such thing as *the* "modern learning theory," only a wide range of competing and, to a considerable degree, incompatible and feuding learning *theories*. Finally, they point out that even these *theories* have been mostly derived from laboratory studies of animal behavior. Apart from the fact that even in the field of animal behavior profound differences exist in theoretical interpretation of the observed empirical data (not to mention conflicts about the data themselves), it is impossible, they argue, to transfer these theories in usable form to the explanation of human behavior, normal or abnormal. Human behavior cannot be accounted for simply in terms of complex interactions among the principles used to explain animal behavior. As a striking instance of this, they refer to Chomsky's (1959) critique of Skinner's (1957) analysis of verbal behavior in terms of constructs derived from the study of *nonverbal* behavior in lower organisms.

"... the basic facts of language learning and usage simply cannot be handled within an S-R approach. It seems clear that an adequate view of language must account for the fact that humans, at a rather early age, internalize a complex set of rules (grammar) which enable them to both recognize and generate meaningful sentences involving patterns of words that they may never have used before. Thus, in language learning, what is learned are not only sets of responses (words and

---

[3] This is not the case, of course, in relation to Wolpe's later work, from about 1959 onward.

sentences) but, in addition, some form of internal strategies or plans (grammar). We learn a grammar which enables us to generate a variety of English sentences. We do not merely learn specific English sentence habits" (Breger and McGaugh, 1965, p. 343).

There are several points that may be made in reply to these criticisms. With respect to the use of learning theory terminology (stimulus, response, conditioning, and so on), their argument is merely an extension of a conflict that has persisted for decades within experimental psychology itself. For, within experimental psychology itself, there exist the purists who reject other experimental psychologists (who would no doubt be accepted as such by Breger and McGaugh for *their* purpose) as interlopers. It is hard to believe that Breger and McGaugh are unaware of the standard discussions in textbooks of learning about the problem of defining and measuring these terms, or that they are unaware of the more specialized discussions of psychologists such as Spence (1956) and Gibson (1960) on precisely this problem. Thus, we are not here dealing with a dichotomy (as Breger and McGaugh imply), with the "pure" experimental psychologists on the one hand and the "impure" behavior therapists on the other, but rather with a continuum of precision of usage. It would be an acceptable argument that behavior therapists often use such terms with less precision, though it is noticeable that Breger and McGaugh are as selective in the examples they choose to illustrate their thesis as they claim behavior therapists are in selecting *their* examples. The writer may perhaps be excused for pointing out that Breger and McGaugh make no reference at this point of their argument to his own work on tics (Yates, 1958b) in which the response variables were specified with reasonable precision and reliability; their examples are deliberately chosen from more difficult and complex areas, such as the behaviors dealt with by Wolpe, using systematic desensitization. The problem of stimulus and response definition is a quite general one in psychology and is nowhere near adequate resolution.

The objection relating to the alleged derivation of behavior therapy from "modern learning theory" has been dealt with adequately by Rachman and Eysenck (1966)[4] and by Wiest (1967). This criticism is simply based on a

misinterpretation of the term "modern learning theory." The word "theory" here is, of course, used in its *generic* sense to cover learning *theories* of various kinds. Thus, it is entirely open to behavior therapists to utilize *any* version of learning theory as the fancy takes them, since theories are merely intended as props from which to derive specific hypotheses from which empirical deductions may be made. There is, of course, no such thing as "the" theory, nor is any theory ever "true." The sole purpose of theories is to be disproved. Thus, this objection is trivial.

As for the criticism that behavior therapists ignore mediational processes, it may be pointed out that this is factually inaccurate. It is, of course, true that behavior therapists have not made as yet a great deal of use of mediational constructs, but the reason for this is the very simple one that the behavior therapists (with the notable exception of Wolpe and a few others) have preferred to concentrate on what *appear* to be simpler forms of abnormal behavior before proceeding to more complex forms. However, again a reference to the present writer's paper on tics will show that mediating constructs such as drive (D), habit strength ($_sH_R$), reactive inhibition (I_R), and conditioned inhibition ($_sI_R$) were an integral part of the theory leading to the derivation of treatment by massed practice and that *the treatment could not have been rationally formulated without the use of these mediational constructs.* As we shall see in the next chapter, it can confidently be expected that more complex mediational variables will be utilized by behavior therapists over the next 20 years. As for the critique of Skinner's analysis of verbal behavior, this has been devastatingly rebutted by Wiest (1967) who points out that the assertion that children learn and utilize a grammar is not (as suggested by Breger and McGaugh) a "fact" which Skinner has to explain, if his theory is to remain viable, but an *inference* or theoretical construct. No one has ever observed a "grammar" and indeed, as Wiest points out, the child usually would be quite unable to specify the nature of the "grammar" he is allegedly using. Wiest also points out that it is quite improper to set up a theoretical construct to account for complex verbal behavior and then demand that Skinner explain this theoretical construct by means of his own theory.

----

[4] See also, however, the riposte of Breger and McGaugh (1966).

2. Faulty Assumptions of Behavior Therapists

Breger and McGaugh discuss three major assumptions on which they allege that behavior therapists base their work. The first assumption is that the overt discrete response is the most meaningful unit of human behavior, that is, for example, that what is learned is a particular response in the presence of a particular stimulus. This "peripheralist" view they regard as dated and outmoded as well as being incompatible with well-known experimental facts such as perceptual constancy, response equivalence, and response transfer. The second assumption has already been mentioned, namely, that behavior therapists apparently believe that complex human behavior can be accounted for in terms of "simple" (Bookbinder, 1962) conditioning. The third assumption is that rewards play an essential role in all learning phenomena. They point out that this position was undermined nearly 40 years ago by the well-known latent learning experiments which showed that reward affects performance, not learning, as well as by more recent experiments on perceptual learning, imitation, and imprinting. They criticize also drive-reduction theory, the circularity of the Skinnerian reinforcement paradigm, and the triviality of the whole concept of reinforcement.

It is interesting to notice—as Wiest (1967) pointed out—how Breger and McGaugh shift their ground according to which particular aspect of behavior therapy they are criticizing. Earlier, as we have seen, they criticized Wolpe for his use of a "stimulus" ("imagining a scene") which, whatever else it may be, could not possibly be described as an "overt discrete response." Now they criticize behavior therapists for allegedly only dealing with "overt, discrete responses." The allegation is, of course, simply untrue. As the reader will by now be well aware, behavior therapists have dealt with the whole spectrum of response complexity. It is quite true that they try to maintain a clear distinction between *observable* and *inferred* responses, since one of their basic assumptions (not mentioned by Breger and McGaugh) is that the development of a scientific account of human behavior is almost entirely dependent on the development of adequate instruments for measuring human behavior. The second assumption is not held by behavior therapists; the problem of higher concepts will be discussed fully in the next chapter. Their criticism of the use of a circular reinforcement paradigm merely reflects a dispute in psychology which is by no means confined to behavior therapists.

As will be seen later, the above criticisms made by Breger and McGaugh are based on the false assumption that behavior therapy is the application of learning theory to the understanding and amelioration of neurotic behavior. Since this definition is an incorrect one, the above criticisms of Breger and McGaugh are fundamentally irrelevant.

3. The Concept of Neurosis in Behavior Therapy

We come now to an objection of more importance and substance. Breger and McGaugh argue that:

"In its essence, the conception of neurosis put forth by the behavior therapists is that neuroses are conditioned responses or habits (including conditioned anxiety) and *nothing else*, though it should be noted that they do not adhere to this argument when they describe the success of their methods. Wolpe, for example, while ostensibly treating overt symptoms, describes his patients as becoming more productive, having improved adjustment and pleasure in sex, improved interpersonal relationships and so forth. The argument that removal of a troublesome symptom somehow 'generalizes' to all of these other areas begs the question" (Breger and McGaugh, 1965, pp. 347–348, italics in original).

And again:

"Much of the behaviorist conception of neurosis rests on a rejection of the distinction between symptoms and underlying causes (Eysenck, 1960) as typified by Yates' (1958a) argument against 'symptom substitution'. By focusing attention on overt symptoms and banishing all underlying causes, however, the behavior therapists are faced with the same problem that has long confronted behaviorism; namely, the difficulty of explaining how *generality* of behavior results from specific learning experiences" (Breger and McGaugh, 1965, p. 348, italics in original).

Their main objections to the behavioristic view of neurosis are that the burden carried by the concept of stimulus generalization is too great unless mediating processes are introduced into the model; that the concept of anxiety as a secondary drive rests on shaky foundations; and that, *in practice*, behavior therapists do not restrict themselves to symptoms or overt responses but surreptitiously introduce much more complex units of behavior (as well as mediating processes) into their actual descriptions of the patient.

The distinction between neuroticism and neurosis was discussed in considerable detail in Chapter 2 and need not be repeated here. The objections of Breger and McGaugh do, however, raise the questions of symptomatic treatment and symptom substitution. Since this author's original paper (Yates, 1958a) appears to have been misunderstood to a considerable degree, it appears relevant to consider afresh this whole set of problems.

The basic misconception (which is no doubt partly, though not wholly, due to lack of clarity in the original paper) appears to have arisen from overgeneralization (if Breger and McGaugh will excuse the use of the term) on the part of the critics. Yates (1958a) argued that psychodynamic psychologists assumed that symptoms were merely the surface indicators of underlying unconscious conflicts; that direct treatment of the symptoms, without treating the underlying conflict, was futile; and that such treatment, even if it succeeded in removing the symptom, would inevitably result in the appearance of new symptoms, since the underlying conflict would become intolerable unless it could be indirectly expressed in symptomatic form. Yates questioned the attribution by psychodynamic psychologists of some fundamental priority of significance or importance to the supposed underlying conflict in relation to treatment procedures, calling this the "vertical" approach. Let us note, first, that there is no doubt whatever that the views attributed to psychodynamic psychologists regarding symptoms and symptom substitution are, in fact, held by the majority of them.[5]

A careful reading of Yates' paper will show beyond doubt that there was no intention whatever to deny the important role of mediational variables. It is difficult to see how anyone could ever have arrived at this interpretation in view of the study referred to in that paper on the application of learning theory to the treatment of tics (Yates, 1958b), where, as was already pointed out, no less than four mediational

constructs (drive, habit, and reactive and conditioned inhibition) were used. The point that Yates was stressing was quite simply that a more adequate conceptualization of abnormal behavior could be achieved by regarding the so-called underlying factors of the symptom as themselves learned responses with no necessary priority over the symptoms in relation to treatment; that a "horizontal" view should be taken instead in which *sequences* of interrelated responses were acquired. It was further pointed out that, while the anxiety (or other mediating) response *could* be treated directly, there were two advantages in starting at the peripheral end of the sequence: first, that the symptoms are directly observable and measurable and hence that hypothesis testing is thereby rendered easier in relation to change in response pattern; and, second, that from the theoretical viewpoint, treating the symptom directly would, at least in some circumstances, have important effects on the anxiety responses, especially in cases where removal of the symptoms produced reality-testing of the anxiety responses as a signal of an impending danger which was, in fact, no longer present. As we have seen, other behavior therapists have preferred to treat the anxiety responses directly.

The misreading of Yates' argument was unfortunately compounded by Eysenck's famous dictum: *get rid of the symptoms and you have eliminated the neurosis.* Eysenck's terminology was perhaps unfortunate, but again a careful reading of his publications shows quite clearly that he was not in any way putting forward a peripheralist argument or denying the significance of mediating variables. In fact, Eysenck has gone out of his way to insist that treatment of both the symptom and the anxiety responses (acting as feedback stimuli) is essential for stable success in treatment.

Since the publication of Yates' discussion of symptoms and symptom substitution, a good deal has been written on this topic,[6] as a result of which it has become clear that some of the differences are entirely a result of semantic problems. It is also clear that some notion corresponding to the term "symptom substitution" is acceptable to most (but not all) behavior therapists, though the use of a different term would probably be preferable since its

---

[5] See Weitzman (1967) for an interesting argument that psychoanalytic theory does *not necessarily* demand symptom substitution following successful symptomatic treatment.

[6] See, for example, Bookbinder (1962), Yates (1962), Costello (1963), Crisp (1966), Kanner (1960), Lazarus (1965), Marks and Gelder (1966), Kraft and Al-Issa (1965), Ayllon et al (1965), and Weitzman (1967).

acceptance does not preclude "symptomatic" treatment whereas, with one notable exception, the idea of symptomatic treatment remains anathema to psychodynamic psychologists.

As Cahoon (1968) has recently pointed out, "the definition of symptom, as reflected by the ways that the word has been used in the literature, reflects gross admixtures of observation, inference, and arbitrary stipulation" (p. 150). He goes on to argue that, provided the concepts of "symptom" and "underlying causes" are redefined so as to have empirical implications of a noninferential kind, the terms should be both acceptable and meaningful to behavior therapists.

"If behaviors judged to be socially or personally maladjustive (symptoms) are decreased in frequency by procedures that do not involve the manipulation of certain classes of independent variables (underlying causes), the formation of new maladjustive behaviors, or an increase in the frequency of existing maladjustive behaviors, is a relatively probable event" (Cahoon, 1968, p. 151).

The question then becomes one of determining the expected fate of treated responses (or response patterns) in relation to a number of "state" or environmental variables. The basic distinctions which it would appear to be necessary to make relate to environmental conditions, personality variables, and the theoretical account of the genesis and maintenance of the response systems being treated.[7]

We may distinguish between three kinds of "new" symptoms. First, it would be predicted, in terms of the distinction made in this book between neuroticism and neurosis, that the development of new symptoms would be rare in low-neuroticism individuals unless they were exposed to some new highly specific and traumatic situation, whereas a person high in neuroticism would be expected to develop new symptoms very readily. In neither case, however, would the new symptoms represent an example of symptom substitution as that term is used by psychodynamic psychologists.

Second, the reappearance of the treated symptom(s) would be expected to occur under either of two conditions: if the untreated anxiety mediating the symptom did not

extinguish spontaneously (through exposure to reality testing) following elimination of the symptom[8] or, alternatively, if treatment were restricted to the laboratory and the environmental conditions mediating the symptom remained unchanged. The latter point has been referred to as a vital consideration in several chapters in this book and will be dealt with in detail in the next chapter. Once again, however, it should be noted that neither of these examples of the reactivation of a successfully treated symptom represents an instance of symptom substitution in the psychodynamic sense.

Third, it may be noted that symptom substitution would not be expected at all in relation to "deficit states." Thus, enuresis has been conceptualized in this book, not as the symptom of some underlying conflict, but as the indication of a failure to acquire cortical control over a powerful natural reflex. Thus, acquisition of such control does not involve *removal* of a symptom, but rather the acquisition of a set of *desirable* responses; the question of symptom substitution logically cannot arise. Similarly, in those instances where the defective response is due to faulty feedback control systems (as in stuttering, for example), there is no question of symptom substitution. Ayllon et al (1965) have also shown that a response (labeled a symptom and interpreted psychodynamically when observed by psychiatrists) may be acquired and extinguished solely by the manipulation of contingencies (reinforcers) entirely extraneous to the patient. Here again, the question of whether symptom substitution will occur is a meaningless one, at least as it is posed by psychodynamic psychologists.

In fact, the *only* condition in which symptom *substitution* would be expected to occur by behavior therapists would be the relatively rare one in which the patient had learned a number of alternative responses to anxiety as a stimulus, with all of the responses except one being inhibited. Removal of the exhibited response would then allow the response next highest in the hierarchy to appear, provided the anxiety stimulus was still present. It may be noted that this case is different from that in which a hierarchy of stimulus situations produces the same response in diminishing strength (as manifested in Wolpe's technique of hierarchy

---

[7] For an alternative but similar account, see Cahoon (1968). The section which follows was written before publication of Cahoon's excellent review.

[8] Yates (1958a, 1962) argued that this would be relatively infrequent.

construction), since all of these responses are manifested under appropriate stimulus conditions. It is rather an instance of *response generalization* (where the same stimulus has attached to it a variety of responses that can be ordered along a generalization continuum). Whether response substitution does occur when the response of greatest strength is eliminated is an empirical question concerning which no evidence appears to be available at present.

4. CLAIMS FOR THE EFFICACY OF BEHAVIOR THERAPY

This section of Breger and McGaugh's paper must be criticized severely for its unfairness. For they dismiss the so-called "case studies" of behavior therapy as just that and therefore irrelevant to the assessment of its efficacy, thus revealing their ignorance of the essential nature of behavior therapy as described in this book. It is true, of course, that many of the individual studies do violate the *experimental* nature of behavior therapy and thus qualify as case studies rather than experimental investigations of the single case. But this is no excuse for the deliberate omission by Breger and McGaugh of those studies which do so qualify.

The criticisms that they bring against the early studies of Wolpe and Lazarus are largely justified (sampling biases, observer biases, and confounding of treatment variables) but give a completely misleading impression of the current state of behavior therapy. It is hoped that the false impression created by Breger and McGaugh's "review" of the efficacy of behavior therapy has been corrected in the previous chapter.

III. CRITIQUES OF BEHAVIOR THERAPY BY BEHAVIOR THERAPISTS

It is, of course, essential that behavior therapists remain as critical as possible of their techniques and results. Here we shall consider briefly some of the suggestions and criticisms that have been made of behavior therapy by behavior therapists themselves and by those who, while not behavior therapists, have been helpful.

1. GENERAL PROBLEMS

In an excellent paper based on much experience, Meyer and Crisp (1966) have considered carefully many of the problems facing behavior therapists in practice. They deny the often asserted proposition that behavior therapy can be applied successfully only to patients presenting monosymptomatic behavior disorders, and they assert, correctly no doubt, that behavior therapy is not always successful with such disorders. They discuss in detail problems related to the selection and order of treatment of symptoms, particularly with respect to the complex interrelations between symptoms. They discuss the importance of motivational level and fluctuation of symptoms during treatment; the problem of discharging successfully treated patients to the same environment from which they came; the need to treat some patients in their family environment rather than in a hospital situation; and ethical problems related to the use of aversion and other unpleasant techniques. In a second part of the paper, they deal with specific treatment problems such as selection of appropriate treatment techniques; the use of SD(R) as against the use of SD(I); and special problems in the use of operant conditioning and aversion therapy. This outstanding paper is a mine of useful information by two very experienced therapists and should be consulted by all behavior therapists.

2. RESPONSE VERSUS STIMULUS CHANGE

Phillips and El-Batrawi (1964) have made an uncompromising plea for a response-oriented behavior therapy, whereas Goodkin (1967) has argued equally strongly against neglect of the stimulus-situation which produces the maladaptive response. Goodkin points out that, at least in some instances, the "maladaptive" response may be the most *rational* response, given the particular stimulus to which it is occurring, and that changing the stimulus situation may be a more rapid means of effecting change in the response than working directly on the response itself. However, it should be pointed out that the dichotomy is a false one. Goodkin, for example, refers specifically to Williams' (1959) study on temper tantrums[9] as a response-oriented study. In fact, however, Williams' study *is* an example of stimulus control rather than response control, since his treatment essentially involved withdrawal of the stimuli maintaining the response, namely, the parental activity of entering the child's room. The question whether the stimulus

---

[9] See Chapter 17 for a description of this study.

situation should be altered or the response itself attacked is one which cannot be resolved on theoretical grounds. In most instances, it seems likely that *both* aspects will need to be attacked. Thus, in the case of the present writer's study of tics, it was suggested that the conditioned inhibition should be attached to as many stimulus situations as possible by having the patient practice the response in ever-widening social situations. The problem is inextricably linked with that of generalization from the laboratory to real life (Walters, 1967) which has already been mentioned and will be dealt with in more detail in the next chapter. Operant conditioning techniques, of course, essentially involve manipulation of the *contingencies* produced by the maladaptive response and thus deal primarily with stimulus control, whether this involves manipulation of stimuli *external* to the patient or with stimuli which are self-produced.

3. INTERACTION OF THEORY AND TECHNIQUE

The relationship between theory and technique in behavior therapy has been considered by several behavior therapists. Arthur (1967), for example, criticizes behavior therapists for confounding practice with theory, arguing that the essential criterion of the validity of behavior therapy as a technique is not dependent on any demonstration that successful results can be tied in with theoretical considerations, but only on the demonstration of effective results. Costello (1967) has suggested that operant conditioning procedures as used with schizophrenics, for example, are *management* procedures, not therapeutic procedures, because *permanent* changes are not produced. He suggests that permanent changes (that is, resistance to extinction) will be produced only if certain considerations (such as the use of partial reinforcement and delay of reinforcement) are incorporated into the procedures. Goldiamond et al (1965), on the other hand, have argued that the behavior therapy practitioner can simultaneously be a research worker by designing his treatment of the individual case to test hypotheses all along the line. Walters (1967) has made a strong plea for the importance of theory in behavior therapy.

Costello's argument that operant conditioning procedures with schizophrenics are management procedures would be rejected by operant conditioners; while Arthur's argument that

practice should be separated from theory would be rejected by many behavior therapists. The position taken by the present author is that the use of theory to derive empirical procedures as against the use of empirical procedures in their own right is again a false dichotomy, depending on a too narrow definition of theory. Behavior therapists working within the framework of operant conditioning do not begin each experiment completely from scratch. If they utilize a particular reinforcement schedule, for example, they do so with the knowledge of previous results obtained in other, more or less similar, situations. If theory is simply more and more refined description, then they are using theory (that is, systematized knowledge). Of course, the term "theory" is often used in a different sense, as in Hull's system of intervening variables, for example. Which particular *kind* of theory (descriptive or postulate) one uses is probably a matter of personal preference at the present time.

4. USE OF MEDIATIONAL CONSTRUCTS

Walters (1967) has recommended that behavior therapists should not ignore the use of mediational processes, even if these cannot be directly observed. It will be apparent to the reader that many behavior therapists do, in fact, use such constructs. In the next chapter this point will be considered in detail and need therefore only be mentioned at this point.

5. MEASUREMENT OF CHANGE AND FOLLOW-UP

Goodkin (1967) has particularly stressed the need for adequate follow-up and the use of objective, real-life measures of change. Both of these points were dealt with in the previous chapter.

6. MISCONCEPTIONS ABOUT BEHAVIOR THERAPY

It is interesting to note that many of the hostile and friendly critics of behavior therapy have failed to point out some of the most serious criticisms that can be brought against it, largely as a result of a failure to appreciate its essential nature. Indeed, a number of serious misconceptions about the nature of behavior therapy exist among many behavior therapists. Most of these have already been mentioned at various points of this book, but it is desirable to recapitulate them here.

(i) The most important misconception arises from the unfortunate definition of behavior therapy by Eysenck as:

"the attempt to alter human behavior and emotion in a beneficial manner according to the laws of modern learning theory" (Eysenck, 1964, p. 1).

It follows directly from the historical account given in Chapter 1 of the development of behavior therapy in England, and the definition of behavior therapy given there, that *behavior therapy is not the application of learning theory or any other kind of theory to the modification of behavior.* Behavior therapy, as it developed in England, was the application of a particular *methodological approach* (the use of the experimental method in the study of the individual case). The distinction is important because it implies that disabilities may arise from causes other than those relating to learning variables, and that theoretical models for explanation and treatment may meaningfully be derived from *any part* of the whole body of psychological knowledge. A classic instance of this, of course, is the feedback control model for stuttering. This is not, of course, to deny that learning theory has played a major role in behavior therapy thus far. But this may well be a historical accident resulting from the fact that empirical knowledge in the area of learning, and theories of learning themselves, are at present more readily utilized for explanatory and treatment purposes than other areas of experimental psychology. To *identify* behavior therapy with the application of learning theory, however, is to commit a gross error which, if perpetuated, may seriously retard the utilization of other equally important areas of knowledge from experimental psychology and the theoretical models derived therefrom.

(ii) A second serious misconception has been perpetuated by Eysenck and Rachman, namely, the identification of abnormality of behavior with neurosis and psychosis. Although this misconception is fortunately absent from the (incorrect) definition of behavior therapy by Eysenck presented above, it is clearly present in the titles of two of his books (Eysenck, 1960; Eysenck and Rachman, 1965) in which it is implied that behavior therapy is concerned with the "causes and cure" of neuroses (and psychoses, though this term is not used in either title). This error is also implicit in the work of Wolpe, where neurotic behavior, as we have seen, is defined as "any persistent habit of un-adaptive behavior acquired by learning in a physiologically normal organism" (Wolpe, 1958, p. 32). It will be noted that Wolpe also perpetuates the error relating to the definition of behavior therapy as the application of learning theory.

The tendency to identify behavior therapy with the modification of neurotic or psychotic behavior is most unfortunate for reasons which have been made clear throughout this book. *Behavior therapy deals with abnormalities of behavior, whether these behaviors define neurotic or psychotic states or whether they occur in essentially normal persons.*

(iii) Misconceptions relating to the alleged peripheral nature of behavior therapy and to the assessment of behavior therapy by means of comparative group studies have also been dealt with elsewhere in detail and need only be mentioned at this point.

In summary, it may be concluded that nearly all of the criticisms, both specific and general, which have been made of behavior therapy derive essentially from misconceptions concerning the nature of behavior therapy, misconceptions which have in part been fostered by behavior therapists themselves. To the extent that the latter point is so, of course, the critics can hardly be blamed for setting up straw men.

IV. THE ETHICS OF BEHAVIOR THERAPY

Behavior therapy has from time to time been attacked on the grounds that it represents an unethical approach to treatment. Some of these critiques unfortunately represent mere abuse as when Glover (1959a) characterizes Wolpe's (1958) book as being "almost as nostalgic as the scent of a late Victorian Wardrobe" (Glover, 1959a, p. 68); or as when he writes that:

". . . some of the practical applications of 'learning theory', though perhaps more detailed in scope and not so glaringly moralistic in intent, do not differ in principle from the earlier Victorian and sometimes Edwardian experiments in therapeutic conditioning. This is especially true of counter-conditioning through shock and suggestion. Perhaps the best example is that of Gwynne Jones's treatment (based on Bykov) of frequency of micturition by the use of a cystometric apparatus in order to apply varying pressures of saline injected into the bladder, using at the same time a manometer the readings of which can be falsified. Though plainly a technique of countersuggestion, this does not differ in principle from the Victorian habit of trying to prevent masturbation, when all moralistic and intimidating suggestions had failed to 'extinguish' the 'habit response', by inserting a safety-pin in the prepuce. And it has the same penal significance which lies behind the application of the death penalty for murder, the therapeutic difference being that the latter conditioning process extinguishes the patient as well as his unadapted synaptic responses, and thereby finally cures him of the homicidal habit" (Glover, 1959a, pp. 73–74).

Along similar lines, behavior therapists have from time to time been characterized as working out possibly sadistic tendencies on their patients when they use aversion therapy (Oswald, 1962) or as indulging in "brainwashing" (Allchin, 1964; Holden, 1965).

These intemperate outbursts could be ignored were it not for the distinction and influence of some at least of those who have made them. It is, of course, outrageous that it should be implied, on the basis of no evidence whatsoever, that behavior therapists are less compassionate toward their patients (Shoben, 1963) than are psychotherapists. Certainly, the present author, on the basis of subjective, personal knowledge of many behavior therapists, has never had any reason to suppose that they were less humanely oriented than any other therapists. The important point surely is that behavior therapists make a clear distinction between *understanding* and *explaining* behavior on the one hand and between the *needs of currently presenting patients* and the *needs of patients who will present for treatment in ten, 20, or 50 years' time.* The behavior therapist believes that, while everything possible must be done for the currently presenting patient with the knowledge available, it is essential also that the advancement of knowledge be always kept in mind so that in treating future patients, forward steps, however small, will have been made. Within the general framework of the definition of behavior therapy as the application of the experimental method to the study of the single case, this means that the treated patient must not only be treated as effectively as possible, but *that the treatment should be carried out in such a way that the next patient to be treated will benefit from*

the results. As an example of the failure to follow such a precept, we may refer again to the use of insulin treatment in the treatment of schizophrenia where probably millions of patients were subjected to a dangerous and unpleasant form of treatment while the opportunity to assess whether the treatment was effective by the use of untreated control groups in a properly designed experiment was denied on the grounds that it was unethical to deny treatment to patients.

The genuine ethical problems in behavior therapy have been considered carefully in a justly famous dialogue between Rogers and Skinner (1956), while more recent papers have discussed the ethics of behavior therapy more specifically (Kanfer, 1965; Krasner, 1965; Lomont, 1964; Ulrich, 1967). Essentially, the issue revolves around the increasing potential for the control of behavior and its possible misuse by behavioral psychologists or by unscrupulous nonpsychologists. The problem is a real one, but it will be argued here that it has been too often posed as if it were a unique problem, that is, a dichotomous division is made between the issue of "control" versus "freedom." It will be shown that the distinction is a false one.[10]

The slightest reflection reveals, of course, that the essence of civilized society lies in the restriction of complete freedom to do as one wishes. Furthermore, control over behavior is exercised by all civilized persons, often without any questioning of the essence of the control. A number of very simple examples will suffice to illustrate the point. Let us suppose, for example, that an individual perceives a two-year-old child crossing a busy highway. Would anyone argue that this activity is not to be interfered with on the grounds that the child must be free to discover that death is the most likely result? Or would anyone refuse to stop the same child from drinking a bottle of poison on similar grounds? The questions have only to be asked for the answer to be apparent. At a slightly less obvious level, it is taken for granted by all parents that their children *must* be taught to speak the language of their parents. No parent ever gives his child a choice as to whether he will learn to speak the parental language or not. Indeed, as we have seen, should the child show signs of not developing any language at all, he is hurried off to the child guidance clinic,

[10] What follows is based on part of an unpublished inaugural address given at the University of New England in 1966.

without being given the choice of not speaking. It is obvious that most children would often prefer not to go to school, yet severe penalties are imposed on parents and child if this is allowed to happen regularly without adequate reason. Most parents go to great pains to indoctrinate their children in religious or, at least, moral principles. At a still higher level, there are countless people incarcerated against their will in mental hospitals and prisons. Indeed, the entire legal system of civilized countries is devoted to defining the limits of personal freedom.

Thus, control of behavior is a daily fact of life and it could be argued that social behavior in general involves mutual control of behavior. Hence, to argue that behavior therapy techniques involve something new is absurd.

There is, however, a very real problem here that is often obscured by the false presentation of the problem as "freedom" versus "enslavement." Control of behavior is a fact of civilized life. But such control at present is very frequently based on quite irrational considerations. Thus, for example, there is no good evidence whatsoever that imprisoning a person for ten or 20 years is other than a primitive action without any remedial or deterrent effects of any kind in most instances. The behavior therapist argues that, if control of behavior is regarded by society as essential in certain cases for the good of society as a whole (as indeed seems to be the case), then at least that control should, as far as possible, be based on rational rather than irrational considerations. The task of the behavioral scientist, then, is to investigate behavior so that the knowledge gained may be applied to the control of behavior in a rational way.

This brings us to the core of the problem, which is the question: who should be authorized to use and apply the knowledge so gained? Here again the answer is quite straightforward. It is essential to distinguish between *knowledge* and the *application of knowledge*. The present author would entirely agree with the proposition that *the psychologist who produces the knowledge of how behavior may be controlled is not necessarily the most competent or appropriate person to decide whether that knowledge should be applied in particular instances.*

This proposition is already accepted fully in other areas of vital concern. Thus, the physicist who knows precisely what will happen if an atom bomb is dropped on a city of 100,000 people is not regarded as necessarily being the person best qualified to decide whether it should be dropped or not. The economist who indicates the effect on the economy of increasing pensions by 20% is not necessarily the person who decides whether pensions will be increased or not. This is so because *each of these decisions has wider implications for society.* Thus, society is entitled to have its say in determining whether a particular action with social implications should or should not be taken.[11] A precisely similar line may be taken in relation to the discoveries made by psychologists. A final example, absurd at present but not necessarily so in principle, will illustrate the point. Suppose knowledge of human behavior had advanced to the point at which, by the use of appropriate tests, it was possible to assert with absolute certainty that a particular child, if not treated in a particular way, would commit murder as an adult but that treatment along certain lines would equally well prevent this event. Would it be unethical for society to subject the individual to compulsory treatment on the grounds that it would interfere with his freedom? Or would it be ethical to submit him to such treatment on the grounds that not to treat him would ultimately interfere with someone else's freedom to stay alive? And who would make the decision? In the present writer's view, the decision would be one which would have to be made by society, not by the psychologist who proffered the empirical facts, though society would no doubt take into account the expert's views.

One further distinction needs to be made here. It is apparently feared that increased knowledge of the factors determining behavior will lead to increased ability to control behavior. However, this fear is dependent on a false correlation of knowledge with control capacity. Let us suppose that a theoretical account of behavior was available as complete as the present theoretical account presented by physics of the inanimate world.[12] Let us suppose further that we have used this system to investigate and control in the laboratory the entire behavior of a single individual. Does this imply that we can now control his behavior perfectly? The answer, of course, is in the negative. No physicist, however

---

[11] One curious exception, which does not appear to have been adequately examined, is, of course, the field of medicine.

[12] Actually, if the history of physics is any guide, such a complete theoretical system will remain an unobtainable goal.

elaborate the system at his disposal, would claim that he could predict the behavior of a single snowflake in a snowstorm as it is occurring. The reason is simply that *perfect scientific control is possible, even in principle, only under very restricted conditions.* Similarly, in the case of humans, it might some day be possible to predict human behavior perfectly under highly controlled conditions. As soon as the subject steps outside the laboratory, however, his behavior becomes subject to so many variables, not all of which could ever be controlled, that perfect prediction is no longer possible.

It is maintained, therefore, that the ethical problem in relation to behavior therapy is no different in principle from other problems relating to actions that affect the individual in society. The psychologist, in so far as he offers *advice* as opposed to *facts*, is entitled to his opinion. But his *opinion* as to what action should be taken in the light of the facts is not necessarily superior to the judgment of a group of experienced and wise laymen making a decision that must be related to society as a whole.

REFERENCES

Allchin, W.H. Behavior therapy. *Brit. J. Psychiat.*, 1964, **110**, 108.

Arthur, A.Z. Behavior therapy versus psychotherapy and applied science. *Canad. Psychol.*, 1967, **8**, 105–113.

Ayllon, T., Haughton, E., & Hughes, H.B. Interpretation of symptoms: fact or fiction? *Behav. Res. Ther.*, 1965, **3**, 1–7.

Barrett-Lennard, G.T. Professional psychology and the control of human behavior. *Aust. J. Psychol.*, 1965, **17**, 24–34.

Bergin, A.E. Some implications of psychotherapy research. *J. abnorm. Psychol.*, 1966, **71**, 235–246.

Bookbinder, L.J. Simple conditioning versus the dynamic approach to symptoms and symptom substitution: A reply to Yates. *Psychol. Rep.*, 1962, **10**, 71–77.

Brady, J.P. Psychotherapy, learning theory, and insight. *Arch. gen. Psychiat.*, 1967, **16**, 304–311.

Breger, L. & McGaugh, J.L. Critique and reformulation of "learning-theory" approaches to psychotherapy and neurosis. *Psychol. Bull.*, 1965, **63**, 338–358.

Breger, L. & McGaugh, J.L. Learning theory and behavior therapy: A reply to Rachman and Eysenck. *Psychol. Bull.*, 1966, **65**, 170–173.

Cahoon, D.D. Symptom substitution and the behavior therapies: reappraisal. *Psychol. Bull.*, 1968, **69**, 149–156.

Cautela, J. Hypnosis and behavior therapy. *Behav. Res. Ther.*, 1966, **4**, 219–224.

Chomsky, N. Review of B.F. Skinner, *Verbal behavior. Language*, 1959, **35**, 26–58.

Coates, S. Clinical psychology in sexual deviation. In I. Rosen (ed.). *The pathology and treatment of sexual deviation.* London: Oxford Univer. Press, 1964, pp. 381–415.

Costello, C.G. Behavior therapy: criticisms and confusions. *Behav. Res. Ther.*, 1963, **1**, 159–161.

Costello, C.G. The problem of extinction in operant therapy. *Canad. Psychol.*, 1967, **8**, 85–89.

Crisp, A.H. "Transference," "symptom emergence," and "social repercussion" in behavior therapy: A study of fifty-four treated patients. *Brit. J. med. Psychol.*, 1966, **39**, 179–196.

Dollard, J. & Miller, N.E. *Personality and psychotherapy.* New York: McGraw-Hill, 1950.

Eysenck, H.J. Learning theory and behavior therapy. *J. ment. Sci.*, 1959, **105**, 61–75.

Eysenck, H.J. *Behavior therapy and the neuroses.* London: Pergamon, 1960.

Eysenck, H.J. Behavior therapy, spontaneous remissions, and transference in neurotics. *Amer. J. Psychiat.*, 1963, **119**, 867–871.

Eysenck, H.J. *Experiments in behavior therapy.* London: Pergamon, 1964.

Eysenck, H.J. & Rachman, S. *The causes and cures of neurosis.* London: Routledge and Kegan Paul, 1965.

Gibson, J.J. The concept of the stimulus in psychology. *Amer. Psychol.*, 1960, **15**, 694–703.

Glover, E. Critical notice of Wolpe's "Psychotherapy by reciprocal inhibition." *Brit. J med. Psychol.*, 1959, **32**, 68–74 (a).

Glover, E. Psychotherapy by reciprocal inhibition: a comment on Dr. Wolpe's reply. *Brit. J. med. Psychol.*, 1959, **32**, 236–238 (b).

Goldiamond, I., Dyrud, J., & Miller, M.D. Practice as research in professional psychology. *Canad. Psychol.*, 1965, **6a**, 110–128.

Goodkin, R. Some neglected issues in the literature on behavior therapy. *Psychol. Rep.*, 1967, **20**, 415–420.

Holden, H.M. Behavior and aversion therapy in the treatment of delinquency: III. Should aversion and behavior therapy be used in the treatment of delinquency? *Brit. J. Criminol.*, 1965, **5**, 377–387.

Kanfer, F.H. Comments on learning in psychotherapy. *Psychol. Rep.*, 1961, **9**, 681–699 (Monogr. Suppl. 6-V9).

Kanfer, F.H. Issues and ethics in behavior manipulation. *Psychol. Rep.*, 1965, **16**, 187–196.

Kanner, L. Do behavioral symptoms always indicate psychopathology? *J. Child Psychol. Psychiat.*, 1960, **1**, 17–25.

Katahn, M. & Koplin, J.H. Paradigm clash: comment on "Some recent criticisms of behaviorism and learning theory with special reference to Breger and McGaugh and to Chomsky." *Psychol. Bull.*, 1968, **69**, 147–148.

Kiesler, D.J. Some myths of psychotherapy research and the search for a paradigm. *Psychol. Bull.*, 1966, **65**, 110–136.

Kraft, T. & Al-Issa, I. Behavior therapy and the recall of traumatic experience—a case study. *Behav. Res. Ther.*, 1965, **3**, 55–58.

Krasner, L. The therapist as a social reinforcement machine. In Strupp, H.H. (ed.). *Second research conference on psychotherapy*. Chapel Hill, N.C.: American Psychological Association, 1961.

Krasner, L. The behavioral scientist and social responsibility: no place to hide. *J. soc. Issues*, 1965, **21**, 9–30.

Kuhn, T.S. *The structure of scientific revolutions*. Chicago: Univer. Chicago Press, 1962.

Lazarus, A.A. Behavior therapy, incomplete treatment, and symptom substitution. *J. nerv. ment. Dis.*, 1965, **140**, 80–86.

Lomont, J.F. Ethics of behavior therapy. *Psychol. Rep.*, 1964, **14**, 519–531.

Marks, I.M. & Gelder, M.G. Common ground between behavior therapy and psychodynamic methods. *Brit. J. med. Psychol.*, 1966, **39**, 11–23.

Meyer, V. & Crisp, A.H. Some problems in behavior therapy. *Brit. J. Psychiat.*, 1966, **112**, 367–381.

Murray, E.J. Learning theory and psychotherapy: biotropic versus sociotropic approaches. *J. counsel. Psychol.*, 1963, **10**, 250–255.

Oswald, I. Induction of illusory and hallucinatory voices with consideration of behavior therapy. *J. ment. Sci.*, 1962, **108**, 196–212.

Phillips, E.L. & El-Batrawi, S. Learning theory and psychotherapy revisited: with notes on illustrative cases. *Psychotherapy*, 1964, **1**, 145–150.

Rachman, S. & Eysenck, H.J. Reply to a "critique and reformulation" of behavior therapy. *Psychol. Bull.*, 1966, **65**, 165–169.

Rogers, C.R. & Skinner, B.F. Some issues concerning the control of human behavior. *Science*, 1956, **124**, 1057–1066.

Shoben, E.J. The therapeutic object: men or machines. *J. counsel. Psychol.*, 1963, **10**, 264–268.

Skinner, B.F. *Verbal behavior*. New York: Appleton-Century-Crofts, 1957.

Spence, K.W. *Behavior theory and conditioning*. New Haven: Yale Univer. Press, 1956.

Ulrich, R. Behavior control and public concern. *Psychol. Rec.*, 1967, **17**, 229–234.

Walters, R.H. Discussion of "Growth of behavior therapies with children" by Leonard Krasner. *Canad. Psychol.*, 1967, **8**, 76–80.

Weitzman, B. Behavior therapy and psychotherapy. *Psychol. Rev.*, 1967, **74**, 300–317.

Wiest, W.M. Some recent criticisms of behaviorism and learning theory with special reference to Breger and McGaugh and to Chomsky. *Psychol. Bull.*, 1967, **67**, 214–225.

Williams, C.D. The elimination of tantrum behavior by extinction procedures. *J. abnorm. soc. Psychol.*, 1959, **59**, 269.

Wolpe, J. *Psychotherapy by reciprocal inhibition.* Stanford: Stanford Univer. Press, 1958.

Wolpe, J. Psychotherapy by reciprocal inhibition: A reply to Dr. Glover. *Brit. J. med. Psychol.*, 1959, **32**, 232–235.

Wolpe, J., Salter, A., & Reyna, L.J. *The conditioning therapies.* New York: Holt, 1964.

Yates, A.J. Symptoms and symptom substitution. *Psychol. Rev.*, 1958, **55**, 371–374 (a).

Yates, A.J. The application of learning theory to the treatment of tics. *J. abnorm. soc. Psychol.*, 1958, **56**, 175–182 (b).

Yates, A.J. A comment on Bookbinder's critique of "Symptoms and symptom substitution." *Psychol. Rep.*, 1962, **11**, 102.

Chapter 20

Future Trends

ANY ATTEMPT to assess the direction that developments in behavior therapy may take over the next decade is bound to involve personal prejudices and preferences. The following discussion therefore represents some of the considerations that have most struck the present author while writing the previous chapters. Interestingly enough, it will be seen that a great deal of stress is laid on the development of more complex models for human behavior, with particular stress on internal mediational processes. It has been repeatedly emphasized in previous chapters that behavior therapists are not peripheralists and have no objection to the use of mediational constructs provided these can be tied to antecedents and consequents or, indeed, measured directly.

I. FROM LABORATORY CONTROL TO ENVIRONMENTAL CONTROL

The definition of behavior therapy adopted in this book has stressed the necessity for the systematic investigation of a particular abnormality of behavior under controlled experimental conditions and the controlled manipulation of the maladaptive behavior so that it is replaced by adaptive behavior. The tendency among behavior therapists has been to exercise such control by bringing the patient into the laboratory and investigating his behavior there. It is now clear, however, that the establishment of control of behavior under such conditions may not only generalize imperfectly to situations beyond the laboratory but that, in fact, the

patient may learn to discriminate between the laboratory and the real-life situation. The former will contain only a small range of the environmental stimuli that control the maladaptive behavior in its natural setting. The problem is not merely one relating to the degree of generalization from laboratory to real life, but rather may involve successive modification of the laboratory conditions so that environmental, real-life stimuli are progressively introduced.

To illustrate the point, we may return again to the study by Yates (1958) on the application of massed practice to the treatment of tics. It is true that, in the laboratory situation, the ability of the patient to reproduce the tics was very markedly reduced; it is also true that this reduction generalized to some degree to the real-life situation (according to the patient's verbal report: no actual measurements were made). The question of how to generalize the laboratory effects more powerfully to the real-life situation was considered carefully by the author[1] at the time. One possible solution to the problem would have been to require the patient to indulge in massed practice in those social situations in which the tics were most strongly manifested (restaurants, buses, interview situations, and so on). In addition to the practical difficulties involved in such a procedure, however, it was clear that adverse consequences might well ensue, due to the possible degree of embarrassment that might be caused. An alternative solution was proposed (but not carried out) along the following lines. The

---

[1] These considerations were not, however, discussed in the article.

common feature of the social situations which increased the frequency and strength of the tics was the presence of other persons. It would, therefore, be desirable to continue the massed practice sessions in the laboratory while introducing more and more observers into the situation. These observers would at first be neutral or sympathetic in their reaction to observation of the patient performing the tics, but would gradually change in the direction of greater hostility and ridicule of the kind met with by the patient in real social situations. In this way, it might be expected that the sI_R generated would become more strongly attached to social situations. This experiment was unfortunately never carried out but remains an interesting possible approach.

As we have seen in an earlier chapter, however, Goldiamond (1965a), in controlling stuttering by reinforcement contingencies, did in fact gradually move from a strict laboratory setting to settings that involved greater and greater approximations to real-life situations involving speech (that is, verbal interactions with other persons) with very considerable success. It may, in fact, be desirable to program the environment of the patient to bring his behavior under real-life control.

The extreme form of environmental control would involve treating the social situation as one which requires control, in which case the social situation becomes the laboratory itself. As we have seen, this approach has been particularly favored by those psychologists who use operant conditioning techniques. It should not, of course, be supposed that laboratory control is ineffective in producing transfer to the real-life situation. Wolpe's procedures, using SD(I), are largely predicated on the assumption that generalization to the real-life situation will take place, an assumption which appears to be fully justified in many instances; and there is experimental support for it (Rachman, 1966). A recent study by Brodsky (1967) indicated some of the limitations of the assumption, however. He found that a positive change in *nonverbal* social behavior produced in a structured setting by operant techniques did indeed generalize to *verbal* behavior in a natural setting, but that a similar increase in verbal statements relating to social behavior in an interview setting similarly produced did not generalize to nonverbal behavior in a natural

setting. It would appear in general to be the case that, while circumscribed control of behavior under strictly controlled conditions is fully justifiable in the initial stages of treatment, at least for some disorders of behavior, behavior therapy must, as soon as possible, move toward the extension of that control in natural settings. The institution of token economies in mental hospital wards represents a major achievement; equally important, however, is the question of advancing beyond this stage to the reproduction and maintenance of adaptive behaviors when the patient is released from the hospital (Agras, 1967), and this may involve manipulation of the behavior of the patient's relatives, friends, and so on.[2]

II. FROM EXTERNAL CONTROL TO INTERNAL (SELF) CONTROL

A striking feature of many of the techniques of behavior therapy (particularly the operant conditioning procedures) is the degree of reliance on external control of the patient's behavior. However, it is quite clear that, while the normal subject's behavior is very frequently under the control of such agencies, a great deal of normal behavior is under internalized control and independent of external rewards and punishments. Indeed, it could be argued that the very essence of a socialized person is his independence of external control. Thus, the law-abiding person certainly does not steal or exceed the speed limit if a policeman is standing by; but it is also true that he is unlikely to steal or exceed the speed limit even when there is no possibility of his being caught and punished. The control of his behavior has been internalized. A major problem for behavior therapists is how to progress from external control of behavior to the point at which the subject controls his own behavior in an adaptive fashion. The problem is not a new one, and a great deal of research has been carried out relating to how this transfer is achieved in children. Here we shall concern ourselves with several aspects of the problem which seem to be of particular relevance for behavior therapy.

1. VICARIOUS LEARNING, PERFORMANCE, AND EXTINCTION THROUGH MODELING

Of particular significance for behavior therapists is the long series of studies on

---

[2] An analogous development in psychotherapy is the move toward milieu therapy in which the patient is treated in his family setting.

vicarious learning by Bandura and his col-leagues.[3] Bandura's achievement essentially has been to show that learning may take place in the absence of opportunity to perform the responses acquired by observation of a model who indulges in the behavior. The behavior ex-hibited by the model (which may involve novel responses unlikely to be in the child's reper-toire) may then be spontaneously reproduced under appropriate circumstances at a later date, even though the model may be absent.

The early studies[4] of vicarious learning involved the transmission of aggressive be-havior through the observation of aggressive behavior by models. Thus, Bandura, Ross, and Ross (1961) subjected preschool children to one of three experimental conditions: observation of male or female aggressive adult models; observation of male or female nonaggressive adult models; and a control condition involving no exposure to model behavior. In this experi-ment the model performed in a real situation. The children were tested for imitation of the aggressive behavior in a similar situation at a later date in the absence of the model. It should also be noted that the aggressive responses were relatively novel responses, that is, the imitation did not merely involve the release of responses already in the child's repertoire. It was found that imitative aggression occurred to a signifi-cantly greater degree in the children exposed to the aggressive model than in the children in the other two groups. The aggressive behavior frequently matched that of the model very closely indeed, both verbally and nonverbally. In two subsequent studies (Bandura, Ross, and Ross, 1963a, 1963b) it was demonstrated that film-mediated aggression (where the model's behavior was portrayed on film rather than in a real-life situation) also produced vicarious learning as measured by subsequent real-life aggressive behavior of the child. It was noted that the children who imitated the behavior of the model often disapproved of the model's behavior verbally, indicating that the success of the model in achieving his aims might be an important factor in producing imitation of the behavior. The fact that expressive behavior that achieved the same result (possession of the objects of aggression) was also imitated sup-ported this finding (Bandura and Huston, 1961).

Subsequent studies have shown that the same techniques may be used to produce vicarious learning of syntactic style (Bandura and Harris, 1966) and moral judgments (Bandura and McDonald, 1963). More recently, the acquisition of vicarious affective arousal has been demon-strated. In a study by Bandura and Rosenthal (1966), a model feigned reaction to shock in a classical conditioning situation with a buzzer as the CS, and GSR as the CR. The subject watched the "conditioning" of the model while his (the subject's) GSR was concomitantly measured during "acquisition," "test" (CS only), and "extinction" trials. Five groups of observers, each with different induced levels of arousal, were used; and it was found that vicarious affective conditioning took place and was related to level of induced activation. The results are shown in Figure 1. Similar results were obtained by Craig and Weinstein (1965) who showed that observation of failure in the model was sufficient to induce vicarious affective arousal.[5]

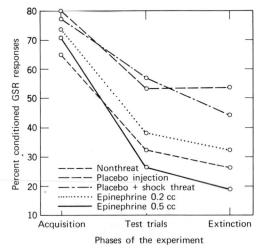

FIG. 1. Mean percentage conditioned GSR re-sponses exhibited by subjects on each of three test periods for each of five treatment conditions representing differential levels of arousal (Bandura and Rosenthal, 1966).

Variables determining the degree to which imitative behavior will be acquired through vicarious learning have been extensively investigated by Bandura and his colleagues. While it is true, for example, that such imitation will occur even if the model is not reinforced or punished directly (Bandura, Ross, and Ross, 1963a), a rewarded aggressive model will induce more imitative learning than a punished aggressive model (Bandura, Ross, and Ross, 1963b). There is usually found to be an interaction between sex of the model and sex of the child (boys will be more influenced by a male model than will girls, but the reverse may not be the case) (Bandura, Ross, and Ross, 1961). It has also been shown that children will imitate a model who controls positive reinforcers in preference to a model who does not (Bandura, Ross, and Ross, 1963c). Other variables studied include the effects of prior nurturant or non-nurturant interaction between model and child (Bandura and Huston, 1961) and the effects of prior success or failure by the child (Bandura and Whalen, 1966).

Bandura, Grusec, and Menlove (1966) tested the theory that implicit symbolization (symbolic matching responses) possess cue-producing properties which are the crucial variables in later elicitation of matching responses. To test the theory, one group of children was exposed to the filmed behavior of models (other children) while engaging in compatible verbal behavior (describing the activities of the model); a second group engaged in competing verbalization (counting); and a third (control) group watched the film passively. The first group indulged in a larger amount of subsequent imitative behavior.

It will be recalled that more matching responses were emitted by children who watched a rewarded as compared with a punished model. Bandura (1965a) examined the question whether the latter children *learned* the matching behavior but did not *perform* it. When the lesser-imitating children (who had watched the punished model) were subsequently offered a reward for producing matching responses, the differences between the groups disappeared, verifying the hypothesis. Grusec and Mischel (1966), however, were able to demonstrate that characteristics of the model could also influence learning as well as performance. Children who

had interacted with a highly rewarding adult model with control over their future resources reproduced significantly more of the model's behavior than children who had interacted with a nonrewarding adult model without control over their future resources, even though both groups were offered rewards for reproducing the model's behavior.

These studies appear to demonstrate unequivocally that vicarious learning may occur, even in the absence of vicarious reinforcement. Bandura (1965b) was led by the results to introduce a most important distinction. He pointed out that operant conditioning procedures based on contingent reinforcement are dependent for their efficacy on the response that is to be strengthened being emitted, at least in some form that approximates to a greater or lesser degree the final form that it is to take. If, however, the required response is not at all in the repertoire of the subject, then operant conditioning procedures are unlikely to be successful. He argued therefore that, while reinforcement procedures might be most appropriate for changing the habit strength of responses already available to the subject, modeling procedures are likely to be most effective in cases where the required response is a completely novel one. While this distinction has very significant implications for behavior therapy,[6] a number of qualifications are in order. First, as we have already seen,[7] it is not in fact *necessary* for the response to be in the patient's repertoire for operant procedures to be successful (treatment of mute catatonics by successive approximation techniques). Second, most modeling procedures do appear to involve a combination of modeling and reinforcement of the model. Third, there seems little doubt that modeling procedures are most unlikely to work in certain situations in which they should theoretically be successful: for example, the reinstatement of speech in mute catatonics.[8] Nevertheless, the importance of the distinction cannot be gainsaid and was well illustrated in the study of Bandura and McDonald (1963), already referred to. They divided children into "subjective" and "objective" responders in terms of the kinds of answers given to requests to judge the moral gravity of a deviant act. "Subjective" responders judged gravity in terms

----

[6] For example, reading retardation based on poor attention (inefficient eye movements, etc.) would be expected to yield to operant procedures and retardation due to inability to make perceptual discriminations might yield to modeling procedures.

[7] See Chapter 14.
[8] It might, of course, be argued here that the verbal behavior is in the repertoire of the mute catatonic but is inhibited.

of the amount of material damage involved and ignored the intentionality of the act; "objective" responders did the reverse. Children falling into each of these categories were allocated to one of three treatment groups. In one group, a model produced judgments of the kind opposite to those characteristically produced by the child who was rewarded if he matched the model's response. In the second group, the same procedure was followed, except that the child was not reinforced for producing a matching response. In the third group (operant procedure), no model was present but the child was reinforced every time he produced a response opposite to that of his dominant tendency. The results of the experiments are shown in Figure 2 (percentage of objective judgments produced by subjective children under the three experimental conditions) and Figure 3 (percentage of subjective judgments produced by objective children). It is clear that the operant reinforcement technique produced significantly less change in performance than the two modeling techniques which did not differ markedly from each other. Examination of the data revealed that, in the operant condition, the children did not produce very many contrary responses and hence received little or no reinforcements.

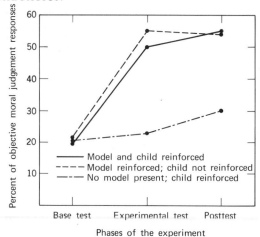

FIG. 3. Mean percentage of objective moral judgment responses produced by subjective children on each of the three test periods for each of three conditions (Bandura and McDonald, 1963).

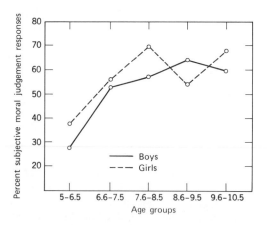

FIG. 2. Mean percentage of subjective moral judgment responses produced by boys and girls at different age levels (Bandura and McDonald, 1963).

As we saw in a previous chapter, early studies of the elimination of fears in children utilised a wide range of techniques, of which the two most successful were direct conditioning and social imitation (Jones, 1924). The latter technique was essentially a modeling technique, in that the fearful subject watched a fearless subject interacting with the object of

fear. Recently, Bandura and his colleagues have reported the results of several systematic experiments that explore the role of modeling in reducing phobias. In the first of these, Bandura, Grusec, and Menlove (1967a) assigned children with three levels of fear of dogs (assessed by a real-life test) to one of four treatment groups: *modeling-positive-context*, in which the children observed a fearless model interact increasingly with the feared animal, while a party atmosphere was maintained; *modeling-neutral-context*, which was similar to the first treatment, except that the party atmosphere was omitted; *exposure-positive*, in which the animal was present in a party atmosphere, but no model was present; and *positive-context*, which involved a party atmosphere in the absence of either dog or model. Post treatment, immediate, and one-month follow-up real-life assessments measured degree of fear manifested toward the original dog and an unfamiliar dog (generalization of fear-reduction). The results, as shown in Figure 4, showed that the two modeling conditions were equally efficacious in reducing real-life fear and that these gains were maintained at follow-up. The two control conditions produced significantly less change. Of the children in the modeling groups, 67% of the children remained alone in the playpen (confined space) with the dog following treatment; of the control groups, only 32% remained alone in the playpen.

Bandura and Menlove (1968) carried out a similar experiment which investigated the relative efficacy of three treatment conditions in

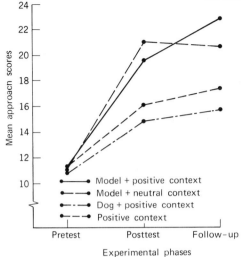

FIG. 4. Mean approach scores achieved by children in each of the treatment conditions on the three different periods of assessment (Bandura, Grusec, and Menlove, 1967a).

reducing fear of dogs in children: *single-model*, in which a five-year-old fearless model interacted progressively with the original feared dog; *multiple-model*, in which several models interacted with several dogs of varying sizes; and a control condition. This study involved film-mediated modeling as opposed to real-life modeling in the earlier study. The control children watched Disneyland films. Both symbolic modeling conditions resulted in a significant increase in real-life approach behavior which was maintained at one-month follow-up. The control group which showed no change in approach behavior was subsequently subjected to the multiple-model treatment condition, after which performance equalled that of the treated groups. There was no difference between the effectiveness of the single and multiple model conditions in reducing fear and the film-mediated modeling appeared to be as effective as the real-life modeling.

Ritter (1968) extended these results by showing the importance of a new technique called contact desensitization. This involves the model first handling the feared object and then the child vicariously handling the same object by placing his hand over that of the model while the model handles the feared object. This technique was contrasted with vicarious desensitization (which is the modeling technique used in the earlier studies) and a test-retest control condition. Contact desensitization was found to be significantly superior to the vicarious condition, and both of these were superior to the control condition, the latter producing no change in the strength of fear.

Bandura, Blanchard, and Ritter,[9] working with adolescents with a fear of snakes, have compared the relative efficacy of four techniques: *self-regulated symbolic modeling*, in which the subject views a film-mediated fearless model and is able to regulate the progress of the film so that anxiety is reduced to zero at each stage of interaction between the model and the snake; *contact-desensitization*, as described above; *Wolpe's SD(I) procedure* with deep relaxation; and a *no-treatment control condition*. The results indicated that all treatments except the control effected substantial fear-reduction, and that the most powerful treatment was contact desensitization. Separate measures of expressed fear and behavior were taken; the SD(I) group experienced less reduction in fear than the modeling groups.

The precise relationship, the degree of overlap between the modeling procedures used by Bandura and his colleagues, and the systematic desensitization techniques—both SD(I) and SD(R) of Wolpe—remain to be elucidated. Certainly, however, as Bandura points out, the modeling procedures provide not only a powerful but a most economical means of eliminating common fears and, of course, may well turn out to be applicable to many other disorders of behavior. It may be added here that independent confirmation of the efficacy of modeling procedures in reducing fear (in this case, of snakes) has recently been provided by Geer and Turteltaub (1967). Students with high fear of snakes observed a fearless model through a one-way vision screen, and a very significant increase in approach behavior was noted on a subsequent real-life test. The two important points to note are that only one modeling session was given, and the posttreatment real-life test was instituted immediately after the modeling session. Geer and Turteltaub also investigated the effects on high and low fear subjects of observing a model manifesting a high degree of fear toward the snake.[10] This condition did not produce a significant increase in fear in the high fear subjects.

----

[9] Reported in Bandura (1968).

[10] The observer did not know the high fear model was feigning fearfulness; while the model did not know whether high or low fear subjects were observing him.

We may conclude by observing that Bandura's techniques of modeling appear to hold exceptionally high promise for therapeutic purposes and that the relative neglect of his work on modeling by behavior therapists is completely unjustified.

2. THE ESTABLISHMENT OF SELF-REINFORCING BEHAVIOR

It has been pointed out that observers will reproduce the behavior of models on a subsequent occasion in the absence of the models. As Bandura and Kupers (1964) point out:

". . . people typically make self-reinforcement contingent on their performing certain classes of responses which they have come to value as an index of personal merit. They often set themselves relatively explicit criteria of achievement, failure to meet which is considered undeserving of self-reward and may elicit self-denial or even self-punitive responses; on the other hand, they tend to reward themselves generously on those occasions when they attain their self-imposed standards" (Bandura and Kupers, 1964, p. 1).

Self-reinforcing behavior may be acquired on the basis of direct, external reinforcements administered by agents who reward the subject for achieving the criterion set. The subject may then receive secondary reinforcement when he achieves these criteria in the absence of the external agent. On the other hand, self-reinforcement schedules may be adopted as a result of observing a model who sets a standard and reinforces himself only when that standard is achieved.

A series of studies by Bandura and his colleagues has investigated the latter phenomenon in some detail. In the first study, Bandura and Kupers (1964) used a miniature bowling alley situation in which the score achieved by the subject could be controlled by the experimenter without the subject's knowledge. The subjects observed a male or female adult or child model who reinforced himself with candy. In one situation, the model reinforced himself only if he surpassed a severe criterion score; in the other, if he surpassed a lenient criterion. The subject then practiced the same task alone and his scores were manipulated. The amount of candy taken was recorded together with the concomitant score. The results for the conditions involving an adult model[11] are shown in Figure 5. Patterns and magnitude of self-reinforcement closely matched those of the model to which the child was exposed. Compared with the control subjects (who were not exposed to any model), the experimental subjects rewarded themselves much less frequently at levels below the criterion for self-reinforcement set by the model, indicating that self-denial (or inhibition of reinforcement) was acquired.

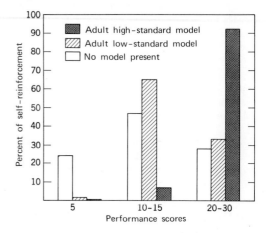

FIG. 5. The distribution of self-reinforcement as a function of performance level by control children and those exposed to adult models adopting high and low criteria for self-reinforcement (Bandura and Kupers, 1964).

The remaining studies to be discussed here amplify and qualify this initial result. Bandura and Whalen (1966) investigated the effects of preexposure success and failure in relation to exposure to a model who either adopted a severe self-reinforcement criterion but who performed better than the subject, or who adopted a more lenient criterion for self-reinforcement but performed at about the same level as the child.[12] The effects of prior success and failure were complex, but it was found that children exposed to the model doing better than they were rejected the self-reinforcement criteria set by the model and adopted a more lenient criterion for reinforcing themselves; whereas children exposed to a model performing at about the same level as they did adopted a higher level of self-reinforcement.

---

[11] The results for the child model were similar.

[12] It will be remembered that performance levels were under the control of the experimenter.

Bandura and Perloff (1967) compared self-imposed and externally imposed reinforcement schedules. One group of children were allowed to set their own performance level and rewarded themselves whenever they reached it; a yoked experimental group was rewarded automatically whenever they reached the performance level of the paired child (the task here involved cranking a handle to produce a visual score). An incentive control group was given token noncontingent reward, and a second control group set its own standard but received no reinforcement. It was found that self-imposed and externally-imposed reinforcement procedures produced equally good performance on the task.

Finally, Bandura, Grusec, and Menlove (1967b) investigated the effect of models who were nurturant or nonnurturant toward the subjects prior to the experiment; who set a high self-reinforcement standard in the presence or absence of a low-standard self-reinforcing peer; and who were rewarded or not with social (experimenter) approval at the end of the performance. The most austere standard of self-reinforcement was set by those children who had no preexperimental nurturant interaction with the model, whose model had no peer competition, and whose model was rewarded. An interesting finding was that nurturance produced less matching of model self-reinforcement standards than nonnurturance, that is, that nurturance does not lead to identification but to self-indulgence and the setting of less severe standards.

Thus, these studies by Bandura and his colleagues show that subjects will adopt self-reinforcement criteria which they observe models adopting but that the matching is complicated by a number of important factors. These studies involve vicarious, not direct reinforcement of behavior and may be contrasted with studies by Kanfer and Martson which show that self-reinforcement standards may be influenced by direct reinforcement administered by an external agent.

Kanfer, Bradley, and Marston (1962) define self control as:

"a process in which S has always available a reinforcing stimulus but administers it only when reinforcement is appropriate to his own behavior" (Kanfer, Bradley and Marston, 1962, p. 885).

They predicted and confirmed that the frequency of appropriate self-reinforcement would increase as a discriminative task was learned.

Marston and Kanfer (1963) trained their subjects to a criterion on a verbal discrimination task with external reinforcement for each correct response and then allowed the subject to dispense a self-reinforcement whenever, in subsequent trials, he was confident he had emitted a correct response. Although, in the subsequent trials, the self-reinforcement group did not perform as well as the external reinforcement group, it did perform better than a control group given neither self-reinforcement nor external reinforcement, indicating that self-reinforcement may increase resistance to extinction.

In both of these studies, the effects of self-reinforcement training were confounded with the effects of task training, but subsequent studies overcame this difficulty. Kanfer and Marston (1963a) trained their subjects to emit self-reinforcements at high or low rates in a situation (pseudo-perceptual task) where learning was not involved. They were then trained on a learning task with external reinforcement to a low criterion of success. One group was then placed on an extinction schedule while the other group rewarded itself for responses felt to be correct. It was found that the group originally trained to emit a high rate of self-reinforcement reinforced themselves significantly more often than the group originally trained to emit a low rate of self-reinforcement. Kanfer and Marston (1963b) investigated the frequency and accuracy of self-reinforcement responses as a function of three factors: the stage of prior learning reached; instructions about the stringency of criteria to be adopted for self-reinforcement; and the similarity of discriminative and reinforcing stimuli in acquisition training and test for self-reinforcement. They found that learning to a higher criterion produced more frequent and more accurate self-reinforcements; more lenient criteria for self-reinforcement produced more frequent but less accurate self-reinforcements; and when the test list differed from the acquisition list, self-reinforcements were fewer but also were less accurate. Marston (1964b) made one of the few attempts to relate self-reinforcement rate during learning to personality factors but without any notable success. On the other hand, Marston (1964a) found that self-reinforcement rate was uninfluenced by the nature of the self-reinforcement obtained. In this study, a link with Bandura's work was obtained, since Marston showed that self-reinforcement rate was increased if the response required agreed with that made by a model. In a later study, Marston (1965) investigated performance on a word association task where the self-reinforcement was saying "good" when the subject thought he had given the most common association. Rate of self-reinforcement was related to the observation of the performance of a model who performed the same task while the subject either did not respond himself, responded but without administering self-reinforcements, or responded with self-reinforcements. The performance of the model was found to influence the self-reinforcement rate significantly whether the subject observed passively on the one hand or participated actively (with or without self-reinforcement).

Since Bandura and Kupers (1964) do not deny the role of external reinforcement in influencing frequency of self-reinforcement, these more recent studies of Marston would appear to represent a significant degree of rapprochement between the two viewpoints. Of course, these studies do not throw light on the stability and maintenance of such self-reinforcing responses. The addition of partial reinforcement techniques to these procedures would be of great interest in relation to stability of the self-reinforcing systems thus set up.

Of course, other approaches to the problem of internalization of control of behavior are possible. Thus, Aronfreed and Rever (1965) adopted Mowrer's passive-avoidance (response-correlated) paradigm to account for internalized suppression of behavior, and they examined the effects of the timing of punishment on suppression of behavior. Their experiment involved the child choosing between an attractive and an unattractive toy and being punished (by verbal reprimand) either just before the toy was picked up or a little while after handling had commenced. The child was then left on his own with an attractive and unattractive toy, and his behavior toward them was observed. The results indicated that the children punished just before they picked up the toy handled the attractive toy in the absence of the experimenter less frequently than children punished while handling the toy and that they picked up the unattractive toy more often.

The elucidation of the genesis and maintenance of internalized control is clearly a problem of the utmost importance to behavior therapists since, as was pointed out earlier, it is obvious that internal adaptive control of behavior represents a more desirable state of affairs than the continuation of external control, once established. The experiments described above represent important contributions to this problem and suggest ways in which such control may be established.

3. INTEROCEPTIVE CONDITIONING

As we have seen, it has proven possible to establish vicarious emotional conditioning in a classical conditioning situation. It may therefore be mentioned here that a large body of literature exists indicating the range of Russian work in interoceptive conditioning which has been largely ignored by behavior therapists. Razran (1960) has defined interoceptive conditioning as:

"classical conditioning in which either the conditioned stimulus (CS) or the unconditioned stimulus (US) or both are delivered directly to the mucosa or some specific viscus" (Razran, 1960, p. 3).

As Razran points out, both CS and US may be interoceptive, or only the CS may be interoceptive, giving rise to two varieties of internal conditioning.[13]

Detailed reviews of the literature on interoceptive conditioning have been published (Bykov, 1957; Razran, 1960, 1961; Voronin, 1962). These studies are of critical significance for behavior therapists and demand far more attention than they have thus far received.

4. FEEDBACK CONTROL OF BEHAVIOR

The importance of feedback control models for behavior therapy has already been discussed.[14] Thus far, behavior therapists have made little use of such models except in special instances, such as stuttering, in spite of the remarkable studies, for example, of Simard and Basmajian (1967), in demonstrating feedback control of fine motor movements. It can be anticipated that such techniques will exert an increasing influence in behavior therapy, particularly in view of the increasing attention being paid by behavior therapists to problems connected with the rehabilitation of physically damaged subjects, to be described later in this chapter.

---

[13] Razran rejects the condition in which the US is internal, the CS external, as a true variety of internal conditioning.

[14] See Chapter 2.

5. Verbal Mediation

In spite of suggestions made occasionally to the contrary, behavioristic psychologists have not neglected internal mediational variables, a fact well documented by Goss (1961, 1964) and Farber (1963). Behavior therapists thus far have, however, not utilized such constructs to any great degree, a notable exception being Staats (1968). It can be confidently predicted that such models will play an increasingly important role as behavior therapists come to investigate more complex disorders of behavior.

III. WIDENING THE SCOPE OF BEHAVIOR THERAPY

The range of disorders to which behavior therapy techniques have been applied is already impressive, but it can be expected that attempts will be made to extend them to many disorders scarcely touched thus far. Brief mention may be made in this connection of recent applications to such disorders as chronic pain (Fordyce et al, 1968), cardiac neurosis (Rifkin, 1968), depression (Lazarus, 1968), psychogenic seizures (Gardner, 1967), and problems associated with geriatrics (Lindsley, 1964; Cautela, 1966). Of particular interest is the discussion of depression and its treatment by Lazarus (1968). After a careful discussion of the problem of deciding what constitutes depressive behavior, he outlines three possible approaches to treatment that he has tentatively applied. The first involves what he calls time projection with positive reinforcement and involves imagining future activities that produce positive reinforcement. The second involves affective expression in an attempt to inhibit the depressive responses, while the third involves essentially the use of sensory deprivation on the assumption that, following a period of such deprivation, almost any stimulus will be reinforcing. Thus far, these techniques are at the exploratory stage.

Behavior therapy could, from one point of view, be regarded as the systematic extension under more rigorously controlled conditions, of techniques which, to a considerable degree, have been in use by experts in other fields for a very long time. Nowhere is this more exemplified than in the field of rehabilitation therapy for the residual effects of physical injury or physiological trauma. Behavior therapists could unquestionably benefit from careful observation of the techniques used by, for example, physiotherapists and occupational therapists in the rehabilitation of victims of road and industrial accidents or those suffering from paralysis as the result of cerebral vascular accidents. It is also true to say, however, that these therapists not infrequently ignore some of the basic principles of behavior control. Several recent studies have given rise to hopes that significant advances may be occurring in these areas. Goodkin (1966), for example, has reported on the use of operant conditioning techniques in one such case where a female with hemiplegia and asphasia was being retrained in a key-punching task but was making slow progress. Goodkin noted that the therapist was providing reinforcement on a noncontingent basis and changed the situation by arranging that verbal reinforcement should be contingent on improvement in performance. Over the short period of nine days, the average response time for ten trials was reduced from 110.6 seconds per card to 71.0 seconds per card. Similar improvement was obtained with the same technique in tasks involving copying letters and words. Goodkin also reported that the same or similar methods were used successfully with a female suffering from Parkinsonism who refused to push her wheelchair. In treating a case of aphasia, Goodkin utilized a variety of ingenious techniques and noted that a modeling procedure with vicarious reinforcement was most successful of all. More recently, Meyerson, Kerr, and Michael (1967) have successfully used operant procedures to improve performance in a post-accident case involving learning to type; a cerebral palsied child who refused to stand or walk without support; and a mentally retarded child who refused to walk, though not physically impaired in this respect. Ince (1968) has applied behavior modification techniques to the reduction of anxiety about speaking in an aphasic.

All of these studies, of course, deal with behavioral disturbance resulting from physical impairment, but they do not actually deal with the rehabilitation of impaired physical functioning as such. Whether organic loss of function can be reduced by such techniques remains a very interesting question on which little work has been carried out by behavior therapists. In an unpublished preliminary study, Ince, Sokolow, and Menon (1966) treated three patients with hemiplegia. Two were treated by instrumental aversive escape conditioning procedures in which the patient could turn off a shock by raising the plegic arm so that it struck a button, the distance to be moved to turn off the shock increasing as training progressed. The third patient was treated similarly, but by instrumental aversive avoidance conditioning in which the patient could avoid the shock if he moved the arm to the CS (buzzer). Only one of the patients (subjected to escape conditioning) showed significant improvement in arm functioning. Trombly (1966) has also utilized operant techniques with quadriplegic patients. In a particularly interesting study, MacPherson (1967) trained a patient suffering from Huntington's chorea in a deep muscle relaxation which was instituted at the onset of an involuntary movement and obtained very significant improvement over a period of one year as assessed both by the husband's report and comparative films. It may be noted that, prior to treatment, the patient tried to inhibit the involuntary movement by increasing muscle tension, a procedure which was successful in delaying the onset of the involuntary movement, the latter, however, manifesting itself with increased strength when it finally occurred. Mention should also be made here of the work of Keenan (1966) who utilized a machine program involving successive approximation training in the rehabilitation of an aphasic patient. The program prototype used with this machine presents auditory and visual stimuli on cards, leading the patient by small steps from easy to more difficult discriminations and then to speaking and writing the names of pictures. Lane and Moore (1962) have shown that it is possible to teach an aphasic patient to discriminate between /to/ and /do/ by means of operant conditioning techniques applied to perceptual discriminatory responses to synthesized variants of these sounds achieved by varying the relative onset time of the first formant.

communalities of behavior between diverse patients may provide clues to communality of treatment that would speed up the study of the single case. The disillusionment with diagnostic procedures (Zubin, 1967; Zubin and Fleiss, 1964; Zubin and Kietzman, 1966; Holt, 1967) has led to alternative approaches based on relationships between behaviors and the environmental contingencies that control those behaviors (Ferster, 1965; Kanfer and Saslow, 1965). The analysis of the problem by Kanfer and Saslow, for example, appears to result in a position midway between the classical diagnostic approach and the rejection of psychiatric diagnosis implied in the experimental study of the single-case approach. The latter approach implies a unique configuration of determining factors in each case, whereas the Kanfer and Saslow approach still retains many features of the shotgun approach. Thus, they stress the importance of investigating all aspects of a patient's functioning, including social relationships, cultural relationships, self-control analysis, and so on, though the necessity for such investigations in the case of, for example, a stutterer or an enuretic child has already been questioned in this book. Ferster (1965),[15] on the other hand, proposes a classification that is essentially made in terms of the relationship between the observed behaviors and the environmental events controlling those behaviors, so that the identical behaviors might be quite differently classified as they are determined to be under the control of different contingencies; while different behaviors may be functionally equivalent if they are under the control of the same environmental contingencies. It must be admitted that little, if any, progress has been made toward the solution of this problem.

IV. DIAGNOSIS, CLASSIFICATION, AND DESCRIPTION OF BEHAVIOR

The dissatisfaction expressed in the first chapter with current diagnostic procedures and the stress laid on the experimental investigation of the single case may appear to lead to the conclusion that, at least at the present time, the problem of the description and classification of behavior is of little interest or usefulness to the behavior therapist. This is not necessarily the case, however, particularly if the phrase "description of behavior" is used in place of the loaded term "diagnosis." The existence of

V. PROFESSIONAL AND SUBPROFESSIONAL TRAINING IN BEHAVIOR THERAPY

Four areas may be considered briefly: the professional training of behavior therapists; subprofessional training; the patient as self-therapist; and parents, relatives, and friends as therapists.

1. PROFESSIONAL TRAINING OF BEHAVIOR THERAPISTS

In spite of the rapid development of behavior therapy over the past 15 years, there has been

---

[15] Although Ferster does not refer to it, a similar analysis had earlier been presented by Lindsley (1962).

virtually no discussion of the training of behavior therapists. Some professional training courses in behavior therapy have been established (Poser, 1967) but, for the most part, behavior therapy has developed like Topsy. In some respects, this is probably fortunate and may have helped to retard the hardening of the arteries which afflicts most new approaches sooner rather than later.

2. SUBPROFESSIONAL TRAINING

Although it has been strenuously maintained throughout this book that the application of behavior therapy is not the simple matter some psychiatrists and others have seen fit to assert it is, nevertheless there seems little doubt that some of the procedures can be taught to, and be effectively applied by, relatively psychologically unsophisticated persons. Thus, Ayllon and Michael (1959) were able to train ward personnel to apply appropriate positive and aversive contingencies to the behavior of psychotic patients; Wetzel (1966) and DeMyer and Ferster (1962) trained childcare workers to employ various social reinforcements to shape new social behaviors in children; Davison (1965) trained students to apply operant conditioning techniques to autistic children; Becker et al (1967) trained teachers to apply the same techniques in the classroom to control anti-social behaviors; Staats et al (1967) trained instructional technicians to teach reading by reinforcement procedures; and Kraft and Al-Issa (1966) consider that SD(I) procedures could be successfully used by general practitioners after minimal practice. Many other examples could be cited. The danger here, of course, lies in the dilution of the experimental approach, the tendency of techniques to be used in a standard, uncritical fashion, and the tendency to conclude that instances of failure invalidate the basic approach of behavior therapy.

3. THE PATIENT AS THERAPIST

Goldiamond (1965b) has systematically explored the possibility of training the patient to be his own behavior therapist. He argues that this may be achieved in one of two ways. On the one hand, the patient may be carefully instructed in the procedures he must follow; on the other hand, he may be trained in the functional analysis of behavior (Goldiamond, of course, is writing within the operant conditioning framework) and, having grasped these,

analyze his own behavior, set his own goals, and determine the appropriate procedures for himself. Goldiamond illustrates these two procedures by reference to patients with difficulty in studying and problems with overeating, marital relationships, and illegibility of handwriting. The technique is, of course, one of transference of control from the experimenter to the patient, discussed earlier in this chapter.

4. PARENTS, RELATIVES, AND FRIENDS AS THERAPISTS

It has been pointed out that parents and others apply operant reinforcement techniques in raising their children, but often produce undesired behaviors that are highly resistant to extinction because of a failure to understand the importance of timing or other relationships in controlling behavior. Thus, the mother may ignore (fail to reinforce positively) the child who plays quietly and may provide reinforcement (attention, whether positive or negative reactions are involved) only when the child becomes excessively demanding. The inadvertent use of partial reinforcement techniques by parents may render the undesirable behavior highly resistant to extinction.

Nevertheless, parents, relatives, and friends may be very powerful allies of the behavior therapist if they are properly trained. Thus, the parents of a psychotic child may be trained to take over from the therapist in the home after initial success has been achieved (Hawkins et al, 1966; Risley and Wolf, 1967). Mothers have also been successfully trained to handle less severe problems of relationships with their children in the home, such as negativism (Wahler et al, 1965; Russo, 1964; Zeilberger et al, 1968), sibling rivalry (O'Leary et al, 1967), or excessive control of the child by the mother (Straughan, 1964). Patterson (1965) trained parents to deal with their school phobic child. In a quite different problem area, Goodkin (1966) trained the wife of an aphasic patient to respond appropriately to the patient's behavior where previously she had been reinforcing the very behavior it was desirable to eliminate. Since the patient must usually live in a social environment, clearly this "treatment" of the patient's relatives can be of crucial importance.

VI. CONCLUDING REMARKS

There can be no denying that behavior therapy has burgeoned enormously during the last 15 years. No attempt has been made to chart the rate of growth of publications directly on behavior therapy during this period, but it would undoubtedly form a positively accelerating curve. The range of disorders covered already and the ingenuity of the techniques used also command respect. Nevertheless, it is fitting to end this book with a strong note of caution. Indeed, in part this book has been written because of a growing uneasiness on the part of the writer that behavior therapy is in serious danger of losing its initial impetus and inspiration and taking the path toward oblivion. It may seem strange to sound such a warning note at the time when behavior therapy appears to be flourishing as never before. Nevertheless, the warning signals have been hoisted and should be heeded. The almost uniform history of all psychotherapeutic "schools," of whatever persuasion, should give grounds for continuing assessment of the position of behavior therapy. The polemical tone of much of the writing (both pro and contra), the increasing emotional involvement of behavior therapists in reacting angrily to criticism of their methods and results, the premature attempts to "validate" behavior therapy by use of medical model designs: all of these signs point to a blurring of the original basic aim of behavior therapy. As was pointed out in an earlier chapter, behavior therapy is *fundamentally* distinguishable from other therapeutic efforts by one mark only: *the application of the experimental method to the understanding and modification of abnormalities of behavior.* There can be little doubt that, if this aim is lost sight of, behavior therapy will rapidly degenerate into just another "school," impervious to and resentful of criticism. The present writer hopes that this will not happen, but is by no means sure that it can be avoided.

REFERENCES

Agras, W.S. Behavior therapy in the management of chronic schizophrenia. *Amer. J. Psychiat.*, 1967, **124**, 240–243.

Aronfreed, J. & Rever, A. Internalized behavioral suppression and the timing of social punishment. *J. Pers. soc. Psychol.*, 1965, **1**, 3–16.

Ayllon, T. & Michael, J. The psychiatric nurse as a behavioral engineer. *J. exper. Anal. Behav.*, 1959, **2**, 323–334.

Bandura, A. Social learning through imitation. In Jones, M.R. (ed.). *Nebraska symposium on motivation.* Nebraska: Univ. Nebraska Press, 1962, pp. 211–269.

Bandura, A. Influence of models' reinforcement contingencies on the acquisition of imitative responses. *J. pers. soc. Psychol.*, 1965, **1**, 589–595 (a).

Bandura, A. Behavioral modifications through modeling procedures. In Krasner, L. & Ullmann, L.P. (eds.). *Research in behavior modification.* New York: Holt, 1965, pp. 310–340 (b).

Bandura, A. Vicarious processes: a case of no-trial learning. In Berkowitz, L. (ed.). *Advances in experimental social psychology* (Vol. 2). New York: Academic Press, 1965, pp. 1–55 (c).

Bandura, A. Modeling approaches to the modification of phobic disorders. *Ciba Foundation Symposium: the role of learning in psychotherapy.* London: Churchill, 1968 (in press).

Bandura, A., Grusec, J.E., & Menlove, F.L. Observational learning as a function of symbolization and incentive set. *Child Developm.*, 1966, **37**, 499–506.

Bandura, A., Grusec, J.E., & Menlove, F.L. Vicarious extinction of avoidance behavior. *J. Pers. soc. Psychol.*, 1967, **5**, 16–23 (a).

Bandura, A., Grusec, J.E., & Menlove, F.L. Some social determinants of self-monitoring reinforcement systems. *J. Pers. soc. Psychol.*, 1967, **5**, 449–455 (b).

Bandura, A. & Harris, M.B. Modification of syntactic style. *J. exp. Child Psychol.*, 1966, **4**, 341–352.

Bandura, A. & Huston, A.C. Identification as a process of incidental learning. *J. abnorm. soc. Psychol.*, 1961, **63**, 311–318.

Bandura, A. & Kupers, C.J. Transmission of patterns of self-reinforcement through modeling. *J. abnorm. soc. Psychol.*, 1964, **69**, 1–9.

Bandura, A. & McDonald, F.J. The influence of social reinforcement and the behavior of models in shaping children's moral judgements. *J. abnorm. soc. Psychol.*, 1963, **67**, 274–281.

Bandura, A. & Menlove, F.L. Factors determining vicarious extinction of avoidance behavior through symbolic modeling. *J. Pers. soc. Psychol.*, 1968, 8, 99–108.

Bandura, A. & Perloff, B. Relative efficacy of self-monitored and externally imposed reinforcement systems. *J. Pers. soc. Psychol.*, 1967, **7**, 111–116.

Bandura, A. & Rosenthal, T.L. Vicarious classical conditioning as a function of arousal level. *J. Pers. soc. Psychol.*, 1966, **3**, 54–62.

Bandura, A., Ross, D., & Ross, S.A. Transmission of aggression through imitation of aggressive models. *J. abnorm. soc. Psychol.*, 1961, **63**, 575–582.

Bandura, A., Ross, D., & Ross, S.A. Imitation of film-mediated aggressive models. *J. abnorm. soc. Psychol.*, 1963, **66,** 3–11 (a).

Bandura, A., Ross, D., & Ross, S.A. Vicarious reinforcement and imitative learning. *J. abnorm. soc. Psychol.*, 1963, **67,** 601–607 (b).

Bandura, A., Ross, D., & Ross, S.A. A comparative test of the status envy, social power and secondary reinforcement theories of identificatory learning. *J. abnorm. soc. Psychol.*, 1963, **67,** 527–534 (c).

Bandura, A. & Whalen, C.P. The influence of antecedent reinforcement and divergent modeling cues on patterns of self-reward. *J. Pers. soc. Psychol.*, 1966, **3,** 373–382.

Becker, W.C., Madsen, C.H., Arnold, C.R., & Thomas, D.R. The contingent use of teacher attention and praise in reducing classroom behavior problems. *J. spec. Educ.*, 1967, **1,** 287–307.

Berger, S.M. Incidental learning through vicarious reinforcement. *Psychol. Rev.*, 1962, **69,** 450–466.

Brodsky, G. The relation between verbal and nonverbal behavior change. *Behav. Res. Ther.*, 1967, **5,** 183–191.

Bykov, K.M. *The cerebral cortex and the internal organs.* New York: Chemical Publ. Co., 1957.

Cautela, J. Behavior therapy and geriatrics. *J. genet. Psychol.*, 1966, **108,** 9–17.

Craig, K.D. & Weinstein, M.S. Conditioning vicarious affective arousal. *Psychol. Rep.*, 1965, **17,** 955–963.

Davison, G.C. The training of undergraduates as social reinforcers for autistic children. In Ullmann, L.P. & Krasner, L. (eds.). *Case studies in behavior modification.* New York, Holt, 1965, pp. 146–148.

DeMyer, M.K. & Ferster, C.B. Teaching new social behavior to schizophrenic children. *J. Amer. Acad. Child Psychiat.*, 1962, **1,** 443–461.

Farber, I.E. The things people say to themselves. *Amer. Psychol.*, 1963, **18,** 185–197.

Ferster, C.B. Classification of behavior pathology. In Krasner, L. & Ullmann, L.P. (eds.). *Research in behavior modification.* Holt, 1965, pp. 6–26.

Fordyce, W.E., Fowler, R.S., & Delateur, B. An application of behavior modification technique to a problem of chronic pain. *Behav. Res. Ther.*, 1968, **6,** 105–107.

Gardner, J.E. Behavior therapy treatment approach to a psychogenic seizure case. *J. consult. Psychol.*, 1967, **31,** 209–212.

Geer, J.H. & Turteltaub, A. Fear reduction following observation of a model. *J. Pers. soc. Psychol.*, 1967, **6,** 327–331.

Goldiamond, I. Stuttering and fluency as manipulatable operant response classes. In Krasner, L. & Ullmann, L.P. (eds.). *Research in behavior modification.* New York: Holt, 1965, pp. 108–156 (a).

Goldiamond, I. Self-control procedures in personal behavior problems. *Psychol. Rep.*, 1965, **17,** 851–868 (b).

Goodkin, R. Case studies in behavioral research in rehabilitation. *Percept. Mot. Skills*, 1966, **23,** 171–182.

Goss, A.E. Early behaviorism and verbal mediating responses. *Amer. Psychol.*, 1961, **16,** 285–298.

Goss, A.E. Verbal mediation. *Psychol. Record*, 1964, **14,** 363–382.

Grusec, J. & Mischel, W. Model's characteristics as determinants of social learning. *J. Pers. soc. Psychol.*, 1966, **4**, 211–215.

Hawkins, R.P., Peterson, R.F., Schweid, E., & Bijou, S.W. Behavior therapy in the home: amelioration of problem parent-child relations with the parent in a therapeutic role. *J. exp. Child Psychol.*, 1966, **4**, 99–107.

Holt, R.R. Diagnostic testing: present status and future prospects. *J. nerv. ment. Dis.*, 1967, **144**, 444–465.

Ince, L.P. Desensitization with an aphasic patient. *Behav. Res. Ther.*, 1968, **6**, 235–237.

Ince, L., Sokolow, J., & Menon, M. *Escape and avoidance conditioning of responses in the plegic arm of stroke patients.* Unpublished paper, 1966.

Jones, M.C. The elimination of children's fears. *J. exp. Psychol.*, 1924, **7**, 383–390.

Kanfer, F.H. Vicarious human reinforcements: a glimpse into the black box. In Krasner, L. & Ullmann, L.P. (eds.). *Research in behavior modification.* New York: Holt, 1965, pp. 244–267.

Kanfer, F.H., Bradley, M., & Marston, A.R. Self-reinforcement as a function of degree of learning. *Psychol. Rep.*, 1962, **10**, 885–886.

Kanfer, F.H. & Marston, A.R. Conditioning of self-reinforcing responses: an analogue to self-confidence training. *Psychol. Rep.*, 1963, **13**, 63–70 (a).

Kanfer, F.H. & Marston, A.R. Determinants of self-reinforcement in human learning. *J. exp. Psychol.*, 1963, **66**, 245–254 (b).

Kanfer, F.H. & Saslow, G. Behavioral analysis: an alternative to diagnostic classification. *Arch. gen. Psychiat.*, 1965, **12**, 529–538.

Keenan, S. A method for eliciting naming behavior from aphasic patients. *J. Speech Hear. Dis.*, 1966, **31**, 261–266.

Kraft, T. & Al-Issa, I. Brief behavior therapy for the general practitioner. *J. Coll. Gen. Practit.*, 1966, **12**, 270–276.

Lane, H.L. & Moore, D.J. Reconditioning a consonant discrimination in an aphasic: an experimental case history. *J. Speech Hearing Dis.*, 1962, **27**, 232–243.

Lazarus, A.A. Learning theory and the treatment of depression. *Behav. Res. Ther.*, 1968, **6**, 83–89.

Lindsley, O.R. Operant conditioning methods in diagnosis. In Nodine, J.H. & Moyer, J.H. (eds.). *Psychosomatic medicine: the first Hahnemann symposium.* Philadelphia: Lea & Febiger, 1962, pp. 41–54.

Lindsley, O.R. Geriatric behavioral prosthetics. In Kastenbaum, R. (ed.). *New thoughts on old age.* New York: Springer, 1964, pp. 41–60.

MacPherson, E.L.R. Control of involuntary movement. *Behav. Res. Ther.*, 1967, **5**, 143–145.

Marston, A.R. Variables affecting incidence of self-reinforcement. *Psychol. Rep.*, 1964, **14**, 879–884 (a).

Marston, A.R. Personality variables related to self-reinforcement. *J. Psychol.*, 1964, **58**, 169–175 (b).

Marston, A.R. Imitation, self-reinforcement, and reinforcement of another person. *J. Pers. soc. Psychol.*, 1965, **2**, 255–261.

Marston, A.R. & Kanfer, F.H. Human reinforcement: experimenter and subject controlled. *J. exp. Psychol.*, 1963, **66**, 91–94.

Meyerson, L., Kerr, N., & Michael, J.L. Behavior modification in rehabilitation. In Bijou, S.W. & Baer, D.M. (eds.). *Child development: readings in experimental analysis.* New York: Appleton-Century-Crofts, 1967, pp. 214–239.

Miller, N.E. & Dollard, J. *Social learning and imitation.* New Haven: Yale Univer. Press, 1941.

O'Leary, K.D., O'Leary, S., & Becker, W.C. Modification of a deviant sibling interaction pattern in the home. *Behav. Res. Ther.*, 1967, **5**, 113–120.

Patterson, G.R. A learning theory approach to the treatment of the school phobic child. In Ullmann, L.P. & Krasner, L. (eds.). *Case studies in behavior modification.* New York: Holt, 1965, pp. 279–285.

Poser, E.G. Training behavior therapists. *Behav. Res. Ther.*, 1967, **5**, 37–41.

Rachman, S. Studies in desensitization: III. Speed of generalization. *Behav. Res. Ther.*, 1966, **4**, 7–16.

Razran, G. The observable unconscious in current Soviet psychophysiology: survey and interpretation of experiments in interoceptive conditioning. *Progress in clin. Psychol.*, 1960, **4**, 1–31.

Razran, G. The observable unconscious and the inferable conscious in current Soviet psychophysiology. *Psychol. Rev.*, 1961, **68**, 81–147.

Rifkin, B.G. The treatment of cardiac neurosis using systematic desensitization. *Behav. Res. Ther.*, 1968, **6**, 239–241.

Risley, T.R. & Wolf, M.M. Experimental manipulation of autistic behaviors and generalization into the home. In Bijou, S.W. & Baer, D.M. (eds.). *Child development: readings in experimental analysis.* New York: Appleton-Century-Crofts, 1967, pp. 184–194.

Ritter, B. The group desensitization of children's snake phobias using vicarious and contact desensitization procedures. *Behav. Res. Ther.*, 1968, **6**, 1–6.

Russo, S. Adaptations in behavioral therapy with children. *Behav. Res. Ther.*, 1964, **2**, 43–47.

Simard, T.G. & Basmajian, J.V. Methods in training the conscious control of motor units. *Arch. physical Med. Rehab.*, 1967, **48**, 12–19.

Staats, A.W. *Learning, language and cognition.* New York: Holt, 1968.

Staats, A.W., Minke, K.A., Goodwin, W., & Landeen, J. Cognitive behavior modification: "motivated learning" reading treatment with subprofessional therapy-technicians. *Behav. Res. Ther.*, 1967, **5**, 283–299.

Straughan, J.H. Treatment with child and mother in the playroom. *Behav. Res. Ther.*, 1964, **2**, 37–41.

Trombly, C.A. Principles of operant conditioning related to orthotic training of quadriplegic patients. *Amer. J. occupat. Ther.*, 1966, **20**, 217–220.

Voronin, L.G. Some results of comparative-physiological investigations of higher nervous activity. *Psychol. Bull.*, 1962, **59**, 161–195.

Wahler, R.G., Winkel, G.H., Peterson, R.F., & Morrison, D.C. Mothers as behavior therapists for their own children. *Behav. Res. Ther.*, 1965, **3**, 113–124.

Wetzel, R. Use of behavioral techniques in a case of compulsive stealing. *J. consult. Psychol.*, 1966, **30**, 367–374.

Yates, A.J. The application of learning theory to the treatment of tics. *J. abnorm. soc. Psychol.*, 1958, **56**, 175–182.

Zeilberger, J., Sampen, S.E., & Sloane, H.W. Modification of a child's problem behaviors in the home with the mother as therapist. *J. appl. Behav. Anal.*, 1968, **1**, 47–53.

Zubin, J. Classification of the behavior disorders. *Ann. Rev. Psychol.*, 1967, **18**, 373–406.

Zubin, J. & Fleiss, J.L. Taxonomy in the mental disorders—a historical perspective. In APA Symposium, *Explorations in typology with special reference to psychotics.* New York: Human Ecology Fund, 1964, pp. 1–12.

Zubin, J. & Kietzman, M.L. A cross-cultural approach to classification in schizophrenia and other mental disorders. In Hoch, P.H. and Zubin, J. (eds.). *Psychopathology of schizophrenia.* New York: Grune & Stratton, 1966, pp. 482–514.

Author Index

Page numbers in boldface refer to end-of-chapter bibliographies.

424

Subject Index